Genocide in Gaza

Voices of Global Conscience

Ahmet Davutoğlu | *Richard Falk*

EDITORS

Clarity Press, Inc.

©2025 Ahmet Davutoğlu | Richard Falk

ISBN: 978-1-963892-02-4
EBOOK ISBN: 978-1-963892-03-1

In-house editor: Diana G. Collier
Book design: Becky Luening

Front cover photos: Courtesy of photojournalist Resul Serdar

Back cover photo, top: November 5, 2023, Washington, District of
Columbia, United States: Protesters gather while holding flags and
signs during the pro-Palestinian demonstration. (Alamy)

Back cover photo, bottom: London, UK. 13/January/2024—Year's First
March for Gaza in London. The first large march in solidarity with the
people of Palestine of 2024 takes place in London. (Roland Ravenhill /
Alamy)

Library of Congress Control Number: 2025931715

Clarity Press, Inc.
2625 Piedmont Rd. NE, Ste. 56
Atlanta, GA 30324, USA
https://www.claritypress.com

Praise for *Genocide in Gaza*

"This courageous and prophetic book is a call for moral conscience and political vision in our grim age of catastrophe! The barbaric genocide against Palestinians in Gaza should fortify us in our struggle for truth and justice!"

CORNEL WEST, Dietrich Bonhoeffer Professor of Philosophy & Christian Practice at Union Theological Seminary

"This book provides a rare, timely, comprehensive. and accurate account of the harm that has befallen the people of Gaza.It is a stark reminder to all humanity that we dare not neglect the urgent call for all of us to join together in utilising international solidarity to actively promote justice for all."

NALEDI PANDOR, former Foreign Minister, South Africa

"This volume, expertly curated by Richard Falk and Ahmet Davutoğlu, demonstrates the breadth and scope of international solidarity with Gaza during the unrelenting genocide, and considers and critiques the vexing international order that insists on the brutalization of Palestinians from many different vantage points. By analyzing law, history, media coverage, and literature, among many other topics, with respect to the Israeli state's attempt to erase the Palestinians' presence in their own homeland, this book offers a multifaceted argument—through an impressive array of contributors—of what the outrages of the past and present have wrought, and what the future may promise, if we continue the fight for true justice in Palestine."

WADIE SAID, Professor of Law, University of Colorado, School of Law

"October 7 shattered the assumptions underlying our understanding of politics in the Middle East, urgently calling for an intellectual and political rethink. With great scholarly imagination and political insight, Richard Falk and Ahmet Davutoğu have put together a remarkable collection of writings from writers and activists, insiders and neighbors. This collection provides us a much needed starting point in this hour of need."

MAHMOOD MAMDANI, Herbert Lehman Professor of Government, Columbia University, author of *When Victims Become Killers: Darfur, Politics, and the War of Terror*

CO-EDITORS

Ahmet Davutoğlu & Richard Falk

IN ASSOCIATION WITH

Abdullah Ahsan

Sevinç Alkan

Büşra Aytekin

M. Selami Çalışkan

Sare Davutoğlu

Hilal Elver

Penny Green

Bilgehan Uçak

For Hind Rajab and all other children of Gaza who were killed, wounded, maimed, and traumatized during Israel's cruel, live-streamed genocide.

&

For Aaron Bushnell, serviceman of the U.S. Air Force, who self-immolated in front of Israel's Embassy in Washington, D.C., on February 25, 2024, whose last words were "Free Palestine!" and for Aysenur Ezgi Eygi, Turkish-American activist killed on September 6, 2024, in the West Bank of Occupied Palestine by an IDF gunshot wound to the head.

Table of Contents

III. Narrations of Genocide

IV. Dimensions of Genocide

VI. INTERNATIONAL LAW AND INTERNATIONAL STATECRAFT: RELEVANCE EXPLAINED & EXPLORED

FOREWORD

Palestine Will Be Free

Dr. Mustafa Barghouti

I WAS HONORED by my dear friends Ahmet Davutoğlu and Richard Falk with the request to write a foreword for the book they are editing on the genocide in Gaza, with contributions from many highly respected scholars and authors. Publishing and editing this book is an immensely meaningful act that serves the ongoing struggle for justice and liberation for Palestinians.

Israel's war on Gaza, which began on October 7, 2023, is unprecedented in modern history. The destruction in Gaza has even exceeded that of World War I and II.

Since October 7, Israel conducted three war crimes in parallel: genocide, collective punishment of a civilian population, and ethnic cleansing.

During the first year of this devastating war, the Israeli army bombed the 2.2 million inhabitants of Gaza, living in less than 140 square miles, with no less than 83,000 tons of explosives. This means 32 kg of explosive for each man, woman, or child. To put this number into perspective, 83,000 tons is four times more than the explosive power of each of the nuclear bombs dropped on Hiroshima and Nagasaki during the second World War.

Nearly 80% of all homes have been partially or completely destroyed. In Germany only 10% of homes were destroyed by the end of the second World War. The Israeli war machine intentionally destroyed all universities, more than 70% of schools, 34 out of 36 hospitals, 165 health institutions, 80 health centers, 137 ambulances, 178 shelters, 611 mosques and all 3 churches in Gaza.

Israeli bombardment killed more than 41,200 Palestinians, in addition to more than 10,000 who are still missing under the rubble. Seventy percent of those killed were children, women, and elderly. Nearly 17,000 Palestinian children have been killed, including 115 children who were born and killed during the war. Some, like the children of Mohamed Abu Elkumsan, lived for fewer than three days. It was heartbreaking to hear him explain how happy he was that his wife had managed to give birth during the war to two healthy twins, how he rushed to get birth certificates for them, and how shocked he was when he returned to his tent to find both his children and wife killed by Israeli bombardment.

Almost 95,000 Palestinians, mostly civilians, were injured. This figure includes 4000 who had amputations, among them 1300 children. On one of the days of this seemingly endless and brutal war, I was heartbroken to see on television a five-year-old Palestinian child who had lost both his hands asking his father, "Father, will my hands grow again when I grow up?" The father could not say a word, his eyes full of tears.

By the end of September 2024, the Israeli army had killed or injured 6.5% of the population of Gaza. Had this happened in the USA it would mean proportionally that more than 20 million Americans had been killed or injured in less than a year.

The Israeli military attack on Gaza that started after the 7th of October was accompanied by a ruthless campaign to dehumanize Palestinians. It was led by Israeli Prime Minister Netanyahu and the Israeli Army Minister Galant, who called Palestinians "human animals." The fascist murderers Smotrich and Ben Gvir, both of whom were previously accused by the Israeli judiciary of belonging to terrorist Israeli groups, ran campaigns to eliminate Palestinians who, according to them, were all terrorists, even the children.

During Israel's bombardment of Gaza, the Israel military not only targeted civilians indiscriminately, but also specifically targeted medical personnel. By the eleventh month of the war, they had killed more than 880 medical doctors, nurses, ambulance drivers and other health professionals. They also arrested and tortured, sometimes to death, no fewer than 200 health workers. This includes Dr. Adnan Al-Bursh and Dr. Iyad Rantisi, previously head respectively of Orthopedic surgery at Al Shifa hospital, and of Obstetrics and Gynecology at the Kamal Edwan hospital, who were tortured to death at the Sde Timan and Ofer prisons.

The Israeli attacks on Palestinian medical and health facilities were clearly intended to destroy medical resources needed for the treatment of the sick and injured. Out of the 95,000 injured, at least 25% could die due to the absence of medical facilities and proper treatment. They are unable to receive proper medical treatment because of Israel's refusal to allow them to leave Gaza.

Journalists and media personnel were also major targets of the Israeli attacks. The aim was and continues to be to prevent the truth about the Israeli war crimes from reaching the world. Foreign journalists were forbidden from entering Gaza (except for one CNN correspondent for 3 hours only), and 173 Palestinian journalists were killed, many with their families, including

Al-Jazeera's correspondents, one of the main media outlets covering Israel's war on Gaza

This was the first war in modern history that international journalists were forbidden from covering, and yet the mainstream Western media made no serious protests against this Israeli behavior of the suppression of the free media. If it wasn't for the courageous Palestinian journalists from Gaza and news outlets such as Al-Jazeera, and Al-Mayadeen, whose offices were closed by the Israeli authorities, or for the young social media activists, the world would not have become aware of the Israeli atrocities in Gaza.

Not only did Israel conduct a genocide through bombardment, but it also allowed targeted Gaza through biological warfare. By depriving people from food, proper nutrition, clean water and all forms of energy such as electricity and fuel, they caused epidemics and diseases. According to Palestinian Medical Relief Society (PMRS), which runs medical operations in Gaza, providing medical treatment to more than 200,000 patients monthly, as of September 2024 there were 1,737,524 sick patients in Gaza, including 112,000 suffering from an outbreak of infectious hepatitis, 3,500 children with severe malnutrition, hundreds of thousands suffering from skin diseases including scabies and impetigo, several children with meningitis and 6 cases of suspected poliomyelitis.

According to PMRS every person in Gaza gets sick an average of 3 times a month, most frequently with respiratory infections, gastroenteritis, or skin diseases.

The WHO was obliged to run a new polio vaccination campaign under Israeli bombardment, since Netanyahu refused to allow a humanitarian ceasefire even for a few days.

Today 10.000 cases of cancer don't receive proper treatment, 12,000 people are in urgent need for medical evacuation, and 350.000 suffer from chronic diseases that require continuous medical care and supply of medications.

Israel is now expanding its genocide to the West Bank. Seven hundred Palestinians, mostly civilians, among them 150 children, have been killed by Israeli settlers and military in the West Bank since October 7, 2023. More than 10,000 prisoners have also been arrested. Israeli bulldozers have caused massive damage in many cities and refugee camps like Jenin and Tulkarem, destroying infrastructure. Moreover, the Israeli government has dismantled most of the areas that are meant to be under the control of the Palestinian authorities, invaded several cities, and stripped the PA of its civil authority in Area B (as established by the Oslo Accords).

The atrocities committed in Gaza by the Israeli army are not only detrimental to the people of Gaza but violate international law as well. The actions of Israel are undermining international and humanitarian law, about which the West claims to care.

Palestinians discovered the double standards of many Western governments when comparing their attitudes towards Russia and Ukraine with that towards Israel and Palestine. Russia was subjected to harsh sanctions after attacking Ukraine while Israel was provided with 50,000 tons of explosives by the United States, in addition to thousands of weapons from other Western countries such as Britain and Germany.

The world order will never be the same after the genocide in Gaza. People everywhere are legitimately asking: "Where are the so-called Western values of human rights, democracy, and international law?"

Why are Palestinians being forced to cope with Israeli occupation, apartheid, and genocide? Why are we Palestinians mistreated by many European and American governments that refuse to treat us as equal human beings because of their racist bias?

What will be the impact of this ongoing genocide on the whole international order created after World War II? Will those in power not be held accountable and enjoy impunity for breaking the most fundamental rules of international law? Will the world continue to be run by the rule of power rather than by the rule of law?

The 7th of October attack was not the cause of the current political situation, rather it is the result of 76 years of ethnic cleansing that the Palestinian people were subjected to by Israel since 1948 when 52 massacres were committed by Israeli military gangs and 520 Palestinian towns and villages were demolished, erased as part of the massive ethnic cleansing operation. Seventy percent of the population of Gaza were already refugees, forcibly displaced by Israel in 1948, and once again internally displaced in 2024, during which they were forced to move 6 to 10 times in the course of one year.

The 7th of October was also a result of 57 years of Israeli military occupation of the West Bank, including East Jerusalem and Gaza, that evolved into the most extreme system of apartheid in modern history. Recently it has featured 17 years of a ruthless Israeli siege of Gaza, which resulted in 94% of its water being polluted or saturated by salt, and a destroyed economy with 80% of young college graduates left unemployed.

The 7th of October was also the result of the declared Israeli government policy leading to the demise of a two-state solution in which Palestinians were expected to build a state on 22% of their homeland, while the UNGA Resolution 181 at least had given them 44% of Mandate or historic Palestine at a time when they actually owned 82% of Palestinian land. This was a result of the Knesset nation-state law of 2018 which declared that the right of self-determination in historic Palestine (Israelis call it Eretz Israel) exclusively belongs to the Jewish people. This legislative act was followed by the Israeli fascist minister Smotrich's declaration "that Israel will fill the West Bank with Israeli settlements till Palestinians lose any hope of a state of their own, and then have to choose between immigration (ethnic cleansing), subjugation to Israelis (eternal apartheid), or death (genocide).

The 7th of October was a direct result of the Israeli shift not only to racism and extremism, but also to fascism, killing all hopes for peace or justice in Palestine.

Many Palestinians once believed that the peace process, international law, and UN Resolutions would render justice. They became disillusioned having watched their homeland be gradually and violently taken over by extremist settlers. They live in a constant state of threat and fear, their children are at risk, while the United Nations and Western governments are failing to implement no fewer than 84 UN Security Council resolutions, and about 800 General Assembly Resolutions that support Palestinians rights.

Over the last 18 years Netanyahu has been implementing Jabotinsky's plans of ethnic cleansing of Palestinians. Palestinians are not only facing the longest occupation in modern history and the worst system of apartheid, but also the same settler colonial Zionist project that established Israel in 1948 through the ethnic cleansing of 70% of the Palestinian people.

It is also clear that the Israel establishment is attempting to annex the West Bank, as well as Jerusalem and the Gaza Strip and to displace Palestinian resident populations.

Netanyahu left no doubt about his intentions when he raised the map of the Middle East in the UN General Assembly, two weeks before the 7th of October, which showed Israel as encompassing the West Bank, Gaza Strip, and the Golan Heights.

No innocent life of any civilian should be lost or killed, and this applies to Palestinians as well. The famous Palestinian poet Tawfiq Ziyad, who happened to be the mayor of Nazareth, once said: "We Palestinians are not better than any other people, but no other people are better than us."

We want to be treated as equals, with our rights to full freedom, dignity, and self-determination.

Whatever it takes we will not be broken, we will not give up till our dreams are fulfilled and Palestine is free.

Preface

Ahmet Davutoğlu | Richard Falk

THIS VOLUME IS DEVOTED to assessing various aspects of Israel's genocidal assault on Gaza that has continued for more than a year in Gaza, and now has spilled over to include comparable Israeli tactics in Southern Lebanon, extending to Beirut. The events are deeply challenging persons of conscience everywhere in the world to respond in whatever way they can, given the failures of the UN and leading governments to act effectively. Israel's leaders seek to justify their behavior as a defensive reaction to the Hamas attack of October 7, but the intensity, persistence, excessiveness, and inhumane character of the political violence called our attention to a more complex causal focus that included contextualizing the Hamas attack. Israel engaged in repeated provocations in the months before Hamas acted, including the undisguised avowal of a territorial expansionist unlawful policy agenda adopted by the extremist Netanyahu coalition government that took over control of Israel at the start of 2023. Some account should also be taken of the well-documented failure by the Tel Aviv government to heed numerous warnings that Hamas was planning and rehearsing an. attack on Israel, suggesting that the Netanyahu knew that the attack was coming and yet failed to tighten border security.

Our initial concern involved whether available evidence justifies considering Israel's rationalization of self-defense to be more properly understood as an instance of the international crime of genocide. Such an inquiry draws a distinction between a civil society assessment of genocide by international law specialists and others and a more legalistic view that allegations of genocide can only be resolved by a duly empowered judicial body after hearing arguments from both complainant and the accused that the elements of genocide have been established in law beyond reasonable doubt. This book is a collective undertaking of a group of concerned individuals that relies on the value of what people know and believe about the deep roots of genocide in a variety of societal malfunctions. It conveys the diverse interests and perceptions of representative of global civil society, without negating the importance of the legal profession and the potential political weight of a subsequent more conventionally legal resolution of the genocide controversy arising from Israel's violence against the civilian population of Gaza over the course of more than ten months.

The contributors to this book do not claim to be non-partisan. None of the chapters defends or to explain sympathetically Israel's behavior. Despite being admittedly partisan, we do claim to be *objective*, abiding by scholarly standards of truthfulness, respect for evidence, and reasonable canons of interpretation. The contributors offer their interpretations guided by a commitment to truth-telling and heeding the eyes and ears of victims, witnesses, and journalists who have themselves resisted the manipulations of state propaganda and self-serving apologists for evil deeds. There are at least two argumentative sides to every human encounter that occurs in the domain of politics, but judgments between right and wrong are still possible, and sometimes, as here, necessary. Rarely in modern times has a people endured more than a century of victimization as have the Palestinian people, reducing them to being persecuted strangers in their own homeland and prolonged refugees denied by Israeli law, contradicting international law, any right of return.

Contributors, most of whom presented preliminary versions of their chapters in a public conference devoted to these themes in London on January 27, 2024, explore the many facets of genocide from different perspectives. Our editorial intention is to be inclusive with respect to the psychological, philosophical, cultural, religious, legal, moral, political, economic. and spiritual dimensions of the Israeli attack and its horrifying impacts on civilian lives, especially Palestinian children, but also the sick, wounded, disabled and elderly, as well as even Palestinian civilians with no special vulnerabilities except personal, family, and national wellbeing. It has also devastated the societal and ecological infrastructure of Gaza, putting in question whether a viable habitat can be restored even if the vast resources needed are made available either by way of Israeli reparations or through international funding.

Part of the impetus for the volume derived from a sense of helpless frustration on our part, after months of failure by governments and the UN to uphold international law and protect the human rights of the deeply abused Palestinians confined to Gaza whose very survival was most precariously hanging in the balance. We drafted a Declaration of Concern & Conscience in December 2023 that was signed by several hundred academic experts on these sensitive issues and by former government diplomats.

The Declaration stimulated anonymous funding that enabled the London conference to take place. We are particularly grateful to Qatar's former Prime Minister, Sheik Hamed bin Jessim, for his generous support. By accident or fate the conference happened on the day after the International Court of Justice handed down its historic near unanimous response to South Africa's allegation of genocide on the basis of Article IX of the 1948 Convention on the Prevention and Punishment of the International Crime of Genocide. The ICJ vote, with the support of several judges with national affiliations to complicit states, not only accepted jurisdiction over the legal dispute, but held oral hearings that led to its Issuance of Interim Orders directed at Israel to stop engaging in activity contributing to "a plausible genocide" in Gaza as well as directing Israel to cease interference with the supply and delivery of humanitarian aid desperately needed by virtually the entire civilian Palestinian population in Gaza estimated as 2.3 million.

As expected, Israel refused to alter its behavior, being shielded from adverse consequences of defying the ruling of the ICJ by the further complicity of the liberal democracies. The highest officials in the U.S. Government went so far as to contend that the South African initiative was "without legal merit," which given the circumstances was an irresponsible blow against not only the Palestinian victims of genocide, but also to the regulative authority of international law and its most respected institutions. Several chapters examine this disturbing linkage between the perpetration of genocide and the complicity of leading governments, which, among other harmful effects on world order, hampered the efforts of the UN to impose a mandatory ceasefire that would produce the release of the Israeli hostages remaining alive and of the large number of Palestinians detained and severely abused in Israeli prisons.

We have been encouraged by many people along the way to completing this journey. Most of all we mention with gratitude those who met virtually to plan every editorial step of the way, with a sense of commitment, in what we came to call "the Gaza Group." The collective nature of this undertaking is signaled by the names of those who worked tirelessly with us during the process, lifting our spirits in the face of daily atrocity images by a sense of common struggle against this genocide transparently unfolding in real time, given its unmistakable signature by the dehumanizing language of the Israeli political leaders and the tactics of IDF military commanders. The dedication that we have together chosen also expresses our solemn sense of shared purpose.

We would also like to warmly acknowledge the dedication and expert editorial assistance of Diana Collier and of the Clarity staff. It has been a great pleasure for us to work with such a supportive publisher. We are especially grateful for Diana's patience in the face of our delays and for the skills she has displayed in her various roles at Clarity.

Once again it is time for persons of conscience and for the love of humanity to raise their voices to shout "Never again!" but this time to do something by way of action, as well of words. A unifying theme during the discussions at the London Conference was that words are not enough, that action is imperative.

Ahmet Davutoğlu and Richard Falk
November 13, 2024, Türkiye

Declaration of Conscience and Concern of Global Intellectuals on Gaza Genocide

ON NOVEMBER 30, the Government of Israel resumed the genocidal onslaught it inflicted on Palestinians in Gaza after a much overdue but brief "humanitarian pause." In doing so, Israel has ignored the worldwide protests of people as well as the fervent pleas of moral, religious, and political authority figures throughout the world to convert the hostage/ prisoner exchange pause into a permanent ceasefire. The overriding intention was to avert the worsening of the ordeal of the Gazan population. Israel was urged to choose the road to peace not only for humanitarian reasons but also for the sake of achieving real security and respect for both Palestinians and Israelis. Yet now the bodies are again piling up, the Gaza medical system can no longer offer treatment to most of those injured, and threats of widespread starvation and disease intensify daily.

Under these circumstances, this Declaration calls not only for the denunciation of Israel's genocidal assault but also for taking effective action to permanently prevent its repetition. We come together due to the urgency of the moment, which obliges global intellectuals to stand against the ongoing horrific ordeal of the Palestinian people and, most of all, to implore action by those who have the power, and hence the responsibility, to do so. Israel's continuing rejection of a permanent ceasefire intensifies our concerns. The accumulated devastation over many weeks caused by Israel's grossly disproportionate response to the October 7 attack continues to exhibit Israel's vengeful fury. That fury can in no way be excused by the horrendous violence of Hamas against civilians in Israel or inapplicable claims of self-defense against an occupied population.

Indeed, even the combat pause seems to have been agreed upon by the Israeli government mainly to ease pressures from Israeli citizens demanding greater efforts to secure the release of the hostages. The United States government evidently reinforced this pressure as a belated display to the world that it was not utterly insensitive to humanitarian concerns. Even this gesture was undercut before the pause started by the defiant public insistence of Prime Minister Netanyahu that he would resume the war immediately after the pause. It is more appropriate to interpret these seven days without combat as a pause in Israel's genocidal operations in Gaza rather than as a humanitarian pause. If truly humanitarian, it would not have crushed hopes of ending the genocide and conjointly resuming efforts to negotiate the conditions for an enduring and just peace between Israelis and Palestinians.

The revival of this military campaign waged by Israel against the civilian population of Gaza amounts to a repudiation of UN authority, of law and morality in general, and of simple human decency. The collaborative approval of Israel's action by the leading liberal democracies in the Global West, particularly the United States and the United Kingdom, accentuates our anguish and disgust. These governments pride themselves on adherence to the rule of law and yet have so far limited their peacemaking role to PR pressures on Israel to conduct its exorbitant actions in a more discreet manner. Such moves do little more than soften the sharpest edges of Israel's genocidal behavior in Gaza. At the same time, their continued endorsement of Israel's false rationale of self-defense, which is inapplicable in a Belligerent Occupation framework established by the UN in the aftermath of the 1967 War, shielded this brazenly criminal conduct from legal condemnation and political censure at the UN and elsewhere.

We deplore the reality that these governments continue to lend overall support to Israel's announced intention to pursue its combat goals, which entail the commission of severe war crimes that Tel Aviv does not even bother to deny. These crimes include the resumption of intensive bombing and shelling of civilian targets, as well as reliance on the cruel tactics of forced evacuation, the destruction of hospitals, bombings of refugee camps and UN buildings that are sheltering many thousands of civilians and the destruction of entire residential neighborhoods. In addition, Israel has been greenlighting settler-led violence and escalating ethnic cleansing efforts in the West Bank. Given these developments, we urge national governments to embargo and halt all shipments of weapons to Israel, especially the United States and the United Kingdom, which should also withdraw their provocative naval presences from the Eastern Mediterranean; we urge the UN Security Council and General Assembly to so decree without delay.

We also support the Palestinian unconditional right as the indigenous people of the land to give or withhold approval to any proposed solution bearing upon their underlying liberation struggle.

The deteriorating situation poses an extreme humanitarian emergency challenging the UN system to respond with unprecedented urgency. We commend UNICEF for extending desperately needed help to wounded children as well as to children whose parents were killed or seriously injured every

continuing effort. We also commend WHO for doing all in its power to help injured Palestinians, especially pregnant women and children, and to insist as effectively as possible on the immediate reconstruction and reopening of hospitals destroyed and damaged by Israeli attacks. We especially commend UNRWA for continuing the sheltering of many thousands of Palestinians in Gaza displaced by the war and for providing other relief in the face of heavy staff casualties from Israeli repeated bombardment of UN buildings. Beyond this, UNESCO should be implored to recognize threats to religious and cultural sites and give its highest priority to their protection against all manner of violation, especially the Masjid al-Aqsa; the Israeli government should be warned about its unconditional legal accountability for protecting these sites.

We also propose that the UN Human Rights Council should act now to establish a high-profile expert commission of inquiry mandated to ascertain the facts and law arising from the Hamas attack and Israel's military operations in Gaza since October 7, 2023. The commission should offer recommendations in its report pertaining to the responsibility and accountability of principal perpetrators for violations of human rights and humanitarian norms that constitute war crimes and genocide.

We also view the desperation of the situation to engage the responsibility of governments, international institutions, and civil society to act as well as to speak, and use their diplomatic and economic capabilities to the utmost with the objective of bringing the violence in Gaza to an end now!

As signatories of this Declaration, we unequivocally call for an immediate ceasefire and the initiation of diplomatic negotiations under respected and impartial auspices, aimed at terminating Israel's long and criminally abusive occupation of Gaza, the West Bank, and East Jerusalem. This process must be fully respectful of the inalienable right to self-determination of the Palestinian people and take proper account of relevant UN resolutions.

Declaration of Conscience and Concern of Global Intellectuals on Gaza Genocide

— Signatories —

1. Ahmet Davutoğlu, Former Foreign Minister and Prime Minister, Türkiye;
2. Richard Falk, UN Special Rapporteur on the Situation of Human Rights in the Palestinian Territories Occupied since 1967 (2008–2014), Professor of International Law Emeritus, Princeton University;
3. Dr. Moncef Marzouki, Former President of Tunisia;
4. Mahathir Mohamed, Former Prime Minister of Malaysia;
5. Hamad bin Jassim bin Jaber Al Thani, Former Prime Minister and Foreign Minister of Qatar;
6. Georges Abi-Saab, Professor Emeritus, Graduate Institute Geneva and Cairo University, Former UN Advisor to the Secretary Generals of the UN; Former Judge of the International Court of Justice, Egypt;
7. Mairead Maguire, Nobel Peace Laureate (1976), Member of Russell Tribunal, Northern Ireland;
8. Amr Moussa, Former Secretary General of the Arab League, Former Foreign Minister, Member of the UN's High Level Panel on Threats, Challenges and Change for International Peace and Security, Egypt;
9. M. Javad Zarif, Professor, University of Tehran, Former Foreign Minister, Iran;
10. Hamid Albar, Former Foreign Minister, First Chancellor of the Asia e University, Malaysia;
11. Brigette Mabandla, Former Minister of Justice and anti-Apartheid Activist, South Africa;
12. Judith Butler, Professor, University of California at Berkeley; Feminist Studies, USA;
13. Kamal Hossein, Former Foreign Minister, Bangladesh;
14. Paulo Sergia, Professor of Political Science (USP) and Former Minister of Human Rights, Brazil;
15. Chris Hedges, Pulitzer Prize Winning Reporter and Former Middle East Bureau Chief for *The New York Times*, USA;
16. Tu Weiming, Member of UN Group of Eminent Persons for the Dialogue Among Civilizations, Professor Emeritus, Harvard University, USA;

Founding Director of the Institute for Advanced Humanistic Studies, Peking University, China;

17. John Esposito, Professor of International Relations and the Founding Director of the Center for Muslim-Christian Understanding, Georgetown University; Member of High Level Group of the UN Alliance of Civilizations, USA;

18. Arundhati Roy, Author of *God of Small Things*, Human Rights Activist, India;

19. susan abulhawa, Palestinian Novelist, Author of *Mornings in Jenin*, USA;

20. Angela Davis, Berkeley, USA;

21. Hans von Sponeck, Former UN Assistant Secretary-General, Faculty Member at Conflict Research Center, University of Marburg, Germany;

22. Hilal Elver, Professor of International Law, UN Special Rapporteur on Right to Food (2014–2020), Türkiye;

23. Abdullah Ahsan, Professor of History International Islamic University Malaysia and Istanbul Şehir University, USA;

24. Phyllis Bennis, Journalist, Author and Social Activist, Institute of Policy Studies, USA;

25. Noura Erakat, Activist and Professor, Rutgers University, New Brunswick, Co-founder of Jadalliyah, USA;

26. Jomo Kwame Sundaram, Former UN Assistant Secretary-General for Economic Development; Deputy Director UN FAO, Malaysia;

27. Victoria Brittain, Former Foreign Editor of the Guardian, worked closely with anti-Apartheid Movement, Founder of the annual Palestine Festival of Literature, UK;

28. Gayatri Chakravorty Spivak FBA, Professor, Columbia University, received Kyoto Prize in Arts and Philosophy 2012, India;

29. Ali Bardakoğlu, Professor of Theology, Former President of Directorate of Religious Affairs, Türkiye;

30. Mustafa Ceric, Grand Mufti Emeritus of Bosnia, President of the World Bosniak Congress, co-recipient UNESCO Felix Houphouet-Bougny Peace Prize, Bosnia and Herzegovina;

31. Maung Zarni, Human Rights Activist, Member of the Board of Advisors of Genocide Watch, Co-founder of Free Burma Coalition, Free Rohingya Coalition and Forces of Renewal Southeast Asia, Myanmar;

32. Joseph Camilleri, Emeritus Professor, La Trobe University, Co-Convener of SHAPE Melbourne, Australia;

33. Mahmood Mamdani, Herbert Lehman Professor of Government Columbia University, Chancellor of Kampala University, Uganda;

34. Dayan Jayatilleka, Former Ambassador to UN (Geneva), France; Journalist, Sri Lanka;

35. Elisabeth Weber, Professor of German Literature and Philosophy, University of California at Santa Barbara, Germany/USA;

36. Marjorie Cohn, Dean of the Peoples Academy of International Law, Professor Emerita, Thomas Jefferson School of Law, USA;

37. Jan Oberg, Chairman of the Transnational Foundation for Peace and Future Research, Sweden;

38. Ramzy Baroud, Author, Academic, Editor of The Palestine Chronicle, Palestine/ USA;

39. Saree Makdisi, Professor of Comparative Literature at the University of California, Author of Pales-tine Inside Out: An Everyday Occupation, USA;

40. Roger Leger, Retired Professor of Philosophy at the Military College of Saint-Jean, Québec, Canada;

41. Usman Bugaje, Professor, Former Adviser to the Vice President of Nigeria, Nigeria;

42. Chandra Muzaffar, President, International Movement for a Just World (JUST), Malaysia;

43. Avery F. Gordon, Professor Emerita University of California Santa Barbara, USA;

44. Arlene Elizabeth Clemesha, Professor of Contemporary Arab History at the University of São Paulo (USP), Brazil;

45. Ömer Dinçer, Professor, Former Minister of Education, Former President of Şehir University, Türkiye;

46. Fethi Jarray, Former Education Minister, current Chairperson of the National Mechanism on Torture Prevention, Tunisia;

47. Alfred de Zayas, Former UN Independent Expert on the Promotion of a Democratic and Equitable International Order, USA;

48. Walid Joumblatt, Member of Lebanese Parliament, Leader of the Progressive Socialist Party, Lebanon;

49. Elmira Akhmetova, Professor at the Institute of Knowledge Integration in Georgia, Russia;

50. Sami Al-Arian, Professor, Director of Center for Islam and Global Affairs (CIGA) at Istanbul Zaim University, Türkiye;

51. George Sabra, Signatory of the Damascus Declaration (2005), Former President of the Syrian National Council, Syria;

52. Ray McGovern, Activist, Veterans for Peace, Supporter of the anti-war group Not in Our Name, USA;

53. Juan Cole, Professor of History, The University of Michigan, Former Editor of *The International Journal of Middle East Studies*, USA;

54. Penny Green, Professor of Law and Globalization, Director, International State Crime Initiative Queen Mary University of London, UK;

55. Bishnupriya Ghosh, Professor of English and Global Studies, UC Santa Barbara, USA/India;

56. Nader Hashemi, Professor, Director of the Alwaleed Center for Muslim-Christian Understanding, Georgetown University, USA;

57. Ahmed Abbes, Mathematician, Director of Research at the Institut des Hautes Etudes Scientifiques Paris, France, Tunisia;

58. Bhaskar Sarkar, Professor of Film and Media, UC Santa Barbara, USA/India;

59. Akeel Bilgrami, Professor of Philosophy at Columbia University, USA, India;

60. Assaf Kfoury, Mathematician and Professor of Theoretical Computer Science, Boston University, USA;

61. Helena Cobban, Journalist, Author, President of Just World Educational, USA;

62. Bilijana Vankovska, Professor and Head of the Global Chnages Center, Cyril and Mehtodius University, Skopje, Macedonia;

63. David Swanson, Author, Executive Director of World BEYOND War, USA;

64. Radmila Nakarada, Professor, Faculty of Political Science, University of Belgrade; Spokesperson of the Yugoslav Truth and Reconciliation Committee, Serbia;

65. Fredrick S. Heffermehl, Lawyer and Author, Norway;

66. Anis Ahmad, Emeritus Professor and President Riphah International University Islamabad, Pakistan;

67. Lisa Hajjar, Professor, University of California, Santa Barbara, USA;

68. Dr. Sayyid M. Syeed, President Emeritus, Islamic Society of North America, USA;

69. Muhammed al-Ghazzali, Professor, Judge Supreme Court of Pakistan, Pakistan;

70. Syed Azman Syed Ahmad, Former Member of Malaysia Parliament, Chairman of Asia Forum for Peace and Development (AFPAD), Malaysia;

71. Osman Bakar, Al-Ghazali Chair of Epistemology and Civilisational Renewal, International Institute of Islamic Thought and Civilization, Malaysia;

72. Ibrahim M Zein, Professor of Islamic Studies, Qatar Foundation, Qatar;
73. Engin Deniz Akarlı, Professor of History Emeritus, Brown University, Türkiye;
74. Francesco Della Puppa, Ca' Foscari University of Venice; Italy;
75. Julio da Silveira Moreira, Professor, Federal University of Latin-American Integration, Brazil;
76. Nabeel Rajab, Founder and former president of the Gulf Center for Human Rights; Former Deputy Secretary-General of the International Federation for Human Rights, Recipient of the Ion Ratiu Award for Democracy and Human Rights, Bahrain;
77. Feroz Ahmad, Emeritus Professor of History and Internatiıonal Relations, Harvard University, USA, India;
78. Serap Yazıcı, Professor of Constitutional Law, MP, Turkish Parliament, Türkiye;
79. Natalie Brinham, Genocide and Statelessness Scholar, UK;
80. Ayçin Kantoğlu, Author, Türkiye;
81. Dania Koleilat Khatib, ME Scholar and President of RCCP TrackII Organisation, UAE;
82. Imtiyaz Yusuf, Assoc. Prof. Dr., Non-Resident Research Fellow Center for Contemporary Islamic World (CICW), Shenandoah University, USA/Vietnam;
83. Kamar Oniah Kamuruzaman, Former Professor of Comparative Religion, International Islamic University, Malaysia;
84. Ümit Yardım, Former Ambassador of Türkiye to Tehran, Moscow and Vienna, Türkiye;
85. Ahmet Ali Basic, Professor, University of Sarajevo, Bosnia and Herzegovina;
86. Kani Torun, Former Ambassador of Türkiye to Somalia, Former Head of Doctors Worldwide, Member of Parliament, Türkiye;
87. Ermin Sinanovic, Center for Islam in the Contemporary World at Shenandoah University, USA/ Bosnia and Herzegovina;
88. Nihal Bengisu Karaca, Journalist, Türkiye;
89. Alkasum Abba, Emeritus Professor of History, Abuja, Nigeria;
90. Hassan Ahmed Ibrahim, Professor of History and Civilization, Former Dean, Faculty of Arts, University of Khartoum, Sudan;
91. Anwar Alrasheed, Khiam Rehabilitation Center (KRC), The Victims of Torture, Representative of the International Council for Fair Trials and Human Rights in the State of Kuwait and the Gulf Cooperation Council Countries, Kuwait;

92. Mohd Hisham Mohd Kamal, Assoc. Prof. Dr., Ahmad Ibrahim Kulliyyah of Laws, Malaysia/ Indonesia;

93. Syed Arabi Bin Syed Abdullah, Former Rector, International Islamic University, Malaysia;

94. Yusuf Ziya Özcan, Former President of Council of Higher Education, Türkiye;

95. Mohamed Jawhar Hassan, Former Chairman and Chief Executive, Institute of Strategic and International Studies (ISIS) Malaysia;

96. Shad Faruqi, Professor of Law, University of Malaya, Malaysia;

97. Mohammad Ahmadullah Siddiqi, Professor Emeritus of Journalism and Public Relations, Western Illinois University, Macomb IL USA/ India;

98. Mohamed Tarawna, Judge at the Cassation Tribunal, Jordan;

99. Etyen Mahcupyan, Author, Former Chief Advisor to Prime Minister of Türkiye;

100. Khawla Mattar, the Director of the United Nations Information center in Cairo, Former UN Deputy Special Envoy for Syria, Bahrain;

101. Aslam Abdullah, Senior Journalist, USA/India;

102. Stuart Rees, Professor Emeritus, University of Sydney, Australia;

103. Hatem Ete, Academic, Ankara Yıldırım Beyazıt University, Department of Sociology, Türkiye;

104. Karim Makdisi, Professor of Political Science, American University of Beirut, Lebanon;

105. Camilo Pérez-Bustillo, National Taiwan University, Taiwan;

106. Bridget Anderson, Professor of Migration, Mobilities and Citizenship, University of Bristol, UK;

107. William Spence, Professor of Theoretical Physics, Queen Mary University of London, UK;

108. Mohammad Hashim Kamali, Professor of Law, Founding CEO of the International Institute of Advanced Islamic Studies, Malaysia/ Afghanistan;

109. Ferid Muhic, Prof of Philosophy, Krill Metodius University, Macedonia;

110. Frej Fenniche, Former Senior Human Rights Officer/UN, OHCHR, Switzerland;

111. Sevinç Alkan Özcan, Associate Professor, International Relations Department, Ankara Yıldırım Beyazıt University;

112. Sigit Riyanto, Professor, Faculty of Law Universitas, Indonesia;

113. Khaled Khoja, Former President of Syrian National Coalition;

114. Tarık Çelenk, Former Chairman of Ekopolitik, Türkiye;

115. M. Bassam Aisha, Human Rights Expert, Libya;

116. Naceur El-Kefi, Academician and Human Rights Activist, Tunisia;

117. Jean-Daniel Biéler, Former Ambassador, Special Advisor, Human Security Division, Federal Department of Foreign Affairs, Switzerland;

118. Fajri Matahati Muhammadin, Faculty of Law, Universitas Gadjah Mada, Indonesia;

119. Ahmet Okumuş, Chairman of The Foundation for Sciences and Arts (BİSAV), Türkiye;

120. Khan Yasir, Dr., Director In-Charge, Indian Institute of Islamic Studies and Research, India;

121. Mahmudul Hasan, Md., Professor, International Islamic University Malaysia/ Bangladesh;

122. Tara Reynor O'Grady, General Secretary for Human Rights Sentinel, USA;

123. Nurullah Ardıç, Professor of Sociology, Istanbul Technical University, Türkiye;

124. Phar Kim Beng, Founder and CEO of Strategic Pan-Pacific Arena, Malaysia;

125. Dinar Dewi Kania, M.M, .M.Sos, Trisakti Institute of Transportation and Logistics. Jakarta, Indonesia;

126. Mulyadhi Kartanegara, Professor of Islamic philosophy at, Universitas Islam Negeri Syarif Hidayatullah Jakarta, Indonesia;

127. Habib Chirzin, Academic and Human Rights activist, IIIT, Indonesia;

128. Avi Shlaim, Historian, London, UK;

129. Moshé Machover, Mathematician, Socialist activist, London, UK;

130. Maivan Clech Lam, Professor of International Law and Indigenous Peoples Rights, Emeritus, City University of New York, Graduate Center; USA;

131. Paul Wapner, Professor of Environmental Studies, Emeritus, American University; USA;

132. Irene L. Gendzier, Professor Emeritus, Boston University, USA;

133. Erol Katırcıoğlu, Professor, Academic, Türkiye;

134. Bekir Berat Özipek, Professor, Academic, Türkiye;

135. Atilla Yayla, Professor, Academic, Türkiye;

136. Ömer Faruk Gergerlioğlu, Member of Parliament, Türkiye;

137. Cengiz Çandar, Journalist, Türkiye;

138. Ümit Kıvanç, Documentary Filmmaker; Türkiye;

139. Izzeldin Abuelaish, Doctor, Author, Palestine/Canada

Framing Genocide in Gaza

Unveiling the Genocidal Mindset
An Examination of Israel's Genocidal Policies and Western Powers' Complicity

Ahmet Davutoğlu

AS OF THE DATE this article was written, Israel has been committing genocide in Gaza for more than a year. Official reports estimate 40,000 deaths, but
The Lancet, a respected British medical journal, places this figure at 186,000,
or about 7.9% of Gaza's population.[1] Scaled to the global population of 8.1
billion, this would be equivalent to 650 million people. Gaza's infrastructure—homes, hospitals, schools, and religious sites—lies in ruins, reducing
the region to near Stone Age conditions.

Unlike past genocides, this one unfolds in full view of the world.
International leaders, who claim to uphold human values, are either complicit
or passively engaged. The Israeli administration is under an illusion of power
like other historical perpetrators of genocide. This illusion, stemming from
a desire to maintain dominance, blinds them to the damage they inflict on
themselves, not just on their victims.

Albert Einstein's words, in a letter to Selig Brodetsky in 1929, capture
the self-destructive consequences of power: "What I have against your talk is
less what you have done but more what you have left unsaid. What's missing,
specifically, is an analysis of the cause of the reaction of the Arab world
against us—without which the question, in my conviction, cannot be solved.
I believe it is my duty to express my opinion. I'm happy that we have no

---

1 Rasha Khatib, Martin McKee, and Salim Yusuf, "Counting the dead in Gaza:
difficult but essential," *The Lancet* 404, no. 10449 (July 2024): 237–38. https://www.
thelancet.com/journals/lancet/article/PIIS0140-6736(24)01169-3/fulltext

Ahmet Davutoğlu, PhD, is a Turkish professor of Political Science and International
Relations who has had a multifaceted career as an academician, political advisor, diplomat, and politician. Professor Davutoğlu served as Chief Foreign Policy
Advisor to the Prime Minister of Türkiye from November 2002 to May 2009, and
later served as Prime Minister of Türkiye's 62nd, 63rd and 64th Governments.

power. If national pigheadedness proves strong enough, then we will knock our brains out as we deserve."[2]

Israel is not just demolishing Gaza's physical structures; it is dismantling the psychological foundation that justified its existence. A vast intellectual framework—built on institutes, museums, research, literature, films, and art about Jewish suffering—disintegrates with every Palestinian child killed and every school or hospital destroyed.

By destroying Gaza, Israel also erodes the "metaphysics of the oppressed" that once underpinned its legitimacy. The gravest harm a previously oppressed people can do to themselves is to become oppressors. Every "formerly oppressed" people that oppresses others destroys their own narrative. Today, with this genocide, not only are Gazans being uprooted from their homes and lands, but Israel is also severing itself from the conscience of humanity.

Albert Einstein's 1929 letter to Chaim Weizmann, President of the World Zionist Congress, resonates today: "If we are not able to find a way to honest cooperation and honest pacts with the Arabs, then we have learned nothing during our two thousand years of sufferings, and deserve the fate which will befall us."[3] Beneath the rubble of Gaza lie not only Palestinian children's bodies but also the psychological legacy of Jewish children killed in Nazi gas chambers.

While Gaza's physical destruction proceeds, a narrative of resistance is being inscribed in humanity's conscience. As the Israeli army attempts to erase "the story of the past" with its technology, Gaza's children write "the story of today." Worldwide, people of all races, religions, and colors are transforming this conflict's meaning. Regardless of the terminology used by Israeli-influenced international media, this conflict is no longer between Israel and Hamas, Israel and Palestine, Israel and Arabs, Israel and Iran or Israel and Muslims; it is between Israel and humanity.

This realization is shared by a significant group of Israeli intellectuals, traditional Jewish communities, and prominent Jewish voices who oppose the genocide, underscoring Israel's break with humanity's conscience and traditional Jewish morality. David Livingstone Smith's reaction to Netanyahu's "Bloodthirsty Monster" rhetoric exemplifies this Jewish intellectual dissent: "I think that this is extremely ominous. This is not because I am sympathetic to Hamas. I am not. It is not because I am an anti-Semite. I am not. In fact, notwithstanding my very Christian name, I am Jewish. (...) The point that

---

2 Fred Jerome, *Einstein on Israel and Zionism: His Provocative Ideas About the Middle East* (New York: St. Martin Press, 2009), 86–87.

3 Jerome, 78

I want to make here—the point that leads me to regard Netanyahu's language as so ominous—is that when we dehumanize others as monsters, we essentialize them in a particular way. (…) Given this pattern of thinking, these racial others, these monsters, must be utterly obliterated—destroyed without quarter. Characterizing the dehumanized other as "bloodthirsty" adds to the picture. A bloodthirsty entity is a vampire—a being that wants to drink human blood. (…) Ironically, it is the basis of the centuries-old "blood libel" that Jews consumed the blood of Christian children."[4]

The genocide in Gaza is under review at the International Court of Justice, but genocide is not simply one group's violence toward another with the intent to annihilate. It is rooted in a mindset that has re-emerged across history and geographies. This mentality, this article argues, enables even genocide survivors to become genocide perpetrators.

Genocide research has developed vast theoretical frameworks, yet Israeli Defense Minister Yoav Gallant's statements during the Gaza assault starkly reveal the core genocidal mindset: "I have released all restraints. …We are fighting human animals. … Gaza won't return to what it was before. …We will eliminate everything."[5]

Netanyahu also employed similar rhetoric, referring to a "battle against the bloodthirsty monsters who have risen up to destroy us."[6] This terminology is not a transient reaction to Hamas's October 7 attacks; rather, it reflects a persistent mindset. Indeed, even in times of relative peace (February 10, 2016), Netanyahu used the same racist and dehumanizing language against Palestinians: "In our neighborhood, we need to protect ourselves from wild beasts."[7]

Phrases like "human animals/wild beasts/bloodthirsty monsters" expose the ontological foundation of genocide. "No restraint" signals methodology of boundlessness, and "eliminate everything" reveals the end goal. Understanding these parameters is essential to grasp the genocide in Gaza.

This analysis is also critical to unpacking the complicity of those who support or ignore this genocide. Legal measures alone are insufficient to

---

4 David Livingstone Smith, "From Human Animals to Bloodthirsty Monsters
The rhetoric of dehumanization in Israel's war against Hamas," *Dehumanization Matters* (Substack blog), October 15, 2023. https://davidlivingstonesmith.substack.com/p/from-human-animals-to-bloodthirsty

5 ICJ Order of 26 January 2024, Document Number 192-20240126-ORD-01-00-EN, p. 17; no. 52 (ICJ, 17, Article 52). https://www.icj-cij.org/node/203447

6 Statement by PM Netanyahu, PM Office, October 25, 2023. https://www.gov.il/en/pages/spoke-statement251023

7 MEE Staff, "Netanyahu calls Arabs 'wild beasts' while announcing Israel wall plan," *Middle East Eye,* February 10, 2016. https://www.middleeasteye.net/news/netanyahu-calls-arabs-wild-beasts-while-announcing-israel-wall-plan

prevent genocide. Since World War II, international norms have failed to stop mass atrocities in Rwanda, Myanmar, Bosnia, and now Gaza. Without addressing the genocidal mindset, preventing future crimes will remain elusive.

Unveiling the Mindet of Genocide

Ontological Base of Genocidal Mindset: "Human Animals"

The definitions of Palestinians as "human animals" by Gallant and as "wild beasts/bloodthirsty monsters" by Netanyahu indicate that the massacres in Gaza have reached the level of genocide. Such definitions highlight the impossibility of legitimizing genocide without establishing an ontological exclusion based on existential differences among people.

David Livingstone Smith describes this phenomenon, seen across various societies throughout history: "The act of conceiving of other human beings as subhuman creatures is not limited to a single culture or just one historical period… The evidence is overwhelming that we human beings periodically view other members of our species as not really people at all, but rather as less-than-human beings that it is morally permissible, or even obligatory, to harm or to kill."[8]

The International Court of Justice references a 16 November 2023 press release by 37 UN Special Rapporteurs and Experts, who expressed alarm over "genocidal and dehumanizing rhetoric" from senior Israeli officials. The United Nations Committee on the Elimination of Racial Discrimination (27 October 2023) noted a "highly concerned about the sharp increase in racist hate speech and dehumanization directed at Palestinians since 7 October."[9] These observations are crucial for identifying the mental framework underpinning genocide.

The notion of "ontological inequality," from ancient Aryan caste systems to modern racism, legitimizes the extermination of one race by another. This idea leads to categorizing communities as "subjects of existence" and others as "objects" whose right to live can be annulled if they do not comply. Terms like "master/superior race" and "chosen people" reflect this mentality.

The principle that "all human beings are born free and equal in dignity and rights," in the Universal Declaration of Human Rights, is founded on "absolute ontological equality." Achieving this principle was challenging.

---

8 David Livingstone Smith, *Making Monsters: The Uncanny Power of Dehumanization* (Cambridge, Mass. & London: Harvard University Press, 2021), xii–xiii.

9 ICJ Order of 26 January 2024, Document Number 192-20240126-ORD-01-00-EN, p. 18; no. 53 (ICJ, 18, Article 53). https://www.icj-cij.org/node/203447

Understanding its significance requires analyzing another concept integral to the mental infrastructure leading to World War II: *Under-Man/Untermensch*. Lothrop Stoddard, who used this term a quarter-century before the Universal Declaration of Human Rights, based the struggle between "Man" and "Under-Man" on ontological inequality: "The idea of 'natural equality' is one of the most pernicious delusions that has ever afflicted mankind...Nature knows no equality. The most cursory evaluation of natural phenomena reveals the presence of a Law of Inequality as universal and as inflexible as the Law of Gravitation." [10]

Stoddard warned white people in the "Man" category about the threat posed by Jews and blacks in the "Under Man" category in his work *The Revolt Against Civilization: The Menace of the Under-man*. After its translation into German as *Der Kulturumsturz: Die Drohung des Untermenschen* in 1925[11], the concept of "Untermensch" became central to Nazi racial discrimination theory, particularly through Nazi theorist Alfred Rosenberg.

While these theories may seem archaic, their relevance persists. The Apartheid regime in South Africa continued nearly half a century after the Declaration, and discriminatory policies in the USA lasted for decades: "This status is similar to that of African Americans in the southern United States until 1964. Legal victimization of the Jews, as of African Americans, was justified because it was condoned by the law. Consequently, it was "legal" to kill an African American in the South; even during the civil rights years, killings of blacks occurred for which no one was convicted. For example, on August 28, 1955, Emmett Till, a young African American from Chicago who was visiting his relatives in Mississippi, was killed for talking to a white woman."[12]

The rise of extreme right-wing populist movements, based on exclusionary frameworks targeting various ethnic and religious communities in the United States and Europe, is significant. Gallant's definition of "human animals" serves as a chilling warning.

It is no coincidence that South Africa reacted most sensitively to the Gaza genocide. President Ramaphosa and Foreign Minister Pandor have personally experienced apartheid's racist historical reality. What stands out even more here is the support by Israel, which was founded supposedly to

---

10 Lothrop Stoddard, *The Revolt Against Civilization: The Menace of the Under-man* (New York: Charles Scribner's Sons, 1923), 30, 31.

11 Lothrop Stoddard, *Der Kulturumsturz: Die Drohung des Untermenschen* (München: J. F. Lehmanns Verlag, 1925).

12 Herbert Hirsch, *Genocide and the Politics of Memory* (Chapel Hill and London: University of North Carolina Press, 1995), 101.

erase the traces of centuries-old ghetto apartheid history, for the apartheid regime in South Africa.

The definition of "human animals" is even harsher and more exclusionary than "under-man." While "under-man" indicates a categorical differentiation between human beings, "human animals" suggests a category between humans and animals. From the perspective of ontological inequality, the difference between "Untermensch" (inferior humans) and "human animals" lies in justification: the former has a pseudo-scientific basis, while the latter has a theological one. Untermensch emerged from evolutionary natural selection. Übermensch, a concept of Nietzsche's misused by Nazi theorists, described a master race monopolizing humanity's future through pseudo-scientific eugenics.

The entire world was seen as the natural "promised land" for this Übermensch. The fate of the *Untermensch* was to be enslaved or liquidated in their own private spaces, without mixing with the Übermensch. Exclusionary ideologies based on ontological inequality commonly perceive different communities living in their "promised land" as a "Question."

It is not a coincidence that, during the time Nazis developed the exclusionary ideological framework based on the "Jewish Question" in Europe, some Zionist leaders also discussed an "Arab Question" in British-mandated Palestine. For example, Serig Bordestky's letter to Einstein on December 4, 1929, mentions: "I have been very much affected by your remark to me at the end of my speech expressing obvious disapproval of my statement on the Arab Question." [13] The apartheid regime in South Africa was built on a similar mentality.

The subconscious behind the term "human animals" attempts to legitimize ontological inequality on theological grounds, deviating from Jewish monotheism, which posits that all humanity descends from Adam and Eve. If humans arose from a single pair, what existential category do "human animals" represent?

A significant consequence of the genocide in Gaza is that this ground of theological legitimacy will be scrutinized. The mental framework of Netanyahu and his team is an exclusionary theological state dominance that denies the existence of another people with both ontological and political equality. This divide underlies the insistence on defining Israel as a "Jewish State" and prevents a two-state solution.

By opposing the idea of a "Jewish state" and advocating for a binational state based on equal rights with Arabs, the predictions of intellectuals like Judah Magnes, Martin Buber, Hannah Arendt, and Albert Einstein have been

---

13 Jerome, 83

vindicated by the genocide that has occurred. As early as January 1946, Einstein testified before the Anglo-American Commission of Inquiry on Palestine, arguing against the idea of a Jewish state: "I am firmly convinced that a rigid demand for a Jewish State will have only undesirable results for us."[14]

This highlights the significant divide between Israeli politicians who advocate for a two-state solution grounded in ontological and political equality, and radical/racist Israeli politicians who view Israel not as an equal nation-state but as a divinely ordained entity. Netanyahu's display of a map at the UN General Assembly on September 22, 2023, declaring all of Palestine, including Gaza and the West Bank, as Israeli territory, violated all UN norms and resolutions. This map, coinciding with the borders drawn for *Eretz Israel* in Hugo Löwy's work *Vom Judenhass zum Judenstadt*[15] ("From Jew-Hatred to Jewish State"), effectively ignores Palestinians' right to statehood. Netanyahu's map was a declaration that the West Bank and Gaza, part of the land promised to Israel, belong to the "Übermensch/Chosen Nation" and will never be abandoned to "Untermensch/Human Animals." Gallant articulated this mentality with his definition of "human animals."

Lasting peace cannot be established with borders and maps based on theological legitimizations stemming from the belief in the "Chosen Nation" and the "Promised Land." Those who claim natural sovereignty "from river to sea" (from the Jordan River to the Mediterranean) based on the belief in the "promised land" could tomorrow, with reference to the Torah (specifically in the Book of Genesis; 15:18),[16] claim sovereignty over "from river to river" (from the Nile to the Euphrates). It is evident that such a claim, which would threaten the borders of at least six countries, would destroy the already fragile regional order.

Israeli leaders may argue this concern is unfounded, citing recent normalization processes as evidence. However, Israel's persistent expansionist policies since 1948 and ongoing colonization by settlers in the West Bank despite the normalization processes of the periods such as the Camp David and Oslo processes have justifiably raised apprehension among regional

---

14 Jerome, 152.

15 Hugo Löwy, *Vom Judenhass zum Judenstadt* [*From Jew-Hatred to Jewish State*] (Wien: Verlag der Renaissance, 1948), 70.

16 "**18** On that day the LORD made a covenant with Abram and said, "To your descendants I give this land, from the Wadi (or river) of Egypt to the great river, the Euphrates— **19** the land of the Kenites, Kenizzites, Kadmonites, **20** Hittites, Perizzites, Rephaites, **21** Amorites, Canaanites, Girgashites and Jebusites" (Genesis 15: 18–21). https://www.biblegateway.com/passage/?search=Genesis%2015

countries. The fundamental question for Israeli politics today is whether it will adhere to international law based on the absolute ontological equality of people and international norms or continue as a theological state on the onto-logical inequality of "humans and subhumans," or "chosen and not-chosen."

The genocides carried out by the Babylonians, Romans, and Nazis against the Jews involved no law, as they saw Jews as a "cursed people" falling into the "under man" category. The Jewish resistance to this men-tality was a struggle for human dignity based on ontological equality. The current political irrationality of Israeli leaders, viewing neighboring people as "human animals," raises a critical issue of self-criticism. To illustrate this, consider how Charlie Chaplin, who achieved a psychological victory for human dignity by satirizing Hitler, would react to Netanyahu and Gallant's actions against Gaza's children today.

In summary, Netanyahu and Gallant see Palestinians not as legitimate participants in peace or conflict, but as "human animals" to be eradicated. Real peace cannot be achieved unless this mentality is overcome by being totally repudiated.

Methodological Aspect of Genocidal Mindset: "No Restraint"

Gallant's phrase "no restraint" extends the doctrine of ontological inequality, granting Israeli security forces freedom from humanitarian norms or legal constraints in conflict. This defies not just Gaza but also the founda-tions of international law, which presuppose equal recognition of opposing parties. In war, laws derive meaning when both sides are equals. However, ideologies that classify people as "human" and "subhuman" remove the sub-human group from legal protection, freeing the superior from ethical limits. Those combating "subhumans," "undermen," "wild beasts," or "bloodthirsty monsters" acknowledge no ethical or legal limitations.

Even those committing genocide recognize human nature, but only when convinced their enemies are "subhuman" or "wild beasts" do they embrace a "no restraint" approach. The human conscience resists harming equals but accepts extermination once the enemy is dehumanized.

Who, then, are Gaza's "subhumans"? Are they extraterrestrial invaders or creatures from dark, unknown realms? Or are they a people who have inhabited these lands for millennia, the rightful owners until the establish-ment of Israel?

When adversaries in conflict are viewed as equals, the legitimacy of the "no restraint" assertion evaporates. The definition of "subhumans" serves as the psychological foundation for the "no restraint" doctrine. Statements by Israeli Minister Israel Katz, quoted by the ICJ, reflect this mindset: " All civilian populations in Gaza are instructed to evacuate immediately. We shall prevail. They shall receive no water or provisions until they leave this world."[17]

This mindset predates October 7. Gilad Sharon, son of Ariel Sharon, voiced it 12 years ago: "Gazans are not innocent; they elected Hamas. They are not hostages; they chose freely and must endure the consequences. Gaza should lack electricity, gasoline, and movement…While images from Gaza might be unpleasant, victory would swiftly follow, sparing our soldiers and civilians. There is no middle ground."[18] Israeli President Isaac Herzog recently echoed the same argument on October 12, 2023, blaming all Gazans collectively, denying civilians' innocence and arguing they should have opposed Hamas: "Unequivocally, it is an entire nation out there that is responsible. It is not true this rhetoric about civilians not aware, not involved. It is absolutely not true. They could have risen up. They could have fought against that evil regime." [19]

This genocidal mindset hinges on "collective guilt," condemning all Gazans for electing Hamas. But the 2006 elections, held under Israeli occupation and backed by the U.S. and international community, were widely considered free and fair. According to the CRS Report for Congress, "The election was monitored by 17,268 domestic observers, supported by 900 accredited international monitors. The conduct of the election was widely deemed free and fair," and "The Bush Administration acknowledged the outcome of the Palestinian legislative elections and commended the PA for conducting free and fair elections."[20] The "no restraint" methodology of genocide requires the deliberate disregard of two clear facts: that 70% of those currently living in Gaza have ancestors who were forced to migrate from within present-day Israeli borders, and that Palestinians, like all peoples, have the right to determine their own future based on "International Covenant on Civil and Political Rights"[21]

---

17 ICJ Order of 26 January 2024, Document Number 192-20240126-ORD-01-00-EN, p. 18; no. 52 (ICJ, 18, Article 52). https://www.icj-cij.org/node/203447

18 Gilad Sharon, "A decisive conclusion is necessary," *The Jerusalem Post,* November 18, 2012. https://www.jpost.com/opinion/op-ed-contributors/a-decisive-conclusion-is-necessary

19 ICJ Order of 26 January 2024, Document Number 192-20240126-ORD-01-00-EN, p. 17; no. 52 (ICJ, 17, Article 52). https://www.icj-cij.org/node/203447

20 Aaron D. Pina (2006). "Palestinian Elections – February 9, 2006" (PDF). Congressional Research Service, The Library of Congress, 14–15.

21 "All peoples have the right of self-determination. By virtue of that right they freely determine their political status and freely pursue their economic, social and cultural development." https://2covenants.ohchr.org/About-ICCPR.html

Within this ideological conditioning, Israeli soldiers did not hesitate to implement the "no restraint" directive received from their superiors, as confirmed by the International Court of Justice (ICJ): Hospitals, schools, refugee camps, and ambulances were indiscriminately bombed to produce complete destruction; tens of thousands of children, elderly, and women of an age not subject to criminal accusation were killed; and hundreds of journalists were killed, apparently under the presumed belief that they would document these crimes.

The Purpose of Genocidal Mindset: "Total Destruction, Extermination"

The ultimate goal of the exclusionary and boundless method of destruction based on the ontological assumption of inequality that forms the foundation of the genocide mentality is clear: the mass murder and annihilation of the excluded communities. The language of extermination employed for this purpose is so destructive that ordinary individuals can over time be transformed into agents of genocidal death: "If the twentieth century is any indication, the end may result from words used to motivate, justify, and rationalize murder on a scale unprecedented in human history. Words can kill—or at least motivate a person to kill. It is through language that the primal impulses, the likes and dislikes, the hatreds and enmities, the stereotypes and degrading and dehumanizing characterizations of those who are not desirable or are rivals for political or economic power or status, are transmitted."[22]

From this perspective, the similarities between the language of the Nazis and the language used by today's perpetrators of genocide in Gaza are chilling. The Nazis' characterization of Jews sent to gas chambers as "vermin," and the descriptions by Gallant and Netanyahu of Palestinians as "human animals" and "wild beasts," serve as legitimizing tools for the goal of "total extermination": "Hitler followed Luther and other proponents of Aryan superiority in the belief in a worldwide Jewish conspiracy and the view that Jews were 'vermin.' It is important that they did not say Jews were like vermin—they were vermin. This assertion was repeated in Nazi propaganda throughout the period of the mass murder."[23]

Former Deputy Speaker of the Knesset Moshe Feiglin's reference to Hitler regarding the purpose of the Gaza genocide clearly illustrates the shared logic of different genocidal ideologies: "As Hitler said, 'I can't live if one Jew is left,' we can't live here if one 'Islamo-Nazi' remains in Gaza." Some may think that by "Islamo-Nazi," Feiglin is referring to Hamas or

22 Hirsch, 97
23 Hirsch, 102

similar groups, rather than Palestinians as a whole. However, a speech he made before the 2019 elections clearly shows that the ultimate goal is the complete cleansing of Palestinian territories from Palestinians: "Don't talk to me about international law, because there is no such thing. You know, the minute you use the word 'Palestinian,' you stop saying the truth. Because there is no Palestinian nation, and they know it ... once you said that this is Palestine, and once you said there are Palestinian people in this Palestine— once you said that you created something that does not appear in reality. And now there is no solution."[24]

The fundamental question here is what the ultimate goal of Zionism, the founding ideology of Israel, truly is. Many Israeli statesmen and thinkers, most notably Ben Gurion who stated, "Zionism in its essence is a revolution-ary movement," have portrayed Zionism as a "perpetual revolution" or an "unfinished revolution." From pre-Zionist thinkers like Nachman Krochmal, Heinrich Graetz, and Leon Pinsker to those who transformed Zionism into a political ideology like Moses Hess and Theodore Herzl, and from Israel's founding fathers to the current political elite what is the ultimate goal of this ongoing revolution? In terms of those implementing the Gaza genocide what stage does this genocide represent in the ultimate goal of the "unfinished revolution"? Using the concepts employed by its pioneers and followers, for Leon Pinsker, it was a matter of *Auto-emancipation* (1882);[25] for Theodore Herzl, it was the establishment of a *Judenstaat*[26] (1896); for Ben Gurion, it was a revolution progressing from class to nation[27]; and for Menahem Begin, it was an expansionist ideal realized by "war of choice." What does the Gaza genocide mean for Netanyahu and Gallant in this ideological journey of Zionism?

The classification made by Anita Shapira in her work titled *Land and Power: The Zionist Resort to Force, 1881–1948*[28], inspired by Menahem Begin's use of the "war of choice" concept for the 1981 Lebanon invasion, could serve as a starting point for us in this matter. For Shapira, viewing war not as a necessity but as a matter of choice represents a revolutionary shift

---

24 "Former Israeli MK Quotes Hitler While Discussing Gaza War," *Haaretz*, June 16, 2024. https://www.haaretz.com/israel-news/2024-06-16/ty-article/former-israeli-mk-quotes-hitler-while-discussing-gaza-war/00000190-224f-d231-a1b2-e65f76fe0000

25 Leon Pinsker, *Autoemancipation! Mahnruf an seine Stammesgenossen* (Berlin: Commissions-Verlag von W. Iasleib, 1882).

26 Theodor Herzl, *Der Judenstaat: Versuch Einer Modernen Lösung der Judenfrage* (Leipzig und Wien: M.Brettenstein's Verlags-Buchhandlung Wien, 1896).

27 David Ben Gurion, Mi-maamad le-am (From Class to Nation), Tel Aviv, 1933

28 Anita Shapira, *Land and Power: The Zionist Resort to Force, 1881–1948* (London: Oxford University Press, 1992).

from a defensive ethos to an offensive ethos in Jewish history. According to Shapira, this argument of "choice of war" was a major departure from previous Zionist ideology in which "war was always viewed as unavoidable, a matter of necessity and not of choice."[29] She emphasized that the transition from the passive, noncombatant position of Jews from the Roman period in 135 AD until the twentieth century to the new ethos of the "fighting Jew" was crucial in the formation of Israel. Before the establishment of Israel, during the Yishuv period, a mindset transformation occurred from a defensive ethos to an offensive ethos, which also laid the intellectual groundwork for current developments. During the Yishuv period, debates shifted from the principle of "Thou shalt not kill" to the slogan "Whoever comes to kill you—kill him first."[30]

These principles and slogans are now far behind. Those carrying out the Gaza genocide today definitely do not see themselves as limited to an "offensive ethos." The mindset attempting to legitimize the Gaza genocide is undergoing a new process of transformation. Netanyahu, Gallant, and Feiglin have formulated a collective annihilation goal resembling Nazi rhetoric, where the killing of children and pregnant women who pose no threat to anyone forms the basis of a genocidal mindset: those who potentially may pose a threat in the future should be killed before they grow up or even before they are born. This understanding of eliminating potential threats is no different from the genocidal mindset rooted in historical events like Pharaoh's order to kill Jewish male infants during the time of Moses or the sending of innocent Jewish children to gas chambers by the Nazis as potential threats.

During the Yishuv period, there was a transition from the understanding that "Zionism could be made reality by a gradual process and without historical breakthroughs that by their very nature tend to be bloody"[31] to the view that "harm to Arabs as individuals was enjoined; yet expulsion, an act on the plane of national confrontation, was permissible."[32] This transition led to the stage where the entirety of the promised land, starting from Gaza, was to be cleansed of Palestinians for the preservation of Israel's Jewish state identity.

Einstein's protest letter to New Times written before Menahem Begin's visit to the United States in December 1948 not only highlights his scientific foresight but also his political insight, as it warns that the transition to an "offensive ethos" could ultimately lead to a mindset reminiscent of Nazi methods:

---

29 Shapira, vii.
30 Shapira, 266
31 Shapira, 130
32 Shapira, 357

Among the most disturbing political phenomena of our time is the emergence in the newly created state, of Israel of the "Freedom Party" (Tnuat Haherut), a political party closely akin in its organization, methods, political philosophy and social appeal to the Nazi and Fascist parties. It was formed out of the membership and following of the former Irgun Zvai Leumi, a terrorist, right-wing, chauvinist organization in Palestine. The current visit of Menachem Begin, leader of this party, to the United States is obviously calculated to give the impression of American support for his party in the coming Israeli elections, and to cement political ties with conservative Zionist elements in the United States. Several Americans of national repute have lent their names to welcome his visit. It is inconceivable that those who oppose fascism throughout the world, if correctly informed as to Mr. Begin's political record and perspectives, could add their names and support to the movement he represents...Today they speak of freedom, democracy and anti-imperialism, whereas until recently they openly preached the doctrine of the Fascist state. It is in its actions that the terrorist party betrays its real character; from tis past actions we can judge what it may be expected to do in the future.[33]

Similarly, the shift from the traditional "war of necessity" principle to Begin's "war of choice" extended to the understanding of "genocide of choice" based on the assumption of "I will eliminate them before they eliminate me" during the Gaza genocide. The genocidal mindset inherently operates on a "zero-sum game" basis of "all or nothing." It views the absolute gain of one side as contingent upon the absolute annihilation of the other, rejecting the Oslo process's envisioned "two-state solution" or alternative proposals for a shared democratic state advocated by peaceful Israeli intellectuals.

Ultimately, all these mindset transformations signify indicators of a "No Ethos" era. So, the Gaza genocide can be seen as transition from "Offensive Ethos" to "No Ethos," where no moral boundaries or human norms are recognized in the aim of annihilating the opponent. During this "No Ethos" era, there is no real commitment to international legal principles or the principle of *pacta sunt servanda*. Indeed, during the ongoing Gaza genocide, the Israeli Knesset voted with an absolute majority against two-state solution declaring that the establishment of a Palestinian State "an existential danger to the state

---

33 Jerome, 213–14.

of Israel" on 18th of July 2024.[34] This resolution signifies not only a rejection of peace with Palestinians but also an official declaration of the demise of the Oslo agreement.

The disaster that the "No Ethos" period will bring is clear: total destruction, total ethnic cleansing, total elimination and total extermination. The "No Ethos" period of genocide experienced in Gaza, if emulated in other regions plagued by ethnic and sectarian conflicts, could lead humanity into a new global war and chaos. The United Nations has failed to prevent these atrocities, and global powers that should be activating UN mechanisms are instead complicit in this genocide, creating a deeply alarming situation.

Unveiling the Mindset of Complicity

The Gaza genocide is distinctive partly due to the open complicity of global actors claiming to represent the international order. Unlike past genocides in Rwanda, Bosnia, and Myanmar, key western powers not only fail to condemn Israel but actively support its actions. Israel's "privileged" status and the perception of Palestinians as "second class" people reflects an underlying mindset of "ontological inequality." This worldview, which aligns with Israeli interests and marginalizes Palestinians, must be questioned and repudiated to establish an objective, genocide-preventing international order based on the firm declaration of "never again."

First, let us present some examples to reveal the discursive background of this complicity mindset, and then we will try to understand the subconscious leading to this mindset.

Joe Biden's remarks following his meeting with Prime Minister Benjamin Netanyahu and Israel's war cabinet on October 21, 2023, highlight a clear stance of complicity: "I don't believe you have to be a Jew to be a Zionist, and I am a Zionist." [35] This statement can be seen as an endorsement of the actions being taken by the Israeli army, signaling tacit approval of the ongoing operations in Gaza. By affirming Zionism—a political ideology centered around "Jewish dominance in the promised land from the Nile to the Euphrates"—Biden risks deepening the psychological divide between the U.S. and the region's peoples, including Muslim American citizens. His

34 Holly Johnston and Nada Al Taher, "Israel's Knesset passes resolution rejecting two-state solution," *The National,* July 18, 2024. https://www.thenationalnews.com/news/mena/2024/07/18/two-state-israel-knesset-palestine/

35 Matt Spetalnick, Jeff Mason, Steve Holland, and Patricia Zengerle, "'I am a Zionist': How Joe Biden's lifelong bond with Israel shapes war policy," *Reuters,* October 21, 2023. https://www.reuters.com/world/us/i-am-zionist-how-joe-bidens-lifelong-bond-with-israel-shapes-war-policy-2023-10-21/

words seem to convey a message to the Israeli forces: "Do as you please; I stand with you," thus implicating him in the act of complicity.

Emboldened by Biden's statement, Netanyahu sought to legitimize his actions, which have been identified as war crimes and genocide by the ICJ and ICC, during his speech to the U.S. Congress. He expressed gratitude, saying: "I thank President Biden for his heartfelt support for Israel after the savage attack on October 7. He rightly called Hamas 'sheer evil.' He dispatched two aircraft carriers to the Middle East to deter a wider war. And he came to Israel to stand with us during our darkest hour, a visit that will never be forgotten. President Biden and I have known each other for over forty years. I want to thank him for half a century of friendship to Israel and for being, as he says, a proud Zionist. Actually, he says, a proud Irish American Zionist."[36]

Similarly, German Chancellor Scholz linked Germany's national identity to Israel's security, emphasizing an unwavering commitment rooted in Holocaust guilt: "Israel's security is part of Germany's raison d'état. Our own history, our responsibility deriving from the Holocaust, makes it our permanent duty to stand up for the existence and security of the State of Israel. This responsibility guides us."[37]

> UK Prime Minister Rishi Sunak also displayed a similar stance, selectively expressing concern for Israeli suffering while omitting mention of Palestinian casualties. At the end of six months during which tens of thousands of Palestinian women, children, and civilians have been killed and injured, most of the population has been displaced, and schools, hospitals, and refugee camps have been devastated, UK Prime Minister Rishi Sunak stated, "Six months later, Israeli wounds are still unhealed"[38]. Families still mourn and hostages are still held by Hamas." In response, Sacha Deshmukh, Chief Executive of Amnesty International UK, highlighted the hypocrisy and complicity of Western leaders when the issue involves Israel:

---

36 "We're protecting you: Full text of Netanyahu's address to Congress," *Times of Israel*, July 25, 2024. https://www.timesofisrael.com/were-protecting-you-full-text-of-netanyahus-address-to-congress/

37 Policy statement by Olaf Scholz, Chancellor of the Federal Republic of Germany and Member of the German Bundestag, on the situation in Israel, October 12, 2023, in Berlin. https://www.bundeskanzler.de/bk-en/news/policy-statement-by-olaf-scholz-2230254

38 AFP and TOI Staff, "Six months since Oct. 7, British PM Sunak says 'terrible' Israel-Hamas war 'must end,'" *Times of Israel*, April 7, 2024. https://www.timesofisrael.com/liveblog_entry/six-months-since-oct-7-british-pm-sunak-says-terrible-israel-hamas-war-must-end/

It is right that Rishi Sunak has expressed horror at the cruel
and brutal crimes against Israeli civilians committed by Hamas a
week ago, which showed a chilling disregard for life and included
war crimes. But for the Prime Minister not to mention the
Palestinian civilians killed due to Israeli airstrikes or include any
call for all parties to the conflict to uphold international humanitarian law, is deeply troubling.[39]

These statements raise critical questions on complicity: Why have some
countries openly supported Israel in the face of the Gaza genocide, committing complicity in this crime? Furthermore, why have almost the same
countries seen Israel, since its establishment, as a state with a special status
that allows it to violate all international legal norms with impunity? Why are
the UN rules applicable to others ignored when it comes to Israel? How did
Europe's "Jewish Question" evolve into an "Israeli Privilege" that exempts
Israel from accountability and get exported to the Middle East after World
War II?

Western complicity in the Gaza genocide can be analyzed through psycho-historical, socio-political, theological, and geopolitical contexts.

Psychological Context: "Sense of Guilt"

History is not composed solely of archival records. It is perhaps directly
shaped by the collective memory passed down from generation to generation.
If the political elites of one or several states adopt a stance that diverges
from the general conscience of humanity to the extent of criminally complicit
genocide being carried out in Gaza before the eyes of the world, the reason for
this should be sought in a common sentiment within the collective memories
of these elites. The psycho-historical background, laden with a deep sense of
guilt is the most important factor behind the complicity crimes committed by
Western leaders—especially those of Germany, the USA, the UK, France,
and Italy—in the face of the Gaza genocide.

When examining the critical junctures of Jewish history in terms of massacres, exiles, and exclusion, it becomes evident that the "Jewish Question"
is entirely a European phenomenon. The greatest theological and socio-political tension from the great exile in AD 137 until the establishment of Israel in
1948 was between Jews and Christians, with Muslims being almost entirely

---

39 "UK/Israel-OPT: Rishi Sunak's failure to mention Palestinian death toll
'deeply troubling,'" Amnesty International UK Press Release, Oct. 14, 2023.
https://www.amnesty.org.uk/press-releases/ukisrael-opt-rishi-sunaks-failure-mention-
palestinian-death-toll-deeply-troubling

uninvolved. Jewish persecution in Europe, culminating in events like the Holocaust, created a deep-seated guilt that now influences Western policies toward Israel. In contrast, such issues had no theological, political, or economic basis in Muslim societies.

For example, the 622 AD agreement[40] between Prophet Muhammad and Jewish communities in Medina granted Jews rights and equality, setting a precedent for later Muslim states. Jews in Islamic territories enjoyed religious autonomy and legal protections, unlike in Europe, where ghettos and exclusions were imposed. In stark contrast, after 557 years, in 1179, the Third Lateran Council convened by Pope Alexander III in Rome formalized restrictions on Jews in Europe, banning them from public office and Christian households, reinforcing social and economic isolation.[41] Such decrees typified medieval European attitudes and laid the groundwork for future discrimination.

During the time of the Third Lateran Council's decisions, the Jewish thinker Maimonides served as Saladin's family doctor and advisor to his vizier, al-Qadi al-Fadil[42]. He also authored the *Mishneh Torah* (1166–1168) and *Guide for the Perplexed* (1186–1190), aiming to reconcile Aristotelian philosophy with Jewish theology. His life and works illustrate the intellectual and cultural exchanges between Muslim and Jewish traditions in the medieval Islamic world. The prominent Jewish historian Salo Wittmayer Baron noted that Judaism reached a "golden age"[43] under Islamic civilization. He observed that Jewish communities from Egypt to Spain found a unique equilibrium in the Dar al-Islam, gaining improved political and economic status.

---

40 This agreement established that these groups formed one community ["They form one and the same community"]; Jews were equal members of this society ["Whosoever among the Jews follows us shall have help and equality; they shall not be injured nor shall any enemy be aided against them"]; they had religious freedom ["The Jews shall maintain their own religion and the Muslims theirs"]; and they had the right to engage in economic contracts ["The Jews shall be responsible for their expenses and the Believers for theirs"], there will be no discrimination in the city/no ghetto ["The valley of Yathrib (Medina) shall be sacred and inviolable for all that join this Treaty"]. https://www.islamawareness.net/Judaism/treaty.html

41 "Jews and Saracens are not to be allowed to have Christian servants in their houses, either under pretence of nourishing their children or for service or any other reason. Let those be excommunicated who presume to live with them. ... those who prefer Jews to Christians in this matter are to lie under anathema, since Jews ought to be subject to Christians." https://www.papalencyclicals.net/councils/ecum11.htm

42 Heinrich Graetz, *History of the Jews*, vol. 3 (Philadelphia: The Jewish Publication Society, 1894), 473.

43 Salo Wittmayer Baron, *A Social and Religious History of the Jews*, vol. 3 (Philadelphia: The Jewish Publication Society, 1957), 119.

Jews contributed actively to Islamic civilization, fostering mutual respect and co-existence.

The Rhineland massacres of 1096, carried out by French and German Christians during the People's Crusade, are often seen as the start of a series of antisemitic actions in Europe leading to the Holocaust. In France and Germany, Jews, viewed as local "non-believers" akin to Muslims, were targeted for their wealth and role in moneylending, which was forbidden to Catholics. Crusaders, often in debt from financing their expeditions, justified violence against Jews as part of their religious mission. In spring 1096, inspired by crusade preaching, knights and peasants set off from France and Germany, persecuting Jews in Magdeburg, Prague, and Bohemia.

In contrast to the Crusaders, who carried out Europe's first pogrom, Saladin's conquest of Jerusalem in 1187 marked a stark difference in treatment of Jews. Eight years after the Third Lateran Council, Saladin encouraged Jews to resettle in Jerusalem, granting them religious freedom and the right to own property, engage in commerce, and contribute to Jerusalem's prosperity. His policies allowed for peaceful coexistence among Muslims, Christians, and Jews, creating a diverse society. Saladin settled the Jews of Ascalon in Jerusalem in 1190, allowing them to build a synagogue and live in designated districts. Over time, more Jewish families arrived from North Africa and France, with 300 families making *aliyah* from France around 1210.[44]

While Jews settled peacefully in Jerusalem under Saladin in 1187, antisemitic violence surged in Europe, exemplified by the 1190 York Massacre in England, where Jews, facing forced baptism, took their own lives. The "blood libel" myth emerged in this period, accusing Jews of using Christian children's blood in rituals. This myth, first appearing in Norwich in 1144 and later reinforced by the case of Hugh of Lincoln in 1255, was used to justify the expulsion of Jews from England in 1290. During the Black Death, Jews were scapegoated as the source of the plague, fueling massacres across Europe, while no similar accusations were made against Jews in Islamic land: "While neither Mahometans nor Mongols, who suffered from the plague, attacked the Jews, Christian peoples charged the unhappy race with being the originators of the pestilence and slaughtered them *en masse*."[45]

Within a quarter-century, the expulsion of Jews and Muslims from Spain (1492), the Lisbon massacre (1506), and the establishment of the first ghetto in Venice (1516) laid the groundwork for systematic, theology-based antisemitism in Europe. Ghettos, walled sections for Jews, quickly spread

---

44 Karen Armstrong, *Jerusalem: One City Three Faiths* (New York: Alfred Knopf, 1996), 299.
45 Graetz, vol. 4, 101.

to cities like Rome (1555) and Prague (1593), creating an ethnically divided urban structure.

In contrast, with the end of Andalusian rule in Spain in 1492, which marked the conclusion of what Hans Küng describes as the "Jewish-Moorish symbiosis,"[46] expelled Jews from Spain found a safe haven in Ottoman lands in the Ottoman Empire. While ghettos were systematically spreading across Europe, Jews living in cities such as Thessaloniki, Istanbul, and Izmir integrated into the sociological fabric of these cities and perhaps experienced the most favorable living conditions since the great expulsion. This was an exemplary civilizational interaction because "until the modern period, a distinctive culture, transplanted from medieval Sepharad, but now in full mutation, could evolve and flourish in the mosaic that was the Ottoman the Levant."[47]

Thessaloniki serves as a notable example, where 20,000 Jews from Granada in 1492, along with others from Sicily, Spain, and Portugal, eventually became the city's largest religious group. By 1913, of Thessaloniki's 157,889 residents, 61,439 were Jewish, 45,867 Muslim, and 40,000 Greek Orthodox, marking the highest concentration of Jews in a city since 70 CE. Unlike Europe, where Jews faced ghettos and pogroms, Thessaloniki offered religious freedom and residential integration, earning it the title "the mother of Israel." Following the Nazi occupation, around 50,000 Jews from Thessaloniki were sent to concentration camps, drastically reducing the Jewish population. The city's cultural landscape shifted as mosques and synagogues were destroyed or converted, mirroring the cultural loss experienced in Córdoba and Granada in 1492.[48]

In summary, from the Great Exile to the Holocaust, European societies—including Germany, France, Italy, England, Spain, Portugal, and Russia—have a long history of antisemitic actions, including accusations, massacres, expulsions, and exclusion of Jews. The Holocaust marked the peak of these atrocities, intensified by scientific advances. During this period, ghettos in occupied Eastern Europe, such as those in Warsaw and Lodz, became centers of severe oppression, overcrowded and lacking basic necessities. The Nazi regime emerged from this antisemitic legacy, and the revelation of their

---

46 "...after the Jewish-Hellenistic symbiosis, the second interaction in world history between the Jewish culture and an alien culture." Hans Küng, *Judaism: Between Yesterday and Tomorrow* (New York: Continuum, 1991), 157.

47 Aron Rodrigue, "The Ottoman Diaspora: The Rise and Fall of Ladino Literary Culture," in David Biale, *Cultures of the Jews: Modern Encounters,* vol. 3 (New York: Schocken Books), 143.

48 Ahmet Davutoğlu, *Pivot Cities in the Rise and Fall of Civilizations* (London: Routledge, 2022), 76.

genocide during World War II instilled a lasting "sense of guilt" among the elites of these European societies, influencing the privileged status granted to Israel during its formation and subsequently.

European antisemitic history has little in common with Islamic societies, where there were no theological justifications for massacres, expulsions, or ghettos. Muslim societies offered refuge to Jews fleeing Christian persecution, focusing on individual responsibility rather than collective guilt. With Israel's founding, Western nations effectively shifted the "Jewish Question" to the Middle East, burdening Palestinians with the legacy of European antisemitism. This "confessional" psychology in Europe, along with Cold War geopolitics, limited criticism of Israel's human rights abuses.

Muslims continued to distinguish between Jews and Israel, refraining from collective punishment. Unlike Europe, where antisemitism was rooted in theological and racial biases, Muslim societies' critiques of Israel were political, focusing on anti-Zionism rather than antisemitism. Jews not espousing Zionist claims of "chosen people" faced no issues in Muslim societies. Islamic teachings, embracing both Semitic and Aryan peoples, historically rejected racism. The Western world, especially Europe, has a legacy of antisemitism, culminating in the Holocaust, which instilled a deep sense of guilt among Western elites. This guilt often leads to uncritical support for Israel to avoid accusations of antisemitism, deterring justified criticism and accountability for actions that would otherwise be condemned.

In diplomatic processes, I have consistently observed this psycho-historical effect in Western diplomats. During the peace negotiations between Israel and Syria, where I mediated, reaching their final stages in December 2008, a significant massacre occurred due to Israel's military attack on Gaza. When I asked a Western diplomat to intervene with Israel, I received a surprising response: "We cannot adopt a stance that criticizes Israel on security matters." I responded by saying, "I understand the mindset you are in, but we, when necessary, issue the most direct warnings to Israel because every time you expelled them from Europe, we provided a safe haven for them; we do not owe them any debt or guilt."

Socio-political Context: Dual Identity and the Power of Jewish Lobby

After centuries of oppression, Jewish communities developed strong solidarity and organizational skills, leading to influential lobbying power in many Western countries. Organizations and individuals within these communities often advocate for policies favorable to Israel. Many maintain a dual identity, balancing connections to their home countries with a strong allegiance to Israel, which can drive support for pro-Israel policies.

Blinken's following statement is a striking example of the impact of this dual identity during a time of a crisis: "I come before you not only as the United States Secretary of State but also as a Jew. My grandfather, Maurice Blinken, fled pogroms in Russia. My stepfather, Samuel Pisar, survived concentration camps—Auschwitz, Dachau, Majdanek."[49] It may be natural for one's personal history and identity to influence their stance on international crises. However, as a foreign minister of a country with a special status for international and regional peace as a permanent member of the UNSC, the political language used is expected to be much more careful. Can the Gaza and Palestinian sides feel comfortable negotiating a ceasefire with Blinken? Similarly, the extent to which Amos Hochstein, an Israeli-born former IDF soldier serving as Biden's special representative for Lebanon-Israeli conflict, can maintain objectivity between the parties involved in the ceasefire efforts and establish a trustworthy relationship during negotiations is also a matter of debate. It is impossible for a mediator who cannot empathize equally with all parties to succeed.

Blinken's statement highlights Israel's privileged position in the eyes of the American political elite, a status that is even more significant for the American elite of Jewish descent. Consider this: Imagine if one day a Muslim American minister or diplomat went to Palestine and said, "I am a Muslim Palestinian, and I am here not just as an American diplomat, but as a Muslim," or if a Chinese American diplomat went to China during a crisis and declared, "I am here with my Confucian Chinese identity." How would this be perceived by the other side of the crisis? More importantly, how would the American public view this Muslim or Chinese American? The uproar caused in the United States by Edward Said, who, as an academic with no official representative mission, made a minor gesture of support as a Palestinian during the peaceful intifada, is still fresh in our memories. The proliferation of such statements and attitudes would most harm America's multicultural identity.

The issue of dual identity has long been a concern, especially for religious minorities like Jews during the formation of European nation-states. Napoleon's questions to a commission of Jewish leaders (*Sanhedrin*) highlight the challenges Jews faced in integrating into emerging nation-states: "Do Jews see the French as equals or foreigners? Do the Jews born in France and subject to French law adopt France as their homeland?"[50] These questions,

49 Tovah Lazaroff, "'I come before you as a Jew,' Blinken tells Israel after Hamas attack," *The Jerusalem Post*, October 12, 2023. https://www.jpost.com/israel-news/article-767997

50 Diogene Tama, *Transactions of the Parisian Sanhedrin* (London: Charles Taylor, 1807), 133–34; cited in Calvin Goldscheider and Alan S. Zuckerman, *The*

aimed at understanding Jewish integration into French society, also inadver-
tently fueled antisemitism by questioning Jewish loyalty and belonging.

The "Jewish Question" in Europe evolved through three major transformations. The first followed the French Revolution, granting Jews political
rights and sparking debates on Jewish identity, as seen in Napoleon's inqui-
ries to Jewish leaders about integration. This period strengthened Jewish solidarity and saw the Jewish Enlightenment flourish, despite rising German and
Slavic nationalism. The second transformation emerged with late 19th-cen-
tury "reciprocal nationalism," where Theodor Herzl's *Der Judenstaat* and the
1897 Zionist Congress laid the groundwork for Zionism, uniting Jews under
a nationalist ideology with a focus on establishing a state in Palestine. The
third phase began with Israel's founding, creating an existential link between
the diaspora and Israel. Many Jews, balancing dual identities, began viewing
their host nations' interests through their lens of its connection to Israel, with
its protection becoming a core reflex.

The influence of the Jewish lobby on U.S. policy is so significant that
discussing it often requires courage. In *The Israel Lobby and U.S. Foreign
Policy*, John Mearsheimer and Stephen Walt highlight the difficulty of
addressing the lobby's impact without facing accusations of antisemitism:
"It is difficult to talk about the lobby's influence on American foreign policy,
at least in the mainstream media in the United States, without being accused
of anti-Semitism or labeled a self-hating Jew. It is just as difficult to criticize Israeli policies or question U.S. support for Israel in polite company.
America's generous and unconditional support for Israel is rarely questioned,
because groups in the lobby use their power to make sure that public discourse
echoes its strategic and moral arguments for the special relationship."[51] One
of the main reasons U.S. Congress members feel compelled to applaud for
minutes after nearly every sentence when being addressed by Netanyahu,
an Israeli leader accused of genocide and crimes against humanity by the
International Court of Justice and the International Criminal Court is likely
their desire to avoid potential accusations of anti-Semitism.

Former U.S. President Jimmy Carter, who led and mediated the most
significant peace agreement in the Middle East at Camp David in 1979 and
received the Nobel Peace Prize for his efforts, has faced accusations of Nazi

---

Transformation of the Jews (Chicago: The University of Chicago Press, 1984), 38.

51 John J. Mearsheimer and Stephen M. Walt, *The Israeli Lobby and U.S.
Foreign Policy* (New York: Farrar, Straus and Giroux, 2008), 9.

collaboration[52] due to his 2006 book titled *Palestine: Peace Not Apartheid*[53] which highlights the new risks of ghettoization through settlers in Palestine. Such accusations reveal the psychological and socio-political climate that influences the complicity of the U.S. political elite in the Gaza genocide.

In many Western countries, the only way to avoid this psychological climate of fear, which feeds on an inherent sense of guilt, and to engage in political activity without risk, is to consistently position oneself as " Israel's lawyer" regardless of the circumstances. Aaron David Miller, who served as an advisor to six American Secretaries of State and took on significant roles at the 2000 Camp David Summit, admitted in his 2005 article published in the *Washington Post* that they acted like "Israel's lawyer"[54] during these negotiations. He emphasized that this pro-Israeli stance played a significant role in the failure of the peace efforts. This clearly demonstrates how this dual-identity diplomacy has captured both American foreign policy and regional and global peace efforts.

The influential roles played by former officials such as Michael Chertoff, Former Secretary of Homeland Security under President George W. Bush, who shaped U.S. counterterrorism policies in the post-9/11 era; Paul Wolfowitz, Former Deputy Secretary of Defense who was pivotal in the lead-up to the Iraq War; and Rahm Emanuel, Former White House Chief of Staff under President Barack Obama who had a decisive impact on U.S. Middle East policy following the Arab Spring, highlight the prioritization of Israeli interests alongside U.S. interests. Anthony Blinken's emphasis on his "Jewish identity" and the Biden administration's continued support for Netanyahu's government despite public outcry over images of genocide reveal the significance of the dense network between the American Jewish lobby and the Israeli government.

This dual approach is evident not only among government officials but also within media and civil society. Mearsheimer and Walt highlight the strong pro-Israel influence in media and lobbying pressures, citing examples such as former *New York Times* executive editor Max Frankel, who admitted in his memoirs that his pro-Israel stance shaped his editorial decisions. Frankel noted, "I was much more deeply devoted to Israel than I dared to assert," acknowledging that his Middle East commentaries often reflected a pro-Israel perspective. Publications such as *Commentary*, *The New Republic*, and *The Weekly Standard* have also consistently defended Israel. Martin Peretz,

---

52 Daniel Freedman, "President Carter Interceded on Behalf of Former Nazi Guard," *New York Sun*, January 19, 2007; cited in Mearsheimer and Walt, 358.

53 Jimmy Carter, *Palestine: Peace not Apartheid* (New York: Simon and Schuster, 2006).

54 Aaron D. Miller, "Israel's Lawyer," *Washington Post*, May 23, 2005.

longtime editor of *The New Republic*, openly stated, "I am in love with the state of Israel," admitting that a "party line on Israel" existed at his journal.[55]

This general attitude in Western media has also directly influenced the descriptions of war victims in Gaza: "More than 500 people *have died* in Gaza after Israel launched massive retaliatory air strikes, according to Gaza's health ministry. More than 700 people *have been killed* in Israel since Hamas launched its attacks on Saturday."[56] These word choices serve to shape perceptions. Palestinians *"die,"* as if death is their fate, with no active subject mentioned in the reports; if a subject were specified, it would reveal the Israeli Army as the perpetrator. Israelis, on the other hand, are *"killed,"* with Hamas necessarily being portrayed as the perpetrator.

Such linguistic choices are not merely stylistic but reflect an underlying "ontological inequality," as identified by the thinker Stoddart. Palestinians are often depicted as a group whose deaths are normalized, while Israelis are portrayed as a group whose deaths are criminal acts. This distinction challenges the fundamental principle of the Universal Declaration of Human Rights, which affirms that "all human beings are born free and equal in dignity and rights."

However, within today's global network of relationships, this link between the diaspora and Israel's security also creates a negative impact. Jews in the diaspora increasingly see that Israel's ongoing genocide in Gaza negatively affects the image of Jews worldwide. Rabbi Alissa Wise vividly illustrates this tight connection between the freedom of Palestinians and the security of Jews: "But I think the most important piece here is that all of this is making Jews less safe in the world. Israel's actions in Gaza, but also not just now but for generations—when Palestinians are not free, Jews are less safe in the world. And that is the crux of the matter. There is no way for Jewish safety to be found when others are being oppressed. That's just the simple truth of it. And organizations that seek to distract from those of us that are trying to realize freedom, democracy, equal rights—it's simple. It's equal rights for Palestinians and Israelis. Those people claim that we are antisemitic, when, in fact, their actions at aiding and abetting genocidal violence in Gaza now, but apartheid and occupation for generations, that is what is making Jews less safe in the world."[57]

---

55 Mearsheimer and Walt, 172.

56 BBC News (World) (@BBCWorld), "More than 500 people have died in Gaza after Israel launched massive retaliatory air strikes, according to Gaza's health ministry. More than 700 people have been killed in Israel . . . ," X, October 9, 2023, 4:19am. https://x.com/BBCWorld/status/1711340677571674567

57 March for Israel Speaker Pastor Hagee Once Said God "Sent Hitler to Help Jews Reach the Promised Land," *Democracy Now!*, November 15, 2023. https://

Theological-political Background: Christian Zionism and the Messianic Role Assigned to Israel.

Theological arguments have historically been a potent tool for legitimizing both genocide and complicity in genocide, as seen from the anti-Semitic atrocities rooted in Christian doctrine, from the Third Lateran Council to Hitler. Today, Israel's actions in Gaza are similarly justified through theological narratives, with claims that they pave the way for Christ's Second Coming via Jewish dominance in Palestine. Thus, both anti-Semitic and pro-Israel genocidal actions draw on interpretations of the same religious texts.

Christian Zionist leaders often invoke biblical prophecy to support Israel, portraying its military actions as part of a divine plan. A prominent example is John Hagee, a Christian Zionist, who in a 2024 interview[58] defended Israel's actions in Gaza as a "prophetic event," asserting that supporting Israel fulfills a divine mandate. Citing Genesis, Hagee claimed that nations supporting Israel are blessed, while those opposing it face ruin, drawing parallels to the fall of ancient empires. For Hagee, Israel's rebirth in 1948 marked the start of the "prophetic clock," aligning Israel's actions with divine prophecy and asserting that Christian identity is inextricably linked with support for Judaism and Israel.

When arguments like Hagee's are accepted, concepts such as human rights, genocide conventions, and peace efforts lose significance. Hagee asserts that "an inevitable peace accord between Israel and Palestinians will be the work of the anti-Christ,"[59] implying perpetual conflict. Sarah Posner, author of *Unholy: How White Christian Nationalists Powered the Trump Presidency*[60], explains that for many Christian Zionists, especially influential evangelicals within the Republican Party, support for Israel is tied to end-times prophecy, anticipating Jesus' return and a climactic battle at Armageddon. She strikingly underlines that "in this scenario, war is not something to be avoided but something inevitable, desired by God, and celebratory."[61]

---

www.democracynow.org/2023/11/15/washington_march_for_israel

58 "John Hagee: THIS Is Why You Should Support Israel," Praise on TBN, July 24, 2024, fundraising video [23:03]. https://www.youtube.com/watch?v=OrmUXoYsJeYY

59 https://www.motherjones.com/politics/2023/11/pastor-john-hagee-says-an-israel-palestinian-peace-deal-will-be-the-work-of-the-anti-christ/

60 Sarah Posner, *Unholy: How White Christian Nationalists Powered the Trump Presidency, and the Devastating Legacy They Left Behind* (New York: Random House, 2021).

61 Sarah Posner, "The dispiriting truth about why many evangelical Christians support Israel," *MSNBC,* October 22, 2023. https://www.msnbc.com/opinion/msnbc-opinion/truth-many-evangelical-christians-support-israel-rcna121481

Such a perspective, framing peace as "anti-Christ" work and war as "divine destiny," could be dismissed as isolated or extreme. However, three key factors suggest that this approach poses substantial risks to both regional and global peace, underscoring that it cannot simply be viewed as an eccentric belief.

First, the relationship between Christian and Jewish Zionism, based on theological arguments about the Second Coming of Christ, is not a recent phenomenon. The alliance between Christian and Jewish Zionism, rooted in theological beliefs about the Second Coming, has developed over the past two centuries, gaining political influence in the early 20th century. This impact became evident in the network that led to the Balfour Declaration. British clergyman William Hechler, who believed that Jewish migration to Palestine fulfilled biblical prophecy necessary for Christ's return, forged a close relationship with Zionist leader Theodor Herzl.

As World War I approached, Christian Zionists intensified lobbying and public campaigns, viewing Jewish migration to Palestine as essential for biblical prophecy. The common theological foundation of the network of relationships among Zionist ideologist Theodore Herzl, Christian Zionist William Hechler, Prime Minister Lloyd George, Foreign Secretary Arthur Balfour, Jewish/British politician Herbert Samuel, and banker Lord Rothschild created the infrastructure for the Balfour Declaration.

The collaboration between Zionists and Evangelicals produced one of its earliest significant outcomes in the Balfour Declaration, which led to the British Mandate in Palestine and the subsequent Jewish immigration: "In addition to the Evangelical members of the War Cabinet, there were two influential Jewish lobbyists; Sir Herbert Samuel, the first Jew to become a Cabinet minister in Britain, and Weizmann, who was said to be able to charm the spots off a leopard."[62]

In this network of relationships, the connections between William Hechler, Herbert Samuel and Lloyd George were particularly significant in establishing both intellectual and practical bridges between Zionist ideals and the British political elite. The relationship between these three figures, each with different backgrounds and influences, is indicative of the dynamics that shed light on the contemporary connections between Zionist Christian pastors, Zionist Jewish leaders, and policymakers of a hegemonic power.

William Hechler, Herbert Samuel, and Lloyd George formed a crucial network bridging Zionist ideals with British political elites. As a Christian clergyman, Hechler promoted Zionism within British politics, using

---

62 Jill Hamilton, *God, Guns and Israel: Britain, the Jews and the First World War* (London: The History Press, 2004), 16.

theological arguments to shape the views of influential figures like Lloyd George and Arthur Balfour. Herbert Samuel, balancing his Jewish identity with his role as a British statesman, translated theological ideas into practical policies, briefing Sykes on Zionism ahead of the Sykes-Picot negotiations: "Sykes therefore contacted Herbert Samuel, the Home Secretary, who was Jewish, hoping to learn about Zionism."[63] Lloyd George, driven by Britain's imperial ambitions, saw Zionism as aligning with Britain's strategic interests, as argued by Samuel in his memorandum, *The Future of Palestine*[64], which portrayed Jewish migration as a strategic asset for the British Empire.

It is unlikely that Lloyd George, an ambitious pragmatist, supported Zionist goals solely out of sympathy for persecuted Jews. His inconsistent stance suggests both theological and power-based motivations. In 1915, he argued against allowing "Agnostic Atheistic France" to control Christian Holy Places in Palestine[65], reflecting his Christian beliefs. Yet, his later praise of Hitler as "the greatest living German"[66] and "the George Washington of Germany" reveals his inclination toward realpolitik.

Herbert Samuel's appointment as the first High Commissioner of the British Mandate for Palestine in 1920, following his 1915 memorandum *The Future of Palestine*, highlights the intersection of Christian and Jewish Zionist agendas. Samuel's influence, combined with Hechler's, brought a theological dimension to Lloyd George and Arthur Balfour's policies: "Just as Samuel had earlier, as home secretary under Asquith, been the first professing Jew to sit in a British Cabinet, now he was the first Jew to govern the Holy Land since Pompey captured the Temple in 63 BCE. Many Jews hoped that he might follow Disraeli and become prime minister."[67]

Ironically, as Jill Hamilton notes[68], Britain—one of the last European countries to accept Jews and the first to expel them *en masse*—ultimately

63 David Fromkin, *A Peace to End All Peace: The Fall of the Ottoman Empire and the Creation of the Modern Middle East* (New York: Henry Holt and Company, 1989), 196.

64 Fromkin, 270

65 Herbert Henry Asquit, Letters to Venetia Stanley, edited by Michael and Eleanor Brock (New York: Oxford University Press, 1982), 406; cited in Fromkin, 270.

66 Thomas Jones, "VII: In Opposition 1923–45," *Lloyd George* (London: Oxford University Press, 1951), 247.

67 Jill Hamilton, *God, Guns and Israel*, p.222.

68 "It was ironic that Lloyd George, a Welshman, let alone the British government, made a cradle in Palestine in which the Jews could create their own state. Britain, one of the last countries in which Jewish people settled in Europe, was also the first European country which forcibly expelled Jews en masse. Jews had not begun migrating to the British Isles until the reign of William the Conqueror, in 1066. Two

provided a foundation for a Jewish state in Palestine.[69] This irony is best understood within the shift from Catholicism to Evangelicalism in Christian theology.

The network of relationships that formed between Evangelical/Zionist Christian pastor William Hechler, the leader of the hegemonic power, British Prime Minister Lloyd George, and the High Commissioner of the Palestine Mandate, Herbert Samuel, to facilitate Jewish immigration to Palestine and the establishment of the State of Israel, has found a striking parallel nearly a century later. This parallel emerged during the process in which the United States recognized Jerusalem as the eternal capital of Israel, one of Zionism's most significant and controversial goals. The key figures in this contemporary scenario were Evangelical Zionist pastor John Hagee, the leader of the current hegemonic power, U.S. President Donald Trump, and Israeli Prime Minister Benjamin Netanyahu who today controls the territories of Palestine under British Mandate.

Secondly, the intense relationships and interactions between Evangelical pastors who adopt this approach and today's political leaders and elites move these arguments beyond the realm of religious debate. Conservative evangelicals have long formed the backbone of the Republican Party's support of Israel.[70] For example, John Hagee, the founder and president of Christians United for Israel (CUFI), which includes prominent Christian Zionist leaders, is a close friend of U.S. President Donald Trump.[71] While not an official advisor, Hagee is influential and has affected Trump's views. Trump's decision to move the U.S. Embassy from Tel Aviv to Jerusalem in 2018 was significantly influenced by Evangelical circles within the Republican Party, rather than rational diplomatic considerations. This decision was supported as a significant fulfillment of biblical prophecy by many evangelical Christians, including Hagee.

Hagee claimed, "he had helped convince Trump by telling him at a White House dinner that Jesus is coming back to Jerusalem to 'set up His throne on the Temple Mount where He will sit and rule for a thousand years

centuries after they had begun to put down roots, King Edward I threw every Jewish man, woman, and child out of his kingdom."

69 Jill Hamilton, *God, Guns and Israel*, p.16

70 Ruth Graham and Anna Betts, "For American Evangelicals Who Back Israel, 'Neutrality Isn't an Option,'" *New York Times*, October 15, 2023. https://www.nytimes.com/2023/10/15/us/american-evangelicals-israel-hamas.html

71 Hagee had previously supported McCain in the 2006 elections, and this support had sparked significant controversy; see Sam Stein, "McCain Backer Hagee Said Hitler Was Fulfilling God's Will (AUDIO)," *Huffpost*, May 29, 2008. https://www.huffingtonpost.co.uk/entry/mccain-backer-hagee-said_n_102892

of perfect peace.'"[72] Describing the embassy move to Jerusalem as "nothing short of a divine miracle," Hagee gave the benediction at the dedication ceremony in May 2018: "We thank you, O Lord, for President Donald Trump's courage in acknowledging to the world a truth that was established 3,000 years ago—that Jerusalem is and always shall be the eternal capital of the Jewish people. ...And because of that courage of our President, we gather here today to consecrate the ground upon which the United States Embassy will stand reminding the dictators of the world that America and Israel are forever united."[73]

The events of October 7, 2023, provided an opportunity for Christian Zionists like John Hagee, who interpret such conflicts as fulfilling prophecy for Jesus' return. In an October 15 sermon, Hagee referenced biblical predictions, claiming that armies coming from China, Russia or Iran opposing Israel would be "wiped out" by God, ushering in "1,000 years of perfect peace" under the sole rule of Jesus. Despite the Biden administration's support for Israel, Hagee criticized it as insufficient, even accusing President Biden of "treason" for not fully aligning with Israel. [74]

The influence of apocalyptic beliefs on U.S. policy poses clear risks, especially if leaders view protecting Israel as divinely mandated. Apocalyptic rhetoric from other religious groups would likely be seen as a global threat, yet similar views from Christian Zionists are often overlooked.

In this biblical prophecy approach, UN Security Council resolutions, the Madrid Process, the Oslo Process, international conventions, and rules are meaningless because, "In this interpretation, settlers' further control of the occupied West Bank, which they call by its biblical names Judea and Samaria, is a fulfillment of God's plan for a Jewish return to Israel—one of a sequence of biblical prophecies that culminates in the Second Coming."[75]

As Sarah Posner underlines, Christian Zionists are not primarily motivated by a concern for Jews who suffered in the Holocaust; rather, "Christian nationalism" lies at the core of their ideology."[76] John Hagee, a prominent figure in this movement, has previously expressed antisemitic views, controversially asserting that God used Hitler—a "half-breed Jew"—to drive Jews to Israel, framing the Holocaust as part of a divine plan. According to Hagee,

---

72 Sarah Posner, "The dispiriting truth about why many evangelical Christians support Israel."
73 Matt Korade, Kevin Bohn, and Daniel Burke, "Controversial US pastors take part in Jerusalem embassy opening," *CNN Politics,* May 14, 2018. https://edition.cnn.com/2018/05/13/politics/hagee-jeffress-us-embassy-jerusalem/index.html
74 Sarah Posner.
75 Sarah Posner.
76 Sarah Posner.

"Hitler was a hunter" sent by God to fulfill biblical prophecy, emphasizing that the priority for Jews was to "return to the land of Israel."[77] This is why his role as a main speaker at pro-Israel events following October 7 has provoked significant reactions within the American Jewish community.[78]

Third, even more dangerous is the widespread societal support for every form of war and massacre enacted by the Netanyahu government as a means of realizing the biblical prophecy. According to a Pew Research Center survey, white evangelical Protestants are notably more likely than other U.S. religious groups to view the Israeli government favorably, with 68% holding a positive opinion. Furthermore, 70% believe that God granted the land of Israel to the Jewish people, and among these believers, 25% support a single state under Israeli governance as a solution to the Israeli-Palestinian conflict—a view shared by only 10% of the general U.S. population.

On October 11, 2023, the Ethics & Religious Liberty Commission of the Southern Baptist Convention, representing Evangelicals, labeled the war aimed at fulfilling biblical prophecy as a "just war." This stance legitimized political complicity in Israel's actions, framing it as a religious duty. The statement, endorsed by 2,000 evangelical leaders, highlighted the "legitimacy of Israel's right to defend itself," citing Romans 13 as justification for wielding power against those who "commit evil acts."[79] Killing of more than 40 thousand Palestinian children, women and civilians by Israeli bombardments were seen as collateral damage of this biblical "just war."[80]

If this way of thinking remained as the view of a religious community, the complicity support given to the genocide in Gaza might not have been considered significant. However, the active and decisive involvement of these Evangelical pastors and churches in politics is laying the theological groundwork for this complicity. The enthusiastic applause and devotional body

77 Sam Stein, "McCain Backer Hagee Said Hitler Was Fulfilling God's Will (AUDIO)," *Huffpost,* May 29, 2008. https://www.huffingtonpost.co.uk/entry/mccain-backer-hagee-said_n_102892

78 Henry Carnell and Sam Van Pykeren, "He Claimed God Sent Hitler to Create Israel. Now He's Speaking at the Pro-Israel Rally. What?" *Mother Jones,* November 14, 2023. https://www.motherjones.com/politics/2023/11/john-hagee-hitler-israel-rally-christian-zionist/; "March for Israel Speaker Pastor Hagee Once Said God 'Sent Hitler to Help Jews Reach the Promised Land,'" *Democracy Now!,* November 15, 2023. https://www.democracynow.org/2023/11/15/washington_march_for_israel

79 *Evangelical Statement in Support of Israel,* Ethics & Religious Liberty Commission of the Southern Baptist Convention, October 11, 2023. https://erlc.com/policy-content/israel/

80 Adam Gabbatt, "'This war is prophetically significant': why US evangelical Christians support Israel," *The Guardian,* October 30, 2023. https://www.theguardian.com/world/2023/oct/30/us-evangelical-christians-israel-hamas-war

language exhibited by congressional members during Netanyahu's speech transcended mere rational support, resembling a ceremonial display rooted in religious fervor and awe. The most notable example of this dynamic is House Speaker Mike Johnson's approach. By standing and applauding enthusiastically behind Netanyahu at nearly every point in his speech, Johnson mobilized other members to join in. When asked about his worldview upon assuming the role of Speaker, Johnson replied, "Well, go pick up a Bible off your shelf and read it. That's my worldview,"[81] emphasizing that, under his leadership, the U.S. Congress would stand firmly with Israel. He cited his Christian faith, stating that "God will bless the nation that blesses Israel."[82]

The alignment in theological rhetoric between Johnson and Evangelical leader John Hagee during pro-Israel demonstrations underscores the religious convictions that drive support for the actions in Gaza. Johnson characterized demands for a ceasefire as "outrageous" and expressed hope that this support would remind both Americans and the global community that "the United States stands proudly with Israel and the Jewish people forever." He noted that "few issues in Washington could so easily bring together leaders of both parties in both chambers," affirming that "the survival of the state of Israel unites us together and unites all Americans."[83]

Members of Congress often approach the Israel-Palestine issue from a theological rather than political viewpoint. In Lee Fang's documentary *Praying for Armageddon,* Representative Pete Sessions, a Texas Republican, frames the matter as based on "the faith of our maker, our creator, but it's also the faith of a chosen people." Similarly, Representative Tim Burchett from Tennessee echoes scripture, saying, "Those who bless Israel will be blessed."[84] Senator Lindsey Graham's views go even further, framing support for Israel as a religious duty. Graham advocates for the "all-out annihilation of Gaza"[85] and has proposed methods more extreme than those used in WWII: "Why is it okay for America to drop nuclear bombs on Hiroshima and

81 Peter Smith, "Evangelical conservatives cheer one of their own as Mike Johnson assumes Congress' most powerful seat," *PBS News,* October 27, 2023. https://www.pbs.org/newshour/politics/evangelical-conservatives-cheer-one-of-their-own-as-mike-johnson-assumes-congress-most-powerful-seat

82 Ibid.

83 Anthony Zurcher, "US Evangelicals Drive Republican Support for Israel," *BBC News,* November 14, 2023. https://www.bbc.com/news/world-us-canada-67422238

84 Adam Gabbatt, "'This war is prophetically significant.'"

85 "Jewish Voice for Peace Calls for Restraint After Sen. Lindsey Graham Urges Israel to 'Level' Gaza," *Democracy Now!,* October 12, 2023. https://www.democracynow.org/2023/10/12/headlines/jewish_voice_for_peace_calls_for_restraint_after_sen_lindsey_graham_urges_israel_to_level_gaza

Nagasaki ... but not for Israel to use similar measures?" he asserted, urging, "To Israel, do whatever you have to do to survive as a Jewish state."[86]

International/Strategic Context: Geopolitical Symbiosis and Complicity

In addition to the emotional and dramatic content of Netanyahu's speech to Congress, the main message to the American public was the argument that they were fighting not against Hamas but against Iran. In this way, Netanyahu aimed to provide a geopolitical rationale to those supporting complicity in the genocide he was accused of, by framing it through a common enemy: "That's why the mobs in Tehran chant 'Death to Israel' before they chant 'Death to America.' For Iran, Israel is first, America is next. So, when Israel fights Hamas, we're fighting Iran. When we fight Hezbollah, we're fighting Iran. When we fight the Houthis, we're fighting Iran. And when we fight Iran, we're fighting the most radical and murderous enemy of the United States of America."[87]

This "geopolitical symbiosis" with Western countries, and specifically with the United States, has been seen as a key factor in the formation of a perception that grants Israel the privilege of ignoring international legal norms. The demonization of leaders such as Nasser during the rise of Arab nationalism, Khomeini after the Islamic revolution in Iran, Saddam after the invasion of Kuwait, nearly every period of Qaddafi, and Hamas after winning the 2006 elections, has been attributed to this "geopolitical symbiosis." Therefore, while preventing Iran from acquiring nuclear weapons, the question of why Israel remains the only country in the region with nuclear arms is not addressed. Similarly, while Iraq's invasion of Kuwait is justifiably opposed and military action is taken to end this invasion with the activation of the UN, Israel's violations of Security Council resolutions to end occupation in West Bank and Gaza have been legitimized for 57 years. Furthermore, the elections held in Iraq under U.S. occupation on December 15, 2005, were presented as a "great victory for democracy," yet the results of the elections held in Palestine a month later on January 25, 2006—described as "fair and free" by all observers—were not recognized. The rationale is clear: developments in the Middle East are viewed primarily through the lens of Israel's interests, and international norms are interpreted accordingly.

---

86 Ben Norton, "US senator says Israel should drop nuclear bombs on Gaza," *Geopolitical Economy,* May 12, 2024. https://geopoliticaleconomy. com/2024/05/12/senator-lindsey-graham-israel-nuclear-weapons-gaza/

87 "FULL TEXT: Netanyahu's 2024 Address to Congress," *Haaretz,* July 25, 2024. https://www.haaretz.com/israel-news/2024-07-25/ty-article/full-text-netanyahus-2024-address-to-congress/00000190-e6c0-d469-a39d-e6d7117d0000

The ambiguity within this "geopolitical symbiosis" raises the question of whether the U.S. sees Israel as a tool for Middle Eastern intervention or if Israel perceives the U.S. as the guarantor of its security. Among certain U.S. theological and political elites, including the Jewish lobby and Evangelical Zionists, Israel, despite its independent status as a UN member, is regarded almost as the "51st state" of the United States.

The view of Israel as a colony or protectorate of a global power, or as a strategic asset, has remained consistent in the Anglo-American tradition, from Herbert Samuel's 1915 memorandum to the British Cabinet through to the current U.S. administration. Samuel's geopolitical rationale, which sought to protect British interests, still underpins Israel's strategic framework:

> The belt of desert to the east of the Suez Canal is an admirable strategic frontier for Egypt. But it would be an inadequate defense if a great European Power were established on the further side. A military expedition organized from Southern Palestine, and including the laying of a railway from El Arish to the Canal, would be formidable. Palestine in British hands would itself no doubt be open to attack and would bring with it extended military responsibilities... A common frontier with a European neighbor in Lebanon is a far smaller risk to the vital interests of the British Empire than a common frontier at El Arish. [88]

This strategy laid the groundwork for the 1948 establishment of Israel, influenced the Sykes-Picot Agreement, and was executed during Samuel's tenure as High Commissioner for Palestine. The alignment between British colonial interests and Israeli geopolitics has seamlessly transitioned into the American-led order (Pax Americana).

The map presented by Netanyahu at the UN General Assembly on September 22, 2023—which disregarded Palestine and may have provoked the Hamas attack—reflects what those in power in Israel consider a geopolitical and theological "existence zone" or *Lebensraum*. This vision underpins the ongoing West Bank settlement policy, pursued in defiance of international conventions. Initially established as a British colony, Israel is now implementing a colonization strategy in the West Bank and Gaza, aiming to make this *Lebensraum* a permanent boundary and incorporated territory. The

---

88 "Future of Palestine" Memorandum by British Cabinet Member, Herbert Samuel, printed for the use of the Cabinet, January 1915. https://www.un.org/unispal/document/future-of-palestine-by-herbert-samuel-government-of-united-kingdom-memorandum/

strategy behind the recent war's goal of cleansing Gaza of Palestinians is also rooted in this context.

Israel's pursuit of its national strategy might seem justifiable from its own viewpoint; however, what stands out as problematic is the U.S.'s support—explicit or implicit—despite its role as a permanent UNSC member with special responsibility for international and regional peace. This support backs Israel's actions, even though they contravene multiple UN resolutions, including UNSC Resolution 242, and key agreements from the Camp David (1979), Madrid (1991), and Oslo (1993) processes. The recent support during the Gaza conflict exemplifies this troubling alignment.

John F. Kennedy articulated the existential strategic nature of the special relationship between the United States and Israel during a personal meeting with Israeli Foreign Minister Golda Meir, stating, "The United States has a special relationship with Israel in the Middle East, really comparable only to that which it has with Britain over a wide range of world affairs."[89] Even Jimmy Carter, who successfully mediated the Camp David Accords between Egypt and Israel, felt the need to publicly emphasize the priority given to Israel: "We have a special relationship with Israel. It's absolutely crucial that no one in our country or around the world ever doubt that our number one commitment in the Middle East is to protect the right of Israel to exist, to exist permanently, and to exist in peace."[90]

The privileged position of Israel has become even more pronounced during wartime. Israeli officials have often regarded the U.S. as almost obligated to provide all necessary logistics while considering themselves free from adhering to their commitments. Interestingly, this attitude has been seen as natural by American officials: "Kissinger was never able to apply much pressure on Israel during his conduct of the 'step-by-step' diplomacy that followed the October War. Kissinger complained at one point during the negotiations, 'I ask Rabin to make concessions, and he says he can't because Israel is weak. So I give him more arms, and then he says he doesn't need to make concessions because Israel is strong.'"[91]

---

89 Mordechai Gazit, "Israeli Military Procurement from the United States," in Gabriel Sheffer, ed., *Dynamics of Dependence: U.S. Israeli Relations* (Boulder, Colorado: Taylor & Francis Group, 1987), 98; cited in Yaacov Bar-Simon-Tov, "The United States and Israel since 1948: A 'Special Relationship'?," *Diplomatic History*, vol. 22, no. 2 (Oxford University Press, Spring 1998), 231.

90 Ibid.

91 Edward R. F. Sheehan, *The Arabs, Israelis and Kissinger: A Secret History of American Diplomacy in the Middle East* (Pleasantville, NY: Reader's Digest Press, 1976), 199; cited in Mearsheimer and Walt, *The Israel Lobby and U.S. Foreign Policy*, 47.

This relationship reached a peak in the 1970s when American diplomats began referring to Israel as the "51st state" of the U.S.:

Last summer, through a series of White House statements, it appeared we extended our commitments to Israel to include the "occupied territories," its continued military superiority, and the preservation of its "Jewish character." . . . Only history can fully explain this unique U.S.-Israel relationship, which now regards Israel's security as vital to our own. Our response to any potential threat to Israel is more immediate than to threats faced by our NATO or SEATO allies. Essentially, Israel has become our 51st state. As one State Department official quipped, "If Israel's survival were seriously threatened, we'd be in World War III in two minutes—whereas with Berlin, it might take several days!"[92]

The strategic alignment between the United States and Israel peaked during the Trump administration, whose policies often contradicted UN resolutions, the two-state framework, and U.S. commitments to Palestinians, emboldening Israel's hardliners. Netanyahu's policies, despite global opposition and legal challenges from the ICJ and ICC, relied on a perceived guarantee of U.S. support. In his Congressional address, Netanyahu praised Trump for actions such as recognizing Israel's sovereignty over the Golan Heights and Jerusalem as Israel's "eternal capital."[93] These moves violate UN Security Council Resolution 242, which includes the provision for the "withdrawal of Israeli armed forces from territories occupied in the recent conflict."[94]

This disregard for UN mandates highlights how powerful nations can bypass international rules, undermining the UN's credibility and effectiveness. If every permanent member of the Security Council starts to unilaterally bypass resolutions to which they themselves are signatories, can we still speak of a functioning UN system?

In this framework, the relationship between the U.S. and Israel shifts from complicity to a shared identity. Viewing Israel as a state with unique privileges, rather than as a nation-state with equal rights and responsibilities,

92 David G. Nes, Israel—The 51st State?," *New York Times,* June 5, 1977 [Approved For Release 2001/03/04]. https://www.cia.gov/readingroom/docs/CIA-RDP80-01601R000300300016-2.pdf

93 Noa Landau, "Netanyahu Welcomes Trump's Recognition of Jerusalem as Israel's Capital," *Haaretz,* December 6, 2017.

94 Resolution 242 (1967), adopted by the UN Security Council at its 1382nd meeting, November 22, 1967.

is perhaps the greatest barrier to achieving sustainable peace in the Middle East. Within this psychological landscape, the repercussions of Israel's actions—such as the recent events in Gaza, which challenge both human conscience and international law—on global perceptions of the U.S. and the rise in anti-American sentiment are rarely scrutinized.

Regardless of the reasons and background, the crime of complicity will remain a dark stain on the historical record of countries and leaders who commit acts akin to genocide. This crime will not be forgotten by future generations, not only of Palestine but of all humanity. To ensure that the principle of "Never Again" is not just a rhetorical statement but is put into practice, both perpetrators of genocide and those guilty of complicity must be held accountable before the collective conscience of humanity and before justice.

The Normative
Global Order after Gaza
Anachronisms, Adaptations, and Transformations

Richard Falk

Point of Departure

THIS CHAPTER analyzes the relationship between international law and world politics in the contemporary historical situation dominated by Israel's response to the October 7, 2023 Hamas attack. Given this purpose, attention is devoted to the nature and assessment of that portion of normative global order, which is dedicated to war prevention, regional and global security, and the realization of basic human rights. The performance of judicial procedures internationally, nationally, and in civil society when recently requested to confirm the genocidal and related allegations against Israel and to propose remedial action that is described and evaluated from juridical, moral, and spiritual perspectives.

The current normative global order combines, without clear lines of delineation, two logics: that of international law and that of geopolitics, with the latter usually given precedence when the logics clash in international political venues. This hierarchy of logics is most explicitly associated with "the primacy of geopolitics" that informs the framework of the United Nations and has been integral to the conduct of world politics since World War II. The human catastrophe being endured by the Palestinian people living in the Gaza Strip, and secondarily by Palestinian residents of the West Bank, exemplifies a controversial operational embodiment of this hierarchy, and makes it imperative to seek humane and effective alternatives to the

Richard Falk is the Albert G. Milbank Professor of International Law Emeritus at Princeton University and Chair of Global Law and Co-Director of Centre of Climate Crime and Climate Justice, Queen Mary University London. Research Fellow, University of California, Santa Barbara. He served as UN Special Rapporteur on Occupied Palestine from 2008 to 2014.

geopolitical management of power and security in arenas of conflict with strategic regional and international ramifications.

Interpreting the Gaza Experience

This discussion of the law dimensions of Gaza makes the broad assumption that the Gaza Genocide is best understood in relation to a larger crisis of humanity centered on the need to live together more benevolently and sustainably on a tightly interconnected planetary social and political reality.[1] In this sense, the genocidal catastrophe visited upon the Palestinian population of Gaza together with the active complicity of the liberal democracies of the Global West is a startling confirmation of the crisis conditions of the global normative order. The United States is leading the complicit engagement of aiding and abetting this deadly Israeli campaign, and by doing so, is revealing fundamental deficiencies of the existing normative global order from the perspectives of law and justice.[2]

The Gaza experience, additional to its unspeakable concreteness as well as its prolonged character and multi-dimensional criminality, can also be usefully interpreted as a *metaphor* for the exposure of vulnerable peoples everywhere to the dangerous and self-destructive systemic features of 21st century world order.

Beyond its metaphoric status, the Gaza Genocide is also an ominous *precursor* of more encompassing future catastrophes if drastic measures are not soon adopted and widely supported to transform the present character of the evolving Westphalian hybrid system of world order. This hybridity arises because, supplemental to routine intergovernmental interactions, the management of power and conflict among sovereign states is overseen and managed by Great Powers, who act as if freed from the constraints of international law and morality to pursue their strategic interests, which are often at odds with humane values and ecological resilience. These so-called Great Powers are global actors long set apart from other states as "geopolitical actors," often acting in collaboration with regional States and local non-state

---

1 See Elisabeth Weber's edited collection of essaysresponding to Jacques Derrida's urgent inquiry into how humans can live together on planet earth in better ways than in the past: Elisabeth Weber, ed., *Living Together: Jacques Derrida's Communities of Violence and Peace* (New York: Fordham University Press, 2013). See also Elisabeth Weber, ed., *Kill Boxes: Facing the Legacy of US-Sponsored Torture, Indefinite Detention, and Drone Warfare* (Goleta, CA: Punctum Books, 2017).

2 The term "normative global order" refers to the legal rules and customs, law-interpreting procedures, and remedial institutions entrusted with implementation in the event that voluntary compliance with the norms and their authoritative interpretation is not forthcoming.

political movements, as is the case in both raging conflicts now taking place in Gaza and Ukraine.[3]

At the same time, of course, it remains imperative to assess the particularities of Israeli behavior from the perspectives of international law and universal morality, and to encourage action on the part of those popular forces around the world that are demanding, as a matter of supreme urgency, an end to genocide and its attendant human suffering. Beyond this, there are growing civil society demands put forward in various populist arenas not only that the genocide be immediately stopped but also that Israel and its leaders be held accountable for the crimes they have committed, and reparations be imposed on the state of Israel. Available evidence strongly supports the belief that Israel, by intention, policies, and practices, is responsible for a wide variety of international crimes, culminating in genocide. As well, Israel and those governments acting in complicity are guilty of a consistent pattern of defiant refusal to respect and comply with the rulings of global tribunals rejecting Israel's arguments advanced in justification of their behavior. The world's highest judicial sources of legal authority, the International Court of Justice (ICJ) and the somewhat less respected and influential International Criminal Court (ICC), have been activated by non-Western governments critical of Israel's behavior.

At a humanitarian minimum that follows from a legal repudiation of its violent assault upon Gaza, Israel should be made to bear an extraordinary burden of reparations sufficient, if this is still possible, to restore Gaza to some semblance of normalcy providing a decent life for the Palestinian people. Israel should be held responsible in the immediate future to ensure that Gaza receives the emergency economic and infrastructural assistance needed to meet the momentous challenges of establishing a viable habitat for the traumatized and otherwise impaired surviving Palestinians who have remained resident in Gaza. However, this minimal and mandatory reassertion of the rule of law, decency, and universal morality in relation to this genocidal pattern of behavior is not likely to be undertaken by the UN or the liberal

---

3 In the contemporary context, the idea of geopolitical actors is often treated as synonymous with the five permanent members of the UN Security Council given a right of veto in a rare formal recognition of their geopolitical status. This UN framing of geopolitics is somewhat anachronistic as it reflects, at least to some extent, the world of 1945. But much has changed in states' relative standing since the end of World War II and the Cold War: the collapse of European colonialism; the rise of India, Brazil, and others; the newly contested U.S. role of being the sole geopolitical actor of global scale; and the emergence of the U.S., China, and Russia as geopolitical rivals. There are further complexities arising from coalitions anchored in the Global South, especially the BRICS, which pose a threat to the economic and political dominance of the American-led West.

democracies. At this point there seems to be far less willingness to mobilize the funding needed for restorative policy initiatives than was the case with respect to the post-conflict diplomacy that helped a devastated Europe, including even Germany, recover from the catastrophic situation that existed at the end of World War II.

Restorative undertakings after 1945 included a legally established reparations regime to compensate racialized victims of Nazi genocidal policies. As well, war crimes trials of surviving German and Japanese political leaders and military commanders were organized, although these trials were flawed by exempting the crimes of the winners ('Victors' Justice') from legal scrutiny. The crimes of the losers were exposed in generally fair trials as measured by due process standards, with the crimes usefully documented, and the perpetrators punished with a sense of justice done and notice served to others in the future.

The victorious countries did endorse a text of the Nuremberg Principles that was drafted in a manner that suggested that in the future *all* sovereign states would be subject to a set of universal constraints. To date there seems scant reason to think that individuals acting on behalf of geopolitical actors or their friends would be held accountable by being prosecuted for international crimes unless defeated in a major war. Also, to avoid the mistake of World War I peace diplomacy of imposing reparations on the German or Japanese nation as a whole causing humiliation and a receptivity to extremist ideology and to avoid repetition punitive measures imposed on the losers by the winners, after World War II punishment was limited to those individuals for whom there was strong evidence of their responsibility for the commission of serious war crimes, including Crimes Against Peace—although by the 1952 Reparations Agreement Between Israel and the Federal Republic of Germany, the latter was compelled to pay reparations to Israel inter alia for the costs of resettling Jews.

In making the case for Gaza as a metaphor for the world crisis, the nature of Israeli criminality is of the greatest relevance. The months of carnage were preceded by ample reliable civic evidence that Israel was guilty of commission of the international crime of apartheid (along with other provocations directed at the Palestinian people).[4] This prior criminality culminated in the commission of sustained genocide as perpetrated in an ecologically destructive

    4 See Richard Falk and Virginia Tilley, *Israeli Practices toward the Palestinian People and the Question of Apartheid,* UN ESCWA, 2017; *A Threshold Crossed: Israeli Authorities and the Crimes of Apartheid,* Report of Human Rights Watch, 2021; *A Regime of Jewish Supremacy from the Jordan River to the Mediterranean Sea,* Report of B'Tselem, 2021; *Apartheid Against Palestine: Cruel System of Domination and Crimes Against Humanity.* Report of Amnesty International, 2022.

manner that left the Gaza Strip bereft of agricultural sustainability and related conditions prohibitive of a viable life experience for its 2.3 million residents.

Suggesting an analogy of the horrifying experience of Gaza to the world situation has become more plausible with each passing month. The disparities of North/South inequality combined with hegemonic patterns of global governance, epitomized by what has been aptly called "nuclear apartheid" and visibly enacted in the hostile anti-migrant public attitudes that have become so prevalent in the Global West, are driving politics in many relevant Western countries to the dark corners of the far right. These international and internal developments are characteristic of a type of world order that depends on an as yet unacknowledged condition of global apartheid. These tendencies are being interpreted throughout much of the Global South as "colonialism after colonialism," that is, the continuing hegemonic dominance of the former colonial powers and even more so, of the breakaway British settler colonial states of North America, Australia, and New Zealand.

As a settler colonial project from its origins in the Zionist movement, Israel is an extension of this breakaway phenomenon, explicitly linked to the British colonial mentality, strategies, and structures established by the Balfour Declaration, and its accompanying encouragement of Jewish settlement in Palestine during the UK period as mandate administrator between the two world wars. Yet because of the violent Zionist revolt against the British administration of Palestine, pre-Israel Zionism managed to present itself to the West as riding the high wave of anti-colonialism, which entailed liberation from foreign rule. For decades this misleading narrative obscured the essential settler colonial Zionist animus of displacement, dispossession, expulsion, subjugation, exclusion, and above all, ethnic dehumanization of the majority native Arab population of Palestine.

As previously mentioned, in the five years prior to October 7, Israel was informally found guilty of the crime of apartheid in Occupied Palestine. A series of well-documented civil society reports by several of the most respected global human rights organizations meticulously documented this delegitimizing allegation.[5] Rather than address such a damning indictment of Israel's management of relationships with Palestinians (most overtly since 1967 in the Occupied Palestinian Territories), pro-Israel elites in Tel Aviv and the West responded with an eerie silence, ignoring this informed consensus of civil society.

Throughout modern colonial history a lethal sequence of events occurs. When apartheid fails to achieve the goals of the dominant settler race due to native resistance, a dire choice is posed for the settler community. This

---

5 See reports cited in note 4.

sequence has happened repeatedly in the Western Hemisphere, most vividly in North America, but also in Australia and New Zealand. Dominance and severe exploitation were not enough to satisfy the greed, address the insecurities of the settlers, and glorify the colonists' sense of destiny through subduing the resistance of the native people. Something more drastic had to be done to hasten the elimination or removal of the native presence to the unwanted geographic and economic margins of the new governance structures and quell any sustained expression of credible resistance.

At such junctures settler colonial entrepreneurs either resort to genocide or dismantle the apartheid regime as was surprisingly done in South Africa. The practical options for the leaders of the settler colonial project become either genocide or peaceful transformation to some constitutional form of inclusive governance based on genuine racial equality. The former option has been playing out in Gaza with the notable complicity of the United States and other Western countries, disguised by misleading language extolling Israel's right to security and self-defense. It is this inter-civilizational confrontation of the West and the Islamically-oriented resistance that links Gaza to the wider global crisis facing humanity, as battleground, as metaphor, and as precursor of a global catastrophe, which recently with increasing frequency is being articulated as the intensifying risk of World War III.[6]

Although ecocide is less integral to genocide than its linkage to apartheid, it is still closely associated with the dynamics of the Gaza genocide, which in this sense is dramatically different from the death camps in Germany designed to achieve racial purity, which did not entail extensive institutional and environmental destruction. The Gaza experience, more than the Holocaust, exposes the root of the current global predicament, which necessitates the generation of a peaceful and resilient form of world order that is capable of sustaining materially tolerable, socially equitable standards of living over long stretches of time.

The conclusion to be drawn is that Israel had recourse to genocide in a global setting in which the normative order constituted by the United Nations and international law was superseded by Western strategic and civilizational priorities. In effect, the Western governments stymied international procedures with potential authority to intervene to prevent severe abuses of human rights, rendering generally laudable efforts impotent and disillusioning. The UN Security Council could not even adopt an authoritative ceasefire resolution and even if it had, there is little reason to believe that Israel would have

---

6 See various manifestations of a rising concern with World War III: Annie Jacobson, *Nuclear War: A Scenario,* (New York: E. P. Dutton, 2024); and Boaventura de Sousa Santos, "Open Letter to Young People on World War III," *Z,* June 2024.

complied. As a result, the killing continued as horrified people throughout the world were daily confronted with unspeakable images of extremes of cruelty, suffering, and devastation, and watched the UN and leading governments reduced to the demeaning role of outraged, yet helpless, spectators.

The Ending of the Post-Cold War Era

There were several signs that the post–Cold War era that commenced with the fall of the Berlin Wall in 1989 and became definite two years later with the collapse of the Soviet Union is now itself either coming to an end or will in the future be regarded as having already ended, with the Gaza experience being perceived as either the end of an era or the beginning of a new one. There is a growing belief that the post–Cold War arrangements are changing, and in the course of being superseded by various international developments. This marks the present as one of radical transitional uncertainty, dramatized by the current genocides in Gaza and Sudan, and a prolonged geopolitical war in Ukraine between Russia and the United States continuing at the expense of the Ukrainian people.

When the Cold War ended a little over 30 years ago the United States suddenly found itself the sole geopolitical actor and quickly moved to fill the vacuum, accepting the responsibility to provide global leadership in ways that obscured tensions between its claims of acting on behalf of the global public good and its representing the ideological and economic interests of those states that endorsed liberal values of national governance and based economic development on market forces minimally regulated by government, a coherent worldview that at the time was labeled "the Washington consensus" or "neo-liberal globalization."

During the early 1990s, while in transition to a new post–Cold War form of world order, there were missed opportunities for enhanced conflict resolution, stronger international institutions, nuclear disarmament, demilitarization of international relations, a multilateral approach to human challenges such as climate change, ecological stability, and global migration. This might also have involved a determined effort to reconcile economic development with a more equitable distribution of the benefits of resilient growth policies, thereby narrowing gaps between the rich and the rest within and among sovereign states. In retrospect, we need to ask why none of this happened or was even seriously considered as an alternative. Yet there are strong reasons to believe, had these alternative paths to global security been chosen, such ordeals as the prolonged Ukraine war, the Gaza and Sudan genocides, and sub-Saharan toxic turmoil would have been much less likely to produce ruptures of world order than what the world has experienced in the form of exposed systemic deficiencies of the contemporary global normative order.

How can we explain, understand, and yet struggle against this failure to take advantage of such an obvious opportunity to be "creative" in an historical situation that posed unprecedented historical challenges to humanity as such, including its ways of living together and its relationship to the challenges of "otherness" that has up to this point served as the principal justification for exploitation, discrimination, wars of aggression, apartheid, and even, genocide.[7] Religion, ideology, and imperial forms of political destiny have obscured the distortions and damage wrought by the inter-civilizational dehumanizing of others as with respect to race, religion, nation, and civilization. The Gaza genocide is both an exhibit of this negative potential and an urgent warning about what the planetary future foretells if remedial action is not taken.

Beyond the Aftermath of the Cold War Era

The emergence of China as a geopolitical rival of the West and the global perception of ecological instability as posing a strategic threat to the future security of the planet were particularly notable features of the post-Cold War era. Yet the transitional morbidity of historical circumstances will long be associated with the outbreak of two high profile violent conflicts in 2022–23, the Ukraine War and the Gaza Genocide, neither of which presently shows signs of being resolved in accord with the imperatives of law, justice, and morality, or even responsible statecraft and the prudent promotions of national self-interests.[8]

These transitional ills have dramatically revealed the fragility and deficiencies of the management of global security in the 21st century. Neither the United Nations nor the geopolitical guardians of world order seem oriented toward new adaptive, let alone transformative, arrangements, and so dark clouds hang over the future horizons of human development. Perceptive

---

7 See Abdullah Ahsan, "Israel's Gaza War: A Symbol of Collapsing Civilization" (page xxxx), for related assessment resting on a postulate of civilizational decline. Particularly relevant is his discussion of Arnold Toynbee's emphasis on the potential role of a "creative minority" in proposing ways to overcome.

8 Irresistible relevance of frequently cited Gramsci quote, variously translated from the original Italian in his *Prison Notebooks*: "The crisis consists in the fact that the old is dying, and the new cannot be born. In the interregnum a variety of morbid symptoms appear."

critics of international relations refer to this dimly discernable future as one of great "disorder" and alarming "entropy."[9]

Dominant trends suggest that the political far right is well situated to gain from this atmosphere of disorder. This would accentuate the dysfunctional over-investment in military capabilities and tighten border controls so that diverse migrant ethnicities will not stage "invasions." Such a process is elevating anti-immigrant politicians to the pinnacles of governmental authority as exemplified by Trump's anti-immigrant agenda. While Rome burns and Nero fiddles, ecological and geopolitical challenges are deflected with cosmetic policies that are at once ineffective or worse and in defiance of every standard of public morality. In the background, is a situation of growing resentment at the degrees of inequality that have left more than 75% of the population of the liberal democracies worse off than were their forebears of the prior century. In a time when billionaires and oligarchs throw their weight around to shape elections and government priorities, perverting decades of economic growth and exerting disproportionate influence on electoral processes in democratic politics, such gross inequalities have become vivid and unacceptable, angering much of the citizenry that have been left to struggle to sustain former living standards.[10]

We have yet to grasp the exploitative and dysfunctional dynamics of post-industrial, digital/cyber/robotic/AI cyber life in the "liberal," affluent, and militarized West, and gradually spreading throughout the world. These countries are mobilized to prepare for and sometimes fight wars that can rarely be won, are costly, and in any event should never be or have been fought. China has comparable capabilities, but as yet has not projected its military reach beyond border island disputes.

As a group, only the young and uneducated are beginning to awaken to these dark realities despite repeated exposure, which even if filtered through brainwashing media platforms can hardly avoid presenting nightly spectacles of bloodshed, barbarism, and dehumanization. Within such a gloomy historical context, there are glimmers of hope. Among these glimmers are an unprecedented recourse by governments of the Global South to international law procedures, especially global tribunals. Of great importance are the enraged outbursts of civic activists everywhere, including in the countries whose governments are complicit with Israel's genocide, staging protests

---

9 Grigory Yavlinsky, "The Collapse of World Order after World War II and the Risks of a Major Conflict," 2024; Parag Khanna, "The Coming Entropy of World Order," *Noema*, May 7, 2024.

10 The "Global West" is not intended as a strictly geographic term but rather more a civilizational marker that includes such breakaway British colonies as Australia and New Zealand, as well as North America and the former European colonial powers.

in whatever spaces they could find and demanding adherence to law and morality. Of course, the established institutions and elites in the West are at odds in foreign policy with large numbers of their citizens, who see more clearly the values, and even the interests, at stake than do political leaders and politicians.

Recourse to Judicial Remedies: The ICJ, ICC, National Courts, and Civil Society or Peoples Tribunals

More than in any prior international conflict since 1945, the Israeli response to the Hamas attack has stimulated recourse to the UN, and when the political organs proved incapable of stopping the violence, to attempts to appeal to established international judicial procedures. Since these procedures supported claims associated with Palestinian grievances, those countries in the West led by the United States and complicit in Israel's assault upon the Gaza civilian population and infrastructure reacted in a manner best described as "jurisprudential nihilism" and were dismissive of the relevance of international law to Israel's behavior. On balance, international law never seemed to offer a way to curtail international crime, and in the end proved vulnerable to geopolitical nullification.[11]

In furtherance of the fundamental UN commitment to war prevention, the pacific settlement of disputes among states is strongly encouraged by a broad range of international approaches available at the discretion of the parties. These include direct diplomacy, mediation, arbitration, and most authoritatively, adjudication. The International Court of Justice (ICJ) is a principal organ of the UN and the highest international tribunal. There are additional specialized tribunals such as the Law of the Sea Tribunal with a mandate to handle specific related disputes, and the International Criminal Court, mandated to address allegations of international crimes directed at individuals.

The emphasis on judicial remedies as a component of a war prevention strategy is particularly associated with the proclaimed peace-mindedness of the liberal democracies with historic roots going back at least to the efforts of post-World War I efforts to construct a more robust global normative order. The developments in Gaza since October 2023 illustrate the relevance of

---

11 This rather surprising aspect of "political realism" in action is best explained by Arab governments in the Middle East fearing challenges from populist religious and political forces more than from Israel, and likewise worry regionally more about meeting the supposed threat posed by Iran than the populist opposition to Israel. Whether Russia/China diplomacy promoting Sunni/Shia reconciliation alters the orientation of Arab governments in the region toward the Israeli abuse of the Palestinian population is not discernable at this point.

judicial remedies and at the same time reinforce the perception that ideals of pacific settlement are subordinated to the strategic interests of geopolitical actors and their friends within the UN framework. The conduct of the Global West liberal democracies is particularly disillusioning, highlighting double standards in responses to Ukraine and Israel, and confirming suspicions that naked power prevails within the UN.

The Gaza genocide unfolded without meaningful interference from either the main states composing the Global West or, for different reasons, its neighboring Arab governments in the Middle East. This pattern did not substantively alter despite more than ten months of accumulating and convincing evidence of the genocidal nature of Israel's military operation. In this respect governments' formal detachment from this cruel genocide gradually disillusioned increasing numbers of ordinary citizens, including in the West, and even some Western governments (most notably Spain and Ireland) about the orientation and functional effectiveness of the normative order operative in international life, and particularly as associated with the United Nations and U.S. managerial governance of global security. This disillusionment extended even to the values claimed to relate to the promotion of human rights and international law championed since World War II *in the abstract* by the liberal democracies in Europe and North America.

This absence of political will on the part of those governments and political leaders influential with Israel and supposedly adherents to liberal values frustrated and angered people in the Global South. Such a situation led to an unprecedented attempt by the Global South to invoke the forces of law. This involved reliance on the relevant actors most insulated from state-centric timidity and regional and global geopolitical alignments with the perpetrators: intergovernmental tribunals and human rights actors within the UN and civil society. Conclusive assessments of the impact of these international law procedures is still not possible, and so what is set forth here must be viewed as tentative and preliminary.

Yet one common reaction is clear, significant, yet often overlooked and unlikely to be altered by subsequent developments—a tendency to adopt a cynical attitude toward the role of international law. This attitude is understandable and commonplace, but wrong. Cynics argue that since international law, regardless of source, has been defied by Israel whenever its impact goes against its national policies of strategic importance, law has little regulative or behavioral relevance. Along this line also is the contention that Israel's continuing non-compliant behavior has had no adverse effects for Tel Aviv, which, for many commentators, reinforces the conclusion that international law is pretty much useless. This pattern leads many casual observers to conclude that recourse to international legal institutions and procedures is a waste of time and energy, yielding no positive effects in global security contexts.

Such a conclusion is prevalent even among sophisticated neo-Machiavellians who run most foreign offices in the West, misunderstanding what makes international law significant even when violated in relation to peace and security, if properly invoked. International law acts as a valuable counter-hegemonic policy tool in high profile situations where defied by targeted states and their allies.[12]

This mainstream disappointment with the impact of international law contrasts with the argument made here that adverse consequences have indeed resulted for Israel because of its refusal to heed international law, even when aided and abetted by complicit geopolitical actors. Compliance would have halted the genocidal assault and mitigated the effects of a deepening humanitarian catastrophe threatening the lives and wellbeing of every Palestinian physically present in Gaza, as well as those living in the West Bank, and even Jerusalem. In reaction to such a disappointment it is reasonable to insist that unless the formal normative order governing international life and state behavior is substantially strengthened, the recurrence of varieties of barbarous behavior toward adversary civilian populations will recur along with a likely increase in tandem with ongoing ecological entropy throughout the world.

It's also arguable that, in light of the Gaza experience, even with the deficiencies of the normative order being exposed by real time imagery of daily atrocities at the core of the Gaza genocide, international law, related procedures, and institutions have constructive and crucial roles in encouraging the peoples of the world to engage in civic activism to address gross injustices and lawlessness when intergovernmental structures fail to do so. Civil society, including even the mainstream media to some extent, is increasingly reacting to the horrors daily unfolding in Gaza and to the disillusioning impotence of the existing formal global networks of states and institutions to do anything effective to stop this transparent genocide carried out at the expense of a helpless, vulnerable civilian population. Populist protests only began to take a radical turn after a waiting period of several months of uncontested Israeli genocide. This gave the established normative order consisting of the UN and the geopolitical managers of global security, largely entrusted to the liberal democracies, an ample opportunity to have restrained Israel's criminality in an effective manner if the political will had been present and strong enough.

---

12 Noura Erakat, *Justice for Some: Law and the Question of Palestine*, (Stanford, CA: Stanford University Press, 2019).

This populist awakening became visible by way of the frequency and geographic dispersal of mass marches, public demonstrations, and college protest activity, as well specific denunciations of Israel's behavior by leading proponents of global morality, including the Secretary General of the UN and the Pope. Such expressions of discontent were accompanied by heightened demands for an arms embargo, as well as calls for boycotts, divestment, and sanctions. In this charged atmosphere several governments, significantly all in the Global South, resorted to institutions and procedures having been in existence since 1945 to elucidate international legal obligations.

Even the vibrant student protests among university students around the world only occurred after it became clear that the UN and governments with leverage over Israel would not use coercive means, including diplomatic leverage and sanctions, to protect victims of this prolonged and unambiguous genocide. The political organs of the UN were blocked from acting robustly, including in their relatively modest efforts to establish a mandatory ceasefire. The complicit governments of the Global West were in varying degrees of agreement with the actions being taken by Israel, or at minimum did not want to oppose Israel openly. This had the effect of nullifying efforts at the UN to stop the genocide, despite plaintive appeals by the normally apolitical UN Secretary General urging the UN to act in the face of a mounting humanitarian catastrophe. In a larger sense, the events should also be interpreted as an enactment of Huntington's "clash of civilizations" thesis, pitting the white and Judeo-Christian Global West against activist Islamic segments of the Global South, which has so far meant non-state movements, not governments other than that of Iran.[13]

Adjudication and Its Limits

Despite disappointing results on the ground to date, an intriguing sideshow during the nine months of savage genocidal violence against the entrapped Palestinian population of an estimated 2.3 million has been the unusual degree of attention given to international law and to international judicial procedures available for its interpretation and enforcement.

To begin with, this attention ended the previous obscurity of these institutions and procedures. Many persons and groups with global concerns have long wondered why two distinct international tribunals—the ICJ and the ICC—even exist and what distinguishes their institutional role from each

---

13 The term "Global West" is not meant to be a geographic marker. It calls attention to a group of States racially associated with whiteness and European colonialism that identified with Israel and vice versa.

other.[14] Beyond this, for many never exposed to an informed explanation of the process by which international law is judicially implemented, the differences between these two tribunals, both located in The Hague, is far from obvious, yet highly relevant. I offer here some brief remarks as to the respective character of the ICJ and ICC with the objective of clarifying the legal proceedings activated by the Gaza attacks by Israel that started a few days after October 7.

Both tribunals are indispensable judicial resources of a functionally effective and equitable international legal order and have exhibited their relevance as well as their limitations in the latter stages of Israel's "war" against Hamas.Their respective positive contributions to law and justice are diminished to the extent that such institutions are suspected of being subject to backdoor geopolitical manipulations and even de facto forms of nullification.[15] To acquire legitimacy and respect such institutions need to build a strong reputation for judicial independence, a respect for their professional competence, and to earn public appreciation through a high rate of compliance with judicial outcomes by participating States and the geopolitical guardians of the global geopolitical order. To achieve these results, it is above all necessary that legal rulings are respected by the losers as well as invoked by the winners and affirmed by the more influential member States at the UN, as well as by global public opinion.

The record of judicial professionalism by the ICJ has been impressively confirmed during the Gaza "war" as to function and outcome. It is somewhat more ambiguous and difficult to evaluate the performance of the ICC. The performance of these tribunals must be assessed within the limits and context set by the wider *geopolitical* ambivalence toward the role of international law within the domain of world politics.[16] International law is used (and abused) in such a hybrid arrangement of power politics when it can be invoked as a policy instrument against adversaries, such as against Russia in the Ukrainian War, while at the same time it is dismissively disregarded if it dares to question Israel's behavior in Gaza. Of course, the cost of double standards makes

---

14 A more comprehensive survey would also consider the role of regional tribunals.

15 A clear case of geopolitical interference has arisen with respect to the role of the UN agency entrusted with the implementation of the Chemical Weapons Convention in relation to the Douma Incident in 2018.

16 The strongest sign of this ambivalence is the inclusion of a right of veto conferred on five of the strongest sovereign state members of the Security Council at the time of the UN's establishment. This can be explained either as "realism" about the extent of authority that could be effectively claimed by international law or as "legal spoils" associated with winning World War II. It also limited accountability for war crimes to the losers in the war.

international law perceived to be more of an instrument of state propaganda than as a universally applicable regulative regime essential for war prevention and the obligatory observance of human rights standards.

It needs to be remembered that the ICJ lacks the mandate and capability to enforce its decisions whenever voluntary compliance is absent and enforcement necessary. Enforcement is entrusted by the UN Charter to the Security Council where the veto can be used without limitation by or on behalf of the non-complying state. In effect, in situations of the sort present when dealing with a strategically significant legal dispute, as in relation to Gaza, a "crisis of implementation" presents itself. The UN has proven incapable of compelling implementation of ICJ decisions in the face of geopolitical resistance, and there is neither the geopolitical willingness nor material capabilities to challenge this form of world order hybridity that is subject under certain conditions to this inhumane and dangerous zone of exception.

While the regional and global intergovernmental responses to the Gaza genocide are equivocal if not deeply disappointing, the pronouncements of these judicial institutions do have the potential to exert a major positive *symbolic* influence even, as here, when their rulings have been scorned and disregarded by Israel and the U.S. The experience of the ICJ in relation to Israel's defiance of judicial issuance of Provisional Orders on three distinct occasions in the case of *South Africa v. Israel* is demonstrative in these widely observed judicial responses to alleged violations of the Genocide Convention. Even these preliminary ICJ actions commanded major worldwide media attention and encouraged civic activism, whether being accepted or condemned by governments depending on their views of Israel's Gaza assault. The pronouncements of the ICJ have had the indirect effect of adding a further intangible element of legitimacy and militancy to worldwide civic activism, including most pointedly among the citizenry in the complicit liberal democracies in the Global West. This judicially stimulated activism focused on opposition to Israel's continuation of the Gaza genocide, and on demands to end the complicity of its supporters by at least imposing an arms embargo.

It seems worth observing, when appraising the symbolic impacts of international law and morality, that the *losers* of every major internal war since World War II have been militarily superior, but on the weaker side of the legitimacy dimensions of these conflicts. In effect, during the last 75 years these symbolic battlefields shaping perceptions of legitimacy seem to have a greater eventual influence on which side controls the political outcome of conflicts more than does the military superiority of the side defeated in the Legitimacy War.

Israel and the United States are partly aware of swimming against this anti-colonial tide. It explains why these governments are willing to sacrifice their liberal and democratic credentials to oppose recourse to authoritative assessments of international law by the ICJ, and even the ICC. It also helps to explain why only governments of the Global South (South Africa, Nicaragua) and outliers in the North (Ireland and Spain) preliminarily expressed positive support for recourse to international law procedures in reaction to the severity of Israel's behavior. Additional states joined later. Again, it needs to be stressed that State actors will not comply, nor does the UN have the will and capability to challenge the primacy of geopolitics in the Gaza context; only the aroused and outraged peoples of the world have this potential to press for and implement international law in their own ways in reaction to such challenges as are present in Gaza.

Against this background the role of the ICJ and ICC in the global normative order can be appraised in relation to the rationales for their establishment under quite different conditions.

International Court of Justice (ICJ)

All states that are members of the UN are *automatically* parties to the Statute of the Court, which sets forth its operational framework. The Court for its part must formally agree that a dispute brought before it for adjudication is of a sufficiently *legal* character and not more properly regarded as a *political* or *moral* dispute. This jurisdictional objection was raised by Israel's contention that South Africa's recourse to the ICJ under Article IX of the Genocide Convention was invalid because there existed no relevant legal dispute between the two countries.[17]

The ICJ rejected Israel's objection to its authority to adjudicate South Africa's allegation of Israeli genocide by a near unanimous vote by its seventeen judges. The ICJ ruled that a legal dispute between South Africa and Israel existed as to the application of the central provisions depicting the international crime of genocide in the 1951 Convention on the Prevention and Punishment of Genocide.

The relationship between the UN and the ICJ is set forth in the Statute of the ICJ as well as Chapter XIV of the UN Charter, Articles 92–96. The Statute frames in technical detail the role, procedure, and scope of concerns of the ICJ. As mentioned, the main function of the ICJ is to decide *legal disputes* between sovereign states as an integral aspect of the UN Charter's

---

17 Some important treaties, including the Genocide Convention, contain what is called a "compromissory clause" in which state parties to the treaty agree in advance to submit all legal disputes for resolution to the ICJ.

emphatic encouragement of "the pacific settlement of disputes," treated as a principal policy instrument relevant to the UN's primary objective of *war prevention* (UN Charter, Articles 2(3), 33–38).

The underlying justification for the establishment of the ICJ was to provide members of the UN with a politically independent, professionally distinguished, and civilizationally representative and diverse panel of judges with strong credentials in the study and practice of international law, with their sole task being to pronounce upon the relevance and interpretation of international law as it bears on the resolution of disputes brought before it, after being exposed to extensive oral and written legal arguments by opposing sides as to its authority to decide, which if affirmed, reflect the respective legal merits of the opposed substantive positions taken. There are additional provisions for third party governments and civil society actors to submit views in the course of pending ICJ litigation. As of October 2024, 14 countries joined the South African submission.

Such a judicial mechanism was hoped to provide sovereign states, large and small, with an alternative to sanctions, war, and diplomatic stalemate, with the desired effect of substituting the assessments of law for conflict resolution in place naked disparities in power. Adjudication was also viewed as a tool to enable states to resolve routine legal disputes in a dignified manner that minimized international friction and contributed to an impartial understanding of respective rights and duties.

The ICJ is also generally limited by legal mechanisms relevant to the submission of a dispute for adjudication. This international judicial remedy is only available if both sides agree in advance to resolve all international legal disputes by recourse to the ICJ (so-called "compulsory jurisdiction") or in specific circumstances reach an ad hoc mutual decision in a particular instance where states disagree about their legal obligations and yet are willing to submit *this* dispute to the Court for settlement by adjudication.[18]

It is helpful to appreciate that the ICJ has no jurisdictional authority with respect to individuals or criminality, its legal authority to adjudicate being limited to the obligations of the governments of states. The ICJ's lack of authority to act with respect to the criminality of individuals who act on behalf of the state or in relation to *political* disputes sometimes raises troublesome questions as to the distinction between law and politics. This especially true when addressing allegations of genocide as law, politics, and morality inevitably overlap. It is a challenge to judicial craftmanship to demonstrate

---

18 See Richard Falk, "Why the World Must Stand Behind the Decision on Israeli Occupation," *Middle East Eye,* July 24, 2024.

their focus on the legal issues present, or risk widespread criticism that the ICJ has become unlawfully politicized, exceeding its treaty authority.

As already indicated, the ICJ as an institution within the UN network of actors has no enforcement capabilities of its own. It is the contention here that legal judgments of respected tribunals possess importance as the most trustworthy source of authoritative declarations of applicable law. This is generally accepted even when the losing State party fails to comply *voluntarily.* The Security Council is given the formal authority in the UN Charter to enforce an ICJ decision that is not being complied with by the losing party, but it has proved useless where strategic interests of veto powers clash with the judicial outcome.

Securing an enforcement mandate is often not a simple matter. It means that the Security Council must have support from nine of its fifteen members, including the affirmative votes or abstentions of its five Permanent Members, each of whom possesses the right to veto any enforcement decision. The General Assembly is vested with a residual authority to recommend compliance with decisions of the ICJ or other measures designed to overcome non-compliance. The General Assembly lacks specific coercive authority to act on its own to implement ICJ decisions, although if the political will existed it could attempt to exert authority to impose a ceasefire in reaction to Security Council paralysis and Israeli defiance.[19]

Yet, as earlier mentioned in general terms, civic activism if sufficiently mobilized can impose punitive responses in high profile instances of non-compliance, as here. More concretely, it can exert various forms of pressure on governments and urge sports and cultural boycotts as well as movements that demand divestment by public institutions and private sector actors (education, labor, human rights) as well as suspension of business relations by corporations with the state targeted by societal sanctions. A telling incident occurred in relation to the 2024 annual observance of the atomic bombings in Japan; the mayor of Nagasaki withheld an invitation to Israel to attend the anniversary event while the mayor of Hiroshima issued an invitation. The U.S. ambassador stayed away from the Nagasaki event in a show of solidarity with Israel. This incident is again illustrates the importance of the symbolic domain of international law and politics in which considerations of legitimacy have political consequences.

The ICJ has certain distinctive features, several of which are worth of comment:

---

19 The vote in the ICJ was 7-7, which according to its rules meant that the President of the Court, who supported the South African legal position, is given a second "casting vote" that broke the tie. *Southwest Africa Cases,* ICJ Rep., 1966.

- Over the course of its history the ICJ has earned a reputation of judicial independence and professionalism but has received criticism for excessive formalism and cumbersome procedures that greatly delay the issuance of judgments. This can result in lengthy intervals of several years between the time of submission and that of judgment. This means that sometimes the ICJ decision comes long after the resolution of the facts giving rise to the dispute. This somewhat restricts interest in judicial outcomes to academic specialists concerned with the ICJ's role in developing international law in previously legally uncharted territory.

  The ICJ has never, before this Gaza genocide litigation, been as deeply engaged with an ongoing legal dispute possessing a major geopolitical dimension, and so far, has received widespread praise for its measured and legally well-reasoned and fully documented generally sympathetic preliminary treatment of South Africa's effort to obtain a ruling that will legally repudiate and judicially order an end to Israel's response to the Hamas attack of October 7 by concluding that Israel is indeed guilty of perpetrating the crime of genocide.

  Israel has already been ordered during preliminary proceedings by the ICJ to take provisional measures in light of the humanitarian emergency imperiling Palestinian lives in numerous ways, while awaiting the decision on the merits of the underlying allegation of genocide that will probably not be forthcoming for several years or, hopefully, long after the probable end of violence in Gaza.

- The judges of the ICJ are elected by the members of the General Assembly and Security Council, but a negative vote by one of the P5 is treated as a normal vote and is not treated as a veto.

- In response to formal requests from the distinct organs and specialized agencies that make up the UN System, including its specialized agencies, the ICJ also has a parallel secondary authority and duty to render what are called in the ICJ Statute "Advisory Opinions." AOs are issued in response to formal requests, but only from organs and specialized agencies of the UN. Again, the authority of the ICJ to act is limited to legal disputes. As the advisory label implies, the legal findings of advisory opinions can be and have been ignored, and there is no expectation that where the issues are controversial, the rulings will change behavior of the government(s) or UN institutions and agencies whose policies and practices are incidentally found to be

unlawful by the ICJ in the exercise of its advisory role. The ICJ is
not permitted to use its advisory opinion role to assess directly the
legality of the behavior of sovereign states. Nevertheless, the legal
assessments of the judges rendering Advisory Opinions may exert
a considerable educational and political influence in relation to the
future development of international law. Diminishing the authority of
opinions about legal questions bearing on the role of the UN is one
example of how the UN balances sovereign rights and the geopolitical
privileges of its most powerful member states while simultaneously
affirming the overriding authority of international law.

The very notion of labeling decisions of the ICJ as "advisory
opinions" is expressive of the overall ambivalence of the post-World
War II architects of the post-war normative architecture when it came
to regulating the behavior of states by their subordination to the
authority of international law.

Perhaps the most significant expression of this ICJ secondary role of
clarifying the relevance of international law to the UN operations was issued
in its advisory opinion of July 19, 2024, on the lawfulness of Israel's occupation of Palestinian Territories, including Gaza but not beyond 2022. The
ICJ examined Israel's occupation policies and practices in the Palestinian
territories only through to the date in 2022 when the General Assembly
requested legal guidance from the ICJ. What makes this AO so important is
the support of a strong majority of the 15 judges for declaring Israel's policies
and practices over the period since 1967 as unlawful. This assessment supported its articulation of the legal duties of Israel, all states, and the UN itself
to implement the various finding by effective action. The judgment deserves
to be read as both an authoritative rendering of international law dimensions
of the occupation and the legal consequences that flow from this conclusion.

The ICJ has rendered some unpopular and dubious decisions in the
course of its history. A good example is the so-called Southwest Africa Case
back in 1966 whereby the outcome favoring apartheid South Africa was
upheld by a close vote. The ICJ upheld South Africa's legal right to govern on
the basis of its authority as the mandatory administrator of Southwest Africa
(now Namibia) by relying on the same kind of racially segregated regime it
relied upon to govern its own national society.

Again, the secondary international effects of an ICJ decision can be significant even if contrary to the legal reasoning and judgment of the majority
decision. This unexpected ICJ outcome shocked many governments of the
Global South and angered anti-racist public opinion because it accepted

South African arguments that apartheid could be extended to administer Southwest Africa. This negative reaction led the General Assembly to terminate abruptly South Africa's administrative mandate. This repudiation of the ICJ judgment had the intended effect of gaining sovereign statehood for Southwest Africa much sooner than if South Africa had been legally required by the ICJ to dismantle the extension of apartheid to Southwest Africa. There was widespread agreement with this outcome. The General Assembly action interpreted the administrative discretion of South Africa as the mandatory power more in accord with international human rights law than the ICJ. The General Assembly action was also more reflective of the anti-apartheid consensus that then existed in international society, which operated as an existential political veto or check upon the unconditional authority normally accorded ICJ decisions.

The contributions of the ICJ to the development of international law through its well-analyzed and researched assessments, including dissents and separate opinions, has been at least as important as its assigned priority of resolving international legal disputes. It has been given very few opportunities during its almost 80 years of existence to render judgment on legal disputes between geopolitical rivals, which is in keeping with the overall UN design that exempts its leading members from the legal duties of "normal" states to obey international law. These exempted states continue to possess a legally endowed national discretion to ignore law based on an insistence of absolute sovereign rights. In major encounters of geopolitics as in the Ukraine War, the U.S. hypocritically undertakes self-righteous recourse to international law and the UN System to condemn a geopolitical challenger.

International Criminal Court (ICC)

The ICC, unlike the ICJ, is still a young institution that did not come into existence until 2002, or 57 years after the UN came into existence.[20] It came about as a project that gained political traction by creating a collaborative coalition of governments from the Global South and many civil society actors or NGOs. To become a member of the ICC it is necessary to become a party to the Rome Statute, a stand-alone international treaty that provides the technical framework for the operations of the tribunal. Unlike the ICJ, the ICC operates without any formal relationship to the UN.

Such a procedure requires states to ratify the Rome Statute as an international treaty in accord with diverse national constitutional procedures

---

20 Even such a time interval is deceptive as the League of Nations included the Permanent Court of International Justice, which in most respects was a direct precursor of the ICJ, although not the ICC.

that typically involve signature by a representative of the executive branch of government followed by legislative approval, sometimes requiring a super-majority. As of 2023, 124 countries have become ICC members, including almost every European state that has supported Israel's claim to act in defense of its security, but to a lesser degree than the U.S. Such important states as the U.S., Russia, China, and India, as well as Indonesia, Türkiye, and Israel have not joined the ICC, many would say for obvious reasons of preserving their respective postures of impunity or non-accountability.

The extent of non-participation is a definite weakness of the ICC as these most important geopolitical actors and other leading states have chosen not to join for pragmatic and ideological reasons, challenging the basic notion that international criminal law should be given precedence over national sovereignty and its legal institutions.[21] Somewhat surprisingly, such leading NATO states as the UK, France, Germany, and Italy became parties to the Rome Statute, and thus potentially subject to the ICC framework.

Unlike the ICJ, the ICC has jurisdiction only over individuals who become physically subject to its authority by arrest or voluntary submission. Members of the ICC are obligated to cooperate with its formal orders, including the arrest of individuals accused of international crimes present on their territory, but only after a thorough investigation of the evidence of alleged criminality has been obtained and evaluated.

A controversial aspect of the Rome Statute is its grant of authority to the ICC to prosecute properly accused individuals who allegedly committed crimes on the territory of member states but were themselves nationals of non-member states. The Global West, especially the U.S. and Israel, have made this issue into a legal and political challenge in current circumstances to the effectiveness, relevance, and legitimacy of ICC operations.

After the Russian attack on Ukraine in 2022 European members pushed hard for the arrest of Putin and others, being cynically encouraged by the U.S. to do so on the basis of unsupported allegations of kidnapping of Ukrainian children. In the context of Israel's genocide, these same governments were outraged when the Senior Prosecutor of the ICC recommended the issuance of arrest warrants for top Israeli leaders, along with Hamas leaders. At this writing, there is no finality as the recommendation awaits action by a chamber of three ICC judges who must decide to approve or reject what the

---

21 The U.S. Congress went so far as to enact the *American Service Members Protection Act* (2002), more familiarly known as the Hague Invasion Act as it authorizes the use of force, if necessary, to liberate Americans and nationals of allies from any effort by the ICC to assert its authority over them. During the George W. Bush presidency, the U.S. Government went so far as to "unsign" Bill Clinton's signature of the Rome Statute during his last days as president in 2000.

prosecutor proposed. In any event, there is no prospect of implementing ICC arrest warrants against the named Israelis (Netanyahu, Gallant) unless they risk visiting ICC member states. Only ICC member states are obliged to give effect to such arrest warrants should they be issued.

Nevertheless, even at this preliminary stage, these recommendations pertaining to arrest warrants have some adverse implications for the individuals targeted and the country of their affiliation. The indicted individuals might hesitate before traveling to countries such as the UK and France, which are ICC members, and obligated to carry out arrests, especially if such states have incorporated universal jurisdiction legislation into their domestic law. It bears on how the political actors are perceived in civil society, tilting the scales of legitimacy and sovereignty ever so slightly, or in some instances giving rise to pushbacks of outrage. This could have serious reputational implications for both the countries involved and for the ICC. It could cause, as here, an angry Israeli/U.S. backlash against all forms of internationalism. Even at this pre-issuance stage Israelis are reported to be shocked and outraged that their leaders could be singled out for arrest due to participation in the crimes alleged, including that of "extermination," but revealingly omitted from the Prosecutor's formal recommendation was any reference to "genocide." As genocide is the most encompassing crime that Israel has been charged with and the basis for worldwide civil society pro-Palestinian activism, this omission is notable.[22]

It should be observed that in the past, the ICC has been sharply criticized for its focus on the alleged criminal wrongdoing of political leaders in countries of the Global South, especially several from Sub Saharan Africa. When the ICC earlier attempted to investigate evidence of crimes by Israel in Occupied Palestine and those of the U.S. in Afghanistan there were furious reactions in Washington and Tel Aviv, including the formal adoption of U.S. sanctions against named ICC officials, and the ICC seems to have been duly intimidated, proceeding no further.

The failure to move forward on genocide, despite the abundant evidence, reinforces the impression that the ICC is a weak institution not capable of

---

22 Although not mentioned in the prosecutor statement recommending the issuance of the arrest warrants by the ICC, forbearance on the genocide charge may exhibit a recognition that the issue was under the remit of the ICJ, which has not reached a decision on the merits of the genocide allegation in the case initiated by South Africa (and joined by Spain and Colombia). At the same time, because of their different judicial functions, there would be nothing inconsistent about the ICC as well as the ICJ both reacting to genocide charges. UN Regional Information Center, "South Africa vs Israel: 14 other countries intend to join the ICJ case," October 30, 2024. https://unric.org/en/south-africa-vs-israel-12-other-countries-intend-to-join-the-icj-case/

consistent professionalism when confronted by geopolitical resistance or of fulfilling the expectations contained in the Rome Statute. Again, in relation to the Gaza genocide there have been calls in the U.S. Congress for "sanctions" against the Prosecutor and other officials of the ICC, should even the recommended issuance of the arrest warrants or other actions against Israelis take place, even though there is no chance that the arrests will be made. The mere issuance, even the pre-issuance recommendation by the Prosecutor, was sufficiently incriminating to produce anger in Israel and Washington and satisfaction elsewhere. While many dissented from equating Hamas leaders with the Israeli perpetrators of genocide, President Biden was shocked that Israeli leaders of a sovereign state would be equated with what he regarded as Hamas terrorist leaders.

The future of the ICC, and indeed the struggle to extend criminal accountability to the strongest political actors, will be seriously affected by the outcome in Gaza and by whether the ICC responds to current geopolitical pressures in ways that improve its reputation for judicial independence. Ever since the Nuremberg and Tokyo war crimes trials international criminal law has been seriously compromised in war/peace contexts by its failures to treat equals equally. The damning fact remains that these widely heralded World War II prosecutions only addressed the crimes of the losers while excluding from consideration the crimes of the winners. Such a double standard has tainted all efforts since 1945 to generally strengthen legal accountability for international crimes. It raises the question as to whether "the primacy of geopolitics" within the UN and elsewhere in managing global security is subject to normative challenge. The planned *UN Summit for the Future,* scheduled for September 22–23, 2024, might have been expected to cast light on this fundamental question.[23] I would be surprised if the UN Summit would dare to touch such a hyper-sensitive topic that is bound to give rise to intergovernmental frictions. Several sophisticated commentators on UN affairs believe the Summit will confine itself to trivial reform issues, thereby resisting any effort to transform the normative architecture created in 1945. If this transpires it will be disappointing to many of us hoping for a brighter UN future in the aftermath of the Gaza experience as well as some major adjustments that respond to the fundamentally changed circumstances and the militarized geopolitics of the U.S.-led Global West. At least some concerted effort by the Global South to propose changes in UN procedures that might pull humanity

---

23 The full formal name is *Summit for the Future: Multilateral Solutions for a Better Tomorrow.* Expectations are not high for UN reform that will overcome the weaknesses of the UN with regard to war prevention or the tendency to entrust the management of global security to geopolitical actors.

back from the brink would have been a welcome sign of creative friction in an otherwise bleak outlook.

National Courts Empowered to Exercise Universal Jurisdiction by Domestic Legal Ennactments

There have also been a variety of legal actions in national courts that are endowed with some variable levels of authority to adjudicate allegations of violations of international criminal law. These include initiatives in several European national courts to prohibit transfers by the territorial government of weapons or military aid to Israel due to credible allegations of genocide. Favorable decisions by such tribunals would generally not encounter the enforcement obstacles that block implementation of ICJ and ICC decisions as the ruling would be implemented by the national legal order that includes measures to coerce compliance. However, these national courts are often reluctant to act in ways that encroach on the domain of foreign policy that is viewed in most constitutional democracies as beyond judicial competence to address. In the U.S. this reluctance takes the form of "the Political Questions Doctrine" by which domestic courts accord deference to the executive branch and decline to adjudicate.

There is currently a notable example of recourse to national courts by the Center for Constitutional Responsibility (CCR) that prepared a detailed, highly professional brief challenging U.S. complicity in the Gaza genocide. On January 31, 2024, shortly after the ICJ approval of Interim Orders in the South Africa case, the U.S. District Court dismissed the CCR complaint on technical grounds associated with "the court's limited jurisdiction." Such a dismissal was ordered despite the acknowledgement by District Court Judge Jeffrey White that Israel actions in Gaza "may plausibly constitute a genocide in violation of international law." This legal reasoning involved the application of the "Political Questions Doctrine," as previously mentioned. The decision of this lower Federal Court has been appealed to the Court of Appeals for the 9th District located in San Francisco. The appellate brief charged named top officials of the U.S. Government (Biden, Blinken, Austin) with criminal complicity associated with a failure to abide by the Genocide Convention's emphasis on the legal duty of parties to the treaty to act in way that *prevents* the commission of genocide.[24]

Two points emerge as central. First, that national court rulings in complicit or wrongdoing in sovereign states may have more enforcement potential than either the ICJ or ICC, especially if deference to foreign policy

---

24 The official name of the 1948 treaty: *Convention on the Prevention and Punishment of the Crime of Genocide.*

is judicially or legislatively curtailed. Secondly, even if the jurisdictional authority of national courts is confirmed or expanded, national partisanship would be likely to overwhelm juridical professionalism in the wrongdoing state or states, but far less so in complicit states where professionalism would be somewhat more likely to prevail. Concretely, an Israeli court would be far less likely to challenge government policy in Gaza than would a U.S. court, although neither has presently accorded a high probability to legal challenges, albeit for different reasons.

This assessment of national courts is concentrated on the situation of complicit governments, all of which seem to be located in the Global West, but further research may uncover evidence of complicity on the part of several Arab governments in the Middle East. From the perspective of civic activism, national courts in progressive countries, if true to their proclaimed adherence to "liberal democracy," offer a promising but much under explored arena for the implementation of international law.

Peoples' Tribunals

Ever since the Russell Tribunal of 1966–67 organized as a project of civil society activism in the middle of the Vietnam War, the ad hoc organization of such tribunals has created a non-state alternative to international tribunals. The dynamic of spontaneously instituting a distinctive judicial approach in situations where controversial international conflicts were not being addressed in a manner that responded to public concerns is an innovation with considerable potential with respect to the depiction of the contours of a just world order. Such tribunals can alter public discourse by media impacts and through the independent documentation and effective dissemination of allegations of criminality, as articulated by individuals with reputations as independent public intellectuals, legal experts, testimony of victims and witnesses, and generally by persons of conscience. Unlike the ICJ or ICC, the emphasis is placed upon morality and politics rather than law, although legal guidelines are examined and treated as relevant to setting a framework for normative thinking and rational assessment.

What would be unusual in the case of Gaza with respect to the establishment of a civically constituted global tribunal is that it would be undertaken while the conflict persists and the existing international tribunals are deliberating on the charges of genocide and other crimes.

It is also possible for civil society representatives to file briefs or make suggestions to the ICJ and ICC in a variety of ways. A particularly interesting initiative has been taken by the Geneva International Peace Research Institute which submitted a long scholarly, prudently phrased statement to the ICC

Prosecutor advancing an argument for why a formal investigation should be undertaken of the complicity crimes relating to the Gaza Genocide allegedly committed by Ursula von der Leyen in her role as President of the European Commission.

This interplay between civil society activism and the working of the formal statist procedures deserves further investigation and commentary. There exists a considerable body of material that has accumulated since the 1960s.

In addition to the seminal role of the Russell proceedings that enlisted some of the leading public intellectuals to pass judgment on charges and testimonies relevant to the U.S. engagement in the Vietnam War, there have been a large number of subsequent occasions where recourse to civil society or people tribunals occurred. The Permanent Peoples Tribunal (PPT), founded in Bologna, headquartered in Rome, has made the most sustained contribution to the basic jurisprudential idea that peoples and minorities can self-constitute law-declaring processes as an aspect of a law-governed *global* democracy. Its many initiatives were inspired by the Russell template but formalized by a normative framework given the name "Universal Declaration of the Rights of Peoples." It was deliberately adopted in 1976 as an acknowledgement of the 200th anniversary of the U.S. Declaration of Independence.

The PPT followed in general the template of the Russell Tribunal, but in the course of more than 50 sessions it has been responsive to the visions and objectives of organizers and sponsors as to the specificities of format. It has embraced a wide range of issues including the Armenian genocide, the Amazonia destruction of the livelihood and traditions of indigenous peoples, as well as U.S. intervention in Nicaragua, the Marcos regime's oppressive treatment of human rights and dissent in the Philippines. and corporate wrongdoing in foreign operations, especially in the course of exploiting Global South resources.

There have been other notable efforts along similar lines but with different organizational auspices. The Russell Tribunal on Palestine in 2010–2011 organized a series of judicial sessions on various Palestinian grievances, including the imposition of apartheid administrative structures.[25]

Of course, the judgments and recommendations of these peoples' tribunals cannot be directly enforced although they can influence public discourse, media treatments, and civic behavior. Widely disseminated reports of the findings and recommendations can encourage support for nonviolent solidarity initiatives such as the BDS Movement. Also, there is educational value in having a well-documented influential account of abusive state behavior, and

---

25 "Russell Tribunal on Palestine": https://www.russelltribunalonpalestine. com/en/sessions/extraordinary-session-brussels.html

the jurisprudential assessment of the work of peoples' tribunals can illuminate the nature of law, as well as the supplemental or complementary roles of these unconventional tribunals in societal struggles for justice, especially by vulnerable peoples.

Strengths and Weaknesses of the Normative Global Order in Response to Gaza Genocide

Never since an institutional matrix of norms, procedures, and institutions was first established in the aftermath of World War I, more than a century ago, have the strengths of normative dimensions of global order been put under greater pressure to perform than during the Gaza genocide. Yet for many, Israel and its supporters exposed its weaknesses, above all, the lack of political traction within the UN and among governments to implement authoritative and objective decisions as to the relevance of international law.

The global remedial resources discussed in prior sections were mobilized, performed mostly with due regard for the primacy of international law, and yet the Gaza genocide has persisted unabated. This can be best explained by both the weakness of mechanisms for enforcing international law and by the parallel meta-legal resistance mounted in this instance by Israel and complicit states in the West relying on their geopolitical capabilities to give priority to their strategic interests when clashing with expectations of compliance with international law. In effect, the primacy of geopolitics embedded in Westphalian world politics since the mid-17th century up to now able to neutralize the concerted challenges to genocide in Gaza posed by international law, impartially interpreted.

The Biden presidency exerted a strong influence on such an outcome by three distinct geopolitical features more recently inserted into post-Cold War global diplomacy: first, the U.S. Secretary of State, Antony Blinken, with obvious approval from Biden, lectured other states, including China, on observing the constraints of "a rules-governed world." Blinken never made clear what he meant by "rules-governed" but it was certainly not a plea to conform behavior to the constraints of international law, and seemed best interpreted as a message or warning to potential geopolitical rivals to refrain from challenging the strategic priorities of American foreign policy.

Secondly, such rules governance was pragmatically adapted to international law, and even the UN Charter, in the aftermath of the Russian attack on Ukraine in 2022, to justify not only condemnation of Russia but to justify joint efforts of self-defense with respect to sovereign rights. Such an identification of "rules-governance" was an implicit departure from American precedents (most notably, U.S. illegal aggression against Iraq in 2003), and became the occasion of moral hypocrisy when Israel's recourse to genocidal violence went unopposed and was in fact aided and abetted. This was preceded by decades of tacit acceptance of U.S. style "rules-governance" as set forth in the Fourth Geneva Convention on belligerent operations. This pattern of systemic noncompliance during the Israeli occupation of Gaza, the West Bank, and East Jerusalem is legally condemned by the strong majority views set out in the historic July 19, 2024 Advisory Opinion of the International Court of Justice.[26]

Thirdly, this reversion to the primacy of geopolitics throughout the more than nine months of devastation in Gaza provided many instances where the U.S., in particular, unconvincingly insisted that international law was irrelevant to the assessment of Israel's behavior in Gaza. This was most spectacularly evident with respect to Washington's scornful dismissal of South Africa's recourse to the ICJ to resolve the legal dispute with Israel arising from its allegations of violations of the Genocide Convention.[27]

In assessing the impact of recourse to judicial remedies, a first reaction would be to observe the presence of a crippling crisis of implementation evidenced by the continuation of Israel's policies in Gaza along with no significant weakening of complicit behavior on the part of several leading liberal democracies. A more comprehensive evaluation would take into account the indirect effects of defying the outcome of authorized judicial tribunals and the civic actions of populist forms of adjudication and assessment. The reputational costs to Israel of its defiant attitude toward international law and the UN seems likely to be high and damaging materially as do the related governmental adjustments and pushbacks demanded by outraged citizenries, especially in the Global South.

The international experience in Gaza poses the question as to whether there exists a sufficient will on the part of peoples and governments to modify the management of power and security by the strengthening of the normative global order. This would entail a corresponding weakening of the geopolitical dimensions of Westphalian hybrid world order which, with historical modifications, provided the normative structures of modernity. It is important to recall that Westphalian hybridity was part of the design of the post-1945 world order as expressed by the ambiguities of the UN Charter with respect to the juridical equality and political inequality of states and the privileged status of the victorious states after World War II.

---

26 See Falk, note 18.

27 See Marjorie Cohn, "Netanyahu's Visit to Congress Underscores U.S. Contempt for International Law," *Truthout*, July 24, 2024. https://truthout.org/articles/netanyahus-visit-to-congress-underscores-us-contempt-for-international-law/

The prospects of a potential non-geopolitical management of global security and the accommodation of powerful states to such transformative developments in the sphere of war prevention and dispute settlement are not bright at present. To the extent transformative prospects exist at all they depend on a convergent mix of civil society activism and non-Western governmental pressure. And most significantly, a rethinking of global security by geopolitical actors, especially the U.S. International law works, as in trade, international navigation, tourism, and diplomatic protocol because of the strong perception of *reciprocity and mutual interests,* creating a bias for stability as opposed to *national advantage.* Such conditions exist with respect to global security and war prevention but are not taken into proper account by political leaders and foreign policy advisors that remain entrapped in the anachronistic mentality of "political realism." Not only is there an immediate challenge to establish and acknowledge the legitimacy of "balance" in place of "hegemony" as the post-Cold War framework is being in any event superseded by existential developments. Even more fundamental is what I would call *the pedagogical challenge,* which involves a new understanding of realism as stressing compliant behavior by sovereign states, including those claiming geopolitical status with respect to law and even morality. Such a shift would almost automatically facilitate an emergent demilitarizing normative order needed to meet traditional security concerns as well as those more recent ecological challenges associated with resilient, equitable, and liberating patterns of human behavior.

SECTION II.
Palestinian and Jewish Voices

Gaza Is Humanity's Moment of Truth

susan abulhawa

The following is an edited transcript of remarks made by susan abulhawa at the May 26, 2024 Conference for SHAPE, Saving Humanity And Planet Earth.

WE DON'T YET HAVE a language to adequately capture the depths of Israeli terrorism. Extermination, holocaust, sadism, depravity—none of the words we know are big enough to convey what an aberration of life this monstrous entity truly is. For the past nine months, they've been implementing a long held colonial fantasy of not only "finishing the job," but doing with a gleeful sadism that echoes the public post of Tzipi Navon, Sara Netanyahu's close advisor and office manager, who wrote:[1]

> *We keep saying to terminate Gaza, terminate Gaza, but I think that's not enough...I want for Palestinians to be centered in one place to live, so that the whole nation of Israel can see, then to take them one by one, torture them well with pork fat and start with humiliation. First removing the fingernails from the hands and feet then removing pieces of flesh from different areas of the body, slowly slowly and carefully not to cause the death, make them to suffer and suffer for a long time. After stripping the scum from their skin, then cut off genitals and let him see how his testicles are fried in canola oil and force him to eat them, and this*

---

1 "Sara Netanyahu's adviser calls for torture of Gaza residents involved in killing Israelis," *Middle East Eye,* October 14, 2023. https://www.middleeasteye.net/news/israel-palestine-war-sara-netanyahu-advisor-torture-gazans-rant

susan abulhawa was born to Palestinian refugees of the 1967 war. Currently based in the United States, she is a human and animal rights activist, author, and frequent political commentator. She is the founder of Playgrounds for Palestine, an organization dedicated to upholding Palestinian children's Right to Play, and the Executive Director of the Palestine Writes Literature Festival.

*is how they slowly and patiently spread it to parts (we have a lot
of time) keep the tongue to the end of the torture session so that
it pleases us with its screams, the ears so that they can hear their
own screams and the eyes so that they can see us smile.*

While these words may sound like the ramblings of a deranged individual, the evidence indicates her sentiments are in fact widespread, entrenched attitudes throughout the Israeli military, and indeed Israeli society.

Macabre Experiment of Empire

In a rare moment of candor, buried in a New York Times article[2] were accounts of Israeli soldiers raping Palestinian hostages with hot metal rods and electrified sticks. The sexual torture of kidnapped Palestinians included being raped by dogs trained to rape; of inserting a fire extinguisher hose in the rectum of a Palestinian young man, then releasing the chemical contents of the extinguisher into his body. Footage of the gang rape of a Palestinian cancer patient at Sde Teiman torture center was leaked to the public after the young man was sent to a civilian hospital, ostensibly to retrieve the cell phone they had shoved inside him to call the number for a laugh. The hospital noted ruptured bowels, ruptured lungs, broken ribs, and a torn rectum with cuts and bruises all over his body. Public outcry ensued to ensure the rapists would not be punished. Then the world got to watch Israeli politicians and pundits extol their right to rape Palestinians.

Many of those who were kidnapped, including prominent surgeons such as Dr. Adnan AlBursh, Director of the orthopedic department at Al Shifa hospital, were tortured to death. Those who made it out of Israeli gulags emerged with such trauma that they had lost all memory and could not recognize their own children and family members. Some emerged unable to speak. All of them returned utterly broken, their mutilated, burned bodies testifying to the unspeakable.

Dr. Mark Perlmutter, an orthopedic surgeon from North Carolina and vice president of the International College of Surgeons said "all the disasters I've seen, combined, forty mission trips, thirty years, ground zero, earthquakes, all of that combined doesn't equal the level of carnage that I saw against civilians in just my first week in Gaza…almost exclusively children. I've never seen that before. I've seen more incinerated children than I've ever

2 Aaron Boxerman, "UN Report Describes Abuse and Dire Conditions In Israeli Detention," *New York Times*, April 17, 2024. https://www.nytimes.com/2024/04/17/world/middleeast/un-report-israel-detainees-abuse.html

seen in my entire life. I've never seen more shredded children in just my first week." He said children were "definitively" being shot by snipers.

The raw footage and sounds of unspeakable carnage are undeniable— whole families buried alive en masse in the rubble of their homes; torn bodies; shredded bodies; broken bodies; burnt bodies; dismembered bodies everywhere; blood and gore in the town squares and roads; unreachable bodies rotting in the streets, picked apart by starving stray dogs; wanton destruction of everything in the entirety of the Gaza strip.

Still, what I witnessed on the ground, even for a small period and even in just a small area of Gaza, is infinitely worse than the worst video broadcast to the world. The enormity of harm beggars belief.

The near total degradation of an entire high-functioning society in a short span is difficult to comprehend. Surely, the widespread lack of adequate sustenance and sanitation, coupled with unceasing terror, testing of new weaponry, and an AI guided death industry has made Gaza the most macabre experiment of empire.

Details and Death Toll of Genocide

I conducted a brief study to estimate the true death toll in Gaza, because the Health Ministry's numbers remained stagnant despite daily slaughter that we can all see. I knew, from speaking with health administrators and physicians alike, that the capacity to keep count of bodies had been decimated. Israel's attack on all hospitals in Gaza destroyed their servers and the cutting off of the internet severely curtailed the ability to log patient data. As well, healthcare workers have been particularly targeted by Israel, further degrading the ability to keep track of data. Paper tracking likewise proved impossible, as records were burned when Israel took over hospitals. Furthermore, the public number itself was already limited even when hospitals were functioning, because they only included those who were martyred by direct Israeli bombs or fire.

My study, published in Electronic Intifada on 27 June 2024, found the true death toll as a range of 193,248—514,464 lives ended. These numbers included martyrs from direct fire, as well as those with chronic illnesses, such as diabetes, cardiovascular, renal, or vascular disease who died from lack of access to medications due to Israel's siege. It also included those who were dead or dying from starvation and dehydration, those who were known to be missing, and those dead from the spread of communicable diseases, such as dysentery, following Israel's destruction of sanitation and water treatment facilities.

As is frequently the case when Palestinians speak, my article was met with skepticism and dismissal. But ten days after its publication, *The Lancet,* one of the most prestigious peer-reviewed medical journals in the world, published their own estimate which corroborated the lower end of my estimated range. They gave a "conservative" number of "at least" 186,000 killed. I believe even that is a gross underestimation.

Israel has dropped the equivalent of six nuclear bombs on Gaza, which is less than 40% the size of Hiroshima. They've dropped more bombs on Gaza than that dropped during WWII on Hiroshima, Nagasaki, and Dresden combined.

The statistics alone are difficult to comprehend, and one's soul collapses when you try to imagine the universe of life, loves, joys and ambitions behind each of those lives. A group of American doctors who were in Gaza wrote a letter saying "everyone in Gaza is sick, injured, or both." But what is yet truly incomprehensible, and terrifying, is the pleasure that Israelis—across nearly all sectors of their society—seem to take from witnessing unimaginable cruelty of their soldiers, and the misery, pain, and terror of Palestinians. Their soldiers post videos of themselves blowing up schools, torching homes and food storage facilities, firing indiscriminately at occupied buildings, and ransacking meager supplies left in Gaza. They set Palestinian pain to music and post on TikTok. Families across Israel dress up in the equivalent of "Black face" to mock Palestinians mourning their dead and bloody children. And people across Israeli society call for greater violence, even a nuclear hit to wipe out all Palestinians in Gaza.

Ram Cohen, a Tel-Aviv school principal spoke in an interview about Israeli culture's attitudes towards Arabs when raising children. He said, "Arabs are inferior to us. That's why we kick Palestinians and slap them. We train dogs so they will bite them strongly and tightly. That's why we shoot them. They're nothing."

Slogans and Impediments of Empire

Israel is committing the holocaust of our time, and they are doing it in full view of a seemingly indifferent world. Their genocidal campaign in what little remains of Palestine is the culmination of decades of capitalist colonial ambitions that have been grooming us all and incrementally pushing the boundaries of our acquiescence since traditional European colonial powers were forced to retreat from their colonies and since the United States was unceremoniously ousted from Vietnam by lightly armed guerilla forces.

Despite the romantic narrative surrounding the establishment of Israel, complete with an aura of a happy ending to Europe's genocide of their own

Jewish citizenry, the reality is that Israel was created as a western colonial outpost in a resource rich region. It was Europe's last hurrah as a colonial powerhouse, which the U.S. adopted in earnest, particularly in the wake of the 1967 war.

The greatest impediment to empire is, and historically has always been, the conscience and consent of masses.

After decades of imperial wars, environmental destruction, the gutting of public services and public institutions and the fleecing of workers, empire is at last having to contend with mass discontent on this occasion of genocide. At some point, the boundaries are pushed too far.

There was a hint of this in the student movements of the 1960s and 1970s that spurred an end America's slaughter in Vietnam and Cambodia. The moral force of Black people rising together in their pain and rage against legislated racism changed the social fabric of America, ending formal segregation and ushering a new era in the struggle against institutional racialism.

Power did what power does, deploying brute force, murder, intimidation, silencing, marginalizing, surveillance and all manner of corrupt policing. We see the outcome and we think we know it. Labels like "victory" and "advancement" are applied. "Civil rights" is a term spoken as an absolute, a singular point of history with a terrible before and liberated after.

It's that "happy ending" reframing of what is indeed a boundless thread of struggle in both directions through time.

Consent and Narrative Construction

The resilience of elite capitalist rule relies heavily on this kind of narrative construction that manipulates public imagination with platitudes and reversible concessions, followed by a rebranding of oppression.

Enslavement becomes mass incarceration and purposeful drug addiction. Segregation is sacrificed to be replaced with conscription of Black faces around the same table of power ethos.

Power adapted since the 1960s, creating new stops, levers, gates and gatekeepers. They lulled us back into their system, rebooted it with greater cruelty and corruption, and retooled it with distractions and celebrity worship while they consolidated and concentrated power in the hands of a tiny minority.

They bought politicians, who in turn work to safeguard and increase the wealth and influence of this elite minority, through various tax loopholes, deregulations, and privatization of public institutions, and all manner of legislations that turned millionaires into billionaires and soon trillionaires,[3] a staggering wealth gap built on the misery of the masses. They created laws to exonerate their criminality and laws to criminalize our dissent. They busted up the unions, subjugated workers and pitted them against each other. Instead of confronting the bosses, workers were manipulated into demanding iron borders and separation of families at those borders.

They scraped environmental regulations and wildlife protections to continue extraction while polluting the planet. The de-regulations allowed this tiny minority to buy up the airwaves; so now they dictate the content of 95 percent of everything we see, hear and read in the way of mainstream journalism, entertainment, education and cultural productions.

It is by no accident that terrorist characters dominate Arab depictions in Hollywood. The unusually high number of casual mentions of Israeli benevolence or Israeli genius in so many television series and films is intentional; and it through such management of public sentiment over decades that Palestinian humanity is shamefully trivialized or ignored in both print and broadcast news media no matter how many atrocities we face at Israel's hands.

This is the reason why people can watch the wholesale vandalizing of our lives without flinching, whether it's Palestine, Iraq, Libya, Sudan, Syria, Somalia, Lebanon. If what's happening to Palestinians were happening to Israelis, well, we all know there would have been zero tolerance for a single bomb.

Instead of paying taxes, this elite ruling class, these billionaires "donate" to universities sufficient sums to impose their vision not only for higher education, but also for the acceptable expression of constitutional rights like the First Amendment. For example, outraged by a Palestinian literature festival—a beautiful celebration of Palestinian excellence and indigenous heritage—the billionaires Marc Rowan, Dick Wolf,[4] and the Lauder family conspired[5] to remove the president of the University of Pennsylvania because she was insufficiently deferrential to their interpretation of academic freedom.

3 Chiara Putaturo, "We are closer to seeing the world's first trillionaire than ending poverty: That's why we need fair taxes now," Oxfam, January 31, 2024. https://views-voices.oxfam.org.uk/2024/01/worlds-first-trillionaire-fair-taxes-now/

4 Ramishah Maruf, "UPenn donors were furious about the Palestine Writes Literature Festival. What about it made them pull their funds?," *CNN Business,* October 25, 2023. https://edition.cnn.com/2023/10/25/business/palestine-writes-literature-festival-what-happened/index.html

5 Rachel Louise Ensign, "The Billionaire Donor Taking On His Alma Mater Over Antisemitism," *Wall Street Journal,* November 3, 2023. https://www.wsj.com/us-news/education/the-billionaire-donor-taking-on-his-alma-mater-over-antisemitism-2d1637cd

Enlisting their hired goons in Congress, they and other billionaires of their ilk, like Bill Ackman, denigrated[6] and/or removed more university presidents for the same reason. This billionaire class even managed to bring the internet—which gave the 1990s generation hope for real democracy—under their nefarious control through monopolies, algorithms, and various forms of surveillance and censorship.

Thwarting Resistance

Americans tried to stop the march of U.S. corporate and Zionist warmongers toward war in the early 2000s, but they marched on, trampling our will and trampling the bodies of millions of Iraqis. And the world watched as the U.S. pulverized that once glorious, high functioning ancient society.

The way they pushed on, ignoring the will of the people, was itself an experiment in how they would continue to "push the envelope," as it were. At the time, I recall analysts saying that Iraq finally broke the stigma of Vietnam and freed Americans to pursue militarism and imperial adventures. An "embedded" media hid the bloody horrors of that naked attack on a sovereign nation, and kept the secrets of U.S. corporate looting of Iraq's treasures and laundering of U.S. tax dollars through rebuilding schemes.[7]

Desensitized or disempowered, Americans didn't bother protesting when the U.S. did the same in Libya,[8] spurring a staggering de-development of one of Africa's most advanced nations into a veritable human slave market.

The enslavement and mutilation of Congolese children and whole families in mineral mines to benefit American tech billionaires[9] (as well as Israel's blood diamond industry[10]) barely elicit a blip in Western media, a shockingly cruel reality they continue to obscure.

There are hundreds more bloody examples of American and Israeli adventures in killing and destroying others in the service of this ruling

---

6 Adam Gabbatt, "'A bully': the billionaire who led calls for Claudine Gay's Harvard exit," *The Guardian,* January 3, 2023. https://www.theguardian.com/education/2024/jan/03/bill-ackman-billionaire-attacks-claudine-gay-harvard-twitter-x

7 "Halliburton Wins Lucrative Iraq Deals," Post reporter Michael Dobbs on *All Things Considered* [radio show clip, 4 mins.], NPR, August 28, 2003. https://www.npr.org/2003/08/28/1414557/halliburton-wins-lucrative-iraq-deals

8 Ali Abunimah, "Columbia students confront Hillary Clinton with her war crimes," *Electronic Intifada Podcast,* February 15, 2023. https://electronicintifada.net/blogs/ali-abunimah/columbia-students-confront-hillary-clinton-her-war-crimes

9 Hanna Le, "Dark Side of Tech," *Medium,* January 28, 2024. https://medium.com/@hanna.le/dark-side-of-tech-73ad0fb20b25

10 Khafre Jay, "Diamonds Drenched in Blood: Unmasking Israel's Role in the Congolese Crisis," *LinkedIn,* November 20, 2023. https://www.linkedin.com/pulse/diamonds-drenched-blood-unmasking-israels-role-crisis-jay-he-him--xqotc/

corporate class. Mass surveillance of the populace followed the gutting and looting of public education in the United States. The rich got richer, and the poor became destitute.

In the name of technology and efficiency, capitalists degraded our food and water—poisoned them even[11]—benefitting pharmaceutical billionaires who keep the masses teetering on the edge of health. Popular gurus pushed philosophies of individualism, contempt for family, and various forms of alienation that shattered community and social or familial bonds, leaving vast swaths of the people unable to cope with life without drug varieties, both legal and illegal.

They have weighed us down with the fake dreams they scripted for us— insurmountable debt as a stand-in for education, a white picket fence and endless consumption as a stand-in for family; blood diamonds as a stand-in for love; and carnage abroad as a stand-in for greatness. They sold us a glorious pile of shit and made us think it was all there is. That such an unnatural and parasitic way of life was the normal—even inevitable.

They glorified obsessive consumerism and obscenely ostentatious lifestyles. And we let them, believing it was our choice. But we had none. Choice, like democracy and free press, is an American illusion, a fairytale they peddle in school, newspapers and songs.

Look how quickly they disbanded, silenced and erased memory of the Occupy Wall Street movement in 2011.[12] Look how we are taught to believe that change can only come through the ballot box, where we're told to "choose" between two war criminals one election after another.

This moment of livestreamed genocide is the culmination of decades of global capitalist criminality and genocidal Western and Zionist imperialism. We watch in horror and perceived impotence.

Gaslighting

Then they gaslight us.

Politicians, spokespeople, pundits, journalists and broadcasters take to the airways to convince us that we hadn't just seen brains, tongues, and eyeballs spilling from the crushed skulls of children and babies. Or worse, that they somehow deserved it.

"Fog of war."

---

11 David Cronin, "Water apartheid in Gaza and Flint," *Electronic Intifada,* March 18, 2016. https://electronicintifada.net/blogs/david-cronin/water-apartheid-gaza-and-flint

12 Kristen de Groot, "Ten years later, examining the Occupy movement's legacy," *Penn Today,* December 13, 2021. https://penntoday.upenn.edu/news/ten-years-later-examining-occupy-movements-legacy

"Collateral damage."
"Hamas. Hamas. Hamas."
"The only democracy."
"Self-defense."

Over and over they use their wicked justifications and obfuscations. They speak to us as if we're stupid because they're accustomed to our silence and acquiescence. And they go on, prancing into the Met Gala in obscene finery, the vulgarity of which is made all the more apparent in juxtaposition to the burned and dismembered small bodies on the same day, pouring into Gaza's few remaining hospitals, screaming, bewildered, in shock and in pain.

Thank God for the Students

But thank God for Palestinian resistance. Thank God for every Palestinian journalist and every Palestinian healthcare worker risking their lives day in and out to serve their people. For every fighter choosing martyrdom over indignity. For the local organizations and activists you never hear about, but whose work has been keeping thousands alive. For the students everywhere,[13] Naledi Pandor[14] in South Africa, Francesca Albanese[15] at the United Nations, and Clare Daly[16] in the European Parliament. For the masses rising up in #Blockout2024.[17] For artists and musicians from Roger Waters[18] and Talib Kweli,[19] to Macklemore[20] and Black Thought,[21] Questlove[22] and more.

---

13 Nora Barrows-Friedman, "Student intifada sweeps U.S. campuses," *Electronic Intifada Podcast,* May 10, 2024. https://electronicintifada.net/blogs/nora-barrows-friedman/student-intifada-sweeps-us-campuses

14 https://electronicintifada.net/tags/naledi-pandor

15 https://electronicintifada.net/tags/francesca-albanese

16 Ali Abunimah, "German EU chief downplays Holocaust while spouting 'infamous Zionist lie,'" *Electronic Intifada,* May 19, 2023. https://electronicintifada.net/blogs/ali-abunimah/german-eu-chief-downplays-holocaust-while-spouting-infamous-zionist-lie

17 https://blockout2024.org/

18 "Stop Gaza genocide, says Roger Waters," *The Electronic Intifada* [YouTube video, 26:19], November 5, 2023. https://www.youtube.com/watch?v=QkfYeo2tIts

19 Palestinian Campaign for the Academic and Cultural Boycott of Israel (PACBI), "Palestinians call for boycott of Open Source Festival in Germany over its censorship of Talib Kweli," BDS Movement, June 17, 2019. https://bdsmovement.net/news/boycott-open-source

20 Aja Romano, "Macklemore's anthem for Gaza is a rarity: A protest song in an era of apolitical music," *Vox,* May 10, 2024. https://www.vox.com/culture/24153524/macklemores-anthem-gaza-protest-song-apolitical-music

21 Open Letter, "Over 600 artists worldwide sign #MusiciansForPalestine letter," *Mondoweiss,* May 27, 2021. https://mondoweiss.net/2021/05/over-600-artists-worldwide-sign-musiciansforpalestine-letter/

22 Randall Roberts, "Patti Smith, Questlove among 600 musicians calling for 'solidarity with the Palestinian people,'" *Los Angeles Times,* May 27,

For Yemen,[23] South Africa and Colombia[24] and Ireland and Spain. For the Hague Group and every courageous country standing on principle. For every person who refuses to remain silent.

Gaza Is All the World Now

This time is different from the uprisings of the 1960s and 1970s. There is a new sense of global interconnection, an emerging class consciousness and foundational political analyses predicated on post-colonial studies and intersectionality, none of which were present decades ago. Back then the white students protesting the war wouldn't unite with the Black Panthers because they were too racist to connect the dots. All dots are connecting now.

Gaza is no longer the enclave sealed and besieged by Israel and Abdulfattah al-Sisi's Egypt into a concentration camp. Gaza is no longer the densely-populated strip of Israeli-occupied land. Rather, Gaza is now all the world. Gaza is our collective moment of truth, the meaning in our lives. It is the clarity we need and seek. It is the definitive divide between us and the ruling class that tramples us. It is us or them. There is no middle place now. All the borders fade, leaving us united to confront this greedy genocidal minority everywhere.

Gaza is the most anguished place on earth at this hour, dimmed by unimaginable Zionist cruelty, set to music for TikTok. And from this tortured place of rubble, death and misery there springs the greatest light we have ever known to guide us out of the darkness in which we've been forced to live. The light of our ancestors—from Palestine and Alkebulan to Turtle Island and Aotearoa.

If we allow the wheels of this genocidal Zionist engine to keep turning, there will be no more limits to fascism. There will be no shame or red lines before which they will halt. There will be no boundaries against which they'll need to push. Saving Gaza is our gateway to save humanity from this insatiable group of humans devouring the planet and its lifeforce. This struggle can no more be just about a ceasefire. It must demand liberation and accountability across our burning planet.

2021.   https://www.latimes.com/entertainment-arts/music/story/2021-05-27/patti-smith-questlove-run-the-jewels-support-palestine-boycott-israel

23 Jon Elmer, "Yemen's naval blockade in support of Gaza," *Electronic Intifada*, December 29, 2023. https://electronicintifada.net/blogs/jon-elmer/yemens-naval-blockade-support-gaza

24 "Colombia to cut diplomatic ties with Israel over Gaza war, Petro says," *Aljazeera*, May 1, 2024. https://www.aljazeera.com/news/2024/5/1/colombia-to-cut-diplomatic-ties-with-israel-over-gaza-war-petro-says

A Graveyard of Slogans

Already they are using the tactics of brute force, violent intimidation, suspension and marginalization. Universities are withholding degrees, deporting students, throwing them into the abyss of policing. They will attempt the same dismantlement, silencing and erasure they did with the Occupy Wall Street movement. They will offer half-baked promises with no teeth, to quiet matters long enough to adopt new strategies and enact new laws.

If we stop they will adapt, and they will do so with artificial intelligence, against which we may well have no defenses, not for a long time to come. So beware of their concessions. Beware of victory that pulls us back into the lanes they made. Israel's genocide against a defenseless and captive indigenous population cannot become a whitewashed, declawed historic moment of before and after.

We cannot leave the lawns and streets and courts and battlefields until Zionism is dismantled and Palestine is free. We must throw all of ourselves and our resources into this moment of global reckoning, and not retreat. We must fight them in courtrooms, in culture, in universities, in our jobs, in how we spend our money. We must boycott, withdraw and withhold our attention from them on social media to affect their bottom lines. We must continue to find creative ways of resistance and employ them until we win. And we most certainly can win through persistence.

Staying the course is the least we can do as brave fighters face the most ruthless and deadly military machines the world has ever known. They do so with extraordinary bravery, resolve, and faith. History promises us that the tides will turn decisively in our favor. We already see it happening, but I believe it will be more dramatic and clearer, even as Israel's genocide becomes more ferocious.

This moment belongs to us, the people. We can dream our own dreams and create a new world in every personal act of refusal to participate in this horrible system predicated on genocide and unending exploitation. We can transform our relationship to the natural world from its current parasitic form to a symbiotic relationship.

Together we are powerful beyond our wildest imaginations. Compassion and defiance are our superpowers, and this is just our origin story. The world we need and want must and will pass through this birthing canal called Gaza, Palestine.

Gaza has been described as "a graveyard for children," and indeed it is, as it is also a graveyard for journalists, healthcare workers, artists, writers, and aid workers—populations most targeted by Israel. But Gaza is also the graveyard for western slogans and mythologies like "democracy," "human rights," "rule of law." And Gaza will be the graveyard of western hegemony and empire.

Taking Gaza from the Political Margins to the Heart of the Palestinian Discourse

Ramzy Baroud

WHAT IS TAKING PLACE in occupied Palestine is not a conflict, but a straightforward case of illegal military occupation, apartheid, ethnic cleansing and outright genocide. Those who insist on using "neutral" language in depicting the crisis in Palestine are harming the Palestinian people beyond their seemingly innocuous words. In the case of Gaza, or more precisely the Israeli genocide in the Gaza Strip, the harm of this "impartiality" is greatest.

"If you are neutral in situations of injustice, you have chosen the side of the oppressor," late South African anti-apartheid activist Bishop Desmond Tutu said. His wisdom will always ring true. While most countries and peoples around the world are certainly not taking the side of the Israeli oppressor, some, wittingly or otherwise, are.

There are those who are taking Israel's side by directly fueling and funding the Israeli killing machine in the Gaza Strip, while blaming the Palestinians for the war and its devastating impact.[1] But supporting Israel not only takes place in the form of weapons provision, trade or shielding it from accountability before international law. Spotlighting Israel's political discourse and expectations while ignoring Palestinian commentary is also a form of supporting Israel and denigrating Palestine.

---

1 Jonathan Masters and Will Merrow. "U.S. Aid to Israel in Four Charts," Council on Foreign Relations, April 11, 2024. https://www.cfr.org/article/us-aid-israel-four-charts

Dr. Ramzy Baroud is a syndicated columnist, the author of six books, and Editor of *The Palestine Chronicle*. Baroud has a Ph.D. in Palestine Studies from the University of Exeter. His latest book, co-edited with Professor Ilan Pappé, is *Our Vision for Liberation: Engaged Palestinian Leaders and Intellectuals Speak Out*. Baroud is currently a Non-resident Senior Research Fellow at the Center for Islam and Global Affairs (CIGA).

Most political discourses on the Gaza war, even by those who outright rejected the unprecedented deadly Israeli campaign, were mostly consumed with Israeli, not Palestinian priorities. Indeed, almost immediately following the October 7 war, questions began arising about what *Israel* wants in Gaza.

Exactly one month later, on November 7, while vowing to destroy Hamas, Israeli Prime Minister Benjamin Netanyahu said that Israel was set to maintain "security responsibility" over the Gaza Strip for "an indefinite period."[2] The Americans were already in agreement. "There is no coming back to the status quo," U.S. President Joe Biden said on October 26, which "means ensuring that Hamas can no longer terrorize Israel and use Palestinians civilians as human shields."[3]

Even the Europeans, who had often presented themselves as equal partners to both Israel and the Palestinian Authority (PA), had a similar attitude. EU Foreign Policy Chief Josep Borrell, for example, envisioned Gaza's future "reinforced" version of the current PA, "with a legitimacy to be defined and decided upon by the (UN) Security Council" not by the Palestinian people themselves.[4]

Even those who admonished Tel Aviv for having unrealistic expectations—i.e. destroying Hamas—failed to ask the obvious question: what do Palestinians want?

As soon as it became obvious that the Palestinian Resistance was far too strong to allow Israel to achieve any of its lofty objectives, government officials, experts and media analysts began warning Israel that no military victory was possible in the Strip.[5] They contended that Israel must also develop a "realistic" strategy to govern the Strip after the destruction of the Resistance there.[6]

---

2 Josef Federman, "Israel Says It Will Maintain 'Overall Security Responsibility' for Gaza. What Might that Look like?" *AP News,* November 9, 2023. https://apnews.com/article/israel-hamas-war-overall-security-responsibility-gaza-b86055806b733f41b6d7b4e2f0974985

3 Jacob Magid, "Biden: There's No Going Back to Prewar Status Quo, There Must Be Vision of 2 States," *Times of Israel,* October 26, 2023. https://www.timesofisrael.com/biden-theres-no-going-back-to-pre-war-status-quo-there-must-be-vision-of-2-states/

4 "EU Foreign Policy Chief Borrell Makes Proposals for Post-war Gaza," *Reuters,* November 13, 2023. https://www.reuters.com/world/eu-foreign-policy-chief-borrell-makes-proposals-post-war-gaza-2023-11-13/

5 Reuters and TOI Staff, "Top US Official Doubts Israel Can Achieve Netanyahu'S Promised 'Total Victory' in Gaza," *Times of Israel,* May 14, 2024. https://www.timesofisrael.com/top-us-official-doubts-israel-can-achieve-netanyahus-promised-total-victory-in-gaza/.

6 Dennis Ross, "Israel Needs a New Strategy." The Washington Institute for Near East Policy, March 13, 2024. https://www.timesofisrael.com/top-us-official-https://www.washingtoninstitute.org/policy-analysis/

Some of these statements were celebrated even by pro-Palestinian Arab and Middle Eastern media as an example of the changing western narrative on Palestine. In actuality, the narrative has remained the same. What has changed is the unprecedented degree of Palestinian steadfastness, *sumud*, which has inspired the world and frightened Israel's allies into foreseeing the grim scenarios awaiting Tel Aviv, should it suffer an outright defeat in Gaza.

Even though many among Israel's Western allies may have seemed critical of Netanyahu, they were still behaving out of concern for Tel Aviv, never out of love or respect for Palestinians. This, however, is not new.

Since the destruction of the Palestinian homeland—known as the Nakba—in 1948, two narratives emerged: An Israeli one, which was fully embraced by Western mainstream media, politicians and academics who became invested in misrepresenting the "conflict."[7] They depicted Israel as a "Jewish state" that valiantly fought for survival against competing Arab interests, factional and disunited Palestinians, who only agreed on one thing: wanting to destroy Israel.

And they ignored a Palestinian priority, which argued that justice is indivisible, and that the cornerstone of any lasting peace in Palestine is the restoration of dispossessed Palestinian refugees to their homeland, what is known as the Right of Return.

As Israel occupied the rest of historic Palestine in 1967 and extended its system of apartheid to reach the newly occupied territories, it was only natural that ending the Israeli military occupation and dismantling apartheid became critical Palestinian demands—without ignoring the original injustice which had befallen all Palestinians in 1948.[8]

Israel's allies in the West used the Israeli occupation as an opportunity to distract from the root causes of the so-called conflict. With time, they reduced the conversation on Palestine to that of the illegal settlements, which Israel began constructing, contrary to international law, after completing its military occupation.

Any Palestinian who contended that the conflict is not a conflict at all, and that the root causes of the crisis go back to the very foundation of Israel, was and continues to be deemed as radical or worse. This reductionist thinking is now being applied to Gaza where every historical reference is

---

israel-needs-new-strategydoubts-israel-can-achieve-netanyahus-promised-total-victory-in-gaza/

7 United Nations, "The Question of Palestine." https://www.un.org/unispal/about-the-nakba/

8 Amnesty International, "Israel's Occupation: 50 Years of Dispossession," June 7, 2017. https://www.amnesty.org/en/latest/campaigns/2017/06/israel-occupation-50-years-of-dispossession/

intentionally pushed aside, and where the Palestinian political discourse is shunned in favor of Israel's deceptive language.

But no matter how often Western media speaks about "Palestinian terrorism" or prioritizes Israeli security—while ignoring Israeli terrorism, Palestinian prisoners, rights and aspirations—there will be no just peace if Palestinian rights are not truly respected.

The reference to Palestinian rights includes all Palestinians, not just those under siege in Gaza. The Strip is not an independent territory from the rest of historic Palestine. Neither its past nor future can be understood or imagined without appreciating the Palestinian struggle in the whole of Palestine—indigenous Palestinians in today's Israel included. This is not an opinion, but the very essence of the political discourse emanating from all of Gaza's political groups. The same assertion can be made about the political discourse of Palestinians in the West Bank, throughout historic Palestine, and those in *shatat*, or diaspora.

Israel and the U.S. may try to imagine whatever future they wish for Gaza, and they may also try to achieve that future through missiles, dumb bombs and bunker busters. But no amount of military might or firepower can alter history or redefine justice.

What Gaza ultimately wants is the acknowledgement of historical injustices, respect for international law, freedom for all Palestinians and legal accountability from Israel. These are hardly radical positions, especially when compared to Israel's practical policy of destroying Gaza, annexing the West Bank and ethnically cleansing the Palestinian people.

Israel remains completely oblivious to these legitimate Palestinian demands, and to their growing global support, which are fully supported by international law as well. Tel Aviv and Washington, along with their military experts and media analysts, are consumed with something else entirely: crushing Hamas, ignoring Palestinian political aspirations and ensuring that Israel restores its so-called deterrence.

"Restoring deterrence," whether against Gaza, Lebanon, Yemen or anywhere else in the Middle East, implies one thing and one thing only: the desire to return to the status quo, regarded as the situation in the region as of October 6, 2023. For Palestinians, however, such a status quo was that of perpetual military occupation, apartheid, colonialism and occasional deadly war, whose time and place was only to be determined by Israel alone.

In fact, the real shock in Israel about October 7 was directly related to the latter point, as it is the first time in Israel's history that an attack of such great proportions was initiated by its enemies, and not by Tel Aviv itself.

Though the Resistance attack, known as Al-Aqsa Flood Operation, may have been a surprise in a political sense, there was nothing surprising about it militarily. Indeed, the entire Gaza Division, the massive Israeli military build-up in the so-called Gaza envelope, exists for the very purpose of ensuring that Gaza's subjugation and siege were perfected according to state-of-the-art military technology.

According to the Global Firepower 2024 military strength ranking, Israel is number 17 in the world, mainly because of its military technology.[9] This advanced military capability meant that no surprise attacks should have been possible, because it is not humans but sophisticated machines that scan, intercept and report on every perceived suspicious movement. In the Israeli case, the failure was profound and multi-layered.

Subsequently, following October 7, Netanyahu found himself in a much deeper hole than the politically embattled Israeli leader had started with. Instead of finding his way out of the crisis by, for example, taking responsibility for what has taken place, or better yet, acknowledging that war is never an answer in the face of a resisting, oppressed population, he kept on digging.

The right-wing prime minister, flanked by far-right ministers Itamar Ben-Gvir, Bezalel Smotrich and Amichai Eliyahu, worsened matters by using the war on Gaza as an opportunity to implement long-dormant plans of ethnically cleansing Palestinians, not only from the Gaza Strip but also from the West Bank. Were it not for the steadfastness of the Palestinian people and strong rejection by Egypt and Jordan, the second Nakba would have been a reality.

Israel has always viewed Palestinians with no regard for their human rights whatsoever. At best Palestinians represented a "demographic threat," at worse "terrorists" to be killed at will. October 7 only worsened the existing fascist sentiments, not only among Israeli politicians and media, but within the broader Jewish society as well.[10]

Mainstream Israeli politicians, despite their ideological and political differences, unanimously outdid one another in their racist, violent, even genocidal language. While defense minister Yoav Gallant immediately announced that "there will be no electricity, no food, no fuel, everything is closed" to the Gaza population, Avi Dichter called for "another Nakba." Meanwhile, Eliyahu suggested the "option" of "dropping a nuclear bomb on Gaza."

---

9 Dean Shmuel Elmas, "Israel Ranked 17th for Military Power" *Globes,* January 10, 2024. https://en.globes.co.il/en/article-israel-ranked-17th-for-military-power-1001467417

10 Amnesty International, "Israel's Apartheid against Palestinians: A Cruel System of Domination and a Crime against Humanity," February 1, 2022. https://www.amnesty.org/en/latest/news/2022/02/israels-apartheid-against-palestinians-a-cruel-system-of-domination-and-a-crime-against-humanity/

Instead of saving Israel from itself by reminding Tel Aviv that the genocidal war on Gaza would also bode badly for Tel Aviv, the U.S. Joe Biden
administration served the role of cheerleader and outright partner. Aside from
generating military packages estimated in the billions of dollars, Washington
became Israel's main, at times only, protector against an enraged international
community that was shocked by the degree of Israeli brutality in Gaza.

According to the United Nations Relief and Works Agency (UNRWA)
nearly all of Gaza's population were displaced, often repeatedly, as a result of
the war.[11] The Israeli rights group B'tselem said that, at one point in the early
phases of the war, 2.2 million were starving. Save the Children reported that
over 100 Palestinian children were killed daily. Gaza's government media
office has said that about 75 per cent of the Strip has been destroyed. Even the
Wall Street Journal, known for its pro-Israeli propaganda, had concluded that
the destruction of Gaza is greater than that of Dresden in WWII.[12]

None of this softened the U.S. administration's position or forced an
American rethink about its policies in the Middle East, or its perception of the
Palestinians. The American idea that only Israel matters, and that Palestinians
are irrelevant to its foreign policy in the region, became even more accentuated after the war.

Such American intransigence, however, had no bearing on the Palestinian
people's perception of themselves as a freedom fighting nation, hell-bent on
achieving its freedom at any cost. Indeed, fathers and mothers, in a scene
repeated countless times, would be carrying the bodies of their dead children while howling in pain, yet insisting that they would never leave their
homeland.

To ensure that our gaze remains fixated at Israel's own sense of victimization, and, subsequently, its priorities, Israel and its Western supporters
have always labored to ensure that the global public looks the other way,
away from suffering, occupied and oppressed Palestine.

October 7 was the Palestinian attempt at imploring humanity to look
their way—at the siege of Gaza, at the military occupation, at the apartheid
regime, at the home demolition, at the expansion of colonies, at the incremen-
tal genocide which pre-dated the Gaza war.

Western governments and media followed Washington's blueprint, prioritizing Israeli language, interests and agendas. This is what led to Al-Aqsa

---

11 Mohammad Sio, "75% of Gazans Forcibly Displaced: UN
Agency," *Anadolu Agency,* May 22, 2024. https://www.aa.com.tr/en/
middle-east/75-of-gazans-forcibly-displaced-un-agency/3227369

12 Jared Malsin and Saeed Shah, "The Ruined Landscape of Gaza After Nearly
Three Months of Bombing," *Wall Street Journal,* December 30, 2023. https://www.
wsj.com/world/middle-east/gaza-destruction-bombing-israel-aa528542

Flood, which the West has insisted on depicting as a despicable, terrorist act with no political or strategic intent, just gory violence for the sake of violence. Look at Al-Fakhoura Schools, Nuseirat Refugee camp, Al-Fallujah, Jabaliya, Khan Yunis—at the many mass graves and every inch of Gaza that has been shelled, bombed or bulldozed.

The Palestinians themselves were pointing us to where we should be looking—in fact, to where we should always have been looking. Relentlessly and with unweakened resolve, ordinary people, often weeping, would point at mass graves, at their dead children in their arms, at mutilated bodies of children in hospital morgues, in parking lots, in the streets, and they would say "Look!," "Look what Israel is doing to us!," "Look what the Nazis have done to our children!," and so on.

The word *look,* here, is key. When they say "look," they actually mean not just look, but understand, help, do something, *anything.* But Palestinian Resistance on the ground—the only actual defenders of those civilians, however uncomfortable this realization makes some of us feel—was also telling us to look, and we did.

In this case, they did not make the announcement "Look" or "*Shufu*" out loud. Instead, they simply used a small, red triangle, the symbolism of which is likely to influence a generation of Palestinians and millions of youth around the world.

Amid massive ruins, half-standing buildings, dust and smoke, a small, red triangle would finally appear within this obvious context. To understand the function of this triangle, we needed to understand the story behind it, thus explaining, without a single word, why Palestinians resist.

The equation then becomes simple to understand: Israeli destruction, red triangle, explosion—followed by triumphant shouts of "God is great," "Palestine will be free," and "The invaders will be defeated." With time, that functionality of the red triangle was transformed to even greater meaning, deeper symbolism.

As millions of people continued to protest Israeli atrocities in Gaza, many carried banners and flags of the red triangle.[13] For them, this symbol not only represented more than the Palestinian Resistance in Gaza, but the need for action everywhere else. Some suggested that the symbolism of the red triangle was inspired by the red triangle of the Palestinian flag, thus arguing that that specific symbol was chosen to purposely delineate a greater national symbol.

---

13 Brooke Anderson, "Millions across the World March for Gaza as Rafah Ground Invasion Looms," *The New Arab,* March 3, 2024. https://www.newarab.com/news/millions-march-globally-gaza-ahead-rafah-invasion

In truth, the origins of the small red triangle do not matter. Sure, maybe it was intended to represent something or maybe it was simply a technical choice made by a young Palestinian tech-savvy fighter, to simply let us know where we needed to look. What truly matters, however, are the deeper meanings of all of this.

For years—in fact decades—Palestinians have been urging us to look: at their lives under Israeli occupation and apartheid; at the destruction of their homes and orchards, confiscated or stolen by the Israeli military and illegal Jewish settlers; at the fate of their prisoners, thousands of them, languishing in Israeli prisons, simply for resisting the Israeli military occupation; at the Israeli siege on Gaza, and that perpetual episode of suffering and pain, which deprived over two million people of their most basic rights; and at so much more.

Unfortunately, and for whatever reason, many of us did not look. Thanks to the courage of the Palestinians themselves, and as a result of the Israeli genocide in Gaza, we are finally looking, and at last we are looking precisely where Palestinians want us to look.

Indeed, it is about time for the Palestinian voice to reclaim its full centrality in the story of oppression and resistance. The reclaiming of the Palestinian voice, and narrative, however, was not a gift granted by mainstream media, or a concession made by Washington and its allies. It was exacted by the Palestinians themselves, those whose steadfastness has awakened the world to the injustices meted out daily by Israel, and the historical injustice that rendered Palestinians stateless refugees with no rights or even a political horizon.

For far too long Gaza has been marginalized, not only in the U.S.-sanctioned foreign policy discourse in the Middle East, but also by the Palestinians themselves. Political factionalism has wreaked havoc in Palestinian society, associated Gaza with Hamas and its clash with its Fatah rivals. The siege on Gaza, however uncomfortable such truth may be for some, was perfected through the collaboration of the PA and Egypt—the first manipulated the salaries of Gaza workers for political gains, and the latter used the Rafah crossing as a political leverage.

The outcome was devastating: complete isolation of Gaza through a hermetic siege; the marginalization of Gaza within the larger Palestinian national struggle, and the empowerment of Israeli policy aimed at further dividing Palestinians.

These factors and more allowed Israel to surpass the Palestinian leaderships, factions and peoples to sign yet more normalization agreements with Arab countries, who too seemed to hold no regard to Palestine and her people. Successive U.S. administrations supported this approach of conspiring to remove Palestine from its Arab environs.[14] What Donald Trump has done to forage diplomatic ties between some Arabs and Israel was the mere culmination of a longstanding U.S. policy in this regard. The Biden administration further invested in this policy simply as it was consistent with all U.S. doctrines in the Middle East since the very start of the so-called "Arab-Israeli conflict."

The genocide in Gaza, however, has brought all illusions to an end, sending messages to all of those concerned that the fate of Palestine lies in the hand of her people, who are willing to endure, starve, die and fight for their freedom. The war and the unprecedented international solidarity around it, including the great and growing role of the Global South, demonstrated that Palestinian allies are not unelected regional governments with self-serving agendas, but ordinary people, civil societies, university students, intellectuals, independent media and an endless list of communities who are willing to turn words into action, even if such actions come at a high price.[15]

Who would have imagined that tiny Gaza, a Strip of isolated land that does not exceed 181 square kilometers, would become the moral compass of humanity; that this supposedly marginal region would mix up all the political and geopolitical cards of the Middle East, in fact of the world; that Gaza would serve as the most earnest attempt at unifying the Global South; that the fight to reclaim Palestine and the freedom of her people would start there. But this did not come as a surprise. Gaza has always been the beating heart of Palestinian Resistance. And without *Muqawama*—Resistance—Zionism would have prevailed decades ago, and the Palestinian quest for justice would have been long crushed under the chains of Israeli Merkava tanks. Deeply wounded, starved, and alone, Gaza fought back, ushering it into a trajectory of history that, not long ago, would have been considered unthinkable.

Gaza is the power of the people, manifesting in unmistakable clarity in the words of Tunisian poet Abu al-Qasim al-Shabbi:

If, one day, the people wills to live
Then fate must obey
Darkness must dissipate
And must the chain give way.

---

14 Marwan Muasher, "Normalization of Arab Countries with Israel: Regional Geopolitical Aspects of the Agreements," IE Med European Institute of the Mediterranean Yearbook (2021). https://www.iemed.org/publication/

15 Columbia Students for Justice in Palestine, and Columbia Jewish Voice for Peace, "Columbia Students for Justice in Palestine Statement of Solidarity," Institute for Palestine Studies (2024). https://www.palestine-studies.org/en/node/1654384

Benjamin Netanyahu's War against Palestinian Statehood

Avi Shlaim

THERE ARE TWO widely held beliefs about Benjamin Netanyahu, Israel's longest serving prime minister and the architect of the war on Gaza that followed the Hamas attack on southern Israel on 7 October 2023. One is that he is deliberately prolonging this war out of narrow political and legal self-preservation. In November 2019, Netanyahu was officially indicted for breach of trust, accepting bribes, and fraud. As long as he is prime minister, he does not have to stand trial. Once he ceases to be prime minister, his trial will resume and, if found guilty, he may end up in jail. In political terms, too, Netanyahu is probably a dead man walking. Once the fighting stops, the pressure will increase for a public inquiry into the failures and possibly the conduct of the Israeli military and government with regard to October 7 and subsequent events, and for the holding of a new election, an election that the public opinion polls predict would end in a catastrophic defeat for Netanyahu and his party. To save his skin and to stay out of prison, so the argument goes, he is deliberately prolonging the war and resisting all the UN and other calls for a ceasefire.

The other common belief is that Netanyahu is prolonging the Gaza war because he is in hock to Israel's ultranationalist far-right. The Likud-led coalition formed by Netanyahu in December 2022 includes two far-right, proto-fascist parties with notoriously Islamophobic as well as homophobic leaders. The minister of national security is Itamar Ben-Gvir, the leader of "Jewish Power," who was considered unfit to serve in the Israeli army on account of his extreme political views, and who was later convicted for inciting racism and supporting a terrorist group. At his home in the violent settler enclave of Kiryat Arba, near Hebron, Ben-Gvir used to hang a portrait of the

Avi Shlaim is an Emeritus Professor of International Relations at Oxford University and the author of *The Iron Wall: Israel and the Arab World* (2014) and *Israel and Palestine: Reappraisals, Revisions, Refutations* (2009).

American Jewish settler Baruch Goldstein, who had massacred 29 Arab worshippers in the Ibrahimi Mosque in Hebron in 1994. The minister of finance, Bezalel Smotrich, the leader of "Religious Zionism," is another settler who openly advocates the ethnic cleansing of the Palestinian territories. Both parties encourage settler violence against Arabs, advocate the formal annexation of the West Bank, and support the resettlement of Jews in the Gaza Strip after the expulsion of its Palestinian inhabitants.

Various considerations no doubt affect Netanyahu's decisions on matters of war and peace; personal interest and political calculation are probably prominent among them. It is patently obvious that Netanyahu is a selfish, mendacious, and thoroughly cynical politician, who is prone to placing his personal advantage above the good of his country. It is also true that, with its inclusion of the Jewish Power and Religious Zionism parties, Netanyahu's coalition is the most right-wing, xenophobic, messianic, apocalyptic, and overtly racist government in Israel's history. But on the other hand, as will be argued here, these explanations for Netanyahu's Gaza policy obscure as much as they reveal. Netanyahu is not a moderate right-wing politician who has fallen among hawks. He himself is a far-right, racist, Jewish supremacist, a devoted proponent of Greater Israel whose life's mission has been to prevent the establishment of an independent Palestinian state. The one consistent theme in Netanyahu's long and chequered political career has been his ideological commitment to an exclusive Jewish state in all of Mandatory Palestine from the river to the sea. In the context of this long war on Palestinian statehood, the Gaza onslaught is not an opportunistic aberration, but a logical terminus.

Foundations

Benjamin Netanyahu grew up in a fiercely nationalistic Jewish home. His father, Benzion Netanyahu, was a historian of Spanish Jewry; an adviser to Ze'ev Jabotinsky, the founder of Revisionist Zionism; and the editor of the Revisionists' daily newspaper *Ha-Yarden*. Jabotinsky was the spiritual father of the Israeli right. He and his party were the main ideological opposition to the mainstream socialist Labor Zionism. The Revisionists advocated a revision of the "practical Zionism" of David Ben-Gurion and Chaim Weizmann. Whereas "practical Zionism" called for Jewish settlement of *Eretz Yisrael* (the Land of Israel), the Revisionists insisted on the Jewish right to sovereignty over the whole of Mandatory Palestine and Transjordan. They were territorial maximalists who rejected the partition of Palestine and laid claim to both sides of the Jordan River, including the east bank which is present day Jordan. The fact that no Jews lived on the east bank of the Jordan made no difference to them.

For Benzion Netanyahu "Jewish history was in large measure a history of holocausts." The core of his belief was that Jews have always been and will always be persecuted by all those around them. To his way of thinking, peace with Arabs was a dangerous illusion because Arabs could not be trusted. He was convinced that, whatever they may say, Arabs remained determined to destroy the Jewish state. From his father Benjamin inherited the notion of Us versus Them, of a preordained and inescapable conflict between Arabs and Jews, and the fear that Jewish history would come to an end unless the Jews could defend themselves. "In the Middle East," he said in 2018, "there is a simple truth: There is no place for the weak."[1] The foundational axiom of both father and son was that military power was the only solution to the Jewish predicament, and the only instrument for attaining and preserving Jewish independence in the ancestral homeland.

Jabotinsky also believed in the primacy of force. In 1923, he published an article under the title "On the Iron Wall (We and the Arabs)." If any one document deserves to be called the bible of Zionist foreign policy, this is it. Its author argued that "there is not even the slightest hope of ever obtaining" a political agreement with the Arab inhabitants of Palestine, because Zionist and Arab aspirations were fundamentally opposed: "Every indigenous people will resist alien settlers as long as they see any hope of ridding themselves of the danger of foreign settlement." From this he concluded that the Zionist goal of an independent Jewish state in Palestine could only be achieved uni-laterally and by military force: behind an iron wall of Jewish military power.

For Jabotinsky, however, the iron wall was not an end in itself but a means to an end. It was intended to compel the Arabs to abandon any hope of defeating the Jews. Once this happened, Jabotinsky predicted, the Arab hardliners would be discredited and the moderates would come to the fore, open to compromise. Then and only then should the Zionists proceed to the second stage of the strategy: negotiations with the local Arabs about their status and rights in Palestine. In other words, Jewish military strength was to pave the way to an eventual political settlement with the Arab residents of Palestine. Jabotinsky did not spell out the endgame but what he appeared to envisage was limited autonomy for the Arabs, under Jewish rule, rather than full sovereignty.

Benjamin Netanyahu was elected leader of the Likud in March 1993. That year he also published a book that set out his political creed, *A Place*

---

1 David Brennan, "The Weak Are Slaughtered, the Strong Prevail: Netanyahu Says Israel Will Not Shy Away from Conflict," *Newsweek,* August 31, 2018.

Among the Nations: Israel and the World. The book was inspired by the teaching of Ze'ev Jabotinsky and Benzion Netanyahu. It presented the most embattled possible version of the history of Zionism and the State of Israel. Its central theme was the right of the Jewish people to the whole Land of Israel, including Judea and Samaria—the biblical names for the West Bank. History was rewritten from a Revisionist perspective in order to demonstrate that it was not the Jews who usurped the land from the Arabs, but the Arabs who usurped the land from the Jews. Britain was portrayed as no friend of the Jews and the chapter on the British Mandate in Palestine was simply called "The Betrayal." The whole world was portrayed as hostile to the Jewish state and antisemitism was said to lie at the root of this hostility.

Netanyahu viewed Israel's relations with the Arab world as one of permanent conflict, as a never-ending struggle between the forces of light and the forces of darkness. His image of the Arabs was consistently and comprehensively negative and it did not admit the possibility of diversity or change. His book did not contain a single positive reference to the Arabs, their history or their culture. Arab regimes were portrayed as ready practitioners of violence against the citizens of their own countries and across their borders: "Violence is ubiquitous in the political life of all the Arab countries. It is the primary method of dealing with opponents, both foreign and domestic, both Arab and non-Arab." In addition, Netanyahu claimed that "international terrorism is the quintessential Middle East export" and that "its techniques everywhere are those of the Arab regimes and organizations that invented it."[2] The Arab world was described as deeply hostile towards the West and to the Western notion of democracy. Netanyahu conceded that a few Arab rulers were friendly to the United States but warned against the delusion that this reflected the real sentiments of the Arab masses. Such rulers, in his view, "frequently represent only a thin crust lying over a volatile Arab and Islamic society."[3]

Much of Netanyahu's vehemence and venom was reserved for the Palestinians. He launched a fierce assault on the notion that the Palestinian problem constituted the core and heart of the Middle East conflict. For him the Palestinian problem was not a genuine problem but an artificially manufactured one. He denied that the Palestinians had a right to national self-determination and argued that the primary cause of tension in the Middle East was inter-Arab rivalry. For Netanyahu compromise with the PLO was completely out of the question because its goal was the destruction of the

---

2 Benjamin Netanyahu, *A Place Among the Nations: Israel and the World* (London: Bantam Press, 1993), 102–103.
    3 Ibid., 121.

State of Israel, and this goal allegedly defined its very essence. This, in his view, was what distinguished the PLO from the Arab states, even the most radical ones. While these states would clearly prefer to see Israel disappear, their national life was not dependent on Israel's destruction: "But the PLO was different. It was constitutionally tied to the idea of Israel's liquidation. Remove that idea and you have no PLO."[4]

Chapter 7 in Netanyahu's book is called "The Wall," alluding to Jabotinsky's 1923 article. In this chapter Netanyahu expanded on the military value of dominating the heights of the (Syrian) Golan and the mountains of (Palestinian) Judea and Samaria. He buttressed his arguments with maps that highlighted Israel's geostrategic vulnerability. Over and over again, he quoted a Pentagon Plan, dated 18 June 1967, in support of his argument that for Israel to protect her cities, she must retain military control over virtually all the territory west of the Jordan River. There was no mention of the many Israeli generals who took the view that control over the West Bank was not a military necessity. Netanyahu's conclusion was that the whole of western Palestine constituted one integral territorial unit: "To subdivide this land into two unstable, insecure nations, to try to defend what is indefensible, is to invite disaster. Carving Judea and Samaria out of Israel means carving up Israel."[5]

The book espoused Jewish sovereignty across Greater Israel, imposed by military force against an Arab populace it depicted as implacably and existentially hostile. It showed that Netanyahu was the Revisionist movement and Benzion's faithful son. These entrenched ideological commitments would underpin Netanyahu's consistent political project: to consolidate Jewish domination, thwart diplomacy with Palestinian leaders, and prevent a Palestinian state.

Power

The iron wall was the basic Zionist strategy in the confrontation with the Arabs under both Labor and right-wing parties from the 1920s onwards. Yitzhak Rabin, the leader of the Labour Party, was the first Israeli prime minister to move from stage one to stage two of the strategy of the iron wall. He did so by concluding the Oslo I Accord with the Palestine Liberation Organisation (PLO) on September 13, 1993, followed by a sequel two years later. In both cases he negotiated from a position of unassailable strength, which enabled him to more or less dictate the terms to the other side. Under the first accord, the PLO gave up its claim to 78 percent of Mandatory

4 Ibid., 232.
5 Ibid., 287.

Palestine in the hope of securing an independent state alongside Israel on the Gaza Strip and the West Bank, with a capital city in East Jerusalem. The accord itself did not mention, let alone promise, an independent Palestinian state at the end of the five-year transition period. Yet, given the scale of the concessions made by the PLO, eventual independence on a fifth of its patrimony was not an unreasonable expectation.

Netanyahu's book, *A Place Among the Nations*, was published six months before the Oslo I Accord was signed. The agreement did precisely what Netanyahu had been warning against: it recognized the PLO, it conceded that the Palestinian people had a legitimate right to self-government, and it began the process of partitioning western Palestine. The Oslo II accord, signed in Washington on 28 September 1995 and approved by the Knesset by a narrow majority a week later, represented another significant step on the stony road to peace. Netanyahu, then Leader of the Opposition, led an inflammatory campaign that did not just criticize the agreement but also delegitimized the democratically elected government that had negotiated it. In a notorious rally of the "nationalist camp" in Zion Square in Jerusalem, he whipped up the crowd to a veritable frenzy. In the crowd were fascist thugs who held up a fake picture of Rabin in an SS uniform. Netanyahu did not call them to order. On the contrary, he played a leading role in the campaign of incitement that culminated in the assassination of Rabin by a Jewish fanatic. At Rabin's funeral, Leah, his widow, refused to shake Netanyahu's outstretched hand. But she received Yasser Arafat at her home when he came to convey his condolences. Arafat's handshake, she explained, symbolized for her the hope for peace, whereas Netanyahu's handshake represented the rejection of peace with the Palestinians.

In the lead up to the elections of May 1996, following Rabin's assassination and the brief premiership of Shimon Peres, Netanyahu repeatedly denounced the Oslo accords as incompatible both with Israel's security and with the right of the Jewish people to the whole Land of Israel. The Likud won the election of May 1996 against the Labour Party by a margin of less than one percent. But on the morrow of this slenderest of electoral victories, Netanyahu declared war on the peace policy of his slain predecessor. He came to power with the self-appointed mission of subverting the Oslo accords and preventing the establishment of a Palestinian state. He spent his first term in office, from 1996 to 1999, in a largely successful attempt to freeze, subvert, and ultimately undermine the fragile peace agreements with the Palestinians. The Oslo accords raised a fundamental question: was Israel ready to accept a Palestinian national entity alongside it? To this question Netanyahu gave an emphatically negative answer.

Throughout his five subsequent terms in office, Netanyahu remained fixated on the first part of Jabotinsky's iron wall strategy—on accumulating more and more military power—while avoiding stage two: serious negotiations with the PLO to find a political solution to the conflict. The official policy guidelines of his first government were pure ethnocentric nationalism. The chapter on education promised to cultivate Jewish values and to put the Bible, the Hebrew language, and the history of the Jewish people at the center of the school curriculum. The foreign policy guidelines expressed firm opposition to a Palestinian state, to the Palestinian refugees' right of return, and to the dismantling of Jewish settlements in the occupied territories. The assertion of Israel's sovereignty over the whole of Jerusalem was explicit and categorical. So was the commitment to continue developing settlements as "an expression of Zionist fulfilment." The guidelines side lined altogether Israel's obligations under the Oslo accords.

On 14 June 2009, in his second term in office, Netanyahu gave a speech at Bar-Ilan University in which he grudgingly accepted a "Demilitarized Palestinian State." This was hailed as a reversal of his opposition to an independent Palestinian state. But he had only made the speech under strong American pressure, and the change of direction was more apparent than real. In the first place, Netanyahu placed conditions—demilitarization, no Palestinian capital city in East Jerusalem, no Jewish settlement removed from the West Bank—that precluded genuine Palestinian sovereignty. At the level of rhetoric, then, Netanyahu's speech was consistent with the position taken by his director of communications and policy planning, David Bar-Illan, back in 1996. Asked whether the Netanyahu government opposed the idea of a Palestinian state, Bar-Illan replied: "Semantics don't matter. If Palestinian sovereignty is limited enough so that we feel safe, call it fried chicken."[6] In practice, meanwhile, Netanyahu remained a stalwart rejectionist on the question of Palestinian statehood. The litmus test of an authentic commitment to a two-state solution is a freeze of settlement activity in the occupied Palestinian territories while negotiations are in progress. Under Netanyahu's leadership, however, settlement expansion went ahead at full tilt, especially in and around Jerusalem.

In 2013 and 2014, Netanyahu obstructed, and ultimately derailed U.S.-sponsored peace talks with the PLO. U.S. Secretary of State John Kerry was a firm friend of Israel. He wanted to resolve the conflict in order to enable Israel to preserve its character as a Jewish and democratic state. In his first year in office, Kerry made no less than eleven trips to the region in search of

---

6 David Bar-Illan and Victor Cygielman, "Palestinian Self-Rule, Israeli Security: An Interview," *Palestine-Israel Journal,* vol. 3, no. 3, 1996.

a breakthrough. Netanyahu, however, was not a genuine partner for peace. He considered the proposed peace process as an American interest, not an Israeli one. So, he entered the negotiations in bad faith and employed characteristically devious tactics to ensure their failure. In private, he told Kerry that he accepted the two basic Palestinian conditions for resuming the talks: a freeze on settlement activity; and the 1967 lines as the starting point for negotiations. But after a year of negotiating in bad faith, Netanyahu publicly went back on his private assurances, making it clear that the shuttle had been an exercise in futility. Publicly humiliated and deeply disappointed, Kerry announced the end of his mission. He blamed Israeli settlement expansion for the diplomatic failure and warned that the Netanyahu government's policies were leading toward an apartheid state.

During the 2015 election campaign, Netanyahu brought his rhetoric back into line with his real stand on Palestinian statehood. He vowed that, if re-elected, no Palestinian state would emerge on his watch. His party, the Likud, had consistently rejected the idea of an independent Palestinian state. Its 1977 platform, the year it first came to power, opened with the declaration that "The right of the Jewish people to the land of Israel is eternal and indisputable and is linked with the right to security and peace; therefore, Judea and Samaria will not be handed to any foreign administration; between the Sea and the Jordan there will only be Israeli sovereignty." The "Peace & Security" chapter of the 1999 Likud Party platform could not have been more explicit. "The Government of Israel," it stated, "flatly rejects the establishment of a Palestinian Arab state west of the Jordan river." In all subsequent elections the Likud strictly adhered to this intransigent, peace-spurning, fundamentalist position.

This record cannot be reconciled with the idea that Netanyahu personally holds the balance between the center-right and the far-right elements in his government. The truth of the matter is that he shares the profoundly illiberal, anti-Palestinian, and Jewish-supremacist views of his far-right coalition partners. His political brand is a noxious blend of anti-democratic, racist-supremacist, and ultranationalist populism. It was he who had introduced the Nation-State Law in July 2018, four years before he formed an alliance with the religious-Zionist parties. Israel has no written constitution, but it has Basic Laws that define the character of the state. This particular Basic Law turned Israel officially into an apartheid state by declaring that "The right to exercise national self-determination in the State of Israel is unique to the Jewish people." What this implied was that even if the Palestinian citizens of Israel became the majority, only Jews would have the right to national self-determination. This is the very definition of apartheid: two classes of citizens and no equality.

The policy guidelines of the 2022 coalition government are even more extreme than the Basic Law of 2018. They open with the stark statement that "The Jewish people have an exclusive and inalienable right to all parts of the Land of Israel." The Nation-State Law refers to the Jewish people's right to national self-determination within the pre-1967 borders; the 2022 policy guidelines assert this right over the whole Land of Israel. This amounts to a flat denial of any Palestinian right to national self-determination anywhere between the river and the sea. This denial should come as no surprise. As this chapter has shown, Netanyahu's commitment to a Greater Israel is long standing. He has never believed in trading "land for peace" with the Palestinians. He advocates instead "peace for peace." According to this formula, Israel can make peace with the Arab states without making any concessions on the Palestinian issue. The Abraham Accords he signed in 2020 with four Arab states—the United Arab Emirates, Bahrain, Morocco, and Sudan—seemed to vindicate his approach. They certainly represented a major foreign policy triumph for Netanyahu. But they were predicated on the assumption that the Palestinian people could be sidelined indefinitely.

Gaza

The Hamas attack on Israel on 7 October 2023, in which 1,200 Israelis, mostly civilians, were killed and 250 taken hostage, disproved this assumption and shattered the entire policy built round it. It was the first time that Hamas fighters had broken down the fence around Gaza and attacked inside Israel's own territory, targeting military bases as well as civilian settlements, including revelers at a musical festival. Members of Islamic Jihad, a small militant organization, and unaffiliated individuals, joined in the violent cross-border raid. The Gaza Strip had often been compared to an open-air prison. On this occasion the angry inmates broke out of the prison and went on a killing spree, committing horrible atrocities in the process. This was an unprecedented and catastrophic Israeli security failure. For decades the Israeli public had been taught that might is right. The Hamas attack exposed this lie but that was not the lesson that the Israeli public drew. It is no exaggeration to say that the whole of Israeli society was unhinged by the trauma of 7 October. The trauma unleashed a tsunami of hatred towards the perpetrators and loud calls for revenge. Revenge followed on a massive scale and out of all proportion to the attack. Revenge, however, is not a policy.

Domestic anger was also directed at Netanyahu, but he, as is his wont, refused to admit any personal responsibility for the egregious intelligence and security failures. Rather than admit that his own policy had been misguided, Netanyahu tried to appease the angry public by promising total victory and the total eradication of Hamas as both a political and a military organization. This entailed a screeching U-turn. Prior to 7 October, Netanyahu's policy had been not to solve but to "manage" the conflict with the Palestinians. To this end it was necessary to separate the West Bank from Gaza, to weaken the Palestinian Authority (PA) on the West Bank, to maintain the blockade of Gaza which had been in force since Hamas assumed power there in 2007, and to allow Hamas to govern Gaza but not to pose a threat to Israel's security. The policy had also entailed a preference for channeling international monetary aid to Gaza via the Qatari government instead of the PA, in order to keep the Palestinian leadership divided and render political negotiations impossible. Acquiescing in Hamas's administration of an isolated Gaza, while seeking to prevent the emergence of a unified and moderate Palestinian leadership, was a cynical ploy in support of the false argument that Israel had no partner for peace.

In March 2019 Netanyahu reportedly told his Likud colleagues: "Anyone who wants to thwart the establishment of a Palestinian state has to support bolstering Hamas and transferring money to Hamas . . . This is part of our strategy—to isolate the Palestinians in Gaza from the Palestinians in the West Bank." The context for this statement was an internal debate within the Likud. The Hamas-Qatar debate was not between allowing some money to be delivered to Hamas versus not allowing any. Everyone recognized that some money had to be transferred to Gaza's administration or else the population would die. The dispute was rather between two different mechanisms for transferring money to Hamas: via the Palestinian Authority or via Qatar. Netanyahu preferred Qatar because it kept Hamas and the PA separate.

By launching the murderous attack on Israel on 7 October, Hamas sent a clear signal that the status quo was intolerable, and that it would continue to lead the national resistance to the Israeli occupation. While Israel regards Hamas as a terrorist organization, Hamas regards itself as a national liberation movement similar to the one that led the Algerian struggle for independence from France. Just as the Algerian struggle involved considerable civilian suffering at the hands of the French forces, the Hamas leaders have factored in serious Palestinian civilian suffering in the struggle for independence.

Hamas is not a secular but an Islamic resistance movement. Its attack on southern Israel was in part a response to the Israeli infringements of Muslim prerogatives in the Old City of Jerusalem. Hence the name of the operation: the Al-Aqsa Flood. The military operation also carried a message to the Kingdom of Saudi Arabia which, under strong pressure from the American administration, was preparing to join the circle of the Abraham Accords by signing a peace treaty with Israel. An Israeli peace treaty with Saudi Arabia, the wealthiest of the Gulf states, would be a serious blow to the Palestinian national movement and, as such, another feather in Netanyahu's cap.

Netanyahu's response to the Hamas attack was to unleash Operation Swords of Iron, a savage military offensive that has been raining death and destruction on the Gaza Strip ever since 7 October. The specific target of the operation was Hamas and its military wing, but it was also conceived as an attack on the entire society of the enclave. It is the civilians who have paid the heaviest price as a direct consequence of this operation. The number of Hamas combatants killed is not known. But the overall toll at the time of writing (15 June 2024) stood at 37,232 people killed and 85,037 wounded. More than 15,000 of the casualties are children. Women and children together account for around two-thirds of the dead. An additional 10,000 people are estimated to be buried under the rubble. 1.9 million out of a population of 2.3 million have been forcibly displaced, most of them several times and some of them were bombed from the air after going to what the IDF designated as "safe areas." By obstructing humanitarian aid from reaching Gaza, Israel is in effect using starvation as a weapon of war. More than a million people, including children, are the victims of a looming, man-made famine, which is a war crime, as is the forcible displacement of civilians.

The "collateral damage" as Israel attempts to frame this indiscriminate act of revenge for the Hamas attack, was colossal. According to the latest data from the UN's Office for the Coordination of Humanitarian Affairs and the World Health Organization, as of June 9: more than half of Gaza's homes have been destroyed or damaged; 80% of commercial facilities; 88% of school buildings; all 12 universities; 16 out of 35 hospitals; 130 ambulances; and 267 places of worship. The unprecedented scale of the destruction has given rise to a macabre terminology: domicide for the destruction of the housing stock; econocide for the wholesale destruction of the economy; ecocide for the destruction of the agricultural land and the natural landscape; scholasticide for the destruction of the educational system; and finally, the crime of all crimes—genocide.

Netanyahu's change of policy toward Hamas—from containment to destruction—reflected the group's decisive rejection of the role he had scripted for it: Israel's enforcer in Gaza. But this tactical switch did not reflect any shift in Netanyahu's ideological commitments or overarching objectives. Before October 7, Netanyahu supported using military might to induce Palestinians to permanently acquiesce in Jewish supremacy across the whole Land of Israel. This remains his project. That is why, even as Netanyahu insists on indefinite Israeli security control of the enclave, he refuses to say how Gaza would be governed after the fighting stops. Israel's U.S. and European allies, along with much of the Arab world, would like to see the PA go back to Gaza and replace Hamas. Netanyahu is opposed to this plan, and this opposition is consistent with his long standing positions. On the one hand, he reflexively champions solutions that are violent and unilateral. On the other hand, he fears that a unified Palestinian leadership would strengthen the case for a two-state solution.

In place of a viable framework for post-war governance in Gaza, Netanyahu's aim seems to be to destroy the Gaza Strip and to render it uninhabitable. In November 2023, the right-wing daily *Yisrael Hayom* revealed that the prime minister seeks to "reduce the number of Palestinian citizens in the Gaza Strip to the minimum possible." One way of reducing the number of Palestinians in Gaza is to push them over the border into Egypt's territory in northern Sinai. A leaked Israeli Ministry of Intelligence paper dated 13 October 2023 suggests that there is an actual plan for depopulating Gaza. Egypt has expressed the strongest opposition to this plan of demographic aggression. However, the IDF capture of the border posts between Gaza and Egypt and the herding of over a million refugees into Rafah at the hideously over-crowded southern tip of the enclave, suggest that the Israeli government has not abandoned its plan for the ethnic cleansing of the Gaza Strip.

Netanyahu's "total war" in Gaza has serious repercussions for the situation on the West Bank. For decades the pressure on the Palestinians in this area has been immense and unrelenting. Since the coming to power of Netanyahu's messianic government in December 2022, this pressure has increased at an alarming pace. During the first half of 2023, his government approved 12,855 new housing units in the illegal settlements on the West Bank. At least 547 Palestinians, including 134 children, were killed by armed settlers and by Israeli soldiers in that year. UN observers recorded 1,227 incidents of settler violence in 2023 that resulted in casualties and/or damage to property. Emboldened by the government, the hard-core ideological settlers exploit the ongoing war in Gaza to push forward their agenda of forcing Palestinians to leave their villages. According to B'Tselem, the Israeli human rights group, settlers have forced at least eighteen Palestinian communities— over 1,000 people—to flee their homes since 7 October.

Again, these developments merely accelerated the systematic colonization and dispossession project that Netanyahu has always promoted. From his first day in office, Netanyahu was determined to push forward the struggle for "the Whole Land of Israel." This was his reason for sabotaging the Oslo accords: he thought they spelled disaster for Zionism. Under his leadership, through six terms spanning sixteen years in power, settlement expansion continued, more and more Arab land was stolen, the ethnic cleansing of East Jerusalem gained momentum, and the settlers were encouraged to behave as if they were the only lords of the land from the river to the sea. At the time of the signing of the first Oslo Accord in 1993, there were approximately 110,000 settlers in the West Bank and around 140,000 in East Jerusalem. Today there are more than 700,000.

It is also unsurprising that Netanyahu has presented the Gaza war as pitting "the sons of light" against "the sons of darkness"[7] and promised "the victory of Judeo-Christian civilization against barbarism."[8] Netanyahu already employed a Manichean moral framing in his 1993 book, while the idea of Arabs as irredeemably hostile traces back to his father. The "Judeo-Christian" refinement draws as well on the idea of a "Clash of Civilizations," popularized by Harvard Professor Samuel Huntington in the 1990s following the end of the Cold War. It posited that after the collapse of the Soviet Union international conflict was no longer between nation states but between the West and the rest. In this scheme of things Israel was regarded not as part of the Middle East but as part of the West, of the "Free World" as it used to call itself. For someone in the business of denying another people their rights and of running a racist regime of horrendous structural violence, this is a clever rhetorical gambit.

The war in Gaza, however, is not a clash of cultures or religions. Nor is it a clash between two opposing sets of values. It is a clash between a brutal colonial power and its victims, between the occupier and the occupied, between the oppressor and the oppressed. It is an indiscriminate, murderous, and genocidal war waged by one of the strongest militaries in the world, not just against Hamas but against the defenseless people of Gaza. If there are any barbarians in this war, it is Israel's political and military leaders, not the long-suffering people of Gaza. Netanyahu's claim of victory, meanwhile, is premature to say the least: so far it has been a moral defeat for Israel, a military failure, and a political disaster, turning Israel into an international pariah.

A Logical Endpoint

Israel's protracted war on Gaza has been attributed to Netanyahu's struggle for personal survival or else his political reliance upon the far-right. The deeper truth is that Netanyahu's resort to unilateral military might, his

---

7 Israel Ministry of Foreign Affairs, "PM Netanyahu Addresses Students in Eli," *gov.il* (30 January 2024).

8 Israel Ministry of Foreign Affairs, "PM Netanyahu in French in TF1 Interview," *gov.il* (30 May 2024).

understanding of the Palestine conflict as zero sum, his refusal to concede that the representatives of Gaza have any legitimate grievances, his resort to genocidal incitement, and his commitment to Jewish sovereignty from the river to the sea are all wholly consistent with his longstanding positions.

Blaming the Gaza onslaught on Netanyahu's current legal predicaments obscures the relentless consistency of his political project over decades, while blaming Netanyahu's dependence on his far-right collaborators ignores the extent to which their respective projects are one and the same. Such explanations also obscure the extent to which the policies and premises of the far-right, including Netanyahu, are shared across Israeli politics and throughout Israeli society. At the institutional level, it defies credibility to suppose that Netanyahu could prosecute a military offensive of such magnitude for purely personal considerations, if he did not have considerable support within the military and intelligence establishments. Politically, the Gaza onslaught was not waged by Netanyahu alone but by a national unity government that included Israel's most popular opposition leader, Benny Gantz.[9] Gantz previously ran for office by declaring that "only the strong survive" while claiming credit for having bombed parts of Gaza "back to the Stone Age"—positions Netanyahu could hardly disagree with.[10] Israeli public opinion has overwhelmingly supported the Gaza campaign, or else believed the violence should be further escalated. More generally, Netanyahu did not become Israel's longest-serving prime minister by standing apart from Israeli Jewish society but by embodying it.

It follows that Netanyahu's vicious incitement and his criminal conduct in Gaza are not personal aberrations. They reflect the steady drift of Israeli society from a semblance of freedom and democracy to utter moral depravity. This process has been going on since the Israeli victory in the June 1967 war. The occupation of the Palestinian territories has eroded the foundations of Israeli democracy, violated core Jewish values, and turned Israel into a nation of oppressors and war criminals. The Labour-led governments were responsible for initiating this process by the building of illegal settlements on Palestinian land but under the Likud it reached its most cruel, indeed genocidal climax. In truth, the origins of Israel's moral decadence go further back even than 1967. Israel has always been a settler-colonial state. The logic of settler colonialism is the elimination of the native. The ethnic cleansing of Palestine is not a discrete event that ended with the 1948 war but an ongoing

---

9   Gantz withdrew from the governing coalition in June 2024.

10   Raoul Wootliff, "'Parts of Gaza Sent Back to Stone Age': Gantz Videos Laud His IDF Bona Fides," *Times of Israel,* January 20, 2019.

process. What is new in the current war on Gaza is that Zionist settler colonialism has gone beyond ethnic cleansing to the brink of genocide.

Francesca Albanese, the UN special rapporteur on the situation of human rights in the Palestinian territories, submitted in March 2024 a report entitled "Anatomy of a Genocide." The context, facts, and analysis of Israel's conduct in the war on Gaza led her to conclude that "there are reasonable grounds to believe that the threshold indicating Israel's commission of genocide is met." "More broadly," she explained, "they also indicate that Israel's actions have been driven by a genocidal logic integral to its settler-colonial project in Palestine, signaling a tragedy foretold." Nothing better personifies the truth of this verdict than the political career of Benjamin, the son of Benzion Netanyahu.

Life in Gaza:
The Duty to Speak Out

Izzeldin Abuelaish

THE WORLD was not created on October 7. The events of October 7 represent the tip of the iceberg.

Understanding and addressing the root causes of violence, conflict, and injustice are critical steps toward preventing the destruction of life, hope, and the future.

The Palestinian people are living one of the most dangerous chapters in their history since the Nakba of 1948, when they were subjected to massacres, slaughter, and forced displacement from their land, stripped of their property and left to face a historical injustice that cannot be erased or overlooked, especially since the Palestinian people are still living the consequences of this historical injustice in the absence of a collective international effort to enable them to exercise their rights, including their right to self-determination and independence and their right to return to their land.

Palestinians are a nation and people with a civilization, history, potential, dreams, and hopes who aspire like other nations for freedom and independence. We are people who want to succeed and be free and we want others to be free. Freedom must not stop at the borders of Palestine. Palestinians harbor no desire for revenge, and we do not hate anyone.

I am a Palestinian refugee who was born, raised, and lived in Jabalia refugee camp in the Gaza Strip, the son of refugee parents who are survival of the Nakba in 1948 where they were expelled from their home. I am the son of refugee parents who lived with successive catastrophes, killing, destruction, loss, homelessness, home demolition, deprivation, and the Nakba. My family

Izzeldin Abuelaish, a Palestinian-Canadian author, academic and researcher, was born and raised in Jabalia Refugee Camp in the Gaza Strip. Dr. Abuelaish is a Professor at the Dalla Lana School of Public Health at the University of Toronto. His autobiography, *I Shall Not Hate: A Gaza Doctor's Journey on the Road to Peace and Human Dignity,* was published in 2010 to worldwide critical acclaim.

—brothers, sisters and extended family—still live in Jabalia Camp where tens of my family were killed since October 7.

I saw the killing of my three daughters Bessan, Mayar, Aya and niece Nour when an Israeli tank shelled my house. There is no reason that can justify the killing of any innocent human being. My answer to the tragedy was: if I could know that my daughters were the last sacrifice on the road to peace between Palestinians and Israelis, then I would accept their loss. Sadly, they were just numbers among the tens of thousands of innocents.

My life continues to be a war and the war follows us. The war and the suffering in this world are manmade by politicians who are selling illusions to us.

In this world people are fighting to live, and others are living to fight. I never tasted my childhood. I found myself a life as challenging as a raging and wild ocean. As life increased my aches, pain and suffering it also amplified my maturity, awareness, strength and I did not allow all the difficulties to kill my dreams.

But what is war? How much of war do we see on the screen? How much of the suffering do we know about in our world? Is it the soldier who is killed or wounded? Or the innocent child, daughter, mother or someone who is old?

War is about our children or grandchildren dying before they are fully adults, or being disfigured, wounded or mentally scarred for life. They are dying in silence, and no one knows or hears about them.

We hear and see just the numbers. It's hundreds of thousands of human beings dying years before their time. It's our children seeing their buddies, limbs blown of their bodies. It's millions of people separated forever from the ones they love.

The physical costs are easier to see: the loss of life, limbs, and other horrible disfiguring injuries. Less visible, but no less damaging, are the other kinds of loss, children abruptly become homeless, orphans. War and injustice are genocide, torture, propaganda, dishonesty and the slavery of humanity. War and injustice are not just to be documented but to be prevented.

Even though we are now in the 21st century, it seems humankind has not learned the lesson. We still have nations, countries dominating, oppressing and occupying other nations and countries. We still have parties, factions, media, groups who want to control how people think and how they live. That's why we still have war and conflict around the globe and the world is endemic with violence, hatred, injustice, poverty. This violence is filling every corner of our world in homes and in streets.

People are people and are equal. We should not be judged based on political interest and we should not be part of it but be part of exposing it.

No one knows loss until it happens. How simple war is when we see it with glasses.

The Palestinian Poet Mahmoud Darwish said:

> He who looks at the sea
> Does not know the sea,
> He who sits on the shore
> Does not know the sea,
> He who comes to see a sight
> Does not know the sea
> Only he who immerses himself, dives, takes risk and forgets
> the sea in the sea.

War is a defeat and failure to overcome arrogance, ignorance, fear and bloodshed. Dwight Eisenhower put it like this:

> Every gun that is made, every rocket fired, signifies in the final sense a theft from those who hunger and are not fed, those who are cold and not clothed.
>
> This world is not spending money alone. It is spending the sweat of its laborers, the genius of its scientists, and the hopes of its children. This is not a way of life at all, in any true sense. Under the cloud of threatening war, it is humanity hanging from a cross of iron.
>
> A nation that continues year after year to spend more money on military defense than on programs of social uplift is approaching spiritual death.

I can add spiritual and human death and bankruptcy. The human suffering is manmade and caused by people and the constitutions which are not made by God or the rules of nature.

Violence happens when we violate someone's dignity, rights and survival. This violence is systemic, structural, cultural, and political human violence. The world's challenges and refugees' crises are manmade. *This is the hope because its manmade.* It's our responsibility to unmake it.

Overcoming our world problems requires honesty and truth. Truth goes side by side with responsibility. It's the responsibility of all to speak the truth and expose the lies.

Truth is a cornerstone of justice. Jesus said in Gospel of John: "and you will know the truth and the truth will set you free."

If the refugee, those killed, the dead, weak and victims cannot cry or speak out, it's the moral, ethical, and human responsibility and duty of the living to speak out.

What scars in the memory of our history while the international community is complicit in the genocide committed and the refugees' suffering! They continue managing and discussing the war and the genocide instead of stopping the war and genocide.

Who can bear the blatant, obvious bias of Western leaders towards the Israeli position, and their reckless involvement in promoting the false narrative of Netanyahu, his advisors, and his Minister of War in an attempt to justify what they planned: the execution of the crimes of genocide and ethnic cleansing against two million and three hundred thousand innocent civilians.

Every day each one of us adds a small drop to the ocean of complicity by watching it, thinking it's not important and saying, "What we can do?" What makes the evil flourish are the good people who do nothing. Any free person will refuse to be killed in silence. You cannot ask people to coexist with or just accept injustice; this is injustice. Injustice leads to violence and violence begets violence and hatred.

The Palestinians have faced and continue to face two Nakbas, one in 1948 and now in 2023 and ongoing.

What about the mass slaughtering, mass murder, mass destruction, mass displacement.

Palestinians wake up, sleep, and live the minutes on news of killing, destruction, deprivation, hunger, and death for our loved ones.

Everyone bids farewell to everyone.

We cry blood for our loved ones.

Oh death, leave us some of our loved ones. We have nothing left.

And the bodies lying on both sides of the road, unknown and decomposing where the world is watching it live, live and in colour.

Gaza is no longer what it used to be, walking between dozens of holes, inhaling the smell of smoke, dust, and death that filled the place. Polluted....... With white phosphorus. suffocating from smoke, dust, and the smell of death emanating from every direction,

Death, blood, pain, and suffering filled every inch of proud Gaza Strip.

The Palestinian people have the right to dream ... and Gazans have the right to live.

Fighting just to survive in a time others are living to fight.

For any human being justice and freedom are essential, crucial to our dignity and our ability to be fully human.

If the dead, weak and victims cannot cry or speak out, it's the moral, ethical, duty and responsibility of the living to act and speak out for them.

Let me tell you about life in Gaza:

Before October 7 it was a hell. Out of 5 children, 4 were mentally disordered. Palestinians in the Gaza Strip are facing continuous, persistent and cumulative intergenerational and transgenerational trauma. Hopeless, lifeless, jobless, lightless, helpless, free less.

After October 7: Once, it was Gaza—it's no longer Gaza!!!!!!!!!!!! Now it's a ghost. Mass murder, mass destruction, mass displacement and mass suffering.

You will find the slaughtered, the wounded, the displaced, the expelled, the hungry, the thirsty, the naked, the cold and the missing.

Corpses scattered in the alleys, side roads.

Now Gaza and Gazans are homeless, waterless, foodless, health less, warm less, childless, parentless, school less, limbless, endless killing, secure less, homeless, futureless, motherless, and lifeless.

A cup of water is more expensive than a cup of blood and all the roads lead to death.

Mass graves. It's a privilege to have a funeral or to be killed and be found and recognized. Not to be dissolved or shattered into pieces.

Facing the silence, indifference, double standards and complicity of the USA and Western countries. You know who uprooted my people from their homeland in 1948. You know who oppresses. Who intimidates and murders my people. You know whose weapons and who is complicit in the suffering and war crimes and genocide being committed even now as you read this in the Gaza Strip.

No nation has been so tested. How many times we have been displaced. A protracted siege for more than 16 years, collective punishment and incitement against Palestinians, being called human animals. What is more heartbreaking is how so much of the world is complicit, indifferent, silent, and biased. Mass graves, collective punishment, field executions, torture, decapitation, bodies dissolved, maimed, disfigured...

We see women, children, men murdered, wounded, traumatized by this ethnic cleansing, this genocide. People treated as animals, caught in this blind colonial revenge.

We should not talk about human rights, Geneva conventions, or world order. Because...... It's hijacked by those very ones who claim advocacy of democracy and human rights.

Israel hit Gaza Strip with three times more firepower than Hiroshima.

More than 80,000 tons. 36 kg of explosives per Palestinian person in Gaza Strip.

Mass graves. Mass executions.

80 million tons of rubble. How do you feel when you are disconnected from the internet for 30 mins? It led to more than 40,000.......... cases of hepatitis.

Gaza Strip and Palestinians in Gaza are limbless, handless, eyeless, skinless, moveless, The World Health Organization estimates more than 22,500 people in Gaza—or a quarter of those wounded in Israel's continuing war crimes—have life-changing injuries and will require rehabilitation "now and for years to come." Those requiring long-term care include people with amputations, head and spinal cord injuries as well as severe burns. Nearly 15,000 people have limb injuries. There are about 4,000 amputations, more than 2,000 major head and spinal cord injuries, and at least 2,000 cases of major burns. More than 22,500 people—a quarter of those wounded in Gaza since Israel's offensive began—have life-changing injuries, requiring rehabilitation services "now and for years to come," the UN World Health Organization (WHO) reported on Thursday.

Take whatever you want from the pleasures of life and your own goals of money and status but have mercy on us and leave us our loved ones and hope for recovery and a future for those who are destined to remain alive.

Everything has a beginning and an end. And it will end.

And it may be written for us to return one day to Gaza, the place of honor and dignity

Gaza, the witness to the betrayal, collusion, injustice, falsehood, lies, mediocracy and hypocrisy of this world.

In the Gaza Strip, for nearly a year, the Palestinian people have been witnessing the most hateful aggression. For 11 months, Israel has continued to bomb densely populated residential neighborhoods, homes, mosques, churches, schools, hospitals, shelters and tents filled with displaced people. Israel does not stop at targeting Palestinian civilians. It has deliberately exacerbated their suffering by obstructing the entry of humanitarian aid, including food, medicine and fuel, spreading famine and using starvation as a weapon of war, in flagrant violation of international law.

The Israeli government's attitudes and aggression have expanded to the West Bank, which translates on a daily basis into massacres as part of their forced displacement policy. In the West Bank, including East Jerusalem, the Israeli occupation forces invade Palestinian cities daily, arrest thousands of Palestinians and subject them to the harshest forms of torture, leading to the martyrdom of prisoners in their cells. Israel also continues to confiscate

Palestinian lands, increase settlement plans and legalize settlement outposts, impose sanctions on the Palestinian government, steal Palestinian tax revenues, and allow settlers to spread their terrorism and carry out their daily attacks against Palestinians, to storm the Noble Sanctuary in Jerusalem, violating the historical status quo of the holy sites in the city. These are weaponized, brutal, criminal and terrorist settlers who are protected by the Israeli army. There is weaponization, militarization and politicization of everything. Collective punishment. But all this reminds us of and strengthens our Palestinianism.

The war of ethnic cleansing and genocide against the Palestinian people continues in its most hideous forms. The war of extermination continues, and the horrific killing continues daily with all kinds of weapons while the whole world fails to deliver humanitarian aid.

International public solidarity: The Palestinian people are living an ongoing catastrophe, and international solidarity and intervention are vital at this particular stage. The international community must rise in its response to a level appropriate to the war crimes committed against the Palestinians, as the occupying state has not left any violation or crime, according to the international law and human rights conventions, uncommitted—before the eyes and ears of the world. What has it done about the dangerous laws passed by the "Knesset," especially in light of the escalating risks resulting from settlement expansion and the terrorism of the colonists, especially now that the legal position issued by the International Court of Justice condemns the occupation and the nature of its practices in the occupied Palestinian territories. International *intervention* is required to hold Israel accountable for its crimes and provide protection for the Palestinian people. Legal and diplomatic action must continue to end this colonial system at all levels. Where are the sanctions? The breaking of diplomatic relations? Why aren't all the actions undertaken against Russia taken against Israel?

A War Against Palestinian Children

"More children have been killed in Gaza in 6 months than the number of children killed in all the other war zones in the world over 3 years, multiplied by 4."

Children who should be in school, learning and playing, are instead thrust into a world of chaos and fear, their childhood stolen by the massacres that surround them. A generation that has lost its education, removing the intellectual wealth of Palestinians.

Imagine dying from the cold because you don't have winter clothes, and you can't find winter clothes. Come and tell me, then, how much you feel for us.

Have you experienced having your sister or wife being pregnant in her last month during a war!!

Have you experienced how she will give birth in the middle of the night or under bombardment.

Do you know that mothers' breastmilk is cut off due to fear and lack of food!!

Have you experienced the feeling of your daughter or son being born in a bathroom, in a car, on the street, or in a tent? Imagine if the little one was your firstborn daughter or son.

Have you experienced the feeling of not finding a single piece of clothing for your newborn son??

Have you experienced a chronic disease with no medicine?

Or your mother having a chronic illness?

Try being in need of medicine you couldn't find!!

Try to forget that you have a life.

Try depriving yourself of your humanity, rights and your future.

Try living in injustice while having others judge you.

Try to be demonized, dehumanized, and intimidated.

Experience the feeling of falling asleep with the sound of drones.

Try facing a continuous cumulative existential threat.

O death, stop for a moment; perhaps we can pick up the pieces of those we lost, so they can sleep without cold and noise.

Our hearts break as we watch the bodies of Gaza's children being torn apart by the shells of the occupation army, and as we hear the painful groans of mothers who lost their children. Closer to death than life. We are always asking our children what they want to be when they grow up. When we ask a Palestinian child what you want to be when you grow up, the answer is: I am not going to grow up. I am born to be killed and not to grow up.

Children as the embodiment of life, the future, and hope can evoke strong emotions and inspire others. In the tapestry of existence children are the vibrant threads that weave together the past, present, and future, creating a masterpiece that resonates with the essence of life. As a father and grandfather, I have been privileged to witness the transformative power that children possess—their laughter echoing through the corridors of our homes, their curiosity lighting up our darkest moments, and their boundless potential serving as a beacon of hope for generations to come.

Children are not merely the beneficiaries of life; they are life itself, breathing vitality into the mundane and infusing our world with unbridled energy. Their innocence is a testament to the purity that resides within the human spirit, and their ability to see the extraordinary in the ordinary is a reminder that life's true beauty lies in the simplicity of being.

The deliberate targeting of children in war is a reprehensible and morally indefensible tactic that goes against ethical principles and international humanitarian laws. Targeting children and the weaponization of children is a strategy—one where hospitals and schools are targeted, one which disrupts the access to health care and education which are essential for the future development and wellbeing of children.

Targeting children in armed conflicts is a gross violation of human rights and is condemned by the international community. International humanitarian law, including the Geneva Conventions and the Convention on the Rights of the Child, explicitly prohibit such acts, and individuals responsible for these crimes can be held accountable by international courts. Efforts to prevent and address these atrocities include advocacy, international pressure, and the establishment of legal mechanisms to hold perpetrators accountable.

In the past 15 years, children in the Gaza Strip have endured six major moments—five escalations in violence and the COVID-19 pandemic—as well as a life-limiting land, air, and sea blockade imposed by the government of Israel. Children make up 47% of Gaza's population of two million, with over 800,000 having never known life without the blockade. a blockade that has sparked a mental health crisis for children and young people, today's research shows. Eighty percent of Gaza children suffer depression after 15 years of blockade, a 2022 report published by Save the Children found.[1] This was even before the Israeli bombardments, post October 7.

The killing and deaths don't hurt the dead or murdered; they hurt the living. And if the murdered, killed, the weak and the victim cannot cry or speak out, it's the moral, ethical, and human duty and responsibility of the living and loving to act and speak out for them.

---

1 Save the Children International, *Trapped: The impact of 15 years of blockade on the mental health of Gaza's children* [report], 2022. https://resourcecentre.savethechildren.net/document/trapped-the-impact-of-15-years-of-blockade-on-the-mental-health-of-gazas-children/

"After 15 years of blockade, four out of five children in Gaza say they are living with depression, grief and fear," Save the Children [news release], June 15, 2022. https://www.savethechildren.net/news/after-15-years-blockade-four-out-five-children-gaza-say-they-are-living-depression-grief-and

Has Humanity Lost Its Humanity?

Humanity forsook, abandoned, gave up its essence. Humanity abandoned its core values. Mankind drifted from its true nature. We lost sight of our humanity. We strayed from our human nature. Humanity lost its moral compass.

And have some Western countries been afflicted with rulers who are subservient to the biased and materialized political agenda and their interests? Or to their blind racism?

Where has the chivalry of the Arabs and Muslims gone? And have not some of their rulers lost their sense of dignity and their duty to defend the future of their people?

Don't they remember the proverb that every Arab child learned in primary school, "I was eaten the day the white bull was eaten"?

What is happening in Gaza is not just a genocide, not just collective punishment and starvation, and not just ethnic cleansing of at more than two million people who were forced to flee and flee under brutal bombardment six times or more. What is happening is not just a biological war that has killed and afflicted thousand people with epidemics and diseases, and revived epidemics such as polio, viral hepatitis and meningitis. Rather, it is a comprehensive and complete atrocity practiced by Zionist fascism and the complicit actions of the USA, UK, France, Germany and Canada against the people, stones, animals, trees and everything living or dead in the Gaza Strip. How have the leaders and advocates of democracy, human rights and international law in the West become so ossified, so turned to stone, so petrified? Are they blind and deaf?

Why do the Western media refuse to even look into what they hear about the suffering of the Palestinians, but instead continue to wait for one or more Israelis to be injured, so that they can glorify the alleged and permanent victim, Israel, even as it slaughters the Palestinian people in Gaza from vein to vein, and expands the crimes of its settlers in Jerusalem and the West Bank?

And why do the leaders of the United States, Germany, Britain and others insist on continuing to supply Israel with weapons, bombs and shells, while it slaughters children and women, and destroys everything that is humane in Gaza? The most horrifying figures at this writing are that Israel has dropped no less than eighty thousand tons of bombs and explosives on the Gaza Strip, equivalent to four nuclear bombs used in World War II, so that every man, woman and child in Gaza received 36 kilograms of American explosives and bombs. Indeed, the United States, which claims to defend democracy, civilization and freedom and punishes Russia under the pretext of its occupation of Ukrainian lands, has sent and approved, since October

7, $45 billion worth of missiles and weapons to Israel, as if it is rewarding Israel with a million dollars for every killing of a Palestinian man, child and woman. The world is witnessing an era of spiritual, ethical, moral and human bankruptcy. Then Blinken crowns his malice for the ninth time by providing cover for the lies and allegations of war criminal Netanyahu, holding the Palestinian side responsible for Netanyahu's refusal to stop the barbaric war on the Gaza Strip.

Everyone knows, and this is even what most Israeli newspapers and most Israeli politicians repeat, that Netanyahu and his fascist government are the ones who are obstructing reaching a ceasefire agreement, and are thwarting every effort and every initiative to reach it, because they prefer to protect their political interests, and do not even care about the lives of the Israeli prisoners who are dying, one after the other, as a result of Israeli bombing. Blinken and Biden are covering up for them, and placing the responsibility on the victim, the Palestinian side. We Palestinians know, based on our life experiences, that all these people will not protect us. Didn't they let Beirut be besieged and destroyed in 1982?

Didn't they let the West Bank and Gaza Strip be invaded and destroyed in 2002?

Didn't they even besiege President Yasser Arafat, who signed the peace agreement with them and then they poisoned him, after they had awarded him the Nobel Peace Prize?

What is happening in Gaza must mobilize every person with honor and dignity, whether Muslim, Christian, Jew, Arab, Westerner, foreigner or Palestinian. There is no cause more just today than saving the Palestinian people in the Gaza Strip from slaughter and genocide. No Palestinian, wherever they may be, should slacken off today in performing their duty, just as no one in Palestinian leadership should continue to hide behind the curtain of division to escape the obligation of national unity on a single program, to stop the war, the aggression and the crimes being committed in Gaza. No street, city or neighborhood in the world should rest until this destructive criminal war stops. Every university, especially in Europe and the United States, must become a hotbed of revolution and rebellion that even surpasses what was achieved in April, May and June. History will not forgive any Arab people who fail to do everything they can to pressure any government that continues to normalize relations with the fascist rulers of Israel, while they commit all these crimes.

The world is endemic with violence, injustice, fear, and hatred. These socioeconomic diseases cross barriers and borders. No one is far from risk, and we all are potential victims.

To endure this world, we need truth, justice, and action. We must protest the indifference, racism, discrimination, silence, apathy, hatred, violence, and injustice We must dissent because we must do better, and we have no choice than doing better for one just, equal, and free human world.

After 11 months of the war crime, aggression and genocide, the demands of the international community have not been met yet. No ceasefire, no safe access for humanitarian aid, no rescue and protection of civilians. The suffering of the Palestinian people is getting worse, and Israel's policy of killing, forced displacement, destruction and deprivation has increased, leading to unprecedented human suffering.

The international community has to impose an immediate ceasefire and asked the international community to act more decisively to impose a permanent ceasefire in Gaza now, and not to allow Israel to continue its genocide by other means.

There is no problem in international law. The problem lies within the international community and the countries that pay lip service to democracy in a selective and bewildered manner. International hypocrisy amounts to complicity in committing these crimes. We need accountability, consistency, transparency.

We must realize that international law and the human rights conventions, democracy, civilization—all are being buried along with the innocent Palestinian women, children and the elderly. It's time for humanity to repudiate a world which is bankrupt humanely, spiritually, ethically and morally. It's time to make our voices heard.

SECTION III.

Narrations of Genocide

Israel's Gaza War: A Symbol of Collapsing Civilization

Abdullah Ahsan

ISRAEL OFFICIALLY declared an all-out war against Gaza following Hamas' surprise attack on October 7, 2023, to "take mighty vengeance" against Hamas.[1] Israel's resentful attitude has blatantly exposed vital weaknesses of Western civilization—the civilization that created and patronized the state of Israel in the historical land of Palestine since 1948. Israel's behavior reminds us of the pattern of collapsing civilizations in history. Prominent civilizational studies scholars such as Ibn Khaldun (1332–1406) and Arnold Toynbee (1889–1975) hold the view that collapsing civilizations usually witness a wide gap between elites and masses. The American society, the society that stands as the prime witness to humanity's progress and prosperity, represents this gap. Toynbee is reported to have predicted in 1945 that, "if a new war broke out, the Americans would be the aggressor."[2] Are we moving to demonstrate that Toynbee was right? Little over two decades later he counted the United States as "one of the two malign imperialist powers in the postwar world; the other was the state of Israel." He justified his claim saying, "must be today the two most dangerous of the 125 sovereign states among which the

---

1 VOA News, "Israel Officially Declares War on Hamas After Surprise Attack," *VOA*, October 8, 2023. https://www.voanews.com/a/israel-officially-declares-war-on-hamas-after-surprise-attack-/7301836.html
2 Arthur Herman, *The Idea of Decline in Western History* (New York: The Free Press, 1997), 285.

Abdullah al-Ahsan is a former professor of comparative civilization in the Department of Political Science and International Relations at Istanbul Sehir University. Earlier, he taught at the International Islamic University Malaysia for almost three decades. A graduate of McGill University, Montreal, Canada, and the University of Michigan in Ann Arbor, Ahsan has written and edited several books and many articles on the relationship between contemporary Islamic and Western civilizations.

land-surface of this planet is at present partitioned."[3] He also suggested that "Israel's occupation of Arab territory constituted as vicious and inhuman an act as Germany's occupation of Czechoslovakia and Poland." In this article, we shall discuss the slow growth of this symbol over the past century or so and examine this issue to demonstrate how America's Israel policy is pushing contemporary civilization toward a total collapse.

The unreserved U.S. support for Israel's genocidal acts in occupied Palestine is already creating a deep crisis in the society. While Israeli actions are producing deep anger and frustration among common Americans, the elites are trying to suppress such popular responses by enacting new laws and imposing their perspective on society using the mainstream academia and media.[4] Out of his frustration, the senior airman Aaron Bushnell self-immolated in front of the Israeli embassy in Washington D. C. declaring that he would "no longer be complicit to genocide."[5] He shouted "Free Palestine" describing in a note his action as "an extreme act of protest." His action has created mixed reactions. The corporate-supported mainstream media depicted the event as an act of suicide with warnings and seeking information about any other potential similar acts while the Israeli spy agency Mossad commented, "Our enemies kill themselves."[6] Some news channels have covered the event with a more rational approach,[7] and many common users of social media channels have declared vigils in appreciation of the act.[8] The overall response to Aaron Bushnell's self-immolation only reflects the wide gap between the masses and the elites in America.[9] As we shall argue later in

3 Ibid., 286.

4 Barbara Sprunt, "House passes bill aimed to combat antisemitism amid college unrest," *NPR,* May 2, 2024. https://www.npr.org/2024/05/02/1247374244/house-passes-bill-aimed-to-combat-antisemitism-amid-college-unrest

5 Kayla Epstein and Angelica Casas, "Aaron Bushnell: Friends struggle to comprehend US airman's Gaza protest death," *BBC News,* March 2, 2024. https://www.bbc.com/news/world-us-canada-68455401.amp

6 Tom Norton: "Fact Check: Did Mossad Celebrate Aaron Bushnell's Self-Immolation?," *MSN,* February 26, 2024. https://www.msn.com/en-us/news/world/fact-check-did-mossad-celebrate-aaron-bushnell-s-self-immolation/ar-BB1iUzHH

7 Rising, "Death Cult? Aaron Bushnell memorialized by 'death cult' Left over self-immolation for 'Free Palestine'," *The Hill,* February 27, 2024. https://thehill.com/video/death-cult-aaron-bushnell-memorialized-by-death-cult-left-over-self-immolation-for-free-palestine/9467686/

8 "Vigils Held for Aaron Bushnell After Self-Immolation Death to Protest Gaza Genocide," *Democracy Now!,* February 27, 2024. https://www.democracynow.org/2024/2/27/headlines/vigils_held_for_aaron_bushnell_after_self_immolation_death_to_protest_gaza_genocide

9 For a good description of the coverage of the situation, see Brett Wilkins, "After Setting Himself on Fire, US Airman Aaron Bushnell Dies Declaring 'Free

this essay, the American elites are not alone; the elites in the Muslim world are equally complicit in this conflict. This is what we call a symbol of the collapse of world order and civilization.

Referring to the event, the Vietnam War veteran David Cortright, who became an academic and a peace activist, commented in *Boston Review*,

> The incident evokes haunting memories of Vietnam, especially for those of us who served during that war and spoke out against it. The fact that Bushnell wore his uniform and called attention to his military service indicates he believed his status as a soldier would lend greater weight and significance to his protest. I feel only sadness that he was compelled to take such drastic action alone.

Cortright ends his article by saying,

> It's tragic that Bushnell felt it necessary to take his life in an extreme manner in order to be heard. His death sends a message for us to take continued action against the war and in support of Palestinian rights, to pressure our government to insist that Israel end the bloodshed. Our success in achieving these goals will depend on building an ever larger and more persistent movement of millions of people determined to work for peace.[10]

It is noteworthy that the voices of conscience and attempts of peace activists are not new in history, but unfortunately, instead of listening to voices of conscience such as Aaron Bushnell, or Rachel Corrie, bulldozed in 2003 by Israeli soldiers, or peace activists such as David Cortright, American elites have become complicit to the current genocide/ holocaust in Palestine. In this essay, we examine Israel's Gaza War in the context of civilizational transformation. We study this symbol of a collapsing civilization and the potential role this event might play in the changing world.

Gaza Crisis in the Context of Civilizational Transformation

The French historian Fernand Braudel has summarized the British historian Arnold Toynbee's theory of change in history: "Arnold Toynbee offered

Palestine'," *Common Dreams,* February 26, 2024. https://www.commondreams.org/news/aaron-bushnell

10 David Cortright, "Aaron Bushnell and the Power of Protest," *Boston Review,* February 28, 2024. https://www.bostonreview.net/articles/aaron-bushnell-and-the-power-of-protest/

a tempting theory. All human achievement, he thought, involved challenge and response. Nature had to present itself as a difficulty to be overcome. If human beings took up the challenge, their response would lay the foundations of civilization."[11] Challenges to humans come not only from nature but from fellow humans too. When humans successfully overcome a challenge, they make progress and their failures lead to decline and fall. A creative minority always plays a prominent role by stimulating core values during its rise and delaying the fall of a given civilization temporarily by reminding its founding values. Where does the Gaza War stand in Toynbee's theory? This question demands a thorough examination of the Palestinian conflict.

Some historians trace the origin of the current conflict in Palestine in 1948 when Israel established itself as an independent nation-state in historical Palestine. Israel created innovative facts on the ground to justify its establishment as a Jewish state in a land where Jews constituted only a tiny minority in the nineteenth century. To understand this complexity, one must evaluate the process by which proponents of Israel created those ground realities. The founding ideology of Israel, Zionism, originated at the end of the nineteenth century when the idea of nationalism dominated the European political horizon. Interestingly although most nationalist ideologies were rooted in non-religious grounds, they heavily relied on religious myths and Zionism was no exception. Here is where one finds a contradiction in the Western civilization's stated claim that it is rooted in rationalism and scientific inquest. Non-religious Zionist leaders effectively used religious myths in support of their newly found ideology and used Christian Zionist messianic ideology very efficiently to promote their case.[12] In his UN Lecture on 100 Years of Balfour Declaration Prof. Rashid Khalidi of Columbia University has rightly pointed out how the current conflict began with the British occupation of Palestine in 1917. The professional chemist but skillful diplomat Zionist leader Chaim Weizmann reached out to British politicians as early as 1914, when the Ottomans joined the Axis, arguing that:

> [w]e can reasonably say that should Palestine fall within the British sphere of influence, and should Britain encourage Jewish settlement there, as a British dependency, we could have in twenty to thirty years a million Jews out there, perhaps more; they would

---

11 Fernand Braudel, *A History of Civilizations* (New York: Penguin, 1994), 11.

12 Motti Inbari and Kirill Bumin, *Christian Zionism in the Twenty-First Century* (New York: Oxford University Press, 2024). For historical connection, see particularly 1–16.

develop the country, bring back civilization to it and form a very effective guard for the Suez canal.[13]

This was a clever move in the light of British colonial and imperialist interests and Weizmann successfully blended the Zionist ideology with the white supremacist mindset of many British politicians. Yoav Litvin, "an Israeli-American doctor of psychology and neuroscience" has rightly pointed out that, "Early Zionists syncretised many aspects of European fascism, white supremacy, colonialism and messianic Evangelism and had a long and sordid history of cooperating with anti-Semites, imperialists and fascists in order to promote exclusivist and expansionist agendas."[14] Here one should note that mostly non-religious (secular) Zionist leaders successfully combined their ideology with (that of?) privileged British political elites, most of whom had little or no concern for Western civilization's basic values such as individual civil liberty, universal human equality and rule of law. Nevertheless, Zionists gradually succeeded in implementing their agenda in creating ground realities for what they called a Jewish state in Palestine. They extensively used religious myths, money, and political influence for the purpose, and the Balfour Declaration laid down an effective mechanism for it.

With the British support, Jewish immigration began the process of demographic transformation in the area. The number of Jews in Palestine increased from about 55,000 during the First World War to about 646,000 in 1948. This reflected from a little over 5 percent to about 31 percent of the total population. The new immigrants increased their land possession from 2 percent to 6.5 percent: thus began the new ground realities. Although most discussions on the subject originate from the birth of contemporary Israel as a nation-state under the auspicious of the United Nations, one cannot ignore the ground realities created during the League of Nations Mandate system.

United States Replacing Britain as the Guardian of Western Civilization

Although the United States came into existence in 1776 after fighting an anti-colonial, war and adopted an isolationist policy following independence, by the end of the nineteenth century it became involved in imperialist design and espoused an expansionist strategy. Nevertheless, many policymakers continued to subscribe to some basic ethical standards and to maintain basic

13 Chiam Weizmann, *Trial and Error: the Autobiography of Chiam Weizmann* (New York: Harper, 1949), 149.
14 Yoav Litvin, "The Zionist fallacy of 'Jewish supremacy'," *Al Jazeera,* January 9, 2019. https://www.aljazeera.com/opinions/2019/1/9/the-zionist-fallacy-of-jewish-supremacy/

civilizational values. In 1917, President Woodrow Wilson decided to join WWI to "make the world safe for democracy" and uphold principles of freedom and justice. He also upheld the principle of self-determination and sought cooperation with all peoples for international peace and security under the platform of the League of Nations. He formed the "Inter-Allied Commission on Mandates in Turkey" to assess the idea of self-determination on the ground. In its report, the Commission known as the King-Crane Commission rejected the Balfour Declaration and the Zionist demand for a homeland in Palestine.[15] However, the U.S. did not follow up the Commission's recommendations and following WWII, the U.S. totally abandoned those recommendations and moved further away from the ideas of democracy and self-determination. The consequential victims were the ideas of accountability and transparency.

The Leagues of Nation's successor institution, the United Nations, came into existence as the guarantor of international peace and security, and as the center of power of Western civilization had already begun to move from Britain to the United States, so did the center of the Zionist Movement. American Zionists began to create pressure to get more Jews migrate to Palestine through their Christian Zionist colleagues even before the state of Israel came into existence. President Truman recognized the State of Israel as an independent nation-state within minutes of its declaration of coming into existence. This swift action of the president indicates bankruptcy of the system: he seems to have been concerned about the subject being debated and rejected in Congress. After all, only a little more than two decades earlier President Woodrow Wilson had rejected the idea. One should also note that his Secretary of State and Secretary of Defense, George Marshall, whom he used to consider "the greatest living American," had strongly opposed the move.[16] Why did the President take such a sensitive action so swiftly? In this connection, one should remember that nineteenth-century German philosopher Frederick Nietzsche, although very controversial, explained the dilemma of the Judeo-Christian tradition very well.[17] One salient point about

---

15 *The King-Crane Commission Report, August 28, 1919,* Official Papers, World War II Document Archive, Brigham Young University. https://wwi.lib.byu.edu/index.php/The_King-Crane_Report

16 *President Truman's Decision to Recognize Israel,* Jerusalem Center for Security and Foreign Affairs (JCFA), May 2008. https://jcpa.org/article/president-truman%E2%80%99s-decision-to-recognize-israel/

17 Jörg Salaquarda, "Nietzsche and the Judaeo-Christian tradition," from Part II - The use and abuse of Nietzsche's life and works, in Bernd Magnus and Kathleen Higgins, eds., *The Cambridge Companion to Nietzsche* (published online by Cambridge University Press, May 28, 2006). https://www.cambridge.org/core/books/abs/cambridge-companion-to-nietzsche/nietzsche-and-the-judaeochristian-tradition/9077DD811EFDE80AFF27A213BD0E966D

President Truman's recognition of the Israel document is that he scratched the typed term the "Jewish State" and wrote the "State of Israel" by hand. Why did he refuse to recognize Israel as a Jewish state although that was the main demand of the Zionists? This seems to be the main dilemma for most Western elites: On the surface, they would like to be liberal, rational, non-religious, and scientific but in the back of their mind, apocalyptic myths seem to drive them. In the current context, President Biden too, like President Truman, seems to have been following Christian Zionist myths. Nietzsche comprehended this internal contradiction among many Christians very well.

Within months, another shocking event occurred. The Israeli terrorist group Lehi, also known as the Stern Gang, assassinated Count Bernadotte, the Swedish diplomat and Red Cross Chief whom the UN had assigned to mediate the Israeli-Palestinian conflict, on September 17, 1948.[18] This event bears another witness to Western civilization's destitution. The United States, along with most other countries, strongly condemned the assassination. President Truman expressed his shock and sorrow over the killing and urged the Israeli government to take immediate action to bring the perpetrators to justice, but no action followed. Is the Biden Administration handling the Netanyahu government differently? In fact, one of the alleged assassins of Count Bernadotte became Israel's prime minister later. This seems to have encouraged Israel to mock international law and all international mediation efforts in conflicts with the Palestinians and other neighboring states since then. South Africa's recent case at the International Court of Justice alleging Israel committing genocide in Gaza is one such instance. Some observers have rightly raised the question of whether Israel is above the law.[19] On its part, Israel has alleged South Africa as being an agent of Hamas.[20]

In 1948, Israel was not yet a member of the United Nations. It applied for UN membership in November, but the world body rejected the application due to its ill-defined border. It also emphasized that Israel did not comply with the UN's demand to address the refugee problem—a problem created during its establishment. The question of the status of Jerusalem too remained unanswered. However, several months later in May 1949 on the insistence of some Western nations, Israel received the UN membership after assuring that

---

18 See, Cary David Stanger, "A Haunting Legacy: The Assassination of Count Bernadotte," *Middle East Journal* 42, no. 2 (Spring, 1988): 260–72.

19 Jameel Hodzic, ed., "Israel: Above the law?," featured documentary [26:00], *Aljazeera*, March 27, 2024. https://www.aljazeera.com/program/featured-documentaries/2024/3/27/israel-above-the-law

20 Jewish News Syndicate, "South Africa acting as Hamas' legal arm, Israel says after ICJ hearing," *National Post*, January 11, 2024. https://nationalpost.com/news/world/south-africa-acting-as-hamas-legal-arm-israel-says-after-icj-hearing

it would follow the world body's recommendations on the stated demands later. Israel never fulfilled its commitment on any of the three issues: it never defined its international border; it refused to define the status of Jerusalem for decades and never allowed refugees to return to their ancestral home. Israel's Western sponsors never tried to enforce international law on these subjects and this is where one finds the total bankruptcy of Western civilization.

It is also imperative to note the swiftness of some Western leaders in endorsing Israel's response to Hamas' October 7 attack. President Biden called the assault "pure, unadulterated evil," and traveled to Israel to declare unequivocal U.S. support for Israel ignoring the fact that Israel was an occupying power in Palestine and actively controlling all necessary items including food, water, electricity, medicine, building materials—literally everything.[21] He also claimed that "American leadership is what holds the world together."[22] "American values are what make us a partner that other nations want to work with," he further explained. These claims demand serious consideration.

Transformation of American Civilization into a Global Civilization

What are the American values that have attracted other nations to become partners with America? This question requires a little wider discussion about the concept and characteristics of civilizations. Scholars agree that civilizations have a long life span and go through various stages in their lives and there are values such as human dignity, equality, justice and rule of law that represent common threads that unite humans in creating a shared heritage of a civilization. Historian Arnold Toynbee has observed that all civilizations in history tended to transform into a "universal civilization" at a certain stage.[23] America now seems to have reached this stage, but how do we evaluate the current Gaza War in light of America's unqualified support for Israel? Let us briefly examine this question.

America came into existence during the last quarter of the eighteenth century based on the principles of civil liberty, equality, democracy, individualism,

---

21 Linda Feldmann and Christa Case Bryant, "After attack on Israel, why US leadership matters profoundly," *Christian Science Monitor,* October 11, 2023. https://www.csmonitor.com/USA/Politics/2023/1011/ After-attack-on-Israel-why-US-leadership-matters-profoundly

22 Joseph Clark, "Biden Says U.S. Leadership Vital, Pledges Support for Israel and Ukraine," U.S. Department of Defense News, October 20, 2023. https://www.defense.gov/News/News-Stories/Article/Article/3564178/ biden-says-us-leadership-vital-pledges-support-for-israel-and-ukraine/

23 "Arnold Toynbee interview (1955)," *Manufacturing Intellect* YouTube channel [30:38]. https://youtu.be/Lp0twnI2gxk

diversity, justice, and the rule of law. American founding fathers learned these principles from the European Enlightenment tradition—a tradition that owes a great deal to both the classical Greek and the Judeo-Christian Biblical tradition. We also should note the extraordinary growth of communication technology during the past few decades that enhanced America's transformation to a universal civilization. Earlier the television industry had created a sort of global culture by facilitating cross-cultural exchange, promoting common languages, disseminating global news coverage, influencing cultural norms and trends, and celebrating cultural diversity. The collapse of the former Soviet Union at the end of the 1980s facilitated America's rise to its current stage.

President Biden has referred to American values while expressing his unconditional support for Israel in this war, but the administration is increasingly encountering student protests against the stance. The Biden administration and powerful wealthy demagogues are actively trying to suppress student uprisings on campuses. Immediately after October 7, some wealthy donors issued statements of warning about student activities on campuses. In this connection, one should also note the British newspaper *Guardian*'s report about "An Israeli diplomat tried to persuade a leading New York college to cancel a course about the growing debate over whether the Jewish state practices a form of apartheid in Palestine."[24] Are these American values? In fact, these efforts demonstrate a violation of the foundational values of the American Republic. Nevertheless, students of civilizational studies know well that such violations are common in human history. By the latter stages of civilizations, those who control power always try to limit elements of civil liberty, equality, and justice to remain in power. Both Ibn Khaldun and Arnold Toynbee have demonstrated this phenomenon very efficiently in their works.

Israel's Gaza war has exposed the double standards of the American elite. After retracting his claim of Hamas decapitating forty Israeli babies, President Biden boastfully declared that "American leadership is what holds the world together." "American alliances are what keep us, America, safe. American values are what make us a partner that other nations want to work with," he insisted. Is he not mocking the dreams of America's founding fathers? We have witnessed mockery and lies in framing the clash of civilizations thesis, in the carpet-bombing of Afghanistan in 2001, in justifying the invasion of Iraq in 2003, and two decades of occupation of Afghanistan. The mainstream academia and media hardly discuss America's humiliating defeat

---

24 Chris McGreal, "Israeli diplomat pressured US college to drop course on 'apartheid' debate," *The Guardian,* November 8, 2023. https://www.theguardian.com/us-news/2023/nov/08/israeli-diplomat-bard-college-apartheid-debate

at the hands of the traditional reluctant Taliban. Why did the most sophisticated army of our time succumb to an ill-equipped and "backward-looking"
outdated force? No accountability for billions, perhaps trillions of dollars of
investment! Contradictions are rampant. President Obama had asked Israelis
in a speech in 2013, "Put yourself in Palestinian shoes,"[25] but in response
in Hamas' October 7 attack, he came out condemning the "brazen terrorist
attacks on Israel and the slaughter of innocent civilians."[26] Did he put himself
in the shoes of Gazans? A few days later, however, he came up with a caution
that, some of Israel's action in its war against Hamas, like cutting off food and
water for Gaza, could "harden Palestinian attitudes for generations."[27] In this
connection, one should also note that a few years earlier, President Obama
had addressed the Muslim youth generating a lot of hope with what he called
"A new beginning," but when the Arab revolutions occurred, the Obama-led
American administration abandoned them.

The Palestinian situation has continuously deteriorated during the past
half a century: From President Carter to President Trump, and now under
President Biden. In 1978, with a good intention, President Carter initiated
reconciliation between Egypt and Israel to legitimize Israel's presence in its
neighborhood, but decades later, he ended up warning that Israel was moving
toward an apartheid state.[28] All administrations following him ignored the
warning. One should note that this is not the first time in history that one
witnesses a decaying power making hollow prerogatives. Decaying powers
throughout history have gone crazy in their killing spree. How terrifying is
it going to be this time? President Biden is already claiming that America is
holding the world together. Holding together for what? To force Gazans to
starve? Arnold Toynbee prophesized America's future based on his studies of
major world civilizations. A culture of fear and intimidation dominates the
atmosphere today.[29] Is the Gaza crisis a symbol of civilizational predicament?
Yes, along with the climate crisis, the current situation has become even more

---

25 "Obama to Israelis: Put yourselves in Palestinians' shoes," *CBS News* video
[3:55], March 21, 2013. https://www.youtube.com/watch?v=MVKWr11oBUE

26 Julia   Mueller,   "Obama   condemns   'brazen'   attacks   against
Israel,"   *The   Hill,*   October   9,   2023.   https://thehill.com/policy/
international/4246382-obama-condemns-brazen-attacks-against-israel/

27 Kanishka Singh, "Obama warns some of Israel's actions in Gaza
may backfire," Reuters, October 23, 2023. https://www.reuters.com/world/
obama-warns-some-israels-actions-gaza-may-backfire-2023-10-23/

28 Jimmy Carter, *Palestine: Peace, Not Apartheid* (New York: ʃ Simon &
Schuster, 2006).

29 David Bauder and Christine Fernando, "Student journalists are covering their own
campuses in convulsion. Here's what they have to say," *AP News,* May 2, 2024. https://apnews.
com/article/campus-protests-student-journalists-b9ff00a494cdb69d45bd1f99db28288b

complex. However, we must note a few basic differences between the current situation and the declining situations in earlier civilizations. The first variance is that this genocide is happening in front of cameras; this never happened in history. Related to this, because of the growth of interpersonal communication, the whole world is witnessing the ongoing abuse of humanity, and this too is happening for the first time in history.

President Biden's claim to be providing leadership holding the world together also relates to the extraordinary growth of communication technology during the past decades. Although civilizations in history also have claimed their universal status, this time around the situation is different because of this growth. The Egyptian Pharaonic civilization, or Mesopotamian, Greek, Indian, or Chinese civilizations were all limited to their geographical territories, but the America-led contemporary civilization is different from this perspective. By the nineteenth century of the Common Era, European colonialism and imperialism had integrated all continents into a kind of one civilizational unit. During the first half of the twentieth century, international organizations such as the League of Nations and the United Nations consolidated this civilizational entity. Although the idea of nationalism has played a role in dividing this phenomenon, most nationalist leaders subscribed to a common worldview that took shape in nineteenth-century Europe. An Indian author has described this development as a colonial educational growth that created "a kind of brown sahibs" among the colonial population. Thomas Macaulay, an English East India Company civil servant working in colonial Bengal, had formulated the education policy that the Indian author is referring to. The objective of this policy was "to form a class of persons, Indian in blood and color, but English in tastes, in opinions, in morals, and in intellect."[30] This British initiative was very successful that later other colonial administrations such as the French and the Dutch espoused. Therefore, President Biden is correct in his claim that the American leadership of keeping the world together, and any observer of international affairs may notice this in the case of Israel's Gaza war. Nevertheless, we have already noted the changing characters of American leadership from the founding fathers to President Woodrow Wilson to President Truman to President Biden. This leads us to raise questions about the future of the current civilization. Is the America-led civilization on the brink of collapse? However, before addressing this question let us briefly examine the possibility of successfully encountering challenges, for most historians including Toynbee have recommended that civilizations may engage in dialogue and exchange of views to rectify themselves.

---

30 Christine E. Dobbin, ed., *Basic Documents in the Development of Modern India and Pakistan 1835–1947* (London: Van Nostrand, 1970), 8.

America's foundational values also demand democratic dialogue and exchange of idea but in practice, its oligarchic power has been actively suppressing criticism from dissenting voices for decades. Let us recall the mechanisms by which the policy makers tried to overturn prominent academics John Mearsheimer and Stephen Walt's valuable contribution *The Israel Lobby and the U.S. Foreign Policy*. After failing to publish their initial findings in the U.S., they first published their article in *the London Review of Books*. This only indicates the influence of money—a characteristic that has been common in all declining civilizations in history. In fact, during the past two decades or so, since the publication of their article on the subject, the influence of money politics has further increased. American politicians, the mainstream media and a powerful segment of academia have marginalized the faculty of critical thinking. The paradox is that modern academic disciplines claim to follow the Socratic Method of inquiry but in reality, they blatantly follow Sophistic relativistic philosophy. I became familiar with comparative civilizational studies at the University of Michigan under the guidance of Professor Stephen Tonsor, a practicing Catholic who had served in the Nixon Administration. I had registered for an undergraduate course entitled European Intellectual History with him. I could easily identify many divinely guided principles such as universal human dignity, equality, and justice that he used to highlight in class discussions. Tonsor used to highlight Toynbee's findings about classical Greece—how aristocrats had corrupted Athens with their money and Sophistic relativity. Following Toynbee's lessons, Tonsor unsuccessfully tried to produce a "creative minority" among conservative Republicans in his dream to save America from money politics.[31] He foresaw the corrupting influence of money, not only in politics but also in higher education.[32] Like all other collapsed civilizations in history, in the current U.S.-led civilization a wide gap has occurred between the wealthy corrupt elite and the common masses.

Is Today's U.S.-led Civilization on the Verge of Collapse?

We now turn to the question if the current U.S.-led civilization is on the verge of a total collapse. In an op-ed in the *Time* magazine, a former European diplomat wrote, "In Gaza we are witnessing the pathologies of a quickly declining America, its role no longer that of an ordering power but

---

31 For a good description of Tonsor's ideas, see Gleaves Whitney, "The Fusionist Mind of Stephen Tonsor," *Modern Age,* January 24, 2019. https://isi.org/modern-age/the-young-stephen-tonsor-teacher-historicist-and-conservative/

32 Rob Copeland, "Warning of 'Grave' Errors, Powerful Donors Push Universities on Hamas," New York Times, October 15, 2023. https://www.nytimes.com/2023/10/15/business/harvard-upenn-hamas-israel-students-donors.html

of a demiurge building a world of private enjoyment."[33] "However, historian Arnold Toynbee held the view that a capable creative and ethical minority not only plays a critical role not only in establishing a given civilization, but also can save the civilization through dialogue and exchange, adaptation, and flexibility following an accountable and transparent method. This, of course, happens at different stages of the civilization. He also pointed out that throughout history civilizations have grappled with questions of meaning, purpose, and the nature of existence. Thought leaders have always sought guidance through philosophical inquiry, religion, and spirituality. This has led many people in recent times trying to identify a creative minority in established religions.[34] However, this in itself has become a major challenge because of the lack of a logical and rational understanding of religion. The rational understanding of religion involves critical thinking rather than solely relying on faith traditions. Let us examine some current trends in this context.

Although President Biden has not presented the reason other than economics for his unconditional support for Israel, the congressional leader, Speaker Johnson has come up strongly to suggest Biblical admonition on the issue.[35] One Republican congressional representative directly asked the Columbia University president in her congressional appearance if "she wanted her university to be cursed by God."[36] Many commentators and observers have raised the problem of anti-Semitism in connection with Israel's Gaza War. Earlier, Prime Minister Netanyahu's reference to Biblical Amalek in justifying his genocidal action in Gaza made headlines.[37] There are also reports of some religious groups preparing to "sacrifice of a red cow, necessary for the construction of a third Jewish temple in Jerusalem." This is creating worries among many religious and political leaders.[38] The use of and abuse of religious ideas have become commonly used in polarizing the

---

33 Bruno Maçães, "Gaza and the End of Western Fantasy," *TIME*, January 10, 2024. https://time.com/6553708/gaza-end-of-western-hypocrisy-essay/

34 Michael Metzger, "The Creative Minority," Clapham Institute, July 2017. https://claphaminstitute.org/the-creative-minority/

35 Elizabeth Elkind, "Speaker Johnson says it's U.S.'s 'biblical admonition' to help Israel," *MSN News*, April 15, 2024. https://www.msn.com/en-us/news/world/speaker-johnson-says-it-s-us-s-biblical-admonition-to-help-israel/ar-BB1lGu4n

36 "WATCH: Columbia University's president testifies at House antisemitism hearing," *PBS News Hour*, April 17, 2024. https://www.pbs.org/newshour/politics/watch-live-columbia-universitys-president-testifies-at-house-antisemitism-hearing

37 Juan Cole, "Netanyahu declares a Holy War of Annihilation on Civilians of Gaza, Citing the Bible," *Informed Comment*, October 29, 2023. https://www.juancole.com/2023/10/netanyahu-annihilation-civilians.html

38 Cécile Lemoine, "In Jerusalem, the "red heifer" worries religious and political leaders," *LaCroix International*, April 25, 2024. https://international.la-croix.com/world/in-jerusalem-the-red-heifer-worries-religious-and-political-leaders

society. In encountering contemporary challenges, while the Catholic Church is undergoing an immense shift toward orthodoxy,[39] the Presbyterian Church (USA) is actively organizing discussions on Christian Zionism in its attempt to clarify Christianity's commitment to its fundamental belief and separating the faith from Zionist abuse.[40]

Israel's Gaza War, along with other issues such as climate change and numerous domestic issues have created a huge gap between the ruling elites and the common people. Many Americans believe that government policies disproportionately benefit the wealthy and powerful at the expense of ordinary citizens, and that is creating feelings of alienation and mistrust. Economic decline, the wide wealth gap between the top two percent and the rest of the population, along with scandals, corruption, and incompetence within political institutions have contributed to a broader erosion of public trust in government. A number of Pew Researches have demonstrated trends in income and wealth inequality in the society.[41] Younger generations, in particular, tend to express lower levels of trust in government institutions as compared to older generations. According to a recent Pew Research Center survey, the public trust in government has significantly declined since 1958 when the Center began such studies.[42] CNN has reported that "President Joe Biden's support for the Israeli military offensive in Gaza mixed with student anger over police crackdowns on anti-war campus protests are complicating the work of Democratic youth groups trying to engage classmates and other Generation Z voters ahead of this year's election."[43] All these indications reflect a deep crisis, not only of the American society and of civilization, but today's global civilization. What is the alternative then?

The Day After

---

39 Tim Sullivan, "'A step back in time': America's Catholic Church sees an immense shift toward the old ways," *AP News,* April 30, 2024. https://apnews.com/article/catholic-church-shift-orthodoxy-tradition-7638fa2013a593f8cb07483ffc8ed487

40 "Confronting Christian Zionism and advocating for peace and justice," *Ekklesia,* February 4, 2024. https://www.ekklesia.co.uk/2024/02/04/confronting-christian-zionism-and-advocating-for-peace-and-justice/

41 Juliana Menasce Horowitz, Ruth Igielnik, and Rakesh Kochhar, "Trends in Income and Wealth Inequality," Pew Research Center, January 9, 2020. https://www.pewresearch.org/social-trends/2020/01/09/trends-in-income-and-wealth-inequality/. Many other similar studies are available.

42 "Public Trust in Government: 1958-2024," June 24, 2024. https://www.pewresearch.org/politics/2024/06/24/public-trust-in-government-1958-2024/

43 Gregory Krieg and Michelle Shen, "Young Democrats face Gaza blowback as they try to mobilize students for Biden," *CNN,* May 4, 2024. https://www.cnn.com/2024/05/04/politics/democrats-young-biden-gaza-war/index.html

The Gaza war has exposed fundamental weaknesses of today's global civilization. As stated earlier, all civilizations in history have gone through similar cycles and although many of those civilizations have perished, the judicious intervention of the creative minority have also salvaged civilizations. However, to find a solution, one must first diagnosis the problem. Both American and Israeli leaders frequently refer to values of Western civilization while justifying their actions and calling for cooperation in the name of democracy, but democracy demands open discussion of what one means by values. All evidence suggests that Israelis are not following the rules of law, they are violating fundamentals of human dignity, they do not allow international investigation of any alleged crimes, deny access of international judicial institutions, and yet claim to be a part of the international civil society. Simple common sense cannot comprehend such behavior in a civilized society.

Israel received UN membership in 1949 with the promise of respecting international law to allow displaced refugees to return and maintain Jerusalem's international status but never fulfilled those promises. Some American elites have now joined Israel in bullying the International Criminal Court (ICC) prosecutor by threatening to invade ICC headquarters.[44] Such conditions are not unique in history, however. What is unique in the current context is that the whole world is directly witnessing the ongoing carnage and Israel's heartless and inhuman behavior. This behavior has sparked a huge outburst among young students in university campuses around the world that began in American campuses. Here again, America has demonstrated its leadership role but not the way President Biden would like to perceive it. Many academics have joined students in their effort to challenge the current elite-controlled governing system. They are standing for freedom of thought and the rule of law. The European Enlightenment tradition and the American founding fathers stood for these values. We have witnessed similar protests during the anti-Vietnam War movement in the 1960s and the South Africa-centric anti-apartheid movement in the 1980s in the recent past that achieved successful outcomes. The current drive too has the potential to achieve a similar goal. Nevertheless, the Palestinian issue that has sparked the current student movement is more complex than the other two issues because this issue involves emotion-clad religious faith.

We have indicated above the relationship between the Palestinian issue and Zionism. Zionism is a form of religious nationalism that motivates not

---

44 Jake Johnson, "GOP Senators Threaten ICC: 'Target Israel and We Will Target You'," *Common Dreams,* May 6, 2024. https://www.commondreams.org/news/republican-senators-icc-israel

only Jews but many Christians as well. How does one academically examine this emotionally tainted ideology? Perhaps one may address this question applying interdisciplinary approaches by critically studying the phenomenon scientifically and engaging in ethical consideration. Researchers may devote themselves to studying the complex relationship between religion and various aspects of human life, fostering deeper understanding and dialogue within both academic and broader societal contexts. This issue relates not only to the Palestinian conflict, but also relates to issues of climate change, wealth inequality, and many other contemporary problems. We all are aware of the Socratic Method that sees critical thinking, intellectual humility, and dialogue as essential tools for seeking truth and understanding. By fostering a spirit of inquiry and open-mindedness, scholars may encourage individuals to engage in rigorous examination of ideas, assumptions, and beliefs, ultimately leading to greater clarity and insight, which has the potential to save the collapsing civilization.

Israel's Gaza war is not going to solve the Palestinian crisis. To initiate a workable solution, Israel must fulfill its commitment that it made in order to gain United Nations membership in 1949: it must allow all Palestinians to return to their ancestral homeland; it must recognize the international status of Jerusalem, and most important of all, it must define its international border. During the formation of the League of Nations in 1920, the Indian Muslim jurist Syed Ameer Ali, a member of the Privy Council (UK), had suggested that Jerusalem be declared the headquarters of the world body. I guess that moving the headquarters of the United Nations to Jerusalem could have facilitated a solution to the question of Jerusalem. I also believe that US based Jewish organizations such as Jewish Voice for Peace or If Americans Knew and Israeli historians such as Avi Shlaim or Ilan Pappe could play constructive role in resolving the problem. Nevertheless, the final solution must address the injustices levied on the Palestinians during the past century to the full satisfaction of all victims. This process must follow all necessary judicial requirements. Let the people who would be living in the territory, be it "from the river to the sea" or larger or smaller than that, decide the name and nature of the state—whether it would be called Israel or Palestine or a combination of both. All citizens of the state must enjoy universal human dignity, equality and justice. Let the nation be, as the Old Testament prophet Isaiah said, "A light to the nations." Let the UN agencies closely monitor the system of governance of the state. These measures will definitely contribute to world peace and continuity of human civilization.

Genocide in Gaza and the
Changing Face of Global Geopolitics

Joseph A. Camilleri

WITH THE DESTRUCTION unleashed on the people of Gaza since October 2023 comes a moment of truth, a moment that lays bare the profound contradictions of our age. Gaza may be regarded as the epicenter of a complex struggle between the old and the new, between the Global West and the Global South, and between contending principles that should underpin international law and the functioning of international institutions.

Some eighty years after the Second World War and the Holocaust, and three decades after the planned campaign of mass murder in Rwanda, the genocidal virus is alive and well. And this, despite the significant body of international law that has come into force since December 1946 aimed at deterring, and where possible, putting a stop to genocide and other war crimes. At first sight, the Israeli state has been able to conduct its military onslaught on the Palestinian people with impunity. Yet, its actions are under legal challenge as never before.

Similarly, it is arguable that Israel has proceeded unhindered with its invasion of the Gaza strip and repeated attacks on the West Bank, shielded by the continued and bare-faced support provided by the United States, including financial aid, weapons, and the shielding from accountability for its illegal use of force. Yet, there are countertrends which, as we shall see, are slowly but surely gathering pace.

One reading of the mayhem that has transpired since October 2023 suggests that the United States remains ascendant in the Middle East, with its imperial presence undiminished. The protection it affords the state of

Joseph Anthony Camilleri OAM is Professor Emeritus at La Trobe University, Melbourne, where he held the Chair in International Relations (1994–2012) and was founding Director of the Centre for Dialogue (2006–2012). He is a Fellow of the Australian Academy of Social Sciences; Convener of Conversation at the Crossroads; and Co-Convener of SHAPE (Saving Humanity & Planet Earth). He has authored or edited some 35 books and numerous journal articles.

Israel rests on foundations which go well beyond the confines of a bilateral relationship. It is able to maintain its dominant role in part by virtue of its alliance arrangements with Europe subsumed under an ever-expanding NATO superstructure and its multiple security partnerships with Arab countries, whose authoritarian regimes are in part sustained by the U.S. connection. Yet, here again, the reality is far more complex than the unipolar thesis would suggest. The sheer barbarism of Israel's military offensive, the resilience of the Palestinian struggle for self-determination and the responses of diverse actors, including governments, international institutions and civil society, are giving rise to a fluid political landscape, the contours of which are slowly beginning to emerge.

The Imperial Connection

The catastrophe that has befallen the people of Gaza in the aftermath of the October Hamas attack on Israel cannot be understood unless placed in its historical context. As a result of the Israeli–Palestinian war in 1948, some 200,000 Palestinians fled or were expelled from their homes, settling in the Gaza Strip as refugees. Since then, Israel has conducted numerous military assaults on Gaza and exercised varying forms of occupation.

Hostilities intensified once Hamas won the 2006 election and solidified its control of Gaza in 2007. Israel quickly imposed a land, air and sea blockade of the Gaza Strip, turning it into what has been fairly described as an "open-air prison." The 2008–2009 Israeli invasion of Gaza resulted in more than 1,000 deaths and widespread destruction of homes, schools and hospitals. A subsequent operation in 2012 killed some 100 people and injured many more.

Another invasion in 2014 led to the killing of an estimated 74 Israelis (mostly soldiers) and some 2,250 Palestinians (mostly civilians). The unprecedented destruction of homes, schools and hospitals was periodically followed by Hamas rocket attacks and further Israeli incursions, culminating in May 2021 in fierce Israeli bombardment with the predictable demolition of buildings and essential infrastructure, and the death of at least 256 Palestinians, including 66 children.

The tale of unrelieved suffering that has been the Gazans' lot over the last twenty or more years is no doubt revealing, but it is just one chapter of a much longer tale of violence that has its origins more than a century ago in the actions of the dominant colonial power of the day, Britain.

The Balfour Declaration of November 1917 committed the British Government to "the establishment in Palestine of a national home for the Jewish People," and to facilitating its achievement.

Control over Palestine was seen as serving strategic imperial interests: retaining Egypt and the Suez Canal within Britain's sphere of influence and gaining the support of influential Jewish communities in other countries for Britain's war aims. The Palestinian reaction, less than lukewarm from the outset, became increasingly hostile. British policies were widely seen as supportive of Zionist objectives, and likely to lead to the displacement of Palestinians from their land. Between 1920 and 1946 some 376,000 Jewish immigrants arrived in Palestine.

Rising Palestinian resistance was soon met by British repression, including mass arrests, administrative detentions, summary killings and punitive home demolitions—practices that the State of Israel would subsequently adopt as key elements in its repertoire of oppression. Though estimates vary, the measures taken to quell the three-year Palestinian revolt are widely thought to have taken the lives of 5,000 Palestinians, with another 15,000 injured and 5,600 imprisoned.

By 1939, with 30,000 troops deployed in Palestine, Britain substantially increased the tempo of its collaboration with the Jewish settler community and facilitated the formation of Jewish paramilitary groups that would later form an integral part of the Israeli army.

But British imperial power would soon decline—a trend greatly accelerated by World War II. A new imperial power, the United States, was now ascendant. Against this backdrop, the newly formed United Nations adopted Resolution 181, which called for the Partition of Palestine into Arab and Jewish states. Palestinian rejection of the plan was inevitable given that it allotted 56 per cent of Palestine to the Jewish state, though Palestinians owned 94 per cent of historic Palestine and comprised 67 per cent of its population.

The ground was thus laid for the "catastrophe," which Palestinians experienced as a "Nakba" (Catastrophe). Even before the British Mandate expired in May 1948, Zionist paramilitary groups set out on a campaign to destroy Palestinian towns and villages and further enlarge the area that would comprise the state of Israel. In the space of two years, an estimated 500 Palestinian villages, towns and cities were destroyed, 15,000 Palestinians were killed, and 750,00 Palestinians were forced to flee. The Zionist movement could now claim control of 78 per cent of historic Palestine.

The rest is history: constant Israeli use of force by the military and by settlers to quell Palestinian resistance and maintain military occupation; rapidly expanding Israeli settler activity in violation of international law; and laws and practices introduced by the Israeli state that have established two categories of citizenship based on race and religion, simply put, an Apartheid state.

Over time, close to 6 million Palestinian refugees have spread across the Middle East, often in squalid camps. Palestinians now comprise the largest stateless community worldwide. Set in this context, events in Gaza since October 2023 may be considered as *déjà vu* in substance, if not in scale.

Why has the international community tolerated such deviant behavior, and for so long? How has the state of Israel evaded the forceful international response that might have led it to change course? The simple answer is that in a relatively short time the United States had stepped into Britain's shoes. Biden's fulsome backing of Israel in the present confrontation continues a special relationship that dates back to the inception of the state of Israel.

In recent years the United States has provided Israel an average of $4 billion annually in foreign military financing and an additional $500 million for cooperative missile defense programs. What is less well known is that between 1946 and 2023 Israel was by far the largest cumulative recipient of U.S. economic and military aid, estimated to total at close to $300 billion (in constant 2022 dollars).

To this must be added joint military exercises, research, weapons development, and importantly the deployment of a wide array of military assets in the Middle East, including the current dispatch of two carrier strike groups to the Eastern Mediterranean. The Israel-U.S. relationship is also anchored by an annual bilateral trade of close to $50 billion, a string of trade, financial and technological agreements, as well as a wide range of cultural, educational and professional programs. In April 2024, the Biden Administration chose to sign off on war assistance to Israel estimated at some $25 billion at the very time that the Palestinian death toll had exceeded 35,000, most of them women and children. This was the strongest signal yet that, words to the contrary notwithstanding, Washington was prepared to give Israel's war machine *carte blanche* to conduct its operations as it saw fit.

The special relationship with Israel served several U.S. objectives. It enabled the United States to extend and justify its military presence in a region of high strategic importance; it kept most Arab states on a leash; and it contained the assertive reach of adversaries, notably Iran, Syria and Hezbollah, and plausibly even China and Russia.

Yet, U.S. support alone does not fully explain international paralysis when it comes to the Palestinian tragedy. By virtue of its alliances and partnerships, the United States could rely on its European allies to place a higher priority on maintaining close economic and military ties with Israel, which helps explain why most of them confined themselves to criticism of illegal settlements, and general expressions of support for a humanitarian ceasefire.

This is not to say that European governments have chosen to continue their support of Israel purely in deference to U.S. wishes. Their policies, euphemistically portrayed as serving "the national interest," have also been dictated by powerful sectional interests in their respective countries. It is worth noting that the European Union (EU) is Israel's biggest trading partner, accounting for 28.8 per cent of its trade in goods in 2022. Moreover, nearly 32 per cent of Israel's imports came from the EU. Germany, Israel's largest European trading partner, has seen the relationship between the two countries steadily deepen, especially since the establishment of bilateral intergovernmental consultations.

A similar pattern is discernible when it comes to many Arab governments. Over the last several years, active Arab support for Palestinian demands has been in visible decline. Perhaps the strongest indication of this trend came in 2020 with the decision by four Arab countries, the United Arab Emirates, Sudan, Morocco, and Bahrain, to establish diplomatic relations with Israel. U.S. pressure was no doubt a decisive factor.

Saudi Arabia was expected to follow suit in due course. Though formally wedded to the creation of an independent Palestinian state, the Saudi government severely curtailed its financial support for the Palestinian Authority and placed restrictions on financial contributions by Saudi charities and individual citizens to the West Bank and the Gaza strip.

It is not altogether surprising therefore that until recently, in reacting to Israel's current military onslaught in Gaza and its continuing attacks in the West Bank, most Arab governments as well as the Arab League and the Organization of Islamic Conference were content to condemn and exhort. They called for an immediate, permanent and sustainable humanitarian truce leading to the cessation of all hostilities. They also repeated their previously stated objective of a just, comprehensive and lasting peace based on the establishment of an independent, sovereign Palestinian state with East Jerusalem as its capital.

Arab officialdom, however, has steadfastly refused to explain how any of these objectives are to be realized, how Israel can be persuaded to stop its armed offensive, or what practical steps the Arab world would take to overcome Israeli intransigence.

The case of Egypt is especially revealing. The standard Egyptian line has been that it opposes any mass exodus from Gaza because this would be tantamount to accepting Israel's use of force to displace a people from their own land. Egyptian President Abdel Fattah El-Sisi has justified his refusal to open Egypt's borders on the grounds that such displacement would "shatter the dream of an independent Palestinian state and squander the struggle of the Palestinian people."

But the underlying concern of the Sisi regime may not be quite so noble. A larger concern is likely related to the unwelcome prospect of a significant influx of Hamas and other Palestinian militants onto its soil. Egypt, it is worth noting, has supported Israel's blockade of Gaza since Hamas took control in 2007. It has restricted the flow of materials and personnel between Gaza and Sinai and destroyed many of the tunnels near the border extensively used by Hamas and other Palestinians.

Like Egypt, Jordan, Saudi Arabia, Bahrain, the United Arab Emirates and Morocco boast authoritarian regimes of different complexion that share a common visceral hostility to Hamas, the Muslim brotherhood, and other radical Islamic movements. In important ways Israel's invasion of Gaza can be said to serve the interests of these regimes.

A second factor helps explain the meagre Arab response to the Palestinian tragedy. For different reasons and to different degrees many of these regimes have come to value closer ties with Israel. Though Saudi-Israeli diplomatic normalization has some way to go, secret contacts and visits involving military and foreign ministry officials, academics and business leaders have been steadily gathering pace.

In October 2018, in a deal mediated by the United States, Saudi Arabia reportedly acquired state-of-the-art espionage equipment from Israel at a cost of over $250 million. In July 2023, Israel announced plans for a $27 billion rail expansion that will connect its outlying areas to metropolitan Tel Aviv and later provide overland links to Saudi Arabia. Two months later, Netanyahu outlined plans for major infrastructure projects, including a 20,000 km fibre optic cable that would link countries in Asia and Europe and run through Israel, Cyprus and the Arabian Peninsula. The prospect of expanding business ties was no doubt a key factor in the signing of the 2020 Abraham Accords and the establishment of diplomatic relations between Israel and four Arab countries: UAE, Bahrain, Sudan and Morocco.

Though the economic and political benefits likely to flow from a less antagonistic relationship with Israel have no doubt influenced the thinking of Arab governments, two other closely related considerations, namely their U.S. connection and their hostility to Iran, have proved decisive. For several Arab countries, the United States has been the primary source of economic and military aid. In 2022, the U.S. disbursed close to $1.4 billion in aid to Egypt, and $1.2 billion to Jordan. For oil-rich countries, it has been the primary source of arms transfers and military training. Between 2017 and 2021,

U.S. military sales to Saudi Arabia and UAE amounted to $34.5 billion and $9 billion respectively.

Simply put, U.S. economic, military, and political support provides an indispensable prop for regime survival. In return these regimes are expected to be sensitive to U.S. diplomatic and strategic interests. In the Middle East, Washington's paramount interests are to support and strengthen the state of Israel, contain Iran, and crush Islamism—all of this within the larger framework of containing China's rise and thwarting Russia's resurgence.

For Arab governments, a cooperative relationship with Israel may be a bitter pill to swallow, but the containment of Iran and the defeat of Islamism are highly prized outcomes. Even the competitive, at times tense relationship between the three major powers holds some attraction in that it allows for a profitable balancing act.

This said, the Arab world cannot wash its hands of the catastrophe that has befallen the Palestinian people. To begin with, pro-Palestinian sentiment in the Arab street is both widespread and enduring. Any regime, however well entrenched, that ignores public support for the Palestinian struggle risks igniting popular opposition to its rule. In any case, as we shall see, the sheer brutality of Israel's invasion of Gaza has severely diminished Israel's and America's diplomatic standing and compounded the strains and stresses of these two deeply fractured and fragile polities.

The Limits of Imperial Power

Slowly, almost imperceptibly at first, Israel's projection of unstoppable brute force has been eroded by the complexities of a deeply fractured world in which U.S. imperial power appears to have reached its limits. The expectation that Israel's military prowess sustained by unflinching U.S. support would bring a swift and decisive military victory in Gaza has dissipated. The evidence suggests that the multiple difficulties encountered by the Netanyahu government as it seeks to reduce Gaza to rubble have exposed and exacerbated political divisions within Israel and placed new limitations on America's ability to shape political developments whether regionally or globally.

Before looking more closely at some of the unintended but not wholly unforeseen consequences of Israel's military expedition and the implications of its genocidal push, it may be worth revisiting recent shifts in America's global strategy. Three decades after the dissolution of the Soviet Union and the initial triumphalism that colored U.S. foreign policy discourse, America's global supremacy is under challenge as never before. Several interconnected factors have been at work.

U.S. military interventionism over many decades has exacted a heavy toll. A succession of military interventions from Vietnam to Afghanistan have failed to achieve their objectives and proved ruinously costly for the invader as much as the invaded. Here it is worth dwelling on the Afghanistan experience. The world's greatest military power battled continuously for twenty years, deployed hundreds of thousands of troops, sacrificed the lives and well-being of its soldiers, spent well in excess of two trillion dollars, lavished hundreds of billions more on nation building, and raised, funded, equipped and trained an army of 350,000 Afghan troops, only to find itself thwarted by a rag tag army of 85,000 fighters. After fighting the longest war in its history, the United States stood defeated and humiliated.

This and previous great power interventions—from Korea to Vietnam, Iraq, Libya, Syria, Chad and Yemen—strikingly demonstrate the diminishing utility of military power. The occupying power may bring about regime change but this invariably comes with highly damaging blowback effects, unintended and often unforeseen, for both occupier and occupied. In Afghanistan, as elsewhere, military intervention, conducted at great human and financial cost, has simply accentuated local ethnic and religious divisions, heightened regional tensions, and provided an opening for other centers of power to establish a foothold, as was the case with Russia in Syria, and in all likelihood, China in Afghanistan.

In today's world, the United States has to contend with a vastly different international landscape, the result in part of its vastly diminished economic clout and, as it turns out, the diminishing utility of its primary asset, military power. Russian, Chinese and Iranian political leaders are all too aware of the limitations of U.S. power.

Faced with these troubling trends, the U.S. security establishment concluded it was time for the U.S. to chart a new strategic direction. The immediate aim was to arrest the decline of U.S. power and influence. The more ambitious goal was to restore American dominance in a rules-based order, where the United States sets the rules and others dutifully comply. In a nutshell the strategy has been to breathe new life into America's strategic alliances and partnerships so that they can more effectively curb Russia's resurgence, China's rise and Iran's flexing of regional muscle. All three were seen as inimical to U.S. interests and, if unchecked, as likely to accelerate the waning of America's economic and political clout.

In the aftermath of the Trump presidency, the strategic imperative was to reach a new consensus with allies and friends that their collective security and economic interests were best served by countering and, where necessary, punishing Russian, Chinese and Iranian misdeeds.

Allies and partners were to be assiduously cultivated as they were deemed crucial to the success of a revamped global containment policy. From America's vantage point, relatively few costs were involved in this exercise. Lofty statements extolling the virtues of democratic alliances, and pledges of support in the hour of need would do for now. Alliances, on the other hand, held the promise of substantial benefits.

First, by marshalling the combined economic and military assets of their members, they presented a more potent bulwark against the expansion of Russian, Chinese and Iranian spheres of influence. Secondly, they could mount a more effective ideological offensive centered on the contrast between democratic and authoritarian principles and practices. For the offensive to have traction, it was crucial for the United States to secure allies who could offer credible renditions of the democratic narrative, hence the importance attached to the strengthening of NATO, and a series of bilateral and multi-lateral security partnerships in the Asia-Pacific region. Israel was considered pivotal to the strategy, especially as a foil to Iran's growing regional influence. Thirdly, alliances could demonstrate in practice the superiority of U.S.-led multilateralism in delivering global public goods, which in the minds of the U.S. political establishment held the key to preserving the Western foothold in the Global South.

The war in Ukraine was to be the first major test of the efficacy of this grand strategy. Russia could be bled dry, economically and militarily, through the coordinated delivery of massive military and economic aid to the Ukraine side and the imposition of a comprehensive suite of sanctions carefully targeted to inflict maximum damage on Russia's industrial and financial sectors.

The strategy has been far less successful than U.S. planners had anticipated. U.S. alliances have proven to be far less cohesive than expected. Few European governments have been willing to pour into the conflict the massive resources needed to sustain an increasingly outmanned and outgunned Ukraine. China has steadfastly refused to criticize the Russian military intervention, and hardly a single country in the Global South has been prepared to join the U.S.-led sanctions regime.

It is in this context that Israel's war in Gaza can be most usefully analyzed. The Hamas attack of 7 October 2023 which resulted in more than 1,200 deaths, primarily Israeli citizens, and more than 240 people taken hostage, was viewed by the Biden administration as a unique opportunity to pursue several key objectives. The relationship with Israel could be safely strengthened, billing this as a country with impeccable democratic credentials that was about to exercise its legitimate right of self-defense. By contrast, Hamas could be exposed as a monstrous terrorist organization that was acting in collusion with, and perhaps under the direction of, Iran's autocratic rulers who had no compunction in authorizing more public hangings per capita than anywhere else in the world.

At the same time, the idea of the Jewish nation placed once again under siege would help galvanize European allies into action and make way for a concerted effort to isolate Hamas and its principal backer Iran, solidify the West's relationship with a number of Arab governments, notably Egypt and the Gulf States, and swiftly move the Israeli-Saudi rapprochement towards diplomatic normalization.

Little of this has come to pass. The ally in this case, Israel, has proved to be a huge embarrassment. In the space of a few months, the portrayal of Israel as the victim defending itself against a ruthless foe had crumbled. The ceaseless rationalizations offered by Prime Minister Netanyahu, Defense Minister Gallant and Head of the Armed Forces Halevi cut little ice on the world stage.

The entire UN system, from the office of the UN Secretary-General to every UN agency, has been unsparing in its condemnation of all aspects of the Israeli military offensive. Quite apart from the number killed (35,709) and injured (79,990) as of 23 May 2024, a joint study released in early May 2024 by the UN Development Programme (UNDP) and the Economic and Social Commission for Western Asia (ESCWA) found that the war in Gaza had thrust nearly 1.74 million additional people into poverty, with the Gross Domestic Product (GDP) sustaining a staggering plunge of 26.9 percent. By the end of April, a detailed assessment prepared by UNESCWA-Statistics, in collaboration with other agencies, estimated that more than 50 per cent of all structures in the Gaza Strip had been destroyed; 360,000 housing units damaged, 5 per cent of the population killed or injured and two million people displaced. A report in early May estimated the level of destruction in northern Gaza had surpassed that of the German city of Dresden, which was firebombed by Allied forces in 1945 in one of the most troubling Allied acts of World War II.

By May, the worldwide response of governments, international organizations and civil society was overwhelmingly critical of the conduct of Israel's military and its senseless disregard for human life. After five months of mayhem in Gaza and five U.S. vetoes of draft resolutions, the UN Security Council adopted a resolution on March 25, 2024 demanding an "immediate ceasefire in Gaza for the month of Ramadan" leading to a lasting ceasefire, the "immediate unconditional release of all hostages," and humanitarian aid access.

Unimpeded by U.S. vetoes, the UN General Assembly was able to act much sooner. On 27 October 2023 it passed a resolution calling for a humanitarian truce with 121 votes for, 14 against (notably the U.S. and Israel) and 44 abstentions (which included most U.S. allies in Europe and Asia-Pacific,). Six weeks later the General Assembly passed a similar resolution but with a much larger majority—153 voting in favor (including Australia, Canada, Denmark, France, Japan, Norway, Sweden and South Korea), 20 against, and 24 abstentions). Then on 10 May 2024 the UN General Assembly voted overwhelmingly in support of the Palestinian bid for full UN membership and called on the UN Security Council to bestow full membership to the state of Palestine. The vote was carried by 143 to 9, with 25 abstentions.

Israel's diplomatic isolation was becoming clearer by the day, and so was America's discomfort as Israel's principal and lonesome backer. The trend gained even greater force with the announcement that Norway, Ireland and Spain would formally recognize Palestinian statehood as of 28 May 2024. In announcing his government's decision, Spanish Prime Minister Sánchez, using the bluntest language yet by a European leader, accused Benjamin Netanyahu of presiding over massacres:

> Prime Minister Netanyahu is still turning a blind eye and bombing hospitals, schools, homes. . . He is still using hunger, cold and terror to punish more than a million innocent boys and girls— and things have gone so far that prosecutors at the International Criminal Court have this week sought his arrest for war crimes.

The number of countries recognizing the State of Palestine now stood at 143, with others likely to follow suit in coming months.

A second arena of contestation, relating to the interpretation and application of international law, pointed in the same direction. Both the International Court of Justice and the International Criminal Court were now the center of attention.

On 29 December 2023, South Africa filed a case with the court alleging that Israel was violating the 1948 Convention on the Prevention and Punishment of the Crime of Genocide. Following hearings held in January, the Court judged that Palestinians in Gaza had plausible rights under the Genocide Convention and concluded that they were at real risk of irreparable damage. Given the "catastrophic humanitarian situation" in Gaza and the real risk of a further worsening of the situation, the Court, while declining to order Israel to stop its military operation, issued interim orders requiring Israel to take all possible measures to prevent the commission of genocide and to punish any incitement to genocide by state authorities, including the military. South Africa returned to the Court in May, arguing that Israel was pressing ahead with its assault in Rafah despite "explicit warnings" of genocidal consequences. It described the planned operation as "the last stage of total annihilation of Palestinian life" .

Since January 2024, a raft of countries have formally joined, or otherwise expressed support for, South Africa's genocide case against Israel, as have several international organizations, including the Arab League and the Organization of Islamic Cooperation. The decision of the Egyptian Government to join the case was noteworthy by virtue of Egypt's longstanding relationship with Israel and its strategic role within the Arab world. It was the first substantial step taken by Egypt to convey its opposition to Israel's escalating assault on Gaza.

No less dramatic was the announcement on 20 May 2024 by ICC chief prosecutor Karim A. A. Khan that he had requested arrest warrants for Prime Minister Netanyahu, his Defense Minister Yoav Gallant and three Hamas leaders, including its chief, Yahya Sinwar. There were reasonable grounds to believe, he explained, that they bore criminal responsibility for war crimes and crimes against humanity. Khan's action had far-reaching ramifications. Apart from the inevitable impact on world opinion, were ICC judges to grant the requested warrants, 124 countries, including every member of the European Union, would be legally obliged to arrest Netanyahu and Gallant on sight. It was the first time in the court's history that a leader of a liberal democracy closely allied to the United States had been targeted in this manner. U.S. President Joe Biden described the legal step against Israel's most senior leaders as "outrageous," while Secretary of State Antony Blinken called the decision "profoundly wrong-headed" and raised the prospect of Congress imposing sanctions on ICC officials. For its part, the French Foreign Ministry expressed France's support for "the International Criminal Court, its independence and the fight against impunity in all situations." The contrast could not be starker.

In giving vent to their displeasure with Israel's conduct in Gaza, several governments went beyond interventions at the UN and international courts and took diplomatic action of one kind or another. Some, including Colombia and Bolivia, severed diplomatic relations with Israel, while others, including Chile, Honduras, Jordan, South Africa and Türkiye, either suspended diplomatic relations or withdrew their ambassadors. In April, Türkiye curbed exports to Israel for blocking its attempt to take part in aid air-drop operations for Gaza. All remaining trade between the two countries was subsequently halted—except for oil.

It remains to say a word about the role of civil society. Hundreds of thousands of people took to the streets across the world to protest against the war in Gaza, calling for a ceasefire, the ending of the Israeli occupation and blockade of humanitarian aid to Gaza, and for Palestinian self-determination. According to one study, at least 7,283 pro-Palestinian protests were held between 7 October and 24 November in different parts of the world. On 27 April well over 100,000 people marched in central London in opposition to the planned offensive in Rafah. It was the 12th pro-Palestinian march in central London since Israel started its campaign in Gaza following the 7 October attacks on Israel by Hamas.

A more recent development that captured global headlines was the flurry of student activism at U.S. college and university campuses, inspired in part by protests at Columbia University. Student demonstrations and sit-ins were also spreading in Europe, Australia and Canada, with increasingly vocal demands for an immediate and permanent ceasefire and calls on universities to terminate their involvement in any research project or financial arrangement which supports Israel and the war in Gaza. University and police attempts to quell or punish student activism, including arrests and suspensions, tended to give protesters additional visibility and, if anything, strengthened their determination to make their voices heard.

A Concluding Note

Israel itself was now at an impasse, with a sharply polarized society, a divided government, a deeply unpopular prime minister whose political survival rested on satisfying the demands of a motely group of extremist parties, and seemingly no clear plan as to how the fighting would end, and what might then follow. International sympathy and support for the State of Israel were at their lowest ebb.

For its part, the United States was saddled with an ally of dubious value, and an excruciating dilemma beyond its capacity to resolve. It could continue to serve as Israel's principal backer, bear the rising costs of economic and military aid, and suffer the diplomatic damage associated with shielding Israeli leaders from the inevitable legal and political fallout. The only other viable option was to make any ongoing support for Israel conditional on ending its military operation in Gaza and accommodating the Palestinian demand for self-determination. This second option seemed beyond the grasp of America's political and military establishment, especially when set against the backdrop of America's polarized political landscape and a looming Biden-Trump presidential contest.

On the international front the United States had to contend with two ongoing conflicts, Gaza and Ukraine, and a third flashpoint, the volatile China-Taiwan relationship. It is doubtful to say the least that allies in Europe, Asia and elsewhere could be relied upon to continue to meekly comply with U.S. directives and priorities on all three fronts. As for the Global South, the Gaza debacle had been a sobering experience. It had reinforced the widely held view that the American ship was in distress, and that its purported commitment to democratic values was highly selective, applied in some cases (e.g. Ukraine) and not in others (Gaza). Governments in the Global South felt increasingly confident about making their own judgements, pursuing an independent course of action, and exploring avenues for collaborative action through the UN and other multilateral settings.

As for Washington's principal adversaries, China, Russia and Iran, they were now better placed to pursue their preferred strategic options, confident in the knowledge that the United States was amply distracted by the paralysis of its political institutions and its engagement in two conflicts (Ukraine and Gaza) which promised much pain and little reward.

In the words of one commentator, "the [Gaza] genocide is doing great damage to American standing not just in the 'Arab street' but across the western world and in the Global South. Israel may be the death of America." A bold prediction perhaps, but by no means implausible.

Genocide in Palestine: A Turning Point?

Chandra Muzaffar

DESPITE PASSIONATE PLEAS from millions of people from all over the world to establish a ceasefire immediately the government of Israel has chosen to perpetuate its bloody, brutal massacre of the inhabitants of Gaza. As of now (July 12, 2024), more than 38,917 have been killed by the Israeli military and allied groups. The majority of the dead are children and women.

Though Gaza has borne the brunt of Israeli wrath, several hundred Palestinians in the West Bank have also been wiped out. Hundreds of thousands of others have been maimed. A large number have been tortured by their occupiers and oppressors.

Gaza itself has been destroyed. Its infrastructure has been reduced to rubble. Hospitals and medical staff have been targeted. Schools have been razed to the ground. People's homes have been demolished.

In the midst of all this, Israel has deliberately restricted the flow of essentials into Gaza. Food, water, fuel, electricity and medicines are in short supply. In early February 2024, there were already signs of starvation in parts of the Strip. UN bodies are warning of the imminent danger of famine on a large scale.

Starving a population, like the planned murder of children and women, is part and parcel of a larger agenda—an agenda that seeks to annihilate the Gazan population and the Palestinian people as a whole. The ethnic cleansing of Palestine has been the agenda of the state of Israel since its establishment in 1948. Wasn't its establishment accompanied by the expulsion of at least 750,000 Palestinians from their homes? Wasn't ethnic cleansing the real aim of not only the expulsions but also the annexations and massacres in the last 76 years? It is as if the Israeli elite is determined to actualize one of the

Dr Chandra Muzaffar is the President of the International Movement for a Just World (JUST). He was Professor of Global Studies at Universiti Sains Malaysia, Penang, Malaysia from 2007 to 2012.

great myths that is associated with the establishment of Israel—that a people without a land had arrived in a land without a people!

It is not just its ability to actualize this myth that reflects Israel's power. Israel has not only held on to the territory it usurped from the Palestinians in 1948, it has also expanded and consolidated the lands it controls. It has a suffocating grip upon Gaza which has been rightly described as the world's largest open-air prison. It occupies the West Bank and East Jerusalem. It regards the whole of Jerusalem as the nation's "eternal capital" in violation of international law. It has also annexed the strategic Golan Heights which is part of Syria and blatantly ignores global public opinion on it.

What explains Israeli power and its arrogant defiance of the world? Israel's steely determination to survive and succeed at all costs is an important factor. I remember the late Jewish scholar, Marc Ellis, once telling me that after securing a State for themselves after 2000 years of exile, the Jewish people would not make any concession to the Palestinians or the Arabs. If accommodating the rights of the Palestinians or any other Arab community is going to lead to a situation where their hegemonic grip over Palestinian land weakens, the Jews will not allow it. This is perhaps why they erroneously equate their dominance with their very survival.

This equation is rendered more complex by a belief that is integral to the Jewish worldview. This is the belief among a significant segment of the Jewish population that they are the "chosen people." As God's chosen, they cannot be judged or evaluated like other people. The land of Israel according to this belief was given to the Jews by God. How they govern Israel including their treatment of the Palestinians cannot be subjected to commonplace scrutiny.

The unflinching support of the American elite for Israel is yet another factor. This support expresses itself through overwhelming military aid to Israel which—in spite of the occasional rebuke of some Israeli leader or other—is guaranteed. The Israeli military has access to the most advanced and sophisticated American military hardware. This is augmented by joint research, joint military exercises and other joint programs. Economic assistance from the U.S. running into millions of dollars constitutes a separate and distinct agenda which is designed to fulfil Israel's multifarious needs.

American elite support for Israel is rooted to a great extent in the religious orientation of the numerically large Christian Zionist community in the United States. This community, whose status within Christianity has always been controversial, provides solid support to the Israeli state and Israeli policies, especially in their confrontation against the Palestinians.

Christian Zionism has moved U.S. domestic and foreign policies more and more towards the Right.

A number of European states such as Britain, Germany and France have also remained committed to Israel for a long period of time. This commitment manifests itself through political support, cultural cooperation and economic assistance. It arises in part from what can be described as "the holocaust syndrome"—a deep sense of guilt for the centuries of discrimination against Jews in various parts of Europe perpetrated by governments and communities which culminated in Nazi Germany's inhuman and ruthless annihilation of a minority before and during World War Two.

The magnitude of Jewish suffering during the Holocaust is one of the reasons why the Western media that emerged after the War has displayed a pro-Jewish and pro-Zionist bias. Wrongdoings associated with the Zionist state of Israel and Jewish leaders are sometimes treated with kids' gloves. Criticisms of Zionism or Israel, on the other hand, are downplayed or sidelined, however legitimate they maybe. It is this attitude that is partly responsible for the projection of an image of Israel that is shorn of warts and pimples. Since Western media channels are more dominant and pervasive than their Asian or African counterparts, the world, as a whole, views the world through the lens of the West. Israel has benefitted from this.

More than the media, it is the intellectual elite of the West that has bolstered the image of Israel. It is these elites and their universities that are perceived as the standard bearers of knowledge and ideas. A number of these academics, it is true, are of Jewish ancestry. Their achievements in both the sciences and humanities are indisputably considerable. Unwittingly, by projecting these individuals and their achievements the impression is created that there is something extraordinary about their national or ethnic identity.

While the role of the universities and the media in creating a positive image of Israel or Jews is huge, without businesses and consumerism that image would not have been perpetuated. Is it a mere coincidence that Starbucks and MacDonalds are linked to entities that have Jewish/Zionist financial interests? There are so many other consumer-oriented enterprises that involve Jewish/ Zionist finance and expertise. Indeed, capitalist structures and interests have played a major role in sustaining Israeli/ Zionist power in individual states and societies and within the global system.

We have shown that in almost every sphere from politics and the military to the media and consumerism, Israel and the interests it represents are formidable. The West oriented international system as we have seen also favors Israel. Besides, Israel's strength has been fortified by the parlous situation prevailing within the Palestinian resistance itself, the disarray within the Arab and Muslim world and the passivity of the Global South. The Palestinian liberation struggle is hopelessly divided between Hamas, and the Islamic Jihad, on the one hand, and Fatah and the Palestinian Authority, on the other. It is not just Israeli Intelligence, the Mossad, and the CIA and MI6 that keep the Palestinian liberation movement split. Antagonism between Palestinian freedom fighters is also a cause. Several Arab and Muslim countries collaborate with the U.S., Britain and even Israel! Isn't the biggest U.S. air force fleet in West Asia located in an Arab country in the region? Who is the host to the U.S.'s largest naval fleet in West Asia? Which country in West Asia (apart from Israel) has the most extensive military ties with the U.S.? Isn't it a Muslim country that is "the protector" of U.S. interests on China's southern borders? And for many Arab states, isn't it true that it is the Islamic Republic of Iran rather than Israel or the U.S. that is the adversary? Doesn't this show that there are deep schisms within the Muslim world that prevent Muslim states from uniting for a common cause—the cause of liberating the Muslim world and humankind from the yoke of U.S. led hegemony?

The failure of Muslim and Arab states to act has been exacerbated by the inability of the Global South as a whole to fight for global justice. We have not been able to do this though we have huge and varied natural resources on our lands and within our seas. It is in the Global South that we have most of the world's oil and gas. The Global South is also the home for most metals needed for manufacturing and industrial production. The world's most strategic sea and land routes are also in the Global South.

And yet we have not harnessed our geopolitical advantages and, as we have noted, we have failed to utilize our resources and wealth for the benefit of our people. Perhaps this is beginning to change. Perhaps we have woken up. It is in this regard we should look at what has been happening after October 7 in Gaza and Palestine and other parts of the world from another angle. Is it a turning point for people in Palestine, in West Asia and the world?

To answer this question, I shall examine briefly Israel's many strengths that I have outlined and its regional and international position to gain an idea of the actual situation confronting the nation. If Israel's determination to survive is such an asset, how does one explain the massive number of Israeli citizens who have left the country since October 7? According to various sources, half a million Israelis have abandoned their country because of prevailing uncertainties and the lack of security. For many of them, their so-called "chosen people" status no longer serves as a protective shield.

There is genuine disillusionment with the Israeli state among millions of Jews living in the United States, Canada and Europe brought about to a great extent by its massacre of tens of thousands of defenseless Palestinians since

October 7. It is significant that young Jews in particular in the West have been in the forefront of huge demonstrations and protests against the Netanyahu government in Tel Aviv for its bestial conduct towards a people who are after all indigenous to the land.

In fact, the injustices perpetrated against the Palestinian people in the last nine months have ignited a new awareness within segments of the West of the root cause of the Israeli–Palestinian/Arab conflict. Many now know that it is the Israeli usurpation of Palestinian ancestral land, Israeli occupation of Palestinian and Arab territories since 1948, the massacres of Palestinians and other Arabs, especially children and women in their thousands, and their continuous expulsion from their homes that have provoked some of the victims to retaliate against the Israeli occupiers and oppressors.

Because their governments and the media have ignored or downplayed the truth about Palestine and other Arab states, citizens in many Western nations are now turning to alternative channels such as social media. Social media were undoubtedly important sources of information and analysis in persuading students in the U.S., Canada, Europe and South Korea to adopt extraordinarily bold and brave positions against not only the Israeli government but also the U.S. government.

Indeed, central to the expanding awareness in a number of countries about the Israel–Palestine/Arab conflict is the realization that it is the U.S. facilitation of arms and money that has enabled Israel to commit unspeakable atrocities in Palestine. To put it more bluntly, it is U.S. hegemony more than anything else that has strengthened Israel's hand in oppressing the Palestinians and other Arabs. If we reflected upon other conflicts since World War Two from Korea and Vietnam to Afghanistan and Iraq, we would very quickly come to the conclusion that the main culprit of war and violence has always been U.S. hegemonic power.

That a lot of people, especially in the West, have now begun to embrace this truth is what endows October 7 or rather the months following that date with special significance. As utterly cruel and inhuman massacres occurred in Gaza on a daily basis, people began to understand that Israel and the U.S. are hell-bent on eradicating an entire people because their very presence is a reminder to the Israeli elite that the state called Israel has no moral legitimacy. Even if the Palestinians did not resist Israeli dominance, even if there was no violence, Palestinians would still be targeted. This is why, as we have observed, the ethnic cleansing of Palestine is a crucial, critical dimension of Israeli state policy.

The ethnic cleansing of the Palestinians, or the ethnic cleansing of any people, is a despicable, diabolical act. It is a shame that we human beings have allowed it to happen so many times in history. Sometimes, it is because we had come to know of the cleansing long after it had occurred as in the case of the eradication of the indigenous people of the Americas and Australia by white colonizers. At other times, we did not have the power or the means or the will to prevent or curb this horrendous act of inhumanity as in the case of the Nazi attempt to eliminate the Jews or the Turkish onslaught on the Armenians or the Serbian attack on the Bosnians. But Israel's attempt to wipe out the Palestinians is happening before our very eyes. We know of the intention of the Israeli elite and the means they are employing to achieve their barbaric goal.

The global consciousness that has erupted in the wake of the tragedy in Palestine and the clarion calls from everywhere to end the genocide are positive developments but much more has to be done. Citizen groups all over the world should pressurize their governments to use the United Nations General Assembly (UNGA) as a platform to achieve two goals, one, short-term and the other, long-term. The short-term goal would be to end the Israel-Palestine/Arab conflict and implement the proposal to establish a Palestinian state adopted by the UN in 1948. Various UN resolutions on the conflict and the establishment of a Palestinian state could guide the UNGA.

The long-term goal would be to get rid of hegemony in global politics and politics at all levels of society. No nation or group of nations should be allowed to control or dominate other nations or states. Inter-state relations should be conducted in such a manner that equality will be upheld in both theory and practice. While differences among nations and states related to, and determined by, their size, resources, history, geography, political acumen and economic management will continue to persist, they must never cease to respect the inherent worth and value of each and everyone them. In reality, this means taking the interests of all into consideration in the decision-making process, consulting them, listening to them and making them feel that they are appreciated. Genuine equality will be possible only if there is sincerity in the relations among nations.

Equality among states will become a living principle if some of its prerequisites are adhered to. These will include recognizing the sovereignty, independence and integrity of individual states while at the same time acknowledging the interdependence of all the constituent parts of the global system. There must be an appreciation of the inevitability of a global system evolving over time that will be more integrated, more harmonious and more unified. And yet it will be a system that will eulogize diversity and uniqueness.

The nation-states that constitute the UN General Assembly today will be able to achieve the laudable goal of unity within diversity only if they have the courage and the vision to eliminate hegemony and hegemonic power in politics, the economy, culture and most of all, in the minds and hearts of people everywhere.

—Kuala Lumpur, 13 July 2024

The Gaza Crisis 2024
Issues, Developments, and the Way Forward

Mohammad Hashim Kamali

Chapter Summary

This chapter is presented in five sections and a conclusion. The first section presents a brief history of the Gaza crisis, to be followed, in section two, by a discussion of the Israeli air raids and bombardment of Gaza that started on 7 October 2023 in response to a Hamas[1] attack of southern Israel and hostage taking of a number of Israelis and foreign nationals. The chapter continues, in section three, to discuss the Genocide Convention and the assertion that Israel has committed genocide in Gaza. The succeeding section discusses the ceasefire talks and the hitherto unsuccessful negotiations over the prospects of a ceasefire in Gaza. The final section, "Call for Action and the Way Forward," discusses peace advocacy efforts by the UN, Amnesty International and other actors proposing actual measures to facilitate conflict resolution and peace between Israel and Palestine.

History in Brief

The Gaza crisis is a localized part of the Israeli–Palestinian conflict. Beginning in 1948, when 200,000 Palestinians fled, or were expelled, from their homes, settling in the Gaza Strip as refugees. Since then, Israel has waged fifteen (15) wars against the Gaza Strip. The number of Palestinians

---

1 Hamas abbreviates the Arabic phrase Harakah Muqawamah Israel or anti-Israel resistance movement.

Dr. Mohammad Hashim Kamali was Dean and Professor at the International Institute of Islamic Thought and Civilization (ISTAC) and the International Islamic University in Malaysia. He then served as Founding CEO of the International Institute of Advanced Islamic Studies in Malaysia (2008–2022) and is currently an Adjunct Fellow of that Institute. The world's leading expert on comparative studies between Islamic and modern law, he is reputed to be the most widely read living author on Islamic law in the English language.

in Gaza killed in the most recent and still continuing 2023–2024 war has exceeded 37,000 (and rising) Palestinians, which is higher than the death toll of all other Arab-Israeli wars since 1948.

Israel fought four wars against the Egyptian-administered Gaza Strip: the 1948 Palestine War; border attacks of 1949–1956; first occupation of Gaza during the Suez Crisis, and the capture of Gaza in 1967. During the first occupation, 1% of Gaza Strip's population was either killed, tortured or imprisoned by Israel. Following two periods of low-level insurgency, a major conflict between the Israelis and Palestinians erupted in the First Intifada (Intifada means uprising—the first Intifada was from 1987–1990) in which 523 Gazans were killed. The 1993 Oslo Accords brought a period of relative calm. However, in 2000 the Second Intifada erupted and continued until 2005. In 2005, towards the end of the Second Intifada, Israel disengaged from Gaza. Hamas won the 2006 general election and seized control of Gaza in 2007.

Israel imposed a land, air and sea blockade of the Gaza Strip, turning it into an "open-air prison." The blockade was widely condemned as a form of collective punishment, which Israel thought necessary to stop Palestinian rocket attacks. Hamas considered it a declaration of war. A 2008–2009 Israeli invasion of Gaza resulted in more than 1,000 deaths and widespread destruction of homes, schools and hospitals. The 2012 Israeli operation killed more than 100 Palestinians.

In 2014, Israel invaded Gaza in a major war that resulted in the deaths of 73 Israelis (mostly soldiers) and 2,251 Palestinians (mostly civilians). The invasion resulted in "unprecedented" destruction, damaging 25% of homes in Gaza City and 70% of homes in Beit Hanoun. After 2014, notable events in the conflict included the "Great March of Return" (2018–2019) and clashes in November 2018, May 2019 and November 2019. The 2021 crisis saw 256 Palestinians and 15 Israelis killed.

On October 7, 2023 a large number of Palestinian militants attacked southern Israel, took hostages and killed some of the 1,139 Israeli and foreign nationals, including 766 civilians and 373 security personnel.[2] Israel responded with bombing Gaza Strip and launching an invasion that as of June

2 Reports are not consistent on the number of Israeli hostages killed by Hamas. Israeli sources maintain that Hamas killed the 1,139 captives it took as hostages. Other sources, including Hamas, give different figures such as 28, 50, etc., Israeli hostages in Hamas custody were actually killed while others were kept in captivity. Israeli forces have also mistakenly killed some of their own nationals in their air strikes. It seems that smaller numbers of Israelis in Hamas custody were killed on different occasions. See for details: "Israel-Hamas war hostage crisis," *Wikipedia.* https://en.wikipedia.org/wiki/Israel%E2%80%93Hamas_war_hostage_crisis

2024 has killed over 37,000 Gazans. The conflict continues and will most likely claim more victims. Media reports indicate that the Israeli military are killing on average 250 Palestinians per day in Gaza. Almost 90 percent of Palestinians have been displaced from their homes, with many moving multiple times in search of safety.[3]

Due to the failure of the international community (esp. America and Western Europe) to fulfil its obligations, the Palestinian people have experienced multiple waves of forced displacement, transfer and land dispossession. During the British Mandate (1922–1947), more than 100,000 Palestinians were displaced in preparation for Zionist colonization.[4] During the Nakba (1947–1949—Nakba lit. means "catastrophe" and refers to the ethnic cleansing of Palestinians in Mandatory Palestine in the 1948 Palestinian war), Israel was created on 78 percent of Mandatory Palestine, after the ethnic cleansing of over 750,000 Palestinians. This was made possible by the UN General Assembly Resolution 181 of 1947 which recommended the (illegal) partition of Mandatory Palestine and granted the colonial Zionist movement 56 percent of the land. In 1967, when Israel occupied the rest of Palestine, another 400,000 to 450,000 Palestinians were displaced, some for the second time.

With the colonial states' ongoing complicity, Israeli genocide in the Gaza Strip is the culmination of 76 years of forced displacement and transfer, colonization and apartheid designed "to acquire the maximum amount of land with the minimum number of Palestinians" to perpetuate the ongoing Nakba.

Since 1948, the Israeli colonial-apartheid regime has gradually established and fortified its three main pillars: Palestinian displacement and transfer, colonization, and apartheid. The ongoing Nakba is sustained by Israeli legislations, policies and practices such as land confiscation, denial of use and access to natural resources and services. The Nakba has also meant denial of residency, segregation, fragmentation and isolation, discriminatory zoning and planning, the permit regime, suppression of resistance and denial of reparations

In the last 30 years, the Oslo Accords and the so-called peace process have only served to further entrench Israel's colonial domination and oppression.

---

3 Britain-based charity Oxfam noted that the daily death toll of over 250 Palestinians in Israel's war on Gaza surpasses that of any other major conflict in the 21st century, while survivors remain at high risk due to hunger, disease, and cold, as well as ongoing Israeli bombardments. Oxfam, "Six months into Gaza conflict, malnutrition and famine emerging," April 5, 2024. https://www.oxfamamerica.org/explore/stories/six-months-into-gaza-conflict-malnutrition-and-famine-emerging/

4 Zionism refers to the idea that the existence of Israel is necessary for the long-term survival of the Jewish people.

It has also served as an example of the international community's failure to ensure the Palestinian people's rights to self-determination and return.

With its ongoing use of force and creation of an unbearable coercive environment, Israel has forcibly displaced over 66 percent of the Palestinian people and controls over 85 percent of Mandatory Palestine

The global pro-Palestine solidarity movement has also played a significant role in countering and challenging Israel's impunity and colonial states' complicity. Through their sustained and strategic efforts, combined with overall resistance, Palestinians hope to put an end to Israel's genocidal war on Gaza, dismantle Israel's colonial-apartheid regime and hold colonial states accountable for their complicity

As the Palestinian people commemorated Land Day during the Israeli genocide, BADIL[5] (the activist youth resistance to the Israeli occupation) called on:

> The Global Solidarity Movement to take strategic and effective direct actions that urge the involved go ernments to end their involvement in the genocide.

Other States are urged to fulfil their obligations and take practical measures to end Israel's genocidal war on Gaza Strip, and 76 years of its colonial-apartheid regime through arms embargoes and military, economic and diplomatic sanctions.

The United Nations is urged to take every available measure under international law to hold Israel accountable under internationally binding mechanisms.

Israeli Air Raids on Gaza

Starting in October 2023 and still (i.e 4 June 2024) continuing, Israeli air raids have killed thousands of civilians, including women and children, in the occupied Palestinian territories. As the world watches in horror, international organizations including the UN, the International Court of Justice, and Amnesty International have been documenting the human rights violations in Gaza. Israeli Defense Forces (IDF) have violated international humanitarian law, including repeated attacks that amount to war crimes and have pulverized Gaza, killing civilians, peace workers and medical personnel in Palestine.

---

5 Cf., BADIL, "On Land Day 2024: People around the World are United against Genocide and Ongoing Impunity," March 29, 2024. https://www.badil.org/press-releases/14836.html

The Global pro-Palestine Solidarity Movement has denounced Israel's disproportionate aggression against Palestine. Israel has not heeded and continues its devastating air raids on Gaza. On December 29, 2023, South Africa filed a case with the International Court of Justice (ICJ) at the Hague saying that Israel is violating the 1948 Convention on the Prevention and Punishment of the Crime of Genocide in Gaza under the Genocide Convention.

On 26 January 2024 the International Court of Justice (ICJ) ordered Israel to take "immediate and effective measures" to protect Palestinians in the occupied Gaza Strip from the risk of genocide by ensuring sufficient humanitarian aid and enabling basic services are reaching Gaza. The Court had given Israel one month to report back on its compliance with the measures. By 26 February, that is a month after the Court order, Israel had not taken even the bare minimum steps to comply. As the occupying power, Israel was under obligation to ensure that life-saving goods and services are reaching the population of Gaza. Gazans are on the brink of famine due also to relentless bombardment and the tightening of a 16-year long blockade. Israel has also failed to lift any of the restrictions it had imposed on the entry of life-saving goods, nor has it opened additional aid access points and crossings or put in place an effective mechanism to protect humanitarians from attack.

Israel has created one of the worst humanitarian crises in the world by displaying a callous indifference to the fate of Gaza's population and by creating conditions which the ICJ has said places them at imminent risk of genocide. "Time and time again, Israel has failed to take the bare minimum steps humanitarians have desperately pleaded for. It is clearly within its power to alleviate the suffering of Palestinian civilians in Gaza," said Heba Morayef, Regional Director for the Middle East and North Africa at Amnesty International. Israel has also blocked the passage of sufficient aid into the Gaza Strip in a clear show of contempt for the ICJ ruling and in flagrant violation of its obligation to prevent genocide.

Furthermore, Israel is using water as a weapon in its war of aggression against Palestinians by denying access to water and destroying its infrastructure. By November 2023, it was clear that the Israeli government had denied Palestinians in Gaza access to water. "Every hour that passes with Israel preventing the provision of safe drinking water in the Gaza Strip, puts Gazans at risk of dying of thirst and diseases related to the lack of safe drinking water," said Pedro Arrojo-Agudo, UN special rapporteur on the human rights to safe drinking water and sanitation. "Israel," he noted, "must stop using water as a weapon of war." Before Israel's most recent attack on Gaza, 97 percent of the water in Gaza's only coastal aquifer was already unsafe for human consumption based on World Health Organization standards. Over the course of its many attacks, Israel has all but destroyed Gaza's water purification system and prevented the entry of materials and chemicals needed for repair.[6]

The scale and gravity of the humanitarian catastrophe Israel has caused by its relentless bombardment, destruction, and suffocating siege puts more than two million Palestinians of Gaza at risk of irreparable harm.

The supplies entering Gaza before the ICJ order have been minimal compared to the needs of Gazan people for the last 16 years. Yet, in the three weeks following the ICJ order, the number of trucks entering Gaza further decreased by about a third, from an average of 500 a day to about 105 carrying food, water, animal fodder, medical supplies and fuel. The only crossings that Israel has allowed to open were also opened on fewer days, further demonstrating Israel's disregard for the provisional measures. Aid workers reported multiple challenges but said that Israel was refusing to take obvious steps to improve the situation.

South Africa further argued that Israel's deliberate denial of humanitarian aid to Palestinians could constitute one of the prohibited acts under the Genocide Convention by "deliberately inflicting on the group conditions of life calculated to bring about its physical destruction in whole or in part."

At its special meeting on Gaza on March 25, 2024, the UNSC called for an immediate ceasefire and the protection of civilians. Israel still did not heed and continued its relentless air raids on Gaza.

Then it was reported on March 29 that the Biden administration had authorized the transfer of additional bombs and fighter jets to Israel despite Washington's expression of concern about an anticipated IDF military offensive on Rafah that could threaten the lives of hundreds of thousands of Palestinian civilians. In his latest announcement, President Biden said the U.S. is sending USD one billion worth of arms and munition to Israel.

The American arms package before this last included more than 1,800 MK84 2,000-pound bombs and 500 MK82 500-pound bombs, according to Pentagon and State Department officials familiar with the matter. The 2,000-pound bombs have also been used in previous instances of Israel's military attacks on Gaza. When Israel actually invaded Rafah during the first week of May 2024, President Biden announced that the U.S. would cut off some weapons to Israel if it invades the crowded city of Rafah.

Some Democrats, including allies of President Biden, said the U.S. government had a responsibility to withhold weapons in the absence of an Israeli

---

6 Vijay Prasad, "How Israel Weaponizes Water," *Transcend Media Service,* April 8, 2024. https://www.transcend.org/tms/2024/04/how-israel-weaponizes-water/

commitment to limit civilian casualties during a planned operation in Rafah, a crowded population center that was on the brink of famine.[7]

According to a Hamas-run media office report, on April 1, Israel withdrew from al-Shifa Hospital in Gaza adding, however, that hundreds of Palestinians were killed in the process.[8] A mass grave of 310 bodies was subsequently discovered in Al-Shifa Hospital, which the IDF had occupied for more than ten days. Forty-nine (49) additional bodies were also discovered in another mass grave in the same hospital.

The ICJ considered South Africa's allegation that Israel was violating the Genocide Convention. In its session of March 26, 2024, the Court adopted binding orders requiring Israel to prevent genocide against Palestinians in Gaza, enable the provision of basic services and humanitarian assistance, prevent and punish incitement to commit genocide.

"Genocide is seen as having under international law this special character that it is relevant to everyone. There are 'reasonable grounds' to believe that Israel is committing genocide against Palestinians in Gaza," the UN Special Rapporteur on the situation of human rights in the Occupied Palestinian Territories, Francesca Albanese, said this on March 26, 2024. She was speaking at the UN Human Rights Council in Geneva, where she presented her report, entitled "Anatomy of Genocide," during an interactive dialogue with the Member States. "Following nearly six months of unrelenting Israeli assaults on occupied Gaza, it is my solemn duty to report on the worst of what humanity is capable of, and to present my findings," she said.

Ms. Albanese defined genocide as a specific set of acts committed with the intent to destroy, in whole or in part, a national, ethnic, racial or religious group.

However, the U.S. State Department spokesman Matthew Miller dismissed out of hand Francesca Albanese's report that found Israel was committing "acts of genocide" in the Gaza Strip.

Reem Alsalem, the UN special rapporteur on violence against women and girls, said "it is deeply concerning" that rather than engaging with the conclusions of the report, the U.S. government "has moved to slander and smear" Albanese, who has also received threats. Alsalem added: "Whereas many of us are attacked for doing the work we were mandated to do [by the

---

7 John Hudson, "The U.S. signs off on more bombs, warplanes for Israel," *Washington Post,* March 29, 2024. https://www.washingtonpost.com/national-security/2024/03/29/us-weapons-israel-gaza-war/

8 Lorenzo Tondo, "Israeli forces withdraw from Gaza's al-Shifa hospital after two-week raid leaving facility in ruins," *The Guardian,* April 1, 2024. https://www.theguardian.com/world/2024/apr/01/israeli-forces-withdraw-from-gaza-al-shifa-hospital-after-two-week-raid

UN Human Rights Council], it is particularly alarming when a member state of the Council does so."

The Israeli onslaught continued unimpeded. According to the Gaza Press Office report of 30 March 2024 the Israeli military killed more than 400 Palestinians and destroyed, burned or otherwise targeted 1,050 homes in the vicinity of Al-Shifa Hospital after laying siege to it for 13 days.

On April 1, 2024, seven people working with the United States-based NGO World Central Kitchen (WCK) were killed in the Gaza Strip in what the group's Founder Chef said was an Israeli air attack.

"We condemn the international silence towards this crime," the Gaza Press Office said that the Israeli military has also arrested and "tortured" hundreds of patients, displaced people and medical staff inside and around the key Al-Shifa hospital in Gaza City:

We once again condemn in the strongest terms the Israeli occupation army's storming of the Al-Shifa Medical Complex, which is a war crime and a crime against humanity.

"We call on all international organizations, all Arab and Islamic countries, and all countries of the free world to move out of the box of silence and verbal condemnation into the box of taking practical positions, real measures, and field action to stop the genocidal war."

Australia's Prime Minister, Anthony Albanese, demanded "full accountability" over the death of an Australian aid worker, Zomi Frankcom, in Gaza who was one of WCK staff.

Frankcom was one of four international aid workers that Palestinian officials say were killed along with their Palestinian driver on Monday 1st April in an Israeli air attack in central Gaza's Deir el-Balah.

The Genocide Convention

Signed in 1948 in the aftermath of World War II, the Convention on the Prevention and Punishment of the Crime of Genocide—the Genocide Convention—codified for the first time the crime of genocide. It signified the international community's commitment to "never again" allow or commit genocide after the atrocities committed during the Second World War—the UN says this on its website. Today, 153 countries are parties to the Convention, confirming that genocide, whether committed in time of peace or in time of war, is a crime under international law which they all undertake to prevent and to punish.[9]

States can meet their obligation to prevent genocide in several ways, including by appealing—as South Africa did—to the ICJ, the UN's top Court. Genocide is seen as having under international law "this special character that it is relevant to everyone," as experts on criminology and criminal justice maintain.

In its filing, South Africa argued that Israel has not only "failed to prevent genocide," but it also "engaged in, is engaging in, and risks further engaging in genocidal acts against the Palestinian people in Gaza." The genocidal acts in question include killing Palestinians in Gaza, causing them serious bodily and mental harm, and inflicting on them conditions calculated to bring about their physical destruction. These acts are all attributable to Israel, which has failed to prevent genocide and is committing genocide in manifest violation of the Genocide Convention.

One can definitely say, on the basis of all the statements and all of the violence and the starvation and the siege and the blockade and the expulsions, air raids and bombardments, that there is a serious risk of genocide, and if there's a serious risk of genocide, the duty to prevent it exists.

South Africa is acutely aware of the particular weight of responsibility in initiating proceedings against Israel for violations of the Genocide Convention. South Africa is also aware of its own obligation—as a State party to the Genocide Convention—to prevent genocide.

The International Court of Justice (ICJ) held hearings on January 11 and 12, 2024 to consider South Africa's request for provisional measures, which also featured the first formal response by Israel that denied before an independent and impartial Court the allegations of atrocities against the Palestinian people. "The World Court's landmark decision puts Israel and its allies on notice that immediate action is needed to prevent genocide and further atrocities against Palestinians in Gaza." Lives hang in the balance, and governments must use their leverage to ensure that the order is enforced.

Back in 2007, the ICJ had expounded that states can act to uphold their obligation to prevent genocide, noting that their responsibility does not solely begin "when perpetration of genocide commences."

"That would be absurd, since the whole point of the obligation is to prevent, or attempt to prevent, the occurrence of the act," said the Court in its decision in a case brought by Bosnia and Herzegovina against Serbia and

---

9 The Genocide Convention has been ratified or acceded to by 153 States (as of April 2022, with Zambia being the last). Other 41 United Nations Member States have yet to do so. See for details: https://www.un.org › genocideprevention › genocide-convention

Montenegro over crimes committed in the former Yugoslavia. Instead, the obligation arises "at the instant that the State learns of, or should normally have learned of, the existence of a serious risk that genocide will be committed," the Court explained.

The ICJ found it "plausible" that Israel has committed acts that violate the Genocide Convention. In a provisional order delivered by the Court's president, Joan Donoghue, the Court said Israel must ensure "with immediate effect" that its forces do not commit any of the acts prohibited by the Convention.

Donoghue said the Court cannot make a final determination right now on whether Israel is guilty of genocide. But she said that given the deteriorating situation in Gaza, the Court has jurisdiction to order measures to protect Gaza's population from further risk of genocide. Donoghue outlined the provisional measures and how each judge voted. The Court voted 15-2 on the order that Israel must take all measures in its power to stop anything in relation to genocide in Gaza. By 16 votes to 1, the Court voted that Israel needs to take all measures within its powers to prevent and punish those involved with inciting genocide against Palestinians in the Gaza Strip.

Also, by a 16-1 vote, the Court held that Israel must take "immediate and effective" measures to ensure the provision of urgently needed humanitarian aid and basic services. The Court further ordered Israel to take effective measures to prevent destruction and ensure preservation of any evidence related to the charge of genocide and gave Israel 30 days to report back on measures taken.

Before delivering the decision, Donoghue read statements from Israeli officials that she said made South Africa's case plausible. She also gave a bleak assessment of the deteriorating humanitarian situation in Gaza.

"In the Court's view, the facts and circumstances mentioned above are sufficient to conclude that at least some of the rights claimed by South Africa and for which it is seeking protection are plausible. This is the case with respect to the right of the Palestinians in Gaza to be protected from acts of genocide and related prohibited acts," the Court declared.

The Palestinian Authority's Foreign Ministry issued a statement welcoming the ruling, thanking South Africa and saying, "The ICJ judges assessed the facts and the law. They ruled in favour of humanity and international law. ... No state is above the law."

South African President Cyril Ramaphosa also said: "the Palestinian people's cries for justice have been heeded by an eminent organ of the United Nations." Since its former President Nelson Mandela's reign, South Africa has long supported the Palestinian cause, saying it sees echoes of apartheid in the situation between the Israelis and Palestinians. "We, as South Africans, will not be passive bystanders and watch the crimes that were visited upon us being perpetrated elsewhere," Ramaphosa said. He also noted that the ICJ affirmed South Africa's right to take Israel to court, "even though it is not a party to the conflict in Gaza."

South Africa brought the genocide complaint to the International Court of Justice in The Hague, Netherlands, in December 2023. During two days of hearings from both sides, South Africa asked the Court to issue provisional measures that would require Israel to immediately halt its assault on Gaza.

The ICJ's provisional order was not a verdict on South Africa's allegation of genocide—that judgment is not expected for years. Israel denies the accusation of genocide and has called it "baseless."

Although the Court's ruling is legally binding, it is not enforceable. "Nobody will stop us—not The Hague," Netanyahu said in a speech after hearing the ICJ's ruling.

However, this order may put pressure on Israel's allies and military backers—including the U.S, which has reiterated its position that the genocide allegations are "unfounded."

The U.S. State Department said in a statement: "We have consistently made clear that Israel must take all possible steps to minimize civilian harm, increase the flow of humanitarian assistance, and address dehumanizing rhetoric."

Gaza Truce Talks

Truce talks between Israel and Hamas were set to resume in Cairo on 31 March 2024 days after the UN Security Council demanded a ceasefire nearly six months into the war in Gaza. As of this writing the ceasefire talks have yet to be held in Cairo—the two sides still seem to be negotiating over the ceasefire details.

Media reports indicate that the Israeli public are protesting against the Prime Minister Benjamin Netanyahu saying that Netanyahu is the main obstacle to signing a deal with Hamas to bring the captives held in Gaza back home. They are urging that a deal should be signed to bring back the captives held for more than 175 days and say that the policies of Israel's government have simply failed. Large scale demonstrations took place near Netanyahu's residence and in other cities across Israel.

Qatar, Egypt and the United States are also trying to reach a captive swap deal and a ceasefire in Gaza, as the first pause lasted only a week in late November 2023. In the meantime, Qatar has ceased to be host country for Hamas and the Hamas leader Ismail Haniyeh currently resides in Türkiye.

Mediators from the United States say they remain optimistic that a deal can be reached. But there are still significant differences between the sides over the terms and duration of a ceasefire while Israeli bombardment of Gaza continues unabated.

Hamas has sought to negotiate a deal to end to the war and the full withdrawal of Israeli forces from Gaza. Israel has ruled this out, however, saying that even if there is a long pause in the fighting, the war will not end until Hamas is defeated. Israel has in the meantime announced its planned invasion of Rafah, independently of the ceasefire talks, which will further complicate the situation.

The French, Egyptian and Jordanian foreign ministers have called for an immediate and permanent ceasefire in Gaza and the release of all captives held by Palestinian armed groups.

Speaking at a joint news conference in Cairo, France's top diplomat Stephane Sejourne said his government would put forward a draft resolution at the UN Security Council setting out a "political" settlement of the war in Gaza. He said the text would include "all the criteria for a two-state solution" of the Israeli-Palestinian conflict, the peace blueprint long championed by the international community but opposed by the Netanyahu government.

The three ministers renewed their governments' support for the UN Palestinian refugee agency UNRWA, which has faced a funding crisis since Israel alleged that a few of its 13,000 Gaza staff were implicated in the October 7, 2023, attack.

Jordan's Foreign Minister Ayman Safadi said that "Israel is not only starving Palestinians but wants to kill the only entity capable of standing in the way of a famine. Egypt's Foreign Minister Sameh Shoukry said that Gaza "can endure no more destruction and humanitarian suffering," and called on Israel to open its land crossings with the Gaza Strip to allow humanitarian aid.

The UN Security Council has also passed a consensus resolution calling for an immediate ceasefire. However, the fighting continues, with Israel still launching aerial and ground attacks across the Strip and has most recently invaded the southernmost city of Rafah where more than one and a half million displaced Palestinians are sheltering.

Call for Action and the Way Forward

United Nations experts have sounded the alarm that Palestinians in Gaza face the risk of genocide. The Israeli army has battered the coastal enclave, forcing most of the population from their homes and imposing a stringent blockade barring food, water and other supplies from getting in.

Amnesty International has also warned of the risk of genocide in Gaza due to the shockingly high death toll among Palestinians, the widespread destruction caused by Israeli air raids and denial of humanitarian aid as part of the ongoing blockade that inflict horrifying levels of suffering on Gaza's civilian population. Other warning signs include the increase in Israel's racist and dehumanizing system of apartheid.

The ICJ concluded in February 2024 that the risk of genocide in Gaza is real and imminent. All states are under an obligation under international law to act to prevent genocide and refrain from export of arms or arm parts to be used by the Israeli Defense Forces (IDF). The new set of provisional measures issued by the ICJ ordered Israel to ensure the unhindered provision of humanitarian assistance to Gaza.

With regard to Israel's invasion of Rafah where close to two million Palestinians have taken refuge, the U.S. has joined the international community's warning to Israel not to attack Rafah—Israel has already invaded Rafah despite the international community's repeated warnings against it.

For a lasting solution to the conflict, it is necessary to address its root causes, including Israel's system of apartheid imposed on the Palestinians. The root cause also lies in the refusal of colonial states to condemn Israeli abuses, hold Israel accountable, and address the systemic issues perpetuating the conflict. The U.S. and Europe have hitherto condoned Israel's war crimes and the crime of apartheid with impunity that encourages repeated cycles of violence and repression of the Palestinian people. The U.S. has not only condoned Israeli atrocities but continued supplying it with more military aid and munitions.

As the people of Gaza face relentless bombardments, death and destruction, all the aid giving governments to Israel must stop export of arms to Israel. For instance, in recent years, Australia has approved hundreds of permits for defense goods to be sent to Israel. The lack of transparency in Australia's defense export policy also means one may not know exactly what was approved for export, but it is important that the government of Australia does not allow arms manufactured in Australia to be used by Israeli Defense Forces.

In face of the ongoing human rights violations and violence in Gaza, civil society and advocacy groups for peace in the colonial states are also called upon to put pressure on their governments to stop arming Israel and financially supporting its attacks on Gaza. America and Europe must also ensure that Israel allows essential food aids and medicine to Gaza and allow essential supplies to go through unhindered so as to minimize the risk of death and disease from the already starvation-stricken population of Gaza.

The UNSC, Amnesty International and other advocacy groups have called on all parties to abide by international law and make every effort to avoid civilian bloodshed and take the following measures:

Put an end to unlawful attacks, including indiscriminate attacks, direct attacks on civilians , civilian objects and disproportionate attacks.

Israel to immediately allow unimpeded delivery of humanitarian aid into the occupied Gaza Strip, lift its 16-year illegal blockade on Gaza, and grant immediate access to independent investigators.

The international community to impose comprehensive arms embargos on all parties to the conflict given that serious violations amounting to crimes under international law are being committed.

The International Criminal Court's[10] ongoing investigation into the situation of Palestine to proceed and to receive full support and all necessary resources.

Hamas and all other armed groups to release unconditionally and immediately all civilian hostages and to treat all those being held captive humanely, including by providing medical treatment, pending their release.

Israel to release all Palestinians it has arbitrarily detained.

The root causes of the conflict to be addressed, including through dismantling Israel's system of apartheid against all Palestinians.

Furthermore, peace negotiations can hardly succeed during an ongoing war. It is essential therefore for the conflicting parties to agree to a ceasefire. America and the leading European countries are also urged to ensure the success of peace negotiations. Past attempts to hold ceasefire and peace talks in Cairo and elsewhere did not succeed due to some issues—mainly the need for

---

10 The International Court of Justice (ICJ) is often referred to as the "World Court" and is the principal judicial organ of the United Nations. Its primary function is to settle disputes between countries (states) based on international law. The International Criminal Court (ICC) is also an international tribunal formed in 2002 for the prosecution of crimes against humanity. Its headquarters are at The Hague. In contrast with the ICJ, the ICC is not affiliated with the United Nations. See for details https://www.icrc.org/en/doc/war-and-law/international-criminal. See also Frank Gardner, "Gardner: ICC warrants 'major blow to Israel's standing'," November 21, 2024, https://www.bbc.com/news/articles/cm273g1jm5lo

Israel to stop air attacks and for Hamas to release the hostages. Both parties have, on the other hand, shown interest in peace talks and must therefore also facilitate its success by minimizing their points of differences. For purposes of confidence building, the conflicting parties may also want to invite the UN to send non-partisan experts to help with the success of ceasefire and peace negotiations.

Witnessing Genocide through Social Media

Narratives, Transnational Memories, and Activism

Meymune Topçu

"HI EVERYONE! This is Bisan from Gaza, I am still alive."
This is how Bisan Owda, a young filmmaker/journalist from Gaza, starts every video she shares on social media. She has more than 4.5 million followers on Instagram. When she doesn't share any content for a few days, her followers start filling her latest posts with comments about her life. This is not only the case for Bisan but almost all Palestinian journalists/content creators who document the Gazan genocide on social media.[1] Since October 7, a complex and deeply interconnected social media network has evolved between Palestinians in Gaza, the West Bank, the diaspora and the wider public across the globe, which has enabled people to get direct information about the events happening on the ground.

As this network continues to grow and connect people across borders, it has also given rise to a new dimension of documenting and remembering atrocities. In this sense, what sets the genocide in Gaza apart from others in history is that it is the first to be "live-streamed" on social media. This real-time documentation is not only critical for recording the atrocities and creating

---

1 Harmeet Kaur, "Palestinians are documenting the war for millions on social media. Their followers have come to see them as family.," CNN, January 19, 2024. https://edition.cnn.com/2024/01/19/world/palestinians-x-tiktok-instagram-gaza-cec/index.html

Meymune N. Topçu is an Assistant Professor of Psychology at MEF University, Istanbul, with a Ph.D. in Cognitive Psychology from the New School for Social Research. Her research focuses on collective memory, anxiety, and future thinking, with publications in leading psychology journals. She has been awarded several prestigious research grants to explore topics such as existential threats, collective future thinking, and perceived agency.

an evolving archive for future legal cases, but it also plays a significant role in shaping the collective memory of the genocide. These memories transcend national borders, influencing global narratives about the Palestinian struggle and fueling activist movements worldwide. In this paper, I explore the effects of social media from a memory studies perspective with a particular focus on the narratives and transnational movements they inspire.

Mainstream Media and Schematic Narratives

The rise of social media as a primary source of news is not a new phenomenon, but in the current case, one of the main reasons why people turn to social media is the mainstream media's failure to provide impartial reports on the events in Gaza. In January 2024, The Intercept published a detailed open-source analysis of three major American media outlets' coverage of Israel's war on Gaza.[2] Their analysis revealed a significant bias favoring Israeli narratives over Palestinian ones. The terms Israel/Israeli appeared more frequently than the words Palestine/Palestinian even though Palestinian death toll far exceeded that of Israelis. More critically, emotive language like "slaughter, horrific, massacre" was nearly always used to describe Israeli deaths but not Palestinian ones; despite the war on Gaza being among the deadliest for children and journalists, these outlets rarely mentioned them in their headlines. News outlets even denied the childhood of Palestinian children by using different terms to describe them. In an article reporting the hostage exchange in November 2023, for instance, *The Guardian* referred to released Israeli hostages as women and children, but Palestinian ones as "women and people aged 18 and younger."[3]

When contrasted with the coverage of the war in Ukraine these biases become even more explicit. Although these newspapers extensively covered personal and sympathetic stories about the plight of children and the dangers journalists face during the Ukraine war, they failed to provide comparable coverage for Palestinian children and journalists.[4] When reporting Palestinian deaths, news outlets notably used passive voice in their headlines without

---

2 Adam Johnson and Othman Ali, "Coverage of Gaza War in the New York Times and Other Major Newspapers Heavily Favored Israel, Analysis Shows," *The Intercept,* January 9, 2024. https://theintercept.com/2024/01/09/newspapers-israel-palestine-bias-new-york-times/

3 Jason Burke, "Benjamin Netanyahu warns war will continue until Hamas is eliminated," The Guardian, November 22, 2023. https://www.theguardian.com/world/2023/nov/22/gaza-ceasefire-due-to-come-into-effect-on-thursday-morning

4 Johnson and Ali, "Coverage of Gaza War."

implicating the Israeli army as the perpetrator, while they explicitly mentioned Russia as the perpetrator when reporting Ukrainian deaths.[5]

These examples illustrate how mainstream media advocate a narrative that minimizes Palestinian suffering and ignores Israeli responsibility, which is an ongoing trend in reporting the Palestine-Israel crisis.[6] Narratives are a critical cultural tool through which people make sense of the events that they experience.[7] Psychological and anthropological works show how certain narratives can take a schema-like form as they are repeated persistently through various cultural reproductions.[8] Bartlett defines schemata as mental structures that summarize people's conception of the world.[9] These schemata are created through experiences within a specific socio-cultural setting, and they assist people to construct simple and straightforward conceptions of the world, which is otherwise complex and ambiguous. Wertsch applies Bartlett's notion of schemata to national narratives and argues that people use *schematic narrative templates* to remember and perceive past and present national events.[10] Once narratives are schematized it becomes very difficult to challenge them. Each new event is perceived and evaluated through those embedded schematic lenses which further contribute to the crystallization of the narratives.

It is possible to detect the traces of such schematic narrative templates in mainstream Western media's coverage of the Palestine-Israel issue. In his detailed analysis of articles published in the *New York Times* and other major news outlets, Greg Shupak identifies three schematic narratives that are prevalent when discussing the

---

5 As an example, BBC News headline for Hind Rajab's killing: "Hind Rajab, 6, found dead in Gaza days after phone calls for help" [https://www.bbc.com/news/world-middle-east-68261286] vs. headline for a Ukrainian baby's killing: "Ukraine War: Baby killed in Russian strike on Kharkiv Hotel" [https://www.bbc.com/news/world-europe-68214631].

6 Noureddine Miladi and Aaya Miladi, "Digital media and the role of narratives in reporting the Palestinian-Israeli conflict," in Noureddine Miladi, ed., *Global Media Coverage of the Palestinian-Israeli Conflict: Reporting the Sheikh Jarrah Evictions* (London: I.B. Tauris, 2023).

7 Jerome Bruner, "Self-making and World-making." in Jens Brockmeier and Donal Carbaugh, eds., *Narrative and Identity: Studies in Autobiography, Self and Culture* (Amsterdam: John Benjamins Publishing, 2001), 25–37.

8 James V. Wertsch, *How Nations Remember: A Narrative Approach* (Oxford University Press, 2021).

9 Sir Frederic Charles Bartlett, *Remembering: A Study in Experimental and Social Psychology* (Cambridge University Press, 1995; original work published 1932).

10 James V. Wertsch, *Voices of Collective Remembering* (Cambridge University Press, 2002).

Palestine-Israel issue.[11] The first such narrative is that "*both sides of Palestine and Israel are victims of, and at fault for, the ongoing violence to a comparable extent*"; the second is that "Palestine-Israel is largely a conflict between *extremists and moderates*," while the third is the framing of Israel's attacks against Palestine as "Israel's *right to defend itself* against Palestinian violence." (8–9, author's emphasis)

The influence of these three underlying schematic narrative templates is easily discernible in the mainstream media's coverage of the war on Gaza since October 7. The analyses of the Hamas attack on October 7 featured:

- the failure to provide context on the continued colonization and illegal occupation of Palestinian lands;
- highlighting the plight of Israeli hostages without consideration of that of the thousands of Palestinian hostages who have been kept in inhumane conditions in Israeli prisons without criminal charge or trial;
- the insistence on Israel's right to defend itself without giving an even nearly comparable coverage of its multitudinous violations of international law; and
- a corresponding continued denial of Palestinians' right to defend themselves and countless other examples are all emblematic of those underlying schematic narratives.[12]

Social Media and the Narrative Shift

As traditional media outlets failed to provide an impartial coverage of the humanitarian disasters in Gaza, people increasingly turned to social media where they can get real-time coverage of the events directly from Palestinian journalists and social media users. In this process, Palestinian journalists like Motaz Azaiza, Bisan Owda, Wael Al-Dahdouh, Plestia Al-Aqad, Saleh Al-Jafarawi, Hind Khoudry and many others gained millions of followers over multiple social media platforms. Most of these journalists work for

---

11 Greg Shupak, *The Wrong Story: Palestine, Israel, and the Media* (New York: OR Books, 2018).

12 Sahar Khamis, "Western Media Has Failed to Properly Cover Gaza Conflict," *Afkār*, December 14, 2023. https://mecouncil.org/blog_posts/gaza-conflict-in-western-media-distortion-of-facts/

Mat Nashed, "Western coverage of Israel's war on Gaza – bias or unprofessionalism?," *Al Jazeera*, October 29, 2023. https://www.aljazeera.com/news/2023/10/29/western-coverage-of-israels-war-on-gaza-bias-or-unprofessionalism

various news outlets, but they also concurrently use their personal social media accounts to share the images and videos of the tragic events that they witness on a daily basis—even though they themselves and their families are under serious threat. So, these journalists work as both traditional journalists and citizen journalists under very difficult circumstances.[13] The fact that the very people who are under targeted attacks are also the ones who report what's going on in Gaza increases the emotional intensity of their content and creates personal bonds between them and their followers. These journalists share images of individual/collective tragedies and acts of resilience, which re-humanizes the Palestinians, who have been continuously dehumanized and reduced to mere numbers by Israel and its allies. Moreover, the images and experiences they post reach millions of people instantaneously all around the world and challenge the deeply embedded schematic narratives that are widespread in the mainstream media.

IMAGE 1. *Etamin artwork depicts Reem and her grandfather Khaled as he bids farewell to her.*

Reproduced with permission from the etamin artist @Ranas_Etamin (Instagram)

There have been countless images/videos from Gaza, recorded and shared by Gazans, that have gone viral in social media, which eventually seeped into the mainstream media's news stories. An example is Khaled Nabhan's video of himself tenderly kissing his 3-year-old granddaughter Reem's eyes good-bye. An Israeli airstrike killed Reem along with her 5-year-old brother Tareq while sleeping in their home.[14] Khaled called Reem "the soul of his soul" and could not hold back his tears as he recounted their memories before the war. Khaled and Reem's story instantly went viral; secondary artistic productions

---

13 Melissa Wall, "Citizen Journalism: A retrospective on what we know, an agenda of what we don't," *Digital Journalism* 3, no. 6 (2015): 797–813.

14 Jomana Karadsheh and Florence Davey-Attlee, "'I kissed her but she wouldn't wake up.' Grandfather grieves for 3-year-old granddaughter killed as she slept in Gaza," CNN, November 29, 2023. https://edition.cnn.com/2023/11/29/middleeast/gaza-truce-israel-grandfather-returns-home-intl-hnk/index.html

like paintings, embroidery, songs, and animations were created in their memory, and protests were organized on Reem's birthday on December 23.

Another video that went viral captured Dr. Amira al-Assouli as she risked her own life and ran through gunfire to rescue a wounded Gazan man who was shot by an Israeli sniper.[15] Dr. Assouli became a symbol of Palestinian women's courage and steadfastness. A most recent viral video was of a Gazan father as he wept when learning that an Israeli airstrike had killed his newly born twins along with their mother while he had gone to get their birth certificates.[16] In the videos, the father, Mohammed Abu Al-Qumsan, is consoled by other Palestinian men who, together, cry with him.

IMAGE 2. *Drawing that depicts Palestinian Dr. Amira Al-Asooli as she rescues a wounded men under gunfire.*

Reproduced with permission from the illustrator, Admir Delić @avet_rio_gribaje (Instagram)

These tragic images and human stories can become ingrained in the memories of those who are exposed to them daily on social media. The psychological term for recollections people form for important life events conveyed to them by someone else, such as a friend or family member, is *vicarious memories.*[17] In most cases vicarious memories involve salient personal events that other people have lived through. Empirical work shows

---

15 "Gaza doctor recalls rescue during hospital raid," *BBC* video [00:56], March 14, 2024. https://www.bbc.com/news/av/world-middle-east-68539701

"Amira Al-Assouli – Palestinians Celebrate Heroic Khan Yunis Doctor in Viral Video," *Palestine Chronicle,* February 11, 2024. https://www.palestinechronicle.com/amira-al-assouli-palestinians-celebrate-heroic-khan-yunis-doctor-in-viral-video/

16 "Palestinian newborn twins killed as father obtained birth certificates," *Reuters,* August 14, 2024. https://www.reuters.com/world/middle-east/palestinian-newborn-twins-killed-father-obtained-birth-certificates-2024-08-14/

17 David B. Pillemer, Kristina L. Steiner, Kie J. Kuwabara, Dorthe Kirkegaard Thomsen, and Connie Svob,"Vicarious Memories," *Consciousness and Cognition* 36 (November 2015): 233–245.

Dorthe Thomsen and David Pillemer, "I Know My Story and I Know Your Story: Developing a conceptual framework for vicarious life sotries," *Journal of Personality* 85, no. 4 (2016): 464–480.

that vicarious memories share similar phenomenological characteristics as autobiographical memories, which are memories that people hold for events they personally experience that are important for their identity. Although to a lesser extent compared to autobiographical memories, vicarious memories are vivid, emotionally intense, and visually salient.[18] Importantly, like autobiographical memories, they serve several key functions like forming a person's identity, helping them understand themselves and the world, impacting their life decisions, and influencing their relationships with others, etc.[19]

To date, psychological work has mostly focused on the vicarious memories people form for life events recounted to them by other people whom they personally know.[20] In the age of digitalization, however, people are daily exposed to strangers' life events through social media. The vicarious memories they construct for those events might not be as phenomenologically rich and functional as regular vicarious memories because of the lack of personal bonds with the source of the memory. In the case of the war on Gaza, however, the circumstances are different. As mentioned before, social media users may well have formed personal bonds with the Gazan journalists/content creators they routinely follow. Unlike regular vicarious events, these Gazans usually directly share the events that they witness by means of images/videos rather than retelling an event they have experienced. As a result, this kind of more direct media witnessing[21] can lead to the formation of strong vicarious memories of genocide among people who follow it via social media. As a result, the vicarious memories formed around the Gazan genocide can be as phenomenologically salient and functional for people's identities as regular vicarious memories.

But it is not only vicarious memories that are created during this process. Whether it is the boy who carried his little brother's remains in his backpack,[22] or the child who looked into the camera with wide-open eyes

18 Emily Pond and Carole Peterson, "Highly Emotional Vicarious Memories," *Memory* 28, no. 8 (2020): 1051–1066.

Pillemer et al., "Vicarious Memories."

19 Ibid.

20 David B. Pillemer, Dorthe K. Thomsen, and Robyn Fivush, "Vicarious Memory Promotes Social Adaptation and Enriches the Self," *Journal of Applied Research in Memory and Cognition* 13, no. 2 (2024): 159–71.

21 Maria Kyriakidou, "Media Witnessing: Exploring the audience of distant suffering," *Media, Culture, and Society* 37, no. 2 (2015).

22 "Al Jazeera's Youmna El Sayed on the boy who had his dead baby brother in a backpack | UNAPOLOGETIC," *Middle East Eye* news video [4:42], April 12, 2024. https://www.youtube.com/watch?v=hLMwNIAkZpg

in shock after an Israeli attack,[23] or the Gazan tailor who uses a bike pedal to power his sewing machine,[24] the personal stories of the Gazan people facing a genocidal onslaught can also facilitate the formation of collective memories.[25] In the most basic sense, collective memories refer to memories that are shared across a community that inform that community's identity.[26] Hence, collective memories can be critical for both personal and collective identity formation.

These vicarious memories and collective memories cumulatively have the potential to challenge the schematic narrative templates that have been prevalent in the mainstream media. The first narrative—that "both sides are responsible for the violence to a comparable extent"[27]—is now much more difficult to contend, as the public constantly was exposed not only to the sheer difference in death tolls but also to the gruesome details of individual tragedies the Israeli army inflict on the Gazan people daily. The power asymmetry is too obvious to hide; people can easily see numerous examples of the devastating consequences of Israel having the capacity to instantly cut Gazans' sources of water, electricity, and food while Palestinians cannot do anything to protect their basic resources.

The second narrative—that "Palestine-Israel is a conflict between moderates and extremists"—has also been challenged strongly during the current assault on Gaza. In this narrative, the label "extremists" is almost exclusive attributed to Palestinians, even though the "terror" inflicted on Palestinians by Israelis is far greater in quantity and intensity.[28] The images in social media of Gazans trying to survive Israeli bombardments and striving to create a sense of "normalcy" while under constant attacks defies the portrayal of Palestinians as extremists.

---

23 "Palestinian Child in Shock after Surviving Israeli Attack in Gaza," *Al Jazeera* NewsFeed video [00:59], October 19, 2023. https://www.aljazeera.com/program/newsfeed/2023/10/19/palestinian-child-in-shock-after-surviving-israeli-attack-in-gaza

24 Fadi Shana, "Gaza Tailor Uses Pedal Power for Sewing Machine as War Grinds On," *Reuters,* January 15, 2024. https://www.reuters.com/world/middle-east/gaza-tailor-uses-pedal-power-sewing-machine-war-grinds-2024-01-15/

25 Maurice Halbwachs, *On Collective Memory,* ed. by Lewis Coser (Chicago: University of Chicago Press, 1952/1992).

26 William Hirst and David Manier, "Towards a Psychology of Collective Memory," *Memory* 16, no. 3 (2008): 183–200.

27 Greg Shupak, *The Wrong Story: Palestine, Israel, and the Media* (OR Books, 2018).

28 Ibid.

One sub-text of this extremism narrative is that Muslim men[29]—and specifically Palestinian men[30]—are inherently and irreversibly violent. This stereotype not only denies victimhood to Palestinian men violently killed by Israel, just as are Palestinian women and children, but also portrays them as incapable of showing human feelings such as compassion, kindness, sorrow etc.[31] Countless videos of Palestinian men shared on social media, however, challenge such stereotypes. Reem's grandfather, Khaled Nabhan, who is now called "Uncle Khaled" in social media, creates a juxtaposition to the Western schema of "terrorist" with his long beard and turban, as he tenderly cares not only for injured and diseased Palestinians, but even for cats suffering from Israeli violence.[32] The images of Palestinian male doctors smiling and singing to their patients to give them moral support,[33] the father who places the biscuits he bought on his deceased son's hand,[34] crying men compassionately consoling each other for their family's deaths,[35] and many others disrupt the long-held schema of Palestinian men as "violent extremists."[36]

The third schematic narrative that underscores "Israel's right to defend itself against Palestinian violence" is also defied by the instances raised previously that emphasize the indiscriminate targeting of civilians and the

---

29 S. Mishra, "'Saving' Muslim Women and Fighting Muslim Men: Analysis of Representations in the New York Times," *Global Media Journal* 6, no. 11 (2007).

30 Khaled Beydoun, "Demonizing Palestinian Men," *Pen>Sword* Substack, December 8, 2023. https://khaledbeydoun.substack.com/p/demonizing-palestinian-men

31 Margherita Cordellini, "The Dehumanization of Palestinian Men by Western Media," *Berkeley Political Review,* April 20, 2024. https://bpr.studentorg.berkeley.edu/2024/04/20/the-dehumanization-of-palestinian-men-by-western-media/

Maya Mikdashi, "Can Palestinian Men be Victims? Gendering Israel's War on Gaza," *Jaddaliyya,* July 23, 2014. https://www.jadaliyya.com/Details/30991

32 See @a7mhisham Instagram post, December 29, 2023. https://www.instagram.com/p/C1cmaoLtlVA/

See @a7mhisham Instagram post, December 12, 2023. https://www.instagram.com/p/C0xG5-jNDCK/

Ahmed Hisham @a7mhisham Instagram page: https://www.instagram.com/a7mhisham/

33 "Gaza doctors sing 'we will remain'," *Middle East Monitor* video clip [00:57], October 26, 2024. https://www.middleeastmonitor.com/20231026-gaza-doctors-sing-we-will-remain/

34 See @middleeasteye Instagram post, December 28, 2023. https://www.instagram.com/middleeasteye/reel/C1asQmLsMpP/

35 See @alximrdch Instagram post, August 13, 2024. https://www.instagram.com/p/C-nJkpGoATh/

36 Tessi Moghaddam, "Heartbreak and Hope: The Unheard Stories of Gaza's Fathers," Euro-Med Human Rights Monitor, June 17, 2024. https://euromedmonitor.org/en/article/6373/Heartbreak-and-Hope:-The-Unheard-Stories-of-Gaza%27s-Fathers

stark asymmetry between the violence inflicted by Israelis vs. Palestinians. Notable here, however, is another social media phenomenon that has been taking place since the beginning of the war on Gaza; namely TikTok videos posted by Israeli soldiers. The schematic discourse that goes hand in hand with the narrative of "Israel's right to defend itself" is that the Israel Defense Forces (IDF) is "the most moral army in the world."[37] The videos/images shared by Israeli soldiers on social media, however, utterly invalidate this discourse. There are countless videos/images that show Israeli soldiers cheering and dancing as they destruct civilian buildings/infrastructures,[38] looting Palestinian homes, shops, vehicles etc.,[39] and toying with and wearing Palestinian women's lingerie found in destroyed homes.[40] Middle East Monitor has collected and recorded a portion of such images/videos, which revealed six main categories of posts: "degradation & humiliation," "wanton destruction of civilian infrastructure," "violating intimate privacy," "looting," "indiscriminate killing," "celebrating genocide."[41] These categories show the various ways Israeli soldiers violate the international conventions of war. To date, there has not been public disciplinary actions taken against the Israeli soldiers who are involved in these social media posts. The only known disciplinary action for social media content has been taken against an Israeli soldier who filmed himself with the bodies of Israeli hostages near Khan Younis.[42] The fact that IDF soldiers continue to share these outrageous images/videos with total impunity—together with numerous other visual

---

37 Neve Gordon, "The myth of Israel's 'most moral army'," *Al Jazeera*, October 16, 2023. https://www.aljazeera.com/opinions/2023/10/16/the-myth-of-israels-most-moral

38 "Israeli soldiers post distressing content out of Gaza," *CNN* news video [3:19], February 20, 2024. https://edition.cnn.com/videos/world/2024/02/20/exp-israel-soldiers-jeremy-diamond-pkg-022009aseg1-cnni-world.cnn

39 Samuel Forey, "Israeli soldiers deployed in Gaza post their abuses on social media," *LeMonde*, February 28, 2024. https://www.lemonde.fr/en/international/article/2024/02/28/israeli-soldiers-deployed-in-gaza-post-their-abuses-on-social-media_6568987_4.html

40 Estelle Shirbon and Pola Grzanka, "Israeli soldiers play with Gaza women's underwear in online posts," Reuters, March 28, 2024. https://www.reuters.com/world/middle-east/israeli-soldiers-play-with-gaza-womens-underwear-online-posts-2024-03-28/

Younis Tirawi @ytirawi on *X*: "Israeli soldiers in Rafah looting and wearing women underwear and dresses belonging to displaced or killed Palestinian women," August 27, 2024. https://x.com/ytirawi/status/1828377369683300584

41 "Misconduct of Israeli Soldiers in Gaza," *Middle East Monitor* special feature. https://www.middleeastmonitor.com/specials/israeli-misconduct/index.html

42 Avi Ashkenaz, "IDF soldier's TikTok video of hostage bodies sparks spread of rumors across Israel," *Jerusalem Post*, July 25, 2024. https://www.jpost.com/israel-news/article-811847

evidence—dismantles the narrative that "Israel—as the most moral army in the world—defends itself against Palestinian violence."

These shifts in long-held narratives have the potential to transform the overall discourse surrounding the Israel-Palestine crisis. Another critical point is that these shifts do not happen just due to an outside force but also because of the direct actions of the Palestinian journalists and content creators who courageously continue to share the details of the Gazan genocide under the most difficult circumstances. So, Palestinians are the main agents driving this narrative shift, which establishes and underlines the agency of Palestinians, who have usually been portrayed as either passive/powerless victims or as violent extremists. Palestinian agency is also re-constituted through images that convey the resilience of Gazans during an on-going genocide.[43] As these memories of genocide travel across the world, the agency of Palestinian people couples with the agency of the wider public to create a wave of trans-national pro-Palestinian activism.

Travelling Memories and Transnational Activism

In the field of memory studies there is an ongoing move from "meth-odological nationalism" towards "transnational memory." Memory studies have long dealt with memories that are contained in and maintained by social units, the most well-studied of which has been the nation.[44] Memory scholars now argue for a transcultural (or transnational) approach to memory that focuses on memory generated beyond national borders.[45] The basic tenet of this theoretical turn is the acknowledgement that memory constantly travels across borders, cultures, nations etc.[46] Erll argues that memories are, in fact, constituted through movement, and that such constant motion is what keeps memories alive.[47] This travelling of memories was always present due to the movement of peoples, ideas, and goods, but now, with new media technologies

---

43 In this chapter, I choose to focus on the positive effects of social media in shifting mainstream narratives. I should, however, also note that being constantly exposed to images of massacres and violent deaths can desensitize viewers to human suffering and can contribute to the further dehumanization of victims. Being exposed to graphic content can also create vicarious trauma, which can debilitate people's capacity to engage in action. It can also lead the victims themselves to feel even more helpless as they witness the world's inaction despite the thousands of images shared in social media that convey their suffering. One needs to be aware of these various aspects of following news through social media.

44 Chiara De Cesari and Ann Rigney, eds., *Transnational Memory: Circulation, Articulation, Scales | Media and Cultural Memory* 19 (2014).

45 Rick Crownshaw, ed., *Transcultural Memory* (Abingdon: Routledge, 2014).

46 Astrid Erll, "Travelling Memory," *Parallax* 17, no. 4 (2011): 4–18.

47 Ibid.

and the age of globalism, this motion has become much more evident and accelerated.

Memories of tragedies that travel across and beyond national borders, however, might not necessarily produce changes in perceptions, attitudes, and action. As Erll points out travelling memories can involve an "idle running: travel without effect."[48] In the case of the memories of the Gazan genocide, however, the motion of memories cannot be characterized as "idle running." As outlined in the previous section, these memories do seem to bring about changes in perceptions and attitudes through the shifts they impel in schematic narratives. More importantly, they can lead to changes in action.

Since the assault on Gaza began, there has been a sustained global pro-Palestine movement that involves diverse groups of people with diverse means. The forms of this activism range from traditional protests[49] to university encampments[50] to blocking of roads/bridges/ports,[51] etc. Although the forms of protests vary as a function of the context, country, social group etc., the transnational character of these demonstrations is manifested in their synchronicity and in the shared symbols (e.g., watermelon), materials (e.g., the keffiyeh), slogans (e.g., "from the river to the sea, Palestine will be free"), songs (e.g., "Leve Palestina" by Kofia), dances (e.g., *dabkhe*), etc.

Another important aspect of these protests is that they almost always include references to individual stories of Gazans that are shared by Gazans, whether in forms of slogans, songs, posters, banners etc. One striking example is the story of Hind Rajab, who was killed together with her relatives when an Israeli tank fired at their family car.[52] Hind's case is especially tragic because she survived the first gunfire, called paramedics to beg for help,

---

48 Astrid Erll, p.15.

49 Beyza Binnur Dönmez, "Protests in Europe demand end to 'genocide' in Gaza," *AA*, January 28, 2024. https://www.aa.com.tr/en/europe/protests-in-europe-demand-end-to-genocide-in-gaza/3120914

50 "List of pro-Palestinian protests on university campuses in 2024," *Wikipedia*. https://en.wikipedia.org/wiki/List_of_pro-Palestinian_protests_on_university_campuses_in_2024

51 Ed Komenda, "Protesters calling for Gaza cease-fire block road at Tacoma port while military cargo ship docks," *AP News*, November 6, 2023. https://apnews.com/article/israel-hamas-gaza-protests-supply-ship-c43e58036416e7e883616d84561a539d

Nadda Osman, "War on Gaza: Pro-Palestine protesters block Israeli ship from port of Melbourne," *Middle East Eye*, January 21, 2024. https://www.middleeasteye.net/news/war-gaza-australia-pro-palestine-protesters-block-israeli-ship-port-melbourne

The Canadian Press, "Gaza protesters blockade truck access to Port of Vancouver," *Global News*, February 1, 2024. https://globalnews.ca/news/10266358/gaza-protesters-blockade-access-vancouver-port/

52 "Israeli tank fired at Hind Rajab family car from metres away: Investigation," *Aljazeera*, June 23, 2024. https://www.aljazeera.com/news/2024/6/23/israeli-tank-fired-at-hind-rajab-family-car-from-metres-away-investigation

and bled to death as she waited for the paramedics to arrive, who were also killed by Israeli soldiers, although they had received permission from Israeli authorities to rescue Hind.[53] On February 3 the Palestinian Red Crescent Society released the recording of Hind begging for help, which instantly spread across social media. Her fate and that of the paramedics became clear 12 days later after the Israeli soldiers withdrew the area. Hind's story become emblematic of the war crimes of the Israeli army.

On April 30th Columbia student protestors occupied Hamilton Hall and renamed it "Hind's Hall," hanging a banner above the building's entrance with her name on it.[54] The history of Hamilton Hall is especially significant because it has been taken over time and again by Columbia students to protest the Vietnam War, apartheid in South Africa, and the demolition of the venue where Malcolm X was assassinated.[55] So, the renaming of the building as "Hind's Hall" not only commemorates Hind's tragic death but also links the Gazan Genocide to other historical injustices against the Vietnamese people, South Africans, Black Americans, and to their various struggles for liberation. Right after the renaming, famous American rapper Macklemore released his single titled "Hind's Hall," which expresses solidarity with university encampments, criticizes U.S. support for Israel, and calls for a ceasefire in Gaza.[56] The song instantly went viral on social media and on other online platforms.

Hind's case illustrates how the memories of genocide now travel around the world, are commemorated in various forms, and inspire individual and collective action. It is important to note that this motion does not happen in one direction only. Activist movements themselves can also lead to the formation of collective memories at both local and global levels. In addition to registering local harms, these memories can involve a more general embedding of various forms of activism or of specific instances of protest. A significant example of transnational memory that has been formed around an act of protest is undoubtedly that of Aaron Bushnell, a member of the U.S. air

---

53 "'The Night Won't End': Biden's War on Gaza," *Fault Lines* feature [1:18:36], Aljazeera, June 21, 2024. https://www.aljazeera.com/program/fault-lines/2024/6/21/the-night-wont-end-bidens-war-on-gaza-2

54 Ali Watkins, "Columbia Protesters Rename Hamilton Hall to 'Hind's Hall'," *New York Times,* April 30, 2024. https://www.nytimes.com/2024/04/30/nyregion/columbia-protesters-hind-rajab-hamilton-hall.html

55 "'Hind Hall': How Columbia's Hamilton Hall became its signature protest hub," *Aljazeera,* May 1, 2024. https://www.aljazeera.com/news/2024/5/1/columbias-hamilton-hall-a-history-of-student-action-at-gaza-protest-hub

56 "HIND'S HALL," *Macklemore* YouTube video [2:48], May 9, 2024. https://www.youtube.com/watch?v=ITVIlr5jUMw

"Hind's Hall," *Wikipedia.* https://en.wikipedia.org/wiki/Hind%27s_Hall

force who set himself on fire in front of the U.S. Israeli embassy, screaming "Free Palestine" seconds after declaring he will "no longer be complicit in genocide."[57] Aaron Bushnell's memory has travelled back to Palestine, with his name given to a street in the Palestinian town of Jericho. The mayor of the town stated: "We didn't know him, and he didn't know us. There were no social, economic or political ties between us. What we share is a love for freedom and a desire to stand against these attacks."[58] Gazans paid tribute to his memory by holding up his pictures in various places in Gaza with statements like "All eyes on Rafah. And Rafah's eyes on Aaron Bushnell" or "From Gaza to Texas we will never forget you Aaron Bushnell."[59] These examples demonstrate the multidirectional movement of memories that is now accelerated to an incredible speed through social media. This accelerated movement of memories of genocide and activism not only inspires and sustains various layers of collective action but also provides an avenue through which communities can envision an alternative collective future.

Future Thinking and Radical Hope

What does the future hold? Psychological work shows that our memory system is not only responsible for remembering the past but also for imagining the future. We rely on our memories when we imagine events that might happen in our future.[60] This characteristic is not only specific to personal memories but also applies to collective memories. The way we imagine the collective future is tightly connected to the way we remember the collective past, especially through the narrative templates that we rely on.[61] Moreover, people usually envision the future to be more positive than the past and this

57 Moira Donegan, "Aaron Bushnell set himself on fire outside an Israeli embassy. It is our loss he is no longer with us," *The Guardian*, February 28, 2024. https://www.theguardian.com/commentisfree/2024/feb/28/aaron-bushnell-self-immolation-gaza-israel

58 Benay Blend, "'Everybody's fight': Palestinians hail the sacrifice of Corrie, Bushnell," *Aljazeera*, March 16, 2024. https://www.aljazeera.com/news/2024/3/16/everybodys-fight-palestinians-hail-the-sacrifice-of-corrie-bushnell

59 "Gaza Pays Tribute to Aaron Bushnell and Honors His Memory," *Middle East Monitor* video [00:22], March 2, 2024. https://www.middleeastmonitor.com/20240302-gaza-pays-tribute-to-aaron-bushnell-and-honours-his-memory/

60 Karl K. Szpunar, "Episodic future thought: An emerging concept," *Perspectives on Psychological Science* 5, no. 2 (2010): 142–62.

Daniel L. Schacter, Roland G. Benoit, and Karl K. Szpunar, "Episodic future thinking: Mechanisms and functions," *Current Opinion in Behavioral Sciences* 17 (2017): 41–50.

61 Meymune N. Topçu and William Hirst, (2022). Collective mental time travel: Current research and future directions. Progress in brain research, 274, no. 1 (2022): 71–97.

is related to the agency they attribute to themselves and their social groups.[62] Such collective future thinking can involve both the act of collectively imagining the future as a group and the act of individually imagining the future for the collective group.[63]

If the analysis here is correct and transnational memories of genocide have indeed created narrative shifts around the world on the Palestine-Israel issue, the next question is what kind of collective future can we imagine through our reliance on these globally formed vicarious and collective memories? A future in which Palestinians are liberated and live in dignity and security as they deserve—or a future in which Palestinians continue to face dehumanization, ethnic-cleansing, and genocide until Palestine is completely eradicated? When addressing this question, the concept of "radical hope" comes into play.

Introduced by Mosley and her colleagues, radical hope differs from traditional approaches to hope with "its focus on a commitment and courage to achieve a vision involving new forms of collective flourishing."[64] They theorize that radical hope has two main components: collective memory and faith/agency. These components orient radical hope in the intersection of past vs. future and individual vs. collective. With its acknowledgment of histories of oppression/resistance and the capacities of agency, radical hope differs from optimism or wishful thinking. In this sense, as French and colleagues argue, "radical hope allows for a sense of agency to change things for the greater good—a belief that one can fight for justice and that the fight will not be futile."[65] Although this concept is discussed in the context of oppression

Meymune N. Topçu, *The Role of Narratives in Collective Future Thinking: The Case of American Exceptionalism* (New York: The New School, 2021).

62 Meymune N. Topçu and William Hirst, "Remembering a nation's past to imagine its future: The role of event specificity, phenomenology, valence, and perceived agency," *Journal of Experimental Psychology: Learning, Memory, and Cognition* 46, no. 3 (2020): 563.

Meymune N. Topçu and William Hirst, (2024). When the personal and the collective intersects: Memory, future thinking, and perceived agency during the COVID-19 pandemic. Journal of Experimental Psychology: General.

63 Piotr M. Szpunar and Karl K. Szpunar, "Collective future thought: Concept, function, and implications for collective memory studies," *Memory Studies* 9, no. 4 (2016): 376–89.

64 Della V. Mosley, Helen A. Neville, Nayeli Y. Chavez-Dueñas, Hector Y. Adames, Jioni A. Lewis, Bryana H. French, "Radical hope in revolting times: Proposing a culturally relevant psychological framework," *Social and Personality Psychology Compass* 14, no. 1 (January 2020 |e12512): 3.

65 Bryana H. French, Jioni A. Lewis, Della V. Mosley, Hector Y. Adames, Nayeli Y. Chavez-Dueñas, Grace A. Chen, and Helen A. Neville, "Toward a

and the resistance of people of color in the U.S., it can easily be applied to the Palestinian context.

Despite the gruesome individual and collective tragedies that have been taking place in Palestine since the Nakba (1948), the narrative shifts happening during the genocide in Gaza enables an active and global stance of radical hope. This has become possible especially due to the agency of Palestinians who initiated and facilitated these narrative shifts not only through relentlessly conveying the realities on the ground but also through their resilience. By definition, a radical hope for Gaza (and Palestine) would involve an understanding of histories and memories of oppression, resilience, and resistance accompanied by an envisioning of future possibilities that is rooted in a sense of moral responsibility.[66] Such "radical hope" is not only an option but a necessity since the perceived hegemony of Western elites over the discourse on human rights, international law, and democracy has also been dismantled during the genocide in Gaza.

---

psychological framework of radical healing in communities of color," *The Counseling Psychologist* 48, no. 1 (2020): 13.

66 Della V. Mosley et al., "Radical hope in revolting times," 3

Dimensions of Genocide

Starvation and Famine in Gaza
Children of Gaza are
the most poignant victims of the war.

Hilal Elver

Prelude

The 13-year-old boy and his 8-year-old sister wandered barefoot in an abandoned semi-destroyed field to hunt vegetables and then went to the bushes to collect sticks for a fire that their mother uses to cook a once-a-day meal. A little further, near the tent city, you see even a five-year-old boy waiting for a meal with an empty pan. The charity food truck might come if he is lucky enough and can get closer to it without bumping up against other children and adults similarly waiting for food aid, or without becoming a target for the IDF's bullets. Sometimes trucks are looted on their way to the distribution centers. Most of the time, half a pita bread is distributed for the entire day, sometimes a can of beans that he is expected to share with the rest of his family. UNRWA workers are forced to restrict their food distribution to one can of tuna and one bottle of water per family; "simply don't have enough" they say. People are surviving on less than 2 liters of water per person per day, falling short by 15 liters of the basic survival level water requirements set by the World Health Organization (WHO).

One of the Gaza residents explained their condition with these words: "If we don't die from bombing, for sure, we will die from starvation or disease."

Hilal Elver is a professor of international law, specializing in human rights and international environmental law, and the co-director of the Climate Change, Democracy and Human Security project at the University of California at Santa Barbara. From May 2014 to May 2020, Elver served as the United Nations Special Rapporteur on the right to food. She is currently serving as a member of the Steering Committee of the High-Level Panel of Experts of the UN World Committee of Food Security (CFS), and a member of the Scientific Advisory Committee of the UN Food Systems Hub.

In late November, a spokeperson for the World Health Organization repeated the same dire prediction: "Without urgent action to repair the Gaza Strip's rapidly collapsing health system, more people would soon die from diseases than from Israel's bombings. There are no medicines, no vaccination activities, no access to safe water and hygiene and no food." [1] *During the most recent four weeks of the war aid agencies, and relevant international institutions are stressing the urgency of the humanitarian aid, to no avail.*

Children in Gaza grow up fast. Far from experiencing an innocent childhood, they find themselves in the most dangerous battlefield in the world. Their life is very unpredictable, leaving them wondering when or if they will get the next meal or be a victim of a bomb that would kill them or leave them disabled for the rest of their lives. Considering that about half of Gaza's entire population, 1.1 million of them, are children, they are the most silent victims of the war. Nearly 15,000 children have died at this writing, thousands are missing under demolished buildings, another several thousands are severely injured, and all can be presumed traumatized. Simply put, Gaza has become a graveyard for children, with their fates unknown and thousands of them missing.

The misery of the Gaza children does not stop there. More than 10 children on average have lost one or both of their legs or arms every day since October 7, with many amputations performed without anesthesia. [2]

Gaza amputation rates according to UNICEF are much higher compared to other conflicts and disasters. In first two months of the war the casualty figure was about 1,000. [3] *In Ukraine, after two years of conflict, there are 30 known cases of child amputees, according to available records.*

If this does not demonstrate Israeli intent—a calculated Israeli plan to eliminate or destroy the generation to come—what is it? Can we not say this is a war against the children of Gaza?

THE PURPOSE of this chapter first is to bring to the attention of readers the fastest and most comprehensive famine conditions that have affected the entire

---

1 Ibtisam Mahdi, "Gaza's health crisis 'catastrophic,' say Palestinian experts," *+972 Magazine,* December 20, 2023. https://www.972mag.com/gaza-health-crisis-disease/

2 Jessie Yeung, Radina Gigova, and Mohammed Tawfeeq, "More than 10 children losing legs in Gaza every day as dire health crisis grows, aid groups say," *CNN,* January 7, 2024. https://edition.cnn.com/2024/01/08/middleeast/gaza-children-losing-legs-disease-intl-hnk/index.html

3 Arafat Barbakh, Maggie Fick and Emma Farge, "Gaza's child amputees face further risks without expert care," *Reuters,* January 4, 2024. As of September 2024, 11,000 children have suffered amputation. https://www.reuters.com/world/middle-east/gazas-child-amputees-face-further-risks-without-expert-care-2024-01-04/

population of Gaza since October 9. We haven't witnessed such a starvation situation turned into famine at such speed in any other conflict in anywhere in the world. One of the causes of the Gaza famine was the culmination of an ongoing planned Israeli policy limiting food access to Gazans ever since the Gaza blockade in 2007. No famine starts in one night, and it is always a result of political decisions and is always man-made. However, each case of famine has its own story. The anathomic picture of the Gaza Famine demonstrates that such a planned control of entire livelihood of the Gazan population not only takes the lives of thousands, but it also goes beyond crime of deliberate starvation to reach the scale of famine, and eventually substantiates the commission of the crime of genocide. This will have a longlasting impact not only on Gaza, but on the entire Palestine Occupied Territories (West Bank, and East Jerusalem), as well as on regional peace. The second part of this chapter focuses on access to food and water used as a weapon of war, and the slow development of international law in addressing the crime of starvation, as well as the ongoing impunity of perpetrators, including a discussion about the possibility of introducing famine crime into criminal law.

Post October 7: Life in the Gaza Strip

After the 7th of October, the Gaza Strip, already besieged for 17 years, has entered into a new regimen, one of absolute islolation and blockade. No food, no fuel, no electricty, no medicines, no vaccination activities, no access to safe water and hygene, and no shelter as per the dehumanizing language of the Israeli Minister of Defence, Chaim Herzog. Approximatelly 2.2 million Gazans area being collectively punished by Israel. In first 100 days, 24,000 people—more than 1% of the entire population, around 70% of them women and children—have been killed by the Israeli Defense Forces (IDF), around 85% of people in Gaza have been displaced from their homes, with many having been forced to flee multiple times.[4]

Basic human needs for survival have been gradually depleted, with severe humanitarian conditions in Gaza quickly reaching catastrophic levels that haven't ever been seen in any known conflicts anywhere. If the war is still going on, a mortality report is difficult to conduct in any ongoing conflict. This is even more difficult in Gaza as there is no access from outside because of heavy fighting and the complete siege of Gaza by the occupying power.

---

4 OCHA, "Hostilities in the Gaza Strip and Israel | Flash Update #95," *reliefweb*, January 17, 2024. https://reliefweb.int/report/occupied-palestinian-territory/hostilities-gaza-strip-and-israel-flash-update-95-enarhe

As of July 22, 2024, according to the Gaza Ministry of Health, the death toll reached 40,000 people. Despite Israel's claim, no evidence of inflated mortality reporting was found.[5] On the contrary, the British medical journal *Lancet* calculated that the true death toll of the Gaza War, if indirect impacts of war are calculated, could be over 186,000 casualties, accounting for 8% of Gaza population.[6] The true number likely includes more than 10 to 20,000 people still trapped under rubble of 35% of buildings in the Gaza Strip,[7] plus those who have succumbed to the secondary effects of the conflict, such as malnutrtion, infectious diseases, lack of medical care, and the negative impact of loss of finance from UNRWA, one of the very few humanitararin organizations still active in the Gaza Strip.[8]

Save the Children estimates approximately 21,000 children are missing in the chaos of the war in Gaza. This includes 17,000 children, unaccompanied, separated or lost from parents, whether detained or buried in unmarked graves, with an estimated 4,000 children buried under the rubble.[9]

Basic necessities, including clean water, food, safe shelter, and sanitation, are scarce for those who are still alive. The massive destruction of basic necessities has contributed to what has become an irreversible humanitarian catastrophe. UN Secretary General Antonio Guterres calls it "humanity's catastrophe, not humanitarian catastrophe," noting that the international community has failed to discharge its responsibility to do all in its power to stop the war.[10]

Gazans are living in tents, partly destroyed school buildings, or on the streets with no shelter from the hot or cold weather and bombing. Life-threatening, water-borne infectious diseases are taking a toll on children and the elderly.

---

5 Zeina Jamaluddine, Francesco Checchi, and Oona M R Campbell, "Excess mortality in Gaza: Oct 7–26, 2023" [Correspondence], Lancet 402, no. 10418 (December 9, 2023): 2189–90. Available at: https://www.thelancet.com/journals/lancet/article/PIIS0140-6736(23)02640-5/fulltext

6 Rasha Khatiba, Martin McKee, and Salim Yusuf, "Counting the Dead in Gaza: Difficult but Essential," *Lancet* 404, no. 10449 (July 20, 2024): 237–38. https://www.thelancet.com/journals/lancet/article/PIIS0140-6736(24)01169-3/fulltext

7 UN Office at Geneva, "10,000 people feared buried under the rubble in Gaza," May 2, 2024. https://www.ungeneva.org/en/news-media/news/2024/05/93055/10000-people-feared-buried-under-rubble-gaza

8 Ibid.

9 "Gaza's missing children: Over 20,000 children estimated to be lost, disappeared, detained, buried under the rubble or in mass graves," Save the Children, June 24, 2024. https://www.savethechildren.org.uk/news/media-centre/press-releases/over-20000-children-estimated-to-be-lost-in-gaza

10 "Gaza humanitarian disaster heralds 'breakdown' of society," *UN News,* December 8, 2023. https://news.un.org/en/story/2023/12/1144547

Besides the high number of casualties, the overall impact of the war has resulted in the destruction of many resources, including infrastructure; simply anything necessary for human life in Gaza has been destroyed. Food systems met with the largest destruction: 80 to 96 percent of agricultural assets, including greenhouses and irrigation systems, have been damaged or destroyed. A total of 81 percent of the Gaza fishing sector has been permamentely destroyed, 98 percent was damaged. The damage and destruction have also extended to 57 percent of wash facilities, 62 percent of roads, with 62 percent of housing having become uninhabitable. What's more—80 percent of the population has been forcefully displaced, most of them multiple times, with the same share of the working population having lost their livelihood and access to income-generating activity.[11] Eighty-four percent of health equipment has been destroyed, and more than 650 000 Palestinian children are out of school. Waste management facilities have been damaged or destroyed, and power has been cut or interrupted.[12] The United Nations Environment Program (UNEP) estimated that at least 100 000 cubic meters of sewage and wastewater are being dumped daily onto the land or into the Mediterranean Sea. As a result, 100 percent of the population is reliant on food aid to survive and subject to acute malnutrition, extreme hunger, and infectious diseases.

The Silent Killer: Severe Malnutrition

Deeper and longer impacts of severe malnutrition on young children, pregnant women, elderly people, and persons who are already sick or have underlying conditions can make malnutrition lethal. The World Health Organization (WHO) and UNICEF warn that young children between 0 to 2 years old cannot tolerate even short periods of malnutrition. A senior UNICEF advisor bluntly says "if a child is malnourished, particularly under two years of age, they are unable to cognitively catch up with other children. The brain is such a big part of caloric and nutrient consumption in a child's development."[13]

In March 2024, a WHO report indicated that 0.8 % of children under 5 had been acutely malnourished; 15% of children between the age of 0 to 2

11 Rob Vos, Ismahane Elouafi, and Johan Swinnen, "Famine in Gaza, questions for research and preventive action," *Nature Food* 5 (2024): 346–48. https://doi.org/10.1038/s43016-024-00990-3.......

12 Food Security Information Network (FSIN) and Global Network Against Food Crises, 2024.

13 Lilia Sebouai and Maeve Cullinan, "Rising hunger in Gaza 'turning children into skeletons'," *The Telegraph,* January 8, 2024. https://www.telegraph.co.uk/global-health/science-and-disease/children-skeletons-rising-hunger-gaza-famine/.

in the North, 5% in South had been acutely malnourished, while 20 children died from malnutrition and dehydration. Infectious diseases and malnutrition were quickly increasing in Gaza as the war entered its ninth month.

Even if the war ends today, the destruction of Gaza's food systems will exert serious negative impacts on the development of current and future generations, and the impact of malnutrition on vulnerable groups will have devastating results. We might not immediately comprehend the importance of the deeper impacts of severe malnutrition deriving from such sustained violence directed at Gazan residential neighborhoods or places of sheltering. The current situation is dire and bloody, making any precise assessment of longer term effects unreliable. Under such circumstances it is not surprising that famine is feared to reach Gaza in the very near future.

A Deadly Combination: Hunger, All Forms of Malnutrition and Communicable Diseases

Another lethal consequence of severe malnutrition is an increase in infectious diseases.[14] Gazans are living in tents, partly destroyed school buildings, or on the streets without any shelter from cold and wet weather and the recently extremely hot summer. When rain arrives, broken sewage canals spill over the streets and onto the floors of buildings.

As a result of clean water shortages and the destruction of sewage systems, water borne diseases skyrocketed. These are treatable under normal circumstances, but for malnourished children with weak immune systems, such diseases can kill. According to UNICEF, intensifying conflict, malnutrition, and disease create a deadly cycle that threatens the entire population of children.[15] There were nearly 419,000 reported cases of infectious disease in Gaza when hostilities continued past its first 100 days. Because the health system has virtually collapsed in Gaza, those facing this deadly combination of hunger and disease are falling further behind in all spheres of life. Even routinely treatable diseases under these conditions can become, and often are, deadly. The largest remaining hospital in Gaza has been bombarded by the

---

14 World Health Organization, "Lethal combination of hunger and disease to lead to more deaths in Gaza," December 21, 2023. https://www.who.int/news/item/21-12-2023-lethal-combination-of-hunger-and-disease-to-lead-to-more-deaths-in-gaza

15 UNICEF, "Intensifying conflict, malnutrition and disease in the Gaza Strip creates a deadly cycle that threatens over 1.1 million children" [press release], January 5, 2024. https://www.unicef.org/mena/press-releases/intensifying-conflict-malnutrition-and-disease-gaza-strip-creates-deadly-cycle

IDF in the North as has the one in the South Kahn Younis, which now cannot function.[16]

A New Crime: Domicide

Since the war started, over 1.9 million people have been internally forcefully removed from North to South, back and forth.[17] In Gaza, on average, there is only one shower for every 4500 people and one toilet for every 220. These conditions are ripe for a continued rise in hunger and infectious diseases. Systematic or widespread bombardment of housing, civilian objects and infrastructure are strictly prohibited by international humanitarian law, criminal law, and human rights law. In a recent report to the UN General Assembly, the UN Special Rapporteur on the right to adequate housing, Balakrishnan Rajagopal, used the term "domicide" to refer to systematic or widespread attacks on housing and civilian infrastructure that cause death and suffering.[18] So far, Israel has destroyed more than 60% of Palestinian homes in Gaza, making the territory unlivable. Such a level of intentional destruction suggests formalization of a new crime against humanity.

From Acute Food Insecurity to Famine

Hunger, starvation, malnutrition and overall acute food insecurity are all risk factors for personal and communal decline. The term famine is used to describe a societal catastrophe that requires an urgent and coordinated humanitarian response to avoid widespread loss of life. Famine is a technical term that applies when a population experiences extreme levels of acute malnutrition and mortality. The most authoritative calculation of famine is done by the Integrated Food Security Phase Classification (IPC) that is periodically conducted by the cooperation of several UN organizations.[19] IPC classifies five stages of food insecurity, and each stage needs appropriate

16 Jason Burke and Heather Livingstone, "Fears grow for largest remaining hospital in Gaza as Israeli forces bombard Khan Younis," *The Guardian,* January 19, 2024. https://www.theguardian.com/world/2024/jan/19/israel-gaza-war-largest-remaining-hospital-nasser-khan-younis-attack-fears-strike

17 World Food Programme, *Food Security Update For Internally Displaced Populations in Southern Gaza Strip,* December 14, 2023. https://docs.wfp.org/api/documents/WFP-0000155014/download/

18 UN Human Rights Office of the High Commissioner, "Gaza: Destroying civilian housing and infrastructure is an international crime, warns UN expert," November 8, 2023. https://www.ohchr.org/en/press-releases/2023/11/gaza-destroying-civilian-housing-and-infrastructure-international-crime

19 Integrated Food Security Phase Classification (IPC) guidelines defining Acute Food Insecurity (AFI), Chronic Food Insecurity (CFI), and Acute Malnutrition (AMN), in *Understanding the IPC Scales* [brochure] available at: https://www.

198 *GENOCIDE IN GAZA*

action to respond the problem: Phase 1: None/minimal; Phase 2: Stressed; Phase 3: Crisis; Phase 4: Emergency and Phase 5: Catastrophe/Famine. Phases 3, and 4 need intervention or external aid to be avoided. Phase 5 defined then experience of an extreme lack of food and/or inability to meet other basic needs. Starvation, death, destitution, and extremely critical acute malnutrition levels are evident.

Between 24 November and 7 December 2023, over 90 percent of the population in the Gaza Strip (about 2.2 million people) was estimated to be facing high levels of acute food insecurity, as classified in IPC Phase 3 or above (crisis or worse). Among these, over 40 percent of the population (939,000 people) was in Emergency (IPC Phase 4), and over 15 percent (378,000 people) was in Catastrophe (IPC Phase 5), which is classified as famine, meaning *dying from hunger.*[20]

The IPC determines a famine to exist when a population reaches stage 5 (Catastrophe) with three indicators having reached those thresholds. Famine occurs when "at least 20% of the population is affected, with about one out of three children being acutely malnourished and two people dying per day for every 10,000 inhabitants due to outright starvation or to the interaction of malnutrition and disease." However, declaring famine is not only a technical decision but also a political decision. Although IPC experts, the Famine Review Committee (FRC), conduct and review the analysis necessary to classify a famine, only government and top UN officials can make an official declaration, which is a complex bureaucratic process. In many cases, countries have hesitated to do so. Therefore, the FRC has been always late in declaring famine, and in many cases when famine declared, it is too late to save lives.[21] In Gaza, the thresholds were existing especially in Northern Gaza since March 2024, but as we discuss below, at the end of July, famine was not yet officially declared.

Testimonies on the ground give us a better understanding than numbers. Humanitarian workers of the UN World Food Program (WFP) indicate that

---

ipcinfo.org/fileadmin/user_upload/ipcinfo/docs/communication_tools/brochures/ IPC_Brochure_Understanding_the_IPC_Scales.pdf

20 GAZA STRIP : IPC Acute Food Insecurity | November 2023 –February 2024, *IPC Global Initiative - Special Brief - Gaza Strip.* https://www.ipcinfo.org/fileadmin/ user_upload/ipcinfo/docs/IPC_Gaza_Acute_Food_Insecurity_Nov2023_Feb2024. pdf

21 Since the IPC was developed in 2004, it has been used to identify only two famines: in Somalia in 2011, and in South Sudan in 2017. In Somalia, more than 100 000 people died before famine was officially declared. In Yemen and Ethiopia, however, IPC analysts expressed grave concern about food insecurity related to the civil wars, but not enough information was available from governments to issue a formal assessment.

many Gazans regularly go up to three days without eating.[22] The chief economist of the WFP, Arif Husain, warned in January 2024, "It is a situation where pretty much everybody in Gaza is hungry... If the war continues at the same level and normal food deliveries are not restored, the population could face a full-fledged famine within the next six months, with widespread outbreak of diseases."

After several months of war, Gazans have exhausted all coping strategies, including consuming livestock fodder, begging, or selling off their belongings to purchase food. Food prices have skyrocketed, and the banking system has collapsed. Hence, as of March 2024, the IPC estimated 2.2 million people were either in a state of crisis (Phase 4) or facing such an emergency catastrophe (Phase 5) that 1.1 million people were at risk of starvation. Oxfam found that 300,000 people in northern Gaza have been surviving on an average of less than a single can of beans, well below the recommended daily intake of 2,100 calories, and 30 percent of children below the age of two are acutely malnourished or wasted.[23]

Devastation, besiegement, the destruction of infrastructure, and severely restricted humanitarian access have put as much as half the population facing the threat of famine, per Phase 5. In April 2024, based on reasonable evidence that all three famine thresholds have been surpassed, the WFP announced that famine was projected to occur any time between mid-March and May 2024 in the governorates of Gaza and North Gaza and that there was a risk of famine across the rest of the Gaza Strip by July 2024.[24]

Many UN and international organizations such as the United Nations Children's Fund (UNICEF), WFP and the World Health Organization (WHO) have called for safe, unimpeded, at scale and sustained access to urgently deliver multisectoral humanitarian assistance throughout the Gaza Strip to avoid Famine. As of 8 June 2024, famine in Gaza had not yet formally been declared by the Famine Review Committee (FRC).[25] However, in its most

---

22 Lilia Sebouai and Maeve Cullinan, "Rising hunger in Gaza 'turning children into skeletons'," *The Telegraph*, January 8, 2024. https://www.telegraph.co.uk/global-health/science-and-disease/children-skeletons-rising-hunger-gaza-famine/

23 Oxfam, "People in northern Gaza forced to survive on 245 calories a day, less than a can of beans – Oxfam," April 3, 2024. https://www.oxfam.org/en/press-releases/people-northern-gaza-forced-survive-245-calories-day-less-can-beans-oxfam

24 *IPC Analysis on the Gaza Strip*, April 4, 2024. https://fscluster.org/sites/default/files/2024-04/IPC_GAZA_for_GFSC_04042024_shared.pdf

25 The Famine Review Committee in March 2024 concluded that "famine is now projected and imminent" in Northern Gaza by the end of May. On June 8, same body rejected this conclusion and said that is not "plausible" that Northern Gaza has entered a state of famine on the grounds that such assertions ignored or underestimated the value of both commercial sources of food and certain

recent of 25 June 2024, the FRC stated that the entire Gaza strip faces a "plausible" risk of famine in the coming months, driven by new evidence.

Pre-existing Food Insecurity in Gaza and Its Impact on Malnutrition

Prior to the current crisis, Gaza was under the blockade since 2007 and it was identified as a major food crisis hotspot. Therefore, following the escalation of violence after 7 October 2023, pre-existing conditions led to Gaza experiencing the fastest decline in a population's nutrition status ever recorded. Over the past 17 years, 35 percent of the Gaza Strip's agricultural land, and as much as 85 percent of its fishing waters, have been restricted due to a range of issues, including creating buffer zones at various points. The inhabitants of the Gaza Strip are confined in one of the most densely populated spaces in the world (5,900 residents per square kilometer), in chronic conflict conditions, with inadequate access to clean water and lack of proper sewage system, and electricity available only for half of a day. In September 2022, 70 percent of the population in Gaza was food insecure, with half of the population relying on humanitarian assistance as their main source of income. (IPC, 2024a).

In September 2023, the International Monetary Fund (IMF) suggested that 53 percent of the population was below the poverty line and 80 percent relied on humanitarian assistance. Per capita income was four times smaller than in the West Bank and the unemployment rate reached 45 percent, with 53 percent of the population below the poverty line.[26] Such conditions contributed to already high unemployment, poverty and food insecurity. While a chronic humanitarian crisis has evolved, 65 percent of the populations of Gaza was food insecure.

Uniqueness of the Gaza Starvation

Starvation and sieges as a means or result of war are common occurrences. Earlier examples include Biafra, Nigeria,[27] Sarajevo, Bosnia,[28]

---

forms of humanitarian aid. See: https://www.fdd.org/analysis/2024/06/17/expert-panel-rejects-claims-of-famine-in-northern-gaza/.

26 HLPE, Conflict and Acute Food Crises, July 2024. Available at: https://www.fao.org/cfs/cfs-hlpe/insights/news-insights/news-detail/new-issues-paper--conflict-induced-acute-food-crises--potential-policy-responses-in-light-of-current-emergencies/en

27 Adaobi Tricia Nwaubani, "Remembering Nigeria's Biafra war that many prefer to forget," BBC, January 14, 2020. https://www.bbc.com/news/world-africa-51094093

28 Blaine Harden, "Starvation Said To Begin in Sarajevo," Washington Post, June 7, 1992. https://www.washingtonpost.com/archive/politics/1992/06/07/starvation-said-to-begin-in-sarajevo/09a44796-ab05-4372-b268-b6271879184f/

Syria,[29] recently in the Tigray region of Ethiopia,[30] Somalia, Sudan, South Sudan, and Yemen. All these populations struggled with starvation and famine during conflict. In Sudan and Yemen famine-like conditions of severe starvation continue, although receiving little attention from mainstream media in the West.

The Gaza famine is unique among those who have suffered from conflict-induced starvation. The current condition in Gaza is far more devastating than the worst sites of hunger during conflicts and starvation in earlier hard-hit places such as Somalia, Afghanistan, Yemen and currently Sudan, where only 40 to 60% of population were in a starvation condition, never 100% as in Gaza.[31] This simply means that an entire generation, 335,000 children under five in Gaza, are at risk of stunting or/and wasting. These conditions adversely affect the physical and mental development of generations to come. Alex De Waal, a renowned scholar on famine, in his recent article states that "... the pace and scale of the destruction of objects indispensable to survival in Gaza surpasses any other case of man-made famine in the last 75 years."[32] He adds: " What's different about the Gaza case is the speed and the comprehensiveness of that destruction. We have not seen a population reduced from an acute stress to an extreme emergency on this scale in a matter of months."[33]

Moreover, the Gaza is the first genocidal battleground in which daily atrocities are shown on TV screens, and in which high level Israeli government personalities repeatedly use dehumanizing, genocidal language in the course of acknowledging their tactics as designed to induce mass starvation.[34]

---

29 Maksymilian Czuperski, Faysal Itani, Ben Nimmo, Eliot Higgins and Emma Beals, "Siege," *Breaking Aleppo,* Atlantic Countil (2017), available at: https://www.jstor.org/stable/pdf/resrep03700.6.pdf.

30 Kalkidan Yibeltal, "Northern Ethiopia facing famine, says Tigray official," *BBC,* December 29, 2023. https://www.bbc.com/news/world-africa-67840422

31 High Level Panel of Experts on Food Security and Nutrition (HLPE-FSN), *Conflict-induced acute food crises: potential policy responses in light of current emergencies,* New Issues paper, July 17, 2024. https://www.fao.org/cfs/cfs-hlpe/insights/news-insights/news-detail/new-issues-paper--conflict-induced-acute-food-crises--potential-policy-responses-in-light-of-current-emergencies/en

32 Alex de Waal, "Gaza's Famine Warning in Perspective," World Peace Foundation, January 3, 2024. https://worldpeacefoundation.org/blog/gazas-famine-warning-in-perspective/

33 Eric Reidy, "Famine expert Alex de Waal on Israel's starvation of Gaza" [interview], *The New Humanitarian,* January 18, 2024. https://www.thenewhumanitarian.org/interview/2024/01/18/israel-icj-gaza-famine-starvation-de-waal

34 "Dangers of Dehumanizing Rhetoric and Its Impact on the Palestinian People," *stratsea,* November 17, 2023. https://stratsea.com/

Legal experts working on crime of starvation and criminal accountability were surprised, if not shocked, that Israeli senior officials "are very clearly publicizing their intent." [35]

Humanitarian Aid: Too Little, Too Late

Israel did not allow water, food, fuel, or medicine until October 21, 2023 into an already blockaded Gaza. The UN Agency for Palestine Refugees (UNRWA) reports that the number of trucks going into Gaza, including those carrying commercial goods, has dropped drastically from its pre-war level, averaging 500 every working day since the war began.

In the last week of December 2023 food assistance only reached 8% of targeted people in need. While the majority of aid distribution is concentrated in the southern governorates, only 21 per cent (5 out of 24) of planned deliveries of aid containing food and other lifesaving supplies reached their planned destination north of Wadi Gaza.[36]

Very limited humanitarian aid was further reduced significantly, because of the IDF's completely arbitrary inspections of cargoes.[37] If only one item is rejected, the truck must return with its entire cargo to be re-packaged, and then start the weeks-long process over again. Some of the rejected goods were water testing equipment, medical kits, oxygen cylinders, gas-powered generators, tents, and nutritious foods for babies, pregnant women and young children. The U.S. senators who visited the Gaza-Egypt Rafah border stated that:"The warehouse was a testament to the arbitrariness" of the process. Israel claims that Hamas is confiscating the aid convoys. There is no credible proof to support such an allegation. When the conflict reached over one hundred days, UN human rights experts issued a press release stating that Israel was destroying Gaza's food system and weaponizing food.[38]

---

dangers-of-dehumanizing-rhetoric-and-its-impact-on-the-palestinian-people/"

35 How Experts Believe Starvation Is Being Utilized in Gaza," Global Rights Compliance, January 8, 2024. https://globalrightscompliance.com/2024/01/08/how-experts-believe-starvation-is-being-utilized-in-gaza/

36 United Nations, Office of the High Commissioner for Human Rights, "Over one hundred days into the war, Israel destroying Gaza's food system and weaponizing food, say UN human rights experts," UN Human Rights, January 16, 2024. https://www.ohchr.org/en/press-releases/2024/01/over-one-hundred-days-war-israel-destroying-gazas-food-system-and

37 Lee Keath, "Cumbersome process and 'arbitrary' Israeli inspections slow aid delivery into Gaza, US senators say," *AP News,* January 6, 2024. https://apnews.com/article/israel-gaza-rafah-aid-us-senators-2bc2a3c5e5f8af8e2d3f0b7242c1a885

38 United Nations, Office of the High Commissioner for Human Rights press release, January 16, 2024.

Unlike other conflicts, humanitarian aid is subject to conditionality and negotiation, as Israel conditioned the humanitarian aid with the release of hostages. Simply, if no comprehensive humanitarian aid reaches Gaza urgently, the risk of famine is raised and becomes imminent. Unfortunately, there will not be sufficient aid if there is no ceasefire. The UN Security Council failed to pass several ceasefire resolutions because of the veto of the U.S.

To speed humanitarian aid, on December 23 UN Security Council Resolution 2720 was adopted, and the Secretary General appointed a Senior Humanitarian and Reconstruction Coordinator for the Gaza Strip, with the new team working around the clock to deliver the desperately needed aid.[39] On January 15, UN agencies (WFP, WHO and UNWRA) called for a fundamental change in the amount of aid entering Gaza, as well as increased access and more efficient security measures from Israel in the combat zones upon entering the territory.[40] However, the harm already had been done by severe malnutrition and starvation and it cannot be reversed.

The delayed delivery of humanitarian aid is also due to heavy fighting. Humanitarian aid requires a secure environment where staff can work safely. Without safe conditions humanitarian aid cannot be delivered. Gaza is one of the most unsafe battle zones in the world. Secretary-General António Guterres said that the real problem was that "the way Israel is conducting this offensive is creating massive obstacles "and he added: "Since October 7, 152 UN staff members have been killed in Gaza, the largest single loss of life in the history of the Organization."[41]

Also, a record number of journalists have been killed in Gaza, as compared to recent conflicts. As of July 31 the preliminary investigation by the Committee to Protect Journalists (CPJ) concluded that at least 111 journalists and media workers have been killed. [42]

Throughout the conflict, humanitarian aid was inconsistent and unpredictable, depending on the calculation to keep Gazans just under the threshold of famine. Gaza was divided between the South and North, with needs and aids constantly shifting, and distribution of aid inside of Gaza controlled to a level of almost impossibility to reach the populations needing it most, because of the destruction of roads and warehouses, as well as Israeli attacks on aid convoys.

---

39 "Security Council adopts key resolution on Gaza crisis; Russia, US abstain," *UN News,* December 22, 2023. https://news.un.org/en/story/2023/12/1145022

40 "Humanitarian ceasefire only way to end Gaza 'nightmare': Guterres," *UN News,* December 22, 2023. https://news.un.org/en/story/2023/12/1145067

41 Ibid.

42 *Journalist casualties in the Israel-Gaza war,* Committee to Protect Journalists. https://cpj.org/2024/07/journalist-casualties-in-the-israel-gaza-conflict/

The escalation in the conflict in May led to a sharp, significant decrease in the volume of food trucked into southern Gaza, while levels of food assistance entering northern Gaza surged to new highs. At the end of June, deliveries dropped even further and, the lowest amount recorded to reach Gaza since October 2023. Conversely, WFP reported that truck deliveries of food and non-food assistance to northern Gaza skyrocketed in May, because of Israeli fear of IPC's report about a coming famine.

It is known that Israel and the U.S. Army use Gaza as an experimental laboratory to test high-tech weapons and tactics, which provides them with an effective marketing strategy for their arms trade industries. For a long time, Israelis have been very forthright about their policy, saying "Gaza is under a subsistence diet." As long ago as 2006, an adviser to then Israeli Prime Minister Ehud Olmert explained that: "The idea is to put the Palestinians on a diet, but not to make them die of hunger."[43] Now, Gaza has become a place for testing the limit of human survival under conditions in which food and water are deliberately withheld. Gaza is being subjected to a famine diet that helps in calculating the durability and resilience of human life without food!

Plenty of Law; Where is the Accontability?

There are distinct categories of international law that pertain to the situation existing in Gaza. The first one is international human rights law, which protects people from violations of fundamental human rights in times of peace or war, such as primarily the right to life, then the right to food, right to housing, right to health, and right to education. Those rights have been gravely violated by Israel during the post October 7 war against Gaza. The second one is international humanitarian law, which protects civilians in times of war. The way in which Israel conducted the war on Gaza has also violated fundamental principles of international humanitarian law. The third category, International criminal law, provides accountability procedures for grave violations of human rights and of humanitarian law, such as various war crimes and crimes against humanity. Finally, the widely ratified Genocide Convention of 1948 holds individuals accountable for crime of genocide based inter alia on bombing, displacing, and removing life supports from civilians intentionally, blocking humanitarian aid to destroy the people in whole or part.

---

43 "Putting Palestinians 'On a Diet': Israel's Siege & Blockade of Gaza," Institute for Middle East Understanding, August 14, 2014. https://imeu.org/article/putting-palestinians-on-a-diet-israels-siege-blockade-of-gaza

Palestinian legal scholar and human rights activist Noura Erakat said in an interview: "There are plenty of crimes unfolding in Palestine, especially the crime of apartheid: a sustained 75 years of settler colonial removal, 56 years of occupation, and 16 years of siege. Apartheid is and will continue to be the greatest crime against humanity."[44] Yet, Israel continues to enjoy impunity as it has since its establishment in 1948, the same year the Genocide Convention became law.

United Nations, International Courts and the Israel Palestine Conflict

It is known that Israel mostly refused to cooperate with the UN or to show respect for relevant international law principles governing its role as the Occupying Power of Palestinian Territories since 1967. Over the years, Israel has rejected numerous resolutions of the UN General Assembly, as well as the UN Human Rights Council investigations into alleged abuses against Palestinians. Israel also did not allow last three UN Special Rapporteurs in the country to investigate human rights violations in Occupied Territories, just as in 2002 it denied UN Secretary-General Kofi Annan access to investigate events surrounding Israeli's military incursion into the Jenin refugee camp.

Nevertheless, various international court decisions and ongoing processes exist dealing with the Israel Palestine conflict. The most recent one is South Africa's application of December 29, 2023 to the International Court of Justice (ICJ), alleging that Israel's conduct in Gaza breaches its obligation under the 1948 Genocide Convention. With this case, the Gaza war entered a new, politically and legally complex and lengthy legal process. Along with the legal process of investigating the crime of genocide, South Africa also requested provisional measures from the ICJ to stop the ongoing war crimes amid the rising humanitarian toll.[45] As a response, the ICJ announced, almost unanimously, three provisional measures (26 January, 28 March, and May 24), indicating that insofar as genocide is "plausible," Israel must stop the ongoing violence that accentuates the perception of genocide and allow humanitarian access. To stop the ongoing war, the second and third provisional measures reaffirmed its previous ones and indicated new measures

---

44 Noura Erakat and Deborah Chasman, "'The Crimes Are Plenty'," *Boston Review,* October 13, 2023. https://www.bostonreview.net/articles/the-crimes-are-plenty/

45 Hyemin Han, "South Africa Institutes ICJ Proceedings Against Israel for Genocide Convention Violations," *Lawfare,* January 3, 2024. https://www.lawfaremedia.org/article/south-africa-institutes-icj-proceedings-against-israel-for-genocide-convention-violations. Read South Africa's application instituting proceedings against Israel here: https://www.documentcloud.org/documents/24252642-192-20231228-app-01-00-en?responsive=1&title=1

to avoid the high risk of famine that should be immediately and effectively implemented.[46] All three of the provisional measures were ignored by Israel.

The ICJ's procedure will not resolve initially the underlying question of whether Israel has committed genocide. This will take several years to decide involving a complex and delicate determination as to whether the State of Israel possessed a specific "intent to destroy, in whole or in part, a national, ethnical, racial or religious group, such" as specified by the Genocide Convention. One should keep in mind that the ICJ is not a criminal court and does not have a jurisdiction over individuals or collective entities accused of war crimes or crimes against humanity. Genocide is considered a state crime of crimes, and the "specific intent to destroy" is difficult to prove.

The South Africa versus Israel case before the ICJ is not the first case to be addressed by the world's most important court dealing with the Israel-Palestine conflict. In 2004 the ICJ delivered an Advisory Opinion at the request of the UN General Assembly on the legality of the construction of those parts of a separation wall between Israel and Palestine located on Occupied Palestinian Territory. The court's non-binding Advisory Opinion affirmed the illegality of the wall. Israel did not accept the outcome and refused to cooperate with the Court.[47]

Twenty years after the Separation Wall decision, the most recent and most important ICJ decision against Israel—another Advisory Opinion of the ICJ, again at the request of the UNGA—was delivered on 19 July 2024 confirming the illegality of the prolonged occupation of the three Occupied Palestinian Territories.[48] The landmark ruling declared that Israel's occupation of the Gaza strip and the West Bank, including East Jerusalem, is unlawful, along with the associated settlement regime, annexation and use of natural resources. The Court added that Israel's legislation and measures violate the international prohibition on racial segregation and apartheid. The ICJ mandated Israel to end its occupation, dismantle its settlements, provide full reparations to Palestinian victims and facilitate the return of displaced people.[49] It remains to be seen whether the ICJ decision will be brought by the member states to the UN General Assembly to have a resolution for the

---

46 International Court of Justice case document filed May 24, 2024. https://www.icj-cij.org/node/204099

47 United Nations, "International Court of Justice Advisory Opinion Finds Israel's Construction of Wall 'Contrary to International Law'" [press release], July 9, 2024. https://press.un.org/en/2004/icj616.doc.htm

48 International Court of Justice, Summary of the Advisory Opinion of 19 July 2024. https://www.icj-cij.org/node/204176

49 United Nations, Office of the High Commissioner for Human Rights, "Experts hail ICJ declaration on illegality of Israel's presence in the occupied Palestinian territory as 'historic' for Palestinians and international law," UN Human

implementation. A reminder: the ICJF ruling as it concerns the crime of genocide is yet to come.

Another set of initiatives was brought by Palestine to the International Criminal Court (ICC) about the criminal responsibility of Israeli leaders. In 2015, when Palestine became a party to the Rome Statute of the ICC, it submitted a complaint to the Court about alleged crimes committed by Israel in the occupied Palestinian territory, including East Jerusalem, since June 13, 2014. Recently, the ICC has begun accepting online reports of war crimes. A civil society organization, *Justice for All,* has issued a tool kit to facilitate the submission by victims and survivors of claims of Israeli criminality to the ICC.[50] Injury, loss of life, and property destruction are all war crimes under certain conditions. Whether the crime happened this year or since June 13, 2014, the International Criminal Court is obligated to accept all credible submissions. However, since its founding the ICC has been subject to sharp criticism for not acting vigorously on allegations against Western states, including Israel and the U.S., while proceeding with great fervor against the enemies of the West, such as accused individuals from Russia or sub-Saharan Africa.

Although Israel is not a member of the ICC and refuses to show respect for the Court's jurisdiction, Israeli families of victims of the October 7 Hamas attacks to Israel appealed to the ICC to order an investigation into killing and abductions of Israelis. The chief prosecutor, Karim Khan, after visiting Southern Israel and Ramallah on December 3, 2023, called for investigations of the actions of the Hamas and Israeli forces against civilians. After a long silent period, on May 2024, the ICC prosecutor announced an arrest warrant for Israeli leaders Prime Minister Benjamín Netanyahu, and Defense Minister Galant, as well as for Hamas leaders Sinwar, Deif, and Haniyeh for alleged war crimes. It is still yet to be seen how this initiative will unfold.[51]

Starvation in International Humanitarian Law

Setting aside this discussion, let us review the international humanitarian law principles. There are three core principles: distinction, proportionality,

---

Rights, July 30, 2024. https://www.ohchr.org/en/press-releases/2024/07/experts-hail-icj-declaration-illegality-israels-presence-occupied

50 Justice For All, "Attention All Palestinians: Submit Your Cases to ICC": https://www.justiceforall.org/icc-submissions/

51 "Statement of ICC Prosecutor Karim A.A. Khan KC: Applications for arrest warrants in the situation in the State of Palestine," International Criminal Court, May 20, 2024. https://www.icc-cpi.int/news/statement-icc-prosecutor-karim-aa-khan-kc-applications-arrest-warrants-situation-state

and precaution designed to protect persons not participating in hostilities.[52] All these core principles are being violated by Israel. Israel failed to differentiate between civilians and combatants since October 7 by indiscriminate bombing, punishing all Gazans collectively, with most casualties being women and children. Collective punishment is also a war crime according to international humanitarian law. Israel used disproportionate force, including allegedly using illegal phosphorus bombs. This violates proportionality principles. Thirdly, Israel did not change its conduct operations despite having clear knowledge of what was happening in Gaza. The war was conducted with the clear acknowledgement of the entire world against the entire Gazan population .

Regarding starvation, international humanitarian law contains a series of food-related rules of a preventive nature that is applicable to the Gaza war. All the principles of international humanitarian law (the Geneva Convention and its protocols) are also considered customary international law and applicable to all conflicts. First and foremost, humanitarian law prohibits the use of starvation as a weapon of war, implemented through denial of food stuffs, destruction of crops and wells and other objects that are essential for the survival of civilians, and forced displacement. If prevention fails and malnutrition and hunger become widespread, rules governing humanitarian assistance become applicable.[53]

Second, parties to an armed conflict have the primary responsibility to meet the needs of the population under their control, including provision of food and water. If a party to conflict is unable or unwilling to provide food, water and basic human needs for survival, it must allow international humanitarian aid/assistance entry to conflict zones to protect non-combatant civilians. Denying or blocking humanitarian assistance is prohibited under international humanitarian law. Humanitarian food aid is the most lifesaving system in war times, and it is to be distinguished from food aid in peace times. For instance, humanitarian aid in war time must be provided in accordance with the principles of humanity, neutrality and impartiality.[54]

52　The four Geneva Conventions of 1949 and two Additional Protocols of 1977 set out the major rules of international humanitarian law, including in Geneva IV setting forth in Article 55 an unconditional obligation to ensure adequate supplies of food to a civilian population living under belligerent occupation, and Article 33 prohibiting collective punishments.

53　See articles 23, 30 and 142 of the Geneva Convention relative to the Protection of Civilian Persons in Times of War and article 70 (1) of Additional Protocol I for the rules on humanitarian assistance in international armed conflict.

54　UNGA 46/182 See.4/2002/58. Cited in Para. 74 of the Interim Report of the Special Rapporteur on the right to food, A/72/188. Submitted pursuant to Assembly resolution 79/54 by UNSR Hilal Elver, 21 July 2017.

Third, there are series of provisions related to humanitarian assistance to civilians required by the occupying power in occupied territories under the Geneva Convention relative to the Protection of Civilian Persons in Time of War (arts. 55 and 59) and additional Protocol I (arts. 68–71).[55] Additionally, states are required to grant the free passage of humanitarian assistance for specific categories of people, such as wounded persons, pregnant women and children, even if such persons belong to an adversary State or enemy non-State party.[56]

Fourth, refusal of the permission to deliver food is possible only in exceptional conditions, such as a credible claim of military necessity. However, this can be invoked only to regulate humanitarian access, not to prohibit definitively the possibility of an impartial humanitarian organization operating in civilian areas. Military necessity can be invoked only to restrict humanitarian assistance temporarily and with specific geographical limits. To refuse passage to delivery vehicles would constitute a flagrant violation of the right to food and right to life, especially if civilians die of hunger as a result.

Finally, forced displacement of civilians is also prohibited under Article 49 of the Geneva Convention and Article 17 of the Additional Protocol II. Unlawful displacement constitutes a war crime under the Rome Statute of the ICC.[57]

International Criminal Law and the Crime of Starvation

Certain gross violations of human rights and humanitarian law have been considered of such gravity that they are also regulated under international criminal law, imposing individual criminal responsibility to perpetrators. These crimes could be prosecuted not only nationally but also internationally. Article 5 of the Rome Statute provides the most complete and updated crimes within the jurisdiction of the court, namely genocide, crimes against humanity, war crimes and crimes of aggression.[58]

The crime of starvation is defined in Article 8(2)(b)(xxv) of the ICC Rome Statute under war crimes, as "Intentionally using starvation of civilians as a method of warfare by depriving them of objects indispensable to their survival, including wilfully impeding relief supplies as provided for

55 Ibid.
56 See article 23 of the Geneva Convention relative to the Protection of Civilian Persons in Time of War.
57 Article 8, para. 2 (a) (vii) and (b) (viii).
58 *Rome Statute of the International Criminal Court, 17 July 1998*, Article 5 - Crimes within the jurisdiction of the Court, International Humanitarian Law Databases, ICRC. https://ihl-databases.icrc.org/en/ihl-treaties/icc-statute-1998/article-5

under the Geneva Conventions."[59] "Objects indispensable to survival" (OIS) include not only food but also water, medicine, shelter, and maternal care for children. The crime of starvation has no requirement that individuals perish of starvation for the crime to have been committed; it is sufficient for persons to have been deprived of OIS. The element of "intent" of starvation crime is not a "specific intent," as is required in establishing responsibility for the crime of genocide.

Israel's actions clearly and squarely constitute a crime of starvation, by way of blocking access to food and clean water as a weapon of war, denying and blocking humanitarian aid, bombing bakeries and food distribution places, depriving the civilan population of objects indispensable to their survival, destroying Gaza's agricultural land by reducing it to mere dirt through repeated bombardment, destroying livestock and the entire fishing sector. This result was confirmed by Human Rights Watch satellite images and by international organizations.[60]

The language used by high-level Israeli officials about starving the entire Gaza population, combined with actions on the ground and blocking humanitarian aid, appear to indicate intentionality of the use of starvation as a weapon of war, a violation of international law.[61]

Famine as a Crime Against Humanity?

Progressively, the situation in Gaza has become more severe, moving from starvation defined as food crises, then a food emergency, which quickly turned into widestread famine. Famine is a virulent form of starvation causing widespread death.[62] A famine is defined as the most severe kind of acute food insecurity. It is very rare, but when it does occur, it means that there is an extreme shortage of food and several children and adults within a certain area are already dying of hunger on a daily basis. However, insofar as famine

---

59 *Rome Statute of the International Criminal Court, 17 July 1998,* Article 8 - War crimes, International Humanitarian Law Databases, ICRC. https://ihl-databases. icrc.org/en/ihl-treaties/icc-statute-1998/article-8. For the entire Rome Statute, see: https://www.icc-cpi.int/sites/default/files/2024-05/Rome-Statute-eng.pdf

60 Human Rights Watch, "Israel: Starvation Used as Weapon of War in Gaza," December 18, 2023. https://www.hrw.org/news/2023/12/18/ israel-starvation-used-weapon-war-gaza

61 Mallory Moench, "How Experts Believe Starvation Is Being Utilized in Gaza," *TIME,* January 6, 2024. https://time.com/6552740/gaza-israel-starvation-hunger/

"'Full-blown famine' in northern Gaza, says World Food Programme executive director Cindy McCain," *NBC News* video [2:26], May 3, 2024. https://www.youtube. com/watch?v=r7QWply967Q

62 Amartya Sen, *Poverty and Famines: An Essay on Entitlement and Deprivation* (Oxford: Oxford University Press, 1981), 40.

is a technical term, it is only officially declared when a series of specific food insecurity, mortality, and malnutrition criteria are met.[63]

Famine is one the oldest weapons of war in history. Yet, there is no formal definition of famine as a crime in international law. Therefore, there is an ongoing lack of legal protection. Yet, if certain conditions are met, it might be included into the legal protection afforded with regard to a crime against humanity. Article 7 of the Rome Statute defines crimes against humanity in a somewhat open-ended manner that can be interpreted as including famine. Art. 7 (1)(k) states that: "…inhumane acts of a similar character intentionally causing great suffering, or serious injury to body or to mental or physical health." A crime against humanity has two components:[64] First, the accused must deliberately perpetrate the acts necessary to accomplish the specific offence, and, secondly, the act must be committed as part of a "widespread or systematic attack" directed against the civilian population. Famine automatically satisfies the second requirement because it is widespread and systematic. The first requirement is harder to satisfy. However, intentionality is not as hard to demonstrate as is "specific intention" for the crime of genocide. Famine becomes a crime if there is sufficient evidence of an intentional or reckless effort to block certain groups from access to food under conditions of conflict or hardship. The crime of famine could result from acts of omission, but also from indirect action such as blocking humanitarian assistance, failing to uphold the relevant laws of war or failing to provide international relief systems with the necessary resources in the context of famine conditions.

Even though international criminal law criminalizes certain conduct that leads to famine, the legal treatment of allegations of famine has not been clear and consistent. Many legal doctrines support an indictment for such behavior (war crimes, crimes against humanity, and Genocide), but the international community has never called for an international criminal trial against government officials or non-State actors for creating, inflicting or prolonging famine as a crime. There are several reasons for this. First, to prove intent as the basis for criminal responsibility might be difficult as death from starvation

---

63 Households experience an extreme lack of food and/or cannot meet other basic needs even after full employment of coping strategies. Starvation, death, destitution and extremely critical acute malnutrition levels are evident. For Famine Classification, an area needs to have extremely critical levels of acute malnutrition and mortality. *Understanding the IPC Scales* [brochure]: https://www.ipcinfo.org/fileadmin/user_upload/ipcinfo/docs/communication_tools/brochures/IPC_Brochure_Understanding_the_IPC_Scales.pdf

64 Article 7 - Crimes Against Humanity: For the purpose of this Statute, "crime against humanity" means any of the following acts when committed as part of a *widespread or systematic attack* directed against any civilian population, with *knowledge of the attack.*

is usually a slow process. Second, famine occurs often results from diverse contributory causes, such as economic hardship, natural disasters such as drought and flood, governing failures, corruption, or extreme weather events. Third, famine normally occurs in conjunction with other severe crimes and as such the judgments rendered often do not identify famine as an independent crime. Finally, prosecutors are reluctant to bring the case about famine as there is no precedent to make the claim strong enough. Therefore, it is important to define famine crime in criminal law to stop ongoing impunity.

Recently, there is a hopeful development that ICC Prosecutor's application for arrest warrant against Netanyahu and Gallant for the first time in the ICC's history mentioned the criminal responsibility for the war crime of starvation as a method of warfare under article 8(2)(b)(xxv) of the Rome Statute as well as other war crimes and crimes against humanity associated with the use of civilian starvation, committed on the territory of the State of Palestine, and more specifically in the Gaza strip, from at least 8 October 2023.

Facts on the Ground: Israel's Accountability for Starvation and Famine

The escalation of violence after 7 October 2023 led to Gaza experiencing the fastest decline in a population's nutritional status ever recorded. Food prices have skyrocketed, and the banking system has collapsed.

In early December 2023, a WFP survey taken during the pause in hostilities showed that "Gazans are simply not eating. Nine out of ten families in some areas spent a full day and night without any food at all. When asked how often this happened, they told us that for up to 10 days in the past month, they had not eaten food."[65] In January 2024 the statements from the World Food Program (WFP), World Health Organization (WHO) and the United Nations Children Fund (UNICEF) warned not only that starvation is happening, but also the coming danger of famine, which is considered a crime against humanity.[66]

The aforementioned Integrated Food Security Phase Classification (IPC) report, the United Nations coordinated early warning system that classifies 5 levels of acute food insecurity adds that "this is the highest share of people facing high levels of acute food insecurity that the IPC initiative has ever classified for any given area or country" The IPC predicted that by February,

---

65 World Food Programme, "Statement by WFP Deputy Executive Director after visit to Gaza," December 8, 2023. https://www.wfp.org/news/statement-wfp-deputy-executive-director-after-visit-gaza

66 World Food Programme, "Famine imminent in northern Gaza, new report warns," March 18, 2024. https://www.wfp.org/news/famine-imminent-northern-gaza-new-report-warns

all 2 million people in Gaza would face crisis levels of acute food insecurity, with at least one in four households facing famine-like conditions.

In its most recent report, in June 2024, the IPC indicated that almost the entire population of 2.15 million people, 96 % of the population, are facing a high level of acute food insecurity and acute malnutrition. The whole territory is classified as Emergency (IPC Phase 4), about 677.000 people are in Catastrophic/Famine condition (IPC Phase 5), where they are starving and have exhausted their coping capacities.[67] Over 1 million people—half of the population—is expected to face death and starvation by mid-July (IPC, 2024a; WFP and FAO, 2024a).

On January 16, over one hundred days into the war, 8 UN Special Rapporteurs issued a press release stating that famine is imminent, as the entire population in Gaza is hungry, completely and quickly in such a short time, and adding that Israel is destroying Gaza's food system and using food as a weapon against the Palestinian people.[68] On July 2024, the same UN Special Rapporteurs declared that famine had spread throughout Gaza Strip.[69] The press releases were criticized by certain states claiming that the UN Special Rapporteurs have no capacity and mandate to declare famine.

The ICJ application by South Africa (29 December) against Israel referred to the IPC report on December 21, 2023, as evidence of the "starvation, death, destitution and extremely critical acute malnutrition levels" in Gaza. The court found in its first provisional decision in January 2024 that Palestinians in Gaza were facing risk of famine. No preventive action had been done, and not enough humanitarian access was allowed by Israel. Therefore, famine gradually spread, first in Northern Gaza, then to the South and the Center. In the third provisional measures in May the court observed that: "Palestinians in Gaza are no longer facing only a risk of famine…but that famine is setting in." At that time, at least 31 people, including 27 children, had already died of malnutrition and dehydration. Palestinians are facing worsening condition of life; famine and starvation are spreading.[70]

---

67 IPC 2024a

68 United Nations, Office of the High Commissioner for Human Rights, "Over one hundred days into the war, Israel destroying Gaza's food system and weaponizing food, say UN human rights experts," UN Human Rights, January 16, 2024. https://www.ohchr.org/en/press-releases/2024/01/over-one-hundred-days-war-israel-destroying-gazas-food-system-and

69 United Nations, Office of the High Commissioner for Human Rights, "UN experts declare famine has spread throughout Gaza strip," UN Human Rights, July 9, 2024. https://www.ohchr.org/en/press-releases/2024/07/un-experts-declare-famine-has-spread-throughout-gaza-strip

70 "ICJ orders Israel to take action to address famine in Gaza," *Aljazeera*, March 28, 2024. https://www.aljazeera.com/news/2024/3/28/

When famine is declared by the IPC, it is already too late and too many preventable deaths will have already occurred.[71] Famines have been declared only twice previously, in Somalia (2011) and in South Sudan (2017). By the time famine was declared, there had already been many deaths and irreversible damage to the population.

As of 8 June 2024, famine had not yet been formally declared in Gaza by the Famine Review Committee (FRC).[72] In the most recent analysis on 25 June 2024, the FRC stated that the entire Gaza strip faces a "plausible" risk of famine in the coming months, driven by new evidence, stating that:

> A high risk of Famine persists as long as conflict continues, and humanitarian access is restricted…The FRC encourages all stakeholders who use the IPC for high-level decision-making to understand that whether a Famine classification is confirmed or not does not in any manner change the fact that extreme human suffering is without a doubt currently ongoing in the Gaza Strip and does not change the immediate humanitarian imperative to address this civilian suffering by enabling complete, safe, unhindered, and sustained humanitarian access into and throughout the Gaza Strip, including through ceasing hostilities. All actors should not wait until a Famine classification is made to act accordingly (UN, 2024a).

---

icj-orders-israel-to-take-action-to-address-famine-in-gaza

71 Although IPC experts conduct and review the analysis necessary to classify a famine, only governments and top UN officials can make an official declaration, which is a complex bureaucratic process. In many cases, countries have hesitated to do so (Gupta, 2024). Since the IPC was developed in 2004, it has been used to identify only two famines: in two regions of Somalia in 2011, and in South Sudan in 2017. In Somalia, more than 100 000 people died before famine was officially declared. In Yemen and Ethiopia, however, IPC analysts expressed grave concern about food insecurity related to the civil wars, but not enough information was available from governments to issue a formal assessment.

72 The Famine Review Committee in March 2024 concluded that "famine is now projected and imminent" in Northern Gaza by the end of May. On June 8, the same body rejected this conclusion and said that it is not "plausible" that Northern Gaza has entered a state of famine on the grounds that such assertions ignored or underestimated the value of both commercial sources of food and certain forms of humanitarian aid. See "Expert Panel Rejects Claims of Famine in Northern Gaza," *FDD*, June 17, 2024. https://www.fdd.org/analysis/2024/06/17/expert-panel-rejects-claims-of-famine-in-northern-gaza/

Conclusion

Since October 9, Israeli military's ground offensive has besieged Gaza from land and the sea, razing farms and destroying agricultural land, including orchards, greenhouses, and Gaza's entire fishing fleet. Gaza was simply turned into rubble. Throughout the war, insufficient and inconsistent humanitarian aid has failed to protect civilans from starvation, famine, and various diseases, most recently polio. Almost everyone in Gaza still lacks food, fuel to cook, and access to clean water. Needed facilities from hospitals to bakeries are not operational due to the lack of fuel and water. Livestock has mostly been killed; the remaining animals are starving and unable to either access or be a source of food. These realities are a textbook example of the grave violation of human rights and humanitarian law, and are subject to international criminal law prosecution for war crimes, crimes against humanity and genocide, including individual criminal accountability.

Causing heavy casualties, the deliberate destruction Gaza's food system and using food as a weapon are clearly war crimes. These indicators should warn Israel to realize the possible legal consequences of its operations and adjust the way in which it conducts warfare and protects its security. So far Israel has failed to do this, and is knowingly "continuing to mount this offensive, that is recklessness, a second degree crime, which qualifies crime against humanity."[73] At this stage, a severe threat to life already seems certain to have lasting harmful effects on the collective physical and mental health of all Gazans, and for generations to come.

All these authoritative reports and circumstantial evidence are sufficient to prove the crime of starvation crime is being committed in Gaza and IDF commanding officers and political leaders should be held responsible.

Israel's impunity for the starvation crime must be ended. We believe and hope the Gaza War will impel the legal and political energy to prosecute crimes long ignored and hold perpetrators individually responsible for this particular heinous crime. The issue of starvation has been addressed on the global stage in the provisional phase of the ICJ response to the South African application, which itself reflects the exercise of a duty to act to prevent as well as punish genocide. The expectation is the Court would include starvation within the compass of genocide during the substantive decision. Another hopeful sign is the recent arrest warrant of the ICC against Israeli leadership in which the prosecutor included the crime of starvation. This is good news for the development of international criminal law in the global effort to stop

---

73 Mallory Moench, "How Experts Believe Starvation Is Being Utilized in Gaza," *TIME,* January 6, 2024. https://time.com/6552740/gaza-israel-starvation-hunger/

long time impunity and start prosecuting the perpetretors of the crimes of starvation and famine.

It is important to acknowledge the gap between what the law prescribes and the feasibility of its implementation, and what steps need to be taken to close the gap. Formal codification of individual responsibility pertaining to famine and severe food insecurity would clarify the conditions of criminality. At present, legal authority is scattered and fragmented. The coherent formulation of the content of the crime in an authoritative treaty text would be an important contribution to the development of international law in this setting, where the most fundamental human rights are currently subject to massive abuses without the prospect of holding perpetrators accountable.[74]

---

74 Interim Report of the Special Rapporteur on the right to food, A/72/188. Submitted pursuant to Assembly resolution 79/54 by UNSR Hilal Elver, July 21, 2017.

Resilient Bonds
Motherhood in the Heart of Palestinian Genocide

Sare Davutoğlu | Ferhan Güloğlu

"WOMEN AND NEWBORNS are disproportionately bearing the burden of hostilities in Gaza," as the World Health Organization states. Hundreds of thousands of pregnant women and children are adversely affected by the atrocities of war.

As of October 7, approximately 50,000 pregnant women resided in Gaza, with over 180 deliveries occurring daily. With 67 percent of the medical facilities destroyed, and miscarriage rates increased by 300%, around 15% of these women are at risk of encountering complications during pregnancy or childbirth, necessitating extra medical attention. Due to the blockage of medical supplies and power, emergency cesarean sections are now performed without anesthesia and the basic sanitary needs. Medically unnecessary hysterectomies are performed to stop bleeding. Pregnant women in Gaza demand early C-sections to give their babies a chance to live, calibrating the risk of uncertain future conditions. The only IVF center in Gaza, housing more than 5000 embryos, has been destroyed. Gaza has been an open-air prison since 2007. Carpet bombing of this impoverished land has destroyed the existing

Sare Davutoğlu is a mother of four and an established medical doctor known for her contributions to both medicine and voluntary non-governmental initiatives. A graduate of the Faculty of Medicine at Istanbul University, she is specialized in obstetrics and gynecology, dedicating her career to women's reproductive and integrative health.

Ferhan Güloğlu is a PhD Candidate in the Sociocultural Anthropology program. She holds an MA in Middle Eastern Studies from Columbia University and a BA in Political Science from Boğaziçi University (Istanbul). She currently works as the coordinator for the Safebirth in Palestine project, which aims to create safe childbirth conditions and maternal health support for pregnant women in Gaza.

infrastructure and terrorized an already traumatized society. As of May 2024, the destruction of Gaza is visible from outer space.

This chapter aims to leave a mark on history by documenting the genocidal targeting of pregnant women and newborns in the Gaza war of 2024. We also claim that these attacks on women and children precede the atrocities starting in 2023. Instead, Israel's settler-colonial regime has always focused on this population as a military strategy, to ruin not only the present of Palestinian political hope but also its future. Thus, here, we first historicize this focus on harming women and children through existing anthropological literature. Then, we share stories of women who lived through the horrors of the 2023–2024 attacks while pregnant or as mothers. Finally, we reiterate our dedication to stand with Palestinian women today and in the future.

As an obstetrics and gynecology specialist and a medical anthropologist, we build on a review of anthropological research, journalistic articles, personal narratives, and scholarly activism to achieve three objectives. First, we aim to historicize reproductive violence and debunk the thesis that the Gaza genocide in 2023–2024 was a response to the October 7 attacks. Second, we seek to support journalistic efforts to document war crimes for future studies, with particular attention to reproductive health-related incidents. Finally, we reiterate our dedication to standing with the indigenous population as an act of conscience.

The Situation in Gaza during the days of Genocide

A study published in May 2024, conducted between January and March of the same year, evaluated the reproductive health of 403 displaced pregnant women and recently delivered mothers across the Gaza Strip, encompassing 65 shelters. The study revealed significant challenges faced by these women, whose average age was 26 years. Notably, 74% of the pregnant participants reported complications, including mental health issues (51%), anemia (22%), physical injuries (9%), and episodes of bleeding (8%). Additionally, many women experienced inadequate access to essential resources such as food, clean water, and appropriate maternal healthcare services. Alarmingly, 42% of the pregnant women did not receive any professional antenatal care.[1]

Regarding the newly delivered mothers, 81.5% gave birth in hospitals, while the remainder delivered in shelters or without the assistance of healthcare

---

1 Hala Allabadi, Celine Maayeh, Umaiyeh Khammash, Bassam Abu Hamad, and Yehia Abed, *Barriers and Access to Maternal Care Among Displaced Pregnant Women and Newly Delivered Mothers Amidst the War in Gaza: A Rapid Assessment* (Juzoor for Health and Social Development 2024). https://www.juzoor.org/cached_uploads/download/2024/05/30/rapid-assessment-report-on-maternal-care-in-gaza-juzoor-1717050181.pdf

providers. Postpartum complications were prevalent, with 13% experiencing severe bleeding and 7.5% suffering from infections. Furthermore, 76% of newborns presented with health issues, including respiratory problems (65%) and malnutrition (20%). Access to healthcare within shelters was severely limited, with only 12% of newborns and 14% of mothers receiving necessary services. While the majority of mothers were able to breastfeed, 35% encountered significant challenges. Both pregnant women and new mothers described the conditions in shelters as inhumane, highlighting the dire state of Gaza's devastated healthcare system.

The report encapsulates the profound struggles faced by women in Gaza, citing on its front page, "During this war and under these pressures and challenges, I don't think there's anything harder than being a woman." This sentiment underscores the ongoing hardships experienced in Gaza and across Palestine, a reality that has persisted since 1948.

According to the World Health Organization (WHO), 84% of all health facilities in Gaza, including 34 out of 36 hospitals, have been severely impacted. In conjunction with ongoing bombardments and the targeted killing of civilians, the rate of miscarriages has increased by 300%, and pregnant women are now three times more likely to die during childbirth.[2]

Even if a woman manages to deliver her baby in one of the two partially functioning hospitals, breastfeeding is likely to be severely impaired due to widespread starvation. This is reminiscent of the Dutch Hunger Winter of 1944–45, when a German-imposed food embargo in the western Netherlands led to severe dietary restrictions for pregnant women.[3] Epidemiological studies in humans and experimental research in laboratory animals have demonstrated a link between intrauterine stressors and the development of diseases in adult offspring. Those who experienced nutritional scarcity during this period exhibited higher incidences of cardiovascular disease, type II diabetes, and mood and personality disorders in adulthood. These effects are attributed to epigenetic changes, which can be inherited by future generations.[4]

---

2 Kvinna till Kvinna Foundation, "Obstetric violence in Gaza: A crisis affecting women's health," May 24, 2024. https://kvinnatillkvinna.org/2024/05/24/obstetric-violence-in-gaza-a-crisis-affecting-womens-health/

3 Suzanne R. De Rooij, Laura S. Bleker, Rebecca C. Painter, Anita C. Ravelli, and Tessa J. Roseboom, "Lessons learned from 25 Years of Research into Long term Consequences of Prenatal Exposure to the Dutch famine 1944–45: The Dutch famine Birth Cohort," *International Journal of Environmental Health Research* 32, no. 7 (2022): 1432–46 (published online May 5, 2021). DOI: 10.1080/09603123.2021.1888894

4 Dipali Goyal, Sean W. Limesand, and Ravi Goyal, "Epigenetic responses and the developmental origins of health and disease," *Journal of Endocrinology* 242, no. 1 (2019): T105-T119 (retrieved August 20, 2024). https://doi.org/10.1530/JOE-19-0009

Tragically, the ongoing atrocities in Gaza are likely to have even more profound and long-lasting consequences than those observed during the Dutch Hunger Winter. The impact of these actions will likely extend beyond the current suffering of Palestinians, affecting generations to come.

Mothering and Birthworkers in Palestine

Houriyah Abdallah Abdulhadi from the Muslih family was a midwife in Gaza, whose labor as well as her life history document instances of motherhood and reproductive health under occupation.[5]

Houriyah was trained by a Malaysian doctor and served all over the Gaza Strip and narrates multiple encounters with the occupation forces during her lifetime. During the Iraq-Iran war, the forces surrounded her house, accompanied by the military commander of Deir al-Balah. She was hiding two soldiers in her house and helped them escape without being seen. The occupation forces forcibly removed her from her house in the Maghazi camp in front of other residents and shot her multiple times. Faking death, she waited till they left and removed one of the bullets with her teeth; the other one remained inside her body, which left her maimed.

In addition to being a birth worker, Houriyah is also a mother of six. One of her sons was tortured and murdered by the Israeli forces at the Erez checkpoint while waiting to enter Gaza. On another instance, when all her village men were taken from their homes and shot, she was the one who took her father and wrapped him in his kefiyyeh to stop the bleeding. They managed to escape to Jerusalem on a donkey cart, and her father survived his wounds. Houriyah took great pride in her service and was still assisting women in her old age, free of charge. She assisted hundreds of births in Khan Yunis, in Maghazi, and other parts of Gaza.

The experiences of motherhood and midwifery in Palestine are intertwined with its subjects' stories and the history of Palestine. Houriyah's story is one marked by oppression and violence, yet also by resistance. The presence of the Malaysian doctor who trained her is emblematic of forcing the Strip to rely on volunteer, temporary medical providers instead of a working, independent health system. She lived and practiced in Maghazi camp most of her life. The camp was designed as a refugee camp but instead became permanent, where she oversaw many children born and die in the camp—usually framed as a temporary setting in the humanitarian imaginary. The instances of violence she narrates are also a part of everyday life under occupation in

---

5 "A Gaza midwife tells her stories," *The Electronic Intifada* video [4:41], December 8, 2020. https://electronicintifada.net/content/video-gaza-midwife-tells-her-stories/31221

Gaza. Her father was assaulted and left to die, surviving due to a piece of kefiyyeh, which in historical Palestine was used to cover their heads from the sun and now has become a symbol of resistance all over the world as people don it to resist genocide. Civilian women were not spared from the occupation forces' violence; Houriyah herself was maimed on such an occasion. Her son's death further underlines the reality of checkpoints. Not only in Gaza but also in the West Bank, Palestinians spend hours at checkpoints and are subjected to discrimination and violence.

Rayna Rapp and Faye Ginsburg claim that reproduction can be used as an entry point to the analysis of social life.[6] Palestine is no exception to this. Settler colonialism and occupation encapsulates every aspect of life, A stark example of this is that 68 pregnant women gave childbirth at checkpoints between 2000–2007; leading to 35 miscarriages and the death of five women[7]. Taking into account that 528 checkpoints existed across West Bank and Gaza, this is only one of the many examples of ongoing targeting of women and children by the settler-colonial regime, the suffering Palestinian women endured long predating the attacks on October 7, which Israel cites as the reason behind the 2023–2024 atrocities. These attacks are in accordance with the temporal plans of the settler-colonial regime, which extends its present control and aims to dominate the future of the indigenous population.

In this part of the chapter, we analyze three themes anthropologists introduced to study reproductive violence and Palestinian women's resistance to it: (a) Political Infertility by Danyah Jaber; (b) Racialized Politics of Reproduction in Colonial Palestine by Frances Hasso; and (c) Sumud by Livia Wick.

Political Infertility

Political Infertility[8] is a quintessential example that the selective violence towards reproductive age women and children in Palestine starts well before conception. Infertility is often thought of as a medical condition, stemming from biological reasons. Reproductive justice and stratified reproduction discussions highlight its economic aspects, that infertility is at times a treatable

---

6 Faye D. Ginsburg and Rayna Rapp, eds., *Conceiving the New World Order: The Global Politics of Reproduction* (Berkeley: University of California Press, 1995)."

7 United Nations Population Fund, "Checkpoints Compound the Risks of Childbirth for Palestinian Women," May 15, 2007. https://www.unfpa.org/news/checkpoints-compound-risks-childbirth-palestinian-women

8 Danyah A. Jaber, *Infertility in the Occupied Palestinian Territories: Women's Narratives* (Doctoral dissertation submitted to University of Exeter, Institute of Arab and Islamic Studies, 2019). Retrieved July 7, 2024. https://ore.exeter.ac.uk/repository/bitstream/handle/10871/122160/JaberD.pdf

condition yet not everybody has access to these treatments.[9,10] Danyah Jaber, a Palestinian ethnographer, introduces the concept of political infertility to describe chronic biological impediments to conception intertwined and encompassed within the lack of a proper healthcare system, economic inabilities and the political atmosphere.

The main protagonist of Jaber's analysis is Karima, a 49-year-old refugee at the time of research from Bethlehem. In 1991, at the age of 23, Karima married her cousin Ahmad, who was a year-and-a-half-year-old. In the first two years of marriage, they couldn't conceive. In 1993, they both were assessed; Karima had ovarian cysts and galactorrhea, which caused her to produce milk whenever she saw a child, Ahmad was diagnosed with varicoceles and a hydrocele, conditions he had since his teenage years but had never been addressed. He underwent surgery to remove varicose veins from his testicles, and Karima received treatment for her ovarian cysts and galactorrhea. However, financial constraints forced them to stop their treatments. The costs were too high, and due to the economic situation in occupied Palestine after the First Intifada, it was difficult for Ahmad to find work.

With the formation of the Palestinian Authority, Karima learned they might provide free fertility treatments. She sent a request to the PA and received approval from Yasser Arafat. However, due to delays and the onset of the Second Intifada, the approval took a long time to reach them, and their financial situation worsened.

For two years, they visited a fertility specialist in East Jerusalem. In 1999, while undergoing treatment at Hadassah, they were told that with six months of treatment, they could attempt IVF. This gave them hope, but a sudden call from the hospital revealed complications with Ahmad's skull, linked to his old injury. Although some doctors believed the injury contributed to his infertility, others disagreed. The uncertainty and financial strain, compounded by the onset of the Second Intifada, made continuing treatment difficult.

Eventually, they decided to seek treatment at a clinic in Haifa, despite the cost and travel difficulties. The journey was grueling and expensive. After months of treatments and financial sacrifices, including selling Karima's car and jewelry, Ahmad needed another surgery due to a failed previous operation at a government hospital. This surgery drained their finances further.

The Second Intifada made their situation worse, with travel restrictions and financial burdens leading to Karima's depression. Ahmad could only

---

9 Kimala Price, "What is Reproductive Justice? How Women of Color Activists Are Redefining the Pro-Choice Paradigm," *Meridians: Feminism, Race, Transnationalism* 10, no. 2 (2010): 42–65.

10 Ginsburg and Rapp, eds., *Conceiving the New World Order.*

find unstable jobs, and as his condition worsened, he began experiencing neurological issues and dementia. Karima took on the full responsibility of his care, enduring extreme physical and emotional stress. Ahmad's frequent night-time wanderings and memory loss added to her burden.

Despite the hardships, Karima found solace in her faith and concluded that their inability to have children was a divine mercy, preventing further suffering. She reflected on her life, acknowledging the pain of their fertility struggles but recognizing that Ahmad's illness brought even greater challenges. She encapsulated her experience by saying that the trials of infertility seemed insignificant compared to the hardships of caring for her husband during his illness.

Karima's story exhibits the entanglements of settler-colonialism, poverty, patriarchy, and disease. Her infertility cannot be attributed solely to biological reasons; the intersectional workings of political and economic factors delayed her treatment. Infertility, like childbirth, is a time-sensitive phenomenon. Thus, making treatment facilities inaccessible without permits or delaying access results in the loss of ovarian reserve for women over time, destroying their possibility of bearing a child.

Karima's is a single story among thousands of other women facing similar struggles, disappointments and oppression. Political infertility is ensured in multiple interrelated ways; unjust imprisonment of Gazan citizens for extended times during their fertile years, blocking access to the treatment facilities, targeted destruction of infertility treatment centers are some of the physical barriers to procreation. In addition to these, occupation creates a constant threat and terror environment that threatens the emotional well-being and mental health of Gazan women, the resulting depression and stress experiences interferes with women's possibility of getting pregnant, though usually this side of warfare remains undocumented. As Holocaust survivor and trauma expert Dr. Gabor Maté aptly observes, "The concept of post-traumatic stress disorder does not apply here, as the trauma is never truly in the past."[11]

Racialized Politics of Reproductive Healthcare in Colonial Palestine

Social historian Hasso documents the historical roots of medical apartheid in Palestine in her monograph.[12] Her detailed analysis of the unequal health infrastructures established during the British Mandate years further

---

11 Zaya and Maurizio Benazzo (hosts), Science and Nonduality (SAND) Podcast episode #78, "The Crisis in Gaza: Gabor & Daniel Maté," aired February 2024. https://scienceandnonduality.com/audio/78-the-crisis-in-gaza/.

12 Frances S. Hasso, *Buried in the Red Dirt: Race, Reproduction, and Death in Modern Palestine* (Cambridge, England: Cambridge University Press, 2021).

demonstrates that the genocidal attacks of 2023–2024 are neither novel nor isolated responses to Palestinian actions against Israel. The racialized health regimes targeting the well-being of Palestinians predate the establishment of the Israeli state.

Disparities in health investment and outcomes are well-documented in UN archives. What Hasso contributed in the re-evaluation of these archives is the understanding that during the British mandate years, the difference between Palestinian and Jewish health investments was not only in scale but also in their inherently different approaches to health. The former employed a public health approach that prioritized the well-being of all communities and improved conditions for the poorest sectors, whereas the latter adopted a social health approach. Zionism's social health project was based on a racialized logic: it not only aimed to outnumber the Palestinian population but also to create modern mothers through "mothercraft," enabling positivist scientific arguments to frame Palestinian mothers as "primitive." As Sherene Seikaly writes, British colonizers assumed that "most nutritional, health, and budgetary problems in 20th-century Palestine were a result of bad cooking, inadequate mothering, and ignorant housekeeping, whether Arab or Jewish."[13]

These Western supremacist sensibilities of civilizational superiority seemed to serve a dual purpose; on the one hand, the demographic transformation of the land was aimed at minimizing infant and maternal mortality among the Jewish population, while on the other hand, the blame for these disparities was attributed to the "ignorance" of Palestinian mothers through gendered, racialized, and pro-eugenics arguments instead of being explained by the obvious infrastructural inequalities.

Hasso also underlines Palestinian elites' early recognition of the Zionist settler-colonial regime's goals of demographic shift in Palestine in favor of the Jewish population through the utilization of colonial civilizational discourse in science and medicine. Palestinian religious and medical officials refrained from participating in British Mandate Department of Health organizations that prioritized improving health by targeting "individuals" instead of "the environment."

The acts of resistance by Palestinians are not limited to refusal of participation but archival records show their academic and professional attempts to fight with British Mandate policies' affect on health in Palestine.

---

13 Sherene Seikaly, "Bodies and Needs: Lessons from Palestine," *International Journal of Middle East Studies* 46, no. 4 (November 2014): 785; as cited in Hasso, 2021.

Tawfik Canaan, a Lutheran Palestinian physician from Bethlehem known for his work to eradicate leprosy in Palestine,[14] wrote prolifically to debunk Zionist claims of superiority and progress. As the cofounder of Palestinian Arab Medical Association, Canaan challenged the Zionist claim of hygienic superiority by analyzing Jewish and Palestinian infant mortality rates separately in 1946. Using British data provided by Zionist health institutions, he argued that "despite the vast sums of Jewish money poured into the country during the 18 years and which were used for Jewish interest, not least for the sanitation of the [Jewish] colonies and the general standard of health of the Jews, [they] were not always able to decrease the mortality among their [own] infants." He demonstrated that "Jewish total infant mortality was higher in 1938 than in any previous year, except 1935 and 1936, while the total infantile mortality among the Arabs was in 1938 the lowest since 1923."[15]

In addition to Dr. Canaan's administrative, professional, and academic acts of resistance, another anecdote Hasso unearthed from British Mandate-era documents concerns a midwife named Alice Butros. A document dated July 17, 1933, in the Israeli state archives, reveals the correspondence between midwife Butros in Ramallah and Vena Winifred Rogers, the prominent superintendent midwife in Jerusalem. In this letter, Butros brought to Rogers' attention that a sick baby named Yasmin, who was acutely suffering, had been referred to the Jerusalem Government Hospital by the doctors in Ramallah but was denied treatment at the Infant Welfare Center operated by the British, and her parents were asked for money. In another document dated July 24, Hasso shares that Butros followed up and noted that the baby was getting worse, with her temperature being over 40 degrees Celsius. Her disappointment is apparent in her words: "What is the point of having a welfare center if babies in these conditions are not offered treatment?"

The last note in the archives about Butros is no longer about baby Yasmin, who most likely died due to her illness and the repeated denial of healthcare. Fed up with the hypocrisy of the mandate regime that denied a terminally ill baby basic care and treatment while providing toy babies to educate the Palestinian population—an extension of their reduction of health system failures to individual shortcomings and the supposed ignorance of Palestinians instead of deliberate infrastructural deficiencies—Butros destroyed the face of the educational toy baby in an act of defiance. This time, midwife Rogers

---

14 Salim Tamari, *Mountains against the Sea: Essays on Palestinian Society and Culture* (Berkeley: University of California Press, 2009); as cited in Hasso, 2021.

15 Tawfik Canaan, *The Hygienic and Sanitary Conditions of the Arabs of Palestine,* The Palestine Arab Medical Association Pamphlet vol. 5747 (March 1946). Jerusalem: Economic Press, Mamilla Road. National Library of Medicine, Bethesda, MD; as cited in Hasso, 2021.

wrote to the Director of Health in Mandate Palestine asking for help in repairing the educational doll that Nurse Alice had smashed. Hasso argues that "the doll symbolizes and materializes colonial prioritization of pedagogical training for Palestinian girls and women over the funding needed for preventative healthcare and treatment. Its destroyed face, moreover, viscerally captures Nurse Alice's sense that the situation was untenable."

Dr. Tawfik Canaan and Midwife Alice Butros were Palestinian subjects who witnessed the hypocrisy of the British Mandate regime as it financially and politically supported the Zionist enterprise. They refused to partake in the colonization of Palestine not only in terms of land occupation but also in the colonization of healthcare and the denial of basic human rights to Palestinians. Their acts of resistance exemplify and embody the practice of *sumud*, literally meaning steadfastness, which will be analyzed in the following section through the work of Livia Wick.

Sumud

Livia Wick's monograph on childbirth narrates a politically different climate than Frances Hasso's heavily politicized reproductive landscape.[16] Adopting a feminist perspective, Wick prioritizes personal stories and the affective experiences of Palestinian women through childbirth stories instead of analyzing grand political changes. The concept which gives the book its title, "Sumud," means steadfastness and has long been used as a strategy of resistance by several groups, ranging from political prisoners to birthing mothers.

The Palestinian Liberation Organization's sumud policy made simply living in Palestine and refusing to emigrate a political act, without needing to join a political party. They supported this by infusing funds to create jobs and sustain the local economy. Motherhood is also often represented as a figure of sumud in literature and art. Wick refrains from romanticizing sumud or instrumentalizing it as a political tool. In this context, she traces sumud in the lives of pregnant and postpartum women as they continue their everyday lives under the occupation, separated from their kin, facing economic challenges, and grieving their past lives while adjusting to new realities. Wick combines these narratives with the stories of medical workers and how they used sumud to build, work with, and expand the infrastructure of childbirth.

They redefined "sumud" as their daily perseverance, working with increased caseloads and reduced staff, and rarely visiting their families due to the closure. An interesting example of sumud is through telehealth work:

---

16 Livia Wick, *Sumud: Birth, Oral History, and Persisting in Palestine* (Syracuse: Syracuse University Press, 2023). https://dx.doi.org/10.1353/book.109933

the birth workers used cell phones to assist with births when women couldn't reach Jerusalem and called their families after shifts to stay connected. This analysis further documents that the history of medical violence in Palestine reaches well before the beginning of the genocide.

Another interesting aspect of this work is Wick's positionality in her field site. Livia Wick, who is not ethnically Palestinian, was born to parents who are immigrants to Palestine from the Soviets as medical professionals to show their support for the Palestinian resistance. Her mother, Laura Wick, herself a midwife, documented the traditional midwifery practices in Palestine. Similar to the limitations in access to health services pre-2023, the Palestinian health system's dependence on temporary foreign workers indicates the eradication of indigenous medical professionals and the limitations imposed on their work. Nevertheless, the presence of foreign medical workers also highlights the global solidarity with the Palestinian cause and people's willingness to serve in Palestine, as seen during the genocide.

The first anecdote Wick recorded as a part of her compelling fieldwork is a comprehensive account of multiple challenges women faced in occupied Palestine. As she told, Maha lived in a typical cement building on the outskirts of Ramallah, where many villagers moved for employment opportunities. She had three children and lived in a modest two-room apartment. On April 14, when she started experiencing mild contractions, she contacted her doctor at Red Crescent Hospital. The doctor, who had been stuck at the hospital for five days, advised her to come to the hospital if she could, as he couldn't leave to assist her.

Maha was hesitant to leave her husband and two children at home, especially since her husband was going through a difficult time due to unemployment. After much contemplation, she decided that going to the hospital during curfew was too risky. Instead, she reached out to a gynecologist who lived nearby and had assisted her previously. The doctor agreed to help and Maha, accompanied by her neighbor, made her way to the doctor's house, carefully avoiding detection.

The doctor informed Maha that she was not yet ready to give birth, but Maha insisted, fearing the risks of traveling back and forth. The doctor administered a drug to speed up her contractions. Despite feeling labor pains, Maha returned home and walked around to ease the process. Later that evening, she returned to the doctor's house and eventually gave birth with the doctor's assistance. However, the doctor, concerned about her own family's discomfort, hurriedly sent Maha home soon after the delivery.

As Maha and her neighbor were returning home, they encountered a tank and sought refuge in a nearby house where they were welcomed and stayed until it was safe to leave. Upon returning home, Maha faced several challenges, including her husband's anxiety and the children's nightmares about soldiers. She struggled to maintain a sense of normalcy despite the constant fear and unrest.

Maha's pregnancy had been fraught with complications and uncertainties. Initially advised to abort due to severe pain, she decided to continue the pregnancy after a second opinion suggested the baby was healthy. Throughout her pregnancy, she faced numerous medical and emotional challenges, including fears of malformations and the need for an incubator, which they struggled to afford.

Despite these challenges, Maha's daughter was born healthy. She named her Waad, meaning "promise," as a tribute to her late uncle's beloved. Though the birth brought some relief, the postnatal period was marked by continued stress and confinement, as Maha navigated life in a small apartment with her anxious husband and three children, longing for the support of her family.

Sumud as it is used in Wick's work signifies the dedication of midwives in Palestine to continue to work, live and hope when there is no proper health infrastructure and the way they develop strategies as they go at the face of constant limitations.

Mothering through Genocide

When does motherhood start? The literature is dominated by the discussions of abortion rights, especially in the U.S., that argues the beginning of life from bioethics, politics and human rights perspectives. This section takes an alternative stance in different aspects of motherhood, by looking at experiences of mothering during 2023–2024 genocide in Gaza.

In 2024, Gaza became the place where babies are orphaned before they are born. The Gaza genocide has been the culmination and crystallization of the Zionist settler-colonial regime's atrocities; yet it is also the time these genocidal acts are broadcast live to the world (Topcu, in this volume). Reproductive violence has been a fundamental part of these humanitarian crimes; it is also important to note that these atrocities are not unprecedented. Political infertility, racial politics of reproduction, and sumud—themes and concepts coined and employed to analyze the Palestinian history of reproductive health—are made evident during the events of the Gaza genocide. In the following examples, it is possible to recount the personal and political experiences of Gazan women as narratives exemplifying the entanglements of these themes.

Danyah Jaber's case study of Karima focuses on blockades and delays as methods of denying Palestinian women access to infertility treatments.

Medical anthropologists studying assisted reproductive technologies typically focus on socioeconomic barriers, citing the high cost of fertility treatments as the primary cause of limited access.[17] However, long-term imprisonment and road blockades present a rare physical barrier to infertility treatments in Palestine. In December, Israel bombed Gaza City's largest IVF center, Al Basma, destroying more than 4,000 embryos and 1,000 additional specimens of sperm and unfertilized eggs. This total destruction of infrastructure is a clear violation of international law and an act of racialized reproduction, as it aims at the killing of Palestinian babies—even embryos in this case—as a method of population control.

Political infertility does not only refer to blocking fertilization but also to the extermination of children born through long and stressful IVF treatments, suggesting an extended reach. Sadly, the settler-colonial regime's targeted attacks on the fertility of Palestinian women have been an ongoing form of violence. Gazan women have devised innovative tactics of resistance in reclaiming their reproductive rights. One of these tactics has been smuggling semen from the prison to artificially inseminate the wives of Palestinian political prisoners. In August 2012, Ammar al-Zaban became the first known Palestinian prisoner to father a child with his wife through the use of smuggled sperm. Since that time, the practice of smuggling sperm has become recognized as a significant aspect of the Palestinian resistance against Israeli occupation.[18]

As argued above, Hasso shows that the apartheid regime, which assumes the racial superiority of Jewish communities in the region, predates the establishment of the state of Israel. It is important to situate the violations of humanitarian law on healthcare grounds during the Gazan genocide within this longer and deeper trajectory. The history and, ultimately, the destruction of Al Shifa Hospital exemplifies the slaughter of Palestinian lives—civilians in a hospital, including newborns, through the denial of safety and resources. This is intricately linked to the racial colonial logic that denied care to Palestinian babies during the Mandate period as a tactical tool for eliminating the Palestinian population. Al Shifa Hospital was converted from British army barracks to a hospital in 1946 and has been the biggest and most advanced medical complex in the Gaza Strip. In November 2024, the Israeli military destroyed Al Shifa Hospital after a fourteen-day siege during

---

17 Marcia C. Inhorn, "Where has the quest for conception taken us? Lessons from anthropology and sociology," *Reproductive Biomedicine & Society Online* 10 (May 13, 2020): 46–57. https://doi.org/10.1016/j.rbms.2020.04.001

18 MEE Staff, "Palestine: Quadruplets born from prisoner's smuggled sperm," *Middle East Eye,* June 13, 2023. https://www.middleeasteye.net/news/palestine-israel-quadruplets-born-prisoner-smuggled-sperm

which the electric and water supply to the hospital was cut. At this point, the hospital was home to 7,000 displaced people from the North, as well as 1,500 patients and medical staff. By November 11, 39 premature babies at the hospital could no longer receive critical care in the incubators. Within a week, eight babies died. All these war crimes were based on Israel's claim that Al Shifa was used as a base by Hamas militants. In an unapologetic act of racial prioritization—saving the potential lives that would be taken by Hamas militants allegedly based in the hospital—the imminent and actual lives of Palestinian civilians were sacrificed.

In the last part of this section, we will analyze an incident of sumud during the Gaza genocide through a personal narrative of a female healthcare worker from Gaza.

Dr. Itimad, who graduated from İstanbul Medical Faculty in 1996 and completed her master's in Obstetrics and Gynecology in Egypt, has preferred to work in Gaza's Shifa Hospital since then. A cancer survivor and mother of four, Itimad was separated from her husband, a radiation oncologist working in Türkiye, for many years. Her son, a dentist, and her son-in-law, a journalist, were both arrested by Israelis on December 8th when their apartment was bombed, and all the men were detained. Both were tortured. Her son was released after two days with many wounds and signs of torture, but her son-in-law is still in an Israeli prison.

She and her nine family members (three daughters, son-in-law, and four grandchildren) applied to be evacuated from Gaza after her colleagues and friends from Türkiye raised the required amount of money, on March 20th. Since they had to head south, she announced on Facebook, and with a group of 120 people, they began the dangerous journey on foot. The group was targeted by gunfire five times, had to pass through many checkpoints, and finally reached Deir al-Balah. They spent two weeks there and left Gaza through Rafah. On April 19, they reached Cairo, where they spent one month on official procedures and visas. On May 19, they finally reached İstanbul and are still trying to make a new start.

After their house was demolished, Itimad and her family had taken shelter in Shifa Hospital for two months. When the IDF attacked Shifa Hospital on February 3, they went to the Sahabe region and stayed there for another two months. In a very small clinic there, Itimad had to perform her daughter's third cesarean section. Using a very small amount of anesthetic, the anesthesiologist administered the spinal block, and without any of the medications routinely used (oxytocin, painkillers, etc.), Itimad completed the surgery on her daughter. The lovely baby girl is now almost five months old. Dr. Itimad embodies Sumud as a Gazan woman, a healthcare worker, a mother and a grandmother.

All concepts analyzed in this paper are lived through during the Gaza genocide in 2023–2024. Yet, it is impossible to identify those events with a singular theme-oppression and resistance, genocide and sumud appear together. As Israerlis bombarded the IVF centers as a case of political infertility, Gazans found ways to smuggle sperm to impregnate the wives of political prisoners. When al-Shifa hospital was surrounded and destroyed amidst all the pain and terror, Palestinian doctors like Itimad did their best to save their people.

Safebirth in Palestine Initiative

One of the goals of this chapter is to document not only the ways in which settler colonial power works and oppress the Gazan people but also to acknowledge and stand with the Palestinian resistance against it.

Since the early days of the genocidal attacks, we have been concerned about the safety and health of pregnant women and newborns in Gaza. Founded by birth professionals in Türkiye, as the Safebirth Palestine initiative we tried several avenues to deliver aid for reproductive and sexual health services. Our initial hope was based on the Turkish Government's possible establishment of a field hospital. We created a volunteer database for this setup, and the Turkish Ministry of Health even completed its feasibility work and started the search for an ideal location. However, these plans failed to materialize. Following this disappointment, we turned our attention to collaborations with several humanitarian organizations. Through established and newly cultivated networks, we were able to offer telehealth services as well as provide support through collaborations via our fundraising efforts. Our call to support pregnant women and halt the attacks in Gaza gained widespread support from multiple organizations, including Spanish doulas, French midwives, Malaysian doctors, and British healthcare workers.

Because we were unable to serve in Gaza in person, we created a confidential database of pregnant women and provided them with telehealth support via WhatsApp. We communicated in English and with the help of Arabic-speaking friends who acted as translators. Without the ability to offer physical examinations, necessary equipment, and medication, the scope of this care was extremely limited. However, the women we contacted expressed that the psychological support and reassurance provided by physicians were a relief for them.

One of the women we communicated with, with the help of an Arabic-speaking colleague, was Amirah, a successful 19-year-old architecture student who was pregnant with her first child. In her seventh month, she was informed that her baby was smaller than expected for its gestational age. By the ninth month, she was surviving only on flour and canned food, leading to weight loss. Additionally, she faced Rh incompatibility due to having different blood types with her spouse. Through the organization Fajr Scientific International,[19] we arranged to send various medications and Anti-D injections to Gaza with a doctor. However, before the medications could arrive, Amirah gave birth naturally at Al-Imarat Hospital to a baby girl she named Noor al Ayn.[20] Fortunately, the baby also had Rh-negative blood, otherwise the medical complications would have been inevitable. After receiving one day of support in an incubator, the baby was safely placed in her mother's arms. After several days of anxious waiting without news, Amirah finally responded, thankfully informing us that, after the attack on Rafah, her family had taken refuge in Khan Younis and were safe.

When specific medications were needed, we procured them from Türkiye or Egypt and did our utmost to deliver them to the patients or families in need. Our desperation and disappointment were somewhat alleviated when we were able to fundraise specifically for the Safebirth in Palestine project. One such fundraising event took place at a Gazan restaurant in Washington, D.C., where the solidarity among the attendees renewed our determination to continue supporting Gazan women.

The Safebirth in Palestine Project was well received by media channels, including The Guardian and CNN. As mainstream media failed to document the horrors of genocide on the ground, their support for the project is not only proof of the presence of pro-Palestinian journalists in these institutions but also indicative of the fact that only certain humanitarian projects are deemed publishable by their administrators.

The Safebirth in Palestine Project follows Kim Tallbear's feminist-indigenous approach at its heart[21]. Determined to distance itself from white feminism that chooses to ignore the pain and terror Palestinian women are experiencing, our efforts are grounded in standing with Palestinian women through constant communication with them. We refrain from framing these humanitarian efforts as "giving back" or isolating women from their families or communities. Instead of apolitically situating the problem as a mere

---

19 One of our collaborators for on ground operations, for more information please visit the website: https://fajr.org.

20 Noor al ayn literally means the light of the eye in Arabic.

21 Kim TallBear, "Standing With and Speaking as Faith: A Feminist-Indigenous Approach to Inquiry" [research note], *Journal of Research Practice* 10, no. 2 (2014), Article N17. https://kimtallbear.com/pubs/standing-with-and-speaking-as-faith-a-feminist-indigenous-approach-to-inquiry/

reproductive health issue, we recognize that the challenges and violations Gazan women face are a direct result of the settler-colonial regime of Israel.[22]

It is impossible to know for certain how many pregnant women, mothers, or babies have been killed or maimed in Gaza, but the estimated death toll by June 19th, 2024, was 186,000.[23] The genocidal regime's specific targeting of pregnant women and children is a stark demonstration of genocide's aims, which extend beyond Gaza to threaten the broader Palestinian population and future generations. In addition to violating international law by targeting civilians and children, these actions are clear evidence of ethnic cleansing in Gaza. Moreover, Palestinian people are not just numbers; women and children are not mere statistics. This essay emerged from our efforts to remember the stories and narratives of Palestinian women from a reproductive health perspective during the days of genocide. In the face of such a horrific situation, which can only be defined as genocide, and deeply disappointed by the silence of our birthworker colleagues, scholars, feminist organizations, and human rights activists, we reiterate our dedication to standing with birth workers and birthing women in Palestine by all means available. Lastly, despite the horrendous genocide unfolding before our eyes, Palestinian women like Dr. Itimad and Amirah's embodiment of sumud renew our faith in Palestinian liberation. Safebirth in Palestine is a result of this hope. To them we dedicate this chapter and our work.

22 Palestinian anthropologist Lila Abu-Lughod reflects on the problematic nature of white feminism's desire to "save Muslim women" without considering our own responsibility in the circumstances that oppress these women. Ilana Feldman offers a similar critique, pointing to humanitarianism as often being depicted as non-political terrain.

23 Rasha Khatiba, Martin McKee, and Salim Yusuf, "Counting the Dead in Gaza: Difficult but Essential," *Lancet* 404, no. 10449 (July 20, 2024): 237–38. https://www.thelancet.com/journals/lancet/article/PIIS0140-6736(24)01169-3/fulltext

Israel Is Waging War on Palestinians Inside Prisons

Basil Farraj | Lisa Hajjar

SINCE ISRAEL LAUNCHED its latest war on October 7, 2023, conditions in Israeli prisons have paralleled the retaliatory and besieging assault on the people of Gaza. At the start of the war, Israel's avowedly fascist National Security Minister Itamar Ben-Gvir and his handpicked head of the Israel Prison Service (IPS), Kobi Yaakobi, instituted a merciless approach towards Palestinian prisoners.[1] Access to water and electricity was drastically reduced, as was the quantity and quality of food which, coupled with the shuttering of canteens where prisoners previously had been able to purchase supplies,

---

1 "Prior to the beginning of Israel's latest genocidal war against Palestinians in 2023, Ben-Gvir decided to limit Palestinian prisoners' visitation rights from once a month to once every two months, a decision that led to threats of a mass hunger strike by Palestinian prisoners. In his attack against prisoners and their rights, [Ben-Gvir] tried to close Palestinian prisoner-run bakeries; attempted to stop funding what he referred to as prisoners' 'non-essential medical treatment'; pushed for a bill that would instate the death penalty as a punishment against Palestinians; and blocked the possibility of early release for Palestinian prisoners, amongst other attempts to withdraw prisoners' rights." Basil Farraj, "Rejecting Defeat and Approaching Liberation: Palestinian Prisoners' Hunger Strikes," *Wasafiri* 39, no. 2 (2024): 20.

Basil Farraj is the Director of the Ibrahim Abu-Lughod Institute of International Studies, and Assistant Professor in the Department of Philosophy and Cultural Studies at Birzeit University, Palestine. His research addresses the intersections of memory, resistance, and art by prisoners and others at the receiving end of violence.

Lisa Hajjar is Professor of Sociology at the University of California at Santa Barbara. She specializes in the relationship between law and conflict. Her publications include *Courting Conflict: The Israeli Military Court System in the West Bank and Gaza* (2005), *Torture: A Sociology of Violence and Human Rights* (2013), and *The War in Court: Inside the Long Fight against Torture* (2022).

amounted to a starvation policy.[2] Personal items, including letters, books, medicine, and radios, were seized. Many prisoners were moved to isolation. Others are held in cells designed for a maximum of five or six that are now overcrowded with twelve or more. The IPS banned prison visits by monitors from the International Committee of the Red Cross, maintaining that this will endure until the ICRC visits Israelis held by Hamas in the Gaza Strip. For West Bank Palestinians, family visits which the ICRC had facilitated have also been banned. Phone calls to relatives have become impossible and lawyers' access to clients has been restricted.

Soldiers and guards have rampaged through compounds, assaulting prisoners and sometimes firing rubber bullets and tear gas. Interrogators have resurrected the crudest forms of physical torture, but brute violence is endemic throughout every prison and detention center. Dozens of Palestinians have died or been killed in custody since October.[3]

FIGURE 1

This war inside Israeli prisons is fueled by escalating arrest campaigns across historic Palestine.[4] Prior to October 7, 5,200 Palestinians were incarcerated.[5] Since then, the numbers have exploded. More than 1,300 Gaza Palestinians—including humanitarian workers, women, and children—were swept up in indiscriminate capture operations and transferred to Israel [see Figure 1]. Others were targeted for arrest. According to the World Health Organization, at least 214 healthcare workers were taken into custody from

---

2 "Palestinians in Israeli Prisons Experience the War," *Jadaliyya,* November 10, 2023. https://www.jadaliyya.com/Details/45487

3 Hagar Shezaf, "27 Gaza Detainees Have Died in Custody at Israeli Military Facilities Since the Start of the War," *Ha'aretz,* March 7, 2024.

4 "Escalation of Arrest Campaigns since the Beginning of the Israeli Aggression... And the Conditions of the Prisoners in Israeli Prisons," Addameer: Prisoner Support and Human Rights Association, N.D. https://rb.gy/5o2o9s

5 "Statistics," Addameer; https://www.addameer.org/statistics

hospitals where they were working when Israeli forces attacked the facilities.[6] After weeks of brutal interrogations in military detention sites, those suspected of having ties to Hamas are sent to prisons and others are deposited at the Kerem Shalom crossing to make their way back into Gaza.

Belying official claims that the primary objective of the war on Gaza is to destroy Hamas, in the West Bank where the Palestinian Authority maintains nominal control, more than 9,000 Palestinians were arrested between October and early June 2024.[7] Inside Israel, two hundred Palestinian citizens were arrested and interrogated, mostly on suspicions of "incitement to terrorism" and "identifying with terror organizations" for expressing opposition to the war and condemnation of its human toll.[8]

As of June 2024, 9,112 Palestinians were being held in Israeli prisons, either as "security prisoners" who have been convicted (2,072) or remanded for trial (2,733) or as "security detainees" who are administratively detained without charges (3,410). Another 899 have been labeled "unlawful combatants."[9]

Testimonies of Torture

People released from custody emerged emaciated, bruised from beatings, and deeply scarred from tight and protracted cuffing. Their testimonies provide glimpses into the abyss.[10] Omar Assaf, 74, was arrested in Ramallah in October 2023 and administratively detained for six months in Ofer prison in the West Bank. After he was released in April 2024, before-and-after photos were posted on social media; the "after" photo, taken as he exited the Ofer military complex, reveals that he had lost a great deal of weight (twenty-nine kilograms) and his hair had turned white [see Figure 2]. As people gathered

---

6 Kavitha Chekuru, "Gaza's Stolen Healers," *The Intercept,* May 24, 2024. https://theintercept.com/2024/05/24/gaza-palestinian-doctors-hospital-detained-missing-disappeared/

7 "Brief on detention campaigns carried out in the West Bank since October 7 until June 3, 2024," Commission of Detainees and Ex-Detainees Affairs. https://cda.gov.ps/index.php/en/51-slider-en/17180-on-the-241st-day-of-genocide-brief-on-detention-campaigns-carried-out-in-the-west-bank-since-october-7-until-june-3-2025

8 "Crackdown on Freedom of Speech of Palestinian Citizens of Israel," Adalah: The Legal Center for Arab Minority Rights in Israel, updated November 16, 2023. https://www.adalah.org/en/content/view/10925

9 "'Security' Inmates in Prisons inside Israel," HaMoked. https://www.hamoked.org/

10 Imad Abu Hawash, "'It would've been better if they shot us': Palestinians Recount Prison Abuse," *+927 Magazine,* December 8, 2023. https://www.972mag.com/palestinians-abused-israeli-prisons-torture/

to greet Assaf, he described the contrast between what he endured during previous periods of imprisonment over the past four decades and the present. "The conditions inside Israeli prisons today are unprecedented,"[11] he said.

FIGURE 2

In May, Euro-Med Human Rights Monitor interviewed approximately 100 people who were seized in Gaza and later released, including twenty-two women, four children, and seventeen elderly men. According to Euro-Med Monitor's findings,[12] the Israeli army routinely commits widespread crimes of arbitrary arrest, enforced disappearance, premeditated murder, torture, inhuman treatment, sexual violence, and denial of a fair trial. It also confirms that the Israeli army used physical and psychological torture against Palestinian civilian detainees, including beatings with the intent to kill, sexual violence, electrocution, blindfolding, and long-term hand and foot shackles.

Euro-Med identified various forms of cruel and degrading treatment and extra-judicial punishments perpetrated against Palestinian detainees, including strip searches and forced nudity; breaking bones and teeth; being stepped, spit and urinated on; punishment for praying; and threats of rape and death.

First-person accounts of torture and abuse are validated by a deluge of photos and videos shot by Israeli soldiers and circulated on Telegram and other social media sites [see Figure 3]. Some of the most gruesome images depict shirtless or naked detainees bound and blindfolded, being dragged across gravel and kicked in their heads and genitals[13] [see Figure 4].

---

11 Basil Farraj visited Omar Assaf following his release in April.
12 Euro-Med Human Rights Monitor, "Hostages of Israeli Revenge in the Gaza Strip," May 21, 2024.
13 See The Listening Post, "Genocide in Gaza through the Eyes of Israeli Soldiers," *Al Jazeera* video [9:10], March 4, 2024. https://www.youtube.com/watch?v=JAT9NQ4WkE0

FIGURE 3

FIGURE 4

Images that shamelessly revel in Palestinians' degradation and pain were intended to be viewed by Jewish Israelis as trophy shots and vindications for the attacks Hamas carried out on October 7. The other obvious intent in taking and disseminating these images was to instill a sense of fear and capitulation among Palestinians.

But photos and videos of Palestinians being abused have circulated internationally and been published in the foreign media,[14] where the condemnations and reproaches they have evoked are a source of consternation and concern for Israeli officials[15] who may have to contend with the threat that material evidence of torture will pose for them in the future.

---

14 See "UN Says Palestinians Detained by Israeli Forces Humiliated, Beaten," *Al Jazeera,* January 19, 2024. https://www.aljazeera.com/news/2024/1/19/un-says-palestinians-detained-by-israeli-forces-humiliated-beaten

"Gaza: Video Appears to Show Palestinian Men Stripped and Detained by IDF," *BBC* news video [00:47], December 8, 2023. https://www.bbc.com/news/av/world-middle-east-67659922

15 Emanuel Fabian and Jeremy Sharon, "IDF Sets Up Committee to Probe Alleged Torture of Palestinian Terror Suspects," *Times of Israel,* May 28, 2024. https://www.timesofisrael.com/idf-sets-up-committee-to-probe-alleged-torture-of-palestinian-terror-suspects/

In order to manage the messaging about the treatment of prisoners while sating domestic appetites for more evidence of retribution, prison authorities have granted access to some reporters. One segment broadcast on Israel's Channel 14 shows an IPS officer boasting about the abusive treatment being meted out in the facility.[16] Panning to prisoners forced to sit on the concrete floor of a courtyard [See Figure 5], he comments, "There are 150 prisoners here. None of them moves…until the shift supervisor approves it." Another scene shows guards opening a cell and shouting at the prisoners to kneel on the ground with their hands on top of their heads. The reporter comments, "What you see now is their daily routine. The days of sweets and meat is over."

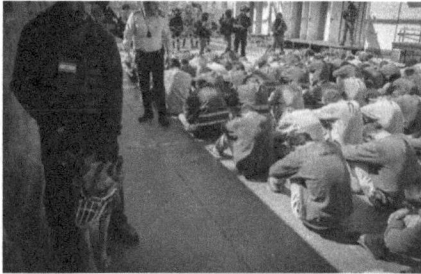

FIGURE 5. *Palestinian detainees in the courtyard of a prison in southern Israel, February 14, 2024.*

A segment broadcast on Channel 13 begins with a scene of armed Israeli guards, accompanied by a dog, entering a cell as one screams, "Head on the floor!" [17] Another scene shows what the reporter refers to as a "secret wing" where prisoners are forced to kneel with their hands and feet cuffed at all times. The reporter comments on a nationalist song playing in the background: "This song 'Am Yisrael Chai' is heard in the wing, repeatedly, non-stop. The prison authorities claim that it is meant to boost the staff's morale. But it is clear that this is another part of the psychological warfare against the prisoners."

---

16 A subtitled video can be accessed through Quds News Network on *X* [formerly Twitter]: "An Israeli television crew was escorted to an Israeli detention camp," February 2, 2024: https://twitter.com/QudsNen/status/1753441486358679852

17 Jonathan Ofir, "Israel Channel 13 prison tour 18.2.2024," YouTube video [10:49], March 1, 2024. https://www.youtube.com/watch?v=jvlIPxxS8Pg

From Bad to Worse

Prison conditions for Palestinians have always been grueling and severe and torture has been a durable feature of Israel interrogations. But in the current period—while Israel wages a genocidal war on Gaza and military assaults and state-supported settler pogroms are rampant across the West Bank—violence and dehumanization perpetrated by Israeli soldiers, security agents, and IPS staff against people in custody have reached a new level. According to Qadura Fares, head of the Palestinian Commission for Detainees and Ex-Detainees Affairs, "During this war, the Israeli authorities are trying to deal with all prisoners in a way that allows them to get revenge on the Palestinians."[18]

Prisoners requiring medical care—whether for new injuries or chronic diseases—have been denied access to prison clinics and outside hospitals. This has exacerbated the long-practiced policy of medical negligence by the IPS and complicit medical professionals. A West Bank man recently released from Ramon prison in southern Israel said there appears to be a standing order to "call on the guards only when prisoners die."[19] One of the medical-negligence deaths in detention was Arafat Hamdan, 25, a diabetic who died two days after he was detained because he was denied insulin or even a handful of sugar; doctors and nurses callously ignored his cellmates' pleas for help when he became unconscious. Adnan al-Bursh, a doctor detained from Gaza's al-Awda Hospital, was tortured to death on April 19; the IPS only acknowledged his fate two weeks later.[20]

At a hearing in the Ofer military court on March 10, 2024,[21] one of the prisoners started talking about the severe beatings he had received at the hands of the IPS's Nahshon, the unit in charge of transporting prisoners between prisons and to court. "I just tried to cover my head when they were beating us," he said before being silenced by a screaming guard. Another

---

18 Ruth Michaelson, Sufian Taha, and Quique Kierszenbaum, "Israeli Abuse of Jailed Palestinian Leader Marwan Barghouti 'Amounts to Torture,'" *The Guardian*, May 18, 2024.

19 Interview with Basil Farraj.

20 "Doctor from Gaza's al-Shifa Hospital Dies in Israeli Prison," *Al Jazeera*, May 3, 2024. https://www.aljazeera.com/news/2024/5/3/doctor-from-gazas-al-shifa-hospital-dies-in-israeli-prison

21 Israeli authorities allowed one member of a prisoner's family to attend court sessions that prisoners join through video conference. These court sessions have become the only way for families to communicate with their loved ones, albeit for a few minutes. Basil Farraj, whose father is imprisoned, was able to attend a session in the Ofer military court on March 27, 2024, in which a number of prisoners appeared on the screen.

prisoner described the violent treatment he received while being transported as a "continuation of interrogational torture through other means."

Israel's war inside its prisons has not been directed only against people captured since October. All Palestinian prisoners have been affected by the vengeance policy of heightened violence and inhumane deprivations. Thaer Abu Assab, who was imprisoned in Ketziot for eighteen years, was beaten to death in his cell by nineteen guards on December 21, 2023.[22]

Marwan Barghouti, a popular political figure who has spent twenty-four years in prison, suffered a dislocated shoulder—untreated—when he was dragged with his hands cuffed behind his back to an isolation cell where he was beaten unconscious. According to his lawyer, Igal Dotan, "He's struggling to see out of his right eye, as a result of one of the assaults." Dotan also commented on Barghouti's dramatic weight loss: "You wouldn't recognize him if you compare his current appearance with the famous photos of him."[23] In December, after Barghouti was transferred to Ayalon prison, he was "dragged on the floor naked in front of other prisoners."[24] Since October, Barghouti has been transferred to three different prisons and held in isolation in each.

Walid Daqqa, a Palestinian citizen of Israel who became a prominent and respected intellectual for his literary and social-philosophical writings, was incarcerated for thirty-eight years. In 2022, he was diagnosed with a rare form of cancer (Myelofibrosis) that would require a bone marrow transfusion. Daqqa died in prison on April 7, 2024, because the IPS refused him medical care and courts rejected petitions from his family for compassionate release in his last days.[25] His body remains in Israeli custody.

State Secrets and Crimes

The Israeli government has labeled some Palestinians detained in the war "unlawful combatants." This concept, an invention of the U.S. government, originated on November 13, 2001, when George W. Bush issued an executive order decreeing that as president, he had the authority to categorize anyone taken into U.S. custody overseas in the context of the "war on terror" as an "unlawful enemy combatant." This status designation has no grounding in

---

22 "Israel Admits 19 Prison Guards Severely Beat Palestinian Prisoner Abu Assab that Led to His Death," *Wafa: Palestine News and Info Agency*, December 12, 2024. https://english.wafa.ps/Pages/Details/140225

23 Michaelson, Taha, and Kierszenbaum, "Israeli Abuse of Jailed Palestinian Leader Marwan Barghouti 'Amounts to Torture.'"

24 Ibid.

25 "Walid Nimer As'aad Daqqa," Addameer, May 15, 2024. https://www.addameer.org/ar/node/5100

the laws of war (i.e., the 1949 Geneva Conventions) because every person is either a combatant or a civilian. The objective in fabricating a new status category was to legitimize secret detention, but the ulterior motive of this secrecy was to enable the use of interrogation techniques that are prohibited and criminalized. Bush's executive order included an across-the-board prohibition for people designated as unlawful combatants to challenge their detention or treatment in any court anywhere which, for all intents and purposes, meant they were disappeared.

Israel copied this contra-legal U.S. model when it passed its own Unlawful Combatants Law in 2002. According to the Israeli version, the unlawful combatant label can be applied to anyone who has directly or indirectly participated in hostile acts against the State of Israel and who is not entitled to prisoner-of-war status according to the Geneva Conventions. After the law was passed, the designation was applied mainly to foreign Arabs who already were being secretly detained in Israel.[26] "No one knew how many captives were held in Israel's Facility 1391, how long they had been there or if there were more such prisons. However, the first testimonies from inmates revealed horrifying conditions. For most of the time, they were kept in a state of sensory deprivation, made to wear blacked-out goggles, except for when being tortured."[27]

On December 18, 2023, the Knesset amended the Unlawful Combatants Law to expand secret detention by enabling the military to hold people for forty-five days without an arrest warrant or any oversight by a court. Under the amended law, detainees can be denied access to a lawyer for up to seventy-five days on the order of the prison official who is responsible for implementing the law. Courts have been granted the prerogative to decide that a detainee can be held for up to 180 days without legal counsel.[28]

Sde Teiman, a military camp in the Negev desert, was partially converted into a detention center after the start of the war; it has been characterized as a "black site" because it is inaccessible to independent monitors and officials regard the identities and treatment of those held there a state secret. Two

---

26 Aviv Lavie, "Inside Israel's Secret Prison," *Ha'aretz*, August 20, 2003. https://www.haaretz.com/2003-08-20/ty-article/inside-israels-secret-prison/0000017f-e76d-d97e-a37f-f76d6c620000

27 Jonathan Cook, "The Message of Israel's Torture Chambers Is Directed at All of Us, Not Just Palestinians," *Middle East Eye*, May 24, 2024. https://www.middleeasteye.net/big-story/israel-torture-chambers-message-directed-us-palestinians

28 Isaac Chotiner, "The Brutal Conditions Facing Palestinian Prisoners," *New Yorker*, March 21, 2024. https://www.newyorker.com/news/q-and-a/the-brutal-conditions-facing-palestinian-prisoners

military bases in the West Bank, Anatot and Ofer, also have had sections repurposed for secret detention.

In late March 2024, a doctor working at Sde Teiman sent a letter to Israel's defense minister, health minister, and attorney general attesting to grotesque abuses. The veil of secrecy shrouding Sde Teiman was lifted in April when *Ha'aretz* reported on this whistleblowing: "'Just this week, two prisoners had their legs amputated due to handcuff injuries, which unfortunately is a routine event,' the physician said in the letter. He said inmates are fed through straws, defecate in diapers, and are held [in] constant restraints, which violate medical ethics and the law."[29] The doctor's letter continues: "I am writing to warn you that the facilities' operations do not comply with a single section among those dealing with health in the Incarceration of Unlawful Combatants Law."

On May 11, the U.S. media corporation CNN published an explosive exposé about Sde Teiman based on accounts by three whistleblowing soldiers who were based there and twelve Gazans who were recently released.[30] According to the whistleblowers, the detention facility has two parts. One section contains a large barbed-wire pen where blindfolded Palestinians are shackled and bound in stress positions for up to sixteen hours a day with no shelter from the desert heat. [See Figure 6] Punishment for talking or moving can involve being zip-tied to the barbed wire fence.

FIGURE 6. *Image of Sde Teiman prison camp shot by a whistleblower, published by CNN.*

---

29 Hagar Shezaf and Michael Hauser Tov, "Doctor at Israeli Field Hospital for Detained Gazans: 'We Are All Complicit in Breaking the Law,'" *Ha'aretz*, April 4, 2024. https://www.haaretz.com/israel-news/2024-04-04/ty-article/.premium/doctor-at-idf-field-hospital-for-detained-gazans-we-are-all-complicit-in-breaking-law/0000018e-a59c-dfed-ad9f-afdfb5ce0000

30 CNN's International Investigations and Visuals teams, "Strapped Down, Blindfolded, Held in Diapers: Israeli Whistleblowers Detail Abuse of Palestinians in Shadowy Detention Center," *CNN*, May 11, 2024. https://edition.cnn.com/2024/05/10/middleeast/israel-sde-teiman-detention-whistleblowers-intl-cmd/index.html

The other section contains a field hospital where wounded detainees are shackled to beds, blindfolded, stripped of their clothes, and forced to defecate in diapers. [See Figure 7] CNN reported that "doctors sometimes amputated prisoners' limbs due to injuries sustained from constant handcuffing; of medical procedures sometimes performed by underqualified medics earning it a reputation for being 'a paradise for interns'; and where the air is filled with the smell of neglected wounds left to rot." One informant told CNN: "I was asked to learn how to do things on the patients, performing minor medical procedures that are totally outside my expertise."

FIGURE 7. *CNN created a model of the Sde Teiman prison infirmary based on testimony by whistleblowers.*

Israeli doctors' decisions to perform medical procedures on detainees without anesthesia is not due to shortages, as is the case facing doctors in Gaza, but a choice that comports with the retaliatory and illegal nature of the broader war. "Sde Teiman is the small torture chamber," writes Jonathan Cook, "mirroring the much bigger torture chamber of Gaza itself, where bombs and starvation are achieving precisely the same ends."[31]

In addition to the Sde Teiman military base, some Gazans are detained in the Ofer and Ketziot prisons. In contradiction to its own timeframe for detainees to see a lawyer, the government has made it virtually impossible for Gazans to do so. According to Qadus Fares, "Israeli prison authorities demand receiving a hard copy of a direct power of attorney made for the lawyer, and signed by the detainee's relatives in Gaza, which is impossible: the lawyer will not access Gaza, and the families of the prisoners cannot enter Israel. Having a power of attorney sent by WhatsApp or email is not accepted by Israeli authorities, and so prisoners aren't allowed legal representation."[32]

---

31 Cook, "The Message of Israel's Torture Chambers."
32 Mohamed Solaimane, "The Systematic Torture of Gazans in Israel's Secret Prisons," *The New Arab*, May 24, 2024. https://www.newarab.com/analysis/systematic-torture-gazans-israels-secret-prisons

A Long History of Torture and Violence

Current conditions inside Israeli prisons and detention centers signal an intensification of the violence and torture practiced against captive Palestinians since 1948. Following the 1967 occupation of the remainder of historic Palestine and the establishment of a military administration in Gaza and the West Bank, interrogational torture became a central component in the trifecta of Israeli control strategies, the other two being arrest and prosecution. Because the government deems all Palestinians to be actual or potential "security threats," most interrogations were conducted by Israel's domestic security agency, the Shin Bet. And because the Israeli military courts are dependent on Palestinians' confessions to secure convictions or to justify extended administrative detention,[33] the use of violence and coercions to elicit incriminating statements became a mainstay of interrogations.

On June 19, 1977, the *Sunday Times of London* published a groundbreaking investigation by its Inside team into allegations of pervasive Israeli torture.[34] The investigation concluded:

1. Israel's security and intelligence services ill-treat Arabs in detention.

2. Some of the ill-treatment is merely primitive: prolonged beatings, for example. But more refined techniques are also used, including electric-shock torture and confinement in specially-constructed cells. This sort of apparatus, allied to the degree of organization evident in its application, removes Israel's practice from the lesser realms of brutality and places it firmly in the category of torture.

3. Torture takes place in at least six centres: at the prisons of the four main occupied towns of Nablus, Ramallah and Hebron on the West Bank, and Gaza in the south; at the detention centre in Jerusalem, known as the Russian Compound; and at a special military intelligence centre whose whereabouts are uncertain, but which testimony suggests is somewhere inside the vast military supply base at Sarafand, near Lod airport on the Jerusalem-Tel Aviv road. There is some evidence too that,

---

33 Lisa Hajjar, *Courting Conflict: The Israeli Military Court System in the West Bank and Gaza* (Santa Barbara: University of California Press, 2005).

34 "Special Report: Israeli Torture," *The Sunday Times of London*, June 19, 1977. The report and the Israeli government's response are reprinted in *Journal of Palestine Studies* 6, no. 4 (Summer 1977): 199–219.

at least for a time, there was a second such camp somewhere near Gaza.

4. All of Israel's security services are implicated: the Shin Beth [sic],…which reports to the office of the Prime Minister; Military Intelligence, which reports to the Minister of Defence; the border police; and Latam, Israel's "Department for Special Missions," both of which report to the Police Minister.

5. Torture is organized so methodically that it cannot be dismissed as a handful of "rogue cops" exceeding orders. It is systematic. It appears to be sanctioned at some level as deliberate policy.

6. Torture seems to be used for three purposes. The first is, of course, to extract information. The second motive, which seems at least as common, is to induce people to confess to "security" offences, of which they may, or may not, be guilty. The extracted confession is then used as the principal evidence in court: Israel makes something of the fact that it has few political prisoners in its jails, only those duly convicted according to law. The third purpose appears to be to persuade Arabs in the occupied territories that it is least painful to behave passively…

Like other torturing regimes, Israel responded to the *Times* report—as it did for accusations by other sources—by denying torture and abuse and claiming that such allegations were lies by "enemies of the state."

One of the first detailed studies of Israeli torture was a 1984 report published by Law in the Service of Man (later renamed al-Haq), *Torture and Intimidation in the West Bank: The Case of Al-Fara'a Prison.*[35] Al-Fara'a, located north of Nablus in the West Bank, was opened as a prison and detention center in 1982. Israel's Chief of Staff Rafael Eitan used the occasion to announce a new policy of *tertur*—an Israeli slang variant of "torture" used to describe military training exercises that are violent and degrading—for dealing with Palestinians who were mobilizing against the occupation. According to Captain Artzi Mordechai, "Population tertur does not mean that you punish those who did something, but you simply round up everyone, just like that."[36] The tertur policy was part of a broader escalation of attempts by the military administration to deter and punish widescale Palestinian protest and political activism.

---

35 *Torture and Intimidation in the West Bank: The Case of Al-Fara'a Prison* (Ramallah, Palestine: Law in the Service of Man, 1985), 3.
36 Ibid.

In 1987, Israel acquired the ignominious distinction of being the first state in the world to *publicly* proclaim the right to torture as a national security necessity, albeit the authorized violent and degrading tactics were euphemized as "moderate amounts of physical pressure." This claim of a right to torture was the enactment of a recommendation by the Landau Commission, a state-established commission to investigate possible wrongdoings by the Shin Bet.[37] The Landau Commission validated long-denied allegations of systematic abuse, but concurred with the Shin Bet that such tactics are necessary in the state's fight against "hostile terrorist activity," which was broadly defined to include not only acts of violence but any resistance—including speech—to the occupation or assertions of Palestinian national rights. The Commission based its recommendation on Shin Bet claims that the tactics they were using were necessary but, because they were legally forbidden, agents were impelled to lie about their use to military judges when confessions were challenged as coerced. The "legalization" of torture enabled agents to avoid perjuring themselves.

Days after the government adopted the Landau Commission's recommendation, the first Palestinian intifada (uprising) began. To put down mass resistance to the endless and brutal occupation, the Israeli military put the trifecta into overdrive as tens of thousands of Palestinians were arrested, interrogated, prosecuted, convicted, and imprisoned. In 1989, Israel had the largest per capita prison population in the world.

The intifada, the mass arrests, and several deaths in detention increased international attention and criticism directed at Israeli interrogation policies and practices. In the early 1990s, the Shin Bet largely shifted from tactics that leave physical marks, like beatings and electric shocks, in favor of "clean" techniques[38] like protracted position abuse, isolation, sleep deprivation, shaking, and confinement in refrigerated or overheated spaces. [See Figure 8] Such tactics are no less torturous, but the difference is that they manipulate the body to target the mind. As Elaine Scarry explains, they cause people subjected to such tactics to think: "my body hurts me."[39] Their advantage for the Shin Bet was that non-scarring techniques are easier to deny, thus avoiding accountability.

---

37 State of Israel, *Commission of Inquiry into the Methods of Investigation of the General Security Service Regarding Hostile Terrorist Activity* (Jerusalem: Government Press Office, 1987), 80.

38 See Darius Rejali, *Torture and Democracy* (Princeton, NJ: Princeton University Press, 2007).

39 Elaine Scarry, *The Body in Pain: The Making and Unmaking of the World* (Oxford: Oxford University Press, 1985), 47.

FIGURE 8

The government's legalization of torture, regardless of the variation in tactics, was challenged by the Public Committee Against Torture in Israel (PCATI) and other Israeli human rights organizations through lawsuits in the High Court of Justice (HCJ). This litigation went on throughout the 1990s. On September 6, 1999, the HCJ issued a unanimous ruling in *PCATI et al v The State of Israel*, finding that certain interrogation tactics used by the Shin Bet—which the Court had not prohibited in the past—were illegal under Israeli and international law. The decision barred the routine use of tactics that the state described as involving "moderate amounts of physical pressure." But the decision included a loophole, enabling such tactics to be used with authorization and not be regarded as illegal if "security officials believe that a suspect is withholding information that could prevent an impending threat to civilian lives"—the so-called "ticking bomb scenario."

Despite this landmark HCJ decision, the use of torture on Palestinians did not cease. But other events and developments altered the centrality of interrogation in Israeli security strategies. The second intifada, which started in September 2000, was more immediately and reciprocally violent than the first intifada. Israeli forces had engaged in targeted killings (i.e., extra-judicial executions) since at least 1988, but denied doing so because it is illegal in militarily occupied territory. In 2001, Israel again acquired ignominious distinction as the first state in the world to publicly declare the legality of target killing as a security necessity (which the United States copied in 2002). The option to kill rather than capture suspects downgraded the importance of the trifecta of arrest, interrogation, and prosecution. Israel's unilateral decision to withdraw from Gaza in 2005, and the sealing of the borders, largely eliminated the need or the possibility to capture and interrogate Gaza Palestinians.

The current war has changed everything in unprecedented ways. The killings are no longer even remotely "targeted" as tens of thousands of

Palestinians have been slaughtered by militarized assaults with high-end and high-capacity ammunition. The importance of interrogation to gather human intelligence about Hamas has been recentered in the state's security strategies. Gone, at least for now, are the days of "clean" torture techniques as brute physical force has prevailed. With the number of imprisoned Palestinians having doubled since October 7, the state's commitment to avenge Hamas's attacks on any and all Palestinians has elevated the vulnerability of those in captivity. Like the *tertur* policy of earlier times, Palestinians are treated as undeserving of humane treatment.

The State of Inhumanity

Israel's conception of national security and the criminalization of Palestinians writ large as inherent security threats is as old as the state. How this has played out on the bodies of Palestinians is an evolving story, but one never free of dehumanization and violence.

Walid Daqqa, the long-time prisoner and social philosopher who died in captivity in 2024, aptly described prisons themselves as "the small prison" and Palestinian society under Israeli rule as "the large prison." He notes that those in the small prison live in "parallel time" to those in the large prison. In a 2021 essay titled "Control through Time," he wrote:

> Israel has managed to impose at least five prisons on Palestinian communities: '48 areas, Jerusalem, the West Bank, the Gaza Strip, and the diaspora. Each of these prisons has its own temporal and spatial reality along with its unique legal and political reality. With the passage of time, these separate entities—at first destined to be temporary in nature—have become near permanent. This reality could create opposing identities. The question thus becomes: how does one ensure that the deconstruction of Palestinian identity does not take place as it grows in these opposing temporal and spatial contexts? What is to be done until liberation?...If time is divided along these contexts, and between various Palestinian spatial and geographical configurations, then what might unite the Palestinian people as to safeguard their identity? How can this be done knowing that the occupation possesses a "time chisel" able to shape the identity of place given that the occupation does not only hold the ability to divide time in relation to physical space, but also controls the division of hypothetical time as well?[40]

---

40 Basil Farraj and Hashem Abushama, "'Parallel Time': Cultural Productions from the Small Prison to the Large Prison, *Jadaliyya*, March 24, 2022. https://www.

In another essay, Daqqa analyzes Israel's carceral regime and its torture practices to argue that what happens inside Israeli prisons "is not just detention and isolation of people considered to be a security threat for Israel, but is part of a general scientifically planned and calculated scheme to remold the Palestinian consciousness."[41] The target of state power and violence is not simply directed toward the imprisoned body; rather, it is the broader political and social body (and mind) that is being targeted. His argument, that prisons are symbolic of the general Palestinian condition under Israeli rule, resonates strongly across Palestinian society, whether among citizens of the state or people living under occupation.

The torture and violence long practiced against Palestinian prisoners thus serve a purpose beyond the infliction of pain and suffering. Israel's carceral practices constitute part of broader tactics designed to eliminate Palestinian existence, re-engineer the Palestinian population, and dissuade them from engaging in resistance or aspiring to liberation. The publication of images depicting the humiliation of Palestinian detainees, the torture practiced inside Israeli prisons, and the stories detailing the horrendous conditions of captivity intend to teach the broader Palestinian population that resisting the occupation is a futile endeavor, one that would certainly end in captivity or death. Indeed, it is through the transformation of imprisonment into "a scenario that keeps repeating itself,"[42] as Daqqa had once noted, that imprisonment had become central to Israel's broader project of eliminating Palestinian existence, and of ensuring that Palestinians are constantly portrayed and treated as dangerous subjects worthy of punishment.

There is no question that the unprecedented level of torture currently faced by Palestinian prisoners represents one dimension of the genocidal war being waged against the Palestinian people. While this chapter seeks to analyze this reality and its relation to longstanding Israeli carceral policies, it is also important to highlight that Palestinian prisoners have, in their parallel time, maintained their tradition of resisting this violent carceral reality. Indeed, Palestinians have engaged in a long history of resistance from their prison cells, through which they managed to secure most of their rights, at least until the start of the ongoing war.

Despite the torture and suffering, the history of resistance continues to reverberate through released prisoners and their families. Nowadays, upon

---

jadaliyya.com/Details/43980

41 Walid Daqqa, "Consciousness Molded or the Re-identification of Torture," in Abeer Baker and Anat Matar(eds.), *Threat: Palestinian Political Prisoners in Israel* (London: Pluto Press, 2011), 235.

42 Abdul-Rahim Al-Shaikh, "The Parallel Human: Walid Daqqah on the 1948 Palestinian Political Prisoners," *Confluences Méditerranée* 117, no. 2 (2021): 84.

the release of each prisoner, dozens of friends, family, and even strangers gather to welcome them home. Prisoners are eager to relay messages from their comrades, given the ongoing communication blackout inside prisons, and to describe the horrifying conditions of captivity while weaving in their stories of daily defiance in the face of the brutality of the Israeli carceral regime. For example, a recently freed prisoner told how she made a cake on a comrade's birthday without access to cooking equipment or ingredients, how she circumvented prison guards' ban on communication between cells, and how she smuggled her favorite pair of boots out of prison.[43]

Since the start of the war, dozens of prisoners have been killed and hundreds have been forcibly disappeared, injured, and maimed. Israel is subjecting Palestinians in custody to genocidal conditions by taking away the rights prisoners have earned through decades of struggle, down to the basics of food, medical care, personal items, and communication with each other and the outside world. What the Israeli government consistently fails to appreciate, however, is Palestinian prisoners' defiance, which stems from their unwavering longing for freedom and belief in their forthcoming liberation.

---

43 Interview with Basil Farraj.

Genocide, *Sanitascide* and the Production of Mass Disability

Israel's Dismemberment of Gaza

Penny Green | Grace Spence Green

Introduction

THIS CHAPTER explores Israel's deliberate production of mass disability and its socio-political debilitation of Gaza as critical components of a genocidal process. Genocide, as we discuss below, must be understood as a *process*, often developing over many decades, which advances particular state organizational goals.[1] We will argue, from within a state crime framework, that genocide, through segregation and apartheid, mass forced eviction, mass killing and mass disablement, has been the means by which Israel has advanced its 76-year settler colonial ambition to impose a Jewish supremacist

---

1 See Penny Green and Tony Ward, *State Crime: Governments, Violence and Corruption* (London: Pluto Press, 2004).

Penny Green is Professor of Law and Globalization at Queen Mary University of London. She has written extensively on state crime theory, genocide, state violence, mass expulsions and resistance to state violence and has a long track record of researching in hostile environments. Recent projects include a comparative study of civil society resistance to state crime in Türkiye, Tunisia, Colombia, PNG, Kenya and Myanmar; forced evictions in Palestine/Israel and Myanmar's genocide against the Rohingya. Her current work explores the humanitarian camp as a potential site of genocidal reproduction.

Grace Spence Green is a doctor working to challenge the narratives surrounding disability, medicine and identity. In 2018, aged 22 and a fourth-year medical student, she sustained a spinal cord injury and is now a full-time wheelchair user. She is passionate about medicine, advocacy for the disabled community and challenging ableism, the stigma surrounding disability and inaccessible spaces.She advocates for inclusive representation for disabled people in all walks of life and particularly in medicine and the media.

state in Palestine. This chapter considers the critical role that the policy and practice of disabling has played in advancing Israel's ambitions through genocide. Genocide, as Daniel Feierstein alerts us, is "a deliberate attempt to change the identity of the survivors by modifying relationships within a given society."[2] Land is intimately connected to identity and attempts to destroy a people by severing their relationship with their land is central to identity destruction.

Disablement, as we show, attempts to destroy the identity not only of Palestinians but of the land that is Gaza. Here, we introduce a new term, *sanitascide*, to capture the centrality that the destruction of healthcare infrastructure has played in Israel's genocidal attempts to weaken, disfigure and destroy Palestinian identity. We will also argue that the production of mass individual disability, and the institutional disablement of a once-functioning Gazan society, are both critical elements of genocide.

Israel's dismemberment of historic Palestine into the ever-increasing fragments of the West Bank, Gaza and East Jerusalem[3] parallels, writ large, what it has done in dismembering Palestinians' bodies. Thousands of Gazans, including a disproportionate number of children, have been subjected to the horror of limb amputation, spinal cord, life changing burns and acquired brain injury by the Israeli occupying forces. A World Health Organisation (WHO) analysis estimates that between 13,455 to 17,550 Gazans have suffered severe limb injuries placing an unimaginable burden on near non-existent rehabilitation services.[4] Jasbir Puar has shown the central role maiming and disabling has played historically in Israel's settler colonial ambitions to eliminate the Palestinians.[5] Our chapter explores the deliberate production of disability and debilitation as once central, and now collateral components, of Israel's genocide of Palestinians in Gaza. In the context of what has taken place since October 7 we argue that total destruction, rather than debilitation, is now Israel's explicit goal but that the mass disablement advances the goal of total destruction.

---

2 Daniel Feierstein, *Genocide as Social Practice: Reorganizing Society under the Nazis and Argentina's Military* Juntas (New Brunswick, NJ: Rutgers University Press, 2014).

3 Jeff Halper, "The 94 Percent Solution: A Matrix of Control," *Middle East Report* 216, MERIP (Fall 2000); Penny Green and Amelia Smith, "Evicting Palestine," *State Crime Journal* 5, no. 1 (Spring 2016): 81–108.

4 World Health Orgnization (WHO), "WHO analysis highlights vast unmet rehabilitation needs in Gaza," September 12, 2024.

5 Jasbir Puar, *The Right to Maim: Debility, Capacity, Disability* (Durham, Maryland: Duke University Press, 2017).

Genocide, State Crime and Disability

Genocide is a state crime, encompassing human rights violations perpetrated by state agents in pursuit of an organizational goal.[6] The state organisational goal of Israel's settler colonial project is, as noted above, the establishment of an exclusively Jewish supremacist state in the land that was historically Palestine. The elimination of Palestinians is central to the achievement of that goal and genocide can thus be seen as both the means and the outcome of this logic.

Disability has not yet explicitly featured in the literature on state crime, although Jasbir Puar's seminal work on Israel's "right to maim" must surely now be counted within its corpus. Similarly, disability has barely featured in the literature on genocide and when it has, the focus has been on the disabled victims.[7] Gaza must surely change that. In this chapter we explore not only the impact of Israel's genocide on the already disabled in the Gazan community and the mass creation of new individual disabilities but more crucially on Israel's orchestration of structural disability in the Gaza Strip as central to its planned elimination of the Palestinians.

The central goal of Israel's 76-year-old settler colonial project throughout the Occupied Palestinian Territories and Israel, has been the erasure not only of the Palestinian population but the complete disablement of Palestinian society and the erasure of the Palestinian identity.[8] The planned erasure or annihilation of a group, "in whole or part" based on the identity of the group

---

6 Green and Ward, 2004.

7 The scant literature on genocide, disability, and state crime has tended to concentrate on the genocidal targeting of disabled people—atrocities perpetrated against disabled people driven by a state organizational goal based on perverse notions of genetic purity and racial superiority. During the Holocaust at least a quarter of a million disabled people were exterminated by the Third Reich [see Suzanne E. Evans, *Forgotten Crimes: The Holocaust and People with Disabilities* (Michigan: Ivan R. Dee, 2004)] and evidence from the Rwandan genocide suggests that the disabled were among the first to die and were frequently targeted [see Pascal Mutabazi, "Focus on Deaf People in Rwanda," *Disability International* (Fall 1998)].

Also see Robert N. Proctor, *Racial Hygiene: Medicine Under the Nazis* (Cambridge, Mass.: Harvard University Press, 1988); and Art Blaser, "From the Field – People with Disabilities (PWDs) and Genocide: The Case of Rwanda," *Disability Studies Quarterly* 22, no. 3 (2002).

8 Ilan Pappé, *The Ethnic Cleansing of Palestine* (Oxford: Oneworld, 2006/2011); Rashid Khalidi, *The Hundred Years' War on Palestine: A History of Settler Colonialism and Resistance, 1917–2017* (New York: Metropolitan Books, 2020).

is genocide,[9] And as Patrick Wolfe so powerfully argued,[10] elimination of the native or indigenous population is the logical, desired and inevitable outcome of settler colonialism. Settler colonialism will thus inherently become a genocidal project.

In order to fully understand the relationship between settler colonialism, genocide and disablement, genocide must first be understood as a process which moves through phases which both contribute to and ultimately secure erasure. It is a process which we know empirically takes place over many years and frequently decades. It begins with dehumanisation and ends in the erasure and social obliteration of the victims' society.[11] In between, and often concurrent, are a number of recognisable phases—occasions of litmus-testing violence (violence without consequence emboldening perpetrators to commit further violence), structural discrimination (through occupation and apartheid), forced isolation (Gaza as the extreme ghetto), and systematic weakening of individuals and communities through the denial of the right to health, adequate food, water, education, movement, livelihood and political equality. The presentation and nature of each of these stages may differ between genocides but they are always present in some form and take place over extended periods of time.

Genocidal elimination, however, can take a range of forms. As the author of the term genocide, Raphael Lemkin, wrote, genocide is not limited to dramatic acts of mass killings nor does it require the "immediate destruction of a nation." "…It is intended rather to signify a *coordinated plan of different actions aimed at the destruction of essential foundations of the life of national groups*, with the aim of annihilating the groups themselves. The objectives of such a plan would be disintegration of the political and social institutions of culture, language, national feelings, religion, and the economic existence of national groups, and the destruction of the personal security, liberty, health, dignity, and even the lives of the individuals belonging to such groups."[12]

---

9 Convention on the Prevention and Punishment of the Crime of Genocide, 9 December 1948, 78 U.N.T.S. 276 (entered into force 12 January 1951). Available at: https://treaties.un.org/Pages/showDetails.aspx?objid=0800000280027fac

10 Patrick Wolfe, "Settler Colonialism and the Elimination of the Native," *Journal of Genocide Research* 8, no. 4 (2006): 387. https://doi.org/10.1080/14623520601056240

11 Barbara Harff and Ted Robert Gurr, "Systematic Early Warning of Humanitarian Emergencies," *Journal of Peace Research* 35, no. 5 (Sept. 1998); Feierstein, 2014.

12 Raphael Lemkin, *Axis Rule in Occupied Europe: Laws of Occupation, Analysis of Government, Proposals for Redress* (Washington, DC: Carnegie Endowment for International Peace, 1944).

By October 9, 2023 when Israel's Defence Minister, Yoav Gallant, announced the complete siege of Gaza with "No electricity, no food, no water, no gas," Gaza's infrastructure had already been weakened to a point which made daily life in the strip almost untenable.[13] For the disabled, newly injured and chronically ill, access to life-saving and life enhancing treatments and assistive devices had been cruelly limited for many years.

Israel's announcement and implementation of a "total siege" of Gaza, cutting off water, food, electricity and medical supplies, precisely fits the Genocide Convention definition of "deliberately inflicting on the group conditions of life calculated to bring about its physical destruction in whole or in part."[14] What else can the intention be of a prolonged total siege?

While every stage of the genocidal process (outlined below) has been pursued by Israel, and all impact the process of disablement, four stages are particularly pertinent to our discussion: dehumanisation, systematic weakening, disabling violence and annihilation.

Dehumanization and the Process of Genocide

As Christopher Browning[15] and others have shown, it is not an easy matter to inspire murderous hatred against a population which includes one's neighbours, friends and acquaintances. Dehumanisation is a central feature of all genocides.

Israel's campaign of dehumanising the Palestinians is decades long,[16] but since October 7, 2023, it has become a publicly celebrated feature of Israel's genocidal state narrative. In a sea of explicitly racist proclamations Defence Minister Yoav Gallant described Palestinians as "human animals" while Yoav Kitsch, Minister of Education declared "Those are animals, they have no right to exist...they need to be exterminated"[17] The "non-human" epithet has always underpinned the mass extermination of the "other" and is a hallmark of all genocides. The Nazis described Jews as "rats," "foxes," and "cockroaches," terms analogous to those now employed by Israeli leaders

13 United Nations, "'Gaza "Unliveable', UN Special Rapporteur for the Situation of Human Rights in the OPT Tells Third Committee – Press Release (Excerpts)," October 24, 2018. https://www.un.org/unispal/document/gaza-unliveable-un-special-rapporteur-for-the-situation-of-human-rights-in-the-opt-tells-third-committee-press-release-excerpts/

14 Genocide Convention 1948, Article 2.

15 Christopher R. Browning, *Ordinary Men: Reserve Police Battalion 101 and the Final Solution in Poland* (New York: Harper Collins, 1992).

16 Khalidi, *The Hundred Years' War on Palestine*, 2020; Pappé, 2006.

17 The patriots on channel 14 episode, posted October 9, 2023 [27:39–27:47] . https://www.youtube.com/playlist?list=PL8E54R76rowCcCOn_HQf36o1RF3_oD3z4

to describe Palestinians. Significantly the Nazis depicted disabled people in terms that removed even "life" from the descriptors—as "useless eaters," "empty human shells," and "life unworthy of life."[18]

Aided by apartheid, occupation, and policies of Judaization, the structural and racist "othering" of Arabs—able or disabled—and the widescale practice of criminalising and casting all Palestinians as terrorists has been devastatingly effective. Israeli polls suggest that the vast majority of Israeli Jews support the war on Gaza[19] as do the widely popular public positions espoused by TV presenters, singers, celebrities and models promoting the genocide. The extraordinary array of racist TikTok and YouTube videos joyously celebrating mass murder, the systemic torture and humiliation of Palestinian prisoners,[20] the mocking of Gazans as they grieve their unspeakable losses, all speak to the same loss of humanity infecting Israeli society. In this dehumanising context the horrific killing of Muhammad Bhar, a young autistic man with Down's Syndrome is simply a ghastly manifestation of Israel's collective loss of humanity animated by pursuit of its settler colonial project. Savaged by an IDF dog, as Israeli soldiers stormed Muhammad's Shujayya family home, leaving Muhammad to die, less human in the eyes of the Israeli soldiers than the dog they allowed to kill him. Here, as in all genocides, the perpetrator, in attempting to dehumanise those targeted for elimination, is actually the one to be truly dehumanised.

By the time the erasure/annihilation stages are reached the perpetrator society has long been inculcated to believe the "threat" that the eliminated group poses. At this point, the impulse of elimination often requires only the smallest trigger.

---

18 Amanda Tink, "Disabled people were Holocaust victims, too: they were excluded from German society and murdered by Nazi programs," *The Conversation,* January 26, 2023. https://theconversation.com/disabled-people-were-holocaust-victims-too-they-were-excluded-from-german-society-and-murdered-by-nazi-programs-198298

19 Amira Hass, "Daily Polls Show That Israelis Continue to Choose This War, Even if They Don't Want Netanyahu," *Haaretz,* April 1, 2024. https://www.haaretz.com/opinion/2024-04-01/ty-article/.premium/polls-show-that-israelis-continue-to-choose-this-war-even-if-they-dont-want-netanyahu/0000018e-98d8-d591-a5cf-9fdddf100000

20 United Nations, Office of the High Commissioner for Human Rights, Detention in the context of the escalation of hostilities in Gaza (October 2023 – June 2024) – Thematic Report by OHCHR (Geneva: UN Human Rights, July 31, 2024). https://www.un.org/unispal/document/thematic-report-detention-gaza-31jul24/

The Systematic Weakening of Gaza

Genocide necessarily involves the prior systematic weakening of the target group. This stage of genocide, as articulated by Daniel Feierstein,[21] is ultimately designed to mark out those for elimination by employing strategies of physical and psychological destruction. Both are part of the process of annihilation and a form of annihilation in itself. The process is attritional and includes state strategies of physical destruction through overcrowding, malnutrition, starvation, targeted disablement, epidemics, denial of health care, torture and rape; and state strategies of psychological destruction through humiliation, abuse, persistent violence, denial of basic rights and the undermining of community solidarity through collective punishment and collaboration. Evidence of both the physical and psychological components of Israel's strategy to destroy Gaza has long been provided by human rights organisations (including Al Haq; Adalah; Bt'selem and Physicians for Human Rights). Systematic weakening is enabled through practices of segregation and apartheid and is most potent once the target group has been physically and socially isolated. Systematic weakening has involved the physical and political fragmentation of Palestine, with the West Bank segregated from East Jerusalem and Israel '48, and Gaza locked behind the apartheid structures of walls, watchtowers and checkpoints, all of which has included wide-scale and repeated house demolitions, forced evictions; settler land-grabbing and violence, the detention without charge of thousands of Palestinians including many children, discriminatory laws and a process of Judaization which seeks to undermine and ultimately erase Palestinian identity.[22]

Gaza's isolation has been extreme. Before the current annihilation phase of Israel's genocide, Gaza had been placed under a brutally restrictive Israeli air, sea and land blockade, which the UN anticipated would make Gaza "unliveable" by 2020.[23] During the 16 years prior to October 7 Israel exerted total control over the movement of goods and people into and out of the enclave. Access to essential items was severely constrained or simply prohibited, including certain medicines, batteries essential for assistive devices, water and sewage pipes, concrete and diesel fuel which Israel claimed had "dual function" and could potentially be used to support "terrorist infrastructure." Israel's prohibition on the import of carbon fibre elements (used to

21 Feierstein, 2014.

22 Jeff Halper, *War Against the People: Israel, the Palestinians and Global Pacification* (London: Pluto Press, 2015); Green and Smith, "Evicting Palestine," 2016.

23 United Nations, "Gaza 'Unliveable,' UN Special Rapporteur for the Situation of Human Rights in the OPT Tells Third Committee – Press Release (Excerpts)," October 24, 2018.

stabilise and treat limb injuries) and epoxy resins (used in the production of light weight and comfortable prosthetics) has meant that the injured and amputees of Gaza were being denied assistive technology that would offer greater comfort and accessibility.

Throughout the years of the blockade access to electricity, water and fuel was sporadic and impacted directly on the capacity of the Strip to generate power and sustain water infrastructure and sewage treatment plants. An estimated 78% of piped water in Gaza became unfit for human consumption.[24] Regular work permits, upon which Gazans relied for employment and crossing into Israel, were almost completely withdrawn until 2022, and travel in and out of the Strip became virtually impossible. By September 2023, Gaza had lost half its GDP, unemployment had reached 50%, and hospitals were denied almost half of what they required to function in terms of equipment and medicine.[25] The blockade, as Israel intended, had a devastating impact on the lives and health of all Palestinians in Gaza, with the UN reporting in 2022 that 80% of the beleaguered population required international aid simply to survive.

Israel had thus achieved an orchestrated humanitarian collapse long before October 7. Its persistent refusal to facilitate the entry of humanitarian aid into Gaza following the Hamas attacks, and its calculated undermining and subsequent disabling of UNRWA[26] are all in keeping with its intention to pursue its genocidal goal and a blatant manifestation of a plan to accelerate death-inducing famine and disease.

A critical element of systematic weakening in Gaza has been Israel's strategy of "mowing the lawn," a strategy Ramzy Baroud has described as "delineating the need for Israel to routinely eradicate or degrade the capabilities of the various Palestinian resistance groups on the street."[27] The routine and relentless aerial bombardment of Gaza and the IOF's weekly military incursions into Gaza, ostensibly carried out to destroy Hamas and forms of Palestinian resistance, have been neither reactive nor spontaneous. They are

---

24 UNICEF, "The Gaza Strip | The humanitarian impact of 15 years of blockade - June 2022" [fast facts]. https://www.unicef.org/mena/documents/gaza-strip-humanitarian-impact-15-years-blockade-june-2022

25 Michael Merryman-Lotza, "5 things you need to know about what's happening in Israel and Gaza," American Friends Service Committee, December 5, 2024. https://afsc.org/news/5-things-you-need-know-about-whats-happening-israel-and-gaza

26 United Nations Relief and Works Agency for Palestine Refugees in the Near East: https://www.unrwa.org/

27 Ramzy Baroud, "'Mowing the Grass' no more: How Palestinian resistance altered the equation," *Mondoweiss,* May 31, 2021. https://mondoweiss.net/2021/05/MOWING-THE-GRASS-NO-MORE-HOW-PALESTINIAN-RESISTANCE-ALTERED-THE-EQUATION/

the manifestation of Israel's 17-year-old Dahyia doctrine—a doctrine premised on laying waste to a defined "enemy area" through overwhelming and
disproportionate force so as to weaken the population to the point where mere
survival completely supersedes resistance.

Decades of systematic and targeted attacks on Gaza's health and rehabilitative structures[28] coupled with almost 2 decades of blockade and now a
crippling total siege have ensured that the newly injured, the chronically ill
and the disabled are denied adequate health care and rehabilitation resources
such that they remain in a state of injury rather than transitioning into a state
of what Puar calls "functioning disability."[29] To be functionally disabled (as
opposed to being in a state of injury) represents for Israel an act of Palestinian
resistance, a resistance that must be suppressed. Any assertion of Palestinian
resilience represents an existential threat to Israel's identity. By disabling the
capacity of Gaza to heal and rehabilitate the injured, to feed the starving,
to educate the young, to house the dispossessed, Israel attempts to weaken
resilience and the possibility of resistance.

Sanitascide in the Process of Genocide

Israel's savage, calculated, wholesale and relentless decimation of Gazan
healthcare represents something hitherto unseen in modern genocides.[30] As
such it demands a new word—a word to capture the particularity of this
unconscionable element of the genocide inflicted on Gaza. *Sanitascide,*[31] the
term we have developed to describe this targeted and comprehensive destruction of healthcare—derived from the Latin terms *sanitas* meaning health and
cide meaning killing—will now join the horrifying array of *cides* Israel has
perpetrated against the Palestinians of Gaza: genocide, ecocide, infanticide,
femicide, domicide[32] and scholasticide.

---

28 Lena Obermaier, "'Disabling Palestine: The case of Gaza's Great March of
Return," *Race & Class* 65, no. 3 (October 16, 2023): 27–46.

29 Puar, 2017.

30 See the Médecins Sans Frontières report, *Gaza's Silent Killings,* April 2024.
https://msf.org.uk/sites/default/files/2024-04/MSF-GazaSilentKillings-Full%20
Report_ENG_April%202023.pdf

31 *Sanitascide*—derived from the Latin terms *sanitas* meaning health and *cide.*

32 See Henrietta Zeffert, *Home and International Law: Dispossession,
Displacement and Resistance in Everyday Life* (London: Routledge, 2024).

Scholars such as Khalidi,[33] Puar,[34] Obermaier,[35] and Gordon and Perugini[36] have documented Israel's long history of targeting Palestinian health infrastructure. In its 2014 war on Gaza, seventeen hospitals, fifty-six primary healthcare facilities, and forty-five ambulances were either damaged or destroyed. Medical workers were targeted, leaving sixteen dead and eighty-three injured.[37] In this war Israel permanently disabled approximately 1,100 Gazan children in just 50 days. Khalidi argues that these attacks were part of Israel's collective punishment "for Gaza's refusal to be a docile ghetto."[38] By debilitating healthcare infrastructure Israel ensured that the injured were more likely to become "permanently wounded," placing even greater strain on Gazan health infrastructure, already disabled by the blockade.

In post October 7 Gaza, Israel has turned hospitals into killing fields. On November 13, 2023, the IDF posted but later deleted a tweet in which they called hospitals and ambulances "legitimate military targets."[39] As well as bombing hospital infrastructure, murdering patients and destroying incubators, ambulances, medications and life support systems, the IOF has tortured and assassinated hundreds of doctors, nurses, physiotherapists and paramedics. As Gordon and Perugini reveal, Israel portrays Palestinian fighters as living in a parallel legal world where "hospitals are command centers, ambulances are transport vehicles, and medics are human shields, in flagrant violation of international law."'[40]

In April 2024 the Gazan Ministry of Health announced that 496 medical sector staff had been murdered and 1,500 injured by Israel since October 7, 2023. Hospital grounds have become mass graves in which men, women and children sheltering in what they believed to be internationally protected spaces have been slaughtered without distinction by targeted aerial bombardments. In April 2024 the Ministry of Health in Gaza announced that 155 health facilities had been damaged, 32 hospitals and 53 health centres had been rendered

---

33 Rashid Khalidi, "Collective Punishment in Gaza," *The New Yorker,* 29 July 29, 2014. https://www.newyorker.com/news/news-desk/collective-punishment-gaza.

34 Puar, 2017.

35 Obermaier, 2023.

36 Nicola Perugini and Neve Gordon, "Medical Lawfare: The Nakba and Israel's Attacks on Palestinian Healthcare," *Journal of Palestine Studies* 53, no. 1 (2024): 68–91.

37 Médecins Sans Frontières, "Aiding & Abetting? The limits of humanitarian aid in the Occupied Palestinian Territories," July 22, 2015. https://www.msf-me.org/media-centre/news-and-stories/aiding-abetting-limits-humanitarian-aid-occupied-palestinian

38 Khalidi, 2014.

39 @CensoredMen post on X, November 13, 2023: https://x.com/censoredmen/status/1724026371511362026?s=21&t=aFnX8cakDpW-3-glmfjfJg

40 Perugini and Gordon, 13.

non-functional. In addition, 126 ambulances had been destroyed or damaged beyond use. The Ministry further reported that 309 medical staff, including hospital directors in Gaza, had been detained by Israeli forces.[41] Two of the most chilling examples of attacks on medics are the cases of Adnan Al-Bursh, Head of Orthopaedics at Al-Shifa Hospital in Gaza City and Iyad Rantisi, Director of the Women's wing at Kamal Adwan Hospital in Beit Lahia. Al-Bursh was disappeared from Al Awda hospital where he was treating patients and, according to the Palestinian Prisoners' Society, tortured to death on April 19 in Israel's Ofer prison in what they described as a "deliberate assassination."[42] According to *Haaretz*[43] Dr Iyad Rantisi, 53, was killed in November 2023 while under interrogation by Israel's internal security service, Shin Bet, in Shikma Prison. In all genocides, healthcare is targeted for destruction. So too are the related intellectual and professional classes, but rarely have leading medics been so visibly selected for public elimination as they have been in Israel's war on Palestinian life.

The significance of *sanitascide* is captured by Médecins Sans Frontières (MSF) in its chilling report, *Gaza Silent Killings*, "Gaza's health system stands shattered; its road to recovery will be long and uncertain—spanning years, if not decades. For humanity to prevail, policymakers must understand the human cost of destroying an entire healthcare system."[44]

Disability Theory in a Time of Genocide

Two models dominate the field of disability studies. The first is the medical model which focuses on the individual and pathologizes that which necessitates medical or rehabilitative intervention. It seeks alleviation or even "cure." Disability within this paradigm rests within the framework of the

---

41 UN Office for the Coordination of Humanitarian Affairs (OCHA), *Hostilities in the Gaza Strip and Israel | Flash Update #132*, March 5, 2024. https://www.unocha.org/publications/report/occupied-palestinian-territory/hostilities-gaza-strip-and-israel-flash-update-132)

42 MEE Staff, "War on Gaza: Prominent Palestinian doctor tortured and killed in Israeli detention," *Middle East Eye*, May 2, 2024. https://www.middleeasteye.net/news/war-gaza-prominent-palestinian-doctor-tortured-and-killed-israeli-detention

43 Hagar Shezaf, Josh Breiner, and Jack Khoury, "Israel Arrested a Senior Doctor in Gaza. Six Days Later, He Died in a Shin Bet Interrogation Facility," *Haaretz*, June 18, 2024. https://www.haaretz.com/israel-news/2024-06-18/ty-article/.premium/israel-arrested-a-senior-doctor-in-gaza-six-days-later-he-died-in-a-shin-bet-facility/00000190-27eb-d14b-a999-27eb9aea0000

44 Médecins Sans Frontières (MSF), "Gaza's silent killings: the destruction of the healthcare system in Rafah" [press release], April 29, 2024. https://www.msf.org/gazas-silent-killings-destruction-healthcare-system-rafah

individual and alleviation of that disability by the medical and allied health professionals.

The social model by contrast presents the case that it is society's infrastructure which presents some of the most disabling factors for a person with an impairment, rather than being innate to their body.[45] It casts disability along a spectrum of what it is to be human and argues that it is primarily environments which limit or disable a person's capacity to enjoy the rights and opportunities afforded the non-disabled. By challenging and transforming the physical (with lifts, ramps, braille signage, assistive devices) and attitudinal barriers (confronting the prejudice of ableism) the social model also accommodates the legally informed human rights framing of disability.[46]

What happens, however, if infrastructure becomes disabling for the able bodied? What if it becomes a weapon? A way of exerting control, of exerting harm? What if this infrastructure in turn injures, ends up both creating and compounding disability?

In the context of Gaza, existing models of disability cannot apply. Western views of disability, of empowerment, of access, are at odds with the environments of genocide and warfare. In a world where prison walls, checkpoints, deliberate deprivation of water, calories, healthcare and mass aerial bombing are all disabling to the entire population, what becomes of the disabled? The chronically ill? The newly disabled?

The social model is inadequate if one's environment has been infrastructurally targeted for dismemberment and obliteration. When the environment which once supported life and community is disabled, when the services and utilities which a society normally provides to ensure the wellbeing of all its citizens, are destroyed or denied, every member of that society becomes disabled. Without access to adequate food, shelter, water, electricity, medical supplies, the opportunity to live healthy and meaningful lives is dramatically diminished.

In Puar's *Right to Maim,* she argues that in Gaza "the infrastructure that ought to sustain life is transformed into a system threatening life itself." By creating a population which is heavily reliant on a healthcare system to survive while simultaneously decimating this system, Israel can create much more damage than caused by the initial injury event, and "has the power to define life after the event of injuring and/or disablement." The perpetrators can exert control beyond the initial injury, initial wounding.

---

45 Mike Oliver, "A sociology of disability or a disablist sociology?," in Len Barton, ed., *Disability and Society Emerging Issues and Insights* (Routledge, 1996).

46 Anna Lawson and Angharad E. Beckett, "The social and human rights models of disability: towards a complementarity thesis," *The International Journal of Human Rights* 25, no. 2 (2002): 348–379. https://doi.org/10.1080/13642987.2020.1783533

Causing an injury that makes one's existence reliant on a certain medical device or treatment vital to their lives—sterile dressings, catheters, stoma bags, feeding tubes, medication, antibiotics, prosthetics, mobility aids—and then denying that resource, spreads the stigmata of injury and disability far further.

Once healthcare and rehabilitative infrastructure have, in effective total-ity, been reduced to rubble the disabled and newly injured move into precar-ious spaces of "bare life" and what Claudia Card has described as "social death." In such a context where the very structures designed to mend, assist and rehabilitate are themselves dismembered, the injured cannot transform into the functioning disabled.[47]

While Majadli and Ziv argue that Israel's attempts to disable the "Palestinian body" signal a deeper intention to use the disablement of Palestine and its healthcare system as part of an "intentional scheme of con-trol"[48] we would argue that Israel's intention is not control but elimination.

Those injured or disabled in these attacks are often not addressed in the media. We may see numbers of "wounded," but there is very little data on what that entails; we don't know the extent of the damage among the injured. How many have acquired disabilities from their injuries? How many of those will die due to injuries sustained days, weeks, months earlier? So, what becomes of the wounded? When numbers are published after each attack, would global readers assume these casualties have sustained a superficial wound or broken a bone rather than a spinal cord injury, an amputation, an abdominal injury resulting in a stoma, a traumatic brain injury, a hearing impairment, blinding?

Disabling Violence: Weapons of Mass Debilitation in Gaza

Violently disabling large numbers of the group and disabling the very infrastructure which supports life in the Gaza Strip are central means by which Israel has advanced its organizational goal of imposing an exclusively Jewish settler state in Palestine. The consequences of using the Gaza Strip as a "weapons laboratory"[49] have been profound. Puar and Obermaier have documented Israel's historic policy of maiming Palestinians.[50,51] During the

---

47 Puar, 2017.

48 Ghada Majadli and Hadas Ziv, "Amputating the body, fragmenting the nation: Palestinian amputees in Gaza," *Health and Human Rights* 24, no. 2 (December 2022): 287.

49 Shir Hever [interview], "Israel turns Gaza into 'Arms Race' laboratory, while Palestinians fly kites (Pt 1/2)," *IMEMC News* (blog), June 23, 2018. https://imemc.org/article/israel-turns-gaza-into-arms-race-laboratory-while-palestinians-fly-kites-pt-1-2/

50 Puar, 2017.

51 Obermaier, 2023.

First Intifada, for example, the deployment of high-velocity fragmented bullets which left a "lead snowstorm" resulted in "multiple cases of 'disability.'"

Although it is difficult to find details on the current weapons Israel is using, what we have is on the ground testimony. Adnan Al-Bursh, before he died, described what he witnessed working as a doctor, and the way in which Israel creates "a disabled generation by using destructive types of bullets and deliberately shooting protesters in their joints."[52] Ghassan Abu Sitta, a plastic and reconstructive surgeon who worked in Al-Shifa hospital for 43 days described in tweets; "Israel's use of a Quadcopter drone with a sniper gun. One night we had 30 injuries when they were sent to shoot at people trying to get to Ahli hospital. We have received over 20 chest and neck gunshot wounds fired from Israeli Quadcopter drones. This is a low flying sniper drone." Reham Shaeen, a humanity and inclusion rehabilitation expert, explains that the types of weapons used in Gaza mean "70 to 80% of the people coming to hospital have been amputated or have spinal cord injuries. The numbers are huge."[53]

These particular injuries require immediate intensive care and rehabilitation and equipment provision. Spinal cord injury rehabilitation in the UK requires a minimum three-month inpatient stay and the involvement of multiple different specialists. In her analysis of the injuries inflicted by Israel during the Great March of Return, Obermaier reports, "Ultimately, by debilitating Gaza's rehabilitative infrastructure, Israel does not need to rely on 'the event of becoming disabled.'" She goes on to describe how "high-velocity bullets have left about half of all Palestinians injured by live ammunition with open fractures of massive wounds and splintered bones." These fractures can end with no choice but to amputate, but also with bone infections requiring an intensive long course of antibiotics that are likely not available. Thus, the stigmata of disease following injury continues.

As well as sniper and gunshot wounds vast quantities of explosives have been rained upon Gaza, all of which directly contribute to traumatic amputations, traumatic brain injuries, spinal cord injuries and other serious internal injuries, often due to collapsing rubble. There have also been eyewitness

---

52 Ali Abusheikh, "Anatomy of a viral photo," *we are not numbers,* May 13, 2019. https://wearenotnumbers.org/viral_photo_doctor_great_return_march_gaza/

53 Humanity & Inclusion UK, "Gaza: Rehabilitation experts fear that massive number of people will be left with permanent disabilities" [press release], March 14, 2024. https://www.humanity-inclusion.org.uk/en/gaza-rehabilitation-experts-fear-that-massive-number-of-people-will-be-left-with-permanent-disabilities

reports of white phosphorus being used in densely populated areas of Gaza, which "poses a high risk of excruciating burns and lifelong suffering,"[54]

According to UNICEF more than 1,000 children underwent limb amputations in the first three months alone of the genocide.[55] An estimated ten children per day have lost one or more limbs[56] through bombardments, crush, or sniper injuries during the course of this genocide. While official sources report at least 2,000 child amputees, Ghassan Abu-Sittah estimates that potentially 5,000 children may have undergone amputations since October 7, 2023[57]—the "biggest cohort of pediatric amputees in history."[58] Abu-Sittah, a London-based plastic and reconstructive surgeon specializing in pediatric trauma reported performing sometimes six amputations a day. "Sometimes you have no other medical option ... The Israelis had surrounded the blood bank, so we couldn't do transfusions. If a limb was bleeding profusely, we had to amputate."[59]

Gaza's Health Ministry reported that by June 19, 2024, Israel's genocide had killed at least 37,396 Palestinians (excluding an estimated 10,000 buried under 35 million tonnes of rubble) and wounded at least 85,532 others.[60] A report published in the *Lancet* in July 2024, reported that up to 186,000 or even more, deaths are likely attributable to Israel's genocidal assault on Gaza.[61] This shocking yet, as acknowledged by the authors, conservative calculation, factors in the indirect and premature deaths caused by reproductive, communicable, and non-communicable diseases that are the inevitable

---

54 Human Rights Watch, "Israel: White Phosphorus Used in Gaza, Lebanon," October 12, 2023. https://www.hrw.org/news/2023/10/12/israel-white-phosphorus-used-gaza-lebanon

55 Arafat Barbakh, Maggie Fick, and Emma Farge, "Gaza's child amputees face further risks without expert care," *Reuters,* January 4, 2024. https://www.reuters.com/world/middle-east/gazas-child-amputees-face-further-risks-without-expert-care-2024-01-04/

56 MEE Staff, "More than 10 children a day lose a limb in 'brutal' Gaza conflict: Report," *Middle East Eye,* January 8, 2024. https://www.middleeasteye.net/live-blog/live-blog-update/more-10-children-day-lose-limb-brutal-gaza-conflict-report

57 Miranda Cleland, "Gaza's youngest generation faces amputee crisis amid war," *TRT World.* https://www.trtworld.com/opinion/gazas-youngest-generation-faces-amputee-crisis-amid-war-18184909

58 Ibid.

59 Cited in Eliza Griswold, "The Children Who Lost Limbs in Gaza," *New Yorker,* March 21, 2024. https://www.newyorker.com/news/dispatch/the-children-who-lost-limbs-in-gaza

60 UN Office for the Coordination of Humanitarian Affairs (OCHA), Reported impact snapshot. Gaza Strip, June 19, 2024. https://www.ochaopt.org/content/reported-impact-snapshot-gaza-strip-19-june-2024

61 Rasha Khatib, Martin McKee, and Salim Yusuf, "Counting the Dead in Gaza: Difficult but Essential," *Lancet* 404, no. 10449 (July 20, 2024): 237–38. https://www.thelancet.com/journals/lancet/article/PIIS0140-6736(24)01169-3/fulltext

consequence of the total siege, mass bombardment, orchestrated starvation, mental and physical trauma and the mass deaths and injuries inflicted by Israel on the population of Gaza.

While equivalent figures for disability and disablement are not available, the implications of the *Lancet*'s projection are striking. The numbers of spinal cord and acquired brain injuries have not yet been formally recorded but it is estimated that those figures will be equal to, if not greater than the number of amputations. Two-thirds of the murdered have been children and women. The real death and injury toll is undoubtedly much higher given the countless bodies buried beneath the 35 million tons of rubble left by airstrikes.

As we write, evidence of hepatitis and meningitis outbreaks have been reported by Gaza's health Ministry[62] and the highly infectious poliovirus has been detected in sewage outlets in Khan Younis and Deir al-Balah.[63] Gazans, particularly children, are now at serious risk of contracting polio which can lead to paralysis, limb deformity and on occasion, death.

Lack of access to sufficient food and water means a whole population becomes slowly disabled. For those members of that population relying on Total Parenteral Nutrition (TPN) and other forms of medical tube feeding the impact is immediately devastating. Muhammad Shehada wrote via *X,* "even if Israel's starvation of Gaza stops NOW & Gaza is 'flooded' with aid, kids who recover from acute malnutrition would show signs of inflammation in the gut & throughout the body, making them more likely to be readmitted to a hospital & die," referencing data on mortality associated with severe malnutrition.[64]

While physical injuries and the consequences of starvation and illness in the context of genocide are so extensive as to be difficult to enumerate, the scale of mental health damage will impact every single Gazan. The first detailed report from Gaza on the genocide and mental health[65] exposed what

---

62 "Gaza Health Ministry reports meningitis, hepatitis outbreak among displaced Palestinians," *Middle East Monitor,* April 24, 2024. https://www.middleeastmonitor.com/20240424-gaza-health-ministry-reports-meningitis-hepatitis-outbreak-among-displaced-palestinians/

63 Agence France-Presse, "Highly infectious poliovirus found in Gaza sewage samples," The Guardian, July 19, 2024. https://www.theguardian.com/world/article/2024/jul/19/israel-gaza-war-polio-sewage-samples

64 Jonathan P. Sturgeon, et al., "Inflammation and epithelial repair predict mortality, hospital readmission, and growth recovery in complicated severe acute malnutrition," *Science Translational Medicine* 16, no. 736 (February 28, 2024). https://www.science.org/doi/10.1126/scitranslmed.adh0673

65 Gaza Community Mental Health Programme, *Nine Months of Israel's war on Gaza: The Mental Health Impacts and the GCMHP's Response* (October 2023 – June 2024). https://gcmhp.org/app_files/publications/aZWl8msyFPM50tT9.pdf

Victoria Brittain has described as "an ocean of need."[66] The scale of mental trauma and its attendant pathologies of PTSD, depression, anomie, and more is incalculable. Nonetheless The Gaza Community Mental Health Program anticipates "…that as the war continues…every child will need mental health support."[67] This figure should come as little surprise given that in 2014 following one of Israel's sustained terror attacks on Gaza, British surgeon Nick Maynard reported that 480,000 children were in need of "urgent psycho-social first aid."[68] That need emerged in 2023 after 50 days of war during which time Israel killed some 2,251—551 of them children—and permanently disabled approximately 1,100 Gazan children.[69]

What of the Disabled at a Time of Genocidal Disablement?

Disabled people are always targeted in conflict, directly or indirectly. Haunting images of families impossibly pushing loved ones in antiquated wheelchairs through rubble and devastation as bombs explode behind them; the starving child with cerebral palsy Yazan El Kafarneh staring from a stretcher in Rafah's Abu Youssef al-Najjar hospital, Nour al-Huda, an 11-year-old girl with cystic fibrosis admitted to Kamal Adwan hospital on March 15 suffering from malnutrition, dehydration, and a lung infection; the deaf sisters Iman and Abir who cannot hear the bombs or the warnings of those around them, or Muhammad Bhar who could not understand the murderous intent of Israeli soldiers and their dog…these are the faces of disability in Israel's genocide.

Available data indicates that "out of 79,562, at least 5,000 people injured were persons with disabilities and that more than 2,000 children have acquired impairment through limb amputation. These figures, however, could be higher as challenges to obtain reliable data and information about persons with disabilities persists. Women and children with disabilities are among the 70 percent of civilians killed and 75 percent of those reportedly injured."[70]

---

66 Victoria Brittain, "Pain, loss, fear, panic, anger: Gaza's Palestinians are suffering psychological torment," *Middle East Eye,* July 17, 2024. https://www.middleeasteye.net/opinion/gaza-war-psychological-torment-palestinians-living-hell

67 GCMHP, 4.

68 @MiddleEastEye post on *X,* May 19, 2024: "British surgeon Nick Maynard said that, while the 2014 war resulted in 480,000 children urgently needing psychosocial first aid to cope with PTSD, he cannot imagine the conditions following the ongoing Israeli war on Gaza." https://x.com/MiddleEastEye/status/1792174395647025215

69 UNRWA, "2014 Gaza Conflict": https://www.unrwa.org/2014-gaza-conflict

70 United Nations, Office of the High Commissioner for Human Rights, "Onslaught of violence against women and children in Gaza unacceptable: UN experts" UN Human Rights, May 6, 2024. https://www.ohchr.org/en/press-releases/2024/05/onslaught-violence-against-women-and-children-gaza-unacceptable-un-experts

Evidence from other genocides suggests that some of the earliest and most damaging effects of genocide are likely to be felt by the disabled community. While the disabled may not have been specifically targeted as victims by the Israelis (as they were by the Nazi regime), they have certainly been disproportionately affected. Following 17 years of an illegal blockade which systematically weakened the whole Gazan population, disabled people have been disproportionately impacted, having been long denied adequate access to liberating assistive devices, including power assisted attachments for wheelchairs, crutches, latest development prostheses and hearing aids.

Gaza's disabled population face a host of extreme barriers. They have become doubly disabled as they experience the destruction of genocide through the lens of their own disability. As Israeli bombs rain down on civilian homes and in the wake of evacuation orders, the medical and physical assistive devices essential to the health, well-being and ultimately life are frequently lost, left behind or destroyed in the chaos of terror and flight. The disabled become separated from their essential caregivers, a terrifying situation for people who rely on trained others for even their most basic daily needs. Without catheters and other continence essentials, adaptive toilet seats, wheelchairs, prostheses, walking frames and other mobility equipment, hearing and sight aids as well as life-saving medications, disabled people become dangerously vulnerable. Electric wheelchairs, and certain devices to assist the blind, require a constant source of power. The siege renders these devices unusable, and the consequences can be devastating. Without electricity lifts do not function, rendering the many physically disabled who live above the ground floor in Gaza's high-rise apartment blocks, unable to evacuate. In an orphanage in Northern Gaza caring for 22 children evacuation was an impossibility given the high need requirements of 12 of its disabled children.[71] For those able to flee, leaving their accessible homes and supportive devices for a future of certain inaccessibility imposed an added terror. Over 90% of the population has been forced to flee their homes, sometimes on multiple occasions and the tents and shelters to which they have fled are inhospitable homes for those who require assistive devices, disabled toilets, medical mattresses and sterilized conditions.

Ziad Amro, a blind West Bank resident and president of the Palestine Association For Visually Impaired Persons, describes disabled people living

---

71 NBC News, *Special Report: Updates on the Israel-Hamas War - October 15,* news feature [1:21:55], aired October 15, 2023. https://www.youtube.com/watch?v=_jj_C9jqBbM&rco=1

in Gaza; "They have no access to sources of life—food, water, communication, internet, phones."[72]

According to Human Rights Watch Gaza was already an inaccessible place for those with disabilities, impoverished as it had become after 17 years of Israel's illegally imposed siege. The genocide has compounded that inaccessibility exponentially. Places of supposed shelter such as hospitals and UNRWA, including for example schools, are limited to squat toilets, impossible for people with mobility issues.[73] The rubble and debris from bombardments make the roads almost impossible to navigate in wheelchairs and mobility devices.

During the Rwandan genocide, Ruwumbra observed that it was rare to see disabled people among the throngs fleeing violence. This, he noted, was because "most of the time they were left behind...."[74] For the disabled whose mobility was impeded death was often the consequence. In Gaza, Israeli orders to evacuate may not be heard, read or understood and even if they are, immobility may still be a sentence of death. The mental health implications of living through genocide also pertain, and possibly more acutely to the disabled. As Jamal al Rozzi, executive director of the National Rehabilitation Society in the Gaza Strip has reported, "Deaf people are not spared the sight of mangled bodies. Blind people are not spared the smell of death."[75]

Annihilation

To mass debilitate through disabling injury and infrastructural collapse, is to deliberately inflict on the Palestinian people "conditions of life calculated to bring about its physical destruction in whole or part."

Disabling Palestinians, as Puar has written, has been a key mechanism in Israel's approach to both punishing and eliminating the "native." The practice of mass disabling in which the Israeli state exerts its "right to maim" and debilitate Palestinian bodies and environments is, as Puar asserts, "a form of biopolitical control."[76] Achille Mbembe describes the power to produce disablement as *necropower*, where "the ultimate expression of sovereignty

---

72 United Nations, Office of the High Commissioner for Human Rights, "Palestinians with disabilities subject to unbearable consequences of the ongoing hostilities and violence in the OPT," UN Human Rights, May 27, 2024. https://www.ohchr.org/en/statements/2024/05/palestinians-disabilities-subject-unbearable-consequences-ongoing-hostilities

73 Human Rights Watch, 2023.

74 Cited in Blaser ""From the Field – People with Disabilities (PWDs) and Genocide," 2002.

75 Jamal al Rozzi, "Shellshocked, attacked, left to die – this is the reality for disabled people in Gaza," *The Guardian*, July 19, 2024.

76 Puar, 128.

resides, to a large degree, in the power and the capacity to dictate who may live and who may die." Mbembe describes the current settler-occupation of Palestine as the most extensive and complete form of necropower, where an entire people have become the ultimate target of the sovereign.

Puar writes of a tension "between *targeting the disabled* and *targeting to debilitate.*"[77] In Israel's indiscriminate genocidal 2023–24 assault on Gaza, however, this tension has been dismantled as the two operate in indiscriminate tandem—Palestinians are killed, maimed, disabled while at the same time the Gaza Strip as a domestic, political, economic, social and ecological space is permanently disrupted, destroyed or debilitated. In this process every Palestinian residing in Gaza has become disabled while those who live with varying forms of individual physical or mental disability are even more vulnerable to the bombardments because accessibility is permanently disrupted. Israel's planned destruction of Gaza through mass bombardment, siege, targeted killings and starvation has challenged the conventional binary between ability and disability, between killing and maiming, between life and death.

Israel's 2023/24 genocidal war against Gaza has redirected state policy from the goal of maiming Palestinians to one of outright erasure by any means. During the course of annihilatory violence, maiming or debilitation has now become a consequence of failed elimination, one which contributes to erasure but is no longer necessarily the key element in Israel's state organizational goal. The slow genocide of the Palestinians has long involved a deliberate strategy of disabling Palestinians and Palestine itself. Majaddli and Ziv observed, during the Great March of Return, that Israel used catastrophic injury to the Palestinian body in order "to fragment the Palestinian land and nation."[78]

In Obermaier's work on deliberate maiming during the Great March of Return[79] she writes of how Israel "strategically" deprived Gazans "of possibilities of being" by rendering them disabled.[80] Through the infliction of mass injuries designed to disable rather than kill (90% of injuries were to the lower limbs) Israel succeeded in overwhelming an already broken healthcare and rehabilitative system. MSF, for example, reported at the time that the acute and complex nature of the injuries sustained by thousands of young men over

---

77 Puar, 2017, xiv.

78 Law for Palestine, "Law for Palestine Releases Database with 500+ Instances of Israeli Incitement to Genocide – Continuously Updated," January 4, 2024. https://law4palestine.org/law-for-palestine-releases-database-with-500-instances-of-israeli-incitement-to-genocide-continuously-updated/

79 The *Great March of Return or Gaza border protests* began on March 30, 2018 to demand an end to the Israeli blockade and the right of return for refugees.

80 Obermaier, 2023.

the course of almost 18 months "overwhelmed" their teams despite trebling their surgical capabilities.[81]

Obermaier and Puar were writing at a time when Israel appeared to register some, albeit limited, concern over international opinion. Maiming Palestinian protesters during the Great March of Return was constructed by Israeli perpetrators as a morally defensive, rather than disproportionate response. Simply disabling Palestinians was presented as humane in the circumstances, given that killing them was, in the eyes of the Israeli state, a politically justifiable response.

In the broader context of a Gaza with drastically diminished and restricted healthcare and rehabilitative resources, maiming could be seen a strategy aimed to further weaken Gazan society. October 7, however, marked a significant change in Israel's genocidal strategy. Elimination now replaced debilitation as Israeli strategy moved from systematic weakening into the annihilatory phase. This was as true for Gazan hospitals and other health and rehabilitative facilities as it was for the whole Gazan population. There is little doubt that this was the planned outcome: On October 9, 2023, Israel's Defense Minister, Yoav Gallant openly declared: "We will end things inside Gaza [...]. I have removed all restraints, attack everything, kill those who fight us, whether there is one terrorist or there are hundreds of terrorists, through the air, land, with tanks, with bulldozers, by all means, there are no compromises. Gaza will not return to what it was."[82] Israel's intention to move to annihilation may also be inferred from statements made by other Israeli political and defense leaders. IDF spokesperson Daniel Hagari declared that "The emphasis is on damage, not accuracy"[83] when referring to Israeli aerial bombardments, while Netanyahu threatened to "flatten" Gaza reducing it "to an island of ruins." Knesset member Arial Kallner revealed that "there is only one goal: Nakba, a Nakba that would dwarf the Nakba of 1948." Israel's President Isaac Herzog declared that "there are no innocent civilians in Gaza."[84]

---

81 "Shattered limbs, shattered lives," *Great march of return*, Médecins Sans Frontières (MSF). https://www.msf.org/great-march-return-depth

82 https://www.youtube.com/playlist?list=PL8E54R76rowCcCOn_ HQf36o1RF3_oD3z4

83 Bethan McKernan and Quique Kierszenbaum, "'We're focused on maximum damage': ground offensive into Gaza seems imminent," *The Guardian*, October 10, 2023. https://www.theguardian.com/world/2023/oct/10/ right-now-it-is-one-day-at-a-time-life-on-israels-frontline-with-gaza

84 Law for Palestine, *Database of Israeli Incitement to Genocide: Decision Makers*, January 15, 2024. https://law4palestine.org/wp-content/uploads/2024/01/1-Database-of-Israeli-Incitement-to-Genocide-15th-January-2024-DECISION-MAKERS.pdf

Conclusion

Israel's genocide of the Palestinians has a long history, but it reached its terrifying denouement in the months which followed October 7. Israel's mass annihilation solution for the Palestinians of Gaza has followed decades of state orchestrated dehumanization, apartheid, sporadic violence and systematic weakening. While this final stage has embodied mass disabling it has exploded any earlier state policy in which physically maiming individual Palestinians in order to control them was the primary goal. We have shown that the destruction[85] and disablement of the Gaza Strip through bombardment, ground invasion and siege mean that every single Gazan trapped within its narrow confines has effectively been disabled. The purposive lives they lived, the places where they loved, worked, socialized, maintained health and were educated have vanished as homes, schools, hospitals, universities and public offices have been obliterated. We have also shown that mass disablement both at the individual and structural level has been a calculated component of Israel's genocide.

Through wholesale sanitascide Israel has ensured that ultimately death rather than functional disability follows injury and trauma. Sanitascide is also in itself, along with domicide, ecocide and scholasticide, a component of genocidal annihilation. By these means and the physical obliteration of Gaza's social and economic infrastructure Israel has attempted to destroy the Gazan national identity "in whole." The prospect of ever rebuilding Gaza for Palestinians has been drastically undermined by what many have described as Israel's orchestrated "ecocide" of the Gaza Strip,[86] where "Olive groves and farms have been reduced to packed earth; soil and groundwater have been contaminated by munitions and toxins; the sea is choked with sewage and waste; the air polluted by smoke and particulate matter."[87]This destruction

---

85 As Francesca Albanese starkly declared in the beginning of her March 2024 report to the UN: "After five months of military operations, Israel has destroyed Gaza." See Francesca Albanese, *Report of the Special Rapporteur on the Situation of Human Rights in the Palestinian Territories Occupied since 1967* (United Nations, March 25, 2024), 1, 11.

86 See for example, Andreas Malm, *The Destruction of Palestine is the Destruction of the Earth* (Verso Books, 2024). https://www.versobooks.com/en-gb/blogs/news/the-destruction-of-palestine-is-the-destruction-of-the-earth

Samira Homerang Saunders, "Environmental devastation and the war on Palestine," *Red Pepper Magazine,* December 1, 2024. https://www.redpepper.org.uk/environment-climate/environmental-justice/environmental-devastation-and-the-war-on-palestine/

87 Kaamil Ahmed, Damien Gayle, and Aseel Mousa, "'Ecocide in Gaza': Does scale of environmental destruction amount to a war crime?," *The Guardian,* March 29, 2023. https://www.theguardian.com/environment/2024/mar/29/gaza-israel-palestinian-war-ecocide-environmental-destruction-pollution-rome-statute-war-crimes-aoe

and disablement, as Andreas Malm asserts, has been conducted as a "transnational effort." Without the material and ideological support of the West's major powers for Israel's settler colonial ambitions this genocide could not have taken the form it has. Israel's armaments, weapons technologies, impunity and hubris have all been endorsed and underwritten by the United States, Germany, France, the United Kingdom and others, all of whom bear culpability. In such a context only the concerted actions of civil society through the Boycott, Divestment and Sanctions (BDS) movement will isolate Israel militarily, economically, culturally, and academically. Civil society has enjoyed widespread legitimacy as an authoritative check on the power and actions of the state[88] and has been at the heart and center of all evidence gathering in relation to Israel's crimes over many decades. And this work by civil society has led efforts to successfully name Israel's crimes as settler colonialism, apartheid and now genocide.

The International Court of Justice's determination that Israel may plausibly be committing genocide[89] provides a powerful discursive resource for activists and legitimacy for actions challenging the complicity of western states in the genocide. Founder and leader of the BDS movement, Omar Barghouti, has stressed that "The most profound ethical obligation in these times is to act to end complicity. Only thus can we truly hope to end oppression and violence."

The role of BDS is to place unremitting economic, cultural, and political pressure on Israel and its supporters by targeting those companies that drive and invest in Israeli industries of violence, annihilation, surveillance, technology, education, culture and sport.

The trauma and injuries following relentless bombardment, mass killings, repeated forced displacement, torture and planned starvation[90] and disease have impacted every member of Gazan society. But the disablement

---

88 Penny Green and Tony Ward, *State Crime and Civil Activism: On the Dialectics of Repression and Resistance (Crimes of the Powerful)* (Routledge, 2019).

89 United Nations, Office of the High Commissioner for Human Rights, "Gaza: ICJ ruling offers hope for protection of civilians enduring apocalyptic conditions, say UN experts," UN Human Rights, January 31, 2024. https://www.ohchr.org/en/press-releases/2024/01/gaza-icj-ruling-offers-hope-protection-civilians-enduring-apocalyptic

90 Israeli Finance Minister Bezalel Smotrich on August 5 2024 declared that starving two million Gazans "to death" may be "right and moral" to do until Israeli hostages held in Gaza are released but that the "world won't let us." See "Israeli Finance Minister Smotrich: Starving Gazans 'To Death' May Be Moral, but World Won't Let Us," *Haaretz*, August 5, 2024. https://www.haaretz.com/israel-news/2024-08-05/ty-article/israeli-finance-minister-starving-gazans-to-death-may-be-moral-but-world-wont-let-us/00000191-22e1-dd23-a7dd-2aed4b050000

of the Gaza Strip as a functioning political, economic, environmental and social entity has been Israel's genocidal goal. To destroy the land in order to sever the bonds that link Palestinian identity with the Gaza Strip is both genocidal and the logical outcome of Israel's settler colonial project. We have shown that disablement both at the individual and structural level has been a calculated component of Israel's genocide. In this process Israel has disabled the relationship between all Gazans and their society, produced tens of thousands of new physically disabled Gazans, further weakened or destroyed the existing disabled population and generated an incalculable number of mental health disabilities.

Israel's genocide in Gaza must be addressed by a structural model of disability, which not only captures the intentional disablement of an entire society but which captures the criminality of states which perpetrate all forms of disablement—individual and structural. Any such model must also include the significance of state organizational goals in the drive toward disablement and strategies of resistance by the target group, which will inevitably be criminalized by the perpetrating state.

The Hamas Question

Walden Bello

IN RECENT discussions among governments and international civil society on the future of Palestine, there now appears to be a consensus around a two-state solution. Where there is disagreement is on the role of Hamas in any future arrangement. Most Israelis opposed to the inclusion of Hamas in any post-Gaza arrangement for the Palestinian people and most liberal two-state supporters are performing all sorts of political acrobatics to justify excluding Hamas.

Shortly after the Hamas military operation in Israel on October 7, 2023, I wrote an article that was reprinted widely globally on the Hamas issue. I am reproducing it here as my contribution to this volume because I believe that progressives must cease to be defensive about Hamas but rather proactively support its inclusion as a leading force in any post-Gaza arrangement since it is, for all intents and purposes, the only effective advocate of the rights of the Palestinian people. No hysterical branding of it as a "terrorist organization" can dispell this reality.

* * *

There was widespread dismay when people learned of the Hamas offensive in Israel two weeks ago. I felt, after talking to people, that perhaps the best way for them to understand what happened, is to ask themselves, as I had asked myself years back, a question. This is a question that I am now proposing to you and other readers of this commentary.

But before I do that, let me give you some background for the question.

The Nakba or Palestinian Catastrophe involved the expulsion of some 700,000 Palestinians from their homes during the 1948 Arab-Israeli War,

Walden Bello is currently Honorary Research Fellow at the Sociology Department of the State University of New York at Binghamton, where he also held until recently the position of International Adjunct Professor of Sociology. He served in the Philippine House of Representatives from 2009 to 2015 and ran for vice president in the Philippine elections of 2022. He was named Amnesty International Philippines' "Human Rights Defender for 2023.

confiscation of their lands and houses, and a permanent ban on their return imposed by Israel. In other words, the state of Israel was born out of the pillage and robbery of somebody else's land, which is the basis of the latter's existence, personality, and culture. That is Israel's original sin. This was the reason that, even before the Nakba, the great Jewish intellectual Hannah Arendt opposed the establishment of the Zionist state, built on the completely binding unity of people, territory, and state, where the original Palestinian Arab majority would be forcibly converted into a minority. At the height of the Second World War, in 1942, Arendt actually equated Zionism with Nazi racism!

In 1967, during the second Arab-Israeli War, Israel seized the West Bank and East Jerusalem, and has since maintained control, though in some parts Israel has allowed nominal authority to be exercised by the Palestinian Authority. The Oslo Accords of 1993 and 1995 were supposed to begin the process leading to a Palestinian state, but instead, in the words of Hamas leader Usamah Hamdan, "it changed the objective from that of securing Palestinian rights to that of providing security for the occupation." Israel has resisted every initiative to create an independent Palestinian state. It has, in fact, annexed East Jerusalem, and now it has a far-right government that is intent on using Israeli settlers to occupy large parts of the West Bank to establish facts on the ground.

According to *The New York Times*, June 29, 2023,[1]

> More than 130 settlements have been built with Israeli govern-ment permission since 1967. In addition, more than 100 settlement outposts have been erected since the 1990s without government authorization. The Israeli authorities are working on authorizing many of them retroactively... Some settlement construction has continued under every Israeli government over the past decades. More than 400,000 Israeli settlers now live in the West Bank alongside more than 2.6 million Palestinians.

Now things have been moving even faster. Again according to the *Times*, which, incidentally, is one of Israel's biggest backers,

> In the six months since Prime Minister Benjamin Netanyahu's coalition government—the most right-wing and religiously

---

1 Isabel Kershner, "Why Israel is Pushing to Expand West Bank Settlements," *New York Times,* June 29, 2023. https://www.nytimes.com/2023/06/29/world/middleeast/israel-west-bank-settlements-expansion.html

conservative in Israel's history—came to power, the country's
planning authorities have advanced or approved permits for
13,000 new housing units in West Bank settlements. The minister
overseeing settlement construction has instructed ministries in
Israel to prepare to improve the infrastructure in settlement areas
of the West Bank to absorb another 500,000 settlers...[2]

So my question, dear reader, is: Imagine you're a young Palestinian who
has grown up in refugee camps, who can't return to your grandparents' home
and lands in Palestine because they have been expropriated by Israelis, who
sees that Israel has no intention of ever leaving the West Bank but, on the
contrary, is intent on annexing it, who watches while Israel spits on peaceful,
legal methods to secure your people's rights, violates international agreements, and tells international public opinion to go to hell—what would you
do?

Would you not be tempted to join Hamas, who says military means are
the only way your people can secure their rights?

But before you answer, let me make a few more comments, this time on
some of the responses to the recent Hamas operation in Israel.

First, there is among progressives and liberals a tendency to blame both
Israel and Hamas in equal measure for the violence. This is a false equivalence. When it comes to violence, Israel is a thousand times more responsible
and accountable for violence than Hamas, since it created the conditions
whereby many Palestinians have come to the conclusion that violence is the
only way they can secure their rights.

Second, there is also, among progressives and liberals, a tendency to separate Hamas from the Palestinian people. They're deluding themselves. The
only reason Hamas can carry out such bold military operations is because it
enjoys tremendous support among Palestinians. When Israel says it is out
to eliminate Hamas, what it is really saying is that it is prepared to commit
genocide by killing off the mass base of Hamas, the Palestinian people, who
will constantly reproduce the children who will join the organization.

Third, some of us may find some of Hamas' methods ethically unjusti-
fiable. I do. But I find them understandable. Understanding is the first step
towards dialogue, towards a peaceful solution. But Israel does not even
want to understand, to acknowledge the reasons why Palestinians have been
cornered into committing the acts they condemn out of desperation. And the
West as a whole is guilty of the same refusal to understand the fundamental
injustice of the Palestinian situation. As in the past, the apartheid state and

---

2 Ibid.

its defenders have in recent days resorted to the inflammatory rhetoric of the Holocaust to shut down any debate.

So back to my question: If you were a young Palestinian, faced with a situation where, except for a handful, Israelis refuse to even hear your case, where dialogue and negotiations with you are alien words in the vocabulary of the Israeli state, where the president of the most powerful country on earth says he backs Israel 100 percent and is prepared to give Israel all the weapons it needs to perpetuate a fundamental historical injustice—what would you do?

Let me give you my answer, and borrow literally from what Max Weber, the famous liberal who was one of the founders of sociology, said he was prepared to do to put "his people back on their feet." If I were a young Palestinian confronted by these conditions, I would most likely be prepared not just to join Hamas but to make a pact with the devil himself to rectify the historical injustice visited on my people.

Israeli Ultra-Orthodox Jews' Attitudes during Coronavirus and Genocide in Gaza:
The "Haredi Factor" in Israeli Politics?

Sevinç Alkan Özcan

Introduction

THE STATE OF ISRAEL constitutes a special combination of religion, secularization and nationalism. Though founded by the secular Zionist movement, religion was not absent as the raison d'etre of the Israeli state. Although only 20% of the population of Israel identify themselves as religious and the remaining 80% as secular, how the state, society and religion are related has been a contested issue. With the creation of the state of Israel, the secular Jewish identity that had arose with the Jewish Enlightenment and the Zionist movement in late 19th century gained strength vis-à-vis traditional Judaism. Israel has become the only place where Jews who do not want to adhere to Jewish law but also do not wish to give up their Jewish identity, feel safe from all other threats. As Avineri said:

> Zionism was the most fundamental revolution in Jewish life. It substituted a secular self-identity of the Jews as a nation for the traditional and Orthodox self identity in religious terms. It changed a passive, quietistic, and pious hope of the Return to Zion

Sevinç Alkan Özcan received her MA and PhD from Marmara University, Department of Political Science and International Relations. She served as advisor to former Minister of Foreign Affairs (2011–2014) and chief advisor to former Prime Minister of Türkiye (2014–2017), Prof. Ahmet Davutoğlu. She teaches on Politics of Caucasus and Central Asia, Religion and Politics in IR and History of Turkish Democracy and Turkish Foreign Policy in Ankara Yıldırım Beyazıt University, Department of International Relations.

into an effective social force, moving millions of people to Israel. It transformed a language relegated to mere religious usage into a modern, secular mode of intercourse of a nation-state.[1]

Stated in a comparative perspective, during the modernization process, secular nationalism served as a disintegrating factor and religious identity as a unifying element in Islamic societies, whereas in the emergence of modern Jewish identity the opposite was the case, with secular nationalist Zionism having a unifying impact, and religious identity a fragmentary one. All the dilemmas of Jewish identity that emerged with the Jewish Enlightenment were transferred to the modern state of Israel. In fact, anti-traditionalist sentiment was stronger in Israel than in the diaspora, but still, political movements and parties always seek the support of religiously devout Jews, especially the Haredim, the ultra-Orthodox Jews. As Y. M. Rabkin stated:

> This hostility to Judaism found diverse expressions among the founders of the state, including the choice of new, Hebraized names: the father of a member of the Knesset gave himself the name Kofer, heretic (Klein). The categorical rejection of Judaism can also be explained by the climate of religious coercion that results from the need of secular Zionist parties to ensure support or at least neutrality of the religious non-Zionists. This coercion weighs heavily on all aspects of life: from the prohibition of bus service on the Sabbath to the almost religious monopoly over weddings and burials. The Israeli press regularly reports incidents of anti-religious hostility. In one such case, the pupils of a secular high school, having completed their final—and obligatory—examination on the Torah, stacked up their copies in the schoolyard and set them a fire, to the delight of all present.[2]
>
> However, in Israel the gulf that separates the secular from Judaism in all its forms has widened. Israeli newspapers are full of caricatures of Haredi Jews, not unlike the anti-Semitic stereotypes current in Europe in the nineteenth and twentieth centuries.[3] The Israeli historian Noah Efron writes: "This kind of hostility is not novel. Nowhere are Haredi Jews as feared and hated as in

---

1 Shlomo Avineri, *The Making of Modern Zionism: The Intellectual Origins of the Jewish State* (2nd edition) (New York: Basic Books, 2017), 12.

2 Yakov M. Rabkin, *A Threat from Within: A Century of Jewish Opposition to Zionism* (Zed Books, 2006), 45.

3 Noah Efron, "Trembling with Fear: How Secular Israelis See the Ultra-Orthodox, and Why," *Tikkun* 6, no. 5 (1991): 15–22, 88–90; quoted by Rabkin, 46

Israel. Israel is a bastion of a classic sort of anti-Semitism, aimed not against all Jews, but against the ultra-Orthodox, the overly Jewy Jews.[4]

In recent years, there has been a growing conflict between the state and the Haredi community who have been exempt from mandatory military service, run schools based on religious study refusing to teach secular subjects, live isolated from non-Haredi groups in the country and away from the secular media. Haredi Jews prefer to be subject to rabbinic authority instead of recognizing the secular authority of the state, even refrain from using the expression "State of Israel" and refuse to speak Hebrew and use the Yiddish language.

The exemption of Haredis from military service dates back to the establishment of the Israeli state in 1948. Israel's first Prime Minister David Ben Gurion implemented an exemption policy at that time to allow the relatively small community of ultra-Orthodox to focus on religious studies and worship. While only a few hundred people were affected by this regulation back then, the growing numbers have made the status quo unsustainable. Today, approximately 60,000 young people benefit from this exemption.[5]

During the coronavirus pandemic (2020–2022) and Gaza genocide, the tension between the secular segments of the society, the governments and the Haredi ultra-Orthodox community seemed to increase. The fragmented structure of Israeli society, including significant lifestyle differences between Haredim and secular groups, has become more apparent and more fragile during the pandemic and the Gaza genocide. In addition to the debates about the exemption of Haredi Jews from military service, which was widely discussed in Israeli politics even before the pandemic period, the Haredi opposition to the measures taken during the pandemic period increased the Haredi-secular tension both socially and politically. During the Gaza war, which started after October 7, as the need for soldiers in the Israeli army increased, the call for Haredim from all segments of society to be drafted into the military made these divisions more sharp. The nature of Israel's political structure and dynamics, which is open to the influence of small groups such as Haredim, became more evident with the Gaza war. Therefore, the fragile structure of Israel's internal dynamics and the increasing number of anti-war and anti-Netanyahu protests have made the Gaza war more important for Israel. Although the coronavirus has been stopped since, there has been a

---

4 Efron, 16; quoted by Rabkin, 46
5 John Strawson, "What will Israel's bombshell court ruling that Haredi Jews must serve in the military mean for Netanyahu?" Expert Q&A, *The Conversation*, June 27, 2024.

continuation of conflict between Haredis and the governments during Gaza genocide. This article aims to analyze the increasing impact of the "Haredi factor" in Israeli politics during the pandemic and the Gaza war in a comparative perspective.

New Front between State and Haredi Jews in Israel: Coronavirus[6]

Since the start of the pandemic, Israel has been one of the places where the conflictual relationship between religion and the state was most evident. The images of clashes between the police and ultra-Orthodox Jews over coronavirus measures have prompted us to rethink the relationship between religion, state and politics in Israel. Since the ultra-Orthodox Jews neighborhood of Mea Sheraim in West Jerusalem and Bnei Brak, a city west of Tel Aviv had the highest rate of infections and the community had insisted on holding communal worship services, many Israelis blamed the Haredim for the rapid spread of the pandemic.[7] Many members of the community have been in defiance of state restrictions and even clashed with the police. Having difficulty in taking precautions, the police used tear gas in the Mea Sheraim neighborhood where residents had set up barricades in the neighborhood to prevent entry to ambulances and security forces. The police were instructed to use force after hundreds of Haredim attended the funeral of a rabbi in Bnei Baraks.[8] Similarly, some Jewish communities in the U.S. have also resisted the restrictions. A Hasidic Jewish school in New York City that did not comply with the coronavirus bans was shut down. In addition, the mayor ordered the dispersal of a crowded funeral held by the Hasidic Jewish community of Brooklyn where social distance rules were not followed.

The growing religious-secular polarization in the 2000s in Israel deepened during the coronavirus pandemic. On the one hand, secular tendencies have been increasing in Israeli society, on the other hand, the Knesset passed the "Jewish nation-state" bill into law on July 19, 2018, amid secular opposition. Critics argued the law would increase discrimination against Arab citizens, pave the way for the implementation of Jewish religious laws, and defined

---

6 This section was published before as a part of the article by Sevinç Alkan Özcan and M. Hüseyin Mercan, "The Impact of Covid-19 On State-Religion Relations: A Study On Israel And Iran," *Insan & Toplum – The Journal of Humanity & Society* 11, no.2 (2021): 169–88.

7 Joshua Sabih, "GOD IS TELLING US SOMETHING: Rabbi Amnon Yitzhak's Pesher and Socio-Political Pantheism of Corona Virus," *Tidsskrift for Islamforskning* 14, no. 2 (2021): 200.

8 Emre Karaca, "Karantinaya Direnen Topluluk: Ultra-Ortodoks Yahudiler," *Anadolu Agency*, May 8, 2020. https://www.aa.com.tr/tr/arastirma/karantinaya-direnen-topluluk-ultra-ortodoks-yahudiler-/1833493

it as an important obstacle to democracy. The legislation that in the words of Netanyahu would ensure "our state's Jewish character for generations to come" was approved with 62 votes in favor, and 55 opposed. The law defines Israel as the "historic national home of the Jewish people," says the right to national self-determination is "unique to the Jewish people," calls Jerusalem as the capital of Israel, and designates Hebrew as the official state language with Arabic having "special status." The law, which can be described as a new apartheid aiming to take away the right of return of Palestinian refugees, as well as the loss of citizenship rights of Palestinians, who make up 20% of the population, is a continuation of President Trump's formal recognition of Jerusalem as the capital of Israel and the United States embassy's move from Tel Aviv to Jerusalem.

The COVID-19 pandemic seemed to have moved the debate triggered by the nation-state law over state-religion relations in new a direction.[9] The pandemic not only led to clashes between the secular state officials and the Haredim but widened the fissures between the secular-liberal/reformist Jews and the ultra-Orthodox Jewish community. Unlike the Haredim, liberal Jews complied with the state's lockdown measures and joined virtual religious services. They have adapted their congregational worship to new pandemic restrictions with solutions such as gathering on balconies at the same time during prayer, celebrated Passover at home without any guests. During this period, the topics of discussion between the two poles of Israeli society were whether the virtual way of performing mass worship such as Sabbath and Passover was in accordance with Jewish religious law and how the burials should be done.[10]

In the early months of 2020, when the first cases of COVID-19 started to emerge, Israel had to hold its third elections in less than a year due to ongoing political crises. One of the most important reasons was the resignation of Avigdor Liberman, the leader of Yisrael Beitneiu (Israel Our Home) party and Minister of Defense, in November 2018, on the grounds that the government was weak against Hamas. However, the main issue that led to the political crisis was the debate over the participation of ultra-Orthodox Jewish population in the mandatory military service. Liberman said that they would

---

9 For a discussion on the theological roots of the ultra-Orthodox groups' reactioanist response to the pandemic, see Sabih, 2021.

10 Özcan Hıdır, "Kovid-19 Teo-Politiği: Evanjelikler ve Ultra-Ortodoks Yahudiler," *Anadolu Agency*, April 15, 2020 https://www.aa.com.tr/tr/analiz/kovid-19-teo-politigi-evanjelikler-ve-ultra-ortodoks-yahudiler/1805863

not back down from a harsher conscription law for Haredim and would not allow Jewish religious law in the state administration.[11]

The ultra-Orthodox Jewish community's share of the population is expected to increase from 12% to 25% by 2065 due to the high birth rates. The Haredim live mostly isolated from the rest of Israeli society and men devote their full time to studying the Torah instead of participating in the labor force and serving in the military, and many families are below the poverty line and rely on state welfare support. Due to these factors, the community draws heavy criticism from the rest of the public. Liberman wanted to implement the conscription law by passing it from the Knesset. However, the ultra-Orthodox Shash Party and Yahadut HaTorah (Union Torah Judaism) coalition, partners of the Netanyahu-led coalition, opposed the bill. Following the elections held in April 2019, a government led by Netanyahu could not be formed because Liberman insisted on the enlistment bill to be passed without any changes. As a result, Israelis went to the polls again in September 2019 and for the third time in March 2020.[12]

Israel's ongoing political crisis due to the debates on the military obligations of ultra-Orthodox Jews has been partly the result of increasing secular-traditionalist polarization. Since the start of the pandemic, the ultra-Orthodox have been held responsible for the rapid spread of the virus, which seems to open a new front for confrontation between the secular right and the far right and may trigger new political crises. Liberman's efforts to split the right by spearheading the opposition to the ultra-Orthodox can further increase the polarization between the secular-right and the far-right. This corresponds to a deeper separation in Israeli politics than the left-right polarization, since the left has declined and almost disappeared, and politics has gradually shifted to the far right. The insistence of the far-right parties on standing by Netanyahu despite the corruption investigations, and the increased anti–ultra-Orthodox sentiment in Israeli society during the coronavirus period, show that the "Haredi factor" in Israeli politics will be discussed more in the coming years. The developments during the Gaza genocide are very significant in this respect because the Israeli army's need for soldiers has significantly increased due to its Gaza attacks.

---

11 Bel Trew, "İsrail'de İktidarın Yeni Belirleyicileri Ultra-Ortodokslar mı?," *Independent Türkçe*, June 11, 2019. https://www.indyturk.com/node/40756/yazarlar/ israil%E2%80%99de-iktidar%C4%B1n-yeni-belirleyicileri-ultra-ortodokslar-m%C4%B1.

12 Ceyda Karan, "İsrail'de Siyaset Aşırı Sağa Kayıyor, Sol Yok Olma Noktasında," *Sputnik Türkiye*, March 4, 2020. https://tr.sputniknews.com/ceyda_ karan_eksen/202003041041540054-israilde-siyaset-asiri-saga-kayiyor-sol-yok-olma-noktasinda/

Ultra-Orthodox Jews, Gaza Genocide and Israeli Politics

After the coronavirus period, discussions on the conscription of ultra-Orthodox Jews resurfaced due to Israel's attacks on Gaza, ongoing clashes with Hezbollah, and possible air operations against Lebanon. On February 28, Israeli Defense Minister Yoav Gallant called for the conscription of Haredi Jews under the new circumstances[13] Benny Gantz, a member of the War Cabinet, also mentioned that they were working on comprehensive conscription legislation that would involve the entire society. Chief of Staff Herzi Halevi expressed similar views. On March 12, 2024, opposition leader Yair Lapid stated that Israel could not continue fighting on multiple fronts without the support of the ultra-Orthodox and that the military had reached its limits.[14]

In Israel, where military service is mandatory for two years and eight months for men and two years for women, Haredis sought legal guarantees for their exemption from military service even before the Gaza war. In September 2023, the Israeli Supreme Court ruled that exempting ultra-Orthodox Jews from military service was discriminatory, bringing the issue back to the forefront just before the Gaza war. The increased need for soldiers during the Gaza war led to clashes reminiscent of the coronavirus period, especially on the streets of Jerusalem. Secular groups protested, demanding that Orthodox religious groups also serve in the military, while Orthodox groups clashed with the police in Jerusalem.[15] Haredis even stated that they would leave the country if forced into military service. A survey conducted by the Israel Democracy Institute earlier this year showed that 70% of Israeli Jews wanted the general exemption for ultra-Orthodox from military service to end.[16]

In 2015, the Israeli Supreme Court's annulment of the law exempting Haredi Jews from military service due to its violation of the principle of equality reintroduced the "Haredi factor" into Israeli politics. Consequently, subsequent governments failed to agree on a new draft law concerning the conscription of Haredis. Thus, decisions extending the exemption of Haredi Jews from military service had to be continued, with the latest extension until

---

13 Amit Elyakam, "Gaza War Is Shifting Ties Between Secular and Ultra-Orthodox Israelis," *New York Times*, March 4, 2024.

14 Bekir Aydoğan, "İsrail'de askerliğe zorlanan Ultra Ortodoks Yahudilerin "ülkeyi terk etme" tehdidi tartışmaya neden oldu," *Anadolu Agency*, March 13, 2024.   https://www.aa.com.tr/tr/dunya/israilde-askerlige-zorlanan-ultra-ortodoks-yahudilerin-ulkeyi-terk-etme-tehdidi-tartismaya-neden-oldu/3163145

15 *BBC News Türkçe*, February 28, 2024.

16 Yolande Knell, "Israel conscription rule stokes ultra-Orthodox fury," *BBC*, June 2, 2024. https://www.bbc.com/news/articles/c6p24expzd5o.amp

March 29. Netanyahu's dilemma on this issue persists. Forced to implement mandatory conscription for Haredi Jews by April 1, 2024, Netanyahu prepared a draft law proposing to raise the exemption age from 26 to 35 and to refrain from prosecuting those avoiding military service for three years.[17]

The representation of Haredis in the Israeli Knesset by "United Torah Judaism" and "Shas" within the coalition alliance maintains the significance of the conscription debates in Israeli politics. Coalition partner Haredi parties aim to pass a law ensuring that those they represent are exempt from military service, asserting that "Torah education is a fundamental right." The statement by Israeli Minister of Construction and Housing and United Torah Judaism Party leader Yitzchak Goldknopf that the government would fall if a law exempting those studying in religious institutions from military service is not passed demonstrates the critical position of Haredis in politics.[18] The government's request for an extension until June to draft a mandatory conscription law in its defense to the Supreme Court's review of the government's decision to extend the exemption for ultra-Orthodox Jews from military service in February highlighted the government's tight spot. Finally with the Israeli army announcement that the recruitment process for Ultra-Orthodox soldiers would begin on July 21, anti-military ultra-Orthodox Jews blocked the road chanting "We will die, we won't go to the military." In the announcement, it was stated that the summoning procedures, which will start on July 21, are for military recruitment next year. In the statement, it was emphasized that the Israeli army "will continue to act in accordance with the decision taken at the political level and the law" and that recruitment from all segments of society continues within the framework of increasing operational needs.[19]

Although Haredis do not oppose Israel's attacks on Palestine, their primary reason for seeking exemption from military service is the fear of not being able to fulfill Jewish obligations in the army. According to them, the military is a secular domain that distances people from Judaism and promotes profanity. They are exempt from military service if they are under Torah courses (Yeshiva) education until the age of twenty-six. A Haredi journalist

17 Arnaout, Abdel Ra'ouf D. A. R. and Muhammed Emin Canik, "İsrail'de ultra-ortodoks Yahudilerin zorunlu askerlik meselesi Netanyahu hükümetini tehdit ediyor," *Anadolu Agency*, March 26, 2024. https://www.aa.com.tr/tr/dunya/israilde-ultra-ortodoks-yahudilerin-zorunlu-askerlik-meselesi-netanyahu-hukumetini-tehdit-ediyor/3175187

18 Bekir Aydoğan, March 13, 2024.

19 "İsrail'den Ultra Ortodoks Yahudiler için celp duyurusu," *TRT Haber,* July 17, 2024, https://www.trthaber.com/haber/dunya/israilden-ultra-ortodoks-yahudiler-icin-celp-duyurusu-868746.html

expressed fears, saying, "Haredi leaders, spiritual leaders ... are very, very afraid of seeing thousands of young Haredi men in uniform in ultra-Orthodox neighborhoods," and "They fear that being a soldier will become normal in the Haredi community. If you join the Israeli Defense Forces, you begin to open up to different ideas. You start opening up to other ideas ... and no one will listen to the rabbis anymore."[20]

Despite their insistence on exemption from military service during the Gaza genocide, news in the Israeli newspaper *Yedioth Ahronoth* suggested that Haredis were trying to participate in the Israeli army's war in the Gaza Strip, which could soften the reactions against them. This news was reported by the London-based Arab World News Agency (AWP), according to Asharq Al-Awsat. The first group to be recruited is said to be a search and rescue and emergency group of 120 people with experience and minimal training requirements. Additionally, it is known that there is a battalion within the Israeli army composed of Haredis under the guidance of Jewish rabbis, called Netzah Yehuda (The Eternity of Judah). This battalion, distinct from other units in the army, allows Haredis to serve in alignment with their religious beliefs for two years and eight months, with no female soldiers and only kosher meals. The number of Haredi Jews volunteering for the army is reportedly around three thousand.[21]

Conclusion

The Gaza War and genocide have had a significant effect on the divisions within Israeli society and politics. Since the Gaza War, various segments of society have organized demonstrations in the streets of Tel Aviv and Jerusalem with different demands. These demands included ending the war in Gaza (not because Palestinians were being killed, but because it jeopardized economic and political stability and security in Israel), securing a ceasefire for the release of hostages, Netanyahu's resignation, ending the military exemption for ultra-Orthodox Jews, and maintaining the exemption for ultra-Orthodox Jews. The Haredi Jews, who make up about 13% of Israel's population, have become a significant element of division during this period of increased military needs. As mentioned in the first section, they also came to the forefront during the coronavirus period due to their opposition to state measures and became a target for the rest of Israeli society, especially secular segments.

---

20 Jo Shelley and Mike Schwartz, "'We will not enlist:' Ultra-Orthodox in Israel vow to defy orders to serve in the military," *CNN International,* July 1, 2024.

21 Asharq Al-Awsat, Turkish, "Israeli newspaper: Thousands of ultra-Orthodox Jews want to join the war in Gaza," October 21, 2023.

From the Haredi community's perspective, there are three different reactions to the potential removal of their military exemption. The first reaction involves leaving the country if Haredi youth are conscripted. The second reaction advocates continued mass protests and resistance. The third reaction believes that Netanyahu and the Haredi parties in the coalition will find a compromise.[22] While the Ministry of Defense sends directives for the forced conscription of men studying in Torah schools, the government also faces threats from Haredi parties. Some of Netanyahu's own coalition members and ministers have joined the opposition's calls for the conscription of the Haredi community, putting Netanyahu in an even more difficult position. Netanyahu's loss of credibility due to the Gaza war, coupled with increased calls for his resignation both internationally and domestically, means that he is unlikely to find the necessary compromise among right-wing and far-right parties. As a matter of fact, the Israeli army's announcement that it will start sending summonses to Haredi men as of July 21, 2024, shows that Netanyahu cannot resist the secular public pressure regarding Haredis under the war conditions. However, according to the news in the Israeli press, it is stated that in the first stage, approximately three thousand Haredi people who are not educated in Torah schools and working life will be called to the military, and also the Israeli army generals, together with the religious leaders of the Haredi section, stated that "female soldiers and officers should not serve in the units in which Haredim will serve, and that they comply with the rules of Judaism." This news also shows that Netanyahu is trying to reduce the Haredim's protests and resentment.

---

22 John Strawson, "What will Israel's bombshell court ruling that Haredi Jews must serve in the military mean for Netanyahu?" Expert Q&A, *The Conversation*, June 27, 2024.

Cultural, Historical, & Global South Perspectives

From a Eurocentric to a Global South Perspective
Paving the Way for Palestinian Solidarity

Arlene Clemesha | *Francesco Schettino*

"Who gave Israel the right to deny all rights?"
—Eduardo Galeano

THE EPIGRAPH ABOVE belongs to a short article written by the great Uruguayan author, Eduardo Galeano, in 2009. His eloquent words, filled with pain, were more than an expression of anguish in face of the brutality of the Israeli attacks against the Palestinian people in the Gaza Strip that year. Galeano's question also reflected a methodological orientation in search of concrete answers.

At the beginning of the twentieth century, the colonization of Palestine was the product of two simultaneous and combined endeavors: a Jewish nationalist settler-colonial project (i.e. Zionism), and a British imperialist project seeking to impose fragmentation and domination over Arab lands for economic and geopolitical purposes. This combined form of colonization was explicitly authorized by the most powerful countries of the time, convened at the Paris peace conferences that followed World War I. The world powers, meeting in Paris, drew up the entire mandate system to enable their own predominance in the region, based on the convenient narratives brought by

Arlene Clemesha Professor of Contemporary Arab History at the University of São Paulo (USP), Brazil, and Director of the Center for Palestine Studies at the same university. Her books include *Brazil and the Middle East: The Power of Civil Society*; *Palestine 48–08*; and *Marxism and Judaism: History of a Difficult Relation*.

Francesco Schettino is Professor of Economics at the Università degli Studi della Campania "Luigi Vanvitelli." Dipartimento di Giurisprudenza. Italy. His main research focuses on inequality and technological change, with articles published in leading journals such as *World Development* and *Journal of Economic Inequality*.

the Zionist movement regarding the alleged "return of the Jewish people" to the holy land following "two thousand years of dispersal."

Three decades later, the countries voting in favor of the partition of Palestine at the United Nations General Assembly session of November 29, 1947, had inevitably a very clear idea that the creation of a Jewish state in Palestine would imply the forceful transfer of a very large number of Palestinians. Since the publication of the Passfield White Paper in 1930, it was already a well-established fact that settler colonialism in Palestine was creating a class of landless Palestinian migrants, and that this was at the root of the Palestinian resistance and revolt. Today, not only are the Palestinians facing a settler colonial project still expanding its borders at the expense of the native population, but there is also an economic and global dimension that is seldom analyzed and that holds the key to understanding where the Palestinian struggle for emancipation and self-determination may possibly find some degree of international support.

The Israeli aggression against the Palestinian people not only responds to the ongoing Zionist project of building a Jewish ethnic state, but also follows the logic of accumulation and exploitation of natural resources that are present in both the Gaza Strip and the West Bank.[1] There is a large amount of gas and oil reserves between the West Bank and the waters opposite Gaza. According to a 2010 estimate,[2] the Eastern Basin appears to contain potentially one of the largest deposits in the world, with a capacity of 1.7 billion barrels of oil and 122 billion cubic feet of extractable gas. Oil and gas resources necessarily stimulate the acquisitive desires not only of Israel, but also of neighboring countries and avid consumers of energy resources located in other parts of the world (Europe, first and foremost).

The history of the exploitation of offshore fields opposite Gaza is clearly intertwined with the periodic invasions of the Strip by the Israeli army. But little has been discussed about the relation between that and the embargo unilaterally implemented in 2007 by Israel against the inhabitants of Gaza and the Palestinians in general, who are unable to access either their natural resources or the revenue generated by them.

---

1 The proliferation of settlements is part of these calculations. Their location is not casual or accidental, but intentionally placed on the lands that are meant to be conquered definitively. See Eyal Weizman, *Hollow Land* (London: Verso, 2012).

2 Christopher Schenk, Mark Kirschbaum, Ronald Carpentier, Timothy Klett, Michael Brownfield, Janet Pitman, Troy Cook, and Marilyn Tennyson, *Assessment of undiscovered oil and gas resources of the Levant Basin Province, Eastern Mediterranean: U.S. Geological Survey Fact Sheet 2010-3014* (USGS, 2010). https://doi.org/10.3133/fs20103014

The Oslo II agreements (1995) granted the Palestinian National Authority (PA) maritime jurisdiction over waters up to 20 nautical miles from the coast. In 1999, the British Gas Group (BGG) discovered a large natural gas field (Gaza Marine) located at a distance compatible with the Palestinian jurisdiction agreements signed just a few years earlier. Subsequent drilling activities generated excellent results. Its estimated flow of up to one billion cubic feet of good quality natural gas would have exceeded Palestinian needs while guaranteeing a good margin for exports. The construction of a pipeline that would take the extracted gas to the Gaza coast was therefore at the heart of an investment plan agreed between the BGG and the PA. The following years, at least until the first half of 2007, were characterized by a substantial sharing of objectives between the Israeli and Palestinian governments of the management of Gaza Marines I and II, with results that seemed to satisfy both parties and also international law.

The big change, however, came the following year, culminating in the December 2008 operation (dubbed "Cast Lead"). Under the pretext of "eradicating Islamic terrorism," this led—in addition to thousands of deaths, injuries and devastation—to the denial of access to the Palestinians' own offshore gas resources, on the grounds that the proceeds would fund "terrorist groups," the pretext for a confiscation clearly in conflict with the agreements signed and international law.

Furthermore, in the occupied territories of the West Bank, there also are oil and gas deposits, but these are managed and exploited entirely by the Israeli authorities. The Meged oil field, discovered in the 1980s, with a potential of around 1.5 billion barrels of oil, as well as natural gas, began its production in the early years of the current century.

The State of Israel is able to meet only 13.4% of the total of its internal demands for energy (2012).[3] It is structurally dependent on the resources of others and since 1999, with the collaboration of North American energy companies, Israeli governments have promoted the search for deposits inside (and outside) their territory, which has led to important discoveries. Although seizure of Palestinian natural resources cannot and should not be considered the sole cause of the violence we have witnessed for decades, the weight of this impetus is certainly real and tangible.

Therefore, it is not an overstatement to say that the confiscation and expropriation of natural resources go hand in hand with the aggressive and, in many cases, genocidal policy of the State of Israel towards the Palestinian territories. The energy issue has been part of Israeli military calculations over

---

3 Natan Sachs and Tim Boersma, *The Energy Island: Israel deals with its natural gas discoveries*, Foreign Policy at Brookings, Policy Paper no. 35 (February 2015).

the past 25 years. However, once again, Israel is not alone. The combined project of displacing the Palestinians with enabling the exploitation of their resources (including international exploitation) has acquired an unprecedented dimension.

It is crucial to acknowledge that the military operation following October 7, 2023, has taken a substantially different shape compared to previous ones. The genocide of the Palestinian people in Gaza is taking place at a time in which the growth possibilities of capital linked to the dollar and the euro are at their historical lows. At least since the beginning of this century, the accumulation of capital at a global level has become increasingly dependent on the performance of the Chinese economy and the Asian economy in general. Compromised by a long crisis of overproduction that originated in the 1970s, the advanced capitalist countries are in fact recording growth rates that tend to worsen, prefiguring a situation of substantial stagnation that alternates with increasingly frequent recessions. At least since the end of the Second World War, the hegemonic capital linked to the dollar has recorded huge setbacks that have become closer and closer over time (that of 2008, which coincided with the controlled collapse of Lehman Brothers, was probably the most important in many respects), outlining a basically inexorable crisis.

What we are witnessing is the ten-year decline of capital linked to the dollar (and the euro) and the rise of Asian economies, as a process of violence and wars. The relative weight of the main economies of the Shanghai Cooperation Organization (China, India, Russia, Iran and Pakistan) has surpassed that of the U.S. since at least 2021,[4] reducing a gap that in the middle of the last century might have seemed insurmountable. Although in crisis, the U.S. dollar is still the main currency of international reserves, although it has fallen by 10% over more than two decades. The Yuan, on the other hand, despite the important weight it has achieved, is still not the object of proportional attention, representing less than 3% of world reserves (the euro remains stable at around 20%, although the 2012 crisis has greatly limited its potential).

Furthermore, if we also consider that China has become the most important trading partner of 61 countries, while the U.S. remains in the 30s, it seems intuitive that this disproportion will naturally have to be reabsorbed, leading inevitably to a reduction in the role of the dollar with an increase in the importance of the currencies of the Shanghai Cooperation Organization countries. Certainly, the formidable investments linked to the so-called "new silk road" (BRI—Belt and Road Initiative) will act as a vehicle for an

---

4 See, among others, Branko Milanović, *Capitalism, Alone: The Future of the System That Rules the World* (Harvard University Press, 2019).

internationalization of the Yuan which, however, does not yet have the ambition to displace the U.S. currency, but which will plausibly act to forward the process of de-dollarization that some analysts take for granted. It should also be added that the process of de-dollarization will inevitably take place through a set of alternative currencies, which will include the Yuan.[5]

The issue has taken on global relevance to such an extent that at the G7 in June 2021, the U.S. president launched a project called "Build Back Better World" (B3W) whose aim was essentially to define an alternative to the BRI by bringing a series of developing countries back into its sphere of influence, removing them from the prospect of an antagonistic Chinese hegemony.

But the project that prior to October 7 seemed to be shaping up most decisively and delineated in the fight against Chinese economic expansion through the BRI was the IMEC (India-Middle East-Europe corridor) which would follow precisely what had already been identified as one of the BRI's Silk Routes but be led by the U.S. The IMEC was launched just a few weeks before the October 7 attack (in the first half of September 2023, on the occasion of the G20 in Doha) and, in short, represented a long network of railroads, ports and energy infrastructures, which would bring together India, the United Arab Emirates, Saudi Arabia, Jordan, Israel, and then reach Europe, placing the Gulf countries at the center of the infrastructure, just as one of the Silk Routes does. What's new here was the projected involvement of Israel as the terminus of a complex and economically strategic structure. Due to mounting global repugnance at Israeli crimes against Gaza, that project may no longer be feasible.

If we also look at how the major powers aligned themselves immediately after October 7, it shapes up like this: Israel supported by the U.S. and Europe, while the other countries—especially those of the BRICS—call for calm, while publicly condemning the massacres perpetrated by the Israeli army against the populations of Gaza and the West Bank. The exceptions are India, which immediately supported Israel (obviously with a view to preserving the 2023 IMEC agreement), and Saudi Arabia, whose ambiguous attitudes in trying to act as a balancer so as not to sacrifice its strategic role gained in both the BRI and IMEC, do not hide its advanced normalization process with Israel mediated by the U.S.—a process, by the way, that is coming at a high cost for the Saudi population, which is allegedly facing crackdown for social media posts that criticize Israel for its ongoing war in the Gaza Strip.

---

5 Serkan Arslanalp, Barry J. Eichengreen, and Chima Simpson-Bell, *The Stealth Erosion of Dollar Dominance: Active Diversifiers and the Rise of Nontraditional Reserve Currencies,* International Monetary Fund Working Paper No. 2022/058, March 24, 2022.

It was due to U.S. diplomatic, economic and military pressure that six Arab countries—Egypt, Jordan, Morocco, Sudan, the United Arab Emirates and Bahrain (the latter four under the Abraham Accords of 2020—established diplomatic relations with Israel: All this diplomatic romance has historically taken place while the Palestinians were being systematically dispossessed of their land, even while they were signing the 1993 Oslo Accords.

Today, in spite of the fact that IMEC has suffered a temporary delay since the beginning of the Gaza carnage, it is impossible to ignore the possibility that it figured in the decision of the U.S. Senate to give final approval (on April 23, 2024) to a package of U.S. $95.3 billion to Ukraine, Israel and Taiwan (of which $17 billion USD in military aid to Israel).[6] This is in addition to the 3.8 billion dollars that the United States provides to Israel every year. The United States has positioned flotillas of aircraft carriers, destroyers and nuclear submarines off the coast of Lebanon and in the Persian Gulf, to help Israel militarily by threatening Hezbollah and Iran. According to the *Financial Times*, the United States has more than 57,000 troops stationed in the Middle East, and Israel is, for the reasons mentioned above, the axis around which its entire strategy in the region revolves. Finally, the anti-missile operation that defended Israel from an approximately 350 drone and missile attack launched by Iran on April 13—in retaliation for the Israeli attack on the Iranian embassy complex in Damascus on April 1 that killed seven Islamic Revolutionary Guard Corps members, including two generals—involved a semi-concealed coalition of countries led by the U.S., and cost more than $1 billion dollars. The process of de-dollarization of the economy will be met by huge military reactions, even before the economic ones, on the part of the U.S. governments.

In terms of support for Palestine, we are witnessing a contrast between the bloc linked to the dollar and that linked to Asian currencies. While the EU has followed the obvious U.S. support for Israel in a substantially uncritical way, the Palestinian cause has received varying degrees of support from China and other BRICS+ countries.[7] However, there is a stark difference between the direct and unconditional military support given by the U.S. to Israel, and

---

6 "'This package will deliver critical support to Israel and Ukraine ... and bolster security and stability in the Indo-Pacific,' Biden said in a statement." Reuters, AP and TOOI Staff, "House okays $17 billion in military aid for Israel under major spending package," *Times of Israel*, April 20, 2024. https://www.timesofisrael.com/house-approves-26-billion-in-aid-for-israel-and-gaza-under-major-spending-package/

7 In 2024, the BRICS+ incorporated Saudi Arabia, Argentina, Egypt, Ethiopia, Iran, and the United Arab Emirates, now representing almost 40% of the global GDP and more than 60% of the population.

the international support Palestine has received, which is usually (in spite of a few exceptions) channeled through international and multilateral forums.

Since the collapse of the Oslo process (2000), we have also seen growing differentiation between international civil society solidarity and governmental support for Palestine. Civil society activism tends to follow Palestinian civil society, academic, and grassroots movements views and their calls for Boycott, Divestment and Sanctions (BDS, since 2005), seeking a region free from apartheid, "from the river to the sea." It demands BDS as a nonviolent means for promoting its goal of dismantling apartheid in the entire region. The model and inspiration clearly reflect the history of the anti-apartheid movement that succeeded in dismantling this system of segregation in South Africa.

On the other hand, governmental support in the Global South has, at least until October 7, followed the directives laid down by the Palestinian Authority and the PLO diplomatic representation,[8] and remained tied to the notion that the final demand should always be for a two-state solution, and that isolating the Israeli apartheid state was not an option. The local civil society call for isolating Israeli apartheid through Boycotts, Divestment and Sanctions has been met with skepticism or very limited consent on the part of Latin American governments.

However, today, in face of the brutality of the war against Palestine, and the recognition on the part of the majority of the Global South, that what is happening in Gaza is a "text-book case of genocide," some degree of divestment is taking place. Governments in Latin America, among other regions, are taking measures that isolate Israel arguably as never before—albeit not as much as necessary—to pressure for a ceasefire. Apartheid has been recognized as a reality in historic Palestine in breach of international law, even as governments continue to believe that calling for a two-state solution is the best way to indicate that they are in favor of a negotiated and peaceful outcome for the region. In practice, governmental support has also been channeled through multilateral forums (mainly the UN), where these countries have voted and argued in favor of the application of international humanitarian law. Seldom had we seen, before October 2023, countries and companies divesting from Israel as we see today—even though few countries have completely severed their diplomatic ties to Israel or renounced all investments and trade.

---

8 At the request of the PLO diplomatic representatives, in 2010 almost all Latin American countries recognized the state of Palestine on the 1967 borders with East Jerusalem as its capital.

In an unprecedented move, China has defended the Palestinian right of resistance at the ICJ hearing on the case concerning the Israeli occupation of Palestinian Territories and has characterized it as "an inalienable right well founded in international law." Russia remains ambiguous at this writing. In spite of the fact that it effectively de-dollarized its economy in 2018—the only country yet to do so—Russia still has commercial and population ties to Israel. Its commercial relations were intensified when Israel decided not to respect the sanctions imposed by Europe and the U.S. on Russia for the invasion of Ukraine. Its populational ties were built through the post-Soviet emigration of more than 750,000 Russians to Israel. Brazil strived but failed to approve a "humanitarian pause" resolution in October 2023, when it held the rotating presidency at the UN Security Council. Not even the temporary and conditional nature of the proposed ceasefire was enough to prevent the U.S. from using its veto power.

But it was South Africa, led by the African National Congress (ANC), with its own history and legacy of anti-apartheid struggle, which took the single most important step to try to halt the massacre of the Palestinian people in the Gaza Strip. On December 29, it presented to the International Court of Justice, a case of genocide against Israel, the *Application of the Convention on the Prevention and Punishment of the Crime of Genocide in the Gaza Strip (South Africa v. Israel)*. Several Global South countries and organizations declared support for the South African case. When the Brazilian president, Luis Inácio Lula da Silva, declared his support for the case on January 10, he simultaneously announced that Brazil would cancel the military contracts established with Israel by his predecessor, the ultra-right-wing, and former president, Jair Bolsonaro. In order to cancel these contracts, and to suspend the Brazilian army's decision of May 2024, to purchase 60 Israeli military vehicles, Lula was obliged to confront both the far-right political parties in Brazil and the Brazilian military itself.[9] Other South and Central American countries, namely, Bolivia, Colombia, and Belize, have completely severed their diplomatic ties to Israel, while Chile, Honduras and Ecuador have called back their ambassadors for consultations. These diplomatic actions, which

---

9 The existence of a strong political opposition to Lula—formed by right-wing political parties and their socio-economic bases, together with important segments of the military, and the local neo-Pentecostal (pro-Zionist) groups—helps to explain why on several occasions, Brazilian policies and positions have taken on a rather zig-zag approach, instead of being straightforwardly supportive of Palestinian liberation. Similar political coalitions including right-wing parties and neo-Pentecostal groups are present in other Latin American countries and tend to be strongly supportive of Zionism and of apartheid.

are mainly symbolic, undoubtedly contribute to the largest isolation Israel has ever faced in its history.

Faced with the unrelenting Israeli refusal to end the war, international support for Palestine is left with the option of demanding the application of international law and international humanitarian law, and international humanitarian law, while, at the same time, resorting more every day to measures that have been called for by the BDS grassroots movement for nearly twenty years.[10] The gap that separates international civil society methods of advocacy from the governmental lines of conduct has narrowed (absence of a political process and negotiations), and the situation is so drastic. However, civil society and governmental Global South positions still operate in very different paradigms, with civil society upholding a view of dismantling settler colonialism through an anti-apartheid struggle, and governments typically supporting the PA, the resumption of a peace process, and the call for a two-state solution. The outcome inexorably depends on the Palestinians themselves, while the obligation and responsibility to pressure Israel to end the genocide falls on global governments, whose historic performance as guarantors of the ethnic cleansing of Palestine since the beginning of the twentieth century must now be viewed as complicity with genocide.

---

10 For a view on the origins and initial years of the BDS movement in Latin America, see Arlene E. Clemesha, "Brazil: the Palestine Solidarity Movement and BDS," *Al Majdal* no. 38 (Summer 2008): 40–43. https://badil.org/phocadownload/Badil_docs/publications/al-majdal-38.pdf

Assassination and Educide
Men of Hope from Lumumba
to Refaat Alareer and Dr. Ahmed

Victoria Brittain

The General's Property
To Ariel Sharon

A flower vase on the general's table
Five roses in the vase
The general's tank has five mouths
Under the tank a boy of five, a rose
A boy and five stars adorn the general's shoulder
In his vase five roses and five boys
The tank has countless mouths[1]

—Samih al-Qasim (1939–2014)

PATRICE LUMUMBA, the first Prime Minister of independent Congo, was assassinated in January 1961 in a remote forest in his country by a firing squad led by a Belgian mercenary, Julius Gat, and his own longtime political rival, Moise Tshombe. Lumumba's body was dug up, reburied deeper

---

1 Ariel Sharon was a general and the 11th Prime Minister of Israel. As Minister of War, he directed the 1982 Lebanon war, and an official enquiry found he bore "personal responsibility" for the Sabra and Shatila massacres of Palestinian refugees in Beirut. Samih al-Qasim was a Palestinian poet with Israeli citizenship who was jailed several times, placed under house arrest, and joined the Israeli Communist Party in 1967.

Victoria Brittain was born in India and has lived and worked in Saigon, Algiers, Nairobi, Washington, and London. She has travelled widely reporting across Africa and in the Middle East, particularly in Gaza, the West Bank and in the Palestinian camps in Syria and Lebanon. She wrote for *The Guardian* for 25 years, and is currently part of the editorial collective of *Afrique XX1*, a specialised website of original reporting and analysis on Africa.

in the forest, dug up again, then cut up with butchers' knives and placed in sulfuric acid in an oil drum and finally burned. Sixty-one years later, a souvenir in a plastic bag kept in Belgium by one of his assassins—one of Lumumba's teeth—was placed in a bright blue jewel case and returned to his three children. Belgium's Prime Minister, Guy Verhofstadt, apologized officially for this colonial crime. Lumumba's carved coffin of dark African wood toured his country and was then placed in a Chinese-built mausoleum in Kinshasa, where all flags were lowered to half-mast in respect. Only now do we know from belatedly released U.S. archives that U.S. President Dwight Eisenhower personally gave the go ahead for Lumumba's killing during a National Security Committee meeting in Washington on August 18, 1960.[2]

Lumumba, born in a village in central Congo, was a bold intense child, an ambitious, charismatic young man, a voracious reader with a tireless work ethic. He burst into the leadership of febrile Congolese politics on the brink of independence under the eye of a Western dominated UN force, which could have saved him, but chose not to.

Lumumba's was a prominent voice of hope and transformational change in a period of sharply contested Western colonial power in Africa and recognized as such by his peers. He forged relations in particular with Kwame Nkrumah, the first president of independent Ghana at the path-breaking All Africa People's Congress in Accra in 1958. He also met there with Franz Fanon, who was representing the Algerian National Liberation Front, then deep in their war of independence from France, and with the future presidents of independent Malawi and Zambia. News of his death in January1961 caused riots in Moscow, Warsaw, Prague, Tel Aviv, Tokyo and Paris. In China, Premier Zhou En Lai addressed a crowd of 100,000 and blamed the U.S. and Belgium. In Cairo, students broke the gates of the Belgian embassy and tore down a portrait of King Baudouin of Belgium and replaced it with one of Lumumba. In the visitors' gallery of the Security Council in New York, a group of women from Harlem heckled its members, and one, Maya Angelou, who would become a famous writer a decade later, shouted "assassins." The Secretary General was escorted out of the session.

Professor Refaat Alareer and Dr. Ahmed, almost half a century later, embodied just such voices of hope and transformational change for Palestinians in the open-air prison of Gaza, in their ever-shrinking lands in Jerusalem, and in the occupied West Bank, where armed and violent Israeli settlers, many from the U.S. and Russia, were installed in huge new settlements erasing Palestinian villages and farms.

---

2 Stuart A. Reid, *The Lumumba Plot* (Alfred Knopf, 2023).

Belgian and U.S. officials demonized and dehumanized Lumumba and marked him out for death as a threat to their dominance and interests in Africa. The Israeli military, twenty-five years later, made the same calculation for Refaat Alareer and Dr. Ahmed in Gaza as the entire Palestinian education system was made an Israeli military target.

Professor Refaat Alareer was assassinated on December 6, 2023, by a targeted Israeli air strike, and Dr. Ahmed al Maqadmeh was assassinated in a hail of bullets by Israeli soldiers near the besieged Al Shifa hospital four months later, as Gaza lay in ruins and the killing of civilians escalated. Collectively in this period, Gazans were dehumanized and described by Israel's most prominent and powerful leaders, such as Defence Minister Yoav Gallant, as "human animals" to be put under a total siege precluding their access to water, food and electricity. Other prominent Israelis called for Palestinians to be eliminated and one suggested the Israel nuclear arsenal should be used in Gaza as in Hiroshima and Nagasaki. Five months later, UN officials declared famine had arrived in the north, and acute hunger was everywhere for Gaza's constantly uprooted families.

As the death toll mounted daily, even in the areas the Israelis ordered Palestinians to move to before repeatedly ordering them to move again once there, the world's civil society alongside UN and Global South leaders called urgently for an immediate ceasefire. But U.S. President Joe Biden, a fervent Christian, continued to authorize the deliveries of massive U.S. armament shipments despite several U.S. government bureaus reporting to Secretary of State Antony Blinken that Israel's assurances that they were complying with International Human Rights Law were "neither credible nor reliable." In the ongoing genocide, Refaat Alareer, Dr. Ahmed and so many thousands of others were marked out for death.

But unlike President Eisenhower, his predecessor all those decades before, President Biden's role in these assassinations, as part of this genocide, will not take sixty-one years to be known. Gaza's assassinations and educide were known to the entire world within hours, thanks to Gaza's extraordinarily brave journalists and social media.

American political leaders came under a strain reminiscent of the Civil Rights Movement and the Vietnam War dissent in campuses and streets across the U.S. in the 1960s. Police violence and more than 2,200 arrests on campus polarized the country. Most media and Congress chose the government's side, falsely called the students antisemitic and violent, and supported their being banned from many of their colleges. The 2024 student encampments, including many Jewish students and public intellectuals, voiced demands for a ceasefire and for disinvestment in arms companies related to Israel. Among prominent Jewish speakers in May 2024 at a huge Brooklyn rally, "Seder on the Streets," the Canadian Jewish writer Naomi Klein said, "Jews must raise their voice for Palestine and oppose the false idol of Zionism—Zionism has betrayed every Jewish value and has brought us to the present moment of cataclysm... it was always leading us here. Look around, we are the exodus from Zionism."[3]

Educide

Refaat Alareer, the poet professor, and Dr. Ahmed, the plastic surgeon, were in professional sectors that Israeli military planners had targeted starting in October 2023 as part of their agenda for the destruction of Palestinian society in Gaza—education and medical care. Both men had high profiles and prestige in Gaza and well beyond. Educide and scholasticide are now key terms in academic and official reporting on the latest Israeli war on Gaza. These two beloved men are symbols of those crimes.[4]

The names of hundreds of distinguished heads of universities, internationally known scientists, mathematicians, artists, musicians, historians, geographers, professors of literature and languages assassinated by the Israeli military in 2023/24 are recorded, spoken, repeated and treasured by Palestinians. Education has always been the passion and pride of Palestinians. In Gaza every single higher education institution has been either destroyed or severely damaged by the Israeli army.

The Palestinian writer and geographer, Salman Abu Sitta, puts it like this:

> Israel took our land and property, renamed our geography, deleted our history, but one thing they failed to do was eclipse our eager desire for education, from the time Palestinian children attended classes under a tree in refugee camps in 1948, til today when most universities in the West have at least one Palestinian professor. Education is the only Palestinian asset Israel failed to rob.[5]

---

3 Naomi Klein, "Jews must raise their voices for Palestine, oppose the 'false idol of Zionism'," *Democracy Now!* April 24, 2024. https://www.democracynow.org/2024/4/24/naomi_klein_seder.

4 "UN experts deeply concerned over 'scholasticide' in Gaza," United Nations Human Rights report, April 18, 2024. Patrick Jack, "Academia in Gaza 'has been destroyed' by Israeli 'educide'," *Times Higher Education,* January 29, 2024, quoting Samia Al-Botmeh, Assistant Professor of Economics, Bir Zeit University in the West Bank.

5 Salman Abu Sitta is a Palestinian researcher, a former member of the Palestine National Council and author of over 400 papers on refugee affairs. His most recent

Following on from this, renowned Palestinian academic, Salim Tamari, describes what he terms "the attack on the Intelligentsia," writing:

> One of the least observed features of Israel's war on Gaza since October 2023 is the attack on the scholarly community, academics, and academic institutions. In the midst of the massive devastation that has engulfed the four major cities of the Gaza Strip focus has been on the destruction of physical infrastructure of the area including electric installations, waterworks, sewage treatment plants, roads, hospitals, public buildings, power plants, schools, mosques and churches. The mass destruction of these public buildings and private habitat resulted in the death of tens of thousands of citizens, now approaching 39,000 deaths, most of whom are civilian women and children. There is today a wide consensus among many observers that a major Israeli objective in these attacks, ostensibly in response to the October 7th 2023 intrusion by Hamas, is a systematic attempt to make the Gaza region uninhabitable. Consequently it will force a large proportion of the refugee population to relocate elsewhere, if Egyptian objections to border crossing could be obtained.

Lost in these horrific details is the direct assault on educational institutions. Not only schools and school yards which have been an important destination for internal displaced refugees, but also institutions of higher education and their cadres. A recent study by two Bir Zeit University academics, Ibrahim Rabaia and Lourdes Habash, show how systematic this attack on the Gaza intelligentsia has been, a process they call "Educide."[6] Eleven out of 19 institutions of higher education have been completely destroyed. By mid-February 2024, four out of six of Gaza's major universities have been eliminated. Four hundred and fifty academic and administrative university staff have been killed. Those include three university presidents, seven deans, and 64 professors. Significantly, much of this physical destruction was undertaken early on during the campaign. Between October 11 and December 7 Al-Azhar University, al Israa' University, Al Aqsa University and al Quds Open University have been substantially destroyed, indicating that they were

book is *Mapping my Return: A Palestinian Memoir* (The American University in Cairo Press, 2016).

6 Ibrahim S.I. Rabaia and Lourdes Habash, "The Hidden War on Higher Education: Unmasking the 'Educide' in Gaza," *The Middle East and Middle East Studies After Gaza Memos*, Project on Middle East Political Science (POMEPS). https://pomeps.org/the-hidden-war-on-higher-education-unmasking-the-educide-in-gaza

primary targets of Israeli attack early on, and not as the Israelis claim, "collateral damage."

In an earlier period, Israelis targeted Palestinian Universities under the guise of fighting terrorism. For example, in 2008 Israel bombed and destroyed the laboratories of the Islamic University in Gaza claiming that those were used for weapons development by Hamas, as reported by Al Jazeera. No such justification is used this time. It is clear that the current onslaught, while largely motivated and even articulated by sentiments of vengeance, is aimed at the physical and logistic destruction of the Palestinian intelligentsia and their institutional base. It should be viewed in the context of the attack on doctors, nurses, aid workers, and technical staff of municipal workers from the start of the war. It gives new meaning to the term genocide.

> The current situation in Gaza recalls the dark days in the spring of 1948, when the bombardment of Jaffa, the largest city in Palestine, led to early exodus of the middle classes from coastal Palestine, which caused the collapse of the economy of the urban sector and facilitated the mass expulsion of the rest of the urban population. The main difference with the circumstances of the Gaza war is that the Israeli assault on the civilian population is indiscriminate and does not distinguish between rich and poor, professional cadres and illiterate segments. However, the critical attack on educators and professionals will mean that if and when the war ends, the restoration of life in educational and other service sectors for the remaining population would face a huge gap for many years to come.[7]

Refaat Alareer was a well-known poet, a popular English literature professor and a creative writing teacher. He received, like so many Gazans, countless death threats by phone and online from the Israeli military as the invasion and bombing of Gaza forced his family to leave their home, just like more than 1.5 million other Palestinians. In fact, on December 7, 2023, he left an UNRWA shelter where he was with his family, after the Israeli military phone warning, "we know where you are." He moved to his sister's apartment in Shujayya, where his sister, Asmara, brother Salah, and their children, Mohammed, Alaa, Yahia and a second Mohammed, were then all killed in the airstrike targeting Refaat.

---

7 Professor Salim Tamari, based in Bir Zeit University, is former director of the Institute of Palestine Studies, and the preeminent Palestinian historical sociologist. He has been a visiting fellow in universities, such as Cornell, Berkley, MIT, Chicago, Cambridge, and is the author of several books.

Among the many, many tributes to Refaat was one from the distinguished Palestinian-American professor Sami Al-Arian, who was a tenured
professor in the University of South Florida until he was abruptly suspended
in 2003. As a prominent voice lobbying the U.S. establishment on civil rights
and liberties, he had been in White House meetings with both Presidents
Clinton and Bush. But a series of scandalously unjust trials on false terrorism
charges saw Al-Arian spend five years in 13 different U.S. maximum security
prisons, and eight years under house arrest, until in 2015 he was deported to
Türkiye. A decade ago, his daughter Laila said to me of her father, "Articulate
Palestinians threaten powerful people."[8] Al-Arian's words about Refaat today
have a poignant echo of his own daughter's words about him. "Refaat was
an amazing poet, an articulate voice for Gazans, and a true bridge to people
outside Gaza. His loss will be missed by many inside Palestine and around
the world."

In a striking example of how easily articulate Palestinians are abused
by powerful U.S. officials and in media misinformation campaigns, Mr.
Al-Arian's wife Nahla was cited by New York mayor Eric Adams as justification for the NYPD assault ordered on students in Columbia University. He
said he gave the order in reaction to "outside agitators" on campus, mention-
ing "one whose husband was arrested for and convicted for terrorism on a
federal level." The mayor's completely false reference to Mrs. Al Arian was
echoed by CBS, CNN, the New York Post, and NPR. Mrs. Al-Arian, whose
father's family is originally from Gaza and whose family had recently lost
200 members there, had visited the student encampment on the Columbia
campus with her two journalist daughters at the end of April for less than an
hour, in order to express her solidarity with the students, whom she called
"the conscience of America" caring about the Palestinian people.[9]

Meanwhile, Refaat's death poem from Gaza, written for his daughter
Shaima, went viral and was read aloud across the world by well-known actors.
It has been translated into a dozen languages. (Shaima and her husband and
her two-month-old baby, Abd al-Rahman, were killed in another air strike
four months after Refaat's death.) In one example of Refaat's world-wide
echo, in Northern Ireland's city of Belfast, which endured decades of British
colonial illegalities and deaths, and has much unfinished business still with
the British army, the poem is the centrepiece of a huge Gaza-inspired mural:

---

8 Victoria Brittain, *Shadow Lives: The Forgotten Women of the War on Terror*
(Pluto Press, 2013).

9 Jeremy Scahill, "NYC Mayor smeared a grandmother as an 'outside agitator' to
justify NYPD assault on Columbia," *The Intercept*, May 3, 2024. https://theintercept.
com/2024/05/03/nyc-eric-adams-columbia-outside-agitator-al-arian/

If I must die
You must live
To tell my story
To sell my things
To buy a piece of cloth
And some strings,
(Make it white with a long tail)
So that a child, somewhere in Gaza
While looking heaven in the eye
Awaiting his dad who left in a blaze –
And bid no one farewell
Not even to his flesh
Not even to himself –
Sees the kite, my kite you made, flying up
Above
And thinks for a moment an angel is there
Bringing back love
If I must die
Let it bring hope
Let it be a tale

Dr. Ahmed was a plastic surgeon in the heroic team which kept Al Shifa hospital operating under extraordinary circumstances, with water and electricity cut, through months of bombardment, and dire shortage of all medical supplies. It was a time of unprecedented numbers of sick and injured patients flooding in due to Israeli shelling and bombing, and with the hospital also serving as a shelter for thousands of uprooted homeless families. In a 15-day siege of the hospital by the Israeli army, 21 patients died. Israel said the army had killed 200 people and arrested 900. Other doctors and other medical staff were arrested in other hospitals. Among them was Dr. Adnan al-Bursh, senior surgeon and head of the orthopaedic unit at Al Shifa, who was taken to Ofer prison where he died on April 19, after torture. Weeks later, many testimonies of torture and near-starvation prison conditions emerged as some men were released and photographs showed them to be almost unrecognizable.

On April 1, Dr. Ahmed and his mother, Dr. Yousra al Maqadmeh, who had also remained in Al Shifa, were found riddled with bullet wounds near the ruins of Al Shifa after the Israeli army forced everyone out and left it destroyed. Beside them was their dead cousin, Bassan al Maqadmeh. Dr. Ahmed had sent his wife and two children south for safety weeks earlier, and in the early weeks of the Israeli attacks had been able to make occasional visits to them. In an earlier life he had won a fellowship from the Royal College of Surgeons in Britain for his pathbreaking work on gunshot wounds, which were then what killed him.

No Accountability

All three of the murdered men in the title of this chapter were young, with young families; they were only in their late 30s or 40s when they were killed. For Refaat and Dr. Ahmed, their future contributions to Palestinian society are incalculable, but the genocide in which they were killed has deeply shaken American political and social life, with consequences yet unknown. In the Middle East too history will be changed profoundly. In the case of Lumumba, his killing probably changed the course of African history over the last 65 years. Congo's people lost their independence hope of post-colonial transformation. Washington used Congo, later Zaïre, as its key tool in the Cold War with the Soviet Union, notably in alliance with the apartheid South African regime, and in U.S.-backed civil wars in Angola and Mozambique both before and after their independence from Portugal in 1975. These unseen post-colonial wars of the 1980s which killed, maimed and destroyed across Southern Africa, were the wars of another U.S. president, Ronald Reagan.

Lumumba is not forgotten, especially for new generations in Africa. But the U.S. President and other officials concerned escaped being held accountable for the crimes of the CIA and others. There was one such attempt, the unprecedented 1975 U.S. Senate investigation into CIA activities, such as Lumumba's death, led by senator Frank Church. Richard Helms, former CIA chief and a senior CIA witness, told the enquiry he "had forgotten" what the Americans had against Lumumba. Mr Helms also handicapped the investigation by ordering the destruction of all files related to the CIA's mind control programme in 1973.[10]

Teams of Palestinian and other human rights lawyers across the world are working hard to follow up on the landmark International Court of Justice (ICJ) hearing of South Africa against Israel in January. The judges ruled that Israel must prevent and punish public incitements to commit genocide against Palestinians in Gaza and said that it was "plausible" that Israeli acts fell within the provisions of the Genocide Convention. Since then, multiple cases for the International Criminal Court (ICC) have been in preparation against Israeli individuals—a reckoning for history. The ICC is investigating the mass graves at hospitals across the Gaza Strip from April and May and reportedly considering issuing arrest warrants for war crimes against the Israeli Prime Minister, Defence Minister and army Chief of Staff. Mr

---

10 Reid, *The Lumumba Plot.*

Netanyahu's enraged response was that this would be "an outrageous assault on Israel's inherent right of self-defence." The ICC Public Prosecutor Karim Khan on May 3 warned that "the court's independence and impartiality are undermined when individuals threaten to retaliate against the Court or against Court personnel, should the Office, in fulfilment of its mandate, make decisions about investigations of cases falling within its jurisdiction."[11]

UNRWA, Another Target

Amid the starvation, famine, bombed homes and infrastructure, invasion, death and ethnic cleansing in Gaza from autumn 2023, Palestinians' indispensable lifeline for food, water, education and medical care was UNRWA, the UN agency set up in 1949. It had a mandate from the UN General Assembly to aid the 700,000 Palestinian refugees expelled from their homes and land following the creation of Israel in 1948, and later included the new wave of Palestinian refugees from the 1967 war, and the descendants of those refugees. It was intended to be a temporary agency until a political solution for Palestinians would be found. But then, as now, Israel and its powerful sponsors lacked the political will to fully pursue a political solution .

UNRWA has been *the* resource in Gaza throughout the 2023/24 horrors of death, starvation and ethnic cleansing. It is, in fact, essential to the lives of nearly six million Palestinian refugees in Gaza, and beyond in Syria, Lebanon, Jordan, the Occupied West Bank, and East Jerusalem. UNRWA has 32,000 employees and 5,000 more part-time. The great majority of them are well-educated Palestinians, products of UNRWA schools themselves. UNRWA schools were the first in the MENA region in the 1960s to achieve gender equality, and to have a slight majority of female students. And, despite three quarters of schools having to squeeze double shifts into the day and design a special emergency programme to anticipate the frequent conflict outbreaks, they usually out-perform government schools in their host counties. Education accounts for 58% of the UNRWA budget.

In January 2024, Israel launched accusations against UNRWA which threatened to kill the organization. Israel announced that a dozen of UNRWA's Gaza employees had participated in the October 7 military breakout into Israel. Accusations followed, notably from Oren Marmorstein, spokesman for the Israeli foreign ministry, that more than 2,135 Hamas employees were Hamas or Islamic Jihad militants. He urged donors not to support UNRWA,

---

11 Nancy Murray, "Gaza's apocalypse 'symbolizes utter moral failure' of the post WWII system of international law," *Medium*, May 6, 2024. https://numurray. medium.com/gazas-apocalypse-symbolizes-utter-moral-failure-of-the-post-ww-ii-system-of-international-law-e9231af4d91e

but to give to private organizations instead. Accusations that guns and ammunition were found by Israeli soldiers in UNRWA's headquarters, and that there was a tunnel beneath the building were reiterated, as against Al Shifa and other hospitals.

In the toxic atmosphere of the moment, despite no evidence being produced by Israel, the UNRWA leadership in New York nevertheless immediately fired the named men and a UN inquiry was opened. Sixteen major donors, led by the U.S., promptly cancelled all funding to UNRWA—still without any proof of the accusations.

Only Palestinians, so thoroughly dehumanized, could have been so punished by the international community, without any proof, in the midst of a recognized genocide, given that UNRWA's employees were known to be regularly vetted by major donor organizations and by Israeli intelligence. Two major international enquiries into UNRWA's work and processes of neutrality were opened. By late March, most donor countries—though not the U.S. and UK—had reversed the hasty damaging decisions.

The U.S. Congress meanwhile had doubled down and approved the ban on funding for UNRWA for a full year. And the European Parliament (EP) in April adopted a resolution condemning textbooks produced by UNRWA and the Palestinian Authority claiming, as Israel has asserted for years, that the textbooks play a role in inciting hatred against Israelis. The EP asserted that "education to hatred" was a factor in Hamas's action on October 7. French MEP, Ilana Cicurel, from President Macron's party, was one of the main promoters of the resolution, "I insisted on keeping the reference to the Hamas terrorist attacks of October 7 in this text because people must understand that they were a direct consequence of this education to hatred that is taught in UNRWA."

Education has been a battleground in every colonial situation under pressure. Each colonial power had their own style. For instance, in 1960, the year Congo attained independence from Belgium and Lumumba became Prime Minister, there were only 15 university graduates in a country of 15.25 million. Belgium expected little challenge to its own economic and political decision making. The British in Kenya imposed English language and punished children for speaking their own languages at school. "English was the official vehicle and the magic formula to colonial elitedom," wrote Ngugi wa Thiong'o, one of Africa's foremost writers.[12] In apartheid South Africa on June 16, 1976, the Soweto uprising of 20,000 school children, in which at least 176 and possibly as many 700 children were shot, was in response to

---

12 Ngugi wa Thiong'o, *Decolonizing the Mind: The Politics of Language in African Literature* (James Currey/Heineman, 1986).

the introduction of Afrikaans language teaching in black schools. That day is now honoured annually as a marker towards the end of apartheid. The 2024 U.S. and European university uprisings for a ceasefire and divestment in Gaza, and freedom for Palestinians, follow in these footsteps.

"This is beyond warfare"

Two million people are under UNRWA's care in Gaza. By May 2024, 160 UNRWA premises had been damaged or completely destroyed, including schools where hundreds of displaced people were sheltering, and warehouses containing food. By April, 175 UN staff in Gaza had been killed, others arrested, tortured and often disappeared by the Israeli military. We are all daily eyewitnesses on our TV and phone screens to the testimony of starving and mutilated children, of humiliated, tortured men and boys and a civilian death toll in mid-May of 10,091 women and 15,780 children in a total of 38,621 civilians. The Israeli government counter-narrative of lies and obfuscation, painting Israel as the victim, is a constant repeated chorus from Israel's supporters in the UN Security Council and U.S. and Western governments and officials through much of the Western media.

On April 23, UN High Commissioner for Human Rights, Volker Turk, an Austrian lawyer, deplored the day's Israeli air strikes on Rafah's million-plus Palestinians, saying, "The latest images of a premature child, taken from the womb of her dying mother, of the adjacent two houses where 15 children and five women were killed—this is beyond warfare….they are protected under the laws of war." That premature child, Sabreen Judah, died after five days in hospital and was buried next to her father, mother and four-year-old sister killed in the strike.

Later in April, horrified by the mass graves found at the destroyed Al Shifa and Nasser hospitals, Mr. Turk called for "independent, effective and transparent investigations into the deaths." One of the graves at Nasser held 392 bodies, including some wearing surgical gowns. Many of the hundreds of bodies had their hands tied behind their backs and a bullet wound to the head, execution style, when the Civil Defense teams found and exhumed them with bulldozers. The dead can be seen in unbearable footage, laid out in lines of earth-stained shrouds, with utterly bereft family members walking beside them, bending to slightly open each shroud, hoping for a glimpse of familiar clothes and the chance of a respectful burial. More mass graves were later found at other hospital sites after Israeli soldiers moved away.

Meanwhile, Israeli minister Bezalel Smotrich declared, "the world now knows that UNRWA is a central element of the war machine of the nazi terrorists of Hamas."

The end of UNRWA, with its unique mandate safeguarding Palestinian refugees' group status, has been an Israeli government strategic goal for years. All other refugees elsewhere in the world are under the care of UNHCR and can be repatriated as circumstances change or be individually resettled.

Now, the political goal of Gaza run by anyone but Gazans is in the open: Jared Kushner, in an interview at Harvard on February 15 praised the "very valuable" potential of "waterfront property in Gaza" and suggested bulldozing a bit of the Negev desert as a place to put people from Gaza; U.S. naval vessels began constructing a giant dock to bring in supplies for delivery outside the UNRWA mechanisms, though one such effort had led to Israeli planes firing three times on three cars of foreign volunteers of the ill-fated World Central Kitchen initiative and their Palestinian driver, killing them all; the American Fogbow group's Blue Beach set out a plan for a sea corridor from Cyprus run by former U.S. special forces, marines, CIA officers, a former diplomat and a former fund manager.

Across Gaza, Israeli bombs fall, ground troops and shelling from the sea claim child and women victims day and night, and the toll of civilian deaths and horrendous injuries rise in plain sight. Ambulance drivers and the Civil Defence staff who searched the rubble of destroyed buildings for wounded people or bodies were targeted by snipers or drones. Children were dying of hunger and suffering amputations without anaesthetic. Women gave birth under fire to babies whose future health was already compromised by their mothers' hunger and weakness in pregnancy. Doctors experienced in war-zone work testified they had never worked in such conditions of deprivation, danger and utter shortages of power and of medical equipment as those in Gaza.

Meanwhile, Palestinian journalists were shooting footage of Palestinian children learning and playing in tent schools in Rafah from kindergarten upwards. UNRWA's Palestinian teachers are doing what they always do to mitigate the effects of the horror of Israel military attacks on children's lives and emotional health. Footage and images show children bent over makeshift desks, sitting on the floor, writing, reading, singing, dancing, playing group games, flying kites and experiencing moments of childhood like any other child.

Educide is a primary aspect of the Israeli attempts to stop the work of UNRWA as the UN agency's schools have been indispensable to the education of Palestinian children across the region for more than seven decades, and therefore responsible for the emergence of remarkable Palestinian intellectual power in universities and specialized medical care across the world.

"Speaking truth to power lies at the core of the intellectual work of Palestinian thinkers," Palestinian academic, Dr. Afaf Jabiri, says:

From Ghassan Kanafani to Refaat Alareer, there is a long list of Palestinian intellectuals who have been targeted by the settler colonial state of Israel. Settler colonial regimes are inherently threatened by the power of truth, by the uncompromising logic, and by the stark realities of oppression faced by the colonised. Through their scholarship, Palestinian intellectuals expose the colonial logic and illegitimacy of the settler colonial regime, posing a direct challenge to its existence. Truth becomes the nemesis of settler colonial regime, and as such, it resorts to extreme measures, including assassination, to silence those who dare to speak it. This ruthless suppression serves as a grim reminder of the lengths to which oppressive powers will go to maintain their control and distort the narrative.[13]

Conclusion

Months spent watching the horrific genocide in Gaza have also been months spent watching the catastrophic failure of the UN system. UN Security Council Resolutions for a ceasefire were repeatedly blocked by the U.S.; the General Assembly decisions were ignored; UN agencies on the ground, like the World Health Organization, the World Food Program, UNICEF, OCHA and most importantly, UNRWA, were deliberately blocked from their legal and moral obligations to supply food, water, healthcare, shelter to starving and wounded Palestinians as they were forcibly displaced multiple times by the Israeli government, military leaders and armed settlers. The Israelis saw themselves as protected by the U.S., and never imagined that accountability would come for them.

After World War Two, under the leadership of Eleanor Roosevelt, the UN accepted the Universal Declaration of Human Rights in December 1948. It is the basis of all International Human Rights Law treaties since. In these months, the obligations of morality and international law have been shredded by powerful, dishonest, hypocritical leaders, alongside their enablers and collaborators in big business, and, more surprisingly, administrators of some of the most prestigious universities in the U.S.

This lawless horror will end.

---

13 Dr. Afaf Jaberi is a Senior Lecturer in Development Studies at the University of East London, UK. Her most recent book is *Palestinian Refugee Women from Syria to Jordan* (Bloomsbury Press, 2024).

It will end because an outraged civil society is mobilized worldwide. This is the motor that will rebuild a humane and moral international legal framework, with the leadership of countries such as those eight, including latterly Egypt, which backed South Africa's successful legal case at the ICJ in January 2024. Those same lawyers, and the next generation who come out of the student strikes and the police repression and Congressional taunting, in the spring and summer of 2024, will be the ones who bring accountability in the highest courts to those with responsibility for the apocalypse in Gaza.

Tens of thousands of Palestinian lives have been taken, from the many professors, poets and doctors, symbolized by Refaat and Dr. Ahmed, to the smallest babies, toddlers, teenagers and their mothers, and the beloved family men who died after torture in Israeli prisons. Every name is known and honored—that is the Palestinian way.

Dr. Jabiri spoke of what happened in the north and Gaza City after the Israeli army pulled out in March, saying they had finished their mission there, leaving massive destruction, with the majority of the population having fled south. But in fact, 700,000 Palestinians had stayed.

> Then the people showed up cleaning the streets, putting hospital equipment back up and running, opening bakeries, and preparing to welcome their loved ones who immigrated to the south. This is a recurring situation with Palestinians simply because we have no choice but to rebuild or revive what is left. We have learned through previous generations and the difficult life they have led, and it has been tested specifically by Palestinians in Gaza more than once, until it became a natural skill they practice. They know that there is no choice but to survive, build and continue, despite fatigue, sadness, terror, loss and exhaustion, their response to the world was clear: they kill us, they destroy. We build.

Reefat Alareer was buried 14 months after his assassination. On February 4, 2025 he was taken with the remains of his brother Salar, his sister Asmaa, and his four nephews to IbnMarwan cemetery near Shujaiya after a two-week daily search for his body by Asem Alnabih, an engineer based in north Gaza, the last person to be with Reefat in his final hours, and who was told by his mother soon before the ceasefire, "I just want to know where he is and give him a proper burial so he can rest in peace."

Many thanks to the three Palestinian academics—Salman Abu Sitta, Salim Tamari and Afaf Jabiri—for their contributions to this piece.

Does Knowing Matter?
Reflections on What the U.S. Knew of
the Conflict in Palestine in 1948[1]

Irene Gendzier

"Israel battled on Saturday to repel one of the broadest invasions of its territory in 50 years after Palestinian militants from Gaza launched an early-morning assault on southern Israel, infiltrating 22 Israeli towns and army bases, kidnapping Israeli civilians and soldiers and firing thousands of rockets towards cities as far away as Jerusalem."[2]

THE ABOVE ACCOUNT appeared on the front page of *The New York Times* of October 8, 2023, in a report that described the scale and surprise of the Palestinian assault on Israel, an "assault without recent precedent in its

---

1 The material that follows is part of a longer study that has roots in numerous earlier works that investigated the question of U.S. policy in Palestine in 1948. Among them is, "Archival Secrets: U.S. Policy in the Postwar Middle East," presented at the Emile Bustani Middle East Seminar, October 8, 1996; "What the U.S. Knew and Chose to Forget in 1948 and Why it Matters in 2009," *ZNet*, January 23, 2009; "September 2011 and May 1948: The Great Fear Now and Then," *Znet*, July 22, 2011; and the presentation offered at Harvard University in honor of Hilda Silverman, *Dying to Forget, Oil, Power, Palestine and the Foundations of U.S. Policy in the Middle East* (Columbia University Press, 2015; 2017).

2 Patrick Kingsley and Isabel Kershner, "Assault Met with Big Strikes on Gaza Cities," *New York Times*, October 8, 2023, 1.

Irene L. Gendzier, currently Prof. Emeritus, Boston University, served in the Departments of History and Political Science, and was associated with the African Studies Center, teaching the history and politics of the Middle East and North Africa and problems of development. Recent publications include *Dying to Forget* [cited above]; *Development Against Democracy;* and *Notes From the Minefield: United States Intervention in Lebanon and the Middle East, 1945–1958*.

complexity and scale," according to *Times'* reporters.[3] Why the surprise? And was it truly "without precedent"? Gideon Levy, Israeli reporter for *Ha'aretz*, underlined the role of Israeli hubris, arrogance and the ignorance that generated as factors directly relevant to Israel's lack of preparedness for the action of Palestinian militants in the October surprise. The U.S. response did not differ.

The Israeli/Palestinian conflict has long been recognized by policymakers, scholars, journalists and those who have repeatedly borne witness to its bitter tenacity, as pivotal to U.S. policy and the instability of the region. New works, moreover, continue to amplify the view that the conflict has been endemic to the turbulent political landscape of the Middle East.[4]

Official U.S. records offer a cautious if no less pessimistic view that clearly identifies the conflicting interests involved. U.S. records obtained through the Freedom of Information Act (FOIA) as well as declassified sources collected in the Foreign Relations of the U.S. series (FRUS) among other sources, including special editions of contemporary media reports such as that printed in *The Nation* magazine in 1947,[5] provide a range of official and unofficial views on the Palestine question before the establishment of the Israeli state in 1948.

What emerges from a review of official U.S. sources is that prior to the end of the British Mandate over Palestine, it was regarded as a troublesome terrain that subsisted in a region irretrievably marked by Anglo-French colonialism. The decade of the 1940s and early 1950s witnessed dramatic transformations. Under nationalist pressure France withdrew from Lebanon and Syria in the mid-1940s; Britain from Palestine by 1948 and from Egypt in 1952. At the root of these seismic shifts marked by the collapse of the ancien regimes of the Middle East, were struggles that led to the emergence of Israel in 1948 and four years later, of Egypt under Gamal Abdul Nasser.

From Washington's perspective, the unprecedented results were alarming, and that included the expansion of the Zionist movement. But as U.S. records indicate initial hostility towards the establishment of the state of Israel changed in accordance with Washington's calculations of its potential benefits to U.S. policy.[6]

---

3 Ibid.

4 Rashid Khalidi, *The Hundred Years' War on Palestine, A History of Settler Colonialism and Resistance, 1917–2017* (New York: Metropolitan Books, 2020).

5 The Nation Associates, *The Palestine Problem and Proposals for Its Solution,* memorandum presented to the General Assembly of the United Nations, April 1947, *Nation Supplement* vol. 164 (May 17, 1947).

6 The question of Palestine is critical to my analysis of U.S. policy in *Dying to Forget: Oil, Power, Palestine and the Foundations of U.S. Policy in the Middle East,*

U.S. records indicate that before the establishment of the state of Israel in 1948, U.S. officials in Washington and the Middle East were wary of the long-range plans of the Zionist movement in Palestine, its implications for U.S. interests in the region as well as its exploitation by the USSR.

Reports of the National Security Council and the Central Intelligence Agency dealing with Palestine in the years 1947–1949 confirm this view.[7] Officials in both agencies were well aware of the place of Palestine in the context of postwar European Jewish immigration, as indicated in the 1946 "Report of the Anglo-American Committee of Enquiry regarding the problems of European Jewry and Palestine" held in Lausanne on April 20, 1946.[8] As to what was to be done, views continued to differ as the liberal U.S. periodical, The Nation, revealed in its special issue on Palestine in November 1947.

Initially hostile to the expansion of the Zionist movement in Palestine as a threat to U.S. oil interests in the years prior to 1948, U.S. policy changed as Washington came to view the new state of Israel as an ally in protecting those very interests against Arab radicalism. The results were indicative of a policy that benefited conservative Arab regimes much as they undermined the possibilities of a Palestinian state. U.S. officials were not unanimous in endorsing such a policy but those who opposed it were overruled by the Departments of State and Defense.

New works continue to amplify the view that the long standing conflict in Palestine is endemic to the turbulent political landscape of the Middle East.[9] Official U.S. records, including those obtained through the Freedom of Information Act (FOIA), and the declassified sources of the Foreign Relations of the U.S. series (FRUS), offer a different view. Far from corroborating the vision of the Palestine conflict as an indelible dimension of a troubled region, U.S. records document the divergent and conflicting interests that shaped U.S. policy before, during and after 1948 with results that persist seventy-five years later.

In their introduction to *The Sacking of Fallujah, A People's History*, the authors remind readers that: "the way in which this

---

Columbia University Press, 2015; 2017.

7 For a work that relies primarily on State Department sources for the same period, consult the instructive study by Josh Ruebner, "Five Things the United States Knew About the Nakba as it Unfolded," Middle East Institute, May 13, 2022. https://www.mei.edu/publications/five-things-united-states-knew-about-nakba-it-unfolded

8 See *Report of Enquiry Regarding the Problems of European Jewry and Palestine,* Lausanne, April 20, 1946.

9 Rashid Khalidi, *The Hundred Years' War on Palestine.*

conflict is remembered is of great political, legal and moral significance, particularly if we are serious about addressing the injustices heaped upon ordinary Iraqis."[10]

The above remarks are no less meaningful when applied to U.S. policy in the Israel/ Palestine conflict, in which how and what is examined and remembered is of political, legal and moral importance in shaping the contemporary history of Israel and Palestine.

The following discussion offers a brief review of the recommendations offered by the Anglo-American Committee of Enquiry in 1946 and that of the U.S. Intelligence agency on Palestine in the period leading up to Israel's emergence in 1948.

"The Report of the Anglo-American Committee of Enquiry Regarding the Problems of European Jewry and Palestine, Lausanne, 20th April 1946," was written in the immediate aftermath of World War II. It was produced at the request of the United States and the United Kingdom with the objective of examining "the political, economic and social conditions in Palestine as they bear upon the problem of Jewish immigration and settlement therein and the well-being of the peoples now living therein."[11]

The 1946 Report reflected the views of postwar administrations in London and Washington, overwhelmed by the urgent requirements of post-war reconstruction in which the place of Europe's Jewish refugees constituted one of a number of critical elements. But as the opening pages of the above Report clearly indicated, the outlook was grim. As the authors of the Report stated, "countries other than Palestine gave no hope of substantial assistance in finding homes for Jews wishing or impelled to leave Europe." As they continued, "Palestine alone cannot meet the emigration needs of the Jewish victims of Nazi and Fascist persecution. The whole world shares responsibility for them and indeed for the resettlement of all Displaced Persons."[12]

In the years that followed, reflected in proposals for a resolution of the crisis over Palestine, Washington faced the question of partition, which it viewed with apprehension,

If the UNGA (UN General Assembly) accepts partition as the best solution of the Palestine problem, it is almost certain that armed

---

10 Ross Caputi, Richard Hill, and Donna Mulhearn, *The Sacking of Fallujah: A People's History* (Amherst, Mass.: University of Massachusetts Press, 2019), 2.

11 See the Preface to the *Report of Enquiry Regarding the Problems of European Jewry and Palestine,* Lausanne, April 20, 1946.

12 Ibid., Chapter 1, "Recommendations and Comments: The European Problem," 2.

hostilities will result in Palestine; that the social, economic, and political stability of the Arab world will be seriously disturbed; and that U.S. commercial and strategic interests in the Near East will be dangerously jeopardized.[13]

The above position was issued in the fall of 1947, when the risks to U.S. interests posed by the seemingly intractable Palestine problem preoccupied U.S. officials, who speculated that it was capable of altering the contours of the Arab world through Soviet supported revolution. In this context, efforts to implement the partition of Palestine appeared only to aggravate existing conditions.

Bearing the above in mind, it is of interest to recall that in the spring of 1947, the President of The Nation Associates, along with a number of progressive colleagues, issued a special edition of the journal titled "The Palestine Problem and Proposals for its Solution." Freda Kirchway, President of The Nation Associates and Henry A. Atkinson, Secretary of The Church Peace Union, offered a critical review of past policies pursued in Palestine, concluding that "all evidence points to the certainty that the establishment of independent Jewish and Arab states is feasible." Further, under the heading, "Possibilities of Expansion," Kirchway raised the question, "would a divided Palestine be equal to supplying the needs of present-day European Jewish life? The answer of experts is in the affirmative." Further, Kirchway reported on her return from a trip to Palestine and the Middle East that "no Arab state or combination of states could start a war in Palestine without British connivance."

The view from Washington differed. By the winter of 1948, U.S. officials concluded that it was "apparent that the partition of Palestine into separate Arab and Jewish states (and an international zone), with economic union between the two states, as recommended by the United Nations General Assembly (UNGA) on November 29, 1947, cannot be implemented."[14]

As Washington looked on—with increasing admiration for Jewish military advances—developments in Palestine were being radically altered by the successful military intervention of Jewish forces, leading in May 1948 to the establishment of the Jewish state. Internal differences in the U.S. policymaking establishment with respect to conditions in Palestine/Israel that followed Israel's emergence did not abate as a result. While the

---

13 "The Consequences of the Partition of Palestine," Central Intelligence Agency, ORE 55 (November 1947), 16. CIA Historical Review Program Release in Full.

14 "Possible Developments in Palestine,"Central Intelligence Agency, February 28, 1948," ORE7-48, CIA Historical Review Program Release in Full.

U.S. president determined to recognize the new state, some of his closest associates took issue with him, to no avail. As the Truman administration quickly recognized, recognition was not the final step in the resolution of the crisis over Palestine. The fact that there were now over 700,000 Palestinian refugees raised new problems that profoundly affected Arab regimes as well as U.S.-Arab relations.

U.S. Intelligence officials, along with their colleagues in the Department of State, were initially cautious if not hostile to the U.S. president's recognition of Israel in the spring of 1948. That changed as U.S. officials across the policymaking spectrum came to realize the relative advantages—as well as the continuing risks of the new configuration of forces in the region.

What they could not have predicted. however, was those seventy-six years after Israel's emergence, the question of Palestine would remain. Knowledge of its history, challenged and contested, was not sufficient to resolve it.

Palestinian Resistance Literature
The Catastrophe Written by the Living

Bilgehan Uçak

ACCORDING TO the etymology dictionary, the word "genre," which means "literary genre," was used for the first time in Turkish by Abdulhak Hamit Tarhan in his book, later published as *Letters*. Hamit, one of the greatest Turkish poets, writes in a letter (1881): "I desire to create a genre in our language other than prose and poetry called *mukaffa*." Over the years, the word "genre" changed its meaning slightly and came to mean a "sub-literary genre" within prose and poetry.

Today, the term "genre" is used to describe various subject or theme associations, both national and international. While "mystery novels in English literature" can be defined as a genre, especially war issues turn into a global genre. The most well-known of these genres is undoubtedly World War II. Countless novels have been written, movies and TV series have been shot on this subject. So much so that it has become necessary to talk about sub-genres such as "concentration camps" within World War II.

The World War II genre was not started by the living. The reason why the first examples appeared in America—and in the Anglo-Saxon world—was that the Nazis had not taken them over though they had taken over the whole of continental Europe. Films like *Casablanca*, made in the middle of the war in 1942, should be considered an exception, because these films—and works of literature—were written as they were heard and felt. Its biggest aim was to raise awareness of Nazi atrocities. That's why nothing was written or shot about concentration camps, which we mentioned as a sub-genre.

Although the Nazis were determined to exterminate everyone who was not one of them, it was the Jewish who suffered the greatest persecution. Yes, dissidents, socialists, communists, people with different sexual orientations, gypsies, even the mentally and physically disabled were sent to concentration

Bilgehan Uçak, a novelist, literary critic, travel book writer and journalist, was born in Istanbul in 1989. He has written nine books and many articles.

camps, but when people think of the Holocaust, they think of the genocide of the Jewish. With the end of the war in 1945, survivors began to tell their stories, they wanted everyone to hear what they had been through, and especially when literature and cinema came into play, everyone became aware of what had happened. Global public opinion condemned fascism. Eighty years later, the use of Nazi imagery is banned. Giving the Nazi salute, carrying a swastika, even using a font called "fraktur" can be a criminal offense.

In the first days of 1945, as the concentration camps began to be liberated one by one, we began to learn about the fate of literary figures. Irene Nemirovsky, one of the symbols of the Holocaust, was killed in 1942 before she could see the end of the war. The same year, Stefan Zweig committed suicide in Brazil, saying he had no hope. Primo Levi was one of the first to describe what happened in the concentration camps, and his book *If This is a Man?*, published in 1947, is considered the beginning of the genre. He told humanity with his own life story that the Holocaust was not a process that ended with survival: He committed suicide by throwing himself down a stairwell. Another survivor was Elie Wiesel, who won the Nobel Prize for Literature in 1986 for his stand against violence and racism. There is no need to multiply examples; these will suffice to show the conditions under which the genre emerged.

Although some argue that Palestinian Resistance Literature did not begin with the Nakba, which resulted in the establishment of Israel, the literary production after 1948 is very decisive in terms of both quality and quantity. *Nakba*, as you know, means "catastrophe." Although May 15 is commemorated as Nakba Day, in the eyes of Palestinians, the Nakba is not a one-day event. The Nakba is used to describe an occupation that has been going on since 1948. Therefore, the Nakba describes a period of seventy-five years. The literary works written during this period always contain various fragments of the Catastrophe.

Palestinian Resistance Literature is a literature that constantly reproduces itself. World War II lasted six years and officially ended in May 1945, but the occupation of Palestine has continued unabated for years. It is spreading. Gaza, one of the three biggest sieges in modern history—the others are Stalingrad and Sarajevo—has been going on for seventeen years in full view of the world.

Just looking at the literature is enough to show that United Nations Secretary-General Antonio Guterres is right when he says that what happened on October 7 "did not happen in a vacuum." [1] It did not happen in a vacuum;

---

1 António Guterres, "Secretary-General's remarks to the Security Council - on the Middle East," United Nations, October 24, 2023. https://www.un.org/sg/en/content/sg/speeches/2023-10-24/secretary-generals-remarks-the-security-council-the-middle-east%C2%A0

in other words, it was not unprovoked, it has a history. While academic disciplines focus on explaining what happened and how it happened, literature aims to "understand" that reason. The power of literature, of understanding, can be found in Palestinian poet Mahmoud Darwish's quote, "Poetry cannot bring down an airplane, but it can confuse the pilot's mind." To continue with Darwish's analogy, if an airplane crashes, a new one will arrive, but if the mindset of the pilots changes, it means that no more airplanes will arrive. The main reason why Nazis and fascism are cursed all over the world is the power of literature. You can write thousands of articles and put up numbers and talk about how horrible the genocide was, but the impact will be nothing compared to a good novel or screenplay.

The leading figures of Palestinian Resistance Literature are striking in the parallels between their life stories and the themes of their works. They have seen the death of their loved ones, their villages have been occupied, they have moved away from their homes, they live in exile... Happiness and peace are far from this literature. If there is hope, it belongs to the past, to times that will never come back.

Ghassan Kanafani, who with *Men in the Sun*[2] (1963) was recognized as one of the greatest writers not only in Palestine but also in Arabic, was murdered in 1972, at the age of thirty-six, when a bomb exploded in his car. Set in August 1958, the following two excerpts from *Men in the Sun* are striking because they show that almost nothing has changed since its publication in 1963.

> (...) she gave birth to a girl he named Hosna, who died two months later. The doctor said distastefully: "She was extremely emaciated." It happened a month after he left his village, in an old house in another village far from the firing line.[27]

When we adapt the novel which was published sixty years ago to today's Gaza, we find a striking result. Since October 7, there are estimated to be sixty thousand pregnant women in Gaza. The novel gives us a snapshot of Palestine in the second half of the fifties. We learn that Hosna, who died at two months old, was "extremely emaciated." Also, the family had left their village. In the last month of pregnancy, the mother traveled, probably on foot, to "another village far from the firing line" and gave birth "in an old house."

Gaza still has both a very high infant mortality rate, and a very high rate of mothers dying during childbirth. Nutrition is again a major problem.

---

2 Ghassan Kanafani, *Men in the Sun and Other Palestinian Stories*, translated by Hilary Kilpatrick (London: Lynne Rienner Publisher, 1999).

Since October 7, the massive famine and starvation in Gaza has been used as an unarmed part of the genocide, an attrition war. In Gaza, where even humanitarian aid supplies can hardly enter, access to any food, let alone food of high nutritional value, has become a major problem. Famine leading to starvation and disease is part of the genocide process.

But if the same Hosna had been born in another city, would the fact that she was "extremely emaciated" necessarily mean that she would have died? It is not easy to say yes to this question, because even if the mother had a good and comfortable pregnancy, if she had a good diet, if she did not have to leave her village to go to a village far away from the battle line, if she gave birth to Hosna in a hospital with proper hygienic conditions, and if, despite all these conditions, her daughter was still extremely emaciated, even then we could not take death for granted. Because the technological possibilities of the day would have been used to the fullest for Hosna to live. She would have been given the necessary medicines and food supplements. It is deprivation that has caused the deaths of thousands of Hosnas over the last sixty years.

There is an inverse correlation between high national income and infant mortality rates. The stronger the health system, the lower the infant mortality rate. In contrast to neighboring Israel, Gaza has one of the lowest per capita incomes in the world.

Just before October 7, The World Bank published its Palestine Economic Monitoring Report, entitled "Racing Against Time." According to this report, one in four Palestinians lives below the poverty line. Of course, it must be said that all these numbers have deteriorated sharply since October 7. The same report also mentions the difficulties Gazans face in accessing health care.

> (...) the Israeli occupation and the broader macro-fiscal context in the Palestinian territories have a significant impact on the Palestinian health system's ability to deliver services, by reducing investments in facilities and infrastructure and restricting the movement of people and goods. (...) A recent official joint WB-IMF mission to Gaza directly observed the critical conditions of the hospitals in the Strip, and—in particular—the challenges faced by cancer patients, especially in relation to the availability of local treatment as well as to the acquisition of timely permits to travel outside Gaza.

A few weeks before October 7, the World Bank wrote that the situation in Gaza is "particularly critical." It is impossible to establish lasting peace or tranquility in a blockaded territory with a collapsed health system.

A few weeks after October 7, another report was published, showing the desperation in Gaza in all its clarity. The report by the United Nations Conference on Trade and Development says that the years-long blockade has left 80 percent of Gaza's population in need of international aid.[3]

Kanafani also describes a forced exile through Hosna. We learn that the reason they left their village was the war. In other words, the Israeli occupation came to their village. Kanafani does not name this "another village far from the firing line" where Hosna was born, but there is no reason not to think that in the following decades this village has joined the occupied territories. Like a stone thrown into the sea, the occupation is spreading like ripples, and by 2024 it covers most of Gaza's territory.

Men in the Sun is about the efforts of Palestinians, frustrated by war and occupation, to leave their homeland. Abu Qais, Assad and Marwan meet with human traffickers to find a way out of Palestine. We learn about Abu Qais, who stands in front of the man "bearing on his shoulders all the humiliation and hope that an old man can carry," that "his head was full of tears." [29] On the day Abu Qais decides to flee, he thinks of Ustaz Selim, the most benevolent character in the novel.

> God was certainly good to you when he made you die one night before the wretched village fell into the hands of the Jews. One night only. O God, is there any divine favor greater than that? (…) You saved yourself humiliation and wretchedness, and you preserved your old age from shame. The mercy of God be upon you, Ustaz Selim. If you had lived, if you had been drowned by poverty as I have, I wonder if you would have done what I am doing now. Would you have been willing to carry all your years on your shoulders and flee across the desert to Kuwait to find a crust of bread? [25-6]

Kanafani does not refrain from a very harsh criticism of Abu Qais: "In the last ten years you have done nothing but wait. You have needed ten big hungry years to be convinced that you have lost your trees, your house, your youth, and your whole village." [28]

---

3 *Preliminary Assessment of the Economic Impact of the Destruction in Gaza and Prospects for Economic Recovery,* UCSTAD Rapid Assessment, January 2024. https://unctad.org/publication/preliminary-assessment-economic-impact-destruction-gaza-and-prospects-economic-recovery

Among those who, like Abu Qais, tried to leave Palestine, we read Assad's name for the first time under the similar conditions. Assad stands in front of the fat man who owned the office that was involved in smuggling people from Basra to Kuwait. Marwan's situation is no different: "Marwan came out of the shop belonging to the fat man who smuggled people from Basra to Kuwait..." [36]

The fatness of the human trafficker is a contrast to Hosna's extreme thinness. It is not without reason that fatness is constantly emphasized. We understand that this smuggler is doing very well. Many Palestinians are trying to find a way to leave the land of their birth. It is even possible to think that this fat smuggler is supported by the occupiers. If the occupiers had not turned a blind eye, he would not have been able to do it so easily, and he would probably be looking for a way to escape.

Marwan decides to flee, but a "tall, familiarly" man grasp him on the shoulder. "Don't be so desperate," he advises him, then says of the fat smuggler, "he is a well-known thief." [38] This man is Abul Khaizuran. We see Abul Khaizuran through Marwan's eyes: "He was very tall, very thin, but his neck and hands had a suggestion of strength and firmness, and for some reason he looked as though he could bend down and put his head between his legs without its upsetting his Spine or his other bones at all." [38]

Abul Khaizuran is thin, not fat. This is important. But his thinness is also different from Hosna's. He is a healthy, strong man. He says he will help Marwan and Assad escape, charges them a third of the fat man's fee, and even reassures them that they can pay him when they arrive in Kuwait. In the following pages, we learn who this character is, who has so far always appeared with positive qualities.

> Abul Khaizuran was an excellent driver. He had served in the British army for more than five years before 1948. When he left the army and joined the Freedom Fighters, he had the reputation of being the best lorry driver one could find. That was why the commandos in Alira invited him to drive an old armored car that the village had captured after a Jewish attack. [47]

The following lines reveal how the Nakba completely changed Abul Khaizuran's life: "Now . . . ten years had passed since that horrible scene. Ten years had passed since they took his manhood from him, and he had lived that humiliation day after day and hour after hour. He had swallowed it with his pride, and examined it every moment of those ten years." [53]

Abu Qais, Assad and Marwan, who had agreed with Abul Khaizuran to flee to Kuwait, lost their lives in the tanker they were hiding in due to an unforeseen delay. They tried to escape but could not.

Men in the Sun is a novel of exile starring escapees and human traffickers. The common characteristic of all the characters in the novel is that the Nakba changed their lives. Some lost their limbs, some lost their homes, some lost the land they had lived in for generations.

Let us look at the life story of Mahmoud Darwish (1941–2008), the most powerful name in Palestinian Resistance Literature in poetry. Mahmoud Darwish was born in the Palestinian village of Berve, in city of Acre, which was among the places occupied during the Nakba. When Mahmoud Darwish was seven years old, he was expelled from the land of his birth and, like many of his compatriots, he settled in South Lebanon and began his life as a refugee. Later, the Dervish family returned home to find Berve destroyed. The village where he was born was wiped out with all its experiences and memories. The deliberate destruction of social memory has been going on since 1948. Today, many places in Gaza have been demolished as a result of this policy of erasing memory. Mahmoud Darwish describes those days as follows.

> "It was one of those summer nights when the villagers sleep on the roofs of the houses: my mother hurriedly woke me up and I found myself running through the forest with hundreds of villagers. Bullets were passing over our heads. I didn't understand what was going on at all (…) We reached a strange village with children I didn't know. "Where are we?" I naively asked. And for the first time I heard the word Lebanon."[4]

The most important element of this policy is consciousness. It consciously aims to completely eradicate a culture, a civilization, to erase it, to destroy it as if it had never existed. According to early 2024 data, Al-Israa University, which the Israeli army demolished after it was used as a military barracks, was the last of Gaza's twelve universities. In the same period, over 100 mosques and churches were bombed. There are strong allegations that names such as Rifat al-Arir, one of Gaza's most prominent poets and writers, as well as a university lecturer, were killed with specific intent (December 6, 2023).

---

4 Ali Eminoğlu, *Mahmoud Darwish in Modern Arabic Poetry and His Poetry Understanding*, unpublished doctoral thesis, 22.

Let us return to Mahmoud Dervish's life story. Dervish's childhood is characterized by all the common features of Palestinian Resistance literature: exile, loss, occupation, deprivation, war. Alhough the Dervishes settled in another village in the Northern Palestine, they could not find peace, because this time they were denied a residence permit on the grounds that they had "entered the country illegally" and became refugees in their own homeland. Dervish's later life was spent in Haifa, Cairo, Beirut, Damascus and Paris. He returned to Palestine in his old age and was buried in Ramallah.

In one of his best-known poems, "Earth Presses Against Us" (1978), Dervish writes:

> Earth is pressing against us, trapping us in the final passage.
> To pass through, we pull off our limbs.
> Earth is squeezing us. If only we were its wheat, we might die and
>   yet live.
> If only it were our mother so that she might temper us with mercy.
> If only we were pictures of rocks held in our dreams like mirrors.
> We glimpse faces in their final battle for the soul, of those who will
>   be killed
> by the last living among us. We mourn their children's feast.
> We saw the faces of those who would throw our children out of the
>   windows
> of this last space. A star to burnish our mirrors.
> Where should we go after the last border? Where should birds fly
>   after the last sky?
> Where should plants sleep after the last breath of air?
> We write our names with crimson mist!
> We end the hymn with our flesh.
> Here we will die. Here, in the final passage.
> Here or there, our blood will plant olive trees.[5]

In his poem "With the Fog So Dense on the Bridge," Dervish expresses the anger of people who have been uprooted from place.

5 Mahmoud Darwish, *Unfortunately, It Was Paradise: Selected Poems* (University of California Press, 2003), 9.

Are we now entering the land of the tale, my friend?
He said to me, I don't want a place to be buried in.
I want a place to live in, and to curse, if I wish.[6]

"We Travel Like All People" is also a very well-known poem which focuses on the theme of exile.

We travel like everyone else, but we return to nothing. As if travel were a path of clouds. We buried our loved ones in the shade of clouds and between roots of trees.
We said to our wives: Give birth for hundreds of years, so that we may end this journey
within an hour of a country within a meter of the impossible![7]

In another poem, he says how important "exile" is in his identity. In fact, even the name of the poem is enough to express the emotion: "Who Am I, without Exile?"

Water binds me to your name.
Nothing takes me away from the butterflies of dream.
Nothing gives me reality: neither dust, nor fire.
What shall I do without the roses of Samarkand?
What shall I do in a square, where singers are
worn smooth by moonstones?
We have become weightless,
as light as our dwellings in distant winds.
We have, both of us, befriended the strange beings in the clouds.
We have both been freed from the gravity of the land of identity.
What shall we do?
What shall we do without exile
and long nights of gazing at the water?[8]

Darwish, a very prolific poet, always included themes of exile, occupation and war in many of his poems and was considered the world-renowned greatest poet of Palestinian Resistance Literature. He is also called "The Poet of Palestine." One of his poems was written to Fadwa Tuqan (1917–2003),

---

6 Mahmoud Darwish, *Almond Blossoms and Beyond* (Northampton, Mass.: Interlink Books, 2009), 73.
7 Darwish, *Selected Poems*, 11.
8 Darwish, *Selected Poems*, 113.

the most important female poet of "Palestinian Resistance Literature." She is
also known as "Mother of Palestinian Poetry."

> Sister, these twenty years
> our work was not to write poems
> but to be fighting
> (...)
> Sister, there are tears in my throat
> and there is fire in my eyes
> Ben özgürüm.[9]

Fadwa's brother Ibrahim Tuqan (1905–1941), who died young, was the
poet who wrote the most passionate poetry of the pre-Nakba period. In his
poem "My Homeland" he says:

> The youth will not get tired
> Their goal is your independence
> Or they die
> We will drink from death
> But we will not be slaves to our enemies
> We do not want
> An eternal humiliation
> Nor a miserable life
> We do not want
> But we will return
> Our great glory
> My homeland
> My homeland[10]

Like her other friends, Fatwa Tuqan's life is woven with the exile and
deprivation brought about by the war. She always carries the hope that the
displaced will one day come together. "Enough For Me" is probably the most
translated poem of the poet.

> Enough for me to die on her earth
> be buried in her
> to melt and vanish into her soil

---

9 Mahmoud Darwish, "Diary of a Palestinian Wound (Quatrains for Fadwa
Tuqan)" in Salma Khadra Jayyusi, ed., *Modern Arabic Poetry: An Anthology* (New
York: Columbia University Press, 1987), 200–202.
10 Ibrahim Tuqan.

then sprout forth as a flower
played with by a child from my country.
Enough for me to remain
in my country's embrace
to be in her close as a handful of dust
a sprig of grass
a flower.

It was stated that this poem, "My Sad City," was written on a day of Zionist occupation.

The day we saw the death and deception, The floods fell back,
The windows to heaven closed,
And the city held its breath.
(...)
The silence in my city –
Silence like mountains at rest,
Like a dark night, a painful silence Burdened
With the weight of death and defeat. Alas! Oh, my sad, silent city
Are you thus at harvest time,
Your crops and fruits aflame?
Alas! Oh, what an end!
Alas! Oh, what an end!

The last poem I want to quote from Fadwa Tuqan is a very powerful one: "And nothing remains."

We are together tonight,
But you'll be hidden from me tomorrow
By the cruelty of this life.
The seas will separate you from me
And oh! If only I could see you;
I'll never know where
Your path led you, which course
You took, and what unknown destination
Your steps pushed you to reach.
(...)
Your scent, your scent has the essence of life
In my heart,
As the earth gulps up the gift of rain

And the fragrance of the trees.
I will miss it when you leave tomorrow,
And nothing remains,
Just as everything beautiful, all that's dear to us,
Is lost, lost, and nothing remains.[11]

Another poet we should mention is Mourid Barghouti (1944–2021). As can be easily seen, Palestine's greatest literary figures belong to the same generation. Kanafani was born in 1936 and Dervish in 1941. Mourid Barghouti is a poet of the generation that faced the Nakba as a child. Exile is one of the most important concepts in Barghouti's life. For thirty years, he was not allowed to return to his country and had to wait until 1996 to return to the land of his birth.

It's also fine to die in our beds
on a clean pillow
and among our friends.
It's fine to die, once,
our hands crossed on our chests,
empty and pale,
with no scratches, no chains, no banners,
and no petitions.
It's fine to have a clean death,
with no holes in our shirts,
and no evidence in our ribs.
It's fine to die
with a white pillow, not the pavement, under our cheek,
with our hands resting in those of our loved ones,
surrounded by desperate doctors and nurses,
with nothing left but a graceful farewell,
paying no attention to history,
leaving this world as it is,
hoping that, someday, someone else
will change it.[12]

---

11 For translations, see Franklin Huntington, *Despite the great distance, existence unites the two: Translating the poetry of Fadwa Tuqan,* Senior Honors Linguistics Thesis, Swarthmore College, 2012. https://www.swarthmore.edu/sites/default/files/assets/documents/linguistics/2012_Huntington.pdf
12 Mourid Barghouti, "It's Also Fine," in *Midnight and Other Poems,* (Lancashire: ARC Publications, 2009).

Mourid Barghouti's memoirs of his return to his homeland thirty years later have been published as *I Saw Ramallah*.[13] Barghouti recalls 1967 when he had to leave his country as follows: "Displacement is like death. One thinks it happens only to other people. From the summer of '67 I became that displaced stranger whom I had always thought was someone else." [14]

In Barghouti's life, too, the scale of occupation is unlike any other. When he encounters soldiers of the occupation army, he asks how those who suffered so much half a century ago could be so cruel to him.

This soldier with the yarmulke is not vague. At least his gun is very shiny. His gun is my personal history. It is the history of my estrangement. His gun took from us the land of the poem and left us with the poem of the land. In his hand he holds earth, and in our hands we hold a mirage. But he is vague in another way. Did his parents come from Sachsenhausen or from Dachau? [23]

The Palestinian Resistance Literature continues to produce new products, new poets and writers. The fact that even eighty years after the Nakba, much remains unchanged makes it possible for this common consciousness to be passed on from generation to generation. Perhaps the most accurate description can be found in Barghouti's words: "The long Occupation has succeeded in changing us from children of Palestine to children of the idea of Palestine." [67]

Today, the first two names that come to mind when we think of young Palestinian writers both live in the UK as a result of the forced exile we see in Palestinian Resistance Literature. Isabella Hammad and susan abulhawa continue to tell the world about Palestine. While Hammad, in *The Parisienne*, focuses on Nablus and describes the transformation before and after World War I, Abulhawa, especially in her books Mornings in Jenin and *Against the Loveless World*, included the Palestinian cry. It is difficult to consider the novels of the two women writers as part of Palestinian Resistance Literature. This is because their circumstances are different and they write in English.

Palestinian Resistance Literature was written during the "catastrophe" and by those who lived it. In this respect, it is a unique genre in world literature.

---

13 Mourid Barghouti, *I Saw Ramallah* (New York: Anchor Books, 2006).

The Sin of Cosmocide[1]

Juan Cole

KILLING AN ENTIRE world is the ultimate act of villainy in science fiction. The most memorable such fictional atrocity occurs in George Lucas's
Star Wars (1977), when the Galactic Empire's imperial officer Grand Moff
Tarkin fires a fatal beam from the newly constructed Death Star at the planet
Alderaan, "the bright center of the universe," to demonstrate its awful power
to captive rebel leader Princess Leia Organa. Jedi Master Obi Wan Kenobi,
in transit to Alderaan aboard the Millennium Falcon, senses the enormity
of this casual murder of two billion individuals. He remarks, "I felt a great
disturbance in the Force, as if millions of voices suddenly cried out in terror
and were suddenly silenced. I fear something terrible has happened."[2] The
Empire had committed what we might term cosmocide, or the extermination
of an entire world. Although it may risk trivializing the massive atrocities our
world has witnessed in the past century to evoke them through a Hollywood
fantasy, we should also acknowledge that the pulverizing of Leia's (and Luke
Skywalker's) home world has shaken millions of filmgoers sheltered by
selective media journalism from exposure to the real thing.

Lamentably, cosmocide in the full sense of the destruction of a whole
planet became a possibility and not merely the stuff of speculative fiction on
July 16, 1945, when the first nuclear device was detonated. On that day, as
physicist (and Sanskritist) Robert J. Oppenheimer witnessed the first successful test of the atomic bomb he had fathered, he famously quoted the Bhagavad
Gita, verse 11:12 (referring to Krishna): "If the radiance of a thousand suns

---

1 This essay first appeared in *Renovatio: The Journal of Zaytuna College.*

2 "I felt a great disturbance in the Force," *QuoteTheGuy* YouTube clip [0:11].
https://youtu.be/EKu7TYWNxqA

Juan Cole is the Richard P. Mitchell Collegiate Professor of History at the University
of Michigan and is past president of the Middle East Studies Association of North
America. He is author of, among other works, *Napoleon's Egypt: Invading the Middle
East* (St. Martin, 2007) and *Muhammad: Prophet of Peace amid the Clash of Empires*
(Bold Type Books, 2018).

were to burst at once in the sky, that would be the splendor of the mighty One." He further recalled in this connection verse 11:32, translating it as, "Now I am become Death, the destroyer of worlds."[3]

Today, a massive exchange of thermonuclear weapons could plunge the earth into long-term darkness, killing most life. Even short of such a planetary slaughter, nuclear-armed states, and even those with extremely powerful conventional weapons, can wipe out "worlds," in the sense of entire cities or regions. We have beheld such orgies of desolation in wars in the Middle East in the twenty-first century that have leveled cities in Syria, Sudan, Gaza, and Israel.

Both the Jewish and Muslim spiritual traditions refer to cosmocide, and interestingly enough, both equate it with the killing of even one human being. In the Qur'an's chapter of The Table, 5:32, it is written,

> For this reason, We ordained for the children of Israel that whoever kills a single soul (except for executing a murderer or a brigand in the land), it is as though that person had killed the whole world. And whoever saves a soul, it is as though that person had saved the whole world. Our messengers came to them with clear signs, but many of them transgressed in the land even after that.

The Islamic scripture here contains an explicit reference to a passage of the Mishnah, the rabbinical oral tradition about Jewish law. Just as the Jewish sages themselves believed that this interpretation flowed inexorably from biblical verses, so too is God depicted in the Qur'an as endorsing the passage as rooted in revelation. The passage was incorporated into the Jerusalem Talmud, completed around 400 CE, which is certainly the edition referred to here in the Qur'an. The later Babylonian Talmud, likely completed sometime in the mid-to-late seventh century—after the Qur'an—contains an alternative version of this sentiment, specifying that killing a Jew is like killing all humankind. The Babylonian Talmud takes precedence for most Orthodox Jews, but the historically minded understand that the earlier text is more primary.

This reference to Judaic lore is only one of many in the Qur'an, where we find numerous episodes from the Hebrew Bible, retold to emphasize distinctive spiritual insights. This scriptural overlap presaged many centuries of fruitful interactions between the scholars and sages of the two religious

---

3 Kai Bird and Martin J. Sherwin, American Prometheus (New York: Knopf Doubleday Publishing Group, 2007), 309; Markandey Katju, "Bhagavad Gita and the First Atomic Explosion," The Times of India, June 10, 2014, https://timesofindia. indiatimes.com/blogs/satyam-bruyat/bhagavad-gita-and-the-first-atomic-explosion

communities. Despite the conflict between Muslims and Jews over territory in the Holy Land in the past century, the two have historically sometimes had warm, if complicated, relations. Before the twentieth century, Muslim rulers sometimes had Jewish ministers in their government, as with the Sassoon family, who served as treasurers for the Mamluk dynasty that ruled over Ottoman Iraq in the eighteenth to early nineteenth century. Jewish and Muslim thinkers debated ideas and learned from one another. Some Jewish thinkers in Muslim lands wrote important works in Arabic. I once visited the Spanish Synagogue in Prague, built by Jewish modernists in 1868 in what was called the "Moorish style," referencing Andalusia. It was a paean by members of the Jewish Enlightenment (Haskalah) to the relative tolerance and ecumenicism of the Umayyad era in southern Spain. And even if Andalusia has been romanticized (the later Almohad era was brutal and intolerant), the Jews of Prague were not entirely mistaken. Talmudic scholar Samuel ibn Naghrillah (d. 1056), for instance, rose to become the first minister of the post-Umayyad Muslim statelet of Granada.

The universalistic and spiritual implications of the Qur'anic verse (5:32) were explored by the great ecstatic Sufi thinker Rūzbihān Baqlī (d. 1209) of Shiraz. He said the verse shows that God

> created souls from a single handful, gathering them together. Then he separated and differentiated them and related them to one another regarding their capacities and creativity. So whoever kills one of them, that murder affects all souls whether they know it or not. And anyone who saves a believing soul with the mention of God and his unity and the description of his beauty and glory—so that he comes to love its creator—and saves it by virtue of his knowledge and the beauty of his witness—then this restored life and its blessings have an impact on all souls. So it is as though he saved the whole world.[4]

Baqlī pointed to the common origins of all people in God's act of creation, to their subsequent diversification, and to the way in which rescuing any of them enriches all the rest.

---

4 Abū Muḥammad Ṣadr al-Dīn Rūzbihān b. Abī Naṣr al-Baqlī, 'Ar'āis al-bayān fī ḥaq'āiq al-Qurā'n, ed. Aḥmad Farīd al-Mizyadī, 3 vols. (Beirut: Dār al-Kutub al-'Ilmiyyah, 2008), 1:311 (my translation). For this figure, see Carl W. Ernst, Ruzbihan Baqli: Mysticism and the Rhetoric of Sainthood in Persian Sufism (London: Routledge, 1996) and Kazuyo Murata, Beauty in Sufism: The Teachings of Ruzbihan Baqli (Albany, NY: State University of New York Press, 2016).

The Sufi tradition of Muslim mysticism was often open to spiritual encounters with adherents of other religions. While Jalāl al-Dīn Rūmī was capable, in his verse narratives, of using Jews and Judaism as symbols for the unbeliever (since after all they declined to recognize either Jesus orMuhammad, who are seen in the Qur'an as successors to the Jewish prophets), he also participated in a trans-religious spirituality that was dismissive of outward markers of sectarian identity, as Elisha Russ-Fishbane argues.[5] R. A. Nicholson translated one of Rūm'īs most celebrated verses this way:

> What is to be done, O Moslems? for I do not recognise myself.
> I am neither Christian nor Jew nor Gabr [Zoroastrian] nor Moslem.
> I am not of the East, nor of the West, nor of the land, nor of the sea;
> … My place is the Placeless, my trace is the Traceless;
> 'Tis neither body nor soul, for I belong to the soul of the Beloved.[6]

Moreover, his followers, at least, alleged that he had warm relationships with the Jews in Konya. Rūm'īs son asserted that, when his father died in Konya,

> The people of the town, young and old, all as one wailed and
>   mourned and sighed.
> The villagers, too, Greeks and Turks alike, tore their collars in pain
>   at his loss…,
> People of every religion were faithful to him,
> Followers of every faith declared their deep love for him,
> The Christians venerated him, the Jews saw him as one of their
>   own,
> The adherents of Jesus said, "He is our Jesus!"
> And the adherents of Moses said, "He is our Moses!"[7]

Traditions of Muslim universalism and expansive spirituality did not end in the medieval period, as they can be observed in modern times as well. For instance, some brave Muslims exemplified the Qur'anic virtue of concern for the life of a single soul during the Second World War. Abdelkader Ben Ghabrit, known as Si Kaddour Benghabrit (d. 1954), of Algerian heritage, served the French Third Republic in various diplomatic roles before becoming the head

---

5 Elisha Russ-Fishbane, "Jews and Judaism in Classical Sufi Literature," Journal of Sufi Studies 6 (2017): 143–64, at 147-53.

6 Reynold Nicholson, Selected Poems from the Divan-i Shams-i Tabriz (Cambridge, England: Cambridge University Press, 1898), 125–26.

7 Russ-Fishbane, "Jews and Judaism," 152.

of the Grand Mosque of Paris. The Nazi occupation of France in 1940 put Benghabrit in an extremely difficult position. His long service to the French state, as an "evolved" Muslim, suggested to Vichy officials that they might be able to recruit him for their purposes, and even the German authorities pressured him, hoping to use him for propaganda purposes in the Middle East. He appears to have maintained stiff but correct relations with Vichy authorities, seeking to protect his minority community, but rebuffed German approaches. It appears from some oral testimonies and family histories that Benghabrit several times risked his life to help North African Muslims who had fallen afoul of the fascist state to escape. It is certain that he also helped Jews on some occasions, hiding them in the mosque or issuing certificates that they were Muslims.[8] It appears that he intervened especially for individuals known to him and his circles but was not always willing to do so for strangers. Likewise, the great Jewish Algerian musician Salim Halali, who partnered with Algerian Muslims in musical productions in the Algerian style that were appreciated by both communities, found himself suddenly isolated and in danger when the Nazis took over Paris. Benghabrit, who loved Halali's music, issued him a certificate saying he was a Muslim in order to protect him from the fascist authorities.

Albert Assouline, a Jew born in Algeria and a resistance fighter, told the story of how he was given refuge in the Paris Mosque. Historian Ethan Katz wrote,

> Assouline explains how, in the first months of the Occupation, he and a Muslim soldier named Yassa Rabah escaped from a German prison camp and found safe refuge at the mosque. They stayed there two or three nights before crossing the demarcation line towards the unoccupied zone, in September 1940. Assouline notes that Si Mohamed Benzouaou, the first imam of the mosque, "took considerable risks to camouflage Jews by providing them certificates attesting that they were Muslims." Benzouaou even personally drove a rabbi, Netter, from Metz to Narbonne, disguising him as a Muslim.[9]

The number of Jews saved by Muslims at the Grand Mosque is hard to estimate. In the Qur'an, however, it is emphasized that if Benghabrit and Benzouaou saved even one Jew from the Nazis (and they certainly saved

---

8 Ethan Katz, "La Mosquée de Paris a-t-elle sauvé des juifs? Une énigme, sa mémoire, son histoire," trans. Anny Bloch-Raymond, Diasporas: Circulations, Migrations, Histoire 21 (2013): 128–155.

9 Katz, "La Mosquée de Paris," 142.

many more), they saved an entire world. Nor were they alone in this endeavor among Muslims in Europe. Iranian diplomat Abdol Hossein Sardari used his country's legation in Paris to protect Jews.[10] Many Bosnian Muslims also protected Jews in that era.[11]

How did the remarkable passage in rabbinical oral tradition equating murder with cosmocide, which the Qur'an references, originate? After the Roman destruction of the Second Temple in 70 CE, the large Jewish community in Roman Palestine gradually reoriented itself toward a more decentralized form of spirituality, one based in local communities and centered on the Bible and the oral teachings of rabbis. These "secondary" rabbinical teachings, the Mishnah, were at first orally transmitted and treated many issues in Jewish law such as prayer, religious taxes, agriculture, the keeping of the Sabbath and holy days, marriage, divorce, civil and criminal law, dietary laws, and rules governing ritual pollution and purification. The Mishnah was complete by about 200 CE, in the reign of the Roman philosopher-emperor Marcus Aurelius. Subsequent rabbis then commented on this text in glosses called the Gemara. The Mishnah, when combined with the commentaries produced in Palestine, eventuated in the Jerusalem Talmud, probably compiled by about 400 CE. As noted above, in the Sasanian Empire of Iran and Mesopotamia, rabbis in Babylon went on commenting for another two or three centuries, producing the Babylonian Talmud in the seventh century, the same century in which the Qur'an appeared.

The passage equating killing a single soul with killing the whole world appears in a universalist form in the earliest manuscripts of the Mishnah Sanhedrin, in the Jerusalem Talmud.[12] In 4:5 of the tractate we find, as translated by early-twentieth-century scholar and Anglican clergyman Herbert Danby:

> For this reason man was created one and alone in the world: to teach that whosoever destroys a single soul is regarded as though he destroyed a complete world, and whosoever saves a single soul is regarded as though he saved a complete world; and for the sake of peace among created beings that one man should not say

10 Fariborz L. Mokhtari, In the Lion's Shadow: The Iranian Schindler and His Homeland in the Second World War (Cheltenham, UK: History Press Limited, 2013).

11 "How Bosnian Muslim Back in 1941 Told a Lie and Saved Hundreds of Jews in BiH?" Sarajevo Times, March 17, 2019, https://sarajevotimes.com/how-bosnian-muslim-back-in-1941-told-a-lie-and-saved-hundreds-of-jews-in-bih/.

12 "The Origins of the Precept 'Whoever Saves a Life Saves the World'," Mosaic, October 31, 2016, https://mosaicmagazine.com/observation/history-ideas/2016/10/the-origins-of-the-precept-whoever-saves-a-life-saves-the-world

to another, "My father was greater than thine," and that heretics should not say, "There are many ruling powers in heaven;" also to proclaim the greatness of the King of kings of kings, blessed be He! for mankind stamps a hundred coins with one seal, and they are all alike, but the King of kings of kings, blessed be He! has stamped every man with the seal of the first Adam, and not one of them is like his fellow. So every single person is forced to say, The world was created for my sake.[13]

This form of the passage appears to be the earliest text, exhibiting the universalist impulses of some of the early sages who emphasized that since all human beings are descended from Adam, murdering him would have forestalled the entire human world from existence. They point out that in the story of Cain killing Abel, the biblical text says that the bloods (plural) of the victim called out—that is, the "bloods" of all his descendants that would not now come into being. Adam is the type of the human being, so killing anyone is killing all members of this class. Jonathan Wyn Schofer explains,

> God's creation of Adam, God's concern for Abel, and God's distinct formation of each person all in the Mishnah highlight the immense importance of each and every person as deserving correct judicial procedure. "Scripture" accounts the preservation of any single life as the preservation of a world. Each person is unique and valued as such, yet all people descend from Adam, so no person has greater ancestry than another.[14]

In the much later Babylonian Talmud, the injunction against killing a soul specifies a Jew, and it is the murder of a Jew that is equated to killing the whole world. The Qur'an paraphrases the universalist version of the Jerusalem Talmud.

Beyond the basic injunctions in the Bible, Jewish ethics have been a set of protracted arguments rather than a static set of precepts. Austrian Jewish philosopher Martin Buber (1878–1965) took a stand against killing anyone, even the notorious Nazi mass-murderer Adolf Eichmann, one of the key officials who plotted out and implemented the Holocaust against Europe's Jews.

---

13 Herbert Danby, Tractate Sanhedrin, Mishnah and Tosefta: The Judicial Procedure of the Jews as Codified Towards the End of the Second Century A.D. (London: Society for Promoting Christian Knowledge, 1919), 80.

   14 Jonathan Wyn Schofer, "Classical Jewish Ethics and Theology in the Halakhic Tractates of the Mishnah," in Imagining the Jewish God, ed. Len Kaplan and Ken Koltun-Fromm (New York: Lexington Books, 2016), 47–62, at 58.

Eichmann was captured at the end of the war but escaped to Argentina. In 1960, Israel's Mossad intelligence agency tracked him down and brought him to Israel for trial. Buber had devoted his life to an existentialist philosophy of mutual human interaction, having authored the key work *I and Thou* (1922), in which he argued that we only become truly human when we treat others as fully human rather than as instrumental objects. He contrasted things, which we experience or instrumentalize (I-it), to the second person address (I-thou), which requires an entirely different attitude: "When thou is spoken the speaker has no thing, he has indeed nothing. But he takes his stand in relation."[15] Buber opposed the execution of Eichmann on the grounds of the biblical commandment, "Thou shalt not kill."[16] Crucially, Buber believed that the Ten Commandments applied to states as well as to individuals. He therefore opposed the death penalty, a common position among leftist and liberal European Zionists. Buber sought an audience with Israeli Prime Minister David Ben-Gurion to urge against Eichmann's execution. Ben-Gurion allegedly averred that he had no personal commitment to such a verdict but that the then president of Israel, Yitzhak Ben-Zvi, was dead set on it.

Buber also feared that the execution of Eichmann might cause German youths to believe that the action had avenged the Holocaust and thus had relieved them of any burden of guilt. He did not seek clemency for the war criminal himself but wished Jews to stand by their own values even in this extreme case.

Buber took the commandment not to kill so seriously that he became a fervent vegetarian and considered most human beings to be engaged in a holocaust against animals. His utopian vision of an Israeli state bound by the commandment against killing contrasted vividly with the militaristic strand in Zionism that led to the Nakba. Despite his Zionism, Buber attempted to intervene in the 1960s on behalf of Palestinian Israelis to ensure that they were fairly compensated for their land the state took over for Jewish settlement projects in the Galilee and that they were given jobs. It was a paternalistic gesture that did not escape a colonial conceptual framework, but it did differ from the more militant forms of Zionism, the adherents of which would have seen nothing wrong with simply displacing these Palestinians, whom the Israelis call merely "Arabs" (haAravim), dismissing their Palestinian-ness.[17]

Buber's legacy of intense engagement with and recognition of the human other can be seen everywhere in modern Judaism, from Israeli NGOs devoted

---

15 Martin Buber, I and Thou, trans. Ronald Gregor Smith (Edinburgh: T. & T. Clarke, 1937), 4.
16 Maurice S. Friedman, Martin Buber's Life and Work, 3 vols. (Detroit: Wayne State University Press, 1988), 3:358.
17 Friedman, Martin Buber's Life and Work, 3:365.

to disaster relief (including in Muslim-majority countries) to organizations such as Jewish Voices for Peace and Rabbis for a Ceasefire, among the more prominent American organizations working for Palestinian rights.[18] Rabbi Brian Walt specifically invoked the Mishnah Sanhedrin in calling for peace in Palestine-Israel, saying, "We insist that in our tradition anyone who destroys a single soul, it is as if they destroy the whole world because each person is a world within themselves."[19]

Yet Buber's vision of a profoundly dialogical existence with respect for and insight into the other has faced fierce headwinds since his death. Toward the end of Buber's life, his colleague Ernst Simon expressed the view that if Israel was not leavened with Buber's pacifism, it would be forever trapped in Ben-Gurion's martial vision, living by the sword and under the sign of Mars.[20]

If extremism and terrorism are a self-evident horror, they do not always come out of nowhere. They can be instruments of overweening ambition and grasping sadism, of the quest for power. They can also be wounded and monstrous reactions to state war crimes and crimes against humanity. States, in their pompous pronouncements on security, indemnify themselves against charges of terror by specifying the term solely for non-state actors, whereas of course it is states that have killed the bulk of innocent civilians in modern conflicts. The ISIS episode, for instance, cannot be detached from the illegal U.S. invasion and occupation of Iraq. The rise of the Taliban Movement of Pakistan likely had more to do with the U.S. invasion and occupation of Afghanistan than with any putative tendency to radicalism of the Pashtun people, who also have produced civil and even pacifist movements. The rounds of violence in Palestine and Israel, in turn, cannot be discussed outside the framework of Israeli occupation and the displacements of Palestinians. Still, just as there can never be any excuse for states to target or recklessly endanger the lives of civilians, there can be no excuse for aggrieved vigilantes to mow down grandmothers and toddlers to make a supposed statement. Jews

18 Samuel Foray, "Morocco Earthquake: Israeli NGOs Are among Those on the Ground," September 12, 2023, https://www.lemonde.fr/en/le-monde-africa/article/2023/09/12/morocco-earthquake-israeli-ngos-are-among-those-on-the-ground_6133536_124.html; "The Growing Jewish Movement for a Ceasefire," Jewish Voices for Peace, November 12, 2023, https://www.jewishvoiceforpeace.org/2023/11/21/jewish-movement-for-ceasefire/

19 "Rep. Rashida Tlaib & Rabbis Call for Ceasefire in Israel-Hamas War," C-SPAN, November 16, 2023, https://archive.org/details/CSPAN_20231117_024100_Rep._Rashida_Tlaib__Rabbis_Call_for_Ceasefire_in_Israel-Hamas_War; see "Rabbi Brian Walt," https://evolve.reconstructingjudaism.org/author/rabbi-brian-walt/

20 Friedman, Martin Buber's Life and Work, 3:368.

and Muslims who kill innocent civilians, whether acting on behalf of a state or taking the law into their own hands, betray the highest ethical imperatives in their own spiritual traditions.

The rise of religious terrorist groups willing to target innocent noncombatants was roundly condemned by the grand imam of Al-Azhar al-Sharīf in Cairo, Ahmed el-Tayeb. Al-Azhar is the preeminent Sunni institution of religious scholarship in the world. In 2019, on the occasion of Pope Francis's apostolic journey to the United Arab Emirates, el-Tayeb and Francis jointly issued the "Document on Human Fraternity for World Peace and Living Together."[21] It begins:

> In the name of God who has created all human beings equal in rights, duties and dignity, and who has called them to live together as brothers and sisters, to fill the earth and make known the values of goodness, love and peace; In the name of innocent human life that God has forbidden to kill, affirming that whoever kills a person is like one who kills the whole of humanity, and that whoever saves a person is like one who saves the whole of humanity....
>
> That is, the pope and the grand imam jointly referenced Al-Mā'idah 5:32 in the Qur'an. In doing so, they implicitly invoked the commentary of the Jewish sages, demonstrating how the passage in the Mishnah Sanhedrin has worked its way into global interreligious dialogue through the Islamic scripture. In a separate legal opinion issued earlier that year, Al-Azhar underlined that this verse of the Qur'an condemns the killing of innocent (ma'sūm) civilians.[22]

The two spiritual leaders went on to lament, "History shows that religious extremism, national extremism and intolerance have produced in the world, be it in the East or West, what might be referred to as signs of a 'third world war being fought piecemeal.' In several parts of the world and in many tragic circumstances these signs have begun to be painfully apparent, as in those situations where the precise number of victims, widows and orphans is unknown."

---

21 Pope Francis and Ahmed el-Tayeb, "Apostolic Journey of His Holiness Pope Francis to the United Arab Emirates (3-5 February 2019): A Document on Human Fraternity for World Peace and Living Together," https://www.vatican.va/content/francesco/en/travels/2019/outside/documents/papa-francesco_20190204_documento-fratellanza-umana.html

22 "Al-Azhar li al-fatwā yufassir qawlahu ta 'ālā faka'annamā qatala al-nās," al-Misrawi, January 17, 2019, http://tinyurl.com/4tyevmu8.

Note their equal condemnation of "religious extremism" and "national extremism." In our own moment, their notion of a staccato and discontinuous third world war seems especially apparent. In country after country, in serial fashion, lawless non-state militias have despoiled entire regions of the globe. At the same time, lethal fighter jets, missiles, and drones have reduced proud buildings and the families dwelling within them to scattered debris. We have seen conflicts in which the megatonnage of conventional explosives aimed at dense urban neighborhoods has exceeded that of the nuclear devices the United States dropped on Hiroshima and Nagasaki in 1945. Moreover, instead of the tomb of the unknown soldier we now see the unmarked graves, beneath rubble, of thousands of innocent noncombatants, whose identities may never be recovered. If each equals a world, then entire clusters of solar systems are being annihilated, even entire galaxies—a cataclysm on a scale not dreamt of in the most audacious Hollywood space operas.

International Law and International Statecraft: Relevance Explained & Explored

A Crack in a 75-year-old Wall of Impunity

South Africa Challenges Israeli Genocide in Court[1]

Craig Mokhiber | Phyllis Bennis

South Africa's painstakingly compiled genocide case against the Israeli government isn't just an important legal document — it's a rallying cry for civil society.

1948 was a year of tragic irony.

That year saw the adoption of both the Universal Declaration of Human Rights and the UN Convention on the Prevention and Punishment of the Crime of Genocide, together promising a world in which human rights would be protected by the rule of law. That same year, South Africa adopted apartheid and Israeli forces carried out the Nakba, the violent mass dispossession of hundreds of thousands of Palestinians. Both systems relied on western colonial support.

---

1 This essay combines two earlier pieces. The first was written jointly by the two authors following the December 29, 2023, South African filing charging Israel at the International Court of Justice with violating the Covenant on the Prevention and Punishment of the Crime of Genocide. It was published first in *Foreign Policy in Focus*. The second part was written by Phyllis Bennis in London on January 26, 2024, just hours after the ICJ's initial ruling that Israeli actions in Gaza "plausibly" constituted acts of genocide, and the Court's imposition of provisional measures against Israel. It appeared first in *In These Times*.

Craig Mokhiber is an international human rights lawyer and former Director of the New York Office of the UN's High Commissioner for Human Rights, who stepped down from his post in October 2023 and penned a now-viral letter on unfolding genocide and the UN's failures.

Phyllis Bennis is a fellow of the Institute for Policy Studies and serves as international adviser to Jewish Voice for Peace. Her books include *Challenging Empire: How People, Governments and the UN Defy U.S. Power*.

In short, the modern international human rights movement was born into a world of racialized colonial contradictions. Seventy-five years later, the world is watching in horror as Israel has continued the Nakba through its months-long, systematic ethnic purge of Gaza—again with the complicity of powerful western governments led by the United States.

The horrors of the original Nakba were met with decades of absolute impunity for Israel, feeding further violence. But this time, three decades since the overthrow of apartheid in South Africa, the post-apartheid "Rainbow Nation" is taking the lead in challenging Israel's genocidal assault.

On December 29, 2023, South Africa became the first country to file an application to the UN's high judicial arm, the International Court of Justice, instituting genocide proceedings against Israel[2] for "acts threatened, adopted, condoned, taken, and being taken by the Government and military of the State of Israel against the Palestinian people."

In wrenching and horrifying detail, South Africa's 84-page document describes a litany of Israeli actions as "genocidal in character, as they are committed with the requisite specific intent ... to destroy Palestinians in Gaza as a part of the broader Palestinian national, racial, and ethnical group."

A Horrifying Civilian Toll in Gaza and the West Bank

2023 was the bloodiest year in the Palestinian territories since the destruction of historic Palestine and the founding of the state of Israel.

In the first half of the year, Israeli assaults on Palestinians in the West Bank had already reached a fever pitch,[3] with successive waves of mass arrests, settler pogroms, and military attacks against Palestinian towns and refugee camps, including the ethnic cleansing of entire villages.[4] At the same time, millions of civilians in Gaza were suffering unbearable hardship under a 17-year-long Israel-imposed siege.

On October 7, Gaza-based militants launched a devastating attack on Israeli military and civilian targets and seized more than 200 military personnel and civilian hostages. In an appalling act of mass collective punishment, Israel immediately cut off all food, water, medicine, fuel, and electricity to the

---

2 Application available at https://www.icj-cij.org/sites/default/files/caserelated/192/192-20231228-app-01-00-en.pdf

3 Omar Shakir, "While a Fire Rages in Gaza, the West Bank Smolders," Human Rights Watch, November 22, 2023. https://www.hrw.org/news/2023/11/22/while-fire-rages-gaza-west-bank-smolders

4 United Nations, Office of the High Commissioner for Human Rights, "UN expert warns of new instance of mass ethnic cleansing of Palestinians, calls for immediate ceasefire," October 14, 2023. https://www.ohchr.org/en/press-releases/2023/10/un-expert-warns-new-instance-mass-ethnic-cleansing-palestinians-calls

2.3 million Palestinian civilians trapped in Gaza. Then it began a relentless campaign of annihilation through massive bombing and missile strikes followed by a ground-level invasion that brought shocking reports of massacres, extrajudicial executions, torture, beatings, and mass civilian detentions.

More than 22,000 civilians and counting[5] have since been killed in Gaza, the overwhelming majority children and women—along with record numbers of journalists[6] and more UN aid workers[7] than in any other conflict situation. Thousands more are still trapped under the rubble, dead or dying from untreated injuries, and now more are dying from rampant diseases[8] caused by Israel's denial of clean water and medical care, even as the Israeli military assault continues. Eighty-five percent of all Gazans[9] have been forced from their homes. And now Israeli-imposed starvation is taking hold.[10]

The Legal Standard for Genocide

Genocide analysts and human rights lawyers, activists, specialists around the globe—no strangers to human cruelty—have been shocked by both the savagery of Israel's acts and by the brazen public declarations of genocidal intent by Israeli leaders. Hundreds of these experts[11] have sounded the genocide alarm in Gaza, noting the point-by-point alignment between Israel's actions and its officials' stated intent on the one hand, and the prohibitions enumerated in UN Genocide Convention on the other.

---

5 "Israel maintains onslaught as Gaza death toll tops 22,000," *Al Jazeera,* January 2, 2024. https://www.aljazeera.com/news/2024/1/2/israeli-bombardment-ongoing-as-death-toll-surpasses-22000

6 Isaac Chotiner, "The War in Gaza Has Been Deadly for Journalists," *New Yorker,* December 12, 2023. https://www.newyorker.com/news/q-and-a/the-war-in-gaza-has-been-deadly-for-journalists

7 Hande Atay Alam and Helen Regan, "UN mourns the deaths of more than 100 aid workers in Gaza, the highest number killed in any conflict in its history," *CNN,* November 14, 2023. https://www.cnn.com/2023/11/14/middleeast/united-nationsstaff-deaths-gaza-intl-hnk/index.html

8 "Diseases spread in Gaza amid health system collapse, Israeli strikes" [picture gallery], *Al Jazeera,* December 15, 2023. https://www.aljazeera.com/gallery/2023/12/15/photos-amid-deadly-israeli-strikes-people-in-gaza-face-a-stormof-diseases

9 Nadia Hardman, "Most of Gaza's Population Remains Displaced and in Harm's Way," Human Rights Watch, December 20, 2023.

10 Mallory Moench, "How Experts Believe Starvation Is Being Utilized in Gaza," *TIME,* January 6, 2024. https://time.com/6552740/gaza-israel-starvation-hunger/

11 "Public Statement: Scholars Warn of Potential Genocide in Gaza" [with 882 signatories], Third World Approaches to International Law (TWAILR), October 17, 2023. https://twailr.com/public-statement-scholars-warn-of-potential-genocide-in-gaza/

The South African application "unequivocally condemns all violations of international law by all parties, including the direct targeting of Israeli civilians and other nationals and hostage-taking by Hamas and other Palestinian armed groups." But it reminds the Court: "No armed attack on a State's territory, no matter how serious—even an attack involving atrocity crimes—can, however, provide any possible justification for, or defense to, breaches of the [Genocide Convention] whether as a matter of law or morality."

Unlike many aspects of international law, the definition of genocide is quite straightforward.[12] To qualify as genocide or attempted genocide, two things are required. First, the specific intent of the perpetrator to destroy all or part of an identified national, ethnical, racial, or religious group. Second, commission of at least one of five specified acts designed to make that happen.

South Africa's petition to the ICJ is filled with clear and horrifically compelling examples, identifying Israeli actions that match at least three of the five acts that constitute genocide when linked to specific intent. Those include killing members of the group, causing serious physical or mental harm to members of the group, and, perhaps most indicative of genocidal purpose, creating "conditions of life calculated to bring about their physical destruction." As South Africa documents, Israel has shown the world, at levels unprecedented in the 21st century,[13] what those conditions look like.

For specific intent, South Africa points to dozens of statements[14] made by Israeli leaders, including the President, Prime Minister, and other cabinet officials, and as well as Knesset members, military commanders, and more.

Accustomed to decades of U.S.-backed impunity, Israeli officials have been emboldened, describing openly their intent to carry out "another Nakba," to wipe out all of Gaza, to deny any distinction between civilians and combatants, to raze Gaza to the ground, to reduce it to rubble, and to bury Palestinians alive, among many other similar statements.

Their deliberately dehumanizing language includes descriptions of Palestinians as animals, sub-human, Nazis, a cancer, insects, vermin—all language designed to justify wiping out all or part of the group. Prime

---

12 United Nations Office on Genocide Prevention and the Need to Protect, *The Convention on the Prevention and Punishment of the Crime of Genocide,* adopted December 9, 1948, entered into force January 12, 1951. https://www.un.org/en/genocideprevention/documents/Genocide%20Convention-FactSheet-ENG.pdf

13 United Nations Palestine, "Gaza: 'Unprecedented and unparalleled' civilian death toll: Guterres," November 20, 2023. https://palestine.un.org/en/253284-gaza-unprecedented-and-unparalleled-civilian-death-toll-guterres

14 "Law for Palestine Releases Database with 500+ Instances of Israeli Incitement to Genocide – Continuously Updated," Law for Palestine, January 4, 2024. https://law4palestine.org/law-for-palestine-releases-database-with-500-instances-ofisraeli-incitement-to-genocide-continuously-updated/

Minister Netanyahu went so far as to invoke a Biblical verse on the Amalek, commanding that the "entire population be wiped out, that none be spared, men, women, children, suckling babies, and livestock."

The U.S. May Also Be Complicit in Israel's Genocide

The petition to the ICJ is sharply focused on Israel's violations of the Genocide Convention. It does not deal with the complicity of other governments, most significantly of course the role of the United States in funding, arming, and shielding Israel as it carries out its genocidal acts.

But the active role of the United States in the Israeli onslaught, while hardly surprising, has been especially shocking. As a State Party to the Genocide Convention, the U.S. is obliged to act to prevent or stop genocide. Instead, we have seen the United States not only failing in its obligations of prevention, but instead actively providing economic, military, intelligence, and diplomatic support to Israel while it is engaged in its mass atrocities in Gaza.

As such, this is not merely a case of U.S. inaction in the face of genocide (itself a breach of its legal obligations) but also a case of direct complicity—which is a distinct crime under the Genocide Convention. The Center for Constitutional Rights,[15] on behalf of Palestinian human rights organizations and individual Palestinians and Palestinian-Americans, has filed a suit in U.S. federal court in California focused on U.S. complicity in Israel's acts of genocide.

South Africa's Genocide Complaint is a Rallying Cry for Civil Society

In a situation such as this, framed by shocking western complicity on one side and a massive failure of international institutions fed by U.S. pressure on the other, South Africa's initiative at the ICJ may hold significance beyond the Court's ultimate decision.

This case comes in the context of the extraordinary mobilization of protests, petitions, sit-ins, occupations, civil disobedience, boycotts, and so much more by human rights defenders, Palestinian and Jewish activists, faith-based organizations, labor unions, and broad-based movements across the United States and around the world.

As such, this move puts South Africa, and potentially the ICJ itself, on the side of the global mobilization for a ceasefire, for human rights, and for

---

15 "Palestinians Sue Biden for Failure to Prevent Genocide, Seek Emergency Order to Stop Military and Diplomatic Support for Israeli Government's Assault on Gaza," Center for Constitutional Rights, November 13, 2023. https://ccrjustice.org/home/press-center/press-releases/palestinians-sue-biden-failure-prevent-genocide-seek-emergency

accountability. One of the most important values of this ICJ petition may, therefore, be in its use as an instrument for escalating global civil society mobilizations demanding that governments abide by the obligations imposed on all parties to the Genocide Convention.

Predictably, Israel has already rejected the legitimacy of the case before the Court. Confident that the U.S. and its allies will not allow Israel to be held accountable, the Israeli government is defiantly continuing its bloody assault on Gaza (as well as the West Bank). If Israel and its western collaborators are once again successful in blocking justice, the first victims will be the Palestinian people. Then the credibility of international law itself may be lost as collateral damage.

But South Africa's ICJ action has opened a crack in a 75-year-old wall of impunity through which a light of hope has begun to shine. If global protests can seize the moment to turn that crack into a wider portal towards justice, we may just see the beginnings of real accountability for perpetrators, redress for victims, and attention to the long-neglected root causes of violence: settler-colonialism, occupation, inequality, and apartheid.

The Legal Implications of Complicity in Genocide

M. Javad Zarif | Reza Nasri

GENOCIDE is often described as an "atrocity crime" that "shocks the conscience of humanity." As such, one would assume that—unlike other complex matters that involve competing strategic ambitions—the prevention of genocide would be a rather uncontroversial task for the global community to tackle. Indeed, it should have been established by now that no security, geopolitical, or ideological imperative ever justifies the commission of genocide and, contrary to the tacit narrative that is often tactfully slipped between the lines of pro-Israeli statements, no "military necessity" or "plea to self-defense" can ever be invoked to give the act any semblance of legitimacy.

In fact, contrary to U.S. and Israeli claims, Israel's brutal military campaign against the people of Gaza was, from the very onset, neither intended as an "act of self-defense" nor a necessary attempt to wage war on alleged "terrorism." It was—and will always be remembered as—an unprecedented violent and ruthless campaign that can best be described as "deterrence through genocide." As a matter of fact, "disproportionate retaliation against civilians" has been a longstanding Israeli policy for which Israel Defense Force (IDF) commander Gadi Eisenkot has even coined a specific term: the "Dahiya Doctrine," which he explains as follows: "We will wield disproportionate

M. Javad Zarif served as the foreign minister of Islamic Republic of Iran from 2013 to 2021. He was Iran's permanent representative to the United Nations (2002–2007) and deputy foreign minister (1992–2002). He received his PhD in International Studies from University of Denver in 1988 and is currently serving as the Vice President of Iran and an associate professor on the Faculty of World Studies, University of Tehran.

Reza Nasri is an international lawyer who received his PhD in International Law from the Graduate Institute of International and Development Studies in Geneva and his LLM from the University of Montreal. Dr. Nasri has written extensively about international law and current affairs.

power against every village from which shots are fired on Israel and cause immense damage and destruction. From our perspective, these are military bases."[1] In reality, in the recent case of Gaza, the "immensity and dispropor-tionality" referred to in this description simply took the form of a "genocide policy" against the Palestinian people—or a "final solution"—whose plausi-ble occurrence has even been established by the International Court of Justice (hereafter "ICJ") in an order in vindication of provisional measures issued on January 26, 2024, in the now well-known *South Africa v. Israel* case.[2]

Aside from the uncontroversial common understanding of the excep-tional nature of the crime and the urgent necessity to prevent it, it should also be pointed out that the global community is rather well-equipped to effectively prevent genocide or to take collective measures to decisively halt its continued commission. In fact, all the necessary legal, political and enforcement mechanisms and frameworks are already in place to enable the global community to embrace a multilayered and multifaceted approach to address and prevent the recurrence of the unparalleled humanitarian crisis in Gaza—and, in a more subtle yet persistent manner, in the West Bank.

At the forefront, there is of course the 1948 *Convention on the Prevention and Punishment of the Crime of Genocide* (hereafter the "Genocide Convention"), which counts 153 State-Parties to this date[3] and whose peremptory customary norms are binding on *all* members of the global community. The Genocide Convention imposes, *inter alia*, a "duty" upon State-Parties to take measures to "prevent" and to "punish" the crime of genocide, which would include enacting relevant legislation and punishing perpetrators "whether they are constitutionally responsible rulers, public officials or private individuals."[4]

Furthermore, as an independent subject of international law, the United Nations (hereafter the "UN") has also its own legal obligations[5] to address

---

1 Amos Harel. "IDF plans to use disproportionate force in next war," *Haaretz,* October 5, 2008.

2 Application of the Convention on the Prevention and Punishment of the Crime of Genocide in the Gaza Strip (South Africa v. Israel).

3 See: https://www.un.org/en/genocideprevention/genocide-convention.shtml

4 Article IV of the 1948 Genocide Convention.

5 It was concluded at the New York session of the Russel Tribunal on Palestine in October 2012 that: "As a subject of international law, the UN is, like a state, bound to fulfill its international obligations in good faith. Significantly, in a recent Declaration of the High-level Meeting of the General Assembly (UNGA) on the Rule of Law at the National and International Levels, the UNGA declared that "the rule of law applies to all states equally, and to international organizations, including the United Nations and its principal organs, and that respect for and promotion of the rule of law and justice should guide all of their activities" (UN Doc. A/67/L.1, 19 Sept.

Israel's blatant violations of *jus cogens* norms, most of which its subsidiary organs and special agencies—like the United Nations Relief and Works Agency (UNWRA) and the World Health Organization (WHO)[6]—have meticulously documented. In this context, the United Nations Security Council (UNSC)—as the UN organ that is vested with the *primary* responsibility for the maintenance of international peace and security—remains also quite well equipped to play a pivotal role in the enforcement of international law and has the prerogative to take concrete measures against Israel—such as demanding a "ceasefire" under Articles 39 and 40 of the Charter of the United Nations, imposing punitive and enforcement measures under Article 41 of the Charter for non-compliance, authorizing peacekeeping missions or even suspending membership from various UN organs—to remedy the exceptionally dire humanitarian situation in Gaza. The International Criminal Court (ICC)—whose jurisdiction extends to the territories occupied by Israel since 1967, namely Gaza and the West Bank, including East Jerusalem following admission of Palestine to the Court—can also provide a key enforcement mechanism in this regard, as it can hold criminally liable those Israeli officials directly responsible in the commission of these heinous crimes.

However, activating such mechanisms and utilizing these and other international tools would require the effective engagement of states (and non-state actors) in genuine multilateralism and diplomacy, which, to the detriment of Palestinian victims, has since the beginning of the crisis been significantly hindered by a major and non-negligeable obstacle: the United States' complicity in the Israeli genocide. A complicity that the United States and some of its Western allies often try to justify on the obscure premises of an emerging "rule-based order," designed to supplant "international law" in an emerging global order.

Multilateral Diplomacy and Its Discontents

Certainly, multilateral diplomacy—often described as mutual "adherence to a common political project based on the respect of a shared system of

---

2012, § 2). The Charter stipulates that the UN's purpose is "To maintain international peace and security," "respect for the principle of equal rights and self-determination of peoples" and "to promote [...] respect for human rights [...] for all" (Art. 1). The Charter provides that the UN must "take effective collective measures" to achieve these goals." See: https://www.russelltribunalonpalestine.com/en/sessions/future-sessions.html

6 See WHO Eastern Mediterranean Region, *Gaza Hostilities 2023 / 2024 - Emergency Situation Reports,* https://www.emro.who.int/opt/information-resources/emergency-situation-reports.html and United Nations Relief and Works Agency for Palestine Refugees in the Near East reports, https://www.unrwa.org/resources/reports

norms and values"—has the potential to accomplish the "seemingly impossible" when employed effectively.

In fact, over the past decades, some of the most intricate, complex, divisive and supposedly insurmountable international crises have been successfully resolved—against all odds—by the collective action of global actors whom—at one point—soberly decided to rely on fundamental principles of international law, the UN Charter and even shared moral imperatives while prioritizing the attainment of mutually beneficial results over zero-sum outcomes.

A case in point, which shares quite pertinent similarities to the issue of Palestine, is the case of Namibia's emancipation from the grip of South African apartheid. Following years of struggle for self-determination, failed international calls, stalled negotiations and even an unheeded Advisory opinion by the ICJ,[7] multilateral efforts finally culminated in the adoption of a binding Security Council resolution[8] that effectively delineated a clear path for a ceasefire, established a peacekeeping force[9] to oversee South Africa's withdrawal from Namibia and ensured "the early independence of Namibia through free elections under the supervision and control of the United Nations."[10]

Another instance of effective multilateral diplomacy—amidst conflicting geopolitical interests during the challenging era of the Cold War—was the attainment of a ceasefire between Iran and Iraq in 1988 following eight years of strenuous armed conflict. Here, too, the conflict was resolved following the pragmatic realization by all parties of the limits of military force and the importance of pursuing regional stability and respective interests through: a) a negotiated settlement, b) third states' commitment to refrain from "any act which may lead to further escalation and a widening of the conflict," and c) a long-term UN-mandated peace plan for the future of region, all being incorporated in paragraphs 5 and 8 of UNSC Resolution 598.[11] Unfortunately, the latter was never implemented, due to resurgence of zero-sum objectives, to

---

7 See: *Legal Consequences for States of the Continued Presence of South Africa in Namibia (South West Africa) notwithstanding Security Council Resolution 276 (1970)*, Advisory Opinion, 1971 ICJ Rep. 16.

8 S/Res/435 (1978).

9 The United Nations Transition Assistance Group (UNTAG).

10 S/RES/435 (1978), [Operative Paragraph 3].

11 S/RES/589 [1988], Paragraph 5 reads: "*Calls upon* all other States to exercise the utmost restraint and to refrain from any act which may lead to further escalation and widening of the conflict and thus to facilitate the implementation of the present resolution.» In paragraph 8 of the Resolution the Security Council "*Further requests* the Secretary-General to examine in consultation with Iran and Iraq and with other states of the region measures to enhance the security and stability of the region."

the detriment of the people of the region, and regional and global peace and security.

The 2001 Bonn Conference, which was crucial for the establishment of a transitional government in Afghanistan after the fall of the Taliban, is also an illustrative example of "true multilateralism in action" in which key stakeholders—including representatives from Afghan factions, regional powers, and international organizations like the United Nations—were brought together to foster consensus and cooperation on yet another highly contentious and difficult matter. In addition to the political determination among stakeholders to reach a settlement, the United Nations played indeed its anticipated institutional role in facilitating the conference and helping define clear objectives—including the establishment of a transitional government and a roadmap for future governance in Afghanistan—fostering discussions and laying the foundation for decision-making.

In a more recent case, the conclusion of the "Joint Comprehensive Plan of Action," or the "JCPOA" (commonly known as the "Iran Nuclear Deal")— negotiated between Iran, China, France, Germany, Russia, the United Kingdom, the United States and the European Union—can also be construed as yet another instance where multilateral diplomacy and positive-sum dialogue—premised upon the belief that "one's security cannot be pursued at the expense of the insecurity of others"—triumphed over unilateral diktat and maximalist positions, producing results that even the most optimistic analysts could not have anticipated.

Thus, with *clear objectives, commitment to international law and principles, positive-sum holistic thinking, adaptability* and the audacity to make right decisions, "multilateral diplomacy" can be—and has indeed proven to be—a quite remarkable way of putting existing international mechanisms and legal instruments to use and producing outcomes that would satisfy both "legal" and "moral" imperatives.

Yet, these faint and fragile components of "multilateral diplomacy" are not to be taken for granted. In fact, gathering all these components in one place often represents, *in and of itself,* the culmination of painstaking efforts that remains susceptible to internal and external disruption. This intricate and volatile arrangement becomes particularly difficult to attain when a superpower decides to deliberately obstruct its formation process. As a matter of fact, when a superpower undermines multilateral efforts, whether through unilateral actions or by eroding trust in international institutions, not only does it stall progress on a current issue, but it also sets dangerous precedents that could discourage future endeavors. This behavior is all the more dreadful and deplorable when the matter at hand concerns the prevention of atrocities, such as the crime of genocide. Regrettably, this is precisely the manner in which the United States conducted itself in the face of multilateral efforts from the start of Israel's genocidal campaign in Gaza!

Clear Objectives

As mentioned above, defining "clear objectives"—or an "endgame" in diplomatic parlance—constitutes one of the indispensable prerequisites for multilateral diplomacy to succeed. However, even after it became quite evident that Israel's 2023 military campaign in Gaza possessed, from the outset, *textbook characteristics* of a genocide, the United States persistently obstructed the global community from defining a "ceasefire" as a common objective that would protect Palestinians from extermination.

Instead, in political milieus, the United States vigorously advanced the flawed narrative that Israel's military operation in Gaza is no more than a legitimate exercise of its "right to self-defense," whose success ultimately depends on the complete "eradication of Hamas." So, under this perspective, the "clear objective" became the impossible task of the "eradication of Hamas," and the mass slaughter that ensued became "occasional transgressions" of International Humanitarian Law (IHL), which in this absurd logic is attributed to Hamas hiding its combatants and assets among civilian populations and structures in Gaza. Taking this absurdity to its logical conclusion, eradication of a popular resistance movement can only be achieved—if ever—through eradication of an entire population.

With this narrative at play, the U.S. opposed a first Security Council draft resolution on October 18, 2003 that called for "humanitarian pauses," which it vetoed on the ground that it "did not mention Israel's right of self-defense."[12] The U.S. subsequently vetoed a second resolution on December 8, 2023, rejecting a draft put forth by the United Arab Emirates and co-sponsored by 97 other states that called for "an immediate humanitarian ceasefire," civilian access to humanitarian aid and "the immediate and unconditional release of all hostages." This time, the U.S. ambassador to the UN vetoed the resolution on the pretext that it did not condemn "Hamas' 7 October attack," adding that "[w]hile the U.S. strongly supports a durable peace in which both Israel and Palestine can live in peace and security, we do not support calls for an immediate ceasefire."[13] On February 20, 2024, the United States

---

12 See: United Nations, "Israel-Gaza crisis: US vetoes Security Council resolution," October 18, 2023. https://news.un.org/en/story/2023/10/1142507

13 See: United Nations, The Question of Palestine, "US vetoes resolution on Gaza which called for 'immediate humanitarian ceasefire'," December 8, 2023. https://www.un.org/unispal/document/us-vetoes-resolution-on-gaza-which-called-for-immediate-humanitarian-ceasefire-dec8-2023/

vetoed yet again a third resolution that called for an immediate ceasefire, this time justifying its obstruction with the claim that "hard diplomacy takes more time," while postulating—quite preposterously—that the resolution "would put sensitive negotiations in jeopardy."[14] Finally, when after 171 days of relentless bombing of Gaza, the Security Council eventually adopted (with 14 members voting in favor and the U.S. abstaining) a resolution demanding an "immediate ceasefire for the month of Ramadan,"[15] the spokesperson for the United States Department of State, Matthew Miller, hastily rushed to provide a novel interpretation of the UN Charter by characterizing the resolution as "non-binding," thus providing Israel the leeway to continue the slaughter with full impunity.

Commitment to International Law and Principles

Of course, these instances were not the first time the United States vetoed UNSC resolutions and deadlocked the institution to shield Israel. The U.S. has vetoed resolutions concerning Israel more than 47 times to this date, accounting for half the total number of negative votes it has cast at the UNSC since 1948.[16] Yet, recent U.S. vetoes diverge from past instances in at least one significant aspect: Unlike previous ones, recent U.S. vetoes have been employed in a situation directly pertaining to the prevention of an ongoing genocide, whose "prevention" and "punishment" constitutes an *erga omnes* obligation for *all* states and a conventional legal duty for all Contracting Parties to the 1948 Genocide Convention. In other words, by obstructing the establishment of a shared objective on preventing the mass killing of Palestinians, not only does the United States impede multilateral diplomacy but it also violates its own obligations under the Genocide Convention while effectively hindering other member-states from utilizing the Security Council to carry out their individual and joint treaty obligations. Furthermore, by essentially rendering the Genocide Convention obsolete in terms of its content, relevance and applicability, the United States is essentially robbing the international community of a well-established legal structure that could have offered appropriate guidelines to tackle the unparalleled humanitarian emergency in Gaza within a proficient and clearly outlined multilateral context.

---

14 See: United Nations coverage of 9552nd Meeting (AM), "Security Council Again Fails to Adopt Resolution Demanding Immediate Humanitarian Ceasefire in Gaza on Account of Veto by United States," February 20, 2024. https://press.un.org/en/2024/sc15595.doc.htm

15 S/RES/2728 [2024].

16 Security Council Veto list from 16 February 1946 to 24 April 2024: See: https://www.un.org/depts/dhl/resguide/scact_veto_table_en.htm

Moreover, preempting the Genocide Convention of its relevance—while preventing the Security Council from serving as an efficient enforcement mechanism in this regard—does not just undermine states' ability to fulfill their positive obligations under the Convention; it also paves the ground for the United States to *proactively assist* Israel in perpetrating genocide against Palestinians by alleviating international pressure, dividing the global community and providing a veneer of legitimacy to its complicity.

The United States government has indeed, from the beginning of the crisis, doubled down on its military aid, economic assistance and diplomatic support for Israel, often circumventing even its own domestic legislations.[17] In fact, the United States' resolve to assist Israel *at all costs* does not just affect legal instruments and those international institutions in which it exercises direct influence due to its legal status or financial contributions; it also extends to independent judicial institutions, such the International Criminal Court, that could in principle intervene on their own initiative to address the situation. The United States' political pressure, intimidatory tactics and extra-territorial sanctions that U.S. lawmakers are often keen to brandish against the Court's staff, officials and even their families[18] are intended to bully and deter the officials of the Court from discharging their responsibilities under the ICC Statute. In fact, one could contend that the United States' "obstruction

---

17 By providing weapons to Israel under the current circumstances, the Biden administration could be in violation of: *The Foreign Assistance Act,* which prohibits aiding governments engaged in consistent patterns of gross human rights violations; *The Arms Export Control Act,* stipulating that U.S.-provided military aid must be used solely for legitimate self-defense and internal security, which may not encompass Israel's actions in Gaza; *The U.S. War Crimes Act,* prohibiting grave breaches of the Geneva Conventions, potentially applicable to actions by Israeli forces in Gaza; *The Leahy Law,* barring U.S. assistance to foreign security units implicated in gross human rights violations; *The Genocide Convention Implementation Act,* which imposes criminal penalties for individuals involved in genocide, raising concerns about complicity in potential genocide against Gaza civilians; and the *Humanitarian Aid Corridor Act,* which prohibit U.S. foreign assistance from going to countries that block U.S. humanitarian aid.

18 A group of 12 Republican U.S. senators sent a letter to International Criminal Court (ICC) Chief Prosecutor Karim Khan on April 24, 2024, threatening repercussions if the court issued arrest warrants against Israeli Prime Minister Benjamin Netanyahu and other officials. The letter reads: "The United States will not tolerate politicized attacks by the ICC on our allies. Target Israel and we will target you. If you move forward with the measures indicated in the report, we will move to end all American support for the ICC, sanction your employees and associates, and bar you and your families from the United States. You have been warned."

See: Team Zeteo and Mehdi Hasan, "EXCLUSIVE: "You Have Been Warned": Republican Senators Threaten the ICC Prosecutor over Possible Israel Arrest Warrants," *Zeteo,* May 6, 2024. https://zeteo.com/p/exclusive-you-have-been-warned-republican

of justice"—as tacitly denounced by a communiqué issued by the ICC's Office of the Prosecutor on May, 03, 2024—constitutes yet another indicator of Washington's deliberate complicity in the genocide committed by Israel and yet another U.S. attempt to dismantle legal regimes that could provide the global community a clear path toward implementing and enforcing international law against the genocidal apartheid regime.

Positive-sum Holistic Thinking

Despite what International Relations Realists may assert, any seasoned diplomat on the ground could confidently posit that a "positive-sum holistic" approach is one of the crucial components of multilateral diplomacy. Holistic thinking involves considering interconnected interests and diverse perspectives in order to address complex global challenges in a comprehensive, effective and sustainable manner. It also involves a strategic foresight that would allow parties to anticipate future behavior, risks and challenges, and to devise an agreement in a manner that would effectively mitigate or prevent their occurrence. In other words, in devising a sustainable solution one must recognize the undeniable fact that—in our interconnected world—one's security and long-term prosperity can no longer be attained at the expense of the insecurity and hardship of the other. Yet again, in the context of the latest crisis in Gaza, it could be shown that the United States has been actively undermining this view in favor of a policy predicated upon the belief that killing, maiming, starving and humiliating an entire nation is somehow susceptible of producing a new reality that would last indefinitely.

The presence of this "zero-sum" belief can be detected in Israeli and American officials' stated goal of "eradicating Hamas" while completely omitting to address the underlying root cause of the problem—i.e. the Israeli occupation—or the profound causes that may have motivated a frustrated segment of the Palestinian society to prioritize armed struggle over any other solution. This shortsighted egocentric belief can also be perceived in the genocidal and often dehumanizing statements made by Israeli officials with regard to the people of Gaza,[19] as well as in Netanyahu's proud admission that

---

19 Israeli officials' statements indicating an intention to commit genocide have been meticulously documented by South Africa in its 29 December 2023 *Application instituting proceedings and request for the indication of provisional measures (South Africa v. Israel)* before the ICJ.

See: https://www.icj-cij.org/sites/default/files/case-related/192/192-20231228-app-01-00-en.pdf

he actively has prevented the establishment of a Palestinian State since the conclusion of the 1991 Oslo Accords despite Israel's commitments.[20]

This myopic conviction is also—one could argue—what may have motivated the United States to singlehandedly veto the State of Palestine's request for full membership at the UN, despite its overwhelming support by the international community. In this instance too, the United States deliberately undermined multilateral diplomacy, reiterating once again the old mantra that its negative vote "[did] not reflect opposition to Palestinian statehood, but instead [was] an acknowledgment that it will only come from direct negotiations between the parties."[21]

Adaptability

The ability to respond to "changing dynamics" is a crucial component of successful multilateral diplomacy. In fact, one of the best qualities of a negotiating partner is his/her ability to understand nuances, recognize changing circumstances, select the proper tools and find creative solutions adapted to the evolving situation. Evidently, this quality cannot be exerted when an influential superpower deliberately and artificially crystalizes the diplomatic process at its desired point by arbitrarily stigmatizing rival stakeholders as "terrorists" and attributing all their motives and actions to their so-called "intrinsic evil nature." Of course, this predetermined conclusion practically prevents the indispensable recognition that the *status quo* can no longer be maintained and that there exists, indeed, an imperative need to proactively search for new solutions. Nothing in the U.S. positioning since October 7, 2023, indicates that it is predisposed to give any credence to such recognition. In fact, neither the events of October 7, nor the genocide that ensued, nor even the massive global mobilization against Israel—which has even spilled over onto American streets and universities—seem to have brought Washington decisionmakers to the realization that "They're not in Kansas anymore."

On the contrary, their proclivity to double down on supporting Israel, their willingness to torpedo any prospect of progress through multilateral diplomacy, their tendency to even aid and abet genocide, along with their unprecedented—and arguably unconstitutional—legislative measures initiated on the domestic front to practically criminalize criticism of Israel in

---

20 See: "Netanyahu boasts of thwarting the establishment of a Palestinian state 'for decades'," *Times of Israel,* February 20, 2024. https://www.timesofisrael.com/netanyahu-boasts-of-thwarting-the-establishment-of-a-palestinian-state-for-decades/

21 See: United Nations, "US vetoes Palestine's request for full UN membership," April 18, 2024. https://news.un.org/en/story/2024/04/1148731

America,[22] all point to the fact that the United States is more concerned with shaping the new regional order to the benefit of Israel *as planned* rather than adapt its approach to the new realities on the ground.

Possible Solutions

Assessing the United States' record since October 7, it seems evident that a substantial portion of Washington's political leadership has aligned with Israel's genocidal policy, viewing it as a viable deterrent tactic, a permanent solution to the Palestinian question and even a costly precondition to outsourcing regional security to Israel through normalization as a prerequisite for the U.S. pivot to Asia strategy. Given this context, from now on, regional stakeholders—along with conscientious members of the Global South, like South Africa—have no other viable alternative than to circumvent Washington and directly assume responsibility for collectively tackling Israel's present and future genocidal behavior, and the underlying cause of the Palestinian issue, namely, the occupation.

In doing so, regional actors must formulate a holistic strategy and accordingly devise a comprehensive plan of action that would involve mobilizing regional organizations, leveraging existing mechanisms, exploring potentials within international bodies where the United States wields lesser influence, devising democratic ways to permanently safeguard Palestinians' status against the Israeli ethnocracy, and collectively initiating a range of political and legal initiatives aimed at fundamentally addressing the issue. In this context, it would be imperative for Arab states to earnestly commit to the plan and adhere to it practically, consistently and credibly. This entails not only initially embracing the plan but also maintaining a coherent and credible approach to its implementation over time. In other words, it requires them to "put their money where their mouth is."

Indeed, by collaborating together, regional countries can exert significant influence on the protracted issue of Palestine. On the political front, a first step would be for Arab countries to realize that resuming the "normalization process" with Israel—which has added to its already abysmal record "the genocide against the Palestinian people"—cannot be considered, by any metrics, a wise policy. In fact, Arab states that still insist on normalizing relations with Israel have—like other members of the international community—a duty under the 1948 Genocide Convention to take measures to *prevent* genocide, not to *reward* genocide through normalization of relations with the perpetrators. As developed by the jurisprudence of the ICJ in the landmark case of *Bosnia v. Serbia* in 2007, States Parties to the Genocide Convention are

---

22 See H.R. 6090, Antisemitism Awareness Act of 2023.

obliged to "employ all means reasonably available to them, so as to prevent genocide so far as possible."[23] Evidently, this obligation to "prevent genocide so far as possible" can hardly be reconciled with the normalization process undertaken by some Arab countries *in the midst of a genocide*, especially considering that most of them acknowledged its occurrence by formally supporting South Africa's position in its application against Israel at the ICJ. In fact, in an official statement issued on December 30, 2023 in support of South Africa's application, the Organization of Islamic Cooperation, which includes Saudi Arabia, UAE and Bahrain, stated that: "The OIC affirms that the indiscriminate targeting by Israel, the occupying power, of the civilian population and the thousands of Palestinians, mostly women and children, killed, injured, forcibly displaced, and denied basic necessities and humanitarian assistance and the destruction of houses, health, educational and religious institutions, in their totality constitute ***mass genocide***"[24] [Emphasis added] This statement raises serious questions about the lawfulness—not to mention the rationale—of the normalization/appeasement process some Arab countries subsequently engaged in relations to the perpetrators of this "mass genocide."

Apart from specific political actions, like halting the normalization process, regional actors might also explore legal avenues to impose costly restrictions on Israel. They could, for instance, start by collectively divesting from companies tied to Israel and adopt national and multilateral sanctions on critical sectors of the Israeli economy. So far, occasional hortatory calls by the Organization of Islamic Cooperation or similar organizations on their members to impose sanctions on Israel have either been neglected or not implemented in a serious manner—often due to considerations related to the prospect of perhaps misperceived benefits to be accrued from normalizing

───────────────

23 *Case Concerning Application of the Convention on the Prevention and Punishment of the Crime of Genocide (Bosnia and Herzegovina v. Serbia and Montenegro)*, 2007 ICJ Rep. 43, para. 430.

24 In a statement issued on 30/12/2023 the Organization of Islamic Cooperation, which includes Saudi Arabia, UAE and Bahrain, declared that "The Organization of Islamic Cooperation (OIC) welcomed the suit filed by the Republic of South Africa at the International Court of Justice for the crime of genocide against the Palestinian people committed by Israel, the occupying power. The OIC has affirmed that the indiscriminate targeting by Israel, the occupying power, of the civilian population and the thousands of Palestinians, mostly women and children, killed, injured, forcibly displaced, and denied basic necessities and humanitarian assistance and the destruction of houses, health, educational and religious institutions, in their totality constitute mass genocide."

See: "OIC Welcomes South Africa's International Court of Justice Suit against Israel Over Genocide," Organization of Islamic Cooperation, December 30, 2023. https://www.oic-oci.org/topic/?t_id=40161&t_ref=26840&lan=en

relations with Israel. In order to produce tangible results, regional countries need to find in themselves the audacity to take decisions on real measures that do not contain within themselves the underlying idea of somehow appeasing the perpetrators of genocide.

In the same vein, regional countries can—in application of Article 4 of the 1948 Genocide Convention which provides that *"Persons committing genocide or any of the other acts enumerated in article III shall be punished, whether they are constitutionally responsible rulers, public officials or private individuals"*—collaborate on taking the necessary coordinated measures to launch criminal proceedings against designated Israeli officials. In doing so, these countries could take measures relying on a "joint list of designated individuals" who would be subject to prosecution upon apprehension—and indicate their willingness to indeed apprehend them on their territories, if successfully prosecuted.

On the international level, regional countries and organizations can also unite as an influential and resolute block to harness the full potential of the UN General Assembly, in view of *inter alia* reviving dormant mechanisms and reinstating rescinded resolutions that could be applied to the case of Israel. One such mechanism is the "UN Special Committee against Apartheid" that was established in 1962 by General Assembly resolution 1761, and later dissolved with the end of the South African apartheid regime in 1994. The Special Committee was mandated to "keep the racial policies of the Government of South Africa under review when the Assembly is not in session" and to "report either to the Assembly or to the Security Council or to both, as may be appropriate, from time to time."[25] It also requested Member States "[to] do everything in their power to help the Special Committee to accomplish its task" and to "refrain from any act likely to delay or hinder the implementation of the present resolution."[26] In addition to its mandated mission, the Special Committee also provided the international community with a solid framework that facilitated the progress of global campaigns against apartheid while greatly contributing to raising awareness among public opinion of the injustice of the South African regime. It could be argued that regional states and organizations opposing Israel's crimes could seek recourse to the UN General Assembly to reconstitute this Special Committee, tailoring it to address the new manifestation of Apartheid in Israel through a new resolution.

Furthermore, regional states and organizations can also act in concert to restore the General Assembly's 1975 resolution determining "Zionism

---

25 A/RES/1761(XVII) [Paragraph 5].
26 Ibid., paragraph 5(b) and 5(c).

as a form of racism and racial discrimination,"[27] which was controversially revoked in 1991 under the pressure of the George H. W. Bush administration, purportedly as a precondition to holding the Oslo conference with the participation of the Palestinian Liberation Organization (PLO). The Oslo agreements were never implemented by Israel and were instead used as a means to advance Israel's objectives of gradually colonizing further Palestinian territories, turning remaining enclaves into new "Bantustans" while consolidating the apartheid system rather than serving as a blueprint for the creation of a Palestinian state or ensuring the Palestinian people's right to self-determination.

In the context of exploring the UN General Assembly's potentiality, another collective initiative by this "regional coalition" could be to reform and improve the current UN procedural practice pertaining to the Security Council's reporting obligation to the UNGA. Article 24 (3) of the Charter stipulates that the "*Security Council shall submit annual and, when necessary, special reports to the General Assembly for its consideration.*" This reporting obligation is corollary to the fact that the Security Council's responsibility was *conferred to it* by the "Charter" (as opposed to "individual members") of the United Nations, to whose Plenary organ it logically became accountable.[28] In this context, the General Assembly serves as the appropriate institutional framework that encompasses all Member-States and thus is the rightful recipient of the Council's reports. It should ensue from this dynamic that the Security Council's reporting obligation should not be viewed as merely a pointless formality but rather as a formal act that effectively subjects the Council's performance to the appraisal of the General Assembly. With this in mind, it seems necessary for regional states and organizations opposing Israel's crimes to collectively impel the General Assembly toward demanding justification for the decisions made at the Security Council, including on those pertaining to the commission of genocide. The proactive involvement of the General Assembly in evaluating the Security Council's performance— which could take the form of a formal response through a resolution—would increase for permanent member of the Council, namely for the United States, the cost of unjustifiably wielding their veto power to obstruct the prevention of atrocity crimes. In the same vein, regional states and organizations may also lend their support to extra-regional countries—such as South Africa, Nicaragua, or Bolivia—that have either taken legal initiatives against Israel,

---

27 A/Res/3379(XXX).

28 Bruno Simma, Daniel-Erasmus Khan, Georg Nolte, Andreas Paulus, and Nikolai Wessendorf (Eds.), *The Charter of the United Nations (3rd Edition): A Commentary, Volume II* (Oxford, England: Oxford University Press, 2012). 1669.

submitted draft resolutions to UN bodies or severed diplomatic relations with Israel following its genocide campaign in Gaza.

In sum, not only could these collective measures leave a real impact on the international scene but, just as importantly, it would convey to populations throughout the region that their governments have at least as much claim to trying to protect Palestinians as American students being brutalized for protesting the Israeli genocide.

Complicity in Genocide

Alfred de Zayas

CIVILIZATION is a process that progressively codifies rules for living together in peace. The United Nations Charter is precisely that law-based international order that should be implemented by all States as a kind of world constitution. Civilization means the rule of law, due process, transparency, accountability, justice, reparation, reconciliation. The survival of mankind depends on cooperation and international solidarity, based on the conviction that we all share the same human dignity, as we share this one planet Earth. With good will and good faith conflicts can be prevented, and grievances can be addressed and resolved.

The UN Charter and civilization itself are under mortal attack by what I would call an open *rebellion* against international law and morals. Provocations, aggressions, escalations, wars culminating in crimes against humanity and genocide as defined in the 1948 Genocide Convention[1] are destroying the fabric of the domestic and international rule of law that humanity has woven and interwoven over the centuries. The deliberate murder of tens of thousands of innocent civilians by Israel in Gaza, the brazen disregard of Security Council and General Assembly Resolutions as well as orders of the International Court of Justice manifest the general breakdown of international morals.

---

1 United Nations, Office of the High Commissioner for Human Rights, *Convention on the Prevention and Punishment of the Crime of Genocide,* General Assembly resolution 260 A (III), adopted Dec. 8, 1948. https://www.ohchr.org/en/instruments-mechanisms/instruments/convention-prevention-and-punishment-crime-genocide

Alfred de Zayas is a former UN Independent Expert on International Order (2012–18), Fulbright Scholar, senior lawyer with the Office of the UN High Commissioner for Human Rights and Secretary of the Human Rights Committee. A U.S. and Swiss citizen, Zayas is author of 12 books and currently teaches at the Geneva School of Diplomacy. He holds a J.D. (Harvard), a doctorate in modern history (Göttingen), and has been visiting professor in the U.S., Canada, Germany and Spain.

This *revolt* against law and justice is further evidenced by the complicity of a number of powerful Western States engaged in aiding and abetting the genocide, not only by delivering lethal weapons used in the genocide, but also by providing political, economic, diplomatic, and academic support to the perpetrators. Some of these accomplices in crime, notably the United States, Germany and the United Kingdom, have heightened their responsibility by endorsing Israel's crimes before the United Nations, blocking effective action by the Security Council, and attempting to negate or banalize the genocide.

Some prominent politicians in the U.S., Germany and UK have engaged in "incitement" to hatred[2] against the Palestinian people, entailing further violations of the 1948 Genocide Convention. This reckless incitement has been echoed and endorsed by many newspapers and media outlets that have thereby become complicit in genocide by contributing to the "culture of hatred" that renders genocide and crimes against humanity possible.

Complicity in the murder of an individual is a grave criminal offence. The legislation of all civilized countries codifies the crime and provides for investigation and prosecution. Facilitating the commission of mass murder, however, is not always perceived the same way. The enablers of crimes against humanity and genocide—the military-industrial complex, the members of the boards of directors of corporations like Lockheed/Martin, Boeing, Raytheon, Northrop Grumman, General Dynamics and other war-profiteers that earn billions from armed conflict[3]—are not always perceived as felons. Their actions are seen as a form of "doing business" and, if at all, perceived as "white collar crimes."

---

2 Tim Hains, "Sen. Lindsey Graham: It Was OK For America To Nuke Hiroshima, So Israel Can 'Do Whatever You Have To Do,'" *RealClear Politics,* May 12, 2024. https://www.realclearpolitics.com/video/2024/05/12/lindsey_graham_it_was_ok_for_america_to_nuke_hiroshima_so_israel_can_do_whatever_you_have_to_do.html

Amanda Yen, "Sen. Lindsey Graham Suggests Nuking Gaza, Calls Hiroshima 'the Right Decision,'" *Daily Beast,* May 12, 2024. https://www.thedailybeast.com/sen-lindsey-graham-suggests-nuking-gaza-calls-hiroshima-the-right-decision

NBC News, "Nikki Haley Tells Israel to 'Finish' Hamas," *New York Times,* November 9, 2023. https://www.nytimes.com/video/us/politics/100000009173179/haley-hamas-israel.html

Patrick Wintour and Alexandra Topping, "David Cameron urges BBC to describe Hamas as terrorist organisation," *The Guardian,* May 12, 2024. https://www.theguardian.com/world/article/2024/may/12/david-cameron-bbc-hamas-terrorist-group-hostage

3 Martin Armstrong, "The World's Largest Arms-Producing Companies," *Statista,* Dec. 5, 2022. https://www.statista.com/chart/12221/the-worlds-biggest-arms-companies/

Article III e of the 1948 Genocide Convention lists "complicity" as one of the prohibited crimes, precisely because complicity frustrates prevention and facilitates the execution of the crime.[4] Professor William Schabas elaborates:

> Article III lists four additional categories of the crime of genocide in addition to perpetration as such. One of these, complicity, is virtually implied in the concept of perpetration and derives from general principles of criminal law. The other three are incomplete or inchoate offences, in effect preliminary acts committed even where genocide itself does not take place. They enhance the preventive dimension of the Convention. The most controversial, "direct and public incitement," is restricted by two adjectives so as to limit conflicts with the protection of freedom of expression.[5]

Complicity may entail military, political, diplomatic, economic, propagandistic, and/or academic support, including the misuse[6] of the veto power in the UN Security Council, e.g. when the veto frustrates the adoption of resolutions aimed e.g. at imposing an arms embargo or enforcing a cease fire.[7] The frequent use of the veto by the United States to shield Israel from censure by the United Nations constitutes a flagrant abuse of the veto power, and in this case has facilitated the continuation of the ongoing genocide in Gaza. Abusing the veto power repeatedly aggravates the crime of complicity further, raising the issue of "conspiracy to commit genocide" pursuant to article III b of the Convention.

The International Court of Justice can make rulings against States concerning State responsibility for genocide and complicity in genocide, as

---

4 Grant Dawson and Rachel Boynton, "Reconciling Complicity in Genocide and Aiding and Abetting Genocide in the Jurisprudence of the United Nations *Ad Hoc* Tribunals," Harvard Human Rights Journal 21 (2008): 241–79. https://journals.law. harvard.edu/hrj/wp-content/uploads/sites/83/2020/06/21.2HHRJ241-Dawson.pdf

See also Schabas, *Genocide in International Law,* 2nd Ed. (Cambridge, England: Cambridge University Press), 2009.

5 William A. Schabas, "Convention for the Prevention and Punishment of the Crime of Genocide," United Nations Audiovisual Library of International Law. https://legal.un.org/avl/pdf/ha/cppcg/cppcg_e.pdf

6 UN Charter, Article 27.

7 Michele Kelemeh and Alex Leff, "The U.S. has vetoed a Gaza cease-fire resolution in the U.N. Security Council," *NPR,* December 8, 2023. https://www.npr. org/2023/12/08/1218332312/israel-hamas-war-us-ceasefire-veto-un

Farnaz Fassihi, Cassandra Vinograd and Thomas Fuller, "U.S. Vetoes Security Council Cease-Fire Resolution," *New York Times,* February 20, 2024. https://www. nytimes.com/2024/02/20/world/middleeast/us-vetoes-ceasefire-resolution.html

well as fix the level of reparation owed to the victims and their survivors. The International Law Commission's Draft Code on Responsibility of State stipulates in its article 16:

> A State which aids or assists another State in the commission of an internationally wrongful act by the latter is internationally responsible for doing so if: (a) that State does so with knowledge of the circumstances of the internationally wrongful act; and (b) the act would be internationally wrongful if committed by that State.[8]

Whereas the ICJ exercises jurisdiction over States, the International Criminal Court, (as its predecessors, the *ad hoc* Tribunals established by Security Council Resolution—the International Criminal Tribunal for the Former Yugoslavia (ICTY) and the International Criminal Tribunal for Rwanda (ICTR)), has jurisdiction over individuals. Moreover, not only governments and government officials, but also officials of intergovernmental organizations like the European Union[9], and private persons can be found guilty of genocide, complicity or conspiracy to commit genocide. The ICTY and ICTR have relevant jurisprudence on the subject.[10]

Article 25 para. 3 of the Rome Statute (Individual criminal responsibility) provides for the criminal responsibility for complicity of those "aiding and abetting or otherwise assisting" the commission of crimes covered by the jurisdiction of the Court, in the following terms: "In accordance with this Statute, a person shall be criminally responsible and liable for punishment for a crime within the jurisdiction of the Court if that person:... (c) ... aids, abets or otherwise assists in its commission or its attempted commission, including providing the means for its commission."

---

8 United Nations, *Responsibility of States for Internationally Wrongful Acts,* 2001. https://legal.un.org/ilc/texts/instruments/english/draft_articles/9_6_2001.pdf

9 Geneva International Peace Research Institute, "Open Letter to the EU Leadership Demanding an Immediate Ceasefire in Gaza," March 15, 2024, reprinted in *Counterpunch,* March 18, 2024. https://www.counterpunch.org/2024/03/18/open-letter-to-the-eu-leadership-demanding-an-immediate-ceasefire-in-gaza/

Geneva International Peace Research Institute, "Follow-Up to an Open-Letter Demanding Accountability From the EU Leadership for Complicity in Genocide," *Counterpunch,* March 25, 2024. https://www.counterpunch.org/2024/03/25/follow-up-to-an-open-letter-demanding-accountability-from-the-eu-leadership-for-complicity-in-genocide/

10 United Nations | International Residual Mechanism for Criminal Tribunal, Case Law Database. https://cld.irmct.org/

The terms "aiding and abetting" in the context of the ICC are not inter-changeable: the wording of Article 25(3)(c) of the ICC Statute indicates that each of them has its own meaning.[11] More specifically, "aiding" refers to the provision of practical or material assistance to the commission of a crime, while "abetting" denotes the provision of encouragement or moral support to the commission of a crime. Aiding and abetting is therefore an accessorial mode of liability where the accused is alleged to have facilitated the com-mission (or, at least, the attempted commission) of crimes by others (i.e. the principals).[12]

The wording of Article 25(3)(c) also makes clear that aiding and abet-ting are just two ways of other possible forms of "assistance," the latter thus serving as a sort of umbrella term. Thus, "providing the means" for the commission of a crime is merely a special example of assistance. As far as the material element (*actus reus*) is concerned, the following elements of "aiding and abetting" liability, as per Article 25(3)(c) of the ICC Statute, and in light of the jurisprudence of *ad hoc* and hybrid international criminal tribunals, are well established: the *actus reus* can occur before, during or after the crime in question is committed;[13] the location of where the *actus reus* takes place can be remote from the time and location of where the crime in question is committed; the accused need not have been personally present during the commission of the crime.[14]

According to Article 25(3)(c) of the ICC Statute, the attempted commis-sion of a crime is sufficient for the "aiding and abetting" liability to arise, i.e. there is no need for the crime in question to have been fully carried out or completed. The underlying rationale is that complicity by assistance is, like instigation, a form of accessorial liability in relation to the principal crime; this means that it must assist the accomplishment (or at least the attempt) of a crime. It has been considered sufficient for " the person [to] provide[] assistance to the commission of a crime" without stipulating the requisite level of contribution to the crimes, or fixing any specific threshold.[15]

---

11 Albin Eser, "Individual Criminal Responsibility," in Antonio Cassese, Paola Gaeta, and John RWD Jones, eds., *The Rome Statute of the International Criminal Court: A Commentary,* Vol. I (Oxford: Oxford University Press, 2002), 798.

12 Manuel J. Ventura, "Aiding and Abetting," in Jérôme de Hemptinne, Robert Roth, and Elies van Sliedregt, et al., eds., *Modes of Liability in International Criminal Law* (Cambridge, England: Cambridge University Press, 2019), 173–256, para. 2.

13 See, e.g., ICTY, Blaškić, Appeals Chamber Judgment, IT-95-14-A, July 29, 2004, para. 48.

14 See, e.g., SCSL, Taylor, Appeals Chamber Judgment, SCSL-03-01-A, September 26, 2013, para. 370.

15 ICC, Blé Goudé, Confirmation of Charges Decision, ICC-02/11-02/11-186, December 11, 2014, para. 167. 45 ICC, Bemba et al., Trial Chamber Judgment,

According to well-established precedent, numerous U.S., UK, and EU politicians and diplomats could be indicted by the International Criminal Court, since article 27 of the Statute of Rome discards the concept of functional immunities, stipulating:

1. This Statute shall apply equally to all persons without any distinction based on official capacity. In particular, official capacity as a Head of State or Government, a member of a Government or parliament, an elected representative or a government official shall in no case exempt a person from criminal responsibility under this Statute, nor shall it, in and of itself, constitute a ground for reduction of sentence.

2. Immunities or special procedural rules which may attach to the official capacity of a person, whether under national or international law, shall not bar the Court from exercising its jurisdiction over such a person. [16]

Such immunities had already been discarded by the International Military Tribunal for Nuremberg, and in Article 7(1) of the Statute of the ICTY and article 6(1) of the stature of the ICTR.

Certainly, the sale of lethal weapons to a country that is committing genocide constitutes complicity in genocide, and a violation of article 6(3) of the 2014 Arms Trade Treaty, which stipulates:

A State Party shall not authorize any transfer of conventional arms covered under Article 2 (1) or of items covered under Article 3 or Article 4, if it has knowledge at the time of authorization that the arms or items would be used in the commission of genocide, crimes against humanity, grave breaches of the Geneva Conventions of 1949, attacks directed against civilian objects or civilians protected as such, or other war crimes as defined by international agreements to which it is a Party. [17]

ICC-01/05-01/13-1989-Red, October 19, 2016, para 93.

16 *Rome Statute of the International Criminal Court* (The Hague, The Netherlands: International Criminal Court, 2021). https://www.icc-cpi.int/sites/default/files/Publications/Rome-Statute.pdf

17 United Nations, *The Arms Trade Treaty,* 2013. https://thearmstradetreaty.org/hyper-images/file/ATT_English/ATT_English.pdf?templateId=137253

Human Rights Now, "HRN signs on to a statement with over 130 other organizations: 'Ending complicity in international crimes: A two-way arms embargo on Israel'," November 16, 2023. https://hrn.or.jp/eng/news/2023/11/16/israel-embargo-statement/

The sale of chemical agents which could be used in armed conflict would also entail a violation of the Chemical Weapons Convention.[18] There are reports of Israel using chemical weapons[19] against the civilian population of Gaza, and not all of these weapons were produced in Israel. Accordingly, corporate board members and other persons engaged in the arms trade could be indicted by the International Criminal Court for violations of articles 6, 7 and 8 of the Statute of Rome.

In this context it is worth noting the Resolution adopted by the Human Rights Council calling for an arms embargo against Israel.[20] On 5 April 2024 the Human Rights Council

> demanded that Israel, the occupying power, end its occupation of the Palestinian territory occupied since 1967, including East Jerusalem. The Council also demanded that Israel immediately lift its blockade on the Gaza Strip and all other forms of collective punishment, and called for an immediate ceasefire in Gaza. The Council called upon all States to take immediate action to prevent the continued forcible transfer of Palestinians within or from Gaza. It called upon all States to cease the sale, transfer and diversion of arms, munitions and other military equipment to Israel and requested the Independent International Commission of Inquiry on the occupied Palestinian territory, including East Jerusalem, and Israel to report on both the direct and indirect transfer or sale of arms, munitions, parts, components and dual use items to Israel, the occupying power, and to present its report to the Council at its fifty-ninth session.[21]

---

18 *Chemical Weapons Convention,* Organisation for the Prohibition of Chemical Weapons, June 7, 2020. https://www.opcw.org/chemical-weapons-convention

19 Alex Kasprak, "Do Photos and Video Confirm Israel Used White Phosphorus Munitions Over Gaza Seaport?," *Snopes,* October 13, 2023. https://www.snopes.com/news/2023/10/13/idf-white-phosphorus-oct-2023/

Areesha Lodhi, "What is the white phosphorus that Israel is accused of using in Gaza?," *Al Jazeera,* October 13, 2023. https://www.aljazeera.com/news/2023/10/13/what-is-the-white-phosphorus-that-israel-is-accused-of-using-on-gaza

"Questions and Answers on Israel's Use of White Phosphorus in Gaza and Lebanon," Human Rights Watch, October 12, 2023. https://www.hrw.org/news/2023/10/12/questions-and-answers-israels-use-white-phosphorus-gaza-and-lebanon

20 United Nations, "Gaza: Human Rights Council resolution urges arms embargo on Israel," UN News, April 5, 2024. https://news.un.org/en/story/2024/04/1148261

21 United Nations, Office of the High Commissioner for Human Rights, "Human Rights Council Adopts Five Resolutions, including a Text Calling for an Immediate Ceasefire in Gaza, Urging States to Prevent the Continued Forcible Transfer of Palestinians Within or From Gaza, and Calling on States to Cease the Sale or Transfer

Which States are complicit in the ongoing genocide in Gaza? Surely the United States, Germany, Canada, United Kingdom, France and all countries that have delivered the weapons used in perpetrating the genocide.

On 1 March 2024 Nicaragua instituted proceedings against Germany[22] before the International Court of Justice, charging Germany with complicity in the genocide of the Gaza populations. Oral hearings were held at the Peace Palace on 8 and 9 April 2024.[23] In its order of 30 April 2024, the ICJ did not issue the provisional measures of protection requested, but also rejected Germany's request that the case be struck from the list. The Court ruled:

> 20. Based on the factual information and legal arguments presented by the Parties, the Court concludes that, at present, the circumstances are not such as to require the exercise of its power under Article 41 of the Statute to indicate provisional measures.
>
> 21. As to Germany's request that the case be removed from the List ..., the Court notes that, as it has held in the past, where there is a manifest lack of jurisdiction, it can remove the case from the List at the provisional measures stage (Legality of Use of Force (Yugoslavia v. Spain), Provisional Measures, Order of 2 June 1999, I.C.J. Reports 1999 (II), p. 773, para. 35; Legality of Use of Force (Yugoslavia v. United States of America), Provisional Measures, Order of 2 June 1999, I.C.J. Reports 1999 (II), p. 925, para. 29; Immunities and Criminal Proceedings (Equatorial Guinea v. France), Provisional Measures, Order of 7 December 2016, I.C.J. Reports 2016 (II), p. 1165, para. 70). Conversely, where there is no such manifest lack of jurisdiction, the Court cannot remove the case at that stage (Armed Activities on the Territory of the Congo (New Application: 2002) (Democratic Republic of the Congo v. Rwanda), Provisional Measures, Order of 10 July 2002, I.C.J. Reports 2002, p. 249, para. 91; Immunities and Criminal Proceedings (Equatorial Guinea v. France), Provisional Measures, Order of 7 December 2016, I.C.J. Reports 2016 (II), p. 1165, para.

---

of Arms to Israel," April 5, 2024. https://www.ohchr.org/en/press-releases/2024/04/le-conseil-adopte-cinq-resolutions-dont-celle-demandant-quun-cessez-le-feu

22 International Court of Justice, *Alleged Breaches of Certain International Obligations in respect of the Occupied Palestinian Territory (Nicaragua v. Germany)* – Latest Developments. https://www.icj-cij.org/case/193

23 International Court of Justice, *Alleged Breaches of Certain International Obligations in respect of the Occupied Palestinian Territory (Nicaragua v. Germany)* – Oral Proceedings. https://www.icj-cij.org/case/193/oral-proceedings

70). In the present case, there being no manifest lack of jurisdiction, the Court cannot accede to Germany's request.

22. The Court recalls that, in its Order of 26 January 2024, it noted that the military operation conducted by Israel following the attack of 7 October 2023 had resulted in "a large number of deaths and injuries, as well as the massive destruction of homes, the forcible displacement of the vast majority of the population, and extensive damage to civilian infrastructure" (Application of the Convention on the Prevention and Punishment of the Crime of Genocide in the Gaza Strip (South Africa v. Israel), Provisional Measures, Order of 26 January 2024, para. 46). In addition, the Court remains deeply concerned about the catastrophic living conditions of the Palestinians in the Gaza Strip, in particular in view of the prolonged and widespread deprivation of food and other basic necessities to which they have been subjected, as acknowledged by the Court in its Order of 28 March 2024 (Application of the Convention on the Prevention and Punishment of the Crime of Genocide in the Gaza Strip (South Africa v. Israel), Provisional Measures, Order of 28 March 2024, para. 18).

23. The Court recalls that, pursuant to common Article 1 of the Geneva Conventions, all States parties are under an obligation "to respect and to ensure respect" for the Conventions "in all circumstances." It follows from that provision that every State party to these Conventions, "whether or not it is a party to a specific conflict, is under an obligation to ensure that the requirements of the instruments in question are complied with."[24] Such an obligation "does not derive only from the Conventions themselves, but from the general principles of humanitarian law to which the Conventions merely give specific expression."[25] With regard to the Genocide Convention, the Court has had the opportunity to observe that the obligation to prevent the commission of the crime of genocide, pursuant to Article I, requires States parties that are aware, or that should normally have been aware, of the serious risk that acts of genocide would have been committed, to employ all means reasonably available to them to prevent genocide so far

---

24 International Court of Justice, *Legal Consequences of the Construction of a Wall in the Occupied Palestinian Territory* – Advisory Opinion, I.C.J. Reports 2004 (I), 199–200, para. 158.

25 International Court of Justice, *Military and Paramilitary Activities in and against Nicaragua (Nicaragua v. United States of America)* – Merits, Judgment, I.C.J. Reports 1986, 114, para. 220.

as possible[26]. Further, States parties are bound by the Genocide Convention not to commit any other acts enumerated in Article III.[27]

24. Moreover, the Court considers it particularly important to remind all States of their international obligations relating to the transfer of arms to parties to an armed conflict, in order to avoid the risk that such arms might be used to violate the above-mentioned Conventions. All these obligations are incumbent upon Germany as a State party to the said Conventions in its supply of arms to Israel.

Personally, I think that the arguments presented by Professor Alain Pellet and Dr. Daniel Müller on behalf of Nicaragua were compelling, and more than sufficient to justify granting the provisional measures requested, *a fortiori* because of the paramount obligation to *prevent* the continuation of the genocide. Personally, I view the decision of the Court as political, not juridical.

Related to the concept of complicity is also the category of "incitement" to commit genocide, which is codified in article III c of the Genocide Convention. The ICTR developed important jurisprudence concerning incitement by some Hutus to commit murder against the Tutsis of Rwanda.[28] Meanwhile, incitement also entails a grave violation of human rights, as it is prohibited in article 20 of the International Covenant on Civil and Political Rights.[29]

---

26 International Court of Justice, *Application of the Convention on the Prevention and Punishment of the Crime of Genocide (Bosnia and Herzegovina v. Serbia and Montenegro)* – Judgment, I.C.J. Reports 2007 (I), 221–22, paras. 430–31.

27 Ibid., 114, para. 168.

28 Angela Hefti and Laura Ausserladscheider Jonas, "From Hate Speech to Incitement of Genocide: The Role of the Media in the Rwandan Genocide," *Boston University International Law Journal* 38, no. 1 (August 2020). https://www.bu.edu/ilj/files/2020/08/Article_HeftiJonas.pdf

Wibke Kristin Timmermann, "Incitement in International Criminal Law," *International Review of the Red Cross* 88, no. 864 (December 2006). https://www.icrc.org/en/doc/assets/files/other/irrc_864_timmermann.pdf

Scott Straus, "What Is the Relationship between Hate Radio and Violence? Rethinking Rwanda's 'Radio Machete'," *Politics & Society* 35, no. 4 (December 2007): 609–637.

29 United Nations, Office of the High Commissioner for Human Rights, International Covenant on Civil and Political Rights, Core Instrument adopted December 16, 1966, by General Assembly resolution 2200A (XXI). https://www.ohchr.org/en/instruments-mechanisms/instruments/international-covenant-civil-and-political-rights

Also related with the concepts of complicity and incitement is the concept of banalization of the crime, that is, the effort to justify or to whitewash genocide. States should adopt rigorously worded legislation aimed at curbing negationism and the effort to ennoble or justify the crime of genocide by confusing it with legitimate "self-defense,"[30] and by completely ignoring the principle of proportionality mandated in international humanitarian law.[31]

Prevention

The cardinal principle of the 1948 Genocide Convention is the obligation to prevent genocide, to adopt all necessary measures well ahead of the unfolding of the tragedy. Some academics like to forget the "prevention" aspect of the Genocide Convention and prefer to focus on punishment. Yet, no one has ever established that deterrence actually works when it comes to geopolitical crimes. Besides, punishment is always *ex post facto* and does not bring the victims of genocide back to life or provide adequate remedies to the survivors.[32]

The International Court of Justice made the point in its judgment of 27 February 2007 in *Bosnia v. Serbia and Montenegro*:[33]

> Has the respondent State complied with its obligations to prevent and punish genocide under Article I of the Convention? Despite the clear links between the duty to prevent genocide and the duty to punish its perpetrators, these are, in the view of the Court, two distinct yet connected obligations, each of which must be considered in turn.

---

30 Marjorie Cohn, "Israel Isn't Entitled to 'Self-Defense' Against the People Under Its Occupation," *Truthout*, May 14, 2021. https://truthout.org/articles/as-an-occupier-israel-isnt-entitled-to-self-defense-under-international-law/

Ralph Wilde, "Israel's War in Gaza is Not a Valid Act of Self-defence in International Law," *OpinioJuris*, November 9, 2023. https://opiniojuris.org/2023/11/09/israels-war-in-gaza-is-not-a-valid-act-of-self-defence-in-international-law/

31 Fareed Zakaria, "Israel's war in Gaza isn't genocide, but is it proportionate?," *Washington Post*, January 12, 2024. https://www.washingtonpost.com/opinions/2024/01/12/israel-gaza-hamas-genocide-netanyahu-response/

"IGH fällt erstes Urteil: Deutschland darf Israel Waffen liefern," *Frankfurter Rundschau*, May 1, 2024. https://www.fr.de/politik/igh-voelkermord-verfahren-nicaragua-deutschland-waffenlieferungen-israel-strafgerichtshof-urteil-zr-93043643.html

32 Alfred de Zayas, "Reflections on Law and Punishment," *Counterpunch*, March 3, 2022. https://www.counterpunch.org/2022/03/11/reflections-on-law-and-punishment/

33 International Court of Justice, *Application of the Convention on the Prevention and Punishment of the Crime of Genocide (Bosnia and Herzegovina v. Serbia and Montenegro)* – Overview of the Case. https://icj-cij.org/case/91

It is true that, simply by its wording, Article I of the Convention brings out the close link between prevention and punishment: "The Contracting Parties confirm that genocide, whether committed in time of peace or in time of war, is a crime under international law which they undertake to prevent and to punish." It is also true that one of the most effective ways of preventing criminal acts, in general, is to provide penalties for persons committing such acts, and to impose those penalties effectively on those who commit the acts one is trying to prevent. Lastly, it is true that, although in the subsequent Articles, the Convention includes fairly detailed provisions concerning the duty to punish (Articles III to VII), it reverts to the obligation of prevention, stated as a principle in Article I, only in Article VIII: "Any Contracting Party may call upon the competent organs of the United Nations to take such action under the Charter of the United Nations as they consider appropriate for the prevention and suppression of acts of genocide or any of the other acts enumerated in article III."

However, it is not the case that the obligation to prevent has no separate legal existence of its own; that it is, as it were, absorbed by the obligation to punish, which is therefore the only duty the performance of which may be subject to review by the Court. The obligation on each contracting State to prevent genocide is both normative and compelling. It is not merged in the duty to punish, nor can it be regarded as simply a component of that duty. It has its own scope, which extends beyond the particular case envisaged in Article VIII, namely reference to the competent organs of the United Nations, for them to take such action as they deem appropriate. Even if and when these organs have been called upon, this does not mean that the States parties to the Convention are relieved of the obligation to take such action as they can to prevent genocide from occurring, while respecting the United Nations Charter and any decisions that may have been taken by its competent organs. This is the reason why the Court will first consider the manner in which the Respondent has performed its obligation to prevent before examining the situation as regards the obligation to punish. (1) The Obligation to Prevent Genocide 428. As regards the obligation to prevent genocide, the Court thinks it necessary to begin with the following introductory remarks and clarifications, amplifying the observations already made above. 429. First, the Genocide Convention is not the only international

instrument providing for an obligation on the States parties to it
to take certain steps to prevent the acts it seeks to prohibit. Many
other instruments include a similar obligation, in various forms:
see, for example, the Convention against Torture and Other Cruel,
Inhuman or Degrading Treatment or Punishment of 10 December
1984 (Art. 2); the Convention on the Prevention and Punishment
of Crimes against Internationally Protected Persons, Including
Diplomatic Agents, of 14 December 1973 (Art. 4); the Convention
on the Safety of United Nations and Associated Personnel of 9
December 1994 (Art. 11); the International Convention on the
Suppression of Terrorist Bombings of 15 December 1997 (Art.
15). The content of the duty to prevent varies from one instrument
to another, according to the wording of the relevant provisions, and
depending on the nature of the acts to be prevented. The decision
of the Court does not, in this case, purport to establish a general
jurisprudence applicable to all cases where a treaty instrument, or
other binding legal norm, includes an obligation for States to prevent certain acts. Still less does the decision of the Court purport
to find whether, apart from the texts applicable to specific fields,
there is a general obligation on States to prevent the commission
by other persons or entities of acts contrary to certain norms of
general international law. The Court will therefore confine itself
to determining the specific scope of the duty to prevent in the
Genocide Convention, and to the extent that such a determination
is necessary to the decision to be given on the dispute before it.
This will, of course, not absolve it of the need to refer, if need be,
to the rules of law whose scope extends beyond the specific field
covered by the Convention.

Secondly, it is clear that the obligation in question is one of
conduct and not one of result, in the sense that a State cannot be
under an obligation to succeed, whatever the circumstances, in
preventing the commission of genocide: the obligation of States
parties is rather to employ all means reasonably available to them,
so as to prevent genocide so far as possible. A State does not incur
responsibility simply because the desired result is not achieved;
responsibility is however incurred if the State manifestly failed
to take all measures to prevent genocide which were within its
power, and which might have contributed to preventing the genocide. In this area the notion of "due diligence," which calls for an
assessment in concreto, is of critical importance. Various parameters operate when assessing whether a State has duly discharged

the obligation concerned. The first, which varies greatly from one State to another, is clearly the capacity to influence effectively the action of persons likely to commit, or already committing, genocide. This capacity itself depends, among other things, on the geographical distance of the State concerned from the scene of the events, and on the strength of the political links, as well as links of all other kinds, between the authorities of that State and the main actors in the events. The State's capacity to influence must also be assessed by legal criteria, since it is clear that every State may only act within the limits permitted by international law; seen thus, a State's capacity to influence may vary depending on its particular legal position vis-à-vis the situations and persons facing the danger, or the reality, of genocide. On the other hand, it is irrelevant whether the State whose responsibility is in issue claims, or even proves, that even if it had employed all means reasonably at its disposal, they would not have sufficed to prevent the commission of genocide. As well as being generally difficult to prove, this is irrelevant to the breach of the obligation of conduct in question, the more so since the possibility remains that the combined efforts of several States, each complying with its obligation to prevent, might have achieved the result—averting the commission of genocide—which the efforts of only one State were insufficient to produce.

Thirdly, a State can be held responsible for breaching the obligation to prevent genocide only if genocide was actually committed. It is at the time when commission of the prohibited act (genocide or any of the other acts listed in Article III of the Convention) begins that the breach of an obligation of prevention occurs. In this respect, the Court refers to a general rule of the law of State responsibility, stated by the ILC in Article 14, paragraph 3, of its Articles on State Responsibility: "The breach of an international obligation requiring a State to prevent a given event occurs when the event occurs and extends over the entire period during which the event continues and remains not in conformity with that obligation." This obviously does not mean that the obligation to prevent genocide only comes into being when perpetration of genocide commences; that would be absurd, since the whole point of the obligation is to prevent, or attempt to prevent, the occurrence of the act. In fact, a State's obligation to prevent, and the corresponding duty to act, arise at the instant that the State learns of, or should normally have learned of, the existence of a serious risk that genocide will be committed. From that moment onwards, if the State has available to it means likely to have a deterrent effect on those suspected of preparing geno-cide, or reasonably suspected of harbouring specific intent (dolus specialis), it is under a duty to make such use of these means as the circumstances permit."

In its judgment, adopted by twelve votes to three, the ICJ found that Serbia had violated the obligation to prevent genocide under the Convention on the Prevention and Punishment of the Crime of Genocide, in respect of the genocide that occurred in Srebrenica in July 1995.

This precedent is applicable to the ongoing genocide in Gaza and imposes obligations on all countries not to deliver lethal weapons that will be used in the genocide. Moreover, all countries must refrain from aiding and abetting the crime by providing political, economic, diplomatic or other support to Israel.

Conclusion

Twenty-nine years after the crime of Srebrenica in 1995, the United Nations, the ICJ and the ICC have not succeeded in stopping the ongoing genocide in Gaza. This impacts negatively on the authority and credibility of these institutions. What does this mean for the viability of international law, of the 1948 Genocide Convention, of the UN Charter, of the doctrine of Responsibility to Protect,[34] or indeed, of civilization at large?

On the positive side, we note that thirty years after the Rwandan geno-cide of 1994, coexistence between Hutus and Tutsis has become possible. This gives us reason for hope, because the way of mutual forgiveness and reconciliation is better than harbouring endless recriminations and hatred.

Professor Isaie Nzeyimana of the University of Rwanda noted in 2024 that while reconciliation after the genocide appeared an impossible task, with good will and good faith a new *modus vivendi* was crafted, because both Hutus and Tutsis started to imagine what a possible future could look like:

> I would say there's no difference between truth and facts, but rather there's a relation of correspondence between them. Facts are the objective face of truth and likewise, truth are the subjec-tive face of facts. Our country started from this premise: What if reconciliation between Rwandans was possible? Rwandans then

---

34 United Nations Office on Genocide Prevention and the Responsibility to Protect: https://www.un.org/en/genocide-prevention

acting from the assumption that reconciliation was indeed possible shifted the general dynamic. The Rwandan reconciliation is a model to follow because it has enabled Rwandans to understand and close one chapter of their history and begin to write a new one.[35]

By contrast, Amnesty International[36] issued a statement that seems to be focused on punishment rather than reconciliation. This idea of "justice" as being co-terminus with punishment is not only wrong, it is inhuman and unethical. Tigere Chagutah, AI's Regional Director for East and Southern Africa stated: "Justice delayed is justice denied. The confirmed deaths of several of the most-wanted genocide suspects before they could face justice, and the indefinite suspension of the trial of another indictee due to age-related illness, show the importance of maintaining momentum to deliver justice for survivors and relatives of victims in Rwanda."

As former Secretary of the UN Human Rights Committee and former UN Independent Expert, I think otherwise. My experience is that victims want a different kind of "justice." They want peace, truth and respect. The way forward cannot be in endless judicial proceedings, but in a change of mindset. Understanding the root causes of a tragedy is far more important than punishing the one or the other perpetrator. I prefer to endorse the words of UN Secretary General Antonio Guterres spoken 28 years after the Rwandan genocide: *"Rwanda today stands as a powerful testament of the human spirit's ability to heal even the deepest wounds and emerge from the darkest depths to rebuild a stronger society."*[37] [emphasis added]

Let us explore a nearly forgotten historical precedent. It was at the Peace of Westphalia[38] of 1648 that the participating diplomats, exhausted after thirty years of slaughter, finally understood that *Pax optima rerum*: peace is the highest good. Precisely because of this, they insisted on making an effort at living together. Like most wars, the "Thirty Years War" (1618–48) was

---

35 CBC Radio, "Why Rwanda is held up as a model for reconciliation, 26 years after genocide," December 15, 2020. https://www.cbc.ca/radio/ideas/why-rwanda-is-held-up-as-a-model-for-reconciliation-26-years-after-genocide-1.5842139

36 Amnesty International, "Rwanda: 30 years on, justice for genocide crimes more urgent than ever," April 5, 2024. https://www.amnesty.org/en/latest/news/2024/04/rwanda-30-years-on-justice-for-genocide-crimes-more-urgent-than-ever/

37 United Nations, "28 years after the 1994 genocide against the Tutsi in Rwanda, 'stain of shame endures'," *UN News*, April 7, 2022. https://news.un.org/en/story/2022/04/1115792

38 Alfred de Zayas, "Westphalia, Peace of" in Rudolf Bernhardt, ed., *Encyclopedia of Public International Law*, vol. IV (Amsterdam: North-Holland, 2000), 1465–69.

eminently preventable. It is instructive to revisit the text of article 2 of the Treaties of Münster and Osnabrück, which stipulated a general amnesty,[39] instead of providing for the continuation of hostilities by means of penal proceedings to attempt to punish those responsible for the eight million deaths, for the torture and rape of thirty years of conflict. They agreed:

> That there shall be on the one side and the other a perpetual Oblivion, Amnesty, or Pardon of all that has been committed since the beginning of these Troubles, in what place, or what manner soever the Hostilitys have been practis'd, in such a manner, that no body, under any pretext whatsoever, shall practice any Acts of Hostility, entertain any Enmity, or cause any Trouble to each other; neither as to Persons, Effects and Securitys, neither of themselves or by others, neither privately nor openly, neither directly nor indirectly, neither under the colour of Right, nor by the way of Deed, either within or without the extent of the Empire, notwithstanding all Covenants made before to the contrary: That they shall not act, or permit to be acted, any wrong or injury to any whatsoever; but that all that has pass'd on the one side, and the other, as well before as during the War, in Words, Writings, and Outrageous Actions, in Violences, Hostilitys, Damages and Expences, without any respect to Persons or Things, shall be entirely abolish'd in such a manner that all that might be demanded of, or pretended to, by each other on that behalf, shall be bury'd in eternal Oblivion."[40]

Is the future of the Israelis and Palestinians in the court room? Must we have endless criminal proceedings against all the criminals of this and other wars? Why cannot humanity learn the lessons of the post-Apartheid South Africa, the post-genocide Rwanda, the post-Thirty Years War Europe?

For now, we need an immediate ceasefire and honest peace negotiations that will aim at reconstruction and rehabilitation with the help of the United Nations and all of its agencies, including UNRWA. There can be a future in peace for both the Israelis and the Palestinians—however repugnant such a notion may seem at present.

---

39 Alfred de Zayas, "Amnesty Clause," in Rudolf Bernhardt, ed., *Encyclopedia of Public International Law,* vol. I (Amsterdam: North-Holland and Elsevier Science, 1992), 148–51.

40 *Treaty of Westphalia: Peace Treaty between the Holy Roman Emperor and the King of France and their respective Allies,* The Avalon Project, Yale Law School, Lillian Goldman Law Library. https://avalon.law.yale.edu/17th_century/westphal.asp

The Collapse of Diplomacy in the Gaza Genocide

Past Experiences and Current Failures

Ahmet Davutoğlu

FOR OVER A YEAR, a genocide has been ongoing in Gaza, where all values of humanity are trampled upon. Equally alarming is the fact that, during this period, no sustainable ceasefire has been achieved. It is shameful from a humanitarian diplomacy perspective that, aside from the one-week temporary ceasefire aimed at exchanging Israeli hostages with Palestinian prisoners, which lasted from November 24, 2023, to December 1, 2023,[1] there has been no brief ceasefire that would allow Gazan civilians, children, and women to catch their breath. During this period, the vetoing of a ceasefire resolution in the UN Security Council by the United States[2] on November 21, 2024, as well as the rejection of ceasefire proposals[3] or the non-implementation of UN decisions[4] by Israel, primarily demonstrates the significant weakness of the UN system.

---

1 A temporary ceasefire was brokered by Qatar, lasting seven days. During this period, 50 Israeli hostages were released in exchange for 150 Palestinian prisoners, and humanitarian aid was allowed into Gaza.

2 "Despite having secured 14 votes in favour, the draft resolution put forward by the 10 elected members of the Security Council (E10), failed to pass owing to the negative vote by a permanent member, the U.S. The text also reiterated the Council's demand for the immediate and unconditional release of all hostages." https://news.un.org/en/story/2024/11/1157216

3 On May 6, 2024, Hamas accepted a ceasefire proposal mediated by Egypt and Qatar, which included provisions for the exchange of captives and prisoners. However, Israel dismissed the proposal, leading to continued hostilities. Negotiations mediated by the U.S., Egypt, and Qatar aimed to broker a ceasefire in August 2024 was also rejected by Israeli Prime Minister Benjamin Netanyahu.

4 For example, the UN Security Council adopted Resolution 2735 on June 10, 2024, proposing a comprehensive three-phase ceasefire to end the war in Gaza and urging both Israel and Hamas to implement it fully and without delay was not implemented.

History has witnessed many wars; however, in an era that claims to uphold international legal norms, there has never been a war characterized by such inequality among the parties and such complicity among the third parties. Without sincerely and openly discussing why a permanent arrangement to guarantee the most fundamental rights of the Palestinian people has not been established since 1948, or why a ceasefire that could at least temporarily halt a genocide lasting over a year cannot be secured, it is impossible to talk about building a regional and global order.

In this context, the experiences gained from past diplomatic initiatives can offer us significant insights. Perhaps the most accurate assessment of the Middle East issue has been made by UN Secretary-General Antonio Guterres: "It is important to also recognize the attacks by Hamas did not happen in a vacuum. The Palestinian people have been subjected to 56 years of suffocating occupation. They have seen their land steadily devoured by settlements and plagued by violence; their economy stifled; their people displaced, and their homes demolished. Their hopes for a political solution to their plight have been vanishing."[5]

Without addressing the grievances mentioned by the UN Secretary-General, it is impossible to achieve a ceasefire or a lasting peace. Neglecting the past and defining the origins of the problem in a manner convenient for Israel is nothing but an effort to legitimize this genocide. If genuine peace is desired, there is a necessity to assess the ongoing processes honestly and objectively. The missed opportunities of the past, unmet promises, and the international norms applied differently to various actors leading to double standards are the root causes of the humanitarian tragedy experienced today.

In this chapter, I present a framework regarding the main reasons for the failure to achieve a ceasefire in Gaza, based on my experiences in mediating numerous international crises,[6] especially contributing to the ceasefires in the Gaza wars of 2009, 2012, and 2014.

Drawing on our varied mediation experiences across different regions, I can state that the success of international mediation efforts depends on the fulfillment of three main conditions: the ability of the conflicting parties to establish an equal status in a common area of interest through peaceful

5 António Guterres, United Nations Secretary-General, "Secretary-General's remarks to the Security Council – on the Middle East," October 24, 2023. https://www.un.org/sg/en/content/sg/speeches/2023-10-24/secretary-generals-remarks-the-security-council-the-middle-east%C2%A0

6 For my approach to mediation efforts, see Ahmet Davutoğlu, "Turkey's Mediation: Critical Reflections From the Field," *Middle East Policy* 20, no. 1 (Spring 2013): 83–90. https://peacemaker.un.org/sites/peacemaker.un.org/files/TurkeysMediation_Davutoglu_2013.pdf

means, the convergence of regional supporters of the parties within this common area of interest, and the compatibility of global actors' regional interests.

Unfortunately, in the context of the Middle East issue, these three elements have never been realized simultaneously. Considering the diplomatic experiences during the ceasefire efforts of 2009, 2012, and 2014, we can summarize the root causes for the failure to implement effective diplomacy to prevent the genocide in 2023–24 as follows: (i.) the asymmetric disparity in the status of Israel and Palestine; (ii.) the exclusion of Hamas that won the democratic elections in 2006; (iii.) the unconditional American support to Israel (iv.) the ineffectiveness of regional actors; (v.) the opportunistic complicity of western powers leading to the paralysis of the UN.

The Asymmetric Disparity in the Status of Israel and Palestine

The most fundamental problem in both the peace process and the ceasefire negotiations regarding the Israeli-Palestinian issue is the disparity in the status of the parties involved. When one party perceives itself as dominant/hegemonic and the other as passive/dependent—particularly in situations where this dynamic is continually reinforced by mediators—it becomes challenging to establish a rational common area of interest. Moreover, if there is a disparity in status between the parties, a rational negotiation relationship becomes nearly impossible.

In last decades, while Israel enjoys the privileges of UN membership and the support of Israel-friendly global powers within the UN Security Council, the Palestinian side is fragmented between the Palestinian Authority, which lacks full control over its own territory, and the Gaza administration under blockade. The primary reason for Israel's initiation of the 2012 war was Palestine's efforts to address this asymmetry by appealing first to the UN Security Council and then to the UN General Assembly for the recognition as a member state. Since the recognition of the State of Palestine by the UN would fundamentally change the dynamics of the Middle East Peace Process, preventing such recognition has been Israel's top priority. The potential for the State of Palestine to be equated with Israel as a subject of international law poses a significant threat that must be thwarted, as it would pave the way for a genuine two-state solution by entailing sovereignty over land, sea, and airspace.

This represents the most significant psychological barrier in the peace and ceasefire efforts between Israel and Palestine. While Israel, bolstered by global power support, views itself as occupying a status above any nation-state, the Palestinian side holds a sub-state status within the framework of sovereignty at the United Nations. Worse still, this status difference is constantly emphasized by the parties claiming to mediate. The United States, which asserts itself as a patron during the Camp David and Oslo processes and related negotiations, acts as "Israel's attorney"[7] in the words of U.S. diplomat David Aaron Miller, while simultaneously opposing Palestine's status as a non-member state at the UN. This approach reflects nothing but an effort to maintain this asymmetry in favor of Israel.

Today, this asymmetry has deepened even further. Israel has not only devastated Gaza but has also launched attacks that have crippled the West Bank, and the institutions of the Palestinian Authority located there. These attacks have nearly completely obliterated the Oslo process, which served as the foundation for a two-state solution, transforming the asymmetry between Palestine and Israel into a chasm that is exceedingly difficult to bridge. Today, a similar gap in status renders any direct negotiations for a ceasefire impossible.

The failure to fulfill any of the commitments made during the Oslo and Camp David processes has increasingly undermined both the credibility and effectiveness of the Palestinian administration under Mahmoud Abbas. Furthermore, the conscious exclusion of Hamas, which won the elections in 2006, has led to a deepening representation crisis within the Palestinian side.

The Quartet, including the U.S. as a guarantor of the Oslo process, has remained unresponsive to this situation, thereby encouraging Israel to persist in its genocidal actions. My call for Palestinian President Mahmoud Abbas to visit Gaza[8] while the genocide was ongoing was fundamentally aimed at reinforcing the legitimacy of the Palestinian Authority as a negotiating party among the Palestinian populace and enhancing its international representation. However, despite Abbas's positive response to my call during his speech at the Turkish Grand National Assembly (TBMM)[9], his visit to Gaza was obstructed by Israel.

Regrettably, the United States and the Quartet, the primary guarantors of the Oslo process and the countries that recognize Mahmoud Abbas as the President of the State of Palestine, failed to exert any pressure on Israel to allow Abbas to travel freely within his own country to empathize with

---

7 Aaron David Miller, "Israel's Lawyer," *Washington Post,* May 22, 2005. https://www.washingtonpost.com/archive/opinions/2005/05/23/israels-lawyer/7ab0416c-9761-4d4a-80a9-82b7e15e5d22/

8 Ahmet Davutoğlu @A_Davutoglu_eng, post on *X,* August 15, 2024. https://x.com/a_davutoglu_eng/status/1824097283278803127?s=46

9 "World media focuses on Abbas' pledge in speech to Türkiye Parliament to visit Gaza," *Middle East Monitor,* August 16, 2024. https://www.middleeastmonitor.com/20240816-world-media-focuses-on-abbas-pledge-in-speech-to-turkiye-parliament-to-visit-gaza/

his people's suffering. Following his address to the Turkish Grand National Assembly, Mahmoud Abbas called me to express his gratitude for my public message suggesting him to visit Gaza one day before his speech and conveyed his profound disappointment at the international community's lack of support regarding this issue. Today Mahmoud Abbas and the Palestinian Authority are in their weakest and most vulnerable position regarding their credibility among the Palestinian people and their international representation since the onset of the Oslo process 32 years ago.

The Exclusion of Gaza and Hamas After the Democratic Elections in 2006

The root cause of Gaza wars in 2006, 2009, 2012 and 2014 is the exclusion of *the Change and Reform* list supported by Hamas, which won the 2006 elections, on charges of terrorism. It contradicts all democratic values for a list that was considered legitimate during the election to be labeled as terrorist afterward. Briefly outlining the background of this hypocritical approach could provide important insights into why a diplomatic intervention to prevent the ongoing genocide in Gaza could not be initiated.

Between June 2005 and January 2006, the elections that took place in Lebanon, Iraq and Palestine created a favorable environment for managing regional crises and initiating a new era. The active participation of Sunni resistance groups in the Iraqi election through our mediation as Türkiye between Sunni resistance groups and the U.S., as well as the participation of all groups, particularly Hezbollah, in elections in Lebanon, and the praise of these elections by the international community, particularly the United States, heightened our hopes for a peaceful process in Palestine, where all groups, including Hamas, participated in the elections. Instead of evaluating this opportunity based on objective and uniform criteria, the inconsistent and hypocritical approach that was followed laid the groundwork for the Gaza issue that persists to this day.

The UNSC celebrated elections in Iraq as a significant victory for democracy declaring a Presidential Statement.[10] President Bush, on the other hand, heralded the elections as the birth of the Arab world's only constitutional democracy.[11] In Lebanon, the elections held under difficult conditions following the assassination of Hariri on February 14, 2005, which triggered

---

10 United Nations, "Press statement on Iraq by Security Council President," December 16, 2005. https://press.un.org/en/2005/sc8606.doc.htm

11 The White House, "President Discusses Iraqi Elections, Victory in the War on Terror," Office of the Press Secretary for President George W. Bush, December 14, 2005. https://georgewbush-whitehouse.archives.gov/news/releases/2005/12/20051214-1.html

a major crisis, were highlighted by the UNSC as a significant historical achievement.[12]

The peaceful conduct of these two elections, along with the positive regional climate, opened a significant window of opportunity for resolving the Middle East conflict, particularly with the elections held in Palestine on January 30, 2006. The participation of *the Change and Reform List* supported by Hamas and the fact that this participation was either directly or indirectly approved by the United States, the Quartet, and Israel, marked an important stage in the transition from conflict to reconciliation in the region following the elections in Iraq and Lebanon.

The elections in Palestine were conducted in accordance with democratic procedures and rules, as confirmed by objective international observers. The conduct of the election was widely deemed free and fair," and "The Bush Administration acknowledged the outcome of the Palestinian legislative elections and commended the PA for conducting free and fair elections."[13] The European Parliament's resolution also clearly stated that the elections were conducted in accordance with democratic procedures.[14]

However, these positive attitudes and comments changed to a hypocritical stance once it was revealed that the *Change and Reform List* had won the elections. Those who had hailed the results of the elections in Iraq and Lebanon could not digest the unexpected outcome in Palestine. It became evident that, for them, democracy was valued not for its essence but for the results it produced. Their reason for allowing the *Change and Reform List* to participate in the elections, despite being aware of its link with Hamas, was their belief that Fatah would win the elections. However, one of democracy's most virtuous aspects is its capacity to surprise those who wish to exploit it for opportunistic purposes. When the election results did not turn out as expected, preconditions were set demanding that Hamas reach the same position as Fatah, which had taken years of negotiations. Nevertheless, Hamas was fully adhering to the ceasefire declared in February 2005, and it was certain that this ceasefire would continue, providing an opportunity for permanent peace talks if the election results were respected.

---

12 United Nations, S/2005/673 Letter dated 26 October 2005 from the Secretary-General addressed to the President of the Security Council.

13 Aaron D. Pina, *Palestinian Elections,* Congressional Research Service Reports, The Library of Congress, updated February 26, 2006, 14–15. https://digital.library.unt.edu/ark:/67531/metacrs9411/

14 European Parliament resolution on the result of the Palestinian elections and the situation in East Jerusalem, February 2, 2006. https://www.europarl.europa.eu/doceo/document/TA-6-2006-0041_EN.html

Since we closely monitored the psychology and approaches of all parties, we sensed the storm that would arise from the cycle of violence resulting from the non-recognition of the election results in Palestine. When Khalid Mashal visited Ankara on February 16, we viewed this visit as an opportunity to prevent such a scenario and to give momentum to Palestinian reconciliation, the Middle East peace process, and regional democratization efforts. Ultimately, Hamas through *the Change and Reform List* could evolve into a political party with democratic legitimacy through a process that functioned as a natural result of this election. Pro-Israel actors, led by neo-cons in the U.S., which promoted the participation of resistant Sunni groups in Iraq and Hezbollah in Lebanon through democratic means, as well as Israel itself, which allowed these elections to take place, chose to disregard the results of these elections.

This stance raised serious doubts about the sincerity and consistency of the United States' commitment to democracy and laid the foundation for the ongoing representation crisis in Palestine. The refusal to acknowledge the Palestinian people's right to elect their own leaders led to a complete psychological collapse of the already dysfunctional Oslo process among Palestinians. Furthermore, Mahmoud Abbas's influence over all Palestinians, who succeeded the charismatic leader Yasser Arafat, was deeply affected from the very beginning of his term.

During my meeting with Khalid Mashal in Ankara, I advised him to eliminate the leverage of those who wished to disregard the election results by referencing the 1967 borders through UN Security Council resolutions. His response essentially confirmed the statement made years later by UN Secretary-General Guterres that "nothing happens in a vacuum": "Out of respect for you, we can make similar statements, but those who exert pressure on us are not pressuring Israel to withdraw from the occupied territories in accordance with UN resolutions. Which of the promises made to the PLO, which has fulfilled all their demands during the Oslo process, has been implemented over time? The PLO, which recognizes Israel's existence, has not attained the genuine sovereign state that Palestinians rightfully deserve and has also lost significant credibility. If we follow the same path, who can guarantee that the promises made will be fulfilled? However, if we are not prevented from exercising the authority granted to us by the Palestinian people, be assured that we will fulfill our responsibilities as the government over time. You can convey this to your interlocutors as well."

Today, leaders and diplomats from various countries must candidly ask: If the results of the Palestinian elections in 2006, which all observers agreed were fair and objective, had been accepted, and if a unified Palestinian government had been allowed to form while Hamas was given a chance to be engaged patiently rather than dictated terms, might the tragedies occurring in the region today have been prevented? If instead of the neo-conservative stance that "Israeli security is the top priority regardless of which principles are violated," a policy of "establishing a fair regional order through granting Palestinians the state they deserve within the framework of UN norms and resolutions" had been adopted, might the radicalization of Israeli politics have been avoided? Due to the Palestinians' inability to exercise their right to elect their own leaders for the past 18 years since 2006, the Palestinian Authority has become significantly weakened in terms of effectiveness and legitimacy. Is the responsibility for the Palestinians resorting to a struggle for existence to take their fate into their own hands attributed to the Palestinian people themselves, or is it the global powers, primarily the United States, that do not respect their political preferences?

The denial of Hamas, which is a natural party to both the war and the ceasefire, as a diplomatic interlocutor in all these processes has rendered it impossible to conduct genuine negotiations that could halt the genocide. This representation issue necessitates a proxy diplomacy that must be synchronized with both Israel and Hamas in efforts to de-escalate tensions and achieve a ceasefire. Establishing a lasting peace agreement or even achieving a temporary ceasefire is not feasible without such a diplomatic initiative that requires effective and coordinated contributions from regional and global powers.

Another critical aspect is the need for mediators involved in these diplomatic processes to be perceived as credible in terms of sincerity and consistency by the relevant parties. The double standards resulting from the application of different criteria in various regional crises undermine the crucial sense of trust required for mediation efforts.

In all Gaza wars in 2006, 2009, 2012 and 2014, the effective involvement of Türkiye and Qatar with Hamas and the establishment of a communication channel facilitated the acceleration of the ceasefire process. Unfortunately, in the recent genocide, the absence of such an effective channel and the deepening trust issues between Egypt and Hamas resulted in a complete breakdown of one the most significant legs of the ceasefire process.

Subsequently, we cautioned all our interlocutors from the Western countries that excluding Hamas would lead to significant regional tensions and new risks of conflict even of widespread war, creating a polarization between Iran-Syria-Hamas-Hezbollah and Egypt-Jordan-Saudi Arabia-Fatah. The primary objective of our active diplomacy was to create a third way to prevent a large-scale regional crisis arising from these tensions. The balanced and coordinated relationships we established between Hamas and Fatah, Hamas and Israel, Syria and Israel, Egypt and Iran, Saudi Arabia and Iran, the U.S. and Iran, the U.S. and Syria, and between Lebanese groups and Syria provided us with the opportunity to open such a pathway.

In the 2023–2024 conflict, Türkiye's lack of prior mediation effectiveness and Qatar's obligation to shoulder this heavy burden alone created a significant void. Consequently, the absence of a reliable and effective channel for Hamas, a party to the war in a practical sense, in mediation efforts, coupled with the undermining of the Palestinian Authority's capacity for representation, obstructed the implementation of diplomacy aimed at preventing genocide.

The Ineffectiveness of Regional Actors

One of the main reasons that both the Hamas attack on October 7 and the Israeli government's ongoing brutal genocide for over a year have not spurred a diplomatic initiative to halt these actions is the attitude of regional actors. Since 1948, Palestinians have perceived the issue as not solely their own but rather as a concern of Arab and Islamic countries, believing that these nations would support their cause. In situations where Arab nations have shown a united front, such as during the 1973 oil embargo and the 2002 Arab Peace Initiative, Palestinians felt a sense of security. However, the silence of regional countries in response to Trump's declaration of Jerusalem as Israel's capital and the subsequent normalization process initiated by the Abraham Accords has led Palestinians to feel abandoned. The increase in Israeli attacks and violations against the Al-Aqsa Mosque throughout 2023, culminating in Netanyahu presenting a map at the UN General Assembly that depicted Palestine entirely as Israeli territory just two weeks before October 7, alongside the lack of response from regional countries, has pushed Palestinians to take control of their own destiny, regardless of the consequences.

While the Palestinian side has entered a phase of existential concern, the Israeli side has adopted an attitude of extreme confidence due to the normalization processes of regional countries, which appear to prioritize these over the genocide in Gaza. Unlike previous wars, the specific abandonment of the people of Gaza and the general neglect of Palestine by Arab countries, along with the resulting gap in mediation processes concerning contacts with Hamas, have provided Israel with a substantial strategic maneuvering space. One factor behind Israel's negative responses to all ceasefire calls is its position to manipulate regional balances on an unprecedented scale.

Israel's strategy of expanding the conflict by activating the geopolitical mechanics of the Middle Eastern issue has become one of the primary obstacles to achieving a peace. The internal circle of the Palestinian-centered Middle Eastern issue consists of Lebanon, Syria, Jordan, and Egypt (particularly the Sinai Peninsula), while the external ring is formed by Egypt, Saudi Arabia/the Gulf, Iran, and Türkiye. Israel fought against the four countries in the inner circle in 1967. After signing agreements with Egypt and Jordan in Camp David process, Israel focused on three goals concerning this inner circle: (i.) to colonize and then annex Palestinian territories through settlers, (ii.) to control Lebanon to eliminate it as a security risk, and (iii.) to isolate Syria.

On the other hand, the Iranian revolution that occurred around five months after the Camp David agreement altered the balances in the outer ring. For Israel, the primary enemy became Iran rather than Egypt. The Iran-Iraq war, which lasted seven years, reinforced the perception of the Iranian threat in the Arab world, making it possible for Israel to manipulate the balances in the outer ring. Today, the ongoing normalization efforts of Arab countries with Israel despite the genocide in Gaza are influenced by this perception of threat. Netanyahu's message to Arab countries during his Congress speech fits into this framework: "America and Israel today can forge a security alliance in the Middle East to counter the growing Iranian theat. All countries that are in peace with Israel and all those countries who will make peace with Israel should be invited to join this alliance.... And we will continue to work with the United States and our Arab partners to transform a troubled region, from a backwater of oppression, poverty and war into a thriving oasis of dignity, prosperity and peace."[15]

So, this regional context has paved the way for Israel's tactic of framing the Gaza genocide within the context of Iranian-Israeli tensions. Israel has propagated the narrative that the conflict is not between Israel and Palestine but rather between Israel and Iran by portraying Hamas as an extension of Iran. The inability of Türkiye and Arab countries to establish a third diplomatic focal point advocating for the rights of the Palestinian people has provided Israel with a significant advantage.

In the ceasefire processes during the wars of 2006, 2009, 2012, and 2014, where I personally participated as a mediator, our first precaution was to advise the Iranian side to act wisely and support the ceasefire processes without directly intervening in the crisis. We were aware that Iran's involvement could be exploited by Israel to delay ceasefires and continue the destruction in Palestine. By initially promoting calm in the early stages of ceasefire

---

15 "FULL TEXT: Netanyahu's 2024 Address to Congress," *Haaretz*, July 25, 2024. https://www.haaretz.com/israel-news/2024-07-25/ty-article/full-text-netanyahus-2024-address-to-congress/00000190-e6c0-d469-a39d-e6d7117d0000

processes in previous wars, and then maintaining continuous contact, we managed to keep Iran out of the crisis as a direct party, thereby preventing the escalation of war and shortening the ceasefire process.

Türkiye's balanced and effective relations with Iran, Egypt, and Saudi Arabia had persuaded Iran to remain outside the conflict. For example, when the indirect talks between Syria and Israel were taking place, our ceasefire agreements in Lebanon and Palestine were disrupted by Israel's attack on Gaza on December 27, 2008. In this process, gaining Saudi Arabia's support in our efforts for ceasefire with Egypt and Qatar and ensuring that Iran refrained from making direct intervention statements had a mitigating effect on the escalation of the situation.

Today, the absence of such an effective third diplomatic channel has hindered the formation of an alternative regional initiative and has enabled the success of the U.S.-backed Israeli tactic of constraining the Gaza genocide within the context of the crisis between Iran and Israel. Qatar's extremely well-intentioned initiatives have not been sufficient to establish such an effective third focal point.

Netanyahu's address in the American Congress was the primary reason for my call[16] for Ismail Haniyeh or a Palestinian representative to address the Turkish Grand National Assembly (TBMM) to reframe the Palestinian issue away from being perceived as an extension of Israel-Iran tension. Unfortunately, the failure of such a visit to occur, coupled with Haniyeh's subsequent trip to Iran for the presidential ceremony after this speech, has provided a false pretext for Israel's strategy to identify Palestinian issue with Iran. The Arab world's silence and lack of a meaningful response to Israel's assassination of Haniyeh also reinforced this perception. Subsequently, Israel's expansion of the war into Lebanon, thereby extracting the issue from the context of the genocide in Gaza and transforming it into a conflict between Iran and Israel, is aimed at legitimizing the genocide.

Another important regional factor is the change in Arab countries' perspectives toward Hamas. Especially Egypt's general stance has significant importance in influencing ceasefire efforts. The dynamics of the relationship between Egypt, the only neighboring country of Gaza and its exit point, and Hamas have directly influenced the ceasefire process in all wars. While there was no trust issue between the democratically elected Morsi administration in Egypt and Hamas, the 2012 war lasted only eight days. In contrast, the 2014 war under Sisi's administration, during which trust issues escalated significantly following the coup, lasted 49 days. The 2009 war during Mubarak's

---

16 Ahmet Davutoğlu @A_Davutoglu_eng post on *X,* July 26, 2024. https://x.com/a_davutoglu_eng/status/1816909755740487686?s=46

regime, when relations were relatively more balanced and stable, lasted 22 days.

The critical mediation roles played by Türkiye and Qatar in facilitating the indirect participation of Hamas in the negotiations during the wars of 2009, 2012, and 2014 have been among the most effective factors leading to these ceasefires. During these processes, the diplomatic channels we established between Hamas and the United States and Israel, first with Qatar's Prime Minister and Foreign Minister Hamad bin Jassem during the 2009 and 2012 wars, and later with Qatar's Foreign Minister Khaled Al-Attiyah during the 2014 war, played a significant role in the successful conclusion of the ceasefire negotiations. During this period, the close dialogue and coordination between Qatari Father Amir Sheikh Hamad bin Khalifa Al-Thani and Prime Minister Erdoğan during the 2009 and 2012 wars, as well as between Qatari Amir Tamim bin Hamad Al-Thani and Prime Minister Erdoğan during the 2014 war, accelerated the ceasefire processes.

This role has been particularly crucial during periods characterized by trust issues between Egypt and Hamas. The mutual lack of trust between Egypt, which views Hamas as an extension of the Muslim Brotherhood that it has designated as a terrorist organization, and Hamas, coupled with the failure of regional actors to fill this gap, has delayed the ceasefire, serving Israel's interests to destroy and dehumanize Gaza.

Moreover, the Arab League and member states of the Organization of Islamic Cooperation have not implemented a single effective measure against Israel beyond harsh rhetoric, emboldening Israel to continue its genocide. On the contrary, the perception that the normalization process will continue regardless of what happens in Gaza and Lebanon has created a conducive environment for Israel to persistently pursue its expansionist policies, particularly the colonization of Palestine.

American Unconditional Support to Israel

One of the primary reasons for the inability to achieve a ceasefire in the genocide in Gaza, is the lack of genuine pressure from the U.S. administration on Israel in this regard. A fact that emerges from all past wars is that the most significant and perhaps the only power that can put sufficient pressure on Israel to achieve any ceasefire and peace agreement is the United States. This is a natural consequence of the 'geopolitical symbiosis' between the two countries, which forms the basis of the U.S. complicity I addressed in my other chapter in this book. Israel cannot initiate an attack without providing information to the U.S. and obtaining its approval, nor can it end a war it has started without U.S. influence and pressure.

The attitude of the U.S. administration, which has the highest influence over Israel, has been decisive. Therefore, there is an interesting timing connection between the start and end of Israel's attacks on Gaza and the U.S. elections. The occurrence of the 2009 and 2012 wars between the U.S. elections and the change of administration, as well as the timing of the 2014 war just before the congressional midterm elections, is no coincidence. Israel's timing for the wars is aligned with periods when the U.S. administration and candidates either felt a significant need for support from the Jewish lobby in the U.S. or wished to remain silent to avoid encumbering the upcoming term. The 2009 war took place during the transition from the Bush administration, influenced by pro-Israel neocons, to the Obama administration, which was determined to abandon neocon policies. The 2012 war occurred just before Obama's second term. The 2014 war happened while the final solution negotiations—which were the most significant initiative of the Obama era—were underway, shortly before the congressional midterm elections. The heavy defeat of the Democrats in these midterms led to outcomes that subsequently opened the way for Trump.

Israel's attempts to prolong the genocide in Gaza until the conclusion of the U.S. elections are also connected to the same reasoning. During the U.S. election campaign, it is impossible for candidates to adopt an anti-Israel stance. Indeed, when the war began, candidate Biden felt the necessity to engage directly with Israel. Biden has not exhibited the willingness to demonstrate the same level of effort as Obama did during the 2012 and 2014 wars, both in terms of his health and his approach to events. Another candidate, Trump, who previously declared Jerusalem as the capital of Israel, has been a significant contributor to one of the primary causes of frustration on the Palestinian side, and he has already made his position clear. Netanyahu's description of the Trump's election victory as "history's greatest comeback"[17] indicates his expectations for the new period.

Conversely, Blinken, who declared from the outset that he would approach the issue through his Jewish identity rather than his American identity, has not shown the efforts that Hillary Clinton demonstrated in 2012 or John Kerry in 2014 for a ceasefire, instead adopting a stance that gives Israel time with each of his actions.

When evaluating experiences from past conflicts, it becomes evident that reducing tensions and establishing ceasefires is more achievable when there is effective synchronization between regional initiatives and global powers. In cases where an adequate and effective regional center of influence cannot

---

17 Gianluca Avagnina, "Netanyahu and Starmer lead congratulations to Trump," *BBC,* November 6, 2024. https://www.bbc.com/news/articles/cly2z812zxvo

be established, exerting any meaningful pressure on Israel proves challenging. During the wars of 2012 and 2014, the influence exerted by the triad of Türkiye, Egypt, and Qatar, in various configurations, along with their impact on the United States, persuaded Israel and Hamas to reach a reasonable ceasefire agreement.

In the 2012 conflict, the synchronization between the joint efforts of Türkiye, Egypt, and Qatar with Hamas, and the diplomatic initiatives of U.S. President Obama and then-Secretary of State Hillary Clinton, was the most critical factor enabling the ceasefire within a brief period of eight days. On November 18, amidst escalating tensions, after discussions with the British, French, German, and Russian foreign ministers, I contacted Clinton, who was in Cambodia for the ASEAN Summit, to inform her of the efforts underway with Egypt and Qatar towards Hamas and outline our three-phase plan for a ceasefire. I emphasized the importance of her presence in the region to initiate diplomatic efforts aimed at pressuring Israel towards a ceasefire. Additionally, Prime Minister Erdoğan also called President Obama, urging him to contribute to an urgent ceasefire.

On November 20, during our visit to Gaza[18] with ten ministers and the Secretary-General of the Arab League, the messages we conveyed, along with the unified messages from Hillary Clinton—who interrupted her East Asia tour to return to the region—in Tel Aviv in the presence of Netanyahu,[19]

---

18 This visit was a historic first for Gaza. However, while we were in Gaza, Israel resumed air bombardments later that evening. As other ministers decided to leave Gaza, I, along with my doctor spouse, went to the Shifa Hospital, which had been devastated in the recent conflict, and stayed there until late at night. During those hours, when a father weeping while cradling the corpse of his 16-year-old daughter rested his head on my shoulder, I felt his pain in my heart. That night, I understood more acutely how easy it is to speak about the war from a distance, yet how difficult it is to live through it at any moment. We must not forget that behind every number reported on television during the ongoing genocide lies a painful story, a mother, father, spouse, child, or sibling who will live with that grief. That day, experiencing the tragedy of a people rendered homeless and stateless, deprived of bread, water, and medicine by blockades, left without a protector, was one of the greatest lessons I have learned in my life.

19 "In the end, there is no substitute for security and for a just and lasting peace, and the current crisis certainly focuses us on the urgency of this broader goal. So in the days ahead, the United States will work with our partners here in Israel and across the region toward an outcome that bolsters security for the people of Israel, improves conditions for the people of Gaza, and moves toward a comprehensive peace for all people of the region." U.S. State Department, Hillary Rodham Clinton, Secretary of State, "Remarks With Israeli Prime Minister Benjamin Netanyahu Before Their Meeting," Prime Minister's Office, Jerusalem, November 20, 2012. https://2009-2017.state.gov/secretary/20092013clinton/rm/2012/11/200911.htm

and U.N. Secretary-General Ban Ki-Moon in Cairo[20], Tel Aviv and Ramallah, had a significant impact in persuading the parties toward a ceasefire. The ceasefire was subsequently declared on the night of November 21, leading into November 22.

During the ceasefire process in the 2014 conflict a similar coordinated diplomatic effort of Türkiye, the United States and Qatar played a significant role. Between November 2012 and July 2014, two significant developments created an opportunity for Israel-Palestine peace: the U.S.-led final negotiation for a two-state solution and Palestinian national reconciliation. The first was the direct negotiations initiated on July 29, 2013, under U.S. auspices, with a nine-month timeline. The Obama administration obtained the Arab League's agreement to amend the "Arab Peace Initiative" to include "minor land swaps" in the context of establishing the parameters for a final agreement, alongside planning a $4 billion program aimed at revitalizing the Palestinian economy. The Palestinian side agreed to suspend initiatives to join international organizations based on rights granted by its observer state status at the UN, in return for Israel's commitment to freeze settlement expansion and release 106 pre-Oslo Accords prisoners.

The second positive development was the reconciliation between the PLO and Hamas on April 23, 2014, offering a unique peace opportunity. Hamas, which had maintained relative calm in Gaza, would gain legitimacy within the Palestinian national authority, bridging the division between the West Bank and Gaza. A unified Palestinian representation could negotiate a two-state solution with Israel.

However, this integration prospect alarmed Israeli radicals, especially Netanyahu. In response, Israel failed to uphold key commitments from the U.S.-initiated negotiations and violated timelines, ultimately refusing to recognize Palestinian reconciliation. Israeli settlers intensified colonization in the West Bank, leading to increased tensions and the abduction of three Israeli settlers. Although Hamas did not claim responsibility for this act, the extensive assaults launched by Israel ultimately ended the final resolution talks initiated by the United States.

Israel's failure to meet its commitments disappointed the Obama administration, particularly Secretary Kerry, motivating them to pressure

---

20 "From Cairo, I will go to Israel, where I will urge the Israeli leadership to end the violence and firmly reiterate that Israel must respect its obligations under international law, including international humanitarian law." Ban Ki-Moon, Former UN Secretary-General, "Remarks at press encounter with the Secretary-General of the League of Arab States," United Nations, November 20, 2012. https://www.un.org/sg/en/content/sg/press-encounter/2012-11-20/remarks-press-encounter-the-secretary-general-of-the-league-of-arab-states

Israel towards a ceasefire. Through intensive contacts within a trilateral mechanism of Türkiye, Qatar, and the United States, efforts were made to create conditions for a ceasefire. Although post-coup tensions with Egypt complicated matters, Türkiye and Qatar played a decisive role in facilitating Hamas's engagement in Cairo for ceasefire talks and the formation of a joint delegation with the PLO.

On July 13, I contacted U.S. Secretary of State Kerry, advocating for intervention based on the 2012 ceasefire agreement to stop Gaza's ongoing violence. Kerry confirmed his similar discussions with Israel. When Israel launched a ground operation on July 17, Türkiye, Qatar, and the U.S. intensified coordinated diplomatic efforts, maintaining regular communication through bilateral and trilateral phone calls. The draft ceasefire agreement was relayed multiple times to Hamas's leadership in Qatar, factions in Gaza, the PLO, Egypt, and Israel. On July 26, further coordination took place in Paris, where two Türkiye-Qatar-U.S. trilateral meetings at the U.S. and Turkish embassies with John Kerry and Khaled Atiyyah marked a turning point towards a ceasefire. A 24-hour ceasefire was declared at midnight on July 27, in coordination with the UN. After intermittent short-term ceasefires, a durable ceasefire was achieved on August 26.

This streamlined diplomatic process, led by Türkiye, Qatar, and the United States, demonstrated the efficacy of trilateral coordination in mediating conflicts. Despite regional tensions and strained relationships, sustained diplomatic engagement facilitated critical steps toward a lasting ceasefire in the 2012 and 2014 Gaza wars.

The absence of a diplomatic mechanism connecting regional actors with the United States—the only nation capable of applying substantial pressure on Israel—has been a significant factor in the inability to secure a ceasefire to halt the 2023–2024 genocide. The reluctance of key Arab states to exert any pressure on the United States, coupled with Türkiye's lack of active mediation efforts, has placed the entire burden on Qatar. This situation has, in turn, enabled the U.S. administration, already inclined towards a pro-Israel stance, to pursue a diplomatic complicity in alignment with Israel's goals.

As a result, Israel has been able to continue its established strategy unimpeded, following the same pattern it has used in previous conflicts: violating UN resolutions and the fundamental principles of the Oslo Accords, escalating tensions to justify war, using pro-Israeli international media to promote their narrative, and securing unconditional diplomatic and military support from the United States.

The Opportunistic Complicity of Global Actors Leading to the Paralysis of the UN

The fourth significant reason for the failure of diplomacy aimed at preventing genocide is that global actors have approached the issue not from the perspective of the international legal principles that impose a responsibility against genocide, but rather from the perspective of their own national strategies. Alongside the United States' unconditional support for Israel, other global actors, particularly the remaining P5 members, have opted for rhetorical and situational stances rather than exerting effective pressure on Israel to halt the genocide.

For Russia, which was expected to balance this U.S. attitude, the genocide in Gaza has served as a shield that relegates the Ukraine war and its associated events to the background. The emergence of double standards applied by Western countries in the cases of Ukraine and Gaza has also become a significant propaganda opportunity for Russia. In contrast to the sanctions imposed on Russia for its aggression against Ukraine, the support extended to Israel—which is facing charges of genocide at the International Court of Justice—has resulted in a striking contradiction that profoundly undermines the fundamental principles of the international order. Russia, a member of both the P5 and the Quartet, has transformed its rhetoric of being anti-genocide into a policy of "passivity" in practice, turning the advantages provided by the Gaza war into strategic opportunism.

The only positive step among the P5 countries came from China, which hosted a national reconciliation initiative involving 14 Palestinian groups on July 23, 2024, and laid the groundwork for a three-phase plan known as the "Beijing Declaration." The first step is to achieve a comprehensive, lasting, and sustainable ceasefire in the Gaza Strip as soon as possible and ensure access to humanitarian aid and rescue efforts on the ground. The second step is to make joint efforts toward post-conflict governance of Gaza under the principle of "Palestinians governing Palestine." Gaza is an inseparable, integral part of Palestine.

China, which has suffered significant reputational damage both in the Islamic world and the international community due to human rights violations against the Uyghurs in East Turkistan, has sought to rehabilitate its image through this initiative concerning Palestine. However, neither China nor any other P5 country, including Russia, has responded appropriately to Netanyahu's speeches at the UN General Assembly, which challenge UN principles by depicting East Jerusalem, the West Bank, and Gaza as within Israel's borders.

The EU has experienced an internal division: countries such as Germany, Italy, and France, which complicitly supporting Israel and countries like Spain, Ireland, and Norway, which have taken a moral stance against the genocide. Norway, which is not a member of the EU, has continued to demonstrate a principled stance as a natural consequence of its historical role in mediation missions.

The countries that have successfully passed this challenging humanitarian test include, primarily, those from the "Global South," such as South Africa, Brazil, Colombia, Bolivia, Chile, Nicaragua, and Malaysia. South Africa's application to the International Court of Justice, along with the uncompromising and principled policies of other "Global South" nations against genocide, has constituted the only commendable stance on behalf of humanity.

In such a context, the United Nations, which has trampled on all its founding principles, has displayed its most helpless image in history in the face of a genocide committed in front of the world's eyes. UN Secretary-General Antonio Guterres has made efforts to reduce tensions and uphold UN principles with great goodwill. Israel's declaration of him as persona non grata and banning his entry into Israel is an overt challenge that disregards the UN system. The silence and ineffectiveness of the UN Security Council members in the face of this brazen challenge has effectively meant the eclipse of the UN system.

The international community, unable to stop a genocide broadcast live before the eyes of the world, along with all its components, states, and institutions, will be remembered with great shame by future generations of humanity. The judgment of history regarding those who committed this genocide, those who entered a complicity relationship with the perpetrators, and those who remained silent about this genocide will be very severe.

A Linkage of UN Human Rights and UN Human Responsibilities

The Impact of Its Absence—What It Implied for Iraq and What It Implies for Gaza

Hans von Sponeck

EXTENSIVE national and international human rights law has been created since the United Nations was founded in 1945. To date there are some 70 treaties and declarations of human rights including the two Covenants on civil, political, economic, social, and cultural rights signed in December 1966, and the Universal Declaration of Human Rights adopted by the UN General Assembly in December 1948. The Declaration recognizes in its Preamble that "...the inherent dignity and the equal and inalienable rights of all members of the human family are the foundation of freedom, justice and peace in the world." The drafters of the Universal Declaration of *Human Rights* struggled over how to handle its possible counterpart, a Universal Declaration of *Human Responsibilities, and* ended up with the vapid conclusion: "Everyone has duties to the Community" (Article 29).

The purpose of this contribution is to review UN operations in Iraq, during the country's 13 years of multilateral sanctions (1990–2003), and in Gaza in war (2023/24) facing annihilation, as examples of how the absence of a universal declaration, and a covenant, on human responsibility has impacted the fate of two peoples; violated international law and prevented the United Nations from fulfiling its humanitarian mandate. The UN should be using

Hans von Sponeck PhD, educated in Germany, the UK and the U.S, served in the United Nations as a civil servant (1968–2000); head of UN missions in Botswana, Pakistan and India; Director, UNDP European Office in Geneva; and UN Assistant Secretary-General and Humanitarian Coordinator for Iraq. Dr. von Sponeck is Faculty Member, ret., Conflict Research Centre, University of Marburg/Germany and Sr. Training Consultant, ret., UN Staff College, Torino/Italy.

its Iraq experience for its interventions in Gaza during the current Israeli onslaught by linking rights with institutional and individual responsibilities.

In 1998, Mary Robinson, the then UN High Commissioner for Human Rights, in a meeting with the author in Geneva, was adamant in insisting that the reference to duties (responsibilities) in Article 29 of the Declaration was sufficient. Including details "would only detract from the Declaration's central focus on human rights." A reminder that in 1997, 47 former heads of state and government including Malcolm Frazer (Australia), Jimmy Carter (U.S.), Lee Kwan Yew (Singapore), Simon Perez (Israel), Pierre Trudeau (Canada), Valery Giscard d'Estaing (France), and Helmut Schmidt (Germany), had thought otherwise and become signatories of a draft Universal Declaration of Human Responsibilities, made no difference to her. In 1998/99 the UN Human Rights Commission had deliberated the issue of "rights and responsibilities" and the General Assembly had adopted, without vote, a resolution which confirmed[1] that "each state has the prime responsibility and duty to protect, promote and implement all human rights and ... enjoy all those rights and freedoms *in practice*."[2] This was an encouraging step towards balancing freedom and responsibility. Many years earlier, Mahatma Gandhi had eloquently supported such a balance by stating "The Ganges of Rights originates in the Himalaya of Responsibility." Today, not much attention, neither politically nor academically, is paid to this debate. Western governments firmly reject any such an initiative. Despite West-centric resistance, the UN GA, encouraged by the accelerating pace of global de-westernization, could decide to resume the discussion of what it would take to establish a partnership between rights and responsibilities.

The annual human development reports the UN Development Program (UNDP) has been publishing since 1990 confirm that civil society in most UN member countries has benefitted over time from more human rights-focussed programs. The UNDP reports show in *quantitative* detail that the rights to life, liberty, and security, to food, access to water, sanitation facilities and housing are reflected in improved living conditions for many, and benefit growing numbers of youth in exercising their right to education. A weakness

---

1 See: UNHRC Res.1998/7 of 3 April 1998 & UN A/Res 53/144 of March 1999.
2 See: A/53/625/Add.2 and also: i. Hans Küng, (1928-2021) Director of the World Ethos Foundation located in Tübingen. In 1997, he prepared a first draft of a Universal Declaration of Human Responsibilities that was published by the InterAction Council. Even though forty-seven world leaders signed it, the UN General Assembly never adopted it.; ii. Samanta Besson "The Bearers of Human Rights' Duties and Responsibilities: A Quiet (R) Evolution," Cambridge University Press, 30 October 2015; iii. Bosko Tripkovic & Alain Zysset "Uncovering the Nature of the European Court of Human Rights (ECHR)," Human Rights Law Review, Oxford University Press, 1 December 2023.

of these UNDP reports is that nothing is ventured about how best to acknowledge legal, ethical, and moral responsibilities that would enhance the ways these human rights should be realized.

Human Rights with Human Responsibilities?

As the world of today is physically more integrated than ever before, and conflicts can occur between parties that are spatially far apart, the call for the linkage between human rights and human responsibilities is becoming louder in civil society in recognition that it "constitutes a basis for a more human and democratic world order." For this reason, the topic of linkage should become an essential part of the agenda of the GA Summit on the Future UN in September 2024. Worldwide, the focus, however, continues to be on human rights and equal opportunities for all. Governments, academia, and civil society are being challenged to accept the idea that the value of a human right ultimately lies in its application. For this reason, the discourse should be broadened. Nowhere is this more obvious than with regard to the current Gaza carnage where the right of response does not lead to the responsibility to implement this right.

The western world, especially the United States, is ideologically preoccupied with *individual* rights. Giving youth opportunities to develop their self-confidence is no doubt a valuable part of learning and socialisation. However, unlike in other parts of the world, neither in North America nor in western Europe are there established linkages to connect individualism with community-mindedness and to give youth in particular the opportunity to learn for themselves that the two should go hand-in-hand.

Two distinctly different anecdotes illustrate the above observations: recently the author travelled by train, sitting next to a teenager who did not hesitate to put his wet shoes on top of the empty seat in front of him. "Why do you do this?" I asked him. "It makes the seat dirty." Without hesitation, he replied: "This is my right; I have a ticket!" Addressing the same issue of individual rights from another perspective, Tariq Aziz, the Deputy to President Saddam Hussein of Iraq told the author in Baghdad in 2000: "You western people associate human rights with individuals. We in the Middle East relate human rights to the family and to the community."

What can be deduced from these two references has to do with: i. the importance of morality and ethics in education and socialisation, ii. the profound relevance of the family and community-based socio-cultural traditions in non-western societies, and the corresponding integration of rights and responsibilities; iii. the existing inter-generational differences of perception of rights and responsibilities, and iv. the ethnocentric approach in western democracies to human rights and human responsibilities which have stymied the development of a mores- and value-based global order. The linkage between rights and responsibilities therefore remains an immensely significant geopolitical issue that needs to be resolved through a globally negotiated social contract involving governments and citizens world-wide.

Human Rights and Human Responsibilities at UN individual and institutional levels

In proceeding, UN policy and UN operations will be reviewed at the individual and institutional levels to demonstrate how the UN identified its rights and how it discharged its responsibilities in dealing with Iraq during thirteen years of sanctions, and currently in Gaza and the occupied West Bank.

The questions that need answers in this context, for both Iraq and Palestine, are: (i.) what challenges do UN civil servants face in exercising their individual rights and how do they implement these rights?; (ii.) how does the UN (the UN General Assembly, the UN Security Council, and the Office of the UN Secretary-General and with it, the UN operational system of Specialized Agencies, Funds and Programs), handle its *institutional* rights?; (iii.) what humane options were available to the UN in Iraq but were ignored, and what options are available to the UN in Gaza?; (iv.) how does the absence of a norm of "responsibility" affect the implementation of rights?; and (v.) what role do ethics and morality play?

In April 1995, the five permanent members of the UN Security Council (P5), addressed a general note to the then President of the Security Council, Ambassador Kavel Kovanda of the Czech Republic, concerning the humanitarian impact of Security Council decisions on countries subjected to multilateral sanctions. In their note, the P5 referred *inter alia* to the importance of: (i.) "collective actions by the SC to minimize unintended adverse side-effects on the most vulnerable"; (ii.) "objective assessments of the short- and long-term human consequences of sanctions"; and (iii.) "allowing unimpeded access to humanitarian aid." The P5 appeared to live up to principled leadership in the Security Council in protecting civil society in crisis situations and war.[3]

This general note, non-binding as it was, also reflected that the P5, consistent with its UN Charter mandate, showed that its members could act as a team and use their right to pronounce on the importance of humanitarian

---

3 Examples of such P5 team-mindedness are unfortunately rare and limited to issues of general concern where individual members could confirm, at no political costs, their alleged commitment to global issues since such support did not involve any geopolitical self-interests.

law and the protection of civilian life. How this general, non-country-specific position, was ultimately implemented at the country level will be reviewed in terms of rights and responsibilities involving UN operations in Iraq and in Gaza.

Following Iraq's illegal invasion of Kuwait on 2 August 1990 and the Hamas attack on Israel on 7 October 2023, the UN Security Council had the right to pass resolutions 660 relating to Iraq and resolution 2712 relating to Hamas[4] It was assumed that subsequent policy decisions and operational actions would be carried out in accordance with UN Charter law.

In the case of Iraq, the UN Security Council had the institutional right to subsequently pass three further resolutions—661 (1990), 687 (1991) and 1284 (1999)—expressing the UN's concern for the welfare of Iraq's civilian population. The UN General Assembly would have had the authority to invoke the "Uniting for Peace" resolution 377 of 1950 in response to the catastrophic conditions prevailing in Iraq but never did so.

On 30 October 2023, the UN GA, in response to similar concerns about the foreseeable human catastrophe facing civilians in Gaza, did, however, use the authority of this resolution to pass resolution ES-10/21, titled "Protection of civilians and upholding legal and humanitarian obligations" relating to the Gaza turmoil, reminding Israeli and Palestinian authorities to respect international humanitarian law; expressing its grave concern for the escalation of violence; condemning all acts of violence aimed at Palestinians and Israelis; and calling for a durable and sustainable truce. The resolution was supported by three P5 members (China, France, and Russia) but rejected by the U.S. with the UK, joining forty-three other countries in abstaining.

The UN Secretaries-General Annan and Guterres had the right, whether asked by the Council or the Assembly to do so or on their own accord, to monitor the impact of these SC resolutions, but concurrently they also had the responsibility to convey to the Council, the GA, and the UN Operational system their assessment on how, in their view, the implementation of these resolutions was affecting human security in Iraq and in Gaza.

It must be remembered that Gaza had been deprived for decades of basics in food, electricity, water and sanitation, housing, education—everything that had to do with human rights and minimal dignified survival. At the time of the Hamas massacre of October 7, 2023, the living conditions in Gaza were therefore already more than precarious and began to further deteriorate rapidly in response to the ensuing war. Immediate UN attention,

---

4 S/RES/660 (2 August 1990) on Iraq – 14 yes votes and Yemen not participating. S/RES 2712 (15 November 2023) on Gaza – 12 yes votes and three abstentions (Russia, UK, U.S.)

at both the political and operational levels, therefore, was urgently needed. Respective UN resolutions and statements by individual SC and GA member governments, including the P5, repeatedly stressed the urgency of help. UN Secretary-General Guterres, UNWRA Commissioner-General Lazzarini, UNICEF, WFP, WHO and other UN entities, all with many years of experience in occupied Palestine, confirmed they were ready to carry out their respective humanitarian mandates hoping to receive the financial and other support they required to do so. It assumed that the Government of Israel would accept this moral responsibility and not stand in their way. As we know, this assumption was false.

The UN right to get involved in Gaza, at policy and executive levels, is consistent with their respective, as it had been in Iraq. In doing so, the UN Security Council, as a legal body, had the concurrent responsibility to abide by the provisions of the UN Charter. Individual P5 and E10 members of the Council, however, had options of choice in determining how they would proceed in implementing this right. Before reviewing options at various levels in reacting to the atrocious conditions in Gaza, it must be remembered that "rights" and "responsibilities" are here referred to with regard to the United Nations only, and not to the Israeli authorities operating in Gaza and the West Bank. It belongs to the ICJ and the ICC and elsewhere to react in detail to the unimaginable disregard for life and law by the Israeli political leadership and the Israeli military, especially Prime Minister Netanyahu, Defence Minister General Gallant, the Minister for National Security Ben-Gvir, and others.[5]

Rights and Their Implementation

The actual implementation of resolutions in Gaza show that the established right of the SC to pass resolutions, in the absence of a covenant on human responsibilities, do not legally oblige Council members to carry out their responsibilities in accordance with UN Charter law, neither in Iraq nor in Gaza. They were at liberty to decide how to implement what they saw as their responsibilities in responding to the Iraq and Gaza crises. UN civil servants, on the other hand, having signed an oath of office, are obliged to perform their duties in full compliance with moral and ethical principles, but again, there exists no legal requirement to do so. There, however, is overwhelming evidence that the "highest standard of efficiency, competence and

---

5 Public statements from political hardliners include: "Palestinians should be 'voluntarily' encouraged to leave Gaza" and "We will initiate conflict" (Minister Gvir); "Don't give them food. Don't give them anything" former (Mayor Weiss); "We are rolling out the Nakba" (Minister Dichter; "Dropping a nuclear bomb is one of the possibilities" (Minister Amihai); "We are fighting human animals and are acting accordingly" (Minister Galant).

integrity," as demanded by UN Charter article 101/3, prevails among staff in the operational UN system in carrying out their respective responsibilities for Gaza with commitment, courage, and endurance as it did for UN staff serving in Iraq. As at mid-May 2024, 196 UN staff had given their lives in the line of duty in doing their humanitarian work in Gaza.[6]

UN Secretary-General Guterres has repeatedly pleaded with Israeli authorities to adhere to the Geneva and Hague Conventions, and that they agree to a ceasefire. He also has condemned, in the strongest terms, the air-strikes on Rafah and other densely populated areas of Gaza and pointed out that the appalling attack by Hamas did not justify collective punishment, and that there was no equivalence between Hamas and Israel. In a statement to the Security Council[7] he, poignantly, and without hesitation, reminded his audience that "It (was) important to recognize that attacks by Hamas did not happen in a vacuum. The Palestinian people had been subjected to 56 years of suffocating occupation!" No Secretary-General before him had used such strong language. In doing so, he linked his right to make a statement on Gaza with his moral responsibility as Secretary-General to condemn acts of unlaw-fulness on the part of the Israeli Government. It was a moving, powerful, and sobering answer to repeated accusations by Israeli politicians that (the UN) "focussed solely on the humanitarian situation and making no mention of what led up to this moment." He certainly mentioned what he thought had "led up to this moment." What emerges shows how the Security Council as a whole, individual Council and GA members *actually* had carried out their responsibilities in Iraq in the 1990s and how they are doing so in Gaza in 2023/24.

In Iraq:

The Security Council's alleged intention was to "meeting the human needs of the Iraqi people" (S/Res 687). While over time the SC had increased the funding for the humanitarian program by permitting the sale of more Iraqi oil, at no time were those amounts sufficient to ensure even a minimal digni-fied standard of survival. Poverty, hunger, and disease remained ever present. The annual value of "humanitarian" aid actually delivered for twenty-three million people during the years 1996 to 2003 amounted to a sobering $185 per capita per year. The SC, in carrying out its *responsibilities,* could have: (i.) allowed early repairs of the oil industry to generate more financial resources; (ii.) unfrozen Iraq Government funds held abroad; and (iii.) unblocked the personal accounts held abroad by Iraqi citizens. Such measures alone would

---

6 *UN News*, 13 May 2924.
7 This statement of the UNSG was made on 24 October 2023 (UN Day)

have significantly increased the opportunities for Iraqis to move from severe ill-being to more well-being.

It had taken five years, and much avoidable death and destruction, from "taking note with grave concern ... of the necessity to meeting urgently the humanitarian needs in Kuwait and Iraq" in 1991 (S/RES/687 of 3 April 1991) to "concern of the serious nutritional and health situation of the Iraqi population" in 1995 (S/RES/986 of 14 April 1995) to belatedly agree to the establishment of a humanitarian programme, the UN "oil-for-food" program.[8]

The procurement of humanitarian supplies for Iraq constituted a nightmare from the very beginning. While the monthly imports of 440,000 tons of food distributed by the UN World Food Programme, and most of the medicines administered by the World Health Organization (WHO), reached households and health facilities in fairly good time, other vital supplies for agriculture, infrastructure, water and sanitation and education, etc. often took a full year before reaching their destinations. On average, twenty-three procurement steps had to be taken for such supplies. These involved foreign ministries, the UN treasury in New York, commercial banks, Baghdad-based UN offices, supplying firms, transport agents, embassies, and often even ministries of defence because of the dual use potential of supplies such as vaccines and fertilizer. In addition, micro-management of the oil-for-food programme by the UN Sanctions Committee in New York, and the resulting slow contract approvals, added significantly to life-affecting delays. What UN agencies operating in Iraq considered as "urgently needed" supplies, were often either temporarily put on hold or permanently blocked by the SC Sanctions Committee. Holds reached a peak in 2001 when within a six-months period supplies worth $5.5 billion (!) were withheld from the people.

In the interest of the welfare of the Iraqi people, a goal of primary importance for the UN as an organisation, the Security Council had a profound and a wide range of humane options to discharge its supply responsibilities but chose not to use these: (i.) for most humanitarian supplies, the highly bureaucratic 23-step clearance process could have been significantly reduced to enable a much faster supply arrival in Iraq; (ii.) reliance on the Iraq-based 2000+ national and international UN humanitarian UN staff and senior UN officials to be left alone to monitor the use of OFFP supplies would have brought relief to the people significantly faster; (iii.) avoiding to put on hold or blocking billions of dollars' worth of supplies could have significantly reduced Iraqi suffering; and (iv.) the consensus principle prevailing in the

---

8 S/RES/986 (14 April 1995) – 15 yes votes and the MOU 986 (20 May 1996), a corresponding operational agreement signed by the UN Secretariat and the Iraqi Mission to the UN.

Sanctions Committee, where decision making was possible only when all committee members were in agreement, could have been replaced by majority voting.[9]

UN Secretary-General Kofi Annan's right to remind the SC that, while it excersized its right to identify the catastrophic conditions of the Iraqi people, it also had the responsibility to support appropriate implementation and to therefore de-link the humanitarian program from geopolitically determined economic sanctions and disarmament. The Iraqi people, he insisted, should not be punished for the policies of their government. The SG argued that the oil-for-food program, as devised, would not be enough "even if it [was] perfectly implemented." China, France, and Russia, three of the five permanent members of the Council, shared this perception.

However, the right of veto prevailed despite its serious implications for the Iraqi people. There was no chance that the U.S. and the UK Governments would even consider such a separation of disarmament and humanitarian exemption for the sake of improving human conditions in Iraq. With respect to (i.) de-linking disarmament and humanitarian relief and (ii.) changing the timing of compensation payments, the SG had the option to impress on the SC that there was also an ethical/morality dimension to be considered. Both Boutro Boutros-Ghali and Kofi Annan did approach the SC in this regard but failed to even get the Council's willingness to discuss such options.

There were additional options the UN Secretariat had to handle its human responsibilities in line with respective UN mandates. These included to: (i.) organize regular briefings by senior Baghdad-based staff of the SC and the SG and his senior staff to get up-to-date information on conditions in Iraq; (ii.) arrange visits to Iraq of the SC, or at least some Council members, to get an in-situ impression of the catastrophic situation Iraqi society was facing and an opportunity to discuss the sanctions situation with the Government; (iii.) correct the flawed management structure of the Office of the Humanitarian Coordinator in Baghdad where two of the management units in that office did not report to the head of the Baghdad office but directly to UN HQ "because this is what the Security Council wants," which, of course, created a serious dysfunctional administrative chaos at the expense of running an effective humanitarian programme; and (iv.) allowing reports on the implementation of the humanitarian program to be written solely by the UN in Iraq rather than drafted in Baghdad but finalized by HQ staff in New York headed by an analyst outposted to the UN from the UK Ministry of Defence in London.

---

9 The consensus approach which assumed that all members of the Iraq Sanctions Committee agreed, allowed the control over decision making by individual members of the Committee.

In a statement to the Security Council in 2000 related to Iraq, the Ambassador of Malaysia, Agam Hasmy, concluded in moving words: "How ironic is it that the same policy that is supposed to disarm Iraq of its weapons of mass destruction has itself become a weapon of mass destruction." (10)

To provide further details to show that some staff in senior positions at UN HQ was submissive to external geopolitical pressure, not free of bias in dealing with Iraq or simply unwilling to carry out their responsibilities with "integrity" as demanded by their appointment (Charter Article 101/3), could be added but would go beyond the scope of this paper.

The UN had unquestionably a wide range of options, at both institutional and individual levels, to carry out its responsibilities for protecting innocent civilians, but more often than not, failed to do so, damaging the credibility of the United Nations, and in the case of the Security Council, even violating Charter and humanitarian law. For P5 Council members, in Iraq and Gaza, geopolitical interests clearly have outweighed humanitarian concerns. Ethical and moral considerations seemed to play at best a marginal role.

In Gaza:

In dealing with the Israeli-Palestinian conflict following the Hamas massacre of October 7, 2023, the Security Council has become dysfunctional by continuous polarized positions involving primarily the Russian Federation and the United States. These P5 members, and the Council as a whole, are fully aware of the dire human conditions in Gaza. Both Russia and the U.S. are cognizant of this reality and have made use of their right to submit draft resolutions on how to de-escalate the confrontation and end this catastrophe. And yet, both have chosen to reject each other's draft resolutions, and made use of their right to veto resolutions. On October 16, 2023, the U.S. rejected a Russian draft resolution, supported by China, which called for an "immediate" ceasefire and "condemning all violence and hostilities directed against civilians and all acts of terrorism" on the grounds that it failed to mention Hamas. On June 6, 2024, Russia, again supported by China, rejected in turn a U.S. draft resolution calling for a two-phased approach to bring an end to the war in Gaza starting with a ceasefire (phase one) followed by a "permanent end to hostilities." Russia indicated it could only support a resolution that would allow phase one to remain in place as long as negotiations for a ceasefire continued before discussing a permanent end to hostilities (phase two).

Two resolutions, both with constructive content, rejected, however, by either side in a retaliatory manner for purely geopolitical reasons and in violation of their Security Council responsibility to act as a team in solving international conflicts. This quid pro quo exchange between the two countries continues with Russia abstaining, rather than vetoing, because of "lack of clarity on the official Israeli agreement" but thereby allowing the U.S. proposed resolution 2735 of 10 June 2024 to pass.

In sum: since October 2023, resolutions on Gaza have been adopted only when P5 members abstained rather than casting a veto. Such irresponsible handling of the Gaza crisis by two permanent members of the Security Council has had its profound human costs. Reminiscent of Iraq resolution S/986 (1995) with which the Security Council, after years of procrastination, finally acknowledged "the serious nutritional and health situation of the Iraq population and 'the risk of further deterioration," the UN oil-for-food programme was established, in the case of Gaza, the United States did not veto resolution A/2728 (March 25, 2024), but instead abstained, allowing it to pass because of "the catastrophic humanitarian situation in Gaza."[10]

Exercising the right to pass resolutions, did, however, not imply that individual members of the Council would carry out their responsibilities in accordance with UN Charter law and in opposition to the Israeli government's illegal military onslaught on Gaza. Despite these profoundly important resolutions raising the hope that conditions of life for the people in Gaza would improve, the catastrophic situation on the ground, if anything, worsened. The Security Council failed to implement the resolutions it had passed. In the words of Ambassador Lana Zaki Nusseibeh of the United Arab Emirates: "Since the start of the conflict, the Council has been unable to produce anything that would alleviate the suffering of the people."

Israel has been ignoring whatever the Security Council decided to advocate in bringing to an end this asymmetrical war; in increasing the inflow of humanitarian assistance and ensuring sustainable security for civilians. Its military offensive has entirely disregarded external appeals from even its key ally, the United States. Prime Minister Benjamin Netanyahu indicated polemically and unrealistically: "If we have to stand alone, we will stand alone!" Israeli General Gvir's motto: "I go my own way. I do not blink. I do not fold."

Palestinians in Gaza have been locked out, routed and often pushed from one location to another, with the Israeli authorities claiming that they did everything to adhere to law and protect civilians, a claim that is brazenly dishonest and disproved by the continuously and dramatically rising numbers of Palestinian casualties. These, according to preliminary UN estimates, stand in early June at 36,586 killed; and 83,074 injured: 1.7 million people (75%) have been displaced and traumatized; and, as estimated by the UN, Gaza is faced with twenty-three million tons of debris that will take years to clear.

---

10 See also: S/RES/2712 (2023); S/RES/2720 (2023); and S/RES/2735 (2024).

Given the fact that Israel has been entirely dependent for decades on the United States for financial and military support, the U.S. is the only country that has the power to force the Israeli government to end its annihilatory military offensive in Gaza. The U.S. authorities decided to pursue a double track approach which they hoped would help multilaterally to improve the humanitarian situation, and at the same time, reassure bilaterally the Israeli government that the U.S. remained a loyal ally and would continue to provide military assistance to Israel. This approach has seriously backfired: the humanitarian conditions in Gaza have worsened; and confrontation in the West Bank between Israelis, especially settlers, and Palestinians has increased, while the Israeli military continues its destruction of the Strip. Additionally, the U.S. government has used its close relations with Israel to negotiate Gaza issues on behalf, and with the agreement, of the UN Security Council. It has done so with some success, most recently in obtaining Israeli agreement for the U.S.-drafted resolution 2728 which was adopted by the Council on 25 March 2024.

The U.S. has often shown leadership in advancing human rights-related initiatives including the drafting of the UN Charter, the nuclear test ban and non-proliferation treaties, climate change and international criminal court agreements, yet, the official United States more often than not, in the end, did not take the ultimate step of joining the majority of nations by ratifying what they had negotiated such as the creation of the ICC, the CTBT, the Convention on the Elimination of Discrimination Against Women and the Convention on the Rights of the Child because of a historic and obsessed fear that it might reduce U.S. sovereignty.

Mention has to be made that both Democrats and Republicans in the U.S. government, until recently, have consistently claimed exceptionalism as an inherent part of what they perceive to be their right for global leadership, but without accepting the international legal responsibilities that would come with this right.

The UN will never forget what Jesse Helms, the Chairman of the U.S. Senate Foreign Affairs committee, conveyed to the UN Security Council in early 2000: "If the UN respects the sovereignty of the American people…it will earn and deserve their respect…but a UN that seeks to impose its presumed authority, it begs for confrontation and eventual U.S. withdrawal."[11]

In the case of Iraq, this presumptuous right of exception meant clandestine U.S. support for the Iraqi opposition; using disinformation about alleged atrocities committed in Kuwait by Iraqi occupation forces as spread by U.S.

---

11 Jesse Helms visited the UN/HQ on 21 January 2000.

PR agencies, e.g., Hill & Knowlton,[12] which were quoted extensively by President George Bush; and the 1995 signing into law of the Iraq Liberation Act by President Bill Clinton, a Democratic President, cooperating with a Republican Congress which in breach of international law but in accordance with U.S. law, allowed interference with Iraq's sovereignty.

With respect to the Israeli/Palestinian war in Gaza, the U.S. government shocked the world by supporting UN efforts to provide more humanitarian assistance to Gaza while at the very same time confirming to supply more military hardware for Israel's war against Hamas which the UN Security Council had not approved.

Had there been a link between formal UN rights and formal UN responsibilities, much death and destruction for the Iraqi and Palestinian people could have been avoided and the credibility of the UN, as an institution, upheld. President Carter might have agreed with this assumption, since he had co-signed in 1997 the heads of state and government draft of a Universal Declaration of Human Responsibilities, as mentioned earlier.

The Link and the GA Summit on the Future of the UN

For the forthcoming reform debate at the UN Summit in September 2024, it is undeniably relevant that the UN's handling of the Iraq and Gaza crises are not standalone examples of UN failure. Such failure was equally apparent in other countries such as (i.) in Libya, when in 2011 the SC passed consensus resolution 1973 authorizing member states, with considerably serious consequences for the Libyan people: "to take all necessary measures to enforce compliance...," leaving it to individual member states, rather than the UN Security Council itself, to decide how to implement this resolution[13]; (ii.) in Syria, where despite frequent illegal airstrikes by the three western P5 members and Israel, and on the ground violations of Syria's sovereignty, the SC has not managed to bring an end to this crisis; and (iii.) in Palestine/

---

12 The Kuwait Government in exile had paid the U.S. PR agency Hill & Knowlton for a story that showed a young girl called Nayirah who allegedly had seen that Iraqi occupation forces had turned off the electricity supply from incubators resulting in the death of several hundred babies. The George Bush administration used this story to gain U.S. public acceptance for the second Gulf war in 1991. As it turned out, Nariyah was the daughter of Nasir Al-Sabah, Kuwait's ambassador to the U.S. and "everything she said was a lie." (see: Indeymedia/UK)

13 S/Res/1973 (17 March 2011) 10 countries supported this resolution, and 5 countries abstained (China, Russia, Brazil, Germany and India). This consensus resolution made it possible that individual Security Council member countries were allowed "to take all necessary measures to enforce compliance" (para. 8) which they did in pursuance of their own bilateral interests rather than in protection of Libyan civilians.

Israel, which has witnessed the most profound UN Security Council failure to adopt a strategy on how to intervene in the worst violation in modern times of UN Charter and international humanitarian law by Israel in Gaza. More generally, the inability of the Security Council to do justice to its mandate has led to growing demands in the General Assembly by an increasing number of governments to demand an end to geopolitical game playing by the Security Council. On April 26, 2022, the GA adopted resolution A/12417, also called the "Lichtenstein resolution," which requires P5 members to justify to the GA their use of veto.[14]

The challenge ahead will be for civil society groups world-wide, among them, a reinvigorated Global Social Forum, Amnesty International, Transparency International, the Stockholm International Peace Research Institute (SIPRI), and also those NGOs that have a consultative status with the UN (ECOSOC), to create a non-governmental forum on "rights and responsibilities." Such a body would have the task to link up with: (i.) the UN General Assembly to pursue initiatives such as the Lichtenstein proposal; (ii.) governments and civil society organisations that have played major roles in preparing the September 2024 GA "Summit of the Future" of the UN,[15] and (iii.) be involved in the post-Summit follow-up. The proposed forum, taking the Iraq and Gaza experience into account, would have the objectives (i.) to encourage the General Assembly to resume its debate on rights and responsibilities and (ii.) to request the International Court of Justice (ICJ) to issue an opinion on a possible partnership between UN human rights and UN human responsibility. Assuming that the September GA Summit will identify a "Pact for the Future" as planned, the hope would be that such a pact will include preparations for a Covenant on Human Responsibility.

---

14 The right to veto by individual P5 member states and the irresponsibility with which they often have exercised this right repeatedly prevented the SC to carry out its mandated rights and responsibilities for the protection of global, regional, national and local peace and security. Ambassador Christian Wenaweser, pointed out to the SC, on behalf of the Government of Lichtenstein, "There has never been a stronger need for innovation in order to secure the central role and voice of the UN in this regard."(15) The Ambassadors and Permanent Representatives to the UN of Namibia and Germany have been appointed by the GA as the facilitators for the preparations of the September 2024 UN Summit. Some 350 civil society organizations from around the world are associated with these preparations.

15 United Nations Summit of the Future, September 20–23, 2024, New York. https://www.un.org/en/summit-of-the-future

Major Documents of International Law Tribunals

- The original statement by Karim Khan with respect to Netanyahu, Gallant, Sinwar, Deif and Haniyeh
  https://www.icc-cpi.int/news/statement-icc-prosecutor-karim-aa-khan-kc-applications-arrest-warrants-situation-state

- Statement in response to Israel's challenge to the arrest warrants
  https://www.icc-cpi.int/news/situation-state-palestine-icc-pre-trial-chamber-i-rejects-state-israels-challenges

- Statement of Karim Kahn on the arrest warrants of Netanyahu and Gallant
  https://www.icc-cpi.int/news/statement-icc-prosecutor-karim-aa-khan-kc-issuance-arrest-warrants-situation-state-palestine

- Statement by Karim Khan on the issue of arrest warrant for Deif
  https://www.icc-cpi.int/news/situation-state-palestine-icc-pre-trial-chamber-i-issues-warrant-arrest-mohammed-diab-ibrahim

- South Africa's full application initiating proceedings against Israel in the ICJ (84 pages)
  https://d3i6fh83elv35t.cloudfront.net/static/2024/01/192-20231228-app-01-00-en.pdf
  https://www.icj-cij.org/sites/default/files/case-related/192/192-20240510-wri-01-00-en.pdf

- South Africa's Request, 26 January 2024 decision of the ICJ
  https://www.icj-cij.org/node/203447

- Order of 26 January 2024 from ICJ
  https://www.icj-cij.org/sites/default/files/case-related/192/192-20240510-wri-01-00-en.pdfICJ

- Nicaragua Submission, 30 April 2024, "Alleged Breaches of Certain International Obligations in respect to the Occupied Palestinian Territory (Nicaragua v. Germany)"
  https://www.icj-cij.org/case/193

- ICJ opinion, 24 May 2024, The Court reaffirms its previous provisional measures and indicates new measures
  https://www.icj-cij.org/node/204099
  https://www.icj-cij.org/sites/default/files/case-related/192/192-20240524-pre-01-00-en.pdf

- Advisory Opinion, 19 July 2024, "Legal Consequences arising from the Policies and Practices of Israel in the Occupied Palestinian Territories including East Jerusalem"
  https://www.icj-cij.org/case/186

- Case 193 – Alleged Breaches of Certain International Obligations in respect of the Occupied Palestinian Territory (Nicaragua v. Germany), Order of 19 July 2024
  https://www.icj-cij.org

Contributors

AHMET DAVUTOĞLU was born in Konya, Türkiye in 1959. He graduated with a double major in Political Science and Economics from Bosphorus University, where he went on to gain a Masters degree, followed by a PhD from the Department of Political Science and International Relations. In 1990 Ahmet Davutoğlu gained his Assistant Professorship at the International Islamic University of Malaysia, where he established the Political Science Department, a body that he chaired until 1993. He became an Associate Professor in 1993, and gained his Professorship in 1999.

Between 1995 and 2002, he lectured and performed senior administrative roles at various universities in Istanbul. Between 1998 and 2002 he was also a visiting lecturer at the Military Academy and the War Academy.

Professor Davutoğlu was appointed Chief Foreign Policy Advisor to the Prime Minister of Türkiye in November 2002 and continued to serve as Chief Advisor until May 2009, in which capacity he played a leading role in the formulation and implementation of Türkiye's foreign policy.

Ahmet Davutoğlu was appointed Minister of Foreign Affairs of the 60th Government of the Republic of Türkiye in May 2009 and continued to serve in this post during the subsequent government's term. Both as foreign policy advisor and Minister, he played an active and prominent role in peace making and mediation efforts to overcome conflicts in the Middle East and the Balkans.

Professor Davutoğlu served as Prime Minister of Türkiye's 62nd, 63rd and 64th Governments.

In the wake of the Turkish general election of November 2015, in which under his leadership the Justice and Development Party won a landslide victory with 49.5% of the ballot, Professor Davutoğlu was reappointed Prime Minister, in which post he served until May 2016.

Ahmet Davutoğlu's influential work in the academic, diplomatic and political spheres has been widely recognized, including by *Foreign Policy Magazine,* which listed him among the Top 100 Global Thinkers in 2010, 2011 and 2012. He was named as one of the 100 Most Influential People in the World by Time magazine in 2012.

Ahmet Davutoğlu has received many awards, including the Woodrow Wilson Award for Public Service in 2010, the AMSS UK Building Bridges

Award in 2010, the 21st Century Statesman Award by the International League of Humanists in 2012, and the Macedonian Friendship Award in 2012.

During a multifaceted career as an academician, political advisor, diplomat and politician, Professor Davutoğlu has published numerous books and articles on foreign policy, principally in Turkish and English, many of which have also been translated into other languages including Japanese, Portuguese, Russian, Arabic, Persian, Italian, Greek and Albanian.

Professor Davutoğlu's published books include *Alternative Paradigms* (Lanham: University Press of America, 1993), *Civilizational Transformation and the Muslim World* (Kuala Lumpur: Quill, 1994), *Stratejik Derinlik: Türkiye'nin Uluslararası Konumu* (Küre Yayınları, 2001), *Küresel Bunalım* (Küre Yayınları, 2002), *Teoriden Pratiğe: Türk Dış Politikası* Üzerine *Konuşmalar* (Küre Yayınları, 2013), *Medeniyetler ve Şehirler* (Küre Yayınları, 2016), and *Duruş: Gençlerle Yüzyüze* (Küre Yayınları, 2017). In addition, he has published many interdisciplinary papers and studies in a wide range of fields including international relations, regional analysis and comparative political philosophy, as well as conducting comparative civilizational historical research in a number of different languages.

Professor Davutoğlu is married with four children and speaks English, German and Arabic.

RICHARD FALK is the Albert G. Milbank Professor of International Law Emeritus at Princeton University and Chair of Global Law and Co-Director of Centre of Climate Crime and Climate Justice, Queen Mary University London. Research Fellow, University of California, Santa Barbara. UN Special Rapporteur on Occupied Palestine (2008–2014). Author of *This Endangered Planet* (1971); *Predatory Globalization: A Critique* (1999); *Religion and Humane Global Governance* (2001); *Public Intellectual: The Life of a Citizen Pilgrim* (2021); *Liberating the UN: Realism with Hope*, (2024) (with Hans von Sponeck); *Patriotism to the Earth* (2025) (with Sasha Milonova). Last nominated for the Nobel Peace Prize, 2023.

SUSAN ABULHAWA was born to Palestinian refugees of the 1967 war. Currently based in the United States, she is a human and animal rights activist and frequent political commentator. She is the founder of Playgrounds for Palestine, an organization dedicated to upholding Palestinian children's Right to Play, and the Executive Director of the Palestine Writes Literature Festival. Her first novel, *Mornings in Jenin*, was an international bestseller, with rights sold in over thirty languages, making Abulhawa the most widely read Palestinian novelist in the world. She is also the author of the novel *The*

Blue Between Sky and Water, set in Gaza, the poetry collection *My Voice Sought the Wind* and, most recently, *Against the Loveless World*, a finalist for the Aspen Words Prize and winner of the 2021 Palestine Book Award and the 2021 Arab American Book Award, among other accolades.

RAMZY BAROUD is a syndicated columnist, the author of six books and the Editor of The Palestine Chronicle. Baroud has a PhD in Palestine Studies from the University of Exeter. His books include *My Father was a Freedom Fighter* and *The Last Earth*. His latest book, co-edited with Professor Ilan Pappé, is *Our Vision for Liberation: Engaged Palestinian Leaders and Intellectuals Speak Out*. Baroud is currently a Non-resident Senior Research Fellow at the Center for Islam and Global Affairs (CIGA).

AVI SHLAIM, Emeritus Professor of International Relations at the University of Oxford and a Fellow of St. Antony's College, is a globally renowned historian of the modern Middle East. He held a British Academy Research Readership between 1995–1997; a British Academy Research Professorship between 2003–2006. He was elected Fellow of the British Academy in 2006, and was awarded a British Academy Medal for lifetime achievement in 2017.

An Arab Jew, Professor Shlaim was born in Baghdad in 1945; grew up in Israel; served in the Israel Defence Forces; and received his university education at Cambridge and the London School of Economics. He is based at the Middle East Centre at St. Antony's College, Oxford where his main research interest continues to be the Arab-Israeli conflict, mostly recently the genocide in Gaza. He became widely known as one of the "New Historians," a small group of Israeli scholars who put forward critical interpretations of the history of Zionism and Israel, from the late 1980s onwards.

His books include *Collusion Across the Jordan: King Abdullah, the Zionist Movement, and the Partition of Palestine* (Winner of the 1988 Political Studies Association's Mackenzie Prize); *War and Peace in the Middle East: A Concise History* (short-listed for the 1995 Lionel Gelber Prize, a Canadian prize for the best book in International Relations); *The Iron Wall: Israel and the Arab World* (2000, updated edition 2014); *Lion of Jordan: King Hussein's Life in War and Peace* (2007); *Israel and Palestine: Reappraisals, Revisions, Refutations* (2009); and *Three Worlds: Memoir of an Arab-Jew* (Winner of the PEN Hessell-Tiltman Prize 2024; runner up for the British-Kuwait Friendship Society book prize for Middle Eastern Studies 2024).

Shlaim is a believer in the subversive function of history, in using archival sources to challenge the received wisdom and to dispel national myths. He believes that "The historian's most fundamental task is not to chronicle but to evaluate... to subject the claims of all the protagonists to rigorous scrutiny and reject all those claims, however deeply cherished, that do not stand up."

Professor Shlaim is a frequent contributor to the print media and commentator on radio and television on Middle Eastern affairs. He has lived in the United Kingdom since 1966; he holds dual British and Israeli nationality; and he lives in Oxford.

IZZELDIN ABULEISH, a Palestinian Canadian, author, academic, and researcher, is a Professor at the Dalla Lana School of Public Health at the University of Toronto Born and raised in Jabalia Refugee Camp in the Gaza Strip.

Prof. Abuelaish' s book, *I Shall Not Hate: A Gaza Doctor's Journey on the Road to Peace and Human Dignity*, a national and international best seller, an autobiography of his loss and transformation, has achieved worldwide critical acclaim. Published in 2010 (translated into 23 different languages).

Prof. Abuelaish has been nominated five times for Nobel peace Prize, and he is fondly known as Nelson Mandela, Mahatma Ghandi and the "Martin Luther King of the Middle East," having dedicated his life to using health as a vehicle for peace.

Prof. Abuelaish' s extensive list of awards and honors include countless national and international awards including 19 honorary doctorate degrees, The order of Ontario, The Meritorious Service Cross, and the Queen Elizabeth II Diamond Jubilee Medal, The Governor General's Medallion, the World Citizenship in Action Award, presented by the Canadian Branch of the Registry; the Mahatma Gandhi Peace Award of Canada; the Foundation P&V Citizenship Award; the Calgary Peace Prize; the Lombardy Region Peace Prize, the Stavros Niarchos Prize for Survivorship; Dr. Abuelaish has been named one of the Top 25 Canadian Immigrants; one of the 500 Most Powerful Arabs; and one of the 500 Most Influential Muslims.

ABDULLAH AL-AHSAN is a former professor of comparative civilization in the Department of Political Science and International Relations at Istanbul Sehır University. Earlier, he taught at the International Islamic University Malaysia for almost three decades. Graduated from McGill University, Montreal, Canada, and the University of Michigan, Ann Arbor, Michigan, USA, Ahsan has written and edited several books and many articles on the relationship between contemporary Islamic and Western civilizations. His books and articles have been translated into Arabic, Bengali, Bosnian, Turkish, and Urdu. He now lives in Chicago.

JOSEPH ANTHONY CAMILLERI OAM is Professor Emeritus at La Trobe University, Melbourne, where he held the Chair in International Relations (1994–2012) and was founding Director of the Centre for Dialogue 2006–2012. He is a Fellow of the Australian Academy of Social Sciences. He is Convener of Conversation at the Crossroads, and Co-Convener of SHAPE (Saving Humanity and Planet Earth).

He has authored or edited some 35 books and written over 130 book chapters and journal articles. covering such areas as geopolitics, governance, the role of culture and religion, intercultural conflict and dialogue, environment, human rights, and the politics of Asia-Pacific.

He has convened several major international dialogues and conferences, including *From the Middle East to the Asia Pacific: Arc of Conflict or Dialogue of Cultures and Religions?* (2008); the *Australia-Malaysia, Australia-China and Australia-Indonesia dialogues* (2010–2013); *Towards a Just and Ecologically Sustainable Peace* (2019); and *Night Falls in the Evening Lands: The Assange Epic* (2024)

CHANDRA MUZAFFAR (PhD) is the President of the International Movement for a Just World (JUST). He was Professor of Global Studies at Universiti Sains Malaysia, Penang, Malaysia from 2007 to 2012.

MOHAMMAD HASHIM KAMALI was Dean and Professor at the International Institute of Islamic Thought and Civilization (ISTAC) and the International Islamic University in Malaysia. Dr. Kamali then served as Founding CEO of the International Institute of Advanced Islamic Studies in Malaysia (2008–2022) and is currently an Adjunct Fellow of that Institute. He is the world's leading expert on comparative studies between Islamic and modern law often describes as "the most widely read living author on Islamic law in the English language." He was conferred with the title Dato by His Royal Highness Sultan Nazrin Shah in November 2020.

MEYMUNE N. TOPÇU is Assistant Professor of Psychology at MEF University, Istanbul, with a PhD in Cognitive Psychology from the New School for Social Research. Her research focuses on collective memory, anxiety, and future thinking, with publications in leading psychology journals. She has been awarded several prestigious research grants to explore topics such as existential threats, collective future thinking, and perceived agency. Her work addresses critical societal issues through a psychological perspective employing rigorous experimental methodologies. Her research seeks to advance interdisciplinary scholarship by establishing critical conceptual and empirical connections between psychology and the broader social sciences. She is also the mother of two daughters, Ayşe Sare and Meryem Hale.

HILAL ELVER is a professor of international law, specialized on human rights and international environmental law, and the co-director of the Climate Change, Democracy and Human Security project at the University of California Santa Barbara. From May 2014 to May 2020, Elver served as the United Nations Special Rapporteur on the right to food. She is currently serving as a member of the Steering Committee of the High-Level Panel of Experts (HLPE) of the United Nations World Committee of Food Security (CFS), and a member of the Scientific Advisory Committee of the UN Food Systems Hub. She taught and maintained several affiliations with academic institutions worldwide. Select publications, UN reports, articles are featured on her website hilalelver.org.

SARE DAVUTOĞLU (PhD), an established medical doctor, is known for her contributions to both medicine and voluntary non-governmental initiatives. A graduate of the Faculty of Medicine at Istanbul University, she specializes in obstetrics and gynecology, dedicating her career to women's reproductive and integrative health. Beyond her medical profession, she is deeply involved in social projects, focusing on education, health, and women's empowerment through non-governmental organizations. In addition to her professional and volunteer work, she is a mother of four, striving to balance her roles while making a tangible difference in healthcare and social development.

FERHAN GÜLOĞLU is a PhD Candidate in the Sociocultural Anthropology program. She holds an MA in Middle Eastern Studies from Columbia University and a BA in Political Science from Boğaziçi University (Istanbul). Her dissertation focuses on childbirth politics in the Middle East. She currently works as the coordinator for the Safebirth in Palestine project, which aims to create safe childbirth conditions and maternal health support for pregnant women in Gaza. Her work has been featured in *Anthropological Quarterly, Scholar and Feminist, AOC Media* (France) and *The Guardian.* She is also the mother of her two kids, Yahya and Vera.

LISA HAJJAR is Professor of Sociology at the University of California at Santa Barbara. She specializes in the relationship between law and conflict. Her publications include *Courting Conflict: The Israeli Military Court System in the West Bank and Gaza* (2005), *Torture: A Sociology of Violence* *and Human Rights* (2013), and *The War in Court: Inside the Long Fight against Torture* (2022).

BASIL FARRAJ is the Director of the Ibrahim Abu-Lughod Institute of International Studies, and Assistant Professor in the Department of Philosophy and Cultural Studies at Birzeit University, Palestine. His research addresses the intersections of memory, resistance, and art by prisoners and others at the receiving end of violence.

PENNY GREEN is Professor of Law and Globalisation at Queen Mary University of London. Professor Green has written 11 books and numerous articles, publishing extensively on state crime theory, genocide, state violence, mass expulsions and resistance to state violence. She has a long track record of researching in hostile environments and recent projects include a comparative study of civil society resistance to state crime in Türkiye, Tunisia, Colombia, PNG, Kenya and Myanmar; forced evictions in Palestine/Israel and Myanmar's genocide against the Rohingya. Professor Green is Founder and Director of the award winning International State Crime Initiative (ISCI) and co-editor in Chief of the international journal *State Crime*. In 2017 she initiated and organized with ISCI, a Permanent People's tribunal on Myanmar State Crimes against Rohingya and other Ethnic Minorities. She is a Steering Committee member of the Gaza Tribunal, a signatory of the Declaration of Global Conscience and an Adjunct Professor at Birzeit University, Ramallah. In 2024 she was appointed a judge for the Palestine Book Awards. Her latest book, co-authored with Thomas MacManus, *Chronicle of a Genocide Foretold: Myanmar and the Rohingya* will be published by Rutgers university Press in early 2025. Her current work, funded by a Leverhulme Major Research Fellowship will explore the humanitarian camp as a potential site of genocidal reproduction.

GRACE SPENCE GREEN is a doctor working to challenge the narratives surrounding disability, medicine and identity. In 2018, aged 22 and a fourth year medical student, she sustained a spinal cord injury and is now a full-time wheelchair user. She is passionate about medicine, advocacy for the disabled community and challenging ableism, the stigma surrounding disability and inaccessible spaces.

She advocates for inclusive representation for disabled people in all walks of life and particularly in medicine and the media. Grace has written for the *British Medical Journal* (BMJ) and the *Guardian* and has appeared on *ITV, BBC* (radio and television) and *Sky News*.

Since 2020 she has been a trustee for BackUp, one of the UK's leading Spinal Cord Injury charities and sits on the Services Committee. She is also a patron for Children Today Charitable Trust, which provides vital, specialized equipment to disabled children across the UK to enable their independence and allow them to have the best quality of life possible.

In the months of rehabilitation which followed her life-changing injury Grace learned that she didn't have to fit into the small and narrowly defined box into which society so often places disabled people. She travels widely and hopes in the future to work in the field of pediatrics and humanitarian aid, advocating for disabled children. Her book, *To Exist As I Am* will be published in 2025 (Wellcome/Profile books).

WALDEN BELLO is currently Honorary Research Fellow at the Sociology Department of the State University of New York at Binghamton, where he also held until recently the position of International Adjunct Professor of Sociology. He served in the Philippine House of Representatives from 2009 to 2015 and ran for vice president in the Philippine elections of 2022. He was named Amnesty International Philippines' "Human Rights Defender for 2023.

An academic with a global reputation, Bello obtained his doctorate in sociology from Princeton University in the United States in 1975 and his Bachelor of Arts from Ateneo de Manila University in 1966. He is the author or co-author of 25 books on topics ranging from the political economy of the Philippines to the rise of the Right globally to the brewing conflict between China and the United States. He received the Right Livelihood Award (aka the Alternative Nobel Prize) in 2003 for his work in exposing the negative side of corporate-driven globalization and was named Outstanding Public Scholar by the International Studies Association in 2008. He has been called "the world's leading no-nonsense revolutionary" by renowned Canadian author Naomi Klein. He was also praised "as the world's best guide to American exploitation of the globe's poor and defenseless," by the late Chalmers Johnson, the world's leading authority on East Asia's economic development.

SEVİNÇ ALKAN ÖZCAN graduated from Marmara University, Department of Political Science and International Relations. She received her MA and PhD from the same department. She was visiting scholar at Oxford Center for Islamic Studies in 2006.

She worked for Foundation for Sciences and Arts, as the director of Center for Global Studies. She served as advisor to former Minister of

Foreign Affairs (2011–2014) and chief advisor to former Prime Minister of Türkiye, Prof. Ahmet Davutoğlu (2014–2017).

She gave courses on Religion and Politics at Istanbul Kültür University. She teaches on Politics of Caucasus and Central Asia, Religion and Politics in IR and History of Turkish Democracy and Turkish Foreign Policy in Ankara Yıldırım Beyazıt University, Department of International Relations.

Sevinç Alkan Özcan is author of the books *Russian Minorities* (2005*), Religion Identity and Politics in Russia and Poland* (2012), *Talks on Eurasia* (edition, 2010), *Glocal Transformations* (edition, 2012), *Religion and Identity in Azerbaijan* (edition, 2014) and several articles on regional politics, Turkish foreign policy and identity and politics.

ARLENE CLEMESHA (PhD) is professor of Contemporary Arab History at the University of São Paulo, Brazil, and Director of the Center for Palestine Studies at the same university (CEPal-FFLCH/USP). Her books include *Brazil and the Middle East: the Power of Civil Society* (co-org./IRI-USP); *Palestine 48-08* (Tehran: DEFC); and *Marxism and Judaism, history of a difficult relation* (São Paulo: Boitempo). She has translated several of Edward Said's works into Portuguese, and her writings have appeared in English, Portuguese, Spanish, French, Italian, Arabic and Farsi.

FRANCESCO SCHETTINO (PhD, 2006) is a full professor of Economics at the University of Campania L.Vanvitelli. His main research focuses on inequality and technological change, with his main articles published in leading journals such as *World Development, Review of Income and Wealth, Cambridge Journal of Economics*, and *Journal of Economic Inequality*. He has also authored books in Italian, Spanish, English, and Portuguese. He is the founder of the Popular University Antonio Gramsci.

VICTORIA BRITTAIN was born in India and has lived and worked in Saigon, Algiers, Nairobi, Washington and London and travelled widely reporting across Africa and in the Middle East, particularly in Gaza, the West Bank and in the Palestinian camps in Syria and Lebanon. She wrote for *The Guardian* for 25 years, where she was latterly Associate Foreign Editor, and for many other English and French media, and also did both radio and TV work. She is currently part of the editorial collective of *Afrique XXI*, a specialized website of original reporting and analysis on Africa. She has written, co-written and edited books on Africa in the Cold War, notably from Angola and was active in the Anti-Apartheid Movement. Later books, and verbatim plays, were on the U.S. war on terror and included Moazzam Begg's Guantanamo memoir,

Enemy Combatant, and *Shadow Lives, the Forgotten Women of the War on Terror.* Her latest book is *Love and Resistance in the Films of Mai Masri.*

IRENE GENDZIER, currently Prof. Emeritus, Boston University, served in the Departments of History and Political Science, and was associated with the African Studies Center, teaching the history and politics of the Middle East and North Africa and problems of development. Recent publications include *Dying to Forget: Oil, Power, Palestine, and the Foundations of U.S. Policy in the Middle East, 1945–1949* (Columbia University Press, 2015; 2016–2017); *Development Against Democracy* (London: Pluto Press, 2017); *Notes From the Minefield: United States Intervention in Lebanon and the Middle East, 1945–1958*; co-editor with Richard Flak and Robert J Lifton, *Crimes of War: Iraq* (2006); *Frantz Fanon: A Critical Study* (1973); currently at work on the manuscript, *Does Knowing Matter: What the U.S. Knew About the Conflict in Palestine in 1948.*

BILGEHAN UÇAK, a novelist, literary critic, travel book writer and journalist, was born in Istanbul in 1989. He has written nine books and many articles.

JUAN COLE is the Richard P. Mitchell Collegiate Professor of History at the University of Michigan and is past president of the Middle East Studies Association of North America. He is author of, among other works, *Napoleon's Egypt: Invading the Middle East* (St. Martin, 2007) and *Muhammad: Prophet of Peace amid the Clash of Empires* (Bold Type Books, 2018).

CRAIG MOKIBER is an international human rights lawyer and former Director of the New York Office of the UN's High Commissioner for Human Rights, who stepped down from his post in October 2023 and penned a now-viral letter on unfolding genocide and the UN's failures.

PHYLLIS BENNIS is a fellow of the Institute for Policy Studies and serves as international adviser to Jewish Voice for Peace. Her books include *Challenging Empire: How People, Governments and the UN Defy U.S. Power.*

JAVAD ZARIF (PhD) is a scholar and career diplomat, who served as the foreign minister of Islamic Republic of Iran from 2013 to 2021. He was Iran's permanent representative to the United Nations (2002–2007) and deputy foreign minister (1992–2002). He also served as Chairman of U.N. General Assembly's 6th (legal) committee (1991–1992), Disarmament Commission (2000) and UNESCO's Cultural Commission (2007–2009). Zarif was appointed by UN Secretary-General's as a member of Group of Eminent Persons on Dialogue among Civilizations (1998–2001). He received his PhD in international studies from the University of Denver in 1988 and has written extensively on international law, international relations, disarmament and international organizations. He is currently serving as the Vice President of Iran and an associate professor at the Faculty of World Studies, University of Tehran.

REZA NASRI is an international lawyer who received his PhD in International Law from Graduate Institute of International and Development Studies in Geneva and his L.L.M from University Of Montreal. He has written extensively about international law and current affairs.

ALFRED DE ZAYAS is a U.S. and Swiss citizen, lawyer and historian, professor of international law at the Geneva School of Diplomacy, former UN Independent Expert on International Order (2012–2018), retired UN official, retired Chief of Petitions at OHCHR, Secretary of the Human Rights Committee, author of 12 book including *Building a Just World Order* (Clarity Press, 2021), *Countering Mainstream Narratives* (2022) and *The Human Rights Industry* (2023).

HANS C. VON SPONECK (PhD), educated in Germany, the UK and the U.S., has served as: UN civil servant (1968–2000); head/ UN missions in Botswana, Pakistan and India; Director, UNDP European Office in Geneva; UN Assistant Secretary-General and Humanitarian Coordinator for Iraq. Faculty Member, ret., Conflict Research Centre, University of Marburg/ Germany and Sr. Training Consultant,ret., UN Staff College, Torino/Italy. Professional interests: political accountability, multilateral sanctions,UN reforms, human rights and human responsibilities; the Middle East and South Asia. Dr. von Sponeck has authored articles and books on multilateralism, and UN affairs, including *A Different Kind of War: The UN Sanctions Regime in Iraq* (University of California Press, 2006); and *Liberating the United Nations: Realism with Vision and Hope* (Stanford University Press, 2024) (co-authored with Professor Richard Falk).

Index